ETHERIZED UPON A TABLE:

FOREWORD

I0681431

POETRY

I, too, dislike it: there are things that are important beyond all this fiddle.
Reading it, however, with a perfect contempt for it, one discovers in
it after all, a place for the genuine.

Marianne Moore

SONG OF MYSELF

I celebrate myself, and sing myself,
And what I assume you shall assume,
For every atom belonging to me as good belongs to you.

Walt Whitman

When we call someone a "modern" poet, we mean, in the broadest sense, that they wrote at some time in the 20th Century. Robert Frost's first book, *A Boy's Will*, was published in 1912, and his second book, *North of Boston*, in 1914. His poetic style was based on what he called "sentence sounds," the natural tones and rhythms of speech cast loosely against standard poetic forms. This was a departure in its time and made Frost a distinctly modern poet. Though poets writing after The Great War used various narrative strategies and lyric devices, what poets like Wallace Stevens, William Carlos Williams, and T.S. Eliot had in common was their use of a natural diction. They wrote the way people talked, in unrhymed, free verse, and avoided the archaic diction of previous centuries. This use of natural speech, more than anything else, characterized the modern poet of the 20th Century.

One gets the impression then, that before the 20th Century all poets wrote in an archaic style. Perhaps this is why Wordsworth felt compelled to call upon all poets to write "in the language really used by men." In 1800, in the preface to his *Lyrical Ballads*, he said that his purpose "was to imitate and adopt the very language of men, to bring my language near to the language of speech." Wordsworth was making an effort to avoid "poetic diction," those "expressions, in themselves proper and beautiful, but which have been foolishly repeated by bad poets." Despite Wordsworth's call, the diction of English poetry since the time of Shakespeare remained much the same until the 20th century. Tennyson's poem "Ulysses" (1847) could easily have fit into any number of Shakespeare's plays.

I cannot rest from travel: I will drink
Life to the lees: all times I have enjoy'd
Greatly, have suffer'd greatly, both with those
That loved me, and alone; on shore, and when
Thro' scudding drifts the rainy Hyades
Vext the dim sea: I am become a name;
For always roaming with a hungry heart
Much have I seen and known. . . .
'Tis not too late to seek a newer world.
Push off, and sitting well in order smite
The sounding furrows; for my purpose holds
To sail beyond the sunset, and the baths
Of all the western stars, until I die.
It may be that the gulfs will wash us down:
It may be we shall touch the Happy Isles,
And see the great Achilles, whom we knew.
Tho' much is taken, much abides; and tho'
We are not now that strength which in old days
Moved earth and heaven; that which we are, we are;   [Robert Kennedy
One equal temper of heroic hearts,   quoted these lines
Made weak by time and fate, but strong in will   the night
To strive, to seek, to find, and not to yield   he was shot]

A hundred years after Wordsworth, Ezra Pound made the call again for poets to write like they talked. In a letter to Harriet Monro, the editor of the newly founded magazine *Poetry*, he sent this famous pronouncement:

Poetry must be as well written as prose. Its language must be a fine language, departing in no way from speech saved by heightened intensity (i.e. simplicity). There must be no book words, no periphrases, no inversions, no straddled adjectives, no Tennysonianess of speech; nothing--nothing that you couldn't, in some circumstance, in the stress of some emotion, actually say. Every literaryism, every book word, fritters away a scrap of the reader's patience, a scrap of his sense of your sincerity.

When the modern poet of the 20th Century adopted the language of speech, it was as if a curtain had been lifted, introducing for the first time the diction of modern man. Was this the first time in the history of literature that poets had brought common speech and syntax to their work? Most poets writing in the 20th century probably thought so, hardly realizing that in his day, Chaucer adopted the spoken dialect of midland England, forever changing the course of English poetry. And let's not forget that "upstart crow," William Shakespeare, scorned by the so-called university wits because he wrote in the language of Everyman and not in the elevated diction sanctioned by university-trained playwrights. One day Ben Jonson was asked about Shakespeare's sloppy penmanship. Was it true, they wanted to know, that in composing his plays, Shakespeare had "blotted" many a word?

ETHERIZED UPON A TABLE:

THE STORY AND EVOLUTION OF MODERN POETRIES

a study guide for the perplexed

Vol. 1

An account of the evolution of poetry
from Homer to the present day,
with particular emphasis on the periods of history
in which poets saw themselves as modern.

Jack Grapes

Bombshelter Press
Los Angeles, 2021

This is a work in progress.

It was begun in 1998, meant to be a short essay on "modern" poetry. Soon, things got out of hand, and the time frame of the book stretched further back into the past until the doorstop of Greek epic and lyric poetry, and then the recovered nuiform tablets of Gilgamesh stretched the canvas beyond my ability to control it. This was before the Internet and Wikipedia, and information and translations of many poets were hard to come by. As the book got bigger, it became two books, and as the writing continued, I found little time to do the kind of editing and proofing I would like to have done. But I've since written several other books, not just my own poetry, but non-fiction essays and historical accounts, and a book on James Joyce's *Ulysses*, all of which have been finished but none fully edited. So I've sort of thrown up my hands and decided to issue these two volumes "as is," like a car that's been sitting in the showroom too long. Take it for what it's worth. If I have time, I will issue a second edition, but for now, forgive the mistypes and incomplete secctions. For now, this edition will have to do. I hope it's enough to satisfy your curiosity about modern poetry, and all the modern poetries that came before, which will provide a blueprint for all the modern poetry yet to be written.

The essay on Charles Bukowski, "This Thing Upon Me," was first published in *Poetry East*.

Cover painting: *The Lamentation of Christ* by Andrea Mantegna, 1480.

With a touch of envy, Jonson replied, "Would that he had blotted them all." So the modern poets of the 20th century weren't the first to use the diction of speech. If avoiding the stilted diction of traditional poetry characterizes the modern poet, we would be correct in saying that Chaucer was a modern poet. The same would be true of Shakespeare.

Granted, the modernism of the 20th century was a revolutionary break from the orthodoxies of the past, and the most obvious orthodoxy was the post-Elizabethan diction still used by most poets. Is the use, then, of a contemporary diction the only criteria for being a modern poet? Just what is Modernism? Is it the rejection of tradition, of the discipline of the classics? Is it the manipulation of narrative form, the experimental, the avant-garde? Is it merely, to use Robert Hughes' term, "the shock of the new?" By mid-century, the whole concept of newness had became a problem for modern poets. If modern art meant being new, modern artists were forced to embrace innovation in order to remain modern. How long, they asked, could modernism last, before it too became the mummified canon of the past? Was there no end to innovation for innovation's sake? Would Modernism come to a dead end? Modern poets continued to face this dilemma throughout the century. Following the brouhaha of T.S. Eliot's *The Waste Land*, Robinson Jeffers avoided the problem altogether by returning to traditional epic narrative (*Roan Stallion*, 1925). Hart Crane's solution was to combine the avant-garde tendencies of High Modernism with the hallucinatory passion of Whitman (*The Bridge*, 1927).

The problem of defining Modernism became further complicated by the fact that various tendencies in art and literature, often at odds with one another, were grouped under the common label Modernism, merely because they were products of the 20th century. Like the word Romanticism, Modernism has been variously defined, and few agree on its time frame. Perhaps modern art is somewhat like pornography—we can't define it, but we know it when we see it.

Or do we? If we confine our definition of Modernism to work produced in the last century, then we must conclude that James Ensor's *The Intrigue* was modern, while Hieronymous Bosch's *Garden of Delights* was not. Kandinsky's *Improvisation No. 30* was modern, while Caravaggio's *Calling of Matthew* was not; Picasso's *Les Demoiselles d'Avignon* was modern, while Géricault's *Raft of the Medusa* was not; George Grosz's *Self-Portrait, Admonishing* was modern, while Rembrandt's *Self Portrait* was not; Boccioni's *States of Mind* was modern, while John Henry Fuseli's *The Nightmare* was not; Gilbert's Woolworth Building was modern, while the Gothic Abbey Church of St. Denis was not; Chester Carlson's invention of xerography was modern, while Guttenberg's use of moveable type to print the *Bible* was not; the Wright brothers' first powered flight and Ford's Model-T automobile were modern, while the use of the wheel was not. Diego Rivera's great mural *The Aztec World,* painted for the Palacio Nacional in Mexico City, was modern, Michelangelo's painting on the ceiling of the Sistine Chapel and the Bison painted on the ceiling of the Altamira cave were not. It's obvious, from the foregoing list, that defining Modern Art solely in terms of the age in which it was produced will not do. Surely those men who first gazed upon the Bison of Altamira felt the shock of the new, as did those who saw the Sistine Ceiling, the paintings of Bosch, and Guttenberg's Bible.

It soon became apparent that neither diction alone nor the "shock of the new" were enough to satisfy the demands of Modernism. Eventually, the movement began to eat its own tail. Modernism gave way to High-Modernism, then to Post-Modernism, then to Neo-Modernism, Neo-Formalism, and a host of other experimental, iconoclastic, avant-garde-isms. No matter how you sliced it, such isms by any other name were still Modern isms. By the end of the century, the entire movement had come full circle. As a historically descriptive term, it was misleading; as a purely descriptive term, it was misleading as well. Art, like politics, has strange bedfellows, and one is forced to conclude that every age has its moderns, poets who break with tradition and take up the banner of newness.

Well, what about the classics? The great poetry of the Greeks, of the Romans, of Dante? Could they be modern? Did the ancients use an archaic diction or, like Chaucer and Shakespeare, the speech of their time? For a good part of the 20th Century, translations of the great poets were rendered into a post-Elizabethan diction, as if Homer, Virgil, and Dante all wrote "thee" and "thou" and "wert" and "whilst." Sappho, for instance, wrote during the late-seventh century BC, sometime after Homer; below is an 18th century translation by Ambrose Philips of one of her "Hymns to Venus."

> Celestial Visitant, once more
> Thy needful Presence I implore!
> In Pity come and ease my Grief,
> Bring my distemper'd Soul Relief;
> Favour thy Suppliant's hidden Fires,
> And give me All my Heart desires.

In 1901, Thomas Hardy translated one of Sappho's poems.

> Dead shalt thou lie; and nought
> Be told of thee or thought,
> For thou hast plucked not of the Muses' tree:
> And even in Hades' halls
> Amidst thy fellow-thralls
> No friendly shade thy shade shall company!

Clearly, based on Hardy's or Phillip's translations, Sappho would not be considered a modern poet. Her diction is archaic, that is, Elizabethan, and what's more, she rhymes. Is that how Sappho sounded to her contemporaries, all those "shalts" and "amidsts?" On the contrary, to someone in her own time, Sappho would not have sounded that way at all. Her Greek was not archaic; she wrote monody in a form of Aeolic Greek, in the natural diction of her day; it was contemporary, and didn't rhyme. Had you lived back then, this is what you would have heard, were Sappho to have read the "Hymn to Venus" in a neighborhood coffee shop.

> Eternal Aphrodite,
> rainbow-crowned,
> you cunning, wily child of Zeus,
> I beg you,
> do not break me, Lady,
> with the pain of misled love.
> But come to me,
> if ever in the past
> you heard my far-off cries
> and heeding, came,
> leaving the Golden home of Zeus.

Or this one, written to the young girl Attis, once Sappho's lover, now engaged to a man picked for her by her parents.

> That man sitting next to you seems to be a God
> as he turns toward you, whispers in your ear,
> and smiles, full of his manhood, confident as he
> listens to your mellow voice,
> then thrills at the sound of your laughter
> that stings my breasts, jolts my heart
> if I dare the shock of catching your eye;
> I cannot speak,
> My tongue sticks to my dry mouth,
> thin fire spreads beneath my skin,
> my eyes cannot see and my aching ears
> roar in their labyrinths.
> Chill sweat slides down my body,
> I shake, turn greener than grass.
> I am neither living nor dead and cry
> out from that no-man's land between.
> But I endure,
>   I endure even this grief
> of love.

Sappho was a modern poet in every sense of the word and the modern impulse is nothing new. Every age had its moderns, and every age, likewise, had those who clung to the classics, imitated their forms, and versified in the cul-de-sacs of tradition. So what's a modern to do? Is it enough to eschew the past and write like one talks, to touch on themes and subjects that reflect one's own time? True modernism is a conscious strategy that includes the treasure trove of the past, the contemporary diction of the present, and the energies of the future toward which all great art and literature moves. To paraphrase Shakespeare, the modern poet's eye, in a fine frenzy rolling, glances from the past to the future, from the future to the past, and as imagination explodes the forms of things unknown, the poet's pen turns them to shapes and gives to airy nothing a local habitation and a name—Modernism! The modern poets of the past continue to live within the modern poets of the present, and the great modern poets of the present cast a net so far into the future that even the poets of the future will have to scramble to keep up with them. Whitman sensed that pulse flowing in his veins when he called out to the poets of the future:

> You will hardly know who I am or what I mean,
> But I shall be good health to you nevertheless,
> And filter and fibre your blood.
>
> Failing to fetch me at first keep encouraged,
> Missing me one place search another,
> I stop somewhere waiting for you.

Whitman and Shakespeare would have clanked tankards of ale with Dante, Virgil and Homer. Moderns—of one time and all time—they were. Homer was a modern poet, blending dialects that had developed over centuries in a display of linguistic magic that produces, when the smoke clears, a superbly modern diction that is both elevated and simple, lucid and stunning in its narrative speed and vivid imagery.

> Achilles had just finished
> His evening meal. The table was still set up.
> Great Priam entered unnoticed. He stood
> Close to Achilles, and touching his knees,
> He kissed the dread and murderous hands
> That had killed so many of his sons.
> Achilles stared in wonder at Priam.
> Was he a god?
> And the others there stared
> And wondered and looked at each other.
> But Priam spoke, a prayer of entreaty:
> "Remember your father, godlike Achilles.
> He and I both are on the doorstep
> Of old age. He may well be now
> Surrounded by enemies wearing him down
> And have no one to protect him from harm.
> But then he hears that you are still alive
> And his heart rejoices, and he hopes all his days
> To see his dear son come back from Troy.
> But what is left for me? I had the finest sons
> In all wide Troy, and not one of them is left.
> Fifty I had when the Greeks came over,
> Nineteen out of one belly, and the rest
> The women in my house bore to me.
> It doesn't matter how many they were,
> The god of war has cut them down at the knees.
> And the only one who could save the city
> You've just now killed as he fought for his country,
> My Hector. It is for him I have come to the Greek ships,

To get him back from you. I've brought
A fortune in ransom. Respect the gods, Achilles.
Think of your own father, and pity me.
I am more pitiable. I have borne what no man
Who has walked this earth has ever yet borne.
I have kissed the hand of the man who killed my son."

(trans.Stanley Lombardo, 1997)

Sappho was a modern poet, writing about erotic love in a way that seems contemporary. In the Hellenistic era, it was Callimachus and his "modern poets" who discarded the grand Homeric epic and wrote shorter verse using the language of the day, laced with irony and personal reference. Centuries later, the Roman poets Lucretius and Catullus were part of the *Poetae Novi*, "the New Poets," who initiated a stylistic revolution by using modern diction, though they were criticized as well for being avant-garde. During the period of the Roman Republic, Lucilius wrote about contemporary life, not myth, and forged a new form—the satire—that Horace and Juvenal would perfect a century later. Both Horace and Juvenal were "moderns," writing in the street vernacular of their day. Writing in the time of Christ, Ovid was not only modern in his own day, but when properly translated, seems as modern as any poet writing now. His poems of love, sex, and exile preserve a tone that seems at home in the 20th century. Poets such as Boethius and Ausonius, who wrote during the decline of the Roman Empire, surprise the reader with their contemporary tone. With the decline of commerce and literacy during the Dark Ages, poets wrote only for a select audience of monks and clerics. Today, those writers are read only by scholars, and most of the work written during this time fell into obscurity. The poets of the 12th century Renaissance were called, in their own time, *moderni*, and their poetry was hip, appealing to the young vagabonds and students flocking to the universities and cathedral schools of learning. During that same period, Provençal poetry written by Troubadour poets in the south of France touched a modern chord; their poetry has been called, by some, the beginnings of modern literature. The culmination of that modern impulse was Dante's *Commedia* (Boccaccio later added the word *Divine* to the title as a reference both to the subject of the poem and to its excellence). Dante wrote it with one ear cocked to the classic diction of Virgil and the other tuned to the speech of his day—his decision to write his epic in the Italian vernacular and not in the Latin usually chosen for important written work was a signal to all his readers that here was a modern poem.

Aside from contemporary diction, writing about oneself is also seen as a 20th century impulse. There is a misconception that "confessional" poetry—the private "I" of Ann Sexton and Charles Bukowski and their legion of imitators—is a passing fad, a fairly recent development in literature. But the personal impulse can be found in poets of every age, beginning with the Greek Archaic age that followed on the heels of Homer, in which poets weaned on the grand epic began to write short lyric poems of great wit and subtly of feeling. Sappho was confessional. So was Ovid, punished for committing an "unspeakable" crime against Augustus Caesar and exiled from Rome to live among the barbarians of Tomis on the edge of the Black Sea.

Yet my talent fails to respond to me as it once did:
it's an arid shore I'm ploughing, with sterile share.
Had Homer himself been consigned to this land, believe me,
he too would have become a Goth. What's more,
my work has fallen off: these days—forgive the confession—
I write scarcely a word.
That divine impulse, inspiration's sustenance,
once always innate in me, now is gone. . . .
Writing a poem you can read to no one
is like dancing in the dark.

Yet for great men, nothing's more fitting
than the homage of poets, offered through their verse.
Poems keep virtue alive, ... Yet the written word
defies the years. It's through *that* you know Agamemmon,
and all who bore arms against him, or on his side.
Even the gods (is this blasphemy?) have their being
through poems: such majesty needs a poet's voice.

Now my poems have stirred up the wrath of this town.
Shall I never stop being injured
by my verse, will I always be taking knocks from this
too tactless talent of mine? Why not chop off all my fingers
to stop me writing, why still crazily pursue
the missiles that maimed me, why steer for those old reef-strewn
waters in which my craft was wrecked before?
But I've done nothing wrong, men of Tomis, I've committed
no crime: you I love, although I loath your land.

Ovid is gone. And I enjoyed a reputation when I was still
alive. Like those who trod Callimachus' primrose path,
and those youngsters whose efforts remain unpublished.
If it's seemly to say so, my *talent* was distinguished,
and among all that competition, I was *fit to be read*.
Don't scatter my ashes after death!
I have lost all: only bare life remains to quicken
the awareness and substance of my pain.
What pleasure do you get from stabbing this dead body?
There is no space in me now for another wound.

The personal impulse continues through such writings as the *Meditations* of Marcus Aurelius, the *Confessions* of St. Augustine, the *History of My Calamities* by the 12th Century poet and philosopher Peter Abelard, the *Confessions* of Jean Jacques Rousseau written near the end of the 18th Century, and Whitman's *Song of Myself* published in 1848. They were all writing songs of the self, assuming the same things you assume. The great poetry of the last three thousand years has always been modern, and the great poets, whether called *poetae novi*, *moderni*, or *avant-garde*, were modern in their own time, and remain modern today.

What does it mean to be modern? The choice to be modern in one's own time can mean the difference between a Cro-Magnum work of literature that runs into an evolutionary dead end, or work that becomes part of the evolutionary line in any age. The great stream of modernity that flows through Homer, Sappho, Virgil, Dante, Shakespeare, Dickenson, Whitman, and the great poets and writers of our own time is neither fashionable nor unfashionable, neither obscure for the sake of obscurity, nor confessional for the sake of sensationalism. Modernism takes them all in; it's a highway blazed by personal vision through the use of a precise and relevant diction, and one travels that highway with one eye trained on the great writers of the past, and the other focused on the future, that place where the new becomes old and the old reinvents itself.

This book is an attempt to chart the currents of that great stream of modern poetries—the modern poetry of the Greeks, of the Romans, of the Middle Ages, of the Renaissance, of the Romantics and post-Romantics, and of the moderns of the last century. It can be read as a history, as an anthology, as a series of critical essays, or as a combination of all three. But I would hope that the ideal reader, a young poet about to enter that great stream, would take note of the essence of modernism. To be modern is not to turn one's back on the classics of the past, nor is it a contemporary fashionableness that avoids or embraces the experimental and the avant-garde, or avoids or embraces common diction, without a conscious sense of what that choice portends. We will see how writers of the past who slavishly followed the formulas of the classics produced work that was insular and unimaginative. Likewise, those writers who displayed a contemporary energy without a knowledge of what came before produced work that was fashionably anarchic but lacking in depth and universality. Modernism is an evolutionary strategy. It's the recursive structure of the old that continually adds the shock of the new. It is a strategic stance, with both feet planted in the now, that scoops up the past and throws it into the future. The poets covered in this book were all modern, each in their own time, and each one modern for all time.

INTRODUCTION (2002)

The purpose of this Study Guide is for use in my Saturday morning class. It is not an anthology, a literary history, or a critical study of Modernism; rather, it is a blend of all three.

Anthologies, by themselves, do not provide the historical and critical overview that helps one manuever through the marshlands of Modern poetry. *The Norton Anthology of Modern Poetry* gives an excellent selection of the poets of this century, but there's no separation into categories that might help the student undertand the poets' relationship to one another. In this study guide, I've separated the poets into chronological categories grouped around the particular movements with which they were associated. There are other ways to group these poets, and other ways to understand their work. I have chosen the most obvious historical connections as a way to begin.

By the same token, a **literary history** of this century's poetry is not an anthology, so one does not get a selection of poems in a literary history. The student would need to keep both a literary history and a comprehensive anthology side by side. I've combined the two.

A book of **literary criticism** may give useful insight into a poet's process and the nature of the product, but without context or familiarity with the poets' works, we're likely to get lost in a theoretical discussion. One would have to read quite a bit of literary criticism to get a feel for the overall development of modern poetries. I hope the overview here will be a good starting point for the student wishing to delve deeper into the critical issues and theories that connect and distinguish these poets.

So I've begun with a little of each. This study guide is not intended to be complete, inclusive, or comprehensive. It's a start. I hope it will give you a picture, blanks you can continue to fill for a long, long time, just as I have in the writing of it.

Why did I feel compelled to start with the ancient classics? Let me quote William Carlos Williams from his poem "Spring and All."

> It is no different from the aristocratic compositions of the earlier times,
> the Homeric inventions. . . . The work the two-thousand year-old poet
> did and that we do are one piece. That is the vitality of the classics.

In his essay "Tradition and the Individual Talent," T. S. Eliot made a case for the idea that a chronological view of literature can be misleading, and that, especially for the artist who is creating works of art, the great works of the past exist in time and space as a contemporary, living stimulus. In fact, there are some works of classical poetry that seem more modern than some of what is being written today. We are informed by the works of the past in a way that can be immediate and *germaine* to the work we are in the process of creating now. Even more to the point, a poet who can make the associative connections to a past work can produce a powerful response in the reader. When T. S. Eliot begins his poem "The Love Song of J. Alfred Prufrock" with the words, "Let us go then, you and I . . . ," one is immediately reminded of Virgil's words to Dante as they begin their descent into Hell. But Eliot is also talking to a companion, or to me, the reader, entreating us to begin a modern journey. He evokes an associational response enriched by both images. Same as in *The Waste Land*, when he notices all the faces passing by him on London Bridge. He says "I had not thought death had undone so many." This is a famous line from Dante's *Inferno*, in which Dante comments on all the great and poor souls he sees before him as he makes his descent. The two images connected like that produce in me, the reader, a startling awareness. Those faces on London Bridge become the souls of those descending into hell. It can even have a comic effect, as when Delmore Schwartz says "Harms and the child I sing," which is a parody of Virgil's opening lines to the *Aeneid*, "Arms and the man I sing."

There are **a few general themes**, or points I have tried to emphasize. One is evolution of verse forms, which did not always stay the same from one period to another. Many of us take for granted rhymed poetry, as if that were the only kind that existed, and the only kind that has changed and died out. The Greek syllabic developed into a stressed accentual meter; that changed over time into the rhythmic alliterative beat of Old English poetry. But form and meter were constantly changing, and subject to the natural evolution of speech and literary fashion. In the Middle Ages, alliterative and syllabic verse gave way to Latin rhyme. We're not even sure where rhymed verse came from, because it had never been used before in poetry. There is evidence that it evolved out of Latin Church hymns. In our own century, we have witnessed one of the great revolutions in verse form: rhymed iambic pentameter, which held sway for centuries, gave way to blank verse and then free verse, which is where we stand today.

Another common development is the way poets have switched from the literary language to the idioms of speech. The other day, Richard Dietmeier wrote to me, saying:

> Over the centuries, several significant revolutions in language have taken place that use the popular [vernacular] voice to challenge the established order and question the nature of things. These revolutions always include a large reading public. One of these was precipitated by Dante and his use of Italian over Latin. And later on, Whitman used the American idiom and rhythms to challenge the official doctrine. What's to come I believe has to rise out of that tradition.

A few weeks ago, I finished a poetry reading by inviting the audience to ask me questions about my work. Many wanted to know about the relationship between the actual events of my life and the content of the poems. One man wanted to know why I didn't write in rhyme.

"You might be asking me the wrong question," I said. "You could ask why I don't write in syllabic verse. It was good enough for Virgil. Or why I don't write in rhythmic alliterative stanzas. It was good enough for the poet who composed *Beowulf*. The answer would be that I don't write in those forms for the same reason Shakespeare didn't, but chose rhyme, and blank verse instead. I'd like to think that if the Bard were writing today, he'd be writing just like the rest of us, in free verse, because it's the form of our time. Verse forms change and evolve. The nature of the stories don't. It's usually—to quote Faulkner's Nobel Prize speech—`the human heart in conflict with itself.'"

I want to thank Cindy Milwe for encouraging me to start the study group and Chana Bell, whose inability to come to the first class prompted me to tape the opening lecture. If I had not taped it, I might not have realized how much information I failed to mention, how much was left out. This led me to typing up a short 16 page summary of what I'd said, and some of what I might have left out. The 16 pages has grown to this, and it is still growing; what you have here is not by any means complete. I would say it's fairly complete through The New Criticism poets. The last 50 pages are more of an outline which I hope to fill out by the time we are ready to cover it in further classes.

I'd like to thank Lynne Zika, Kathy Goldman, and Richard Dietmeier for their proof-reading, copy-editing, and perceptive suggestions. I want to thank all of you who have given me encouragement. Your insights and suggestions have been and will continue to be invaluable. I have appreciated those of you who have taken the time to give me specific comments on what parts worked best, and what parts did not. My ultiamte purpose is to turn you on to the writers that will enrich your understanding and love for poetry.

There is no way I can adequately thank my wife Lori, "the better craftsman," for her help with this. She takes those sentences of mine that try to scale tall buildings with a single bound, and with a few cuts and a few additions, enables them to swoosh right in the bullseye. Her probing questions have helped me get to the root of what I was trying to say. In some cases, she has said it for me, and I humbly accept the generous gift of her expertise. Furthermore, she has been patient and understanding in my obsession with this project, giving me the extra time to get some of this work done. If she is this good at supporting my art, imagine what she does for my life.

ॐ

Keep in mind that many of the longer poems have been drastically edited. You should go back to the complete originals reprinted in anthologies to get the whole thing. I've done my best to give a sense of what the poem was about, or more importantly for our purposes, what it's strategies were.

I've also printed certain lines of poetry in bold. You will discover those lines, or variations of those lines, used by 20th century poets in their own work.

And finally, I think of this study guide as a story of modernism because I want to emphasize that works of literature function in relation to each other as characters in a story do. The development of a single work of art, or the evolution of a literary movement is not isolated from all that has gone before it, and all that follows. Dante's *Commedia* speaks to us now in a way that is different from when it first appeared. When we read of the poet's descent into the underworld, we hold in our minds not only Odysseus' similar journey, but Stephen Daedelus' nightown experience and Bloom's day in Dublin in James Joyce's *Ulysses*, as well as Pound's own journey through the *Cantos*. Such reference points give resonance to a reading of the *Commedia*—indeed, to most 20th Century works of literature.

It is also the story of how one kind of verse evolved into other kinds of verse; how a new verse form emerged, only to be changed again. What were the forces and pressures that caused these verse patterns to change? In many cases, it was the evolution of vernacular speech infiltrating the literary style. It's also the story of the development of genres, from epic to romance, from romance to lyrical meditation, from the post-romantic lyrical meditation to the deconstruction of style and the subversion of communication itself. And it is a story of how individual artists confront their own relationship with their art.

If someone else had written this guide, they may have told a different story. Many of the characters would be the same, but their importance, influence and even relationships to one another would likely have been presented differently, depending on who was telling it. That's what makes literature so fascinating: It changes as we do. With each reading, a book changes; as we grow, it does too. And so, as you read and reread these poets and writers, they will become a part of your own history, your own story. And when you sit down to write, they will sit down with you—Pound and Eliot, Williams Moore, Rich and Frost, Stein and Stevens, Whitman and Dickinson, Virgil and Dante, Sappho and Ovid, Homer and Shakespeare. Their constellations are as various as you are. Don't believe me. Find out for yourself.

❄

Jack

moᴅᴇʀɴɪsᴍ: 20ᴛʜ ᴄᴇɴᴛᴜʀʏ ᴘᴏᴇᴛʀʏ
OVERVIEW

Poetry does not exist apart from the other arts. What goes on in poetry, goes on in all the arts. Toward the end of the 19th Century, a modernist revolution was taking place, and English poetry began to change radically. The typical subject matter and the style in which it was written no longer served the modern poet. There was a desire to break with the past, to embrace the new century with a "modern" gusto, to write in a natural idiom, the way people spoke.

Prose writers were exploring new techniques of naturalism and realism, especially Flaubert in France, Henry James in America, and James Joyce in Great Britian. Whitman's expansive style encouraged poets to bring the energy of the new democracy to writing, and poets such as Edgar Lee Masters, Edward Arlington Robinson and Robert Frost were beginning to write in a more American English. The "Genteel Tradition" in American poetry—characterized by poets such as Henry Wadsworth Longfellow, James Russell Lowell, John Greenleaf Whittier, Oliver Wendall Holmes—was slowly giving way to a flexible line and bolder, more personal subject matter.

By the second decade of the 20th Century (1910-1920), it was obvious a revolution was taking place. Robert Frost, T.S. Eliot, Gertrude Stein, Ezra Pound, Wallace Stevens, William Carlos Williams, Marianne Moore, and e.e. cummings were all to publish their early poems in this period, launching the Modernist revolution. William Butler Yeats was another poet whose work at that time could be called <u>Popular Modernism.</u> Whereas the others were just beginning their careers, Yeats, with the publication of his *Collected Poems* in 1908, had seemed to be at the end of his. But he transformed himself and began to write with a direct and natural power. He is often credited (along with Ezra Pound) with laying the foundations for the Modernist Revolution. <u>The major works of Popular Modernism were:</u>

> **T.S. Eliot**, "Prufrock," (1911) and his book *Poems* (1919)
> **Ezra Pound**, *Hugh Selywn Mauberly* **(1920)**
> **Robert Frost**, *A Boy's Will* (1913) and *North of Boston* (1914)
> **Marianne Moore**, *Poems* **(1921)**
> E.E. Cummings, *Tulips & Chimneys* (1923)
> **William Carlos Williams**, *Poems* (1909) and *Al Que Quiere!* (1917)
> **Gertrude Stein**, *Three Lives* (1909), *Tender Buttons* (1914)
> **Robinson Jeffers**, *Roan Stallion* (1924)
> **Wallace Stevens**, *Harmonium*

Furrthermore, Pound, Williams, and Stevens were to suffer somewhat of a decline in the '30s and '40s, as <u>T.S. Eliot</u> became the towering influence into the '50s, having won the Nobel prize in 1948. But it was the resurrected, rediscovered, and/or revitalized work of <u>Ezra Pound</u>, <u>William Carlos Williams</u>, and <u>Wallace Stevens</u> that led to another revolution in American poetry in the '50s that is still going on today.

In a sense, one could symbolize the entire evolution of Modern American poetry by the 4 different strands represented by those poets. Eliot would be responsible for both wild, syntactical experimentation and the more conservative, well-wrought, well-made poem;

Pound remained for most of his life the avant-garde modernist encouraging other writers. One of those writers, Charles Olson, became the figurehead in the '50s & '60s for poets writing long, fragmented experimental poems. Williams also influenced a generation of poets in the '60s who strove for natural verse, writing of everyday objects and events in a very spare style. Stevens' work was philosophical and meditative, and poets like John Ashbery seemed to take their cue from that impulse, writing intellectually challenging poems in language surprisingly fresh, if somewhat distancing.

Robert Frost became the most recognized poet in America during the '50s and '60s, and his influence has continued, stressing the cadences of speech as the real music of poetry, what he called "sentence sounds." His work was distinctive because of the way he combined those "sounds" with a more standard poetic meter and rhythm. Marianne Moore flaunted the conventions of poetic rhythm and meter by writing poems that were not only prose like and looked like prose, but often veered off into a "written" kind of prose one found in unliterary kind of documents. Even prose often sounded lyrical, but Moore purposefully defied convention by writing poems that were blatantly unpoetic. Gertrude Stein cracked the normal structure of the sentence in a way that was not spoken or written, but clearly an attack on the use of words in any communicative process. Frost, Moore, and Stein made an impact that was more subtle and less flashy, and their influence was spread over the entire span of the century. They didn't *seem* as revolutionary as the big four, but in ways that went deeper, set the tone for a fundamental change in the way poetry was written in this century.

These poets who started the Popular Modernist Revolution in 1910, were the same poets who in the '20s launched what is called High Modernism, a movement parallel to the experiments in abstract, cubist, and expressionistic art. With the publication of Eliot's *The Waste Land* in 1922, poets felt free to write poems that were disjointed, highly experimental and avant-garde. These poems were characterized by wild changes in voice, literary allusions to Greek myth and anthropological studies, cinematic montage and fragments—they challenged the reader's intellect, as well as making bold assaults on the senses. It was a time when "the shock of the new" rattled people's assumptions about art and excited the artists themselves to explore the many possibilities suddenly opened to them. The major works of High Modernism were all published in a space of two or three years:

T. S. Eliot, *The Waste Land* (1922)
Wallace Stevens, *Harmonium* (1923)
William Carlos Williams, *Spring and All* (1923)
Ezra Pound, *A Draft of XVI Cantos* (1925)
Gertrude Stein, *The Making of Americans* (1925)

High Modernism was so intoxicating that poets found themselves confronted with a fundamental problem: either to imitate the structural fragmentation and experimental effects, or find a new way to manipulate the surface form of the poem and deconstruct the content. Poets not wishing to imitate realized that the other approach would only take them further into the narrow cul-de-sac of structural experimentation for experimentation's sake.

Hart Crane tried combining T. S. Eliot's High Modernism with Walt Whitman's exuberant American free verse, and the poems that make up his great work—"Voyages," "The Marriage of Faustus and Helen," and his long poem *The Bridge* (1930)—are unique. **Robinson Jeffers** took another tack: He decided that there was no use attempting to follow High Modernism's lead; instead he returned to the roots of narrative poetry, poetry that told a story and did so with the intensity of Greek drama. *Roan Stallion* was published in 1923 to great popular success.

During the '30s and '40s, High Modernism took a conservative turn, led by T. S. Eliot's critical essays calling for a more traditional poetry that suppressed the personality and emotion of the poet and focused on a more contemplative approach to subjects that were not personal or everyday, but closer to philosophical examinations of a higher order.

This impulse was taken up by other poet-critics, notably **William Empson**, who wrote a book showing how poems could be analyzed and explicated for multiple meanings. His book, *The Seven Types of Ambiguity*, was published in 1930 and influenced a generation of poets studying in Universities, many of whom went on to write their own critical extensions of this theory. In 1938, **Robert Penn Warren** & **Cleanth Brooks** wrote *Understanding Poetry*, a textbook used in college courses. Students were not learning to read poems for pleasure, but in order to "understand" them. Poems were studied and analyzed for their meaning; or, since there were seven types of ambiguity, it was possible for a poem to have many different interpretations.

Three years later, when **John Crowe Ransom** published *The New Criticism*, the entire movement was dubbed "The New Criticism." Not only was another generation of poets studying how to analyze and explicate a poem, but they began writing poems that *could be* analyzed for their deep and multiple meanings, a kind of poetry that only other poets, critics and scholars could appreciate. The popular base that poetry had enjoyed decades earlier was eroded completely; it was now something college students learned to hate.

It wasn't until the late '50s, with the influence and rediscovery of Williams, Pound, and Stevens, that poetry began to claim a larger audience. Once again, a revolution was in the making, and it came with the Beat Poets and the Confessional Poets. Not only were poets writing in a natural, spoken idiom, à la Williams, but they were writing poems that were more personal and daring than anything that had come before. The major books of Confessional Poetry were:

> **Robert Lowell**, *Life Studies*, 1959
> **W.D. Snodgrass**, *Heart's Needle*, 1960
> **Ann Sexton**, *To Bedlam and Part Way Back*, 1960
>   *All My Pretty Ones*, 1962
> **Sylvia Plath**, *Ariel*, 1961
> **Charles Bukowski**, *It Catches My Heart in its Hands*, 1964

Since then, there have been reactions to this so-called confessional poetry. The Language Poets began writing in the '70s a poetry devoid of apparent meaning. Their object was to suppress assumed meaning, and therefore cliché—the obliteration of meaningfulness. One way of achieving this was by using certain High Modernist techniques practiced by the 20th Century avant-garde—such as William Burroughs's "cut-up" method—to disrupt conventional narrative and syntax. Another way was the removal of the self—a deconstruction of what language poets uniformly believed to be the false consciousness of individualism that has evolved in the Euro-American poetic traditon. To avoid "communication," they focused on language as an end in itself, so that representations of the self in poetry are replaced by chains of self-referential language, a practice showing the influence of Gertrude Stein.

The Neo-Narrative movement called for a return to narrative poetry, telling a story without any side commentary, the poet's thoughts or feelings. Finally, a whole umbrella began to be applied to all of the movements that arose after WWII, Post-Modernism. But this term can be defined in several different ways, as we shall see, and it often depends on who is using it and what poets are being discussed.

Perhaps out of the umbrella term Post-Modernism will come the new strategy and tactic for the poetry of the 21st Century. Exactly what that will be, I'm not sure, but I think, in our own way, without realizing it, we are beginning to do just that. Walt Whitman and Emily Dickinson still stand as the greatest of all modernists, from whom we have still much to learn. Furthermore, as poets, we need not feel compelled to follow any one school or movement. Each approach offers tools we can use to fashion writing that has the human breadth, the cosmic depth, and the poetic height necessary for work that will be true and lasting.

This study guide is meant to be used in conjunction with a few basic anthologies of modern poetry. I have tried to include poems here that are infrequently anthologized, but often I couldn't avoid the more famous examples. This study guide combines what you'd find in an anthology, a literary history, and a work of critical comment, but it cannot replace any one of those. I think it essential that the student go to the anthologies that give substantial samples of the poets' best works, and from there to the individual volumes of poetry by the poets themselves. Nevertheless, The best and most inclusive anthologies are:

The Norton Anthology of Modern Poetry, *ed. Elman & O'Clair*
I jokingly refer to this as "the phone book." It's about as comprehensive an anthology as you're going to get, but what makes it even better are the biographies and critical essays that precede each poet's selection.

The Vintage Anthology of Contemporary Poetry, *ed. McClatchey.*
This one covers the more recent period in American poetry, and consequently includes a great many poets not found in the Norton. It too has biographies of the poets and some critical remarks, but nowhere near as extensive as the Norton book.

Three anthologies that include the work of many Language poets and poets who have tended to steer clear of either Confessional or traditional verse are:
   Postmodern American Poetry, *edited by Paul Hoover (Norton)*
   From the Other Side of the Century: *A New American Poetry: 1960-1990,*
      edited by Doug Messerli (Sun & Moon Press)
   American Poetry Since 1950, *edited by Eliot Weinberger (Marsilio Publishers).*

I would also make sure you have a copy of three excellent collections:
   Stand-up Poetry, *ed Charles Webb (Cal State U. Press, Lng Beach)*
   The Maverick Poets, *ed. Steve Kowit (Gorilla Press)*

Before we launch into the modern era, however, I think it important to explore the background from which it sprang. This will be helpful when we get to the modern poems, which often use imagery and references from classical work. How far back shall we go? Well, one logical starting point is the beginning of English poetry written in a language that is close to our own—the work of Elizabethan poets of the late 16th century. We could get an earful of Shakespeare & a few of his contempories like Christopher Marlowe and John Webseter, then sample a few 17th & 18th Century poets such as John Milton, William Blake, Christopher Smart, and Thomas Gray. Following that, we might take in the Romantic poets of the 19th century—Wordsworth, Keats, Shelley, etc., on up to Tennyson—to see how different modern poetry was from an English verse that had stayed much the same for four centuries. Someone in Shakespeare's day could have easily read Tennyson's *Ulysses*, but Eliot's "Prufrock" would have seemed strange and somewhat incomprehensible.

Or we could go further back than that to the beginnings of Old and Middle English verse in poems like *Beowulf* and Chaucer's *Canterbury Tales*. After all, we live in a time when spoken and written English is undergoing a major transformation, and in those poems we can see the same vital impulse at work.

But why confine ourselves to English. The revolution we see in literature in this century, in which the written work reflects the inclusion of a developing vernacular and new speech patterns is a recurring pattern in all literatures. Writers such as Chaucer in 14th England and Dante in late 13th century Italy chose to write their greatest work in the vernacular of their time—not in the Latin that dominated the verse of the Middle Ages. Dante's decision to use Italian instead of Latin was a bold choice at the time, a daring choice considering the fact that those guardians of Latin literature could easily have dismissed his great poem.

The period from the decline of the Roman Empire to the 12th century renaissance was not as rich in great poetic achievements as what came before and after. Latin poems written during this time were usually composed by monks or clerics, and with the great decline in learning of the Dark Ages and the Early Middle Ages, poetry lost a vital edge that characterized the great poems of Greece and Rome. If we're going to go back, if we're going to look at Dante and Chaucer, and one or two poets of the Middle Ages, hell—we might as well go further back and touch on a few of the great poets of the Roman era, Virgil and Ovid—and what the hell—let's not stop now, we're on a roll—we might as well dip into the great Greek poetry and literature that in some ways is more modern than anything since. The epic of the *Odyssey* and the story of Oedipus and Antigone contain themes and issues that inform our time with a psychological truth that is as exciting as our action movies and as revealing as that confessional impulse found in both poems and the sleaziest of television talk shows

But the real place to start is at the beginning, with the oldest piece of literature in the Western world,* Book XI of the *Odyssey* by the blind poet, Homer. As Virgil said to Dante in the *Inferno*, "let us go, then."

* Of course, the oldest surviving epic poem is the ancient Sumerian tale of ***Gilgamesh*** (c. 2000-3000 BC), written in Akkadian on clay tablets in a complex cuneiform alphabet. It's the story of a great king and his doomed friend Enkidu. Written not much later than the invention of true writing, the tale was passed on to the Babylonians, who made it their national epic. It recounts the exploits of the hero Gilgamesh, the son of the goddess Ninsun and a mortal, priest of the city of Uruk. He attempts to reconcile himself to death and journeys to the underworld to bring his friend back. But after searching the world over, he realizes that he is unable to avoid death. The hero's quest for immortality—a necessarily failed quest—is one that has recurred in the literature of every age. The story has often been described as a revolt against death, but its greater themes are the nature of love, friendship, and loyaly. The poem is at once a dramatic narrative, yet is also striking for its emotional, mythic, and philosophic content.

> The one who saw the abyss I will make the land know;
> of him who knew all, let me tell the whole story
> . . . in the same way . . .
> [as] the lord of wisdom, he who knew everything, Gilgamesh
> who saw things secret, opened the place hidden,
> and carried back word of the time before the Flood —
> he travelled the road, exhausted, in pain,
> and cut his works into a stone tablet.

Many ancient poetic narratives were written about the creation and the flood that in some resepcts bore a striking resemblance to the oral narratives that were eventually incorporated into the Hebrew Torah. The Babylonian poem known as ***Enuma Elish***, which seems to have been recited once a year (if not oftener) contained enough parallels to the first two chapters of the Hebrew Bible to have become known rather loosely as "the Babylonian Genesis." It was recovered by Austen Henry Layard in 1849 (in fragmentary form) in the ruined Library of Ashurbanipal at Nineveh (Mosul, Iraq), and published by George Smith in 1876. The Enûma Eliš has about a thousand lines and is recorded in Old Babylonian on seven clay tablets, each holding between 115 and 170 lines of text. Most of Tablet V has never been recovered, but aside from this lacuna the text is almost complete. A duplicate copy of Tablet V has been found in Sultantepe, ancient Huzirina, located in Turkey.

The Enûma Eliš exists in various copies from Babylon and Assyria. The version from Ashurbanipal's library dates to the 7th century BCE. The composition of the text probably dates to the Bronze Age, to the time of Hammurabi or perhaps the early Kassite era (roughly 18th to 16th centuries BCE), although some scholars favour a later date of ca. 1100 BCE. The first tablet begins:

> When the sky above was not named,
> And the earth beneath did not yet bear a name,
> And the primeval Apsû, who begat them,

And chaos, Tiamat, the mother of them both,
Their waters were mingled together,
And no field was formed, no marsh was to be seen;
When of the gods none had been called into being.

The discovery of the Rosetta Stone in 1799 and its deciphering by Jean-François Champollion, which led to the "cracking" of the code of Egyptian hieroglyphics, opened up four thouand years of Egyptian literature, of which the world had been ignorant before that time.

The written record is almost continuous from 3700 to 200 B.C. *The Book of the Dead* is generally considered the most significant of ancient Egyptian writings, preserved in about 2000 papyrus rolls which contain prayers, hymns, confessions, etc. The various chapters range from *c*. 4266 to *c*. 2000 B.C. Its purpose is to tell men how to obtain eternal life.

The oldest sacred literature of India is found in the four Vedas ("Books of Knowledge") written as poetry about 1400 B.C. Their two great epics are the *Mahabharata* and the *Ramayana* (both begun about 500 B.C.) The *Mahabharata*, nearly eight times as long as the *Iliad* and the *Odyssey* combined, concerns the battle between those representing good and those representing evil. Among it's 200,000 lines and eighteen books are two notable interpolations: the *Bhagavad-Gita* ("divine song"), a long, didactic poem (18 cantos) in which Krishna discusses philosophy and the good life with Arjuna (one of the Pandavas representing the principle of good), and *Nala and Damayanti*, a love story concerning conjugal patience and fidelity.

The literature of ancient China is extensive and includes almost every known form, including the philosophy of **Lao-tzu** (b. 604 B.C.) and **Confucius** or **Kun'g Fu-tzu** (551-479 B.C.) Considered "the founder of Chinese literature," Confucius wrote numerous books, including *The Analects*, the *Ta Hio*, and *The Unwavering Middle* (or *The Unwobbling Pivot*). Following the death of Confucius there flourished a school of poets noted for passionate expression, irregular meter, allusiveness, and allegory. There was some rhyme in early Chinese poetry (before 600 A.D.), but thereafter the seven-syllable lines was employed. **Mei-Sheng** (d. 140 B.C.) is famous for five-syllable verse and love lyrics; **Liu Ling** (3rd century A.D.) was one of the Seven Sages of the Bamboo Grove, a hard-drinking school of poets (perhaps Bukowski was one of the Seven Sages of the Asphalt Groove); **T'ao Ch'ien** (365-427 A.D.) wrote technically brilliant poems full of strong emotion. He resigned a magistracy because he could no longer "crook the hinges of his back for five pecks of rice a day." **Wang Chi** (7th century A.D.) was known as the Five-Bottle Scholar, and one of his noteworthy poems tells of a visit to "Drunk-Land." But this is too extensive a subject to cover here.

The scope of this book will be Western literature, and more specifically, poetry. We'll start with Homer, the blind poet of the *Illiad* and *Odyssey*, move through the lyric poets of early Greece, the epic and lyric poets of Latin Rome, then follow that line through the Dark and Middle Ages, where both Secular Latin poetry and Christian Latin poetry vie for prominence, as both eventually merge into the poetry of the Renaissance, the Enlightenment, the Romantic Age, and finally modern poetry of the 20th century. This is not meant to imply that the poetry of India, China, etc., are not worthy of study; they are.

Ancient China was an empire that lasted longer than Rome, and which produced great art and literature. But ancient Greece and Rome have a special claim on the West, because our own culture has grown directly out of them. Thus, from the vantage point of the 20th century, especially for English and American poets, our starting point is Homer and the poetry of the ancient Greeks.

But even though the Sumerian literature, especially the *Epic of Gilgamesh*, did not have a direct influence on Western poetry (except how parts of it found their way into the Hebrew Bible), it seems fitting that now is as good a time as any to discuss it, before moving on to Homer. In some ways, the same might be said for the Hebrew Bible, whose impact did not come until a few centuries after Christ, but was composed in parts over a period of 500 to 900 years (depending on one's theory of when certain books of the Bible were composed). So I will treat *The Epic of Gilgamesh* as a "food for thought" first, before we look at Homer's epics, and I will deal with the various books of the Bible around the time of their composition, even though their greatest impact did not occur until the Middle Ages.

Food for Thought

THE CONJURING WORD: THE EPIC OF GILGAMESH

This Sumerian poem about friendship, death and Gilgamesh's descent into the underworld touches upon a fundamental theme, the mystery of death and the search for eternal life. Friendship, death, and a descent into the underworld: sounds like a writer's life. Poor arrogant pig-headed warrior king Gilgamesh loses his friend and shadow-self Enkidu, whose life the gods took because Gilgamesh spurned the goddess Ishtar's advances. Maybe it was the way he said no. He called her "a back door which does not keep out the wind; pitch which fouls the man who touches it; a water-skin which leaks over the man who carries it; a shoe which throws its owner down." Then, as if that wasn't enough, he pointed out her fickleness:

> What lover did you ever love constantly?
> Come! I will enumerate your lovers:
> For Tammuz, the lover of your youth,
> you have brought about repeated weeping year upon year;
> You used to love the pied allalu-bird,
> yet you struck him and broke his wing.
> And he stands in the woods and cries, "My wing!"
> You used to love the lion, perfect in strength,
> yet you have dug innumerable pits for him.
> You used to love the horse, renowned in battle,
> yet you have assigned to him the whip, the goad and the lash.
> You used to love the herdsman,
> who daily slaughtered kids for you,
> yet him you struck and turned into a wolf,
> so that his own shepherd boys chase him,

and his dogs snap at his shanks.
You would love me too,
and then throw me like a piece of meat to the wolf.

So Ishtar gets the gods to show Gilgamesh who's boss, and they take Enkidu's life. Gilgamesh, overcome with grief and despair, heads into the Netherworld to bring Enkidu back, and to discover the secret of immortality. He finds Utanapistim, the survivor of the Great Flood, who was granted eternal life by the Gods. Utanapishtim cannot give him the secret, but as Gilgamesh is leaving, down-trodden and despairing, Utanapishtim takes pity on him. "Even if you were given immortality," he says, "you'd be unable to bear it." Utanapishtim challenges Gilgamesh to remain awake for six days and seven nights, but as soon as Gilgamesh sits down, "Sleep wafts over him like a mist." Upon waking, he acknowledges that he had utterly failed in his test, and accepts death as his lot:

The Snatcher has hold of my flesh,
Death sits in my bedchamber,
And wherever I set my feet there is Death.

Utanapishtim's wife takes pity on Gilgamesh and tells her husband to give Gilgamesh some reward for his wearisome journey. He's given a plant with thorns, found beneath the sea, a plant called "the old man becomes young," which restores to an ageing man his youth and virility. But on his return journey, Gilgamesh foolishly sets the plant down by the bank of a pool. While he's skinny-dipping, a snake comes along and takes it away, shedding its skin as it slithers off. Gilgamesh sits down and weeps, realizing there's no way he can escape Death, it comes for all. When he returns, he finds his only consolation in the great wall he built around the city of Erech, the fields and lands belonging to the Great Temple of the patron goddess Ishtar.

Gilgamesh is the oldest work of epic literature in the world, written at least a millennium before the first books of the Bible were written, a millennium even before Homer's *Odyssey*, yet for more than two thousand years all traces of it were lost. If you were to mention Gilgamesh to Homer or Virgil or Ovid or Dante or Shakespeare or Goethe, they'd say "Gilgamesh Who?" It wasn't until 1843 that the first fragments of Sumerian writing were discovered among the ruins of Nineveh, and many of the clay tablets weren't restored, much less deciphered or translated, for several decades afterwards. (Actually, parts of it are still being recovered and deciphered.)

In the last few decades, numerous translations and renderings have appeared, each one trying to find the right balance between the literal cuniform meaning and the nuances of sound and rhythms. To read even a few different versions is to fall into the netherworld of *The Epic of Gilgamesh* and the Sumerian and Akkadian names:

ANU, the sky god; (the original goodness gracious Great Ball of Fire).
EA, the cleverest of the gods, god of the intellect, creation, wisdom, magic, and medicine, as well as god of the subterranean ocean, often called the Great Deep; (don't mess with Ea!)
ENLIL, Lord of the Winds; (ate too many beans)
ENNUGI, sheriff of the gods; (but who shot the sheriff!)

ISHTAR, queen of heaven; (a J-Lo Knock-off)
NAMTAR, Decider of Fate and Gatekeeper of the Underworld; (the muscular guy outside the Roxy)
NINURTA, Lord of the Earth; (great grandfather of Darth Vadar).
SHAMASH, the sun god; (sells hot dogs at the beach);
S N, Moon God of Fertility; (fuckin' A!);
TAMMUZ, lover of Ishtar; (thinks he's a big shot, has rebirth in his veins).
URSHANABI, Boatman of the Underworld; (also works the Ferris Wheel at Magic Mountain)
UTANAPISHTIM, immortal survivor of the Great Flood; (still has his life-preserver & flares)
LUGALBANDA, father of Gilgamesh; (still can't work the remote)
HUMBABA, the monstrous guardian of the Ceder Forest (also works the door at the Whiskey)
SHIDURI, Goddess of Brewing and Wisdom, who keeps a tavern at the edge of the world; (well-drinks at half price);
SUMUQAN, God of the Wilderness; (always carries a Swiss knife and snake-bite kit);
AYA, Goddess of Dawn; (knows my Uncle Louie);
BELET-SERI, Lady of the Desert, official scribe of the underworld (watch what you say, she's taking notes.)

Each translation of the Epic brings a different viewpoint and poetry to the experience, a different understanding of this ancient and complex work of literature:

One translation by Stephen Mitchell (1992) lies under my pillow,
another translation by David Ferry (1992) sits on my desk,
another rendering by Maureen Kovacs (1989) is in the car,
another by John Gardner (1984) in the living room,
and another by Herbert Mason (1970) in the kitchen,
one by Andrew George (1999) next to the bed,
and one by Danny Jackson in my underwear.

In my dreams, I meet up with Urshanabi, boatman of the underworld, and say to him, "Take me to Gilgamesh, through the Cedar Forest and the Heavenly Bull and all the other Monsters of the Deep. Take me to the poem that speaks of Gilgamesh's sad and futile journey to find the secret of eternal life."

There is so much about this poem that is compelling. Many 20th century poets have become obsessed with this poem including Rilke, Gregory Corso, and Charles Olson. I just got an email from David Booth who admitted that he too became obsessed with it when he was in college, and still has his tattered, well-annotated John Gardner translation of the Standard Version, the one written in Babylonian in 1300 BC by Sin-Leqi Unninni, which he based on the Akkadian version written in 1800 B.C., which was based on the Sumerian versions written down somewhere between 2500 and 2100 B.C. Rilke declared in 1916, reading one of the earliest of translations in German, that it was "stupendous!" He went on to write: "I have immersed myself in these truly gigantic fragments and experienced measures and forms that belong with the supreme works that the conjuring Word has ever produced." I like that, "The Conjuring Word." A good title for a book.

A few decades after Rilke first read the German translation, there appeared the first useful English translation by R. Campbell Thompson (1930), but Corso and Olsen were most likely using Herbert Mason's 1970 translation, each based on the discovery, restoration, and decipherment of more of those clay tablets. Stephen Mitchell's recent translation, which is quite good, has very illuminating notes, and is the one I'd recommend for first-timers. Mitchell has also done a fine verse translation of the *Book of Job*, the *Bhagavad Gita*, and the *Selected Poetry of Rilke*, so he really does a great job with Gilgamesh (by the way, for those of you who read Philip Roth's *The Great American Novel*, you might remember that the main character was named Gil Gamesh. Hmmmmmm, hint hint. One can compare John Gardner's 1984 masterful rendition of the Babylonian Standard Version first written (or, might one say, cuniformed) by the Akkadian poet S n-Leqi-Unninni in 1300 B.C., not to mention Maureen Kovacs 1989 translation (the one on my desk), David Ferry's 1992 rendering in free verse, (the one in my car), Benjamin Foster's 2001 edition (the one in the living room), and a nifty French translation by Jean Bott ro, *L' pop de Gilgames: Le grande homme qui ne voulait pas mourir* (The Great [or tall] Man Who Didn't Want to Die), and a German version by Albert Schott, *Das Gilgamesch-Epos, neu herausgegeben von Wolfram von Soden*, and the most recent and monumental two-volume edition by Andrew George who gives us both the original cuniform and current translation of all three versions:

> 1) the five original Sumerian tales of Gilgamesh, cuniformed on clay tablets around 2100 BC;
> 2) the Akkadian compilation done 400 years later by an unknown poet, often called the Old Babylonian version;
> 3) and the Babylonian Standard Version which was written by Sin-Leqi-Unninni in 1300 BC.

(Sometimes, S n-Leqi-Unninni functioned as an editor, following the older version line for line, but more often than not, he embellished, added, and rewrote passages, functioning as an original poet himself. Much of what he did has the vividness and density of great art.) Andrew George's two volume set (2003) is available from Oxford University Press for $500, but there's a nifty penguin paperback version not as complete or as up-to-date as the 2003 two-volume edition, but it's pretty affordable. $10 vs $500.

The story of the discovery of Gilgamesh—you couldn't make this stuff up—reads like a tale right out of *The Thousand and One Nights*. When Henry Layard was on his way to Ceylon in 1844, he heard that there were antiquities buried in the mounds of what is now the city of Mosul, so with his assistant Hormuzd Rassam he began excavations the following year (suffice it to say, he never got to Ceylon). These mounds turned out to contain the ruined palaces of Nineveh, the ancient capital of Assyria, including what was left of the library of the last great Assyrians king, Ashurbanipal, grandson to Sennacherib, who ruled 700 years before Christ. Image if he hadn't valued his artistic and intellectual legacy and not collected all those ancient Sumerian and Akkadian clay tablets! Most of what we have we owe to Ashurbanipal. We take for granted how the great works of literature often hang by a thread in terms of their survival. Ninety-percent of Sappho's poems were discovered in the 19th century preserved on manuscript pages used to line someone's coffin. Lucretius' ancient Latin poem written a century before Christ, *On the*

Nature of Things, had been almost entirely lost to history for more than a thousand years and probably would have been lost forever were it not for Poggio Bracciolini, the greatest book hunter of the Renaissance, who in the winter of 1417 plucked a very old manuscript off a dusty shelf in a remote monastery, saw with excitement what he had discovered, and ordered that it be copied. The book's return to circulation changed the course of history, shaping the thought of Galileo and Freud, Darwin and Einstein, and—in the hands of Thomas Jefferson—left its trace on the Declaration of Independence. Were it not for this short, genial man in his thirties, that last copy of Lucretius' work may well have been lost forever. Poggio, we who are at the mercy of Amazon.com, salute you.

Anyway, what Layard and Rassam found when the roof of the library caved in were endless corridors and seventy rooms lined with two full miles' worth of carved reliefs, along with tens of thousands of clay tablets inscribed with the curious, and then undeciphered wedge-shaped cuniform script, and over twenty-five thousand of these tablets were shipped back to the British Museum. Remember, these tablets were not all intact, most were in fragments, so we're talking hundreds of thousands of fragments along with some that were intact. Most of these tablets contained accounting information, business and trading transactions, letters from one king's envoy to another, and some historial accounts—what one would expect in the highly organized bureaucratic society going back to the Third Dynasty of Ur, which endured for centuries. Today, there must be hundreds of thousands of these clay tablets in museums, the majority of which are still unrestored, undeciphered and unpublished. Some of the clay tablets still bear the palm and fingerprints of the scribes who were molding the wet clay in preparation for documentation and baking. These clay tablets recorded almost every economic and administrative information possible: Documentation seemed obsessive. One tablet contains an exact accounting of the number of fish (2,740 of them) delivered as food for the temple dogs. Two sheep, dead from natural causes, were regarded as a matter requiring record. There were even documents recording that there was nothing to record. Sounds like an old diary entry: "Dear Diary, nothing happened today, nothing happened yesterday, nothing will probably happen tomorrow. Life goes on one dreary day after another."

And among the mass of these clay tablets, about ten percent of them contained poems, hymns, myths, lamentations, proverbs, moral instructions, incantations, historical narratives, folk tales, riddles, snippets of cultural history, travelogues, lists of kings since the beginning of time, school essays, and literary epics, all written to instruct, entertain, or mystify. These texts show that well before the middle of the Third Millenium writing was already being applied far beyond the mere keeping of records for which it had been originally intended. It was the beginning of creative literature. *The Epic of Gilgamesh* was written out on eleven of those tablets (well, twelve, but that's another story, both figuratively and literally). So out of those thousands of fragments, from hundreds of thousands of clay tablets, first they had to be pieced together. There was no color coding so you'd know which piece went with which tablet. At least with a puzzle you get in a box, you know there's only one puzzle. This was like hundreds of thousands of puzzles, each puzzle composed of dozens of pieces. Imagine trying to find eleven needles out of one hundred thousand needles in a haystack the size of Mt. Everest, and gluing those eleven needles together.

This is really mind-boggling when you think of it. Imagine buying a steamer trunk full of puzzle pieces, only there's no picture on them, they're just puzzle pieces with funny markings on them, those curious wedge-shaped symbols. Since you don't know what they mean, it's rather hard piecing anything together, other than by shape. Easier to reconstruct a copy of *War and Peace* that's been fed through a shredder! Out of tens of thousands of puzzle pieces, cradled in the crates and drawers of the British Musuem's massive collection, you've got to find those that make up the eleven tablets of Gilgamesh. But wait, you don't even know there *is* such a collection of tablets comprising the epic of Gilgamesh. You've never even *heard* of Gilgamesh! Or for that matter, of any Sumerian literature. There are many books of ancient and classical literature that are mentioned or summarized in other books of those periods, so even when we don't have the book itself, at least we know it existed, what others thought of it, even perhaps a summary of it. But there is not one mention of the epic of this Sumerian king in any other source, so it's loss to succeeding generations was comlpete. As a matter of fact, until the discoveries of those caly tablets, we didn't even know there was a Sumerian literature. For decades those fragments and clay tablets, looking much like terra-cotta roofing tiles, sat in the British Museum, about as mysterious and curious to human beings as a few pages from Einstein's paper on "The Special Theory of Relativity" would be to a monkey.

Just as the Sumerians were superceded by the Akkadians, the Akkadians were soon superceded by the Babylonians, who were eventually conquered by the Persians. So many of those clay tablets were copies of original documents written in Akkadian, and many of the Akkadian tablets were copies of Sumerian. The Babylonians themselves made catalogues of their literature, some items of which they believed to be "from before the Flood." Some were attributed to specific authors, either legendary humans or actual people. Other texts had a more unusual origin: thus, we find one ascribed directly to the god Ea, and another is said to have been written "at the mouth of a horse."

When the formidable Sir Henry Creswicke Rawlinson, the original Indiana Jones, came upon the scene, those thousands of fragments were sitting undeciphered in the British Museum. Rawlinson had been knighted after a distinguished military career in India, Persia, and Iraq (where ancient Sumer, Akkadia, and Babylonia existed in the land between the two rivers, the Tigris and the Euphrates, thus the meaning of the term Mesopotamia, Land Between Two Rivers). It was Rawlinson who made the decisive breakthrough in the decipherment of cuniform writing thanks to a combination of Indy Jones type insight and sheer physical daring. He was famous for feats of strength and endurance, making great journeys on horseback, such as 750 miles within 150 consecutive hours. He was distinguished as much by his intellectual passion, learning Eastern languages during his tour of duty at the Persian court and could recite long passages of Persian poetry from memory. While in Persia he learned of a trilingual text, carved on a cliff three hundred feet above the valley floor, purported to be an inscription detailing Persian King Darius's invasion of Babylon in the 6th century B.C. It was pretty hard reading the inscription from the ground below—the only access to the carvings, after a harrowing climb up an almost sheer rock face, was a narrow, crumbling ledge maybe 18 inches wide. So Henry Creswicke "Indiana Jones" Rawlinson scales the cliff wall carrying a ladder, which he perches on the ledge below the inscription, climbs the ladder, and with the left arm he balances the ladder, with the right hand he holds a pencil, and proceeds to copy the inscription into a notebook held in his left hand. He said he was so intent on the inscription, he lost all sense of danger. Now comes the cool part. The inscription was written in three different languages: Sumerian, a language no one could understand, Akkadian (a dialect of Babylonian), also undecipherable, and Old Persian, each text carved side by side, very much like the Egyptian Rosetta Stone, which was deciphered a decade earlier by Jean-Francois Champillon, who was able to decipher hieroglyphics because he could read the other two parallel texts written in Greek and an older Egyptian language. Champollion worked backwards from the Greek, and voila, he was able to decipher the hieroglyphics, which he gradually began to reconstruct and published his translation in 1824. And Rawlinson figured that maybe he could do the same with this trilingual text written in three languages, including Old Persian.

Rawlinson could read Old Persian. It took like 15 years of steady work before he could declare that he had deciphered most of the inscription, partly because of his knowledge of Old Persian, but also because Akkadian bore a close relationship to Hebrew and Arabic. "Dog," for instance, is keleb in Hebrew, kalb in Arabic, and kalbum in Akkadian. To make matters more difficult, the intricacy of the Akkadian cuneiform system was represented by over six hundred different characters. Rawlinson concluded that they weren't pictorgraphic, but they certainly weren't basic sounds, like our current alphabet. They were logographic, or syllabic, and since Mesopotamian scribes didn't leave spaces between words or supply any kind of punctuation, Rawlinson spent years making charts of signs, looking for patterns, making informed guesses when he had to. A great deal of trial-and-error, made even more difficult by the fact that the Sumerians spoke a language competely unrelated to any other known language. But the Akkadians used the Sumerian cuniform system to express themselves in their own language, just as we do today, using Roman letters, not to write Latin, but to write English (and French, Spanish, Italian, Rumanian, etc.). So Rawlinson's work was a start, but it was Rawlinson's assistant, George Smith, who decades later, discovered and deciphered the first of the tablets from the Epic of Gilgamesh.

George Smith happened to be working on one of the tablets, which he had painstakingly pieced together from among those twenty-five thousand fragments, and realized that he was reading a portion of the Chaldean account of the Deluge and the Baylonian Noah. George realized that he was the first man to read these after more than two thousand years of oblivion. He was so excited that he jumped up and ran around the room, and to the astonishment of those who were there, began to take off his clothes piece by piece, flinging them into the air. Whether he got down to his skivvies, or his birthday suit, the account doesn't say. But if he did end up running around stark naked, it would be fitting, emulating Gilgamesh's friend, the wild-man Enkidu.

As more tablets were deciphered, more complete translation appeared over the years, and even now only about 75% of the epic is complete, many parts still missing, and many passages and lines illegible or missing. But when comparing the different translations (some should rather be called versions, or renderings), I especially enjoy comparing certain key passages, especially the different translations of the erotic and sexual passages, seeing how different translators from different times tried to convey the explicit passages into more appropriate English, including Thompson's (1930) choice to translate any offending passages into German or Latin (god forbid he would have to write those words in English!) and he even supplied a footnote that the lines in question were too inappropriate for the cultured reader (I guess those Sumerians were not too cultured).

Mitchell's version finds a nice balance between explicit imagery and suggestive eroticism when he renders the scene where the sacred prostitute (some just call her the temple whore) entices the wild-man Enkidu:

> "She stripped off her robe and lay there naked,
> with her legs apart, touching herself.
> Enkidu saw her and warily approached.
> He drew close, Shamhat touched him on the thigh,
> touched his penis, and put him inside her.
> She used her love-arts, she took his breath
> with her kisses, held nothing back, and showed him
> what a woman is. For seven days
> he stayed erect and made love with her.
> He knew that his mind had somehow grown larger,
> he knew things now that an animal can't know."

But it can also be quite comic, the lengths some translators go to keep the description from bordering on the pornographic, and since I don't read cuniform, who's to know if "fuck" and "vagina" that Gardner uses in his translation is a more accurate translation than "sexual intercourse" and "between her legs," or as another editor wrote, "laid on top of her" and "her female mystery," or if the cuniform is saying she "spread her legs" or "spread her vulva," two quite different and distinct images from other more recent translations. Maybe Foster's version (2001) is correct, maybe those wedge-shaped symbols really said "she laid bare her charms." Who's to say? Next time I need a good pick-up line, I'll try, "Hiya beautiful, what say we go back to my mud-hut and you can lay bare your charms."

But what really is making a profound impression on me is the fact that this is the first great work of literature ever written, two thousand years before the the the ILIAD, a thousand years before the first books of the Bible, nearly five thousand years before Lincoln's Gettysburg Address. And it occured at the very beginning of the invention of writing itself, the use of cuniform (those wedge-shaped symbols) inscribed on clay tablets that were just discovered 150 years ago and not really begun to be deciphered until the early 20th century, meaning that the poem of Gilgamesh had been lost to history for over three thousand years—think of that! And there is little doubt that hundreds of thousands more of those clay tablets lie buried in the ground, awaiting a future excavator, and future decipherers and future translators. Is there a chance we'll discover another ancient epic on a literary par with GILGAMESH?

I mean, let's face it, one of the outstanding contributions of this century to the humanities is the recovery, restoration, translations, and interpretation of the Sumerian literary documents, the majority of which were composed from about 2500 to 1800 B.C. So far, we got 20 myths, 9 epic tales, 100 hymns, 12 disputations and school essays, a dozen collections of proverbs and fables, all totaling some 28,000 lines. And the vast majority of those lines are arranged in poetic form, characterized primarily by the skillful use of repetition and parallelism——Read and Sung, anyone?

There was nothing quaint about these poetic forms. Check this out, from several clay tablets. each one about the size of a standard sheet of typewriter paper on which the scribe divided the text into twelve columns, six hundred lines of a Sumerian heroic poem called "Enmerker and the Lord of Aratta," told in a style that is characteristic of epic poetry the world over: repetition and parallel lines, or as we say, "Read & Sung." And in this epic poem, there's a remarkable passage, which, if correctly interpreted, informs us that Enmerker, the lord of Kullab, was in the opinion of the poet, the first to write on clay tablets, and he did so because his messenger seemed "heavy of mouth," and unable to repeat the message, probably because it was so long. Eventually, after its discovery, and then after decades of sitting in the Istanbul Museum of the Ancient Orient for nearly a century, the text of this epic "cuniformed" across twenty tablets and fragments was finally restored by the famous Sumeriologist Samuel Noah Kramer, who copied them in 1946 and published a translation in 1952. Here's a "read & sung" passage that will raise the hairs on the back of your neck– no simpering whimpering fools these Sumerian poets:

> May your groves be heaped up like dust,
> May your clay bricks return to their abyss,
> May they become clay bricks cursed by Enki,
> May your trees return to their forests,
> May they become trees cursed by Ninildu.
> Your slaughtered oxen—
> May you slaughter your wives instead, Your butchered sheep—
> May you slaughter your children instead,
> Your poor— May they be forced to drown their precious children,
> Agade, may your palace built with joyful heart,
> be turned into a depressing ruin,
> May the fox who haunts the ruined mounds glide his tail,
> May your canal-boat towpaths grow nothing but weeds,
> May your chariot-roads grow nothing but the "wailing plant,"
> May no human being walk because of the wild-goats vermin,
> snake, and mountain scorpion,
> May your plains where grew the heart-soothing plants,
> grow nothing but the "reed of tears,"
> Agade, instead of your sweet-flowing water,
> May the bitter water flow,
> May dust be heaped upon your lives,
> May you not find in any city a good dwelling place,
> May you not find in any city a good sleeping-place.

But when we come to the epic of *Gilgamesh*, we're talking about one of the great works of literature lost for nearly three thousand years, like, in 1850 they're excavating in Nippur and the roof of some building under layers of earth caves in and they discover thousands—hundreds of thousands clay tablets, most of them broken in pieces, and on them something even more undecipherable than hieroglyphics– and the decipherment of those wedge-shaped symbols takes nearly 50 years and is still going on. And tablet VII of the Gilgamesh Epic contains the story of the Deluge, the Flood, written at least a thousand years before the Biblical version. The Noah character in Gilgamesh is named Utanapishtim, and he's the one Gilgamesh seeks out in the Netherworld to ask him for the secret of immortality.

I tried to imagine what I would do if there were no such thing as writing. Sure, we could tell each other stories and remember tales of heroic deeds and stuff, myths and legends and lamentations and proverbs and stuff, all that "oral" literature passed down from one generation to the next, and maybe some of it forgotten and not passed down, but there was no way to make marks on papyrus or wet clay tablets, so either you memorized it or it was forgotten. So at some point someone had to set in motion this idea of making marks that someone else could decipher and "read." What if I were that someone, sitting in my mud-hut and trying to think of how I could construct a system that would represent my thoughts and feelings? Like, say I wanted to write something in my "journal." What would that journal even be, a clay tablet, a piece of dried sheep skin, the rock face of a cliff wall high enough to read? Like, where would I start? I could draw a picture of an ox and that would mean ox. But a picture for every possible word?!?! I'd have to learn like thousands of pictures. I mean, think about this. Forget what you know about the alphabet and all that. How would you begin to figure this out? Would I use pictures, which they did for centuries, called pictographic writing. That's how the cuneiform script actually began, each sign was a picture of one or more concrete objects and represented a word whose meaning was identical with, or closely related to, the object pictured. Imagine the number of signs you'd have to learn to say "Meet me by the river where the big boulder sits on the land across from the tree with the broken trunk and bring a loaf of rye bread." Yeah, granted, the Sumerians scribes learned to simplify the signs, but still, we're talking at least hundreds of signs the scribe would have to learn. Pictographic symbols do not represent "sounds." To represent sounds, you'd have to break down the sounds into units of speech, syllables perhaps. But what about pictures representing syllables? How about that. A logographic system of writing, in which I'd have to figure out the hundreds of different syllable sounds and represent them with a specific mark of some kind. As a scribe, I'd have to learn hundreds, maybe a thousand sounds. A scribe would be treated almost like a nuclear physicist. But how would I write I love you, or Happy Birthday, or Take me to your leader? Someone had to go into his laboratory with test tubes and bunsen burners and magic potions and different colored viles of magical kaka and come up with something simpler, something everybody could learn to use.

We take the alphabet so much for granted, but even that is a late invention, when you consider the use of hieroglyphics, cuneiform, and phonetic and syllabic symbols, often numbering in the hundreds if not thousands, which were used to represent speech for over a thousand years. Becoming a royal scribe was an occupation akin to studying physics, only a rare few could go to the eddubas, or "tablet schools," to learn hundreds if not thousands of ways to represent language. Schoolboys sat at their tables or benches and practiced "cuniforming" or "hieroglyphiking" from sunrise to sunset, and if they made mistakes, were often whipped with a cane and made to stand in the corner. Yep, we know this because one of those cuniform clay tablets discovered in the palace library of Ashurbanipal whose roof caved in, when finally pieced together like a puzzle, turned out to be an "essay" written by a young school boy, describing his punishments, and how he got his father to invite the teacher over for dinner so he could get a better grade. The clay tablet is even signed! Nabi-Enlil. The essay was only recently pieced together from seventeen clay tablets and fragments going back some 3,700 years, and these were probably copies, its original composition may go back several centuries earlier. Talk about writing in your journal! Wrote Nabi-Enlil when his father asked what he did in "tablet school": "I recited my tablet, ate my lunch, prepared by new tablet, wrote it, finished it, then they assigned me my written work, then school was dismissed."

Little did Nabi-Enlil dream that his literary vignette on school life as he knew it would be resurrected and restored some four thousand years later by a 20th century professor in an American university. It must have been a popular essay in ancient days, as can be seen from the fact that twenty-one copies, in various states of preservations, have come to light: thirteen are in the Univeristy Museum of Philadephia, seven are in the Museum of the Ancient Orient in Istanbul, and one is in the Louvre in Paris (I got to see it when I was there in September).

When compared to those attempts at constructing a system to represent ideas and the sounds and syllables of speech (I wonder if their teacher ever said to them, "write like you talk!), the alphabet (yeah Phoenicians!) with it's 22 to 28 "letters," which stand for basic sounds (not syllables), is pretty amazing. And here I am right now, typing away on this computer, and there you are, just zipping along reading it. It's a miracle, don't you think. And to think we have Homer's *Odyssey*, Virgil's *Aenid*, Dante's *Commedia*, Shakespeare's *Hamlet*, Cervantes's *Don Quixote*, Goethe's *Faust*, James Joyce's *Ulysses*, Mann's *Magic Mountain*, Proust's *Remembrance of Things Past*, and the poems of Robert Frost, Sylvia Plath, Ann Sexton, etcetera, etcetera, etcetera.

> In honor of that messenger who was "heavy of mouth,"
> In honor of Enmerker, the lord of Kullab,the first to write on a clay tablet,
> In honor of that Sumerian schoolboy Nabi-Enlil,
> in honor of that first anonymous Sumerian poet
> who first wrote the tales of Gilgamesh,
> in honor of S n-Leqi-Unninni, the Babylonian poet who took the tales
> recorded by that Sumerian poet and put them into coherent epic form,
> and especially in honor of the Phoenicians who first E=mc-quared the alphabet,
> I'm gonna take my moleskin journal and go sit in a cafe on Third St.,
> and write something with my Gel Retractable 07 Pen.
> Not because I have an epic up my sleeve,
> but because I want to celebrate this amazing invention called writing:
> better than an electric can-opener,
> handier than a pair of jumper cables,

more powerful than a speeding locomotive.
I can spell C-A-T,
and I can spell L-O-V-E,
and I can spell M-O-O-N,
and I can spell
S-U-P-E-R-C-A-L-A-F-R-A-G-A-L-I-S-T-I-C-E-X-P-I-A-L-I-D-O-S-H-U-S.

The next time someone asks you who thought of it, you can say, "Well, it began with a messenger who was heavy of mouth." Ofi eir ieir, bongo eogj totot98e moon hthe, "Coe tgz tjtjt," said gkjot jk meouit. That's cuniform for, "Have a great new year."

The cylinder seal, known as the Temptation seal from post-Akkadian periods in Mesopotamia (c. 23rd–22nd century BCE), has been linked to the Adam and Eve story. Assyriologist George Smith (1840–1876) describes the seal as having two figures (male and female) on each side of a tree, holding out their hands to the fruit, while at the back of one is a serpent, giving evidence that the Fall of man legend was known in early times of Babylonia.

POETRY

I, too, dislike it: there are things that are important beyond
                        all this fiddle.
    Reading it, however, with a perfect contempt for it, one
                        discovers it
    it afterall, a place for the genuine.

                                        -- *Marrianne Moore*

IN DISPRAISE OF POETRY

When the King of Siam disliked a courtier,
He gave him a beautiful white elephant.
The miracle beast deserved such ritual
That to care for him properly meant ruin.
Yet to care for him improperly was worse.
It appears the gift could not be refused.

                                        -- *Jack Gilbert*

from ASPHODEL, THAT GREENY FLOWER

Of asphodel, that greeny flower,
                I come my sweet,

                                to sing to you!
My heart rouses
                thinking to bring you news
                                of something
that concerns you
                and concerns many men. Look at
                                what passes for the new.
You will not find it there but in
                despised poems.
                                It is difficult
to get the news from poems
                yet men die miserably every day
                                for lack
of what is found there.

                                —*William Carlos Williams*

ORPHEUS IN GREENWICH VILLAGE

What if Orpheus,
confident in the hard-
found mastery,
should go down into Hell?
Out of the clean light down?
And then, surrounded
by the closing beasts
and readying his lyre,
should notice, suddenly,
they had no ears.

                    —*Jack Gilbert*

more quotes can go on this page, but will do that later.

ETHERIZED UPON A TABLE:

THE STORY AND EVOLUTION OF MODERN POETRIES

a study guide for the perplexed

**An account of the evolution of poetry
from Homer to the present day,
with particular emphasis on the periods of history
in which poets saw themselves as modern.**

ROOTS

1) Homer (late 8th Century B.C.)

> Seven wealthy towns contend for Homer dead
> Through which the living Homer begged his bread.
> — *Anonymous*

It was a story as old as the hills. One can easily imagine it being pitched today to a big Hollywood producer. In walks Homer, fresh from film school. Handshakes all around. Pleasantries about the business, the weather. Finally Homer opens his lyre-case and sets the instrument on his lap. His long hair falls around his shoulders.

"Two warriors, one woman," he says. The producers nod. Already they're casting it in their minds.

"One of the warriors is a sly, crafty general. Quick-witted, you might say." This is good, one of the producers thinks. A wise-cracking hulk, it brings in a bit of the comedy. "His name is Odysseus, which means long journey."

"I like that," one of the producers says. "Sequels."

"The other guy's invincible. I call him Achilles. Strong-willed, courageous, powerful, fast, feared by everyone." The producer thinks, we could get Brad Pitt to play him.

"He's gotta have some kind of weakness," one of the producers says. He's right, thinks Homer. Gotta have a weakness. He admonishes himself, why didn't I think of that before? Stalling for time, he strums the lyre and hums.

"Well, it's a weakness, but no one knows about it." The producers nod their heads. "See, the reason why he's invincible, is because when he was a baby, his mother dipped him in the River Styx to protect his body from harm. But she was holding him by his heel, so that part of his body remained vulnerable." Homer strums the lyre again and arches his eyebrow. The producers nod some more. Good gimmick. Already they're counting the box-office.

We have the wall paintings of four horses created 30,000 years ago and recently discovered in a huge limestone cavern near the Ardèche River in southern France. There's the winged human figure found at Galgenberg, Austria, carved out of stone around 33,000 years ago. In 1991, divers at Cap Morgiou, France, explored a small cave 121 feet below the surface of the Mediterranean, swam through a tunnel that rose 600 feet, and suddenly emerged into a cavern above sea level with limestone walls decorated with a playful auk and other animal images. This prehistoric bird became extinct about 150 years ago. The painting of these prehistoric creatures, done with manganese and charcoal diluted with saliva, was executed nearly 17,000 years ago, but the charcoal handprints found there go back even further, about 25,000 years ago. The handprints are all the same size, indicating the work of a single artist who probably worked by the light of a flickering lamp fueled with animal fat. During the upper Paleolithic period between 42,000 and 37,000 years ago, long before the development of writing, our human ancestors created sculptures and cave paintings that have survived into our own time. Scholars, historians, and anthropologists have argued for years, offering countless theories to explain the meaning of the images painted on the cave walls in Lascaux and Altamira. Were they part of some religious expression, totemistic ceremonies, fertility rites, expressions of "sympathetic magic" in order to insure a successful hunt, or did the artist-hunter simply paint what he or she observed while lying in the grass in late summer—a herd of bison "dust wallowing" during mating season.

Huge prehistoric stone chamber tombs imbedded in the earth were constructed near the western European coast nearly a thousand years before the building of the Great Pyramids that were begun some twenty-six centuries before the birth of Chrst. Within another few centuries, freestanding megalithic monuments (Stonehenge) were built by the local population of southern Britain. By the fourth millennium BC, metalsmiths developed copper metallurgy, and started alloying bronze by learning to add 10 percent of tin to the copper being fired. Out of the end of the Stone Age, conventionally subdivided into the Paleolithic ("Old Stone") and Neolithic ("New Stone"), people began to develop agricultural technology, and it was this invention of agriculture about ten to twelve thousand years ago that opened the way for the growth of cities and the emergence of political states.

The first of what we might call "civilizations" emerged between 3500 BC and 500 BC. The river valleys of Meopatamia in 3500 BC, and Egypt about 3100 BC, India about 2500 BC, and China around 1500 BC; Minoan civilization on the island of Crete emerged around 2000 BC, and following the collapse of the Mycenean civilization around 1250 BC and the Dark Ages that followed, Greek civilization emerged in the 8th century BC (around the time of Homer). The eastern Mediterranean and Near East was a distinct region where various cultures influenced and interacted with one another in complex ways. (The emergence of a meso-American civilization in Central and South America are also important early civilizations, but they had no direct bearing on Western civilization and literature). Meopatamia, Egypt, China and India were basically river-type civilizations; meso-America, Minoan Crete, and Greece were not. Though all these civilizations were distinct and different from each other other in many ways, they shared a similar depenendence on agriculture, the rise of cities as a new kind of social organization (the word civilization comes from a Latin word meaning "city"), and lastly, the achievement of writing.

With the emergence of cities, a critical population mass was achieved, allowing innovation to occur, for accumulation of surplus wealth to maintain a complex religious structure and the construction of large buildings and monuments. The invention of writing was first used to keep track of accounts and inventory supplies, tools, and weapons. But eventually a way was found to preserve and crystallize the experience of the accumulated culture, a way that could be more far-reaching and more intensive than the oral tradition of tale and song.

The Sumerians used cylinder seals with pictures engraved on them. The seals were rolled onto soft clay, forming a continuous pattern, and this eventually evolved into a form of writing called cuneiform. The priests were the first to learn and control this early form of visual communication, and palace scribes were given the job of keeping track of the use of agricultural resources. They also began to preserve their oral literature. The epic story of *Gilgamesh* was written down soon after 2000 BC. Gilgamesh appears to us as a real person as well as a fictional hero in world literature. The harsh ruler of the city of Uruk, Gilgamesh travels to the realm of the underworld in order to bring back his friend Enkidu and to discover the mysteries of death. The goddess Ishtar offers Gilgamesh immortality, but he rejects it. Versions and parts of the Epic may well have spread throughout the Near East, but it was eventually lost until modern times when twelve incomplete Akkadian-language tablets were found at Nineveh in the library of the Assyrian king Ashurbanipal (who reigned 668-627 BC). Later, various fragments were found elsewhere in Mesopatamia and Anatolia (modern day Turkey), partly filling some of the gaps in the original text. The most complete version that exists today is pieced togather from nearly 30,000 tablets or fragments in three languages. Just as Latin was preserved in monasteries after the fall of the Roman Empire, the Sumerian langauge lived on in temples and scribal schools, influencing the pictographic form of writing called hieroglyics, developed by the Egyptians. It took another 1500 years before picture-writing evolved into syllabic-writing—the use of signs which stood for the sound of part of a word. Egyptian hieroglyphics were inscribed on soft clay with a reed-stalk. But hieroglyphics were difficult to write, and their use did not spread as cuneiform did. It soon died out, and inscriptions on tombs, monuments, and papyrus that survived were not translated until the discovery at the beginning of the 19th century of the "Rosetta Stone,"which was inscribed in Greek, "demotic" Egyptian, and hieroglypic.Though hieroglyphics failed to work as an efficient system of writing, the invention of papyrus proved to be a major contribution. Strips of reed-pitch were laid criss-cross and pounded together until a uniform sheet was made. Cheaper than animal hide (from which parchment was made), papyrus proved to be more convenient than clay tablets or slate. Not until the arrival of paper from China during the early Middle Ages was papyrus supplanted as a material for written correspondance. In a sense, we could credit the Egyptians with the invention of the book, though the book as we know it—the codex, with separate sheets bound on one side—did not come into use until late in the Roman era. Before that, writers pasted sheets of papyrus together into a long continuous roll. An epic such as the *Iliad* would have taken several dozen such rolls to complete.

Literacy for the most part was confined to the great river valley civilizations, though cuneiform was common in Mesopatamia, and several different languages were written in it. But in the Near East, Crete and Greece, new scripts were being invented. The still-undeciphered Linear A was based on a Semitic language that was borrowed from the Phoenicians. Linear B was an early form of Greek, which eventually became the script of the first western literature used to record the story of the fall of Troy, perhaps the last great victory of the Mycenaea civilization before its collapse at the end of the 13th century. The tale of the fall of Troy evolved over five centuries of bardic improvisation before it was written down and put into final form in the 8th century BC. (At least, that's the theory. It may have been orally carried forth by a family of singers knows as Homeraids, passed down from generation to generation, like a family of actors performing the works of Shakespeare. Finally, in the 6th century, an Athenian tyrant had them all assebled for a week's performance, with scribes at the ready, writing down every spoken word.)

Eight centuries later, the Kingdom of Hammurabi flourished, with cities such as Nineveh, Ashur, and Nimrod along the upper Tigris, and Kish, Nippur, and Babylon along the Euphrates. Egypt was under Asian domination then, and Babylonia and Assyria had become great powers. Hittite Asia Minor was about to become another.

The first population in Greece that spoke Greek was not the Minoans, who had grown rich through complex agricultural and seaborne trade with the peoples of the eastern Mediterranean and Egypt, but the Mycenaeans of the second half of the second millennium BC, whose civilization was destroyed in the period from about 1200 to 1000 BC as part of the widespread turmoil throughout the eastern Mediterranean region. The descendants of the Greeks who survived these catastrophes eventually revived Greek civilization. The original Indo-European language had virtually disappeared by evolving into its different descendant languages well before the invention of writing, though traces of that language survive in certain words common to Greek, Latin, Vedic, English, Spanish, French, German, and Russian (the word for night in those langauges are respectively: *nux, nox, nakt, night, noche, nuit, Nacht,* and *noch*). The Greeks constituted one linguistically identifiable group descended from Indo-Europan ancestors. While its language had Indo-European origins, the relation between Greece and the Near East, especially Egypt, is a much discussed question. Egyptian culture obviously had a deep influence on Greek civilization, indicated by the seminal religious ideas that Greek adopted from Egypt, like the geography of the underworld, the judgement of the souls of the dead, the use of fire in initiation ceremonies, etc.

Out of a long oral tradition of story-telling and song, writing developed in the Near East and Egypt long before the skill reached Greece. Probably influenced by Egyptian hieroglyphs, the Minoans at first develpoped a pictorgraphic script, but this system evolved into a more linear form of writing that expressed phonetic sounds. The Linear A script found on clay tablets (which has yet to be fully deciphered) appears to have been a true syllabary form of writing in which characters stood for the sound of the syllables of words. We know from the Linear B script that the earliest writing was used to make official inventories, tallies and pedestraian lists of soldiers, slaves, serving women, military units, jars, bowls, weapons, pottery, clothing material, chariot wheels, animals—even occasional "doodles." It was a world not so much geared toward heroic deeds as focused on good accounting. Sometimes, it is possible to see the fingerprints of the scribe on the reverse where a tablet was held, and some large tablets have depressions corresponding to the positions of the thumb and fingers. These clay tablets were not literary productions, but, as John Chadwick, who assisted Michael Ventris in the original decipherment of Linear B, called them, "the account books of anonymous clerks." Nevertheless, certain names also crop up, the names of Homer's heroes: Achilles, Hector, and Aeneas. From Knossos comes another tablet with the words "To all the gods—a pot of honey." It was in the crossroads of cultures among the coastal peoples known as the Phoenicians that the first alphabet was developed from about 1700 to 1500 BC, and its later form eventually became the base of the ancient Greek and Roman alphabets and hence of modern Western alphabets.

The Greeks apparently lost their knowledge of writing when Mycenaean civilization was destroyed, though the loss may not have been total. With the destruction of the palaces and economic strongholds, there was no longer a need for keeping written records, but the oral transmisson of cultural events and traditions were probably passed on as stories, history, legends and myth. From one generation to the next, storytelling and oral performances of poetry were an integral part of Greek life. As the Greeks came through the end of their Dark Age, they came in contact once again with literate civilizations of the Near East. Greek traders who traveled to Crete, Cyprus, or even as far as the western Mediterranean, probably began to use the Phoenician alphabetic script for bookkeeping and instructional purposes, listing names and goods as the palace scribes had done on those clay tablets centuries earlier. The Greeks relearned the technology of writing. But in so doing, they made a significant addition. The Phoenician alphabet consisted of some twenty-odd consonants, though like similar alphabets of the Near East, there were no vowels. The letter *k*, for instance, could have sounded *ka*, *ke*, *ki*, *ko*, or *ku*. The Greeks adapted several Phoenician consonants, and turned them into vowels. Without vowels, it would have been nearly impossible to have written Greek satisfactorily. There were countless different Greek communities that emerged out of the Dark Age, and each used slightly different letter shapes, but despite the variations in script, all the Greek alphabets incorporated vowels, making the Greek alphabet more accessible and useful than the consonantal alphabets of the ancient Near East. Furthermore, despite the variations of script, and the development of different Greek dialects throughout the mainland and the islands of the Aegean, there emerged a cultural coherence within the Greek world that allowed for the development of a distinct cultural identity. The newly acquired skill was quickly used to write down the names of their gods, along with elaborate dedications that included a few lines of verse. As they mastered the new technique, it would have been logical, though difficult, to begin the transcription of their sophisticated oral literature. It's likely that many of the so-called Homeric bards who sang of the deeds of Achilles, Odysseus, Hector, and Agamemnon, were each able to memorize only specific parts of what we now call The Epic Cycle. Perhaps each "rhapsode" specialized in certain parts of The Epic Cycle, and in time, became identified with that part of the story, the same way we identify certain actors in movies with the characters they portray. A better analogy might be the scene at the end of Ray Bradbury's *Farenheit 491* in which different people memorized specific outlawed books, thus becoming identified with that particular classic—the oral tradition come full circle.

The origins of those epic poems are lost, but they probably went back to Mycenaean times, and there must have been a corpus of sagas on which a bard could draw, just as the western movie in our time draws upon the true or legendary deeds of men like Jesse James, Billy the Kid, Wyatt Earp, Bat Masterton, Doc Holliday, Butch Cassiday and the Sundance Kid. Like the Greek Epic Cycle, we have our Western Cycle, with all the variations of the shootout at the O.K. Corral (over half a dozen such films, *My Darling Clementine*, *Gunfight at the O.K. Corral*, *Tombstone*, and *Wyatt Earp*, to name just four) and the killings of Jesse James and Billy the Kid. There was no fixed text (and before literacy, no written text), just an existing body of myth, legend, and history which could be arranged so as to make a chronological narrative extending from the beginning of the world to the end of the heroic age. Each bard would have improvised some part of the story, depending upon the occasion—a royal feast, a festival that was part of athletic contests, a wedding, the celebration of a victory after a battle. The Epic Cycle was divided into two main sequences: the Trojan Cycle, which dealt with all aspects of the Trojan War, and the Theban Cycle, which comprised a narrative of the legends of the city of Thebes, the third most important city in Greek history after Athens and Sparta. Sophocles described it as "the only city where mortal women are the mothers of gods" (i.e. Dionysus and Heracles). The reason you won't find Thebes mentioned by Homer in the famous catalogue of Greek cities which fought against the Trojans is because it was destroyed a generation before the Trojan War by the Epigonoi, the sons of the Seven against Thebes, who were the subjects of the tragedy by Aeschylus. Their story was told in the *Thebais*, one of the tales of the Epic Cycle.

The Trojan Cycle probably consisted of seven or eight epic poems dealing with the seige and capture of Troy and the events that followed: The *Iliad*, the *Odyssey*, the *Cypria*, the *Ilias Parva* (the "Little Iliad"), the *Iliupersis*, the *Aethiopis*, the *Nosti*, and the *Telegonia*. The *Iliad* would have been the second of the seven, and the *Odyssey* seems to have been the second of three epics dealing with the heroes of Troy and their return home. Excluding the *Iliad* and the *Odyssey*, only some 120 lines belonging to the rest of the Trojan Cycle, written down by various poets in the seventh and sixth centuries, now survive. *The Cypria* recounted in eleven books the events that led up to the point in the Trojan War at which Homer's *Iliad* begins, including the wedding of Peleus and the goddess Thetis (Achilles' parents) and the "Judgement of Paris," which set in motion the events that started the Trojan War. (Hera, Athena and Aphrodite asked Paris to decide which of them was the most beautiful of all the goddesses. For picking her, Aphrodite, helped him abduct the most beautiful of mortals, Helen of Troy. In the whole of the *Iliad*, Homer never explains why Hera and Athena were hostile to Troy, assuming his listeners and readers already knew the reason.)Another of the epic poems that form part of the Epic Cycle is the *Cypria*, which also describes the assembly of the Greek fleet, the rescue of Iphigenia by Artemis at the moment of sacrifice, the fight with Telephus, and the first engagements at Troy. The epic is sometimes ascribed to Stasinus of Cyprus, hence the title (otherwise unexplained). Homer does not tell the entire story of the Trojan War; he picks up after the seige is in its tenth year, and concentrates on the rivalry between Achilles and Agamemnon, Hector's slaying of Achilles' friend Patroclus, the fight between Hector and Achilles, and the funerals of Patroclus and Hector. To find out what happened afterwards, we must look to the *Ilias Parva*, or the "Little Iliad," attributed to Lesches of Pyrrha. It was a sequel to the *Iliad*, in four books, and according to a summary made by Proclus (412-485 AD), the Neoplatonist philsopher, it covered the awarding of the arms of Achilles to Odysseus; the madness and suicide of Ajax; the ambushing of Helenus and his prophecy about the capture of Troy through the agency of Philoctetes, who kills Paris, the arrival at Troy of Achilles' son, Neoptolemus, the secret entry of Odysseus into Troy and his stealing of the Palladium, and the entry of the Wooden Horse. The lost poem *Iliupersis*, the "Sack of Troy," attributed to Arctinus of Miletus, was a sequel in two books to the *Little Iliad*, and covers the episodes of the Wooden Horse, the Greeks burning the city of Troy, Neoptolemus killing Priam, Menelaus finding his wife, Helen, Odysseus murdering Astyanax, son of Hector, and Neoptolemus taking Hector's wife, Andromache as prize. Arctinus was also supposed to have written another sequel to the *Iliad*, the *Aethiopis*, also lost. The *Nostoi* dealt with the homecoming of the heroes, and the *Telegonia* concerns its main character, Telegonus.

Around the middle of the 8th century BC, two of these epic poems began to be written down and put into final form by the blind poet the ancients called Homer. In a sense, he would have been the final author of these tales that grew out of centuries of oral performance by countless Greek poets glorifying the stories of Bronze-Age warrior-heroes and the significant deeds of war and peace. Some have even suggested that the adaptation of the Phoenician alphabet and the use of vowels to facilitate song were done for the express purpose of recording the poems. To recite the entire story of the *Iliad* or the *Odyssey* would have taken all night, but it's not improbable that such special recitations occured. Perhaps two or three different rhapsodes were needed to recount the portion of the tale they knew. Of course, a written text would have made it easier for the traveling rhapsode to retain larger portions of the story. Did Homer present a portrait of himself in the *Odyssey* when Alcinous, king of the Phaeacians, a land "out in the surging sea, off at the world's end," orders a feast with songs and games to welcome Odysseus, "the unlucky wanderer who strayed our way."

> Alcinous rose and addressed his island people:
> "Hear me, lords and captains of Phaeacia,
> hear what the heart inside me has to say.
> This stranger here, our guest—
> I don't know who he is, or whether he comes
> from sunrise lands or the western lands of evening,
> but he has come in his wanderings to my palace;
> he pleads for passage, he begs we guarantee it.
> So now, as in years goen by, let us press on
> and grant him escort. . . .
> Come to my royal halls so we can give
> this stranger a hero's welcome in our palace—
> no one here refuse. Call in the inspired bard
> Demodocus. God has given the man the gift of song,
> to him beyond all others, the power to please,
> however the spirit stirs him on to sing."

With those commands Alcinous led the way
and a file of sceptered princes took his lead,
while the herald went to find the gifted bard.
    .   .   . In wise Alcinous' high-roofed halls,
colonnades and courts and rooms were overflowing
with crowds, a mounting host of pople young and old.
The king slaughtered a dozen sheep to feed his guests,
eight boars with shining tusks and a pair of shambling oxen.
These they skinnned and dressed, and then laid out a feast
to fill the heart with savor.
                                In came the herald now,
leading along the faithful bard the Muse adored
above all others, true, but her gifts were mixed
with good and evil both: she stripped him of sight
but gave the man the power of stirring, rapturous song.
Pontonous brought the bard a silver-studded chair,
right amid the feasters, leaning it up against
a central column—hung his high clear lyre
on a peg above his head and showed him how
to reach up with his hands and lift it down.
And the herald placed a table by his side
with a basket full of bread and cup of wine
for him to sip when his spirit craved refreshment.
All reached out for the good things that lay at hand
and when they'd put aside desire for food and drink,
the Muse inspired the bard
to sing the famous deeds of fighting heroes—
the song whose fame had reached the skies those days:
The Strife Between Odysseus and Achilles, Peleus' Son . . .
how once at the gods' flowing feast the captains clashed
in a savage war of words, while Agamemnon, lord of armies,
rejoiced at heart that Achaea's bravest men were battling so.
For this was the victory sign that Apollo prophesied
at his shrine in Pytho when Agamemnon strode across
the rocky threshold, asking the oracle for advice—
the start of the tidal waves of ruin tumbling down
on Troy's and Achaea's forces, both at once,
thanks to the will of Zeus who rules the world.

That was the song the famous harper sang
but Odysseus, clutching his flaring sea-blue cape
in both powerful hands, drew it over his head
and buried his handsome face,
ashamed his hosts might see him shedding tears.
Whenver the rapt bard would pause in song,
he'd lift the cape from his head, wipe off his tears
and hoisting his double-handled cup, pour it out to the gods.
But soon as the bard would start again, impelled to sing
by Phaeacia's lords, who reveled in his tale,
again Odysseus hidhis face and wept.

[the irony here is that
the Phaeacians do not
know that
the "unlucky
wanderer" is
none other than
Odysseus, an irony
made even more
delicious by the fact
that within the story
of Odysseus
Homer has the
blind bard tell the
story of Odysseus,
and Odysseus,
hearing the story
of his being
so far from home
must hide
his own tears.

Later, after more tales and games, Odysseus cuts a choice strip of loin from a cooked boar and sends Demodocus a plate,

> "so he can eat his full—with warm regards
> from a man who knows what suffering is . . .
> From all who walk the earth our bards deserve
> esteem and awe, for the Muse herself has taught them
> paths of song. She loves the breed of harpers."
>
>   The herald placed the gift in Demodocus' hands
> and the famous blind bard received it, overjoyed.
> Odysseus, master of many exploits, praised the singer:
> "I respect you, Demodocus, more than any man alive—
> surely the Muse has taught you, Zeus' daughter,
> or god Apollo himself. How true to life,
> all too true . . . you sing the Achaeans' fate,
> all they did and suffered, all they soldiered through,
> as if you were there yourself or heard from one who was.
> But come now, shift your ground. Sing of the wooden horse
> Epeus built with Athena's help, the cunning trap that
> good Odysseus brought one day to the heights of Troy,
> filled with fighting men who laid the city to waste.
> Sing that for me—true to life as it deserves—
> and I will tell the world at once how freely
> the Muse gave *you* the gods own gift of song."

The story contained in the *Iliad* may well be an amalgam of numerous wars and many such adventures that took place during this period of history. Homer's epic probably tells the story of one such military expedition which took place four or five centuries before his own time in which warriors (called Acheans) from all over Greece led by the king of Mycenae sailed across the Aegean to lay seige to a walled-citadel named Troy situated near the south shore of the Hellespont in northwestern Anatolia (present day Turkey). With its commanding position at the entrance to the Hellespont and hence to the Black Sea, Troy would have been a strategic prize, controlling as well the land route between Europe and Asia. It's doubtful the Greeks were invading Troy just to avenge the abduction of Helen. Homer's *Iliad* tells only a part of the story of the ten-year seige of Troy and the eventual destruction of the citadel in 1230 BC. More than Troy was lost. Because of the widespread violence and destruction throughout the Meditteranean, society collapsed and a complex economic system was shattered. The fall of Troy signaled the end of the Mycenean civilization, a Bronze Age culture of great prosperity and rich palace societies. The four centuries following the fall of Troy has been called the Greek Dark Age (*c.* 100—*c.* 750 BC), and it was at the end of this period that Homer began to set down the story in the *Iliad*. However, Homer was actually recalling a time nearly a thousand years before when he "sang" of an Aegean culture in which a great civilization existed, its "ninety cities, and the land of Crete in the midst of the wine-dark sea." It was a Golden

Age, in one of the most artistic civilizations in history. In this Minoan Age, named after a mythical King Minos, tin and copper were mixed for the first time, marking the beginning of Bronze Age culture in which oral literature and art flourished. As successor to the Minoans on the island of Crete came the prosperous Mycenaean monarchies on the mainland. That civilzation ended in a mysterious episode of destruction, entering a period of decline during the Dark Age which followed, characterized by widespread poverty and depopulation, its final decay marked by the destruction of Cnossus, the greatest of the "90 cities."

> But he sent him to Lycia with a folding tablet
> On which he had scratched many evil signs,
> And told him to give it to Anteia's father,
> To get him killed.
>   Homer, the *Illiad* (Book 6)

Despite Homer's obscure reference to the act writing in the *Iliad* (quoted above), archaeological and literary evidence suggests that writing did not become widespread in Greece until the first half of the 8th century BC. Writing materials convenient for literary composition—papyrus or parchment and some kind of stylus or reed pen—are thought to have first become available in the late 7th century. The script would not have been that easy to read, consisting of capital letters only. The codex or the book as we know it in which leaves of parchment (or later, paper) are folded and stitched at the spine wasn't invented until the first century AD. We know for sure that papyrus came into general use in Greece no later than the time of the poet Archilochus (c. 680-640 BC) when it seems that poetry in general came to be written down, especially shorter personal poems. Sheets of papyrus were pasted together side by side so as to form a continous roll, which would have been convenient for reading, but not for reference. Committing 16,000 lines of the *Iliad* and 12,000 lines of the *Odyssey* to writing in the script available at the time would have been an arduous task, and would have taken a number of rolls. We get our word "book" from the word "papyrus," originally imported into Greece from the Phoenician town of Byblos. The Greeks took that name for papyrus and thence for book (*biblos*—hence "bible," or to be precise, bibles, or books. The Bible is really many "books," as when we say the "books of the Bible."). The work was written in verticle columns, but scribes seem not to have been concerned to keep regular number of lines to a column or of letters to a line. The minimum of help is given to the reader: punctuation and even spacing between words are non-existenet or at best erratic, and enlarged initial letters are not used. Papyrus rolls were difficult to use. Athenian vase-paintings show readers having a hard time with twisted rolls that were easily torn. Ink was made from a dense carbon black, and scribes had to get up early to grind the ink before work. In some cases, rolls were coated with wax and the writing scratched on with a stylus—thus one of the Latin verbs "to write or jot down," *exaro*, originally meant "to plow or dig up," because the stylus furrowed the wax like a plough-share. Afterwards, the scribe would smooth the wax with the blunt end of the stylus.

Books to the classical Greeks were essentially a substitute for recitation, and only centuries later do we find a thriving book trade. From the fifth century onward authors such as Thucydides, Plato, Xenophan, Aristotle, etc., refer to the Homeric poems in terms that assume that they are works whose content is common knowledge and that verbatim quotations will be recognized by an ordinary cultured man. We also possess evidence to support the belief that from the latter part of the sixth century BC a continuous recitation of the *Iliad* and *Odyssey* was an officially regulated feature of the Panathenaic Festival held at Athens every four years—the literary equivalent, one might say, of the Olympic Games, which began in 776 BC.

Writing was not welcomed by everyone. Just as television has its detractors today, many felt that the invention of writing was a detriment to the powerful and flexible engine of memory. Plato's *Phaedrus* involves a dialogue between Socrates and Phaedrus about the theme of love, but in it Socrates tells a tale about the invention of the art of writing by the legendary Theuth, and his conversation on the subject with the king of Egypt.

Socrates:
Enough appears to have been said by us of a true and false art of speaking.

Phaedrus:
True.

Socrates:
But there is something yet to be said of the propriety and impropriety of writing. . . . . At the Egyptian city of Naucratis, there was a famous old god, whose name was Theuth; the bird which is called the Ibis is sacred to him, and he was the inventor of many arts, such as arithmetic and calculation and geomerty and astronomy and draughts and dice, but his great discovery was the use of letters. When Theuth came to that great city of Upper Egypt which the Hellenes call Egyptian Thebes, he showed his inventions to king Thamus, who inquired about the invention of letters. This, said Theuth, will make the Egyptian wiser and give them better memories; it is a specific both for the memory and for the wit. Thamus replied: O most ingenious Theuth, the parent or inventor of an art is not always the best judge of the utility or inutility of his own inventions to the users of them. And in this instance, you who are the father of letters, from a paternal love of your own children have been led to attribute to them a quality which they cannot have; for this discovery of yours will create forgetfulness in the minds of those who learn it, because they will not use their memories; they will trust to the external written characters and not remember of themselves. The specific which you have discovered is an aid not to memory, but to recollection, and you give your disciples not truth, but only the semblance of truth; they will be hearers of many things and will have learned nothing; they will appear to be omniscient and will generally know nothing; they will be tiresome company, having the show of wisdom without the reality.

Of course, Plato had an even greater disdain for poets, and in *The Republic*, he would have them banished from any ideal state. Elsewhere in the *Phaedrus* Socrates discusses various kinds of madness. The first two are noble and have divine attributes for prophecy.

The third kind is the madness of those who are possessed by the Muses; which taking hold of a delicate and virgin soul, and there inspiring frenzy, awakens lyrical and all other numbers; with these adorning the myriad actions of ancient heroes for the instruction of posterity. But he who, having no touch of the Muses' madness in his soul, comes to the door and thinks that he will get into the temple by the help of art—he, I say, and his poetry are not admitted; the sane man disappears and is nowhere when he enters into rivalry with the madman.

Perhaps because of centuries of oral tradition that lay behind it, literary composition seems to have leapt from the simplest inventories of wine jugs and grain jars to the two epic masterpieces of the blind poet. It's an astonishing event, to imagine the development of epic poetry, not in stages, but full-blown as it were, like Minerva from the head of Zeus. The following statement is not meant to minimize the great power and dignity of those cave paintings, like the *Wounded Bison* found at Altimira that shows such an uncanny sense of life. But going from those Minoan palace inventories and administrative records to the stateliness of Homer's hexameters and the passion of the narrative in the *Illiad* and the *Oddysey*, with the vivid and subtle humanity of its characters, is a little like looking up at the images incised, sculpted and painted on the rock surfaces of the caves of the Aurignacian and Magdalenian cave painters, then walking into the Sistine Chapel and gazing up at the frescoed ceiling, the hundreds of figures rhythmically distributed across the architectural framework depicting scenes from The Creation of the World to The Drunkenness of Noah.

We will discuss later this question of when the *Iliad* and *Odyssey* were actually written down, made into a text, and whether there was one actual author named Homer, or many authors each contributing portions of the oral epic until it was finally written down as a text, as opposed to a memorized performance that was shaped and edited during a long period of oral composition and transmission. This "Homeric Question" has vexed classicists for generations. Whether seen as part of an evolutionary oral process that led to the writing down of the text, or whether there was a written text around 750BC and that text became the basis for the oral transmission until it was finally written down for the Athenian games around 550BC is a matter of speculation and controversy. If the text that was finally written down was the product of centuries of oral transmission, we lose our cherished author, the blind poet named Homer. But if many Homeric Rhapodes had a hand in creating a text that grew out of the oral transmission, what accounts for the consistency of voice and style, the structural unity of both the *Iliad* and the *Odyssey?*. How could so many contributing voices over several centuries achieved such a unity of tone and structure, which was finally made into a definitive text in the 6th century BC? There are many such "Homeric Questions," and no one has arrived at a definitive answer. A great deal of evidence for different points of view has been offered, and will continue to be offered based on new discoveries, but the jury is still out; we can only speculate on a final verdict, if there will ever be one.

T hough the *Iliad* was brought intoan approximation of a final state (oral or written) in the 8th century BC, the tale of the fall of Troy in 1230 BC takes place during the end of the

Mycenaean Age, an age Homer and the Greeks looked back upon with reverence. Between 1450 and 1150 BC, Mycenaean Greece reached its height, with cities such as Mycenae, Tiryus, Pylos and Mycenaean Athens, Thebes, & Corinth reaching the end of their prosperity and influence in the 13th-11th centuries BC—their downfall gradually occuring during the 12th. Writing as we know it first made its appearance, only to be forgotten in the Dark Age that followed. Evidence of Mycenaean expansion can be found in the decorative motifs from 15th century Ireland and the successive cultures of Los Millares in Spain which show the influence of Crete, Mycenae and perhaps Troy. Around the Aegean, Troy—once a mythical city perched on the edge of Asia Minor (present day Turkey)—was destroyed twice in the 13th century, once by earthquakes, the other as a result of raids and mass migrations which plunged the entire near and middle east into turmoil, chaos, and destruction. It was during this century that Moses led the Israelites back to the Promised Land.

Bronze Age civilization was destroyed by invasions of barbaric nomads who came from two different directions: The "sea peoples" came from the northwest and raided the eastern coasts of the Mediterranean in the late 13th century. A century later, new waves of barbarians—the Dorian Greeks—swept over the mainland, destroying for good Mycenae, Crete and Rhodes. Greek speaking peoples who were displaced by these invasions overran the central Aegean islands and the western coast of Asia Minor. Troy was one of the cities burned and ravaged. Other invaders from the southeast and the fringes of the Arabian desert conquered Palestine, Syria, and Babylonia, the lands of the Fertile Crescent. The two areas affected were the lands forming an arc from Greece to Egypt, and the lands forming an arc from Palestine to Babylonia. It was a time of warring cities and tribes, with each little city and each little band of invaders being a law unto themselves. No single nation was able to impose unified control over these cities or petty states. The political history from 1150 BC—when Mycenea was destroyed, a century after the destruction of Troy—to 750 BC—the approximate time when alphabetic writing began in Greece and Homer brought together the various tales of the burning of Troy into the *Iliad* and the *Odyssey*—was one of numerous cities and states without a major national identity. But cultural achievements grew out of this period of darkness. The art of writing had been lost, but was recovered by the end of this period. The so-called barbarian invaders slowly built a new civilization, though it was far different from the old one. Stories that glorified a past golden age gave people a sense of belonging to a great tradition toward which they were once again aspiring. Though he "wrote" centuries later, Homer's epic poems looked back to the great age of Mycenean civilization, but the ideals celebrated were "heroic," reflecting the warrior culture of the invaders in which a man's fighting ability was highly esteemed, and prophets who led their tribes across the deserts were glorified for their gift of prophetic speech.

Homeric Langauge

Language is always changing, and there is no evidence—despite the protestations of those language purists (sad to say, I'm probably one of them) who shake their heads at the corruptions of language they witness daily—that overall progress or decay results from such change. Within a language, there are subdivisions tradtionally known as dialects, which are most commonly geographical but may also be social. A dialect is more than a simple difference of pronunciation, but can involve different accents. Often one dialect becomes socially prestigious and is adopted as the norm. Variation in language may be due to social class, ethnic origin, age, and/or sex, and can change depending on the social situation. Language is constantly shifting through dialect and idiom, often with one community leading the way as a forerunner of change. Occasionally formal and informal varieties of the same language may differ to such an extent that they are used virtually as different languages.

Food for Thought

A NEW KIND OF ENGLISH

"What will Americans be like linguistically in a century from now? Given that America will still be a world-spanning empire and civilization, we can look for cultural clues in earlier empires and civilizations.

Dialects are variants of established languages. Pidgins are amalgams of two languages. English is a pidgin. In the 14th century English storytellers, notably Chaucer, decided to fuse French, the language of the Norman conquerors of Britain, with the common Anglo-Saxon language (itself a pidgin of two Germanic languages).

But a more dramatic pidginization occurred two centuries later when the Mughal (Mongol) conquerors of India created an empire that lasted three centuries. Now, despite many cultural variants, the current official languages, Hindi for India and Urdu for Pakistan, both have their origins in "Hindustani," the pidgin name used by the Mughals and then by the imperial British.

American troops in Iraq and Iraqi merchants are already creating pidgins of English and the Iraqi dialects of Arabic. That is similar to what Mughal soldiers did when they went into town to haggle. Urdo/Urdu is a Turco-Mongolian word that meant a "military encampment." If American soldiers and merchants should still be stationed in Iraq in 2104 then it's a good chance that a new language will have arisen, e.g. "Amerarab." And then some writers, like Chaucer, will see if they can sell a novel written in Amerarab.

When the Western Roman Empire officially fell in 476, Britain's Latin-speaking population, mostly soldiers, were worried what to do. But contemporary English archeologists found out what Roman soldiers did. The archeologists carried out diggings in all towns that had the suffix "chester," an Anglo-Saxon variant of Latin "castrum," for military encampment. There are dozens of cities and towns in England with the suffix "chester." Since most of the Roman military encampments were built by a single plan, the archeologists could judge what happened before and after 476. The archeologists concluded that most soldiers remained in Britain and became merchants.

In the heartland of the USA a new pidgin is arising called "Spanglish." Harvard Professor Samuel P. Huntington warns Americans that Spanglish already poses a mortal threat to English. But there is a good chance that in 2104 Spanglish storytellers will replicate the historical formation of English. They will create a new pidgin language that has a Spanish syntax, just as English is based on an Anglo-Saxon syntax.

African Americans speak English as do their millions of kinfolk in Africa and the Caribbean. But they also speak dialects of English that other Americans have difficulty understanding. Some linguists classify the Gullah language, spoken in the North Carolina islands, as a pidgin that is based on West African syntax. But others say Gullah is a dialect of English, just as French, Spanish and Romanian began as offshoots of Latin.

African Americans, especially from the South, have family get-togethers that can include many hundreds of participants. They, too, according to African-American friends, speak two kinds of English. Yet, the attempt by many African Americans to get Ebonics, a dialect of English, recognized as a valid language failed because Ebonics is a private, not a public, language.

Back in the early 1800s the "Massachusetts Reformers" like Horace Mann had educational visions of what the new America should be. The reformers were deeply affected by ancient Greek civilization, what they overlooked was that the Greeks could not get together to face a mortal danger coming from Macedonia. Not long after they preached their visions of the new America, the Civil War broke out and the North came close to losing at Gettysburg.

The Massachusetts Reformers wanted to create a new nation and nationality. They wanted all people to become part of one national identity. But African Americans in the east and south, Latinos and Asians in the west, and indigenous people everywhere in the USA, have insisted that their identities must also be preserved. From these peoples, who now are a majority in California, the core issue is language, and their efforts to retain their collective identities will lead to the transformation of American English as the language of all."

By Franz Schurmann, Pacific News Service. Posted August 13, 2004. Franz Schurmann is emeritus professor of history and sociology at UC Berkeley.

✳

The evolution of Homeric Greek over the course of several centuries involved not only the normal shift of language in time, but the development of various dialects spoken throughout the Greek world. Not only do we experience in the Homeric poems the Ionic dialect set against the Attic dialect, but we might see two different versions of the Ionic dialect, one older than another, just as the cockney dialect would show variations depending on the different stages of its development. There's hardly anything to compare to the experience of Homeric Greek. The form that appears in the Homeric poems is a standardized, artificial amalgam, combining forms from different dialects and from different stages in the history of the spoken langauge. The Doric dialect of Sparta and

Corinth is more rustic, whereas the Attic, the dialect of Athens and closely related to Ionic, became the basis for standard Greek. The Ionic dialect was spoken mainly on the coast of Asia Minor, whereas the Aeolic was spoken on many of the islands (including Sappho's Lesbos). Homer's poetic idiom is based primarily on the Ionic dialect, but it also includes the Aoilic, and in some cases, forms that go back as far as Mycenaean times. Many older forms and dialects survived in the poetic diction because it was metrically convenient My wife and I were driving in the car yesterday and I asked her to recite Clement Moore's famous Christmas poem. She began, "Twas the night before Christmas, and all through the house . . ." Why not say, "*It was* the night before Christmas?" I asked. Modernize the diction, so to speak. The "twas" was a holdover from a previous langauge contraction for the sake of the meter, but no one speaking today would say "twas" in a normal spoken sentence. Yet, that dictional element will remain in the poem no matter what changes occur in the English language because "twas" is metrically correct. But it also reamins for reasons that transcend metrics, but have to do with a certain musicality, an eloquence that comes from its very archaic nature, just as we prefer certain parts of the King James translation of the Bible to more modern renderings.

> Futility, utter futility, says the Speaker, everything is futile.
> What does anyone profit from all his labour and toil here under the sun?
> Generations come and generations go, while the earth endures for ever.
> > "Ecclesiastes," The Revised English Bible, 1989

> Vanity of vanities, saith the Preacher, vanity of vanities; all is vanity.
> What profit hath a man of all his labor which he taketh under the sun?
> One generation passeth away, and another generation cometh,
> But the earth abideth forever.
> > "Ecclesiastes," Authorized King James Version 1611,

Yes, you might say, but would one use an archaic diction on purpose when writing in the modern vernacular? The choice to do so would be telling. Ezra Pound mixes a slew of dictional variations in his *Cantos*, written over the course of 50 years from 1915 to the 1950s. Yet nothing is more beautiful than one section written in Elizabethan/Biblical diction, that would become flat if rendered in the modern vernacular:

> What thou lovest well remains,
> > > the rest is dross
> What thou lov'st well shal not be reft from thee
> What thou lov'st well is thy true heritage
> Whose world, or mine or theirs
> > > or is it of none?
> First came the seen, then thus the palpable
> > Elysium, though it were in the halls of hell,
> What thou lovest well is thy true heritage
> What thou lov'st well shall not be reft from thee.

Thus, before the invention of writing, stories told again and again over the course of several centuries were subject to extension and embellishment, and may even have reflected the use of both a spoken and a "literary" idiom. How would a literary, poetic idiom develop even before the conventions of writing? For instance, a story I made up for a group of 1st graders has evolved over the course of the last few years. I've yet to transcibe it, but when I tell it, I'm aware of the fact that I've practically got it memorized. Each time I tell it, I add a detail, incorporate a better way of telling a certain section. For the most part, I tell the story as I would speak, but there are touches where a "literary" phrase attains a separate embellishment. None of it originated in writing, but through heighted langauge and poetic embellishment, I found I was able to create a certain effect that delighted the kids, especially when that particular phrase with its internal rhyme and syntactical paralellism was repeated several times throughout the story. In the beginning I tell how "the anger in the heart of the tree with three hearts traveled through the vein in the grain of the wood and into the vein in the arm of the man with the heart of fear and changed his fearful heart into a heart of anger." It's a mouthful, and has an obvious internal rhyme. Each time the man touches a piece of the wood that came from the tree with three hearts, I repeat the phrase with the proper change in plot, and by the third time, the kids are able to say it along with me—and do. It's an obvious poetic device, and departs considerably from the way I would talk, just telling a story. The sentence grew out of the telling, not out of writing, yet it is not a spoken sentence, but a "literary" one. The same would have been true of the tale of Ilium, the story of the fall of Troy. Much of the tale would have been told in the language of speech, but over time, phrases and sentences would have evolved using literary devices for the purposes of embellishment and poetic elevation. The phrases themselves may have been characteristic of the language idiom of the time, but as the tale was passed on from generation to generation, the spoken language would have continued to evolve, while the phrases themselves that were rooted in a poetic device might well have remained as they were. Thus, we'd get a kind of mixture. The result is a langauge that is metrically flexible, archaic, elevated, using both the spoken dialects and heightened phrasing that would resemble—for us, speaking English—the Elizabethan diction of the King James version of the Bible mixed with the stentorian Latinity of Milton's *Paradise Lost* and the modern idioms of everyday speech. Imagine Homer's tale evolving over several centuries, in which certain poetic expressions were added to the poem, then frozen in place as the poem grew over time. Rendering the first line of the *Iliad* is in itself a complex task, since the Greek words

mênin	aeide	thea	Pêlēïadeô	Achilêos
Anger	sing	goddess	son of Peleus	Achilles

involve various language forms from normal spoken Greek, the Ionic form, an archiaic feminine form of the word goddess that survived only in religious formulas, and Achilles' name preceded by his patronymic reference in a dialect that violates the meter, and thus adds an older form for metrical convenience, and a non-Ionic archaic genitive ending remote from any contemporary spoken dialect. Nevertheless, in Homeric Greek, it's quite musical, something of which is lost in Chapman's 1611 translation and Pope's 1717 version

> Achilles' banefull wrath resound, O Goddesse
> > (George Chapman, 1559-1634))

> Achilles' wrath, to Greece the direful spring
> Of woes innumerable, heavenly goddess, sing!
> > (Alexander Pope, 1688-1744)

Imagine how varied the translations judging by the rendering of that one line:

> I thee beseech, O Goddesse mild, the hateful hate to plaine,
> whereby Achilles was so wrong, and grewe in such disdaine.
> > (Arthur Hall, 1539-1605)

> O Goddess sing what woe the discontent
> Of Thetis' son brought to the Greeks.
> > (Thomas Hobbes, 1588-1679)

> The wrath of Peleus' son, O Muse, resound
> Whose dire effects the Grecian army found.
> > (John Dryden, 1631-1700)

> The wrath of the son of Peleus, -- O goddess of song, unfold,
> The deadly wrath of Achilles.
> > (James Macpherson, 1736-1796)

> Achilles sing, O Goddess! Peleus' son,
> His wrath pernicious.
> > (William Gowper, 1731-1800)

Other translators, when referring to the wrath of Achilles, called it the "destructive wrath," the "implacable wrath," the "fatal wrath," the "ruinous wrath," and the "maniac wrath."

Best known today for his fairy tales, Andrew Lang (1844-1912), was one of the most prolific and versatile writers of his day. Many of his poems were written in the old French forms of rondeau, triolet, etc., but when his ambitious narrative poem, *Helen of Troy* (1888) received such poor notices, he turned to lightweight verse and devoted his scholarly efforts toward anthropology. As a Greek scholar, he collaborated with Walter Leaf and E. Myers on a prose translation of the *Iliad*, wrote several books arguing the unity of Homer, and disputed any notion that Shakespeare was not the author of Shakespeare's plays (see his *Shakespeare, Bacon and the Great Unknown* (1912). His 1883 opening of the *Iliad* serves Homer's five words in proper Victorian prose.

> Sing, goddess, the wrath of Achilles, Peleus' son

Samuel Butler (1835-1902), whose most revealing work was his semi-autobiographcal novel, *The Way of All Flesh*, published posthumously in 1903, developed a theory of the feminine authorship of *The Odyssey*, and translated both epics into vigorous colloquial prose a few years before his death. His opening to the *Iliad* is simple and straightforward.

> Sing, O Goddess, the anger of Achilles

Richmond Lattimore's 1951 opening takes a literal approach, but there's no hint of any complex idiomatic variation, which is probably impossible anyway with five English words.

> Sing, goddess, the anger of Peleus' son Achilleus
> (Lattimore)

Robert Fitzgerald's 1974 version retains the word order, hints at the archaism, but lacks a simplicity that Homer somehow manages:

> Anger be now your song, immortal one,
> Akhilleus' anger, ...

The 1990 translation by Robert Fagles is both poetic and forceful, as typified by his opening which presents the invocation as more of a command, mimicking the force of Achilles' anger.

> Rage—Goddess, sing the rage of Peleus' son, Achilles,

When we get to Stanley Lombardo's 1997 rendering, we find a thoroughly modern tone. He dispenses with the reference to Achilles' father, and goes for the dynamic thrust one might find, not in a recitation, but in a dramatic performance.

> Rage: Sing, Goddess, Achilles' rage.

The most recent translation into English by Barry S. Powell, one of the twenty-first century's leading Homeric scholars, appeared in 2015. Powell's translation is graceful, lucid, and energetic, rendering the Homeric Greek with a simplicity and dignity reminiscent of the original. He admits that many ancient and classical Greek words and phrases have "slippery meanings," and it is not always easy to guess at the exact equivalent in English. In some cases, we're not really sure what Homer meant. But every translator in every age tries to capture what the poem would have sounded like to the average Greek at the time it was being recited. And that's the rub. The recitation of the *Iliad* was passed down from traveling poets, minstrels, or rhapsodes, as they were called, who would themselves had a hand in both performance and translation themselves, not only retaining certain archaic phrases and words from prior recitations, but supplying their own updated expressions to make the story clearer. This process went on for centuries following the Trojan War, which occured around 1250 B.C. By Homer's time, due to the introduction of alphabetic script imported by the Phoenicians, it became possible to transcribe the rhapsodes' performance. Homer lived in the 8th Century B.C., and probably dictated his memorized recitation to a scribe -- thus becoming a link between the Bronze age Mycenean era of the Trojan War and his own pre-classical time. Between those two eras the Greek world had fallen into a period called the Greek Dark Ages, or the Dark Times. But the recitation and performance of the poem over the course of those centuries kept alive words and phrases dating back to the Trojan War, as well as words and phrases that evolved into more contemporary idioms, as language always does. You might say the *Iliad* preserved the collective memory of the Greek people, first as oral performance and then as a text that was memorized and recited by Homeric Rhapsodes. Because papyrus decomposed easily, scribes produced many versions over the centuries, and it wasn't unusual for each scribe to make their own interpolations. It wasn't until the Alexandrian age of the 3rd century *B.C.* that parchment came into use, creating a standard text that remained pretty consistent into the Middle Ages.

Powell's recent engrossing translation is noted for its tight and balanced rhythms, while the incantatory repetitions evoke a continuous "stream of sound" that offers as good an impression of Homer's Greek as one could hope to attain without learning the language. His rendering is accessible, poetic, and as accurate as can be, considering the "slipperiness" of so much of Homer's Greek. With swift, transparent language that rings both ancient and modern, Powell's *Iliad* captures all of the rage, pleasure, pathos, and humor characterized by Homer's *Iliad*. But language stands still for no man. Future translations will strive once more to update Homer's fluid diction, while at the same time preserving some of the archaic phrases that go back over three thousand years to the time of the Trojan War itself.

There's no equivalent in English poetry that could fully capture the texture of Homeric Greek. The idioms and dialects are there, but they're not usually mixed in a literary composition. Even translators tend to render everything into contemporary English, but Homer's Greek audience, as well as the generations after Homer, would have heard many archaic words and expressions popping up throughout the poem, because the oral transmission through the centuries tended to modernize most portions while retaining certain words and expressions that had become fixed into the poem, just as we continue to begin the poem with "Twas the night before Christmas," rather than modernizing it with "It was the night before Christmas." Imagine a poem in English that combined Upper Crust London English with cockney, mixing that with various American dialects from Brooklyn, Charleston, Dallas, Boston, Iowa, and Southern California, and added to that were phrases in Chaucer's Middle English and Shakespeare's Elizabethan English, maybe even throwing a well-know phrase from Beowulf's alliterative Old English, such as "whale road" instead of ocean. Just for the fun of it, I've pieced together a poem I'll call "On Spring," combining lines from Chaucer, Shakespeare, T.S. Eliot, and William Carlos Williams' famous 1923 poem *Spring and All*.

> It is Spring! but miracle of miracles a miraculous miracle . . .
> everything is new.
> He capers, he dances, he has eyes of youth,

he writes verses, he speaks holiday, he smells April and May.
It is spring: life again begins to assume its normal appearance as of "today."
O, how this spring of love resembleth
The uncertain glory of an April day,
Which now shows all the beauty of the sun,
And by and by a cloud takes all away!
What are the roots that clutch, what branches grow
Out of this stony rubbish. Son of man,
You cannot say, or guess, for you know only
A heap of broken images, where the sun beats,
And the dead tree gives no shelter, the cricket no relief,
And the dry stone no sound of water.
Our orchestra is the car's nuts.
The farmer in deep thought
is pacing through the rain
among his blank fields, with
hands in pockets,
in his head
the harvest already planted. And
whan that Aprille with his shoures sote
The droghte of Marche hath perced to the rote,
And bathed every veyne in swich licour,
Of which vertu engendred is the flour.
Meanwhile, SPRING, which has been approaching for several pages,
is at last here.
Such comfort as do lusty young men feel
When well-apparell'd April on the heel
Of limping winter treads.
For you have been absent in the spring,
When proud-piedApril dress'd in all his trim
Hath put a spirit of youth in every thing,
Breeding lilacs out of the dead land, mixing
memory and desire, stirring
Dull roots with spring rain,
like an envious sneaping frost
that bites the first born infants of the spring.

April, methinks, is the cruellest month.

To compare this with Homer's diction might be a stretch, but it's an impression, in English, of what Homeric Greek might have sounded like to those who heard it recited and sung over the course of centuries. Just as we easily accept the dictional shift from "Twas" to "the night before Christmas;" just as the kids accept the shift from everyday, spoken, colloquial phrasing to "the vein in the grain of the heart of the tree to the vein in the grain of the arm of the man . . . ," Homer's listeners were able to absorb the various dictional shifts from one part of a verse to another. Homer's diction, despite the variations, is uniformly dignified, immediate on the one hand, "poetic" and remote on the other. Despite the eloquence and richness of the language, its imagery is never so elaborate as to require a great effort to understand. There is something natural about the way the narrative flows, a lucid and plain word order with logical connectives that make for effortless clarity.

Homeric poetry set a standard that poets were to imitate—or attempt to break away from—throughout the history of Greek poetry.

During the past nine centuries, English has undergone more dramatic changes than any other major European langauge. A modern speaker of English would have a difficult time understanding Old English or Anglo-Saxon, whereas Medieval Icelandic would be easily accessible to the modern Icelander. The structure of Old English was more like Latin in that words had various inflectional endings to indicate their grammatical function. Word order in Old English was more flexible, whereas in Modern English grammatical relations are indicated largely by word order, and not by case or gender, etc. Begun soon after 1386, Chaucer's *Cantebury Tales* was written in a language close to modern English, but not close enough to be easily understood. Shakespeare's English is modern, in the sense that we can comprehend him, though the diction and idioms are Elizabethan, with lots of thou's, methinks and forsooths. Most readers need to read Chaucer in translation; Shakespeare, on the other hand, is still comprehensible, but in another fifty years, given the language's tendency to evolve, he may need to be "translated" much like Chaucer.

Food for Thought
METER, PROSODY, AND THE GUNS OF NAVARONNE

There are probably many modern and contemporary poets who continue to count syllables and accents, who pay close attention to the metrics of their poems. But most modern poets pay attention to the natural rhythm of the spoken langauge, to the talking voice, not the sing-song voice of regular meter based on a metric patter of stressed and unstressed accents. This is a historical fact, but there are several reasons for this.

In ancient times, the poet was a "singer." In fact, the Homeric bards who traveled and recited the story of the *Iliad* and the *Odyssey*, actually accompanied themseves on a lyre; it was more of a sung performance than a spoken recitation. In the 12th century, when rhyme finally came into its own, the troubadour poets were writers and singers of song. Today, when we refer to vocal artists like Bob Dylan or Paul Simon, who write and sing their own material, we sometimes call them "troubadours." The Romantic poets like Keats and Shelley, Victorian poets like Tennyson and Longfellow, may not have "sung" their poems, but the recitation depended on the rhythms they used, whether iambic pentameter or dactylic hexameter. If a poet was going to write poems that rhymed and made metric sense, they had to know how to use the various meters available.

Toward the end of the 19th century, popular song and the influence of "Tin Pan Alley" began to change the nature of modern poetry, just as the camera had a revolutionary effect on painting. Since the camera was literally capable of holding a mirror up to nature, it was no longer necessary for painters to do so; they began to give their "impression" of nature, or to render reality "expressionistically," where the emphasis was not on the subject so much as on how the picture was painted, expressing the emotional/psychological state of the painter. Artists began to delve into the geometric or abstract nature of landscape and portraiture. Likewise, rhymed poetry was channeled into popular song, something that could be played on the piano, and "interpreted" by popular singers. The phonograph was the beginning of the end of poetry as mere rhymed entertainment. Whether they were conscious of it or not, serious poets turned in the same direction other modern artists did, in that they began to write impressionistically, expressionistically, using words and phrases the way the abstract or cubist artist did in their paintings. Today, the poet can either become a writer of "song" and enter the field of popular music, or she can write from the deeper tone of the speaking voice, the isolated, meditative individual plowing his way through the nature of reality. The contemporary poet must listen to the music of the voice, not the beat of a metronome.

But Greek verse was more song than we can imagine. For one thing, Greek verse is not equivalent to the English verse, in that Greek verse pays attention to the number of syllables in a line, not the number of stressed beats. That's why we call Greek (and Latin) verse quantitative. When we compare Greek epic poetry to English verse in terms of their metrical aspect—i.e., epic poetry uses dactylic hexameter, English poetry uses iambic pentameter—they're not exaclty parallel comparisons.

The hexameter established itself at a very early date as the meter of epic and didactic poetry, besides being used for some hymns, for bucolic (pastoral) poetry, and for satire. It consists of six metra or feet, each of which is a dactyl or, its metrical equivalent, a spondee. A dactyl is one stressed (or long) beat, followed by two unstressed (or short) beats. The word "carefully" is dactylic. Tennyson's "The Charge of the Light Brigade" uses the dactylic,

> Half a league, half a league,
> half a league onward,
> All in the valley of Death
> Rode the six hundred.
>
> . . . .
>
> Cannon to right of them,
> Cannon to left of them,
> Cannon in front of them
> Volleyed and thundered;
> Stormed at with shot and shell,
> Boldly they rode and well,
> into the jaws of Death,
> Into the mouth of hell
> Rode the six hundred.

as does Thomas Hardy's "The Voice," which begins

> Woman much missed, how you call to me, call to me,
> Saying that now you are not as you were
> When you had changed from the one who was all to me,
> But as at first, when our way was fair.

Even this anonymous ditty gives a sense of the musicality—in English—of the dactylic mater:

A was an archer, who shot at a frog;
B was a bitcher, and had a great dog;
C was a captain, all covered with lace;
D was a drunkard, and had a red face.

The dactyl, like the trochee, produces a falling rhythm, and since this is not the natural rhythm of English verse, which favors "rising rhythm," poems in English composed entirely of dactylics are rare.

But in the above cases, we're really counting accented, or stressed syllables, as we would the beat of a drum. This gives a misleading impression of what quantitive meter in Greek verse sounds like. In Greek and Latin , syllables are classified according to the length of time it takes to pronounce them, and are called long or short, or "ambivalent, i.e., either long or short. A syllable is long or short "by nature," whether or not it contains a long vowel or diphthong, or a short vowel. It's the vowel, and the length of time it takes to sound it that gives Greek verse it's musical quality, not the beat of the consonants.

When I acted in my first musical, I took singing lessons. The very first lesson focused on holding the note on the vowel sounds, not on the consonants, especially at the end of a line, as I had been incorrectly doing. For instance, when singing the line "Young at heart," I had been holding the note on the "rt," instead of on the "ar," and hitting the "rt" to close off the note. It makes sense, and makes for better phrasing. Even the opening note, on the word "young," sounds better if you hold the sound on the "ou" and round off the note at the end with the "ung" sound. (Of course, a singer like Frank Sinatra, will often break this rule and give the note a unique sound. When he holds the "ung" in his throat, it's a characteristic Sinatra sound, but most of us amatuers should not try it at home alone without proper supervision).

Thus, when Homer, or the homeric bard sang parts of the *Iliad*, accompanying himself on the lyre, it was more of a song, than a recitation. When I began to compose the title for this "food for thought," I started with "Meter, Prosody, and the . . . ." My ear was looking for a balanced number of syllables or beats for the second part of the phrase. I plucked out the title of the movie *The Guns of Navarrone*, mostly as a joke. It sounds unexpected, and anacronistic. In English, though, if we read the whole phrase metrically for the beat, we give emphasis on the consonants—"the **G**uns of **N**a-va-**r**onne." Three beats, seven syllables. But if we said it the way the homeric bard would have said it, we stress the vowels, and hold them to give the line a musical quality—"the **Guuuuuuuuuuu** u ns of **Naaaaaaaaaa** va **Rooooooooooo** ne."

Later, when we get to Latin poetry, we'll see that spoken Latin had a stress accent which classical Greek apparently did not have, yet the metres of classical Latin poetry were quantitative, as in Greek. On the whole, Latin poets avoided conflict between stress accent and quantity. All Latin metres were borrowed from Greek (except perhaps the saturnian metre).

✳

From 1100 BC to 750 BC, the heroic ideal became the subject of stories, poems, and legends that were eventually brought together and written down. Only two incomplete collections survive to our day: the Homeric epics—the *Iliad* and the *Odyssey*—put into written form during the 8th century BC (well, it's possible those two epic poems weren't actually written down as text until the 6th Century BC, but we'll talk about that later), and the books of the *Old Testament* from Genesis through Kings II, which reached its present written form by the 5th century BC. Both collections celebrated similiar ideals of the new primitive societies, personified by specific men who embodied these qualities: power and bearing (Samson, Ajax), the beauty of the body (Absalom, Achilles), masculine friendship (David, Patroclus), quick thinking and skill at deception (Jacob, Odysseus), generosity toward others (Abraham, Menelaus), and most of all, faithfulness to a god that guided them (Moses, Odysseus). The Homeric poems were recited and sung in the courts of petty kings, as part of the seasonal celebrations of small towns and villages, and eventually, in the marketplace and tavern where they were made available to the whole people.

Until the 4th century BC, the literature of early Greece was transmitted orally, through the human voice, since papyrus was expensive and cumbersome. The poets who sang or recited these epic tales made use of a vast tradition, often stitching pieces of stories together, weaving them into a new poem at each performance.

Homer's *Iliad* takes its title from Ilios or Ilion, which he used as alternative names for Troy: the *Iliad* being the "poem about Troy." According to Homer, Troy was a great city surrounded by powerful walls which made capture of the city by direct assault nearly impossible. Inside the walls were streets, palaces, temples, and the houses of the Trojans and their allies. For the last few centuries, historian have dismissed the lost world of Troy as nothing more than myth and epic fantasy. Few individuals believed Troy actually existed. And were it not for the pioneering excavations and astounding discoveries of a grocer's apprentice turned self-aggrandizing industrialist-cum-adventurer and amateur archeologist named Heinrich Schleimann (1822-1890), the real Troy might never have been found. He began excavating in 1870 on a hill lying about four miles inland from the Dardanelles, found the lost gold of Priam, king of ancient Troy, and continued digging until his death in 1890. This hill, now named Hissarlik, is generally identified with ancient Troy. Several settlements occupied the site one after the other, leaving a deposit some fifty feet deep. These settlements were labeled Troy II through Troy VI. Troy II belongs to the early Bronze Age, and was made up of a strongly fortified citadel about the size of a football field. The fortifications of the citadel were made of brick and stone, and massive walls strengthened by rectangular towers surrounded the citidel. In the southwest section of the wall there was a gateway leading into three small rooms. A larger gateway was also located on the southeast side. A series of small houses surrounded a main hall similar to the *megaroon*-complex later known in Mycenaean Greece. This *megaroon* contained ceremonial rooms. Objects found in this strata were bronze and copper weapons and domestic utensils. Most striking were the ornaments of gold, silver, and other precious jewelry, elaborate gold necklaces, lapis lazuli, carnelian, faience, rock-crystal, and nine-thousand gold chains that were later called "Schliemann's Treasure," a play on the cache called "Priam's Treasure." Schliemann contrived to smuggle the Treasure to his government in Berlin, where it was lost when pillaged by the Nazis during the Second World War. In 1993, the Treasure was revealed to be residing in Moscow, having been looted in 1945 by the Russians. Troy II was destroyed in a violent conflagration. Troy III, IV, and V were comparatively insignificant, but when we get to Troy VI, we come to the most imposing of the settlements, with walls surrounding a citadel that seemed to have flourished for centuries and was twice as large as Troy II. Five gateways led into the citadel, and on the east side stood a great tower with handsome masonry and a cistern. The homes within were built on terraces ascending from the circuit walls to the center of the citadel. Considerable amounts of imported Mycenaean pottery were found in later phases of the city, attesting to the close relations they must have had with the Mycenaeans of southern Greece. Like Troy II, Troy VI was destroyed in a great catastrophe, possibly an earthquake. Though rebuilt, it was again sacked and devastated by fire during the first half of the thirteenth century BC. It's successor, Troy VIIa, the Troy of the large storage jars, identified by some as the Troy of Helen, Priam and Homer's epic poems, was sacked at some time between the middle of the thirteenth century and the early part of the twelfth century BC. The destruction of rich and prosperous Troy, with its thousand or so citizens dwelling inside the fortified walls, and some five thousand in the city below, was one of the last great exploits of the Mycenaean world, remembered and sung by the bards as the Mycenaean world descended into a dark age of poverty and isolation. Excavations are still under way, and the discoveries that continue to be made have given rise to numerous controversies as new methods and attitudes in archeology are brought to bear on the work. Schliemann had turned, as a friend put it, the heroes of the *Iliad* and the *Odyssey* into "men of flesh and bood." He had given archaeology a whole new world. But had he discovered Priam's Troy? Of the many settlements unearthed at Hissarlik, which one was the fabulous Troy written about by Homer? Schliemann favored Troy II, but recent dating indicates that it existed around 25000-2200 BC, much too early for Homer's poem. Based on the Mycenaean pottery found there, Troy VI or Troy VIIa may well have come to an end around 1300 BC, close enough to Homer's date of the destruction of the city by Achaeans in 1230 BC.

Schleiman grew up hearing the story of the *Iliad*, and was convinced that Ancient Troy had actually existed. Thanks to him, and the archeologists that followed, cities such as Troy, Mycenae and Cnossus described in the *Iliad* are no longer the stuff of myth, but history. Archeologists exhumed a Mycenaean civilization that bears striking resemblance to the one we conjure when reading the lines of Homer. If the cities were real, could the characters have been real, too: Agamemnon, who returned to Mycenae after the victory over Troy only to be butchered by his wife, Clytemnestra; Helen, whose abduction by her lover, Paris, began the Trojan War; wrathful Achilles, whose quarrel with Agamemnon set in motion the crucial confrontations of the *Iliad*; and beloved Hector, the hero whose tragedy is the tragedy of all Troy? Were the two warriors who escaped the destruction of the city real as well: nimble-witted Odysseus and his Trojan counterpart, Aeneas? Unlike Achilles, whose passions clouded his intellect, Odysseus made maximum use of both passion and intellect. Aeneas, the Trojan warrior who battles Achilles at the end of the *Iliad*, was about to meet his death when, just in the nick of time, Homer had Poseidon rescue the young hero for Virgil's use a millenium later as the hero of the great Latin epic, the *Aeneid*.

Homer's Achaeans—the Greeks of the Heroic Age—were beautiful and fair-haired women, tall and handsome men with long hair and wild beards. Before the body of Patrocolus was set atop his funeral pyre, his companions expressed their love by "covering the corpse under the locks of their hair, which they cut off and dropped on him." Their dress was simple, a garment folded over the shoulder reaching nearly to the knees, and held with a pin. The wealthier wore costly robes, like the one Priam brought to Achilles in ransom for the body of his son, Hector. Their world was rural, toiling over the land and against the rivers that "in their swift course shatter the dykes." Everyone drunk diluted wine, even the children. "Cities" were but small villages hugging a hilltop fortress. Messengers carried important news, and were sometimes slain with the message. Over long distances, communication by signal fires flashed from peak to peak. In Aesclylses' *Agamemnon*, Clytemnestra recounts how she knew the fall of Troy was complete.

Clytemnestra:
> The men of Argos have taken Priam's citadel.
> The Achaeans are in Troy.

Chorus:
> How long, then, is it since the citadel was stormed?

Clytemnestra:
> It is night, the mother of this dawn I hailed.

Chorus:
> What kind of messenger could come in speed like this?

Clytemnestra:
> Hephaestus, who cast forth the shining blaze from Ida.
> And beacon after beacon picking up the flare
> carried it here; Ida to the Hermaean horn
> of Lemnos, where it shone above the isle, and next
> the sheer rock face of Zeus on Athos caught it up;
> and plunging skyward to arch the shoulders of the sea
> the strength of the running flare in exultation,
> pine timbers flaming into gold, like the sunrise,
> brought the bright message to Macistus' sentinel cliffs,
> who, never slow nor in the carelessness of sleep
> caught up, sent on his relay in the courier chain,
> and far across Euripus' streams the becaon flare
> carried to signal watchmen on Messapion.
> These took it again in turn, and heaping high a pile
> of silvery brush flamed it to throw the message on.
> And the flare sickened never, but grown stronger yet
> outleapt the river valley of Asopus like
> the very moon for shining, to Cithaeron's scaur
> to waken the next station of the flaming post.
> These watchers, not contemptuous of the far-thrown blaze,
> kindled another beacon vaster than commanded.

The light leaned high above Gorgopis' staring marsh,
and striking Aegyplanctus' mountain top, drove on
yet one more relay, lest the flare die down in speed.
Kindled once more with stintless heaping force, they send
the beard of flame to hugeness, passing far beyond
the promontory that gazes on the Saronic strait
and flaming far, until it plunged at last to strike
the steep rock of Arachnus near at hand, our watchtower.
And thence there fell upon this house of Atreus' sons
the flare whose fathers mount to the Ideaean beacon.
These are the changes on my torchlight messengers,
one from another running out the laps assigned.
The first and last sprinters have the victory.
By such proof and such symbol I announce to you
my lord at Troy has sent his messengers to me.

Chorus:

The gods, lady, shall have my prayers and thanks straightway.
And yet to hear your story till all wonder fades
would be my wish, could you but tell it once again.

Clytemnestra:

The Achaeans have got Troy, upon this very day.
I think the city echoes with a clash of cries.
Pour vinegar and oil into the selfsame bowl,
you could not say they mix in friendship, but fight on.
Trojans are stooping now to gather in their arms
their dead, husbands and brothers; children lean to clasp
the aged who begot them, crying upon the death
of those most dear, from lips that never will be free.

The Achaeans have their midnight work after the fighting
that sets them down to feed on all the city has,
ravenous, headlong, by no rank and file assigned,
but as each man has drawn his shaken lot by chance.
And in the Trojan houses that their spears have taken
they settle now, free of the open sky, the frosts
and dampess of the evening; without sentinels set
they sleep the sleep of happiness the whole night through.

The Achaean culture that Homer paints is in many ways lawless and violent. Achilles is generous to Priam when the latter comes to ransom his son's body. He suggests they both weep for their lost loved ones. But Achilles' courteous manner comes after he has dragged Hector's body in mangled dishonor around the walls of Troy.

Reading Homer's epics, we get the impression that writing is something left to lowly scribes. The Heroic Age is a time of flesh and blood, not clay and ink. The only time writing is mentioned in the *Iliad* is when a folded tablet is given to a messenger. The message he delivers instructs the recipient to kill the messenger. For the Achaeans, epic verse is both poetry and history rolled into one. When the king or prince holds a feast or victory celebration, the wandering minstrel is brought in to entertain with poetry that glorifies the deeds of valorous warriors.

Nothing whatever is known about Homer the man, including the crucial point of whether he existed. Several schools of thought differ over whether the *Iliad* and the *Odyssey* were written by the same person, two authors, or several. Epic poetry of the Homeric age was the end product of a long period of growth during which historical events, legends, and folk tales were stitched together by many generations of bards. In the case of the *Iliad* and the *Odyssey*, this process probably covered four centuries, from shortly after the series of events known as the Trojan War (set off by Helen of Troy, "the face that launched a thousand ships") in the early 13th century BC to the mid-9th century BC, which seems the most likely date for Homer.

The most widely held position today is that, although both the *Iliad* and the *Odyssey* are made up of traditional materials, each bears the unmistakable imprint of a single artistic intelligence. This belief is supported by the remarkable structural, dramatic, and stylistic unity achieved in both epics. The *Odyssey* is even more remarkable for its extraordinary modern structure, which employs the techniques of the "flashback" and parallel lines of action common in the novel and film.

A The Wrath of Achilles—"a poem about Ilium" (i.e. Troy).
nyone who sets out to translate Homer must reconcile two opposing elements: the directness and immediacy of Homer's narrative, and the artificial poetic diction developed over generations of oral performance before it was finally written down. Each generation of translators has to find a diction that corresponds to the poetic tradition of its day, while at the same time using the right colloquial tone, especially in the set speeches that account for almost half of the *Illiad*'s lines.

Homer's language is not the everyday speech of his time. It's a poetic idiom, heightened and stylized in some instances, simple and natural in others. As the language of the King James Version of the Bible or of Milton is removed from the ordinary speech of the seventeenth century, so the dactylic hexameter of Homer's poetic idiom is the product of a long tradition, a coalescence of the various Greek dialects of the time: the sweet cadences of the Ionic, which never uses contractions and resolves the diphthongs into two syllables so the words sound elevated and sonorous; the Attic dialect, with its flexible contractions and blunt expressions; the broader Doric with its enobling diction; and the feebler Aeolic, which rejects its aspirate, or takes off its accent. Thus, Homer's lines are flexible yet dignified, simple and direct yet capable of great power and majesty of sound. Anyone translating Homer must keep alive the fire and spirit that animates his characters' speeches, while preserving the stylistic modulations of his narrative, which seem to bolt directly into the action. Imagine a clown playing a king, a weightlifter leaping into the air like Nijinsky, Louis Armstrong playing Mozart. Or imagine someone telling a story that leapt from the Elizabethan diction of the King James Bible to the modern colloquialisms of rap, to the stentorian voice of a New England politician to the Southern drawls of a Tennessee Williams. Because the *Iliad* developed over centuries, and because the Homeric rhapsodes who transmitted the tale through recitation incorporated the various dialects of their region and of their day, the epic became a masterpiece of tonal dynamics and dictional variations. Though there have been prose translations that stress the narrative, they often miss the eloquence and music of Homer's diction. As a story-teller, he knew how to keep his audience awake; as a poet, he knew how to make them dream.

If, as Alfred North Whitehead contended, that all western philosophy is a footnote to Plato and Aristotle—that is, that we are all either Platonists or Aristotelians—then one might also contend that all European literature is merely a commentary on the first of its masters—Homer. In his *Erotic Poems*, Ovid (43 BC–17 AD) called him, "Great Homer, perennial well-spring of inspiration for poets." Theocritus has one of the characters in his pastoral idylls say, "Homer is enough for everybody." In Homer we find a richness of language that is both elevated and contemporary, eloquent and colloquial; every nuance of tone between majestic solemnity and off-beat satire presents itself for poets to use in their own work. Homer's famous similies serve a function that goes well beyond clever decoration; they're extended imagistic devices that help weld the elements of Homer's narrative into a unified structure, illuminating the nuances of characters as diverse as Achilles and Penelope, Agamemnon and Hecuba, King Priam and Odysseus' herdsman. A poem in mixed meter attributed to Homer but now lost featured a hero who was inept and comical, a parody of the isolated warrior as Simple Simon.

Not only did Homer's imitators miss his human dimension in mechanically copying the externals of his style, but his translators through the ages have failed to convey the astonishing range of language in reducing his style to a one-dimensional poetic idiom. This misunderstanding and simplification of Homer's legacy was common, partly because the range of poetic devices available to translators in the literary langugage of their own day was somewhat limited, and many translators were misguided in their hesitancy to use the idioms of current speech, focusing instead on Homer's elevated idioms.

In Book III of his *Rhetoric*, Aristotle (384-322 BC) reverses his earlier theory on tragedy and decides that modern poets and dramatists should reject the use of over-ornamentation and archaic language, but instead should use the diction and vocabulary of current speech, except in specific instances where an outworn poetic phrase used in the context of natural speech might jolt the reader and bring life to the text. For centuries after Homer, no Greek epic poet was as famous and as influential as Callimachus (310-240 BC), who reminded poets of his own day to model Homer's great accomplishment by using both the living language of their contemporaries—that plain style that aimed for clarity and eschewed obscurity—mixed with the literary poetic gloss that produced an emotional and intellectual response. By the same token, the poet using a literary language, Callimachus warned, had to be careful not to lapse into bombast and inflated diction for its own sake, to avoid the hackneyed phrase and tiresome cliché.

Every English translator since the Elizabethan age has tried to bring Homer into the prevailing idiom of the day. It's an almost impossible task, and can, at best, approximate the experience the original Greek would have had on those hearing it. The accepted Greek text of the *Iliad* is based on poems edited in the 6th century BC for use in Athens, and revised in the 2nd century AD by Aristarchus of Samothrace. The first printed editions were made in 1488 by Chalcondyles and in 1504 by the great Venetian editor and printer Aldus Manutius (to whom we owe the sloping type known as *italic*, said to be a copy of contemporary handwriting). Homer's tale of Troy had its place in Tudor myth, and the original text was increasingly studied in early manuscripts. Shakespeare used Caxton's *Recuyell of the Historyes of Troye* (printed in Bruges, 1473-74) as a source for *Troilus and Cressida* as well as for the mention it gets in *Hamlet*. It's remarkable that Caxton's version remained popular for over a century. Caxton's translations contributed to the development of 15th century prose style, though his own style is somewhat rambling and ill-constructed, manifesting the weaknesses of the elaboration of courtly writing without its virtues. In 1581 Hall's version of ten books appeared, but it was George Chapman who first translated the entire *Iliad* into English (1616) and Hobbes and Ogilby offered their renditions in the century that followed.

When I was in high school, I had to memorize the famous invocation that opens the poem and states the subject and theme: Paris abducting Menalaus's wife Helen and bringing her back to Troy, which precipitated the war between Troy and Greece, and the quarrel between two of the Greek heroes, Achilles, son of the goddess Thetis, and Agamemnon, son of Atreus and leader of the Greek forces. Below is Chapman's rendering, but the one I had to learn was Alexander Pope's version.

A*chilles* banefull wrath resound, O Goddesse, that imposd
Infinite sorrowes on the greekes; and many brave soules losd
From breasts Heroique: sent them barre, to that invisible cave
That no light comforts: and their lims, to dogs and cultures gave.
To all which, *Joves will* gave effect; from whom, first strife begunne,
Betwixt *Atrides*, king of men; and Thetis godlike Sonne.
(George Chapman, 1611)

Chapam claimed to have been directly inspired by the fiery breath of Homer himself, but just as likely he was influenced by the second hand breath of Andreas Divus, whose Latin translations of the *Iliad* and *Odyssey* were published in the 1530s. It was this Latin translation that centuries later, Ezra Pound bought in a Paris bookstall for four francs, and from which he made his own English translation for the opening poem of the *Cantos*.

George Chapman (1559-1634), poet and dramatist, was just a few years older than Shakespeare, and despite numerous non-dramatic poems, seven comedies, two two-part tragedies, and several other dramatic collaborations, he is best remembered for his translations of Homer, the first of which appeared in 1598, comprising only the first seven books in a hasty publication devised to mark the Earl of Essex's embarkation for Ireland; twelve books of the *Illiad* appeared in 1608, and the complete *Iliad* and *Odyssey* were published together in 1616 as *The Whole Works of Homer, Prince of Poetts*.

Two centuries later, Keats's famous sonnet commended Chapman's Homer to another generation of readers.

ON FIRST LOOKING INTO CHAPMAN'S HOMER

Much have I travell'd in the realms of gold,
　　and many goodly states and kingdoms seen;
　　Round many western islands have I been
Which bards in fealty to Apollo hold.

Oft of one wide expanse had I been told
    That deep-brow'd Homer ruled as his demesne;
    Yet did I never breathe its pure serene
Till I heard Chapman speak out loud and bold;
Then felt I like some watcher of the skies
    When a new planet swims into his ken;
Or like stout Cortez when with eagle eyes
    He star'd at the Pacific—and all his men
Look'd at each other with a wild surmise—
    Silent, upon a peak in Darien.

Swinburne praised the translations for their "romantic and sometimes barbaric grandeur, their freshness, strength, and inextinguishable fire." T.S. Eliot called Chapman "potentially the greatest artist" of the Elizabethan dramatists, despite his lack of academic rigor. Many have guessed that he was "the rival poet" of Shakespeare's *Sonnets*. Using the distinctive 14-syllable lines of Chapman's *Iliad*, Shakespeare may have attempted to acount for the great rhetorical sweep of his poetry in Sonnet #86, the most famous of the "rival-poet" group—"Was it the proud full sail of his great verse"—the reference, then, to the "affable familiar ghost" would have been a reference to Homer's spirit.

Was it the proud full sail of his great verse,
Bound for the prize of (all-too-precious) you,
That did my ripe thoughts in my brain inhearse,
Making their tomb the womb wherein they grew?
Was it his spirit, by spirits taught to write
Above a mortal pitch, that struck me dead?
No, neither he, nor his compeers by night
Giving him aid, my verse astonished.
He nor that affable familiar ghost
Which nightly gulls him with intelligence,
As victors, of my silence cannot boast;
I was not sick of any fear from thence.
    But when your countenance fill'd up his line,
Then lack'd I matter; that enfeebled mine.

The only lines of Chapman's own poetry still quoted from time to time are these from his two-part tragedy *Bussy D'Ambois*:

Man is a torch borne in the wind; a dream
But of a shadow, summ'd with all his substance.

Despite the off-putting sound of his Elizabethan inversions, Chapman's translation retains a vigorous and inspiring boldness. In places, he adds whole lines of his own that function as personal commentary on the story, and occasionally uses strange and unfamiliar words, though Shakespeare's verbal innovations in his own plays were more numerous than Chapman's. When he began translating the epic, Chapman favored Achilles, but gradually, as his understanding of the epic became clearer to him, he gained a new vision of the heroic ideal as finding its greatest embodiment in Hector, or even in the crafty Ulysses. The "fourteener" he chose was not even well-suited for English metrics, tending to degenerate into a monotonous drum-beat, jog and trot, thumping along best when used for the ballad, not the epic. But his translation inspired English poets for centuries after his time, and it is one of the major poetic achievements of an age that was already rich in poetic achievement.

In 1715, Alexander Pope (1688-1744) issued the first volume of his translation of Homer's *Iliad* in heroic couplets, and completed it by 1720. The work was supplemented in 1725-6 by a translation of the *Odyssey*. The two translations brought him financial independence, and were reprinted in numerous collections in the following centuries. In his introduction, Pope confessed that he felt "utterly incapable of doing justice to Homer," but hoped to make "a more tolerable copy of him than any entire translation in verse has yet done." He did not find Chapman's version suitable, to say the least.

> Chapman has taken the advantage of an immeasurable length of verse, notwithstanding which, there is scarce any paraphrase more loose and rambling than his. He has frequent interpolations of four or six lines; and I remember one where he has spun twenty verses out of two. He is often mistaken in so bold a manner, that one might think he deviated on purpose, if he did not in other places of his notes insist so much upon verbal trifles. He appears to have had a strong affectation of extracting new meanings out of his author; insomuch as to promise, in his rhyming preface, a poem of the mysteries he had revealed in Homer; and perhaps he endeavored to strain the obvious sense to this end. . . . In a word, the nature of the man may account for his whole performance; for he appears, from his preface and remarks, to have been of an arrogant turn, and an enthusiast in poetry. His own boast, of having finished half the *Illiad* in less than fifteen weeks, shows with what negligence his version was performed.

Of his own attempt to translate Homer, Pope noted that "one could sooner pardon frenzy than frigidity."

> Homer not only appears the inventor of poetry, but excels all the inventors of other arts, in this, that he has swallowed up the honour of those who succeeded him. He showed all the stretch of fancy at once; and if he has failed in some of his flights, it was but because he attempted everything. It is certain no literal translation can be just to an excellent original in a superior language: but it is a great mistake to imagine (as many have done) that a rash paraphrase can make amends for this general defect; which is no less in danger to lose the spirit of an ancient, by deviating into the modern manners of expression. If there be sometimes a darkness, there is often a light in antiquity, which nothing better preserves than a version almost literal. It is not to be doubted, that the fire of the poem is what a translator should principally regard. It is a great secret in writing, to know when to be plain, and when poetical and figurative; and it is what Homer will teach us, if we will but follow

modestly in his footsteps. Where his diction is bold and lofty, let us raise ours as high as we can; but where he is plain and humble, we ought not to be deterred from imitating him by the fear of incurring the censure of a mere English critic. Nothing that belongs to Homer seems to have been more commonly mistaken than the just pitch of his style. There is a graceful and dignified simplicity, as well as a bold and sordid one. It is one thing to be tricked up, and another not to be dressed at all. Simplicity is the mean between ostentation and rusticity.

More Augustan than Homeric in spirit and diction, Pope's achievement was admired for centuries, prompting Coleridge to call it "an astonishing product of matchless talent and ingenuity." This was the version I had to memorize in high school.

Achilles' wrath, to Greece the direful spring
Of woes unnumber'd, heavenly goddess, sing!
That wrath which hurl'd to Pluto's gloomy reign
The souls of mighty chiefs untimely slain;
Whose limbs of unburied on the naked shore,
Devouring dogs and hungry vultures tore:
Since great Achilles and Atrides strove,
Such was the sovereign doom, and such the will of Jove!
(Alexander Pope, 1720)

Chapman and Pope's works have long been considered the greatest English translations of Homer, though certainly not in American English. For catching the contemporary diction of modern American English, both Fagel's and Lombardo's recent translations are excellent. Many still consider Pope's work a classic, echoing Samuel Johnson's assessment that it was "a performance which no age or nation can pretend to equal." Statements like that often confer distinction upon the hyperbolicker, not the hyperbolickee. The scholar Richard Bentley kept things in perspetive with his admonishment, "It is a pretty poem Mr. Pope but you must not call it Homer."

A few years prior to Pope's translation, John Dryden (1631-1700) had translated Virgil's *Aeneid* into heroic couplets, which became a standard version for centuries. He began a version of the *Illiad* but never completed it. Pope noted that it was "a great loss to the poetical world that Mr. Dryden did not live to translate the *Iliad*. He left us only the first book, and a small part of the sixth. Had he translated the whole work, I would no more have attempted Homer after him than Virgil: his version of whom (notwithstanding some human errors) is the most noble and spirited translation I know in any language." Below is Dryden's version of the opening.

The Wrath of Peleus' Son, O Muse, resound;
Whose dire Effects the Grecian Army found:
And many a Heroe, King, and hardy Knight,
Were sent, in early Youth, to Shades of Night;
Their Limbs a Prey to Dogs and Vultures made;

So was the Sov'reign Will of *Jove* obey'd:
From that ill-omen'd Hour when Strife begun,
Betwixt *Atrides* Great, and *Thetis* God-like Son.
(John Dryden, 1700)

It was in the 19th century that Homer came into his own as a popular "classic." Samuel Butler considered the Lang, Leaf, and Myers translation to be "the best yet made," having been reprinted eighteen times between 1883 and 1914. As Chapman's and Pope's were typically Elizabethan in diction, Andrew Lang's prose version was quite Victorian, and even today retains an eccentric effectiveness, especially when the mannered alliterative effects rise to the poetic occasion.

Sing, Goddess, the wrath of Achhilles Peleus' son, the ruinous wrath that brought on the Achaians woes innumerable, and hurled down into Hades many strong souls of heroes, and gave their bodies to be a prey to dogs and all winged fowls; and so the counsel of Zeus wrought out its accomplishment from the day when strife first parted Atreides king of men and noble Achilles.

But though Samuel Butler admired Lang's translation, he still felt there was room for improvement. In his preface, he discussed his guiding principals and why he felt he could imporove on Lang's version.

The genius of the language into which a translation is being made is the first thing to be considered; if the original was readable, the translation must be so also, or it is not a translation. It follows that a translation should depart hardly at all from the modes of speech current in the translator's own times. . . . We know the charm of the Elizabethan translations, but he who would attempt one that shall vie with these must eschew all Elizabethanism that are not good Victorianisms also. . . . The Elizabethan did not lard a crib with Chaucerisms, and think that they were translating. They aimed fearlessly and without taint of affectation at making a dead author living to a generation other than his own. To do this they transfused their blood into his cold veins, and quickened him with their own livingness.

Dr. Leaf has in the main kept more closely to the words of Homer, but I believe him to have lost more of the spirit of the original through his abandonment (no doubt deliberate) of all attempt at stately, and at the same time easy, musical, flow of langauge, than he has gained in adherence to the letter—to which, after all, neither he nor any man can adhere.

Butler begins the tale of Troy thusly:

Sing, O Goddess, the anger of Achilles, son of Peleus, that brought countless ills upon the Achaeans. Many a brave soul did it send hurrying down to Hades, and many a hero did it yield a prey to dogs and vultures, for so were the counsels of Zeus fulfilled from the day on which the son of Atreus, king of men, and great Achilles first fell out with one another.

For Lang, it was "strife first parted" Agamemnon and Achilles; for Butler, they had a falling out. When Richard Lattimore's translation appeared in 1951, it was considered the best modern *Illiad* ever made into the English language. In his note on the translation, he said, "I have used the plainest language I could find which might be adequate, and mostly this is the language of contemporary prose." Using a six-beat hexameter line, Lattimore's rendering is rapid, plain, and direct, unrhymed, but not without poetical effect.

Sing, goddess, the anger of Peleus' son Achilles
and its devastation, which put pains thousandfold upon the
Achaians,
hurled in their multitudes to the house of Hades strong souls
of heroes, but gave their bodies to be the delicate feasting
of dogs, of all birds, and the will of Zeus was accomplished
since that time when first there stood in division of conflict
Atreus' son the lord of men and brilliant Achilles.
(Richard Lattimore,1951)

The same year, W.H. D. Rouse went at it in modern, colloquial prose.

An angry man—there is my story: the bitter rancour of Achilles, prince of the house of Peleus, which brought a thousand troubles upon the Achaian host. Many a strong soul it sent down to Hades, and left the heroes themselves a prey to dogs and carrion birds, while the will of God moved on to fullfilment. It began first of all with a quarrel between my Lord King Agamemnon of Atreus' line and the Prince Achilles.
(W. H. D. Rouse, 1951)

In 1974, Robert Fitzgerald's translation was seen as something of a landmark, solving many of the problems that had plagued previous translations. It won the Harold Morton Landon Translation Award two years later, and set a standard for its swift rhythms, vivid imagery, and crisp English that gave dignity and life to the texture of Homer's original.

Anger be now your song, immortal one,
Akhilleus' anger, doomed and ruinous,
that caused the Akhaians loss on bitter loss
and crowded brave souls into the undergloom,
leaving so many dead men—carrion
for dogs and birds; and the will of Zeus was done.
Begin it when the two men first contending
broke with one another—
the Lord Marshal
Agamémnon, Atreus' son, and Prince Akhilleus.

When Robert Fagles' brilliant new translation appeared in 1990, it was hailed as an astonishing and powerful version, destined to become a standard for a new generation.

Rage—Goddess, sing the rage of Peleus' son Achilles,
murderous, doomed, that cost the Acheans countless losses,
hurling down to the House of Death so many sturdy souls,
great fighters' souls, but made their bodies carrion,
feasts for the dogs and birds,
and the will of Zeus was moving toward its end.
Begin, muse, when the two first broke and clashed,
Agamemnon lord of men and brilliant Achilles.
(Robert Fagles, 1990)

A few years later, Michael Reck chose a ten-syllable iambic line, and translated the poem line for line, almost word for word.

Sing, Goddess, Achilles' maniac rage:
ruinous thing! it roused a thousand sorrows
and hurled many souls of mighty warriors
to Hades, made their bodies food for dogs
and carrion birds—as Zeus's will foredoomed—
from the time relentless strife came between
Atreus' son, a king, and brave Achilles.
(Michael Reck, 1994)

It is impossible not to be impressed by Fagles' achievement, a version imbued with humanity and eloquence. But here's a vote for Stanley Lombardo's pulsing account which jumps off the page with a hard-edged, racy idiom that brings an Iron Age passion to the urgency of our Electronic Age.

Rage:
    Sing, Goddess, Achilles' rage,
Black and murdcrous, that cost the Greeks
incalculable pain, pitched countless souls
Of heroes into Hades' dark,
And left their bodies to rot as feasts
For dogs and birds, as Zeus' will was done.
    Begin with the clash between Agamemnon—
The Greek warlord—and godlike Achilles.
(Stanley Lombardo, 1997)

It is apparent reading these samples from various versions, that the real Homer, like Dante perhaps, exists only in the original, and at best, can only be conveyed as an amalgam of different renderings. Each translation is but another spice thrown into the strew. The reader stirs them together and, in his own mind, imagines for himself the power and luminosity of the original.

In this great epic, Homer celebrates the Greek heroes and their victory over Troy, a grand city on the Hellespont and the rich lands lying about the Black Sea. Yet, the noblest portrait is that of Hector, the Trojan leader who fights to the very end. His wife will be sold into slavery, his young son thrown from the walls of Troy. The Greeks heard this story told century after century, first by traveling singers and poets—ancient jongleurs, and then several centuries later by the blind poet who brought the various tales together and wove them into a grand, unified design. While they may have been awed by the mighty deeds of their Achaean heroes, they must have been disturbed at the way Achilles dragged Hector's dead body before the Trojan wives and children looking down from the ramparts, and they must have been touched by the nobility of Hector's purpose, his relationship with his family, and his affection for his people.

The background of the *Iliad* is the story of the twenty-year seige of Troy, though Homer concentrated on a specific episode that took place in the tenth year of the seige. The cause of the conflict falls upon the so-called Judgement of Paris. When asked by the goddess Aphrodite to name the fairest of them all, Paris picked Helen, wife of Menalaus. It was the gods who set the conflict in motion by having Helen fall in love with Paris and run away with him to Troy. Agamemnon, commander-in-chief of the Greek forces, calls upon all the Greek-speaking nations to seek vengeance. They assemble a thousand ships and sail across the Aegean. All Greece and all western Asia saw it as a decisive conflict, with reinforcements sent to Troy from Asia Minor and the various nations of Greece. This struggle for control of the Hellespont would be renewed throughout history—from the battle of Marathon against the Persians in 490 BC (Athens was saved when a Greek runner traveled 26.3 miles with crucial information, then dropped to his death), to the Battle of Gallipoli in World War I. Compare the invasion and twenty-year seige of Troy with a similar modern-day assault, the Normandy Invasion. Operation Overlord, code name for the Battle of Normandy, began on June 6, 1944, now known as D-Day (although the term "d-day" is a military term for the beginning of any military offensive, it has now become synonymous with the invasion by Allied forces of Europe to end World War II. American-British forces crossed the English channel and landed on the beaches of German-occupied Normandy, the largest and most difficult amphibious operation ever mounted in the history of warfare. 8,000 ships and craft and 13,000 aircraft broke through the German defenses of the Atlantic Wall, landing over beaches rather than at a major port. Fighting was bitter, but by late July, the Allies broke through the weakened German defences and made rapid progress inland, liberating Paris at the end of August and Brussels on September 3. Our modern day epic poets—screenwriters and film directors—have "sung" of this event in numerous movies: *The Longest Day, Saving Private Ryan*, etc. Where the Troajn war had its controversial episode—the fued between two of its "generals," Agamemnon and Achilles—the Normandy Invasion had its Anglo-American friction, and the controversial failure at Arnhem, the largest airborne battle in history, and General Montgomery's only major defeat.

Every epic poet and filmmaker knows that within the sweep of large action, it's the minor episodes and personal stories that really convey the truth about war. Through the eyes of Steven Spielberg, the Normandy Invasion could best be told by focusing on the attempt by a small squad of soldiers to find and bring back Private Ryan. In the Iliad, though there is both the joy and agony of battle, and the celebration of individual courage, Homer avoids glorifiying war as such. The war was essentially a calamaty for both sides, perpetuated by fate and the whims of the gods . The story Homer tells is personal, a petty squabble between an arrogant general, Agamemnon, and Achilles, the strongest and most effective fighter in the Greek army. The story also includes a more heroic fight to the death between Achilles and the great Trojan warrior, Hector. The first dispute begins when Agamemnon refuses to return his captive mistress, Chryseis, to her father, despite the ensuing pestilence which will continue to ravage the Greek forces.

> And why should I? I like her better than
> My wife Clytemnestra. She's no worse than her
> When it comes to looks, body, mind, or ability.
> Still, I'll give her back, if that's what's best.
> I don't want to see the army destroyed like this.
> But I want another prize ready for me right away.
> I'm not going to be the only Greek without a prize. [Lombardo]

When Agamemnon grudingly agrees to release her, he decides to take Achilles' mistress, Briseis as compensation. Publically humiliated, Achilles explodes in rage, vowing to withdraw his services and praying that the Greeks suffer defeat in the field.

> You shameless, profiterring excuse for a commander!
> How are you going to get any Greek warrior
> To follow you into battle again? You know,
> I don't have any quarrel with the Trojans,
> they didn't do anything to me to make me
> Come over here and fight, didn't run off my cattle or horses
> Or ruin my farmland back home in Phthia, not with all
> The shadowy mountains and moaning seas between.
> It's for you, dogface, for your precious pleasure—
> And Menelaus' honor—that we came here,
> A fact you don't have the decency even to mention!
> And now you're threatening to take away the prize
> That I sweated for and the Greeks gave me.
> I never get a prize equal to yours when the army
> Captures one of the Trojan strongholds.
> No, I do all the dirty work with my own hands,
> And when the battle's over and we divide the loot

You get the lion's share and I go back to the ships
With some pitiful little thing, so worn out from fighting
I don't have the strength left even to complain.
Well, I'm going back to Phthia now. Far better
To head home with my curved ships than stay here,
Unhonored myself and piling up a fortune for you."
(Stanley Lombardo, 1997)

Agamemnon says, "I couldn't care less about you or your famous temper," and proceeds to tell him that he plans to go to Achilles' hut and take Briseis for his own.

Achilles' chest was a rough knot of pain
Twisting around his heart: should he
Draw the sharp sword that hung by his thigh,
Scatter the ranks and gut Agamemnon,
Or control his temper, repress his rage?
(Stanley Lombardo, 1997)

At this point, Athena shows herself to Achilles and counsels him to forego violence. Instead, he should tell Agememnon off, which he does with typical Achillean anger.

Food for Thought

JUVENAL MEETS ALLEN GINSBERG, LENNY BRUCE & GEORGE CARLIN

I think comparing several different translations of this scene demonstrates the relative accuracy of such renderings, each appropriate to their own time. Several years ago I was lecturing on the classic poets and read aloud one of Juvenal's satires. I read from a recent translation that so captured the tone of his biting satire that it sounded almost like a modern stand-up comedian in a night club, which is exactly as it should have, since Juvenal's Rome was very much like our modern era. Someone in the audience wanted to know if that's how Juvenal really wrote. After all, he was a classic Latin poet, writing in the 1st century AD. He should sound archaic, shouldn't he. People didn't really write like that, did they? Didn't all poetry sound like the English poetry written in the centuries following Shakespeare, up to the beginning of the modern era, when poets began to write in a more natural idiom?

"You mean like this?" I asked, and proceeded to read from Juvenal's tenth satire, from a translation by Samuel Johnson (1709-1784)

Must hapless man, in ignorance sedate,
Roll darkling down the torrent of his fate?
Must no dislike alarm, no wishes rise,
No cries invoke the mercies of the skies?
Inquire, cease: petitions yet remain,
Which Heaven may hear: nor deem religion vain.
Still raise for good the supplicating voice,
but leave to Heaven the measure and the choice.

"Like that?" I said.

Nods all around. That's what poetry, they supposed, written before the 20th century sounded like, before all that modern "write like you talk" stuff. Especially the great classics. I read another selection from Juvenal's first satire, a translation by the Rev. M. Madan, published by J.B. Lippincott & Co in 1860.

> Shall I always be only a hearer? — shall I never repay,
> Who am teas'd so often with the Theseis of hoarse Cordus?
> Shall one (poet) recite his comedies to me with impunity,
> Another his elegies? shall bulky Telephus waste a day
> With impunity? or Orestes — the margin of the whole book already full,
> And written on the back too, nor as yet finished?
> No man's house is better known to him, than to me
> The grove of Mars, and the den of Vulcan near
> The Aeolian rocks: what the winds can do: what ghosts Aeacus may be
> tormenting: from whence another could convey the gold
> Of the stolen fleece: how great wild-ash tree Monychus could throw:
> The plane-trees of Fronto, and the convuls'd marbles complain
> Always, and the columns broken with the continual reader:
> you may expect the same things from the highest and from the least poet.

Then I read the same passage from a recent translation by Peter Green, published in 1967.

> Must I *always* be stuck in the audience at these poetry readings, never
> Up on the platform myself, taking it out on Cordus
> For the times he's bored me to death with ranting speeches
> From that *Theseid* of his? Is X to get off scot-free
> After inflicting his facres on me, or Y his elegies. Is there
> No recompense for whole days waster on long-winded and drawn-out
> Versions of *Telephus*? And what about that *Orestes* —
> Each margin of the roll crammed solid, top and bottom,
> More on the back, and *still* it wasn't finished!
> I know all the mythical landscapes like my own backroom:
> The grove of Mars, the cave near Aelous' island
> belonging to Vulcan. The stale themes are bellowed daily
> In rich patrons' colonnades, till their marble pillars
> Crack with a surfeit of rhetoric. The plane-trees echo
> Every old trope — what the winds are up to, whose ghost
> Aeacus has on his hellish rack, from what country
> The other fellow is sneaking off with that golden sheepskin,
> The monstrous size of those ash-trees the Centaurs used for spears:
> You get the same stuff from them all, established poet
> and raw beginners alike.

"This is what Juvenal actually sounded like to his contemporary audience," I said. He was funny, biting, topical, and when he was pissed off, he sounded modern, like someone who's pissed off today. He's making fun of pompous poets and tedious poetry readings, and his audience knew just what he was talking about. He was stand-up comic and social critic rolled into one, a cross between Allen Ginsberg and George Carlin. The translation made over a century ago might have worked then, but not now. The modern poet needs to see how modern a poet writing two millennia ago really was. And a translation that fails to capture the true tone and diction does a disservice to modern poets, struggling with their own voice. In time, Peter Green's translation will no longer sound modern, and someone else will have to bring Juvenal up to date. Both language and speech change over time, but all great poets and writers tend to write in the diction of their day. Translations tend to lock them into one era. There's an old saying that poetry "is what gets lost in translation." Well, given that no translation can do complete justice to any poem, that only by going back to the original can we glean it's true essence, those of us who are unable to do that must depend on a translation, however imperfect any translation is bound to be. But to base our sense of what a poem sounded like in it's original form in it's own time on a translation that captures the diction of the time in which it was translated would be to do injustice to the original. Thus, we are constantly in need of new translations. In the world of science, we often hear people advising the young to go into "biology," or "physics," or "chemistry,"or "paleonthology,"—"that's the up-and-coming field." Well, one could easily say that to any poet, "go into translation, that's the up-and-coming field." Translations will always be "up-and-coming." Of course, the modern poet may wish to write her own original stuff and leave the translations to others.

There was a general assumption that the Greek and Roman classical poets wrote in rhyme, with the usual inversions of natural syntax and lots of thou's and whence's and methinks's and forsooths's. Common sense alone should tell you otherwise. Except for special cases and rare exceptions, most great poets in their own day spoke in the voice and idiom of their time. No one would purposefully write in an archaic diction unless it was for a specific character, or tone, and then it would clearly be meant to sound archaic. Every age since Homer has had modern poets, and each in their own day sounded modern. Furthermore, poetry was meant to be heard and memorized, and so certain devices were used to aid in memorization, rhyme being only one such device. The Greeks and Romans wrote, for the most part, using the dactylic hexameter for epic, and various other metrics for lyric poetry, but hardly ever rhymed. Rhyme as we know it began to filter into poetry in the Middle Ages, coming into full blossom with the 12th century Renaissance. Anglo-Saxon and Old English poetry was written using the principal of alliteration; again, not rhyme. And for the most part, except where tradtitional literary conventions were used for special effect, the language was a natural, spoken idiom. For the poet, language is key, and it is the most difficult thing to convey in translation. Each age has to use the conventions of its own time to give a flavor of the diction, tone, and the meaning. John Dryden's translation of the *Aeneid* is rendered in heroic couplets, rhymed decasyllables in iambic pentameter, the commonest metrical form in English poetry for centuries. Thus, most of the ancient classics were translated into heroic couplets, even though the classic poets did not rhyme, nor did they use the often lofty style characteristic of English poetry in the 17th and 18th centuries. The origin of the heroic couplet is a matter of speculation. Chaucer may have been influenced by the Old French decasyllabic rhymed couplets, and by adapting and modifying the old alliterative meters, he became the first English poet to make extensive use of the heroic couplet. But it was not until the 16th and 17th centuries that it became firmly established in English poetry, used and exploited by Spenser and Shakespeare among others. But it was Dryden and Pope who made it their own. If Dryden shaped it into perfect form, it was Pope, with his subtle wit and elegance, who polished it to near perfection.

Their translations of Homer and Virgil may have been appropriate in their own time, but it is misleading today in that it gives the reader a false impression of Homer's langauge and diction. True, Homer's dialect is often literary, and he uses archaic forms and words, which, by a long process at which we can now only guess, became especially suited to his narration. But there is nothing stilted about Homeric manner. The various dialects, combined with hints of colloquialism on the one hand and a dignified passion on the other—all combine to create an experience that touches on all the genres of western literature: tragedy, epic narrative, comedy, lyric poetry, fanstasy adventure, even the dramatic soliloquey in which characters debate their own fate with themselves.

Unfortunately, a stilted, archaic translation of Homer—of any classic work of literature—that fails to account for the changing idioms of lanaguage, conveys a damaging message to the modern poet, who must seek, as Homer did, to combine various idioms, ways of speaking, and literary devices into a coherent, "modern," tone. Modern, because in the context of their own time, every great poet was modern, and throughout the millennia, every poet has challenged the petrified literary langauge of their day and sought to invoke the speech of their own time. As Ezra Pound proclaimed at the beginning of this century, the poet must "make it new." The irony, or the paradox, is that, while inculcating the spoken idiom, poets must also not throw out the baby of all the great literature before them with the bathwater of archaic diction and outworn literary conventions. Homeric epic stands at the beginning of our literature, and poets who pay attention to its contribution will have a great advantage over those who merely "write as they talk," without ingesting subtlies of language and vivid imagery, not to mention the elements of the story itself. To borrow Homer's penchant for complicated similies, it's like a fisherman casting his net into the ocean of classic literature, bringing up the silvery flapping words of the poets who came before, then preparing a dish of his own making.

So here we are. Agamemnon's going to take Brisies, Achilles' prize. Achilles is about to draw his sword against Agamemnon when Achilles hears war-goddess Athena, patron goddess of Athens and personification of wisdom.

Food For Thought

GODDESS OF WAR / GODDESS OF PEACE

Whether Athens is named after the goddess or the goddess after Athens is an ancient argument, but the latter is generally considered more probable. She is sometimes known as Pallas Athena for reasons which remain obscure; Pallas was sometimes understood to mean "maiden," sometimes "brandisher" (of weapons). In Homer, despite the fact that she is the enemy of Troy, she is still the goddess of the Trojan citadel. She was *par excellence* a war-goddess, but in addition she was the patronness of all urban arts and crafts, and so ultimately the personification of wisdom.

The principal myth concerning her relates to her birth. She was the daughter of Zeus and Metis. Zeus swallowed Metis ["cunning intelligence"] for fear she should give birth to a son stronger than himself. In due time the God Hephaestus (or Promoetheus, it was sometimes said) opened (a pregnant) Zeus' head with an axe and Athena emerged, fully armed and uttering her war-cry, a child born without a mother.

Minerva was an Italian native deity, goddess of crafts and trade guilds, and often identified with Athena. [to "spring full-blown, like Minerva from the head of Zeus" is the well-known expression]

Later in the *Iliad*, Homer describes how Athena took off the finelywrought robe "which she herself had made and worked at with her own hands" and "armed herself for grievous war." This passage typifies the paradoxical nature of a goddess who is as skilled in the preparation of clothes as she is fearless in battle, who thus unites in her person the chracteristic excellence of both sexes. Her virginity is a bridge between the two sides of her nature. In warfare she expreses rational force, in contrast to the mindless violence of Ares (Mars). As a palace- or city-protecting goddess, there is the tantalizing reference in a Mycenaean Linear B tablet from Knossus to *A-ta-na po-ti-ni-ja*.

Athena tells Achilles that she was sent from Hera (Juno) to remind him that greater reward awaits if he can refrain from physical violence. Tell him off, instead, she counsels. If the main theme of the *Illiad* is "the wrath of Achilles," this is the scene where Homer delivers the goods. "You want wrath, you want rage, I'll give you wrath and rage." Even those in the cheap seats would have no problem hearing the action. Let's begin with the translation by Chapman, who uses the Roman names for the Greek deities (Athena=Minerva, Hera=Juno, Zeus=Jupiter, or Jove in English).[Remember, Achilles is the son of Thetis, Agamemnon the son of Atreus]

> Thetis' sonne at this stood vext. His heart
> Bristled his bosome and two waies drew his discursive part—
> If, from his thigh his sharpe sword drawne, he should make roome about
> Atrides' person, slaughtering him, or sit his anger out
> And curb his spirit. While these thoughts striv'd in his bloud and mind
> And he his sword drew, downe from heaven Athenia stoopt and shind
> About his temploes, being sent by th'Ivorie-wristed queene
> Saturnia, who out of her heart had ever loving bene
> And careful for the good of both. She stood behind, and tooke
> Achilles by the yellow curles, and onely gave her looke
> To him apparance—not a man of all the rest could see.

He, turning backe his eye, amaze strooke everie facultie,
Yet straight ke knew her by her eyes, so terrible they were
Sparkling with ardor, and thus spake: "thou seed of Jupiter,
Why com'st thou? To behold his pride, that bosts our Emperie?
Then witnesse, with it, my revenge, and see that insolence die
That lives to wrong me." She replied: "I am sent from Juno, whose affects
Stand heartily inclined to both. Come, give us both respects
And ceasse contention. Draw no sword. Use words, and such as may
Be bitter to his pride, but just. For, trust in what I say,
A time shall come when thrice the worth of that he forceth now
He shall propose for recompence of these wrongs. Therefore throw
Reines on thy passions, and serve us." He answered: Though my heart
Burne in just anger, yet my soule must conquer th'angrie part
And yeeld you conquest. Who subdues his earthly part for heaven,
Heaven to his prayers subdues his wish." This said, her charge was given
Fit honor. In his silver hilt he held his able hand
And forc't his broad sword up. And up to heaven did reascend
Minerva, who in Jove's high roofe that beares the rough shield tooke
Her place with other deities. She gone, againe forsooke
Patience his passion, and no more his silence could confine
His wrath, that this broad language gave:
                                   "Thou ever steep't in wine,
Dog's face, with heart but of a Hart, that nor in th'open eye
Of fight dar'st thrust into a prease, nor with our noblest lie
In secret ambush. These works seeme too full of death for thee.
Tis safer farre, in th'open host, to dare an injurie
To any crosser of thy lust. Thou subject-earting sking,
Base spirits thou governst — or this wrong had bene the last fowle thing
Thou ever author'dst. Yet I vow, and by a great oath sweare,
Even by this scepter — that, as this never againe shall beare
Greene leaves or brances, nor increase with any growth his sise,
Nor did since first it left the hils and had his faculties
And ornaments bereft with iron, which now to other end
Judges of Greece beare and their lawes receiv'd from Jove defend
(For which my oath to thee is great), so, whensoever need
Shall burne with thrist of me thy host, no prayres shall ever breed
Affection in me to their aid, though well-deserved woes
Afflict thee for them, when to death man-slaughtering Hector throwes
Whole troopes of them, and thou torment'st thy vext mind with conceit
Of thy rude rage now and his wrong, that most deserv'd the right
Of all thy armie." Thus he threw his scepter gainst the ground,
With golden studs stucke, and took seate.
                                   (Chapman, 1616)

Pope's version using rhymed heroic couplets:

    Achilles heard, with grief and rage oppress'd,
His heart swell'd high, and labour'd in his breast;
Distracting thoughts by turns his bosom ruled;
Nor fire by wrath, and now by reason cool'd:
That prompts his hand to draw the deadly sword,

Force through the Greeks, and pierce their haughty lord;
This whispers soft his vengeance to control,
And calm the rising tempest of his soul.
While half unsheated appear'd the glittering blade,
Minerva swift descended from above,
Sent by the sister and the wife of Jove
(For both the princes claim'd her equal care);
Behind she stood, and by the golden hair
Achilles seized; to him alone confess'd;
A sable cloud conceal'd her from the rest.
He sees, and sudden to the goddess cries,
Known by the flames that sparkle from her eyes:

    "Descends Minerva, in her guardian care,
A heavenly witness of th e wrongs I bear
From Atreus' son—Then let those eyes that view
The daring crime, behold the vengeance too."

    "Forbear (the progeny of Jove replies)
To calm thy fury I forsake the skies:
Let great Achilles, to the gods resign'd,
To reason yield the empire o'er his mind.
By awful Juno this command is given;
The king and you are both the care of heaven.
The force of keen reproaches let him feel;
But sheathe, obedient, thy revenging steel.
For I pronounce (and trust a heavenly power)
Thy injured honour has its fated hour,
When the proud monarch shall thy arms implore,
And bribe thy friendship with a boundless store.
Then let revenge no longer bear the sway;
Command thy passions, and the gods obey."

    To her Pelides: "With regardful ear,
'Tis just, O goddess! I thy dictates hear.
Hard as it is, my vengeance I suppress:
Those who revere the gods, the gods will bless."
He said, observant to the blue-eyed maid;
Then in the sheath return'd the shining blade.
The goddess swift to high Olympus flies,
And joins the sacred senate of the skies.

    Nor yet the rage his boiling breast forsook,
Which thus redoubling on Atrides broke:
"Oh monster! mix'd of insolence and fear,
Thou dog in forehead, but in heart a deer!
When wert thou known in ambush'd fights to dare,
Or nobly face the horrid front of war?
'Tis our, the chance of fighting fields to try;
Thine to look on, and bid the valiant die:
So much 'tis safer through the camp to go,
And rob a subject, than despoil a foe.
Scourge of thy people, violent and base!
Sent in Jove's anger on a slavish race;
Who, lost to sense of generous freedom past,

Are tamed to wrongs;—or this had been thy last.
Now by this sacred sceptre hear me swear,
Which never more shall leaves or blossoms bear,
ON the bare mountains left its parent tree:
This sceptre, form'd by temper'd steel to prove
An ensign of the delegates of Jove,
From whom the power of laws and justice springs
(tremendous oath! inviolate to kings);
By this I swear:—when bleeding Greece again
Shall call Achilles, she shall call in vain.
When, flush'd with slaughter, Hector comes to spread
The purpled shore with mountains of the dead,
Then shalt thou mourn the affront thy madness gave,
Forced to deplore when impotent to save:
Then rage in bitterness of soul to know
This act has made the bravest Greek thy foe."
    He spoke; and furious hurl'd against the ground
His sceptre starr'd with golden studs around.
                              (Alexander Pope, 1716)

An edition of Pope's translation was issued in 1943 by the George Macy Companies in New York, perpetuating to the average reader of that generation the notion that Homer sounded as old fashioned and archaic as the Romantic and Elizaethan poets they had to read in school. The Macy edition is being used today by the Easton Press (thus, no royalties to the translator necessary) to make their leather bound Collector's Edition of the Classics that people are buying to give their home library an expensive, dignified look (at $50 a pop). One night, they'll get a fire going in the fireplace, settle down into their red leather wing chair, open the book, begin to read the story of Achilles' rage, and after a few stanza, fall asleep. Another classic cure for insomnia.

Well into the 20th century, these translations of the *Iliad* by Chapman and Pope represented to readers of English what Homer must have sounded like. Both translations rhyme, giving the impression that rhyme was a three thousand year poetic device, which is false. Greek and Latin poets did not use rhyme, nor did poetry written in Old English, which used alliterative verse. Though rhyme began to be used in the Middle Ages, mainly from folk and vernacular tales, it wasn't until the 12th century Troubadour poets of the south of France that rhyme makes it boldest appearance, and does not become standard until Dante and Chaucer in the 14th century. Yet, even today, rhyme may be the best English device to redner the music of Homer's dactylic hexameter. But even if the diction is modern, what kind of rhyme?—the "listen my children and you shall hear / of the midnight rhyme of Paul Revere? kind of rhyme? What about a rhyme that sallies forth like "it was the night before Christmas and all through the house / not a creature was stirring, not even a mouse." The opening of the *Iliad* might go:

Sing Oh Muse, of Achilles rage,
that doomed the bitter and the sage,
those Greeks who died and went to Hell,
God's will was done and great Troy fell.

Well, this is pretty lame, and the meter is accentual, four beats to a line. It might work for a short poem, but in time, the reader will die of poetic exhaustion. "Casey at the Bat"'s longer metric line—"it looked extremely rocky for the Mudville nine that day,/ the score stood two to four with but an inning left to play"—or "The Shooting of Dan McGrew"'s—"A bunch of the boys were whooping it up in the Malamute saloon;/ The kid that handles the music box was hitting a jag-time tune"—might work for a while, but not for 600 pages.

Modern translators have correctly resisted using rhyme, but have held to a regular metric that appoximates Homer's six-foot hexameter, using a variety of accentual meters: dactylic, trochaic, iambic, anapests, and spondees. Richmond Lattimore's 1951 tranlation has a certain nobility, though he strove as well for plain langauge when it suited the dramatic situation. Throughout, he does his best to keep to a free six-beat line, though not as regular as Longfellow's or the Smith-Miller translation that came out a few years earlier.

> .... And the anger came on Peleus' son, and within
> his shaggy breast the heart was divided two ways, pondering
> whether to draw from beside his thigh the sharp sword, driving
> away all those who stood between and kill the son of Atreus,
> or else to check the spleen within and keep down his anger.
> Now as he weighed in mind and spirit these two courses
> and was drawing from its scabbard the great sword, Athene descended
> from the sky. For Hera the goddess of the white arms sent her,
> who loved both men equally in her heart and cared for them.
> The goddess standing behind Peleus' son caught him by the fiar hair,
> appearing to him only, for no man of the others saw her.
> Achilleus in amazement turned about, and straightway
> knew Pallas Athene and the terrible eyes shining.
> He uttered wingined words and addressed her:
> "Why have you come now,
> o child of Zeus of the aegis, once more? Is it that you may see
> the outrageousness of the son of Atreus Agamemnon?
> Yet will I tell you this thing, and I think it shall be accomplished.
> Bu such acts of arrogance he may even lose his own life."
> Then in answer the goddess grey-eyed Athene spoke to him:
> "I have come down to stay your anger — but will you obey me? —
> from the sky; and the goddess of the white arms Hera sent me,
> who loves both of you equally in her heart and cares for you.
> Come then, do not take your sword in your hand, keep clear of fighting,
> though indeed with words you may abuse him, and it will be that way.
> And this also will I tell you and it will be a thing accomplished.
> Some day three times over such shining gifts shall be given you
> by reason of this outrage. hold your hand then, and obey us."
> Then in answer again spoke Achilleus of the swift feet:
> "Goddess, it is necessary that I obey the word of you two,
> angry though I am in my heart. so it will be better.
> If any man obeys the gods, they listen to him also."

He spoke, and laid his heavy hand on the silver sword hilt
and thrust the great blade back into the scabbard nor disobeyed
the word of Athene. And she went back again to Olympos
to the house of Zeus of the aegis with the other divinities.
    But Peleus' son once again in words of derision
spoke to Atreides, and did not yet let go of his anger:
"You wine sack, with a dog's eyes, with a deer's heart. Never
once have you taken courage in your heart to arm with your people for battle, or
go into ambuscade with the best of the Achaians.
No, for in such things you see death. Far better to your mind
is it, all along the widespread host of the Achaians
to take away the gifts of any man who speaks up against you.
King who feed on your people, since you rule nonentities;
otherwise, son of Atreus, this were your last outrage.
But I will tell you this and swear a great oath upon it:
in the name of this sceptre, which never again will bear leaf nor
branch, now that it has left behind the cut stump in the mountains,
nor shall it ever blossom again, since the bronze blade stripped
bark and leafage, and now at last the sons of the Achaians
carry it in their hands in state when they administer
the justice of Zeus. And this shall be a great oath before you:
some day longing for Achilleus will come to the sons of the Achaians,
all of them. Then stricken at heart though you be, you will be able
to do nothing, when in their numbers before man-slaughtering Hektor
they drop and die. And then you will eat out the heart within you
in sorrow, that you did no honour to the best of the Achaians."
    Thus spoke Peleus' son and dashed to the ground the sceptre
studdeed with golden nails, and sat down again.

                                    (Richmond Lattimore, 1951)

After reading several different translations, it should be clear to the reader that what comes through every version is Homer's ability to capture both the larger-than-life dimensions of epic warfare, and the human pettiness of outrage, the petulance and vengeful nature of righteous anger. The *Iliad* is not the story of the twenty year war against Troy, but a specific incident involving the wrath of one warrior and the enmity between two epic heroes. Centuries later, the poets of Greece celebrated the victories, not of war, but of athletic contests between those heroes of the Olympics, which began in 776 BC, around the time of the composition of the *Iliad*. Pindar and Bacchylides sang of individual feats of athleticism and pride in competition. Reading those lyric odes today, we are reminded of the gladiators who take the field on Super Bowl Sunday, the instant replays capturing on tape the deeds that—were it not for the electronic techonology—would be celebrated by lyric poets. By the same token, the war of words between Achilles and Agamemnon reminds us of modern day warrior-athletes who refuse to play because they're not being paid as much as another super star. Like Achilles, these free-agent hold-outs sulk in their palatial tents, and send word through their agent-emissaries that one day, in the Super Bowl, when the team is down by two touchdowns, they'll beg their star halfback to save the day, but it'll be too late. Homer's greatness as a poet is this ability to paint small hearts on the large canvas of epic, and at the same time to paint the great souls of men like Hector and Priam on the small stamp of the human heart.

Robert Fitzgerald's 1974 version has some oddities in it, words and epitephs that seem anachronistic in the wrong way. At one point, Achilles calls Agamemnon a coward, or a brazen coward, depending on the translation. Fitzgerald uses the word "poltroon." But except for these mishaps, his translation is supple, and at times, almost iridescent.

> A pain like grief weighed on the son of Pêleus,
> and in his shaggy chest this way and that
> the passion of his heart ran: should he draw
> longsword from hip, stand off the rest, and kill
> in single combat the great son of Atreus,
> or hold his rage in check and give it time?
> And as this tumult swayed him, as he slid
> the big blade slowly from the sheath, Athêna
> came to him from the sky. the white-armed goddess,
> Hêra, sent her, being fond of both,
> concerned for both men. And Athêna, stepping
> up behind him, visible to no one
> except Akhilleus, gripped his red-gold hair.
>
> Startled, he made a half turn, and he knew her
> upon the instant for Athêna: terribly
> her grey eyes blazed at him. And speaking softly
> but rapidly aside to her he said:
>
> "What now, O daughter of the god of heaven
> who bears the stormcloud, why are you here? To see
> the wolfishness of Agamémnon?
> Well, I give you my word: this time, and soon,
> he pays for his behavior with his blood."
>
> They grey-eyed goddess Athêna said to him:
>
> "It was to check this killing rage I came
> from heaven, if you will listen. Hêra sent me,
> being fond of both of you, concerned for both.
> Enough: break off this combat, stay your hand
> upon the sword hilt. Let him have a lashing
> with words, instead: tell him how things will be.
> Here is my promise, and it will be kept:
> winnings three times as rich, in due season,
> you shall have in requital for his arrogance.
> But hold your hand. Obey."
>
>   The great runner,
> Akhilleus, answered:
>   Nothing for it, goddess,
> but when you two immortals speak, a man
> complies, though his heart burst. Just as well.

Honor the gods' will, they may honor ours."

On this he stayed his massive hand
upon the silver pommel, and the blade
of his great weapon slid back in the scabbard.
the man had done her bidding. Off to Olympos,
gaining the air, she went to join the rest,
the powers of heaven in the home of Zeus.

But now the son of Pêleus turned on Agamémnon
and lashed out at him, letting his nager die
in execration:

                              "Sack of wine,
you with your cur's eyes and your antelope heart!
You've never had the kidney to buckle on
armor among the troops, or make a sortie
with picked men—oh, no; that way death mught lie.
Safer, by god, in the middle of the army—
is it not?—to commandeer the prize
of any man who stands up to you! Leech!
Commander of trash! If not, I swear,
you never could abuse one soldier more!

But here is what I say: my oath upon it
by this great staff: look: leaf or shoot
it cannot sprout again, once lopped away
from the log it left behind in the timbered hills;
it cannot flower, peeled of bark and leaves;
instead, Akhaian officers in council
take it in hand by turns, when they observe
by the will of Zeus due order in debate:
let this be what I swear by then: I swear
a day will come when every Akhaian soldier
will groan to have Akhilleus back. That day
you shall no more prevail on me than this
dry wood shall flourish—driven though you are,
and though a thousand men perish before
the killer, Hektor. you will eat your heart out,
raging with remorse for this dishonor
done by you to the bravest of Akhaians."

He hurled the staff, studded with golden nails,
before him on the ground. Then down he sat,
and fury filled Agamémnon, looking across at him.
                              (Robert Fitzgerald, 1974)

Homer's language is an amalgam of words and grammatical forms reflecting not only
different dialects, but dialects that became part of the poem over the course of several
centuries of oral transmission. At best, a translator can hope to give the reader an
"impression" of Homer's unique combination of high formality and narrative vigor,

careful not to let the archaic phrases sound ridiculous to a contemporary reader, while at the same time not letting idiomatic naturalism lapse into hip vulgarity.

Translators of the *Illiad* have generally tried to balance two opposing tensions: the oral nature of the composition, meant to be read aloud, and the written, "literary" form, which in Greek uses the dactylic hexameter. Alexander Pope said, "*Homer* makes us Hearers; *Virgil* leaves us Readers." But when translating Homer, translators have too often tried to balance the oral and literary nature of the composition, and based too much, it seems to me, on the metrical pattern.

Robert Fagles admits in his introduction that he tried to find a middle ground between these two features, the expectations of performance and the demands of a contemporary reader. As regards the word-for-word, line-for-line approach, he opted for more flexibility. "For the more literal approach would seem to be too little English, and the more literary seems too little Greek. I have tried to find a cross between the two, a modern English Homer." Thus, he opts for a flexible range between Homer's hexameter line and the tighter line more suited to English. Sometimes he used a five- or six-beat line, and sometimes expands that to seven beats, a "tug-of-war," he confesses "between trying to encapsulate the meaning of the Greek on the one hand and trying to find a cadence for one's English on the other."

> Anguish gripped Achilles.
> The heart in his rugged chest was pounding, torn . . .
> Should he draw the long sharp sword slung at his hip,
> thrust through the ranks and kill Agamemnon now? —
> or check his rage and beat his fury down?
> As his racing spirit veered back and forth,
> just as he drew his huge blade from its sheath,
> down from the vaulting heavens swept Athena,
> the white-armed goddess Hera sped her down:
> Hera loved both men and cared for both alike.
> rearing behind him Pallas seized his fiery hair —
> only Achilles saw her, none of the other fighters —
> struck with wonder he spun around, he knew her at once.
> Pallas Athena! the terrible blazing of those eyes,
> and his winged words went flying: "Why, why now?
> Child of Zeus with the shield of thunder, why come now?
> To witness the outrage Agamemnon just committed?
> I tell you this, and so help me its the truth —
> he'll soon pay for his arrogance with his life!"

> Her gray eyes clear, the goddess Athena answered,
> "Down from the skies I come to check your rage
> if only you will yield.
> The white-armed goddess Hera sped me down:
> she loves you both, she cares for you both alike.
> Stop this fighting, now. Don't lay hand to sword.
> Lash him with threats of the price that he will face.
> And I tell you this — and I *know* it is the truth —
> one day glittering gifts will lie before you,

three times over to pay for all his outrage.
Hold back now. Obey us both."
                                        So she urged
and the swift runner complied at once: "I must—
when the two of you hand down commands, Goddess,
a man submits though his heart breaks with fury.
Better for him by far. If a man obeys the gods
they're quick to hear his prayers."
                                        And with that
Achilles stayed his burly hand on the silver hilt
and slid the huge blade back in its sheath.
He would not fight the orders of Athena.
Soaring home to Olympus, she rejoined the gods
aloft in the halls of Zeus whose shield is thunder.

But Achilles rounded on Agamemnon once again,
lashing out at him, not relaxing his anger for a moment:
"Staggering drunk, with your dog's eyes, your fawn's heart!
Never once did you arm with the troops and go to battle
or risk an ambush packed with Achaea's picked men—
you lack courage, you can see death coming.
Safer by far, you find, to foray all through camp,
commandeering the prize of any man who speaks against you.
King who devours his people! Worthless husks, the men you rule—
if not, Atrides, this outrage would have been your last.
I tell you this, and I swear a mighty oath upon it . . .
by this, this scepter, look,
that never again will put forth crown and branches,
now it's left its stump on the mountain ridge forever,
nor will it sprout new green again, now the brazen ax
has stripped its bark and leaves, and now the sons of Achaea
upholding the honored customs whenever Zeus commands—
This scepter will be the mighty force behind my oath:
someday, I swear, a yearning for Achilles will strike
Achaea's sons and all your armies! But then, Atrides,
harrowed as you will be, *nothing* you do can save you—
not when your hordes of fighters drop and die,
cut down by the hands of man-killing Hector! Then—
then you will tear your heart out, desperate, raging
that you disgraced the best of the Achaeans!"
                                        Down on the ground
he dashed the scepter studded bright with golden nails,
then took his seat again.
                        (Robert Fagles, 1990)

There's a cadence to this version that still plugs into the voltage of Achilles' anger and sizzles with the force of the original. Fagles' translation is a magnificent tour de force, likely to be read for a long time. But I still believe the reliance on the metrical line to solve the problem of oral vs. literary a mistake. Let's face it, we do not live in an age of oral recitation. We read Homer, we do not listen to him being read. Furthermore, if we did listen to him being read, we would lose the sweep and power of Homer's narrative drive because it would be a "reading," or a performed reading, but the effect would be the same. If we lived in an age in which rhyme were still contemporary, we'd probably feel more at home hearing it read in a metrical equivalent of "Listen my children and you shall hear, of the midnight ride of Paul Revere," or even "Twas the night before Christmas, and all through the house, not a creature was stirring, not even a mouse." In English, the metre chosen must relate to rhyme, or it's pointless. The end-rhyme combined with the force of the consonants would help carry the power and speed of Homer's diction. The style must serve the narrative character of the *Iliad*, and only a strong metrical rhyme in English can do that. Unfortunately, it might work for "Paul Revere's Ride," or "The Night Before Christmas," but after awhile, in the Homeric drama, it's going to sound rather trivial. What to do?

The key lies in another duality, narrative vs. dramatic speeches, each accounting for half of the poem. To get at the real Homeric experience, one that captures the contemporary feel of both the oral and literary nature of the composition, the translator must approach the *Iliad* as a dramatic piece of theatre. Not a "reading," but a dramatic performance. Without rhyme, the translator should avoid any consistent metrical pattern, and turn instead to the dynamics of the spoken voice, especially considering the fact that our contemporary poetic idiom is not the heroic couplet, but a poetics based on natural langauge that can be heightened and stylized in a dramatic context. Stanley Lombardo's 1997 translation uses a "living poetry, [which] means a living speech, certainly in the speeches that account for almost half of the *Iliad*'s lines." The speeches are dramatic, not subject to the metrical regularity of a "reading," but the sudden shifts in tone and diction that characterize an emotional speech. And modern readers are accustomed to reading drama, and can hear in their heads the literature of the lines meant to be spoken out loud in a dramatic context. Lombardo's translation blends both the literary and the oral, the lyric and the spoken, the narrative and the dramatic. In his version, Achille's monologue seems to jump off the page, and the entire work reads like a screen-play.

> Achilles' chest was a rough knot of pain
> Twisting around his heart: should he
> Draw the sharp sword that hung by his thigh,
> Scatter the ranks and gut Agamemnon,
> Or control his temper, repress his rage?
> He was mulling it over, inching the great sword
> From its sheath, when out of the blue
> Athena came, sent by the white-armed goddess
> Hera, who loved and watched over both men.
> She stood behind Achilles and grabbed his sandy hair,
> Visible only to him: not another soul saw her.
> Awestruck, Achilles turned around, recognizing
> Pallas Athena at once — it was her eyes —
> And words flew from his mouth like winging birds:
>
> "Daughter of Zeus! Why have you come here?
> To see Agamamnon's arrogance, no doubt.
> I'll tell you where I place my bets, Goddess:

Sudden death for this outrageous behavior."

Athena's eyes glared through the sea's salt haze.

"I came to see if I could check this temper of yours,
Sent from heaven by the white-armed goddess
Hera, who loves and watches over both of you men.
Now come one, drop this quarrel, don't draw your sword.
Tell him off instead. And I'll tell you,
Achilles, how things will be: You're going to get
Three times as many magnificent gifts
Because of his arrogance. Just listen to us and be patient."

Achilles, the great runner, responded:

"When you two speak, Goddess, a man has to listen
No matter how angry. It's better that way.
Obey the gods and they hear you when you pray."

With that he ground his heavy hand
Onto the silver hilt and pushed the great sword
Back into its sheath. Athena's speech
Had been well-timed. She was on her way
To Olympus by now, to the halls of Zeus
And the other immortals, while Achiles
Tore into Agamemnon again:

                                        "You bloated drunk,
With a dog's eyes and a rabbit's heart!
You've never had the guts to buckle on armor in battle
Or come out with the best fighting Greeks
Or any campaign! Afraid to look Death in the eye,
Agamemnon? It's far more profitable
To hang back in the army's rear—isn't it?—
Confiscating prizes from any Greek who talks back
And bleeding your people dry. There's not a real man
Under your command, or this latest atrocity
Would be your last, son of Atreus.
Now get this straight. I swear a formal oath:
By this scepter, which will never sprout leaf
Or branch again, since it was cut from its stock
In the mountains, which will bloom no more
Now that bronze has pared off leaf and bark,
And which now the sons of the Greeks hold in their hands
At council, upholding Zeus' laws—
                                        By this scepter I swear:
When every last Greek desperately misses Achilles,
Your remorse won't do any good then,
When Hector the man-killer swats you down like flies.
And you will eat your heart out
Because you failed to honor the best Greek of all."
                                        (Stanley Lombardo, 1997)

This is a verse rendering that moves with the speed of prose, yet at the same time suggests dramatic performance, which in our time, carries the pulse and rhythms of the Greek long and short vowels, and the kind of rhetorical effectiveness that musicality served. The poetic diction modulates between eloquent formalisms and everyday idioms, adapting itself to changing voices and situations with the utmost versatility and grace.

Food for Thought:

HOMER, HERMOGENES, POUND, AND ALL THAT.

Finding one's "voice" is an age-old goal for all writers and artists. The concept has become simplified, but there's more to it than just "writing like you talk." Un fortunately, most writers and poets are not aware of the difference—writing like one talks and writing in a literary style—and so are unable to make the deeper discovery of "finding their voice," which goes to the heart of developing a unique style. It's a bit like the Supreme Court Justice's comment on pornography—he couldn't define it, but he knew it when he saw it. The concept of "voice" is hard to define, but we know it when we see it, or hear it. Poet and teacher Jack Gilbert called it the "invisible form."

> The poet must listen hard to the voice in the poem. [Because] the invisible form is not just a reflection of the material; it is an intrusive, enterprising, meddling, subversive, active, intervening form. In order to effectuate. It is the major craft of all writing.

Read Shakespeare's earliest plays and compare them to his later, mature ones. Did he become a better writer, or did he find a voice, his voice? Of course, he became a better writer, but that's a simplification, and misses the point. The same can be said for his contemporaries like Webster, Kydd, etc. Their best plays are better written than some of Shakespeare's early plays, yet Sheakespeare's early plays still have a life that makes them accessible even today, where the others seem laboured. It's a question of "voice," not writing style. In his own day, of course, Shakespeare was criticized by those university poets and playwrights because his work was not as "well-written" as theirs was. Perhaps Ben Johnson had some part of his tongue in his cheek when he responded to a question about Shakespeare's sloppy writing, namely that he "blotted" (scratched out) many words when he wrote. "Would that he had blotted them all," said Johnson. I'm sure there was a good deal of good-natured envy behind the comment. Johnson grudgingly realized that despite his common touch, Shakespeare "was not of an age, but for all time."

When we talk of Homer's use of various dialects and changes in diction and tone, it's hard for the contemporary reader to fully grasp what this means, or feels like. Modern translators do a fair job of conveying it, but we live in an age which is uncomfortable with these kinds of tonal shifts which can create a "carnivalesque" effect. I'll talk more about this when we get to the Hellenistic poet Callimachus, but for now suffice it to say that what Homer did (or how the style of the *Iliad* and *Oddysey* evolved over the course of their oral transmission before being written down) was set a standard for dramatic verbal effects that have been used ever since by only a handful of writers, and often their readers were unable to fully comprehend their purpose. Ezra Pound was one 20th century poet who grasped this effect. This Callimachian ideal and how it influenced Menippean satire will be discussed in a later "food for thought" section, but here I'd like to comment on one aspect of it.

What's important to realize is that Homer was aware that he was mixing and matching dialects, switching from a formal archaic tone to modern contemporary diction. Many contemporary poets and writers slide into archaic and cliché forms without realizing it. They go from formal diction to natural speech without knowing how to manipulate its affects, and if asked, would probably think they're just writing "like they talk." It's important for writers to know when they are using stylistic devices, and for what purpose.

Hermogenes of Tarsus was a 1st century AD child prodigy known for his oratorical skill. Before he was barely twenty-three years old, he wrote numerous books on writing and speaking that became influential both in Byzantine and in Renaissance times. The most famous and influential of his works is the treatise *On Types of Style*, in which he outlines, with almost mathematical precision, seven basic types or ideal forms of style: Clarity, Grandeur, Beauty, Rapidity, Character, Sincerity, and Force (*sapheneia*, *megethos*, *kallos*, *gorgotes*, *ethos*, *aletheia*, and *deinotes*).

Hermogenes actually goes on to investigate twenty basic types of style, discussing choice of diction, figures of speech, clauses, word order, cadences, and rhythm. By combining these basic elements, the orator or poet can create dramatic effects in narrative and lyric composition. Hermogenes systematic approach was a further extension of stylisitc analysis from Homer down to Hellenistic times, most notably in the *Rhetoric to Herennius*, written in the first century BC, from which Cicero quoted frequently when he wrote *On the Orator* in 55 BC. Cicero defined three styles: the plain style was basically conversational, and avoided literary affectation and ornamental phrases; the middle style could use poetical effects, metaphors, figures of speech, paralelism and antithesis, rhythm and periodic structure, but it should do so only in moderation, so that the effect was smooth and natural; the grand style was forceful and passionate, combining the first two styles in dramatic ways and vigorous exclamations of poetic intensity. The plain style, Cicero noted, could be used to instruct, or to bring the reader along narrative action. The middle style was more for pleasure, a way of charming the reader. The grand style was meant to rouse the emotions. The secret was in how each poet combined all three, knowing when and where each style should be used, and to what extent. Hermogenes' system soon replaced Cicero's concept of three styles, and his work became a standard textbook used in schools for centuries. In 1426 it was introdfuced into the West by George Trebizod, eventually translated into Latin by Gasparis Laurentius in 1614, and was studied again by humanist scholars and poets well into the Renaissance.

When discussing Solemnity, he focuses on a verbal effect that is characteristic of Greek, but not of English, and helps us understand the nature of a syllable counting meter that uses long and short voewl sounds for their effects, and an accentual meter, which counts stresses, not syllables, as is done is English iambic pentameter.

> The diction that is appropriate for Solemnity consists of braod sounds that make us open our mouth wide when we pronounce them. We are thus forced by the nature of the words

themselves to speak broadly, which some speakers do anyway. There are other possibilities, but long *a*'s and *o*'s especially produce this effect. That is why, according to Plato *(Phdr.* 244d), some people call *oionistiké* (augury) *oonistike*, to make it sound more solemn by adding an extra long *o*. The same is true with long *a*. Theocritus (15.88), for example, depicts a man who is angry with whomen who, because they speak Doric, use lots of broad *a*'s in their speech. Long *a*'s and *o*'s elevate and broaden speech especially if they occur in the final syllables of the words, as in Plato when he says, *ho men dé megas hégemon en ourano Zeus*, "Zeus, the great leader in heaven" (Phaedrus. 246e).

When Hermogenes discusses Clarity (*sapheneia*), he emphasizes that a clear sentence must be conversational; its clauses should employ the loose rhythms of speech, especially the natural iambic meter. Ironically, Hermogenes' own style is pretty bad. Many of his sentences are tortured exercises in redunant language, hackneyed compression, and atrocious verbal displays. It's conjectured that he wrote the book when he was a teenager, filled with the swaggering self-confidence and exuberance one finds in a high-school essay. As a literary work, it has no intrinsic merit, but the ideas are sound, and his comments on Homer are quite instructive in that they give us a glimpse of how well-understood were the stylistic devices used by the blind poet. The previous and following passages were tanslated by Cecil W. Wooten, who confesses to clearing up Hermogenes' school-boy style. [I've marked certain sentences in bold for emphasis]

> .... Here we must also repeat what we said earlier and keep the same "proportion," to use the geometric term: what, in our opinion, Demosthenes is to practical oratory, both deliberative and judicial, and Plato is to panegyric oratory in prose, Homer is to poetry. If anyone says that poetry is panegyric in meter, I cannot say that he is mistaken. Here you could simply invert the propositions as we did in the case of Plato and Demosthenes: the best poetry is that of Homer, and Homer is the best of poets. I would also say that he is also the best of orators and speech-writers, although perhaps this is implicit in what I have already said. Poetry is an imitations of all things. The man who best imitates, in a suitable style, both orators delivering speeches and singers singing panegyrics, such as Phemius and Demodocus and other characters engaged in every pursuit, this man is the best poet. I have made a statement that is tantamount to saying that he is also the best of orators and the best of speech-writers. He is perhaps not the best general or craftsman or other such professional, although he represents their pursuits in the best way. Their skill does not reside in the use of speech and words. But as for those whose business is with the use of speech, such as orators and speech-writers, the one who represents them best describes how the best of them would speak, is surely himself the best of them. **Thus of all poets and orators and speech-writers Homer is the best at using every kind of style**. Indeed he is the man who more than any other poet has created passages of Grandeur and those that produce pleasure and those that exhibit a carefully wrought style and Force. He has also produced a vivid representation of reality that is suitable to the circumstances that he is describing, both in the style that he uses and in the way he presents his characters, as well as in vivid narrations of mythical stories. He uses different kinds of caesura, or pauses in the line of verse, in his poetry, and as a result of this **the verses are varied**. And a sense of porpriety in reference to a specific passage always governs the various kinds of verse that he uses. Moreover, he has also chosen a meter that is by nature the most noble of them all [dactylic hexameter]. **Finally, he has turned variety and diversity into the most beautiful unity**. These comments are sufficient to characterize the best kind of poetry and Homer himself.
>
> [paragraph #389]

Hermogens concludes his section on Homer's diction:

> It should be clear to everyone what kind of diction is typical of poetry, and that the most beautiful of poetic dictions is that of Homer. His diction is probably the only one that is pure, so far as poetry allows, with the possible exception of Hesiod. Unlike the thoughts and at least one approach and the diction, there are no figures [of speech] that are particuary characteristic of poetry, but it uses the same ones that are typical of panegyric oratory, although their use is determined by the demands of various styles required by the nature of what is being represented—since poetry is a representation of reality.
>
> It is easy to see that the clauses and word order and rhythms and cadences that are typical of poetry are determined by the meter, and one can see that this is true so long as the poetry is nothing but verse. But when we discuss Homer, we must add that we cannot descirbe his meter simply by saying that it is dactylic hexameter catalectic. **Nor can we say that Homer uses one kind of cadence or rhythm or word order.** Just as we said that various figures must be used because epic poetry is a representation of reality, so the same observation could be made in the case of the meter used. Whenever Homer describes the emotional state of a speaker or imitates some peculiar characteristic of a person in the poem or even narrates various deeds on his own, in each of these situations he must vary the kind of style that he uses and employ appropriate cadences and feet and word order and rhythms, so that he can produce passages that are solemn or harsh or simple or very beautiful and carefully wrought or that illustrate any other kinds of rhythm and styles that we have discussed. These various effects are easily produced because of the large number of patterns that a hexameter can take—the grammarians teach us that there are thirty-two. The effect produced also depends on what kind of cadence is used, and that is very important in such questions. Often a metrical impression that is different from what one expects in epic poetry is produced because of the logical divisions within the line of poetry and the cadences of the clauses in which a thought is completed. Take the followed line, for example, from the opening of the *Iliad*: [1.4]
>
> *heroon, autous de heloria teuche kynessin*
>
> of warriors, and made themselves spoils for the dogs
>
> That the preceding clause is completed at the beginning of this line, with the word *heroon*, produces the same impression that an anapaest does. Anyone who has carefully studied all my previous comments about the various types of style would have no difficulty in understanding why this rhythm is necessary in this passage or why some other rhythm is appropriate in another passage. This will be even clearer to anyone who has also studied our discussion about the approach that is characteristic of Force.
>
> [paragraph #393]

In modern terms, Hermogenes is talking about a form of enjambment, the running over of the sense and grammatical structure from one verse line or couplet to the next without a punctuated pause, which became typical of English poets writing in blank verse who did not always want to emphasize the word at the end of a line, called end-stopped. Keats is an example of a poet who rejected the 18th century closed, end-stopped couplet by using frequent enjambment in his poem *Endymion*. Many contemporary poets of the Neo-Formalist school use enjambment, not for its effect, but by default, in failing to make consistent end-stopped rhymes when that is the whole purpose and rationale for their composition, to promote a return to formalistic rhyme. Enjambment defeats that very purpose while striving for other effects, but if the rhymed word at the end of a line is enjambed, and therefore not stressed, the whole point of the rhyme becomes academic, rather than melodic. This would be akin to praising an actor's performance, however inept, just because he was wearing authentic underwear.

This is why, finally, in a modern verse translation of Homer, the metrical consistency of a line is of less importance than the lyric or narrative cadence as it relates to an oral performance, which to our modern ears, must mimic the dramatic monologue or soliloquey, and not the rhythmic recitation of formal poetry. One might be faithful to Homer's metric, but not to the effect such metrical variations had in the original Greek. Many translators have sacrificed the literal in favor of the metrical, and I believe this is unfortunate. We want to know what Homer said, but we also want to get an impression of how that Greek must have sounded to listeners back in Homer's day, and why Homer's poetry was so enjoyed and admired. His metrical verse certainly wasn't monotonous, or sing-song rhyme, but a forceful dramatic performance noted for its various verbal effects and tonal dyanamics. Which is why I favor Stanley Lombardo's translation, though the successful blending of poetic and dramatic elements characteristic of Fagles' translation is marvelous as well. I enjoy comparing various translations of my favorite passages, and in my imagination blending the best of each. That is why I went to such lengths to give you various examples of the scene in the first book between Agamemnon and Achilles.

HEY, WHAT ABOUT EZRA POUND & ALL THAT JAZZ

Ina roundabout way, one of the best examples I can give of Homer's effect is by pointing not to a specific translation, but to the *Cantos* of Ezra Pound, which not only mimicks the variety of dialects and tonal dynamics in Homer, but in many cases exaggerates those effects. The *Cantos* begins with a translation of Book 12 of Homer's *Odyssey*.

> And then went down to the ship,
> Set keel to breakers, forth on the godly sea, and
> We set up mast and sail on that swart ship,
> Bore sheep aboard her, and our bodies also
> Heavy with weeping, and winds from sternward
> Bore us out onward with bellying canvas.

Then after several pages he breaks off mid-translation and writes:

> Lie quiet Divus. I mean, that is Andrea Divus,
> In officina Wecheli, 1538, out of Homer.

He's addressing Andrea Divus, who translated Homer into Latin in 1538. Pound was not translating Homer from the Greek, but from this Latin translation he bought in a Paris bookstall for four francs. Pound then renders that in Old English alliterative verse, as if to sweep two centuries of versification into his handbasket. He breaks off again, ending Canto I,

And he sailed, by Sirens and thence outward and away
And unto Circe.
        Venerandam,
In the Cretan's phrase, with the golden crown, Aphrodite,
Cypri munimenta sortita est, mirthful, orichalchi, with golden
Girdles and breast bands, thou with dark eyelids
Bearing the golden bough of Argicida. So that:

So that what? Typical of Pound to leave us hanging like that. Who's not going to turn the page to read Canto II. And when we do, we are blasted by a diction so far removed from the "and thence outward and away . . . . bearing the golden bough of Argicida." Pound drops the persona of the Homeric/Victorian poet declaiming verse, grabs his suspenders and throws his voice into the modernism of the 20th century:

Hang it all, Robert Browning,
there can be but the one "Sordello."
But Sordello, and my Sordello?
Lo Sordels si fo Mantovana.
So-shu churned in the sea.
Seal sports in the spray-white circles of cliff-wash,
Sleek head, daughter of Lir,
            eyes of Picasso
Under black fur-hood, lithe daughter of Ocean;
And the wave runs in the beach-grove:
"Eleanor, ελενουσ and ελεπτολισ!"

This is not the place to explicate the meaning of the above text, but the shifts from one tone to another, one diction to another, one langauge to another, as well as the use of various poetical devices such as Anglo-Saxon alliteration and Homeric hyphenated epitephs produce an effect similar to hearing a singer begin with a few lines of a romantic ballad, suddenly shift into progressive jazz rhythms, then slide into a country twang and a rock-and-roll Little Richard squeal, topped off with a few lines of rap followed by a French *chanson d'amour* and a boogie-woogie calypso version of Henry 'Iggins from *My Fair Lady*. The effect is so exxagerated in the opening salvo of the *Cantos*, that the reader is both put off, and put on guard that this is going to be a Homeric *tour de force* like no other. It's debatable whether Pound in his *Cantos* achieved the kind of overall unity that Homer is credited with achieving in the *Iliad*. Even Pound finally admitted that his work, written over several decades, "didn't cohere." But there are passages in the *Cantos* of great humour, philosophical important, narrative drama, and great lyric beauty. For our purposes here, The *Cantos* also gives a sense of the range of dialects and poetic and rhetorical variations that characterizes Homer in the original Greek.

There are passages using Shakespearian eloquence set against a contemporary conversational idiom that give the Elizabethan diction a beauty that is profoundly haunting, and would be lost if rendered in standard English. But the effect is deliberate; it isn't as if Pound is unconsciously using an archaic idiom, or worse, a clichéd, hackneyed poetic phrase. In that part of the *Cantos* written while Pound was detained in a wire cage in a Pisan prison camp awaiting execution for treason after the war—called "The Pisan Cantos"—he offers a haunting, yet tonally eccentric lament for the masterful dead whom he had known and loved in his lifetime. Here's a sampling from "The Pisan Cantos" of the shifts from one idiom to another, one dialect to another, one   lanaguage to another, and changes in tone with passages that mimick and exaggerate the same kinds of effects Hermogenes notes were characteristic of Homer:

. . . . That was Padre José Elizondo   [the Spanish priest who helped
         in 1906 and in 1917   [Pound get a photostat of the
or about 1917   [Cavalcanti mss. in Madrid]
         and Dolores said, "Come pan, niño,"   eat bread, me lad
Sargent had painted her   [John Singer Sargent, Am. painter
         before he descended
(i.e. if he descended
         but in those days he did thumb sketches, . . .
         goat bells tinkled all night
         and the hostess grinned: Eso es luto, *haw*!
mi marido es muerto
         (it is mourning, my husband is dead)
when she gave me paper to write on
with a black border half an inch or more deep, . . .
Possum observed that the local portagoose fold dance   [Possum was nickname
was danced by the same dancers in divers localities   [for T.S. Eliot]
         in political welcome . . .
Yet
Ere the season died a-cold
Borne upon a zephy's shoulder
I rose through the aureate sky
         Lawes and Jenkyns guard thy rest
         Dolmetsch ever be thy guest,
Has he tempered the viol's wood   [Henry Lawes(1596-1662: set to music
         [Wallers "Go, Lovely Rose."]
To enforce   both the grave   and the acute?   [John Jenkyn (1592-1678,
Has he curved us the bowl of the lute?   [English composer to Charles I and II
         Lawes and Jenkyns guard thy rest
         Dolmetsch ever be thy guest
Hast 'ou fashioned so airy a mood   [Arnold Dolmetsch foundation 1928
         To draw up leaf from the root?   [encouraged int. in old music]
Hast 'ou found   a cloud   so light
         As seemed neither mist nor shade?   [these 4 lines derive from Ben Johnson's
         ["The Triumph of Charis"]
And for 180 years almost nothing.

Ad escoltando al leggier mormorio   ["and listening to gentle murmur"]
         there came new subtlety of eyes into my tent,
whether of spirit or hypostasis,
         but what the blindfold hides
or at carneval
         nor any pair showed anger

Saw but the eyes and stance between the eyes,
colour, diastasis,
        careless or unaware it had not the
      whole tent's room
nor was place for the full Ειδωξ   [seeing or knowing]
interpass, penetrate
  casting but shade beyond the other lights
        sky's clear
        night sea
        green of the mountain pool
        shone from the unmásked eyes in half-mask's space.

What thou lovest well remains,
                          the rest is dross
What thou lov'st well shall not be reft from thee
What thou lov'st well is thy true heritage
Whose world, or mine or theirs
                  or is it of none?
First came the seen, then thus the palpable
      Elysium, though it were in the halls of hell,
What thou lovest well is thy true heritage
What thou lov'st well shall not be reft from thee

The ant's a centaur in his dragon world.
Pull down thy vanity, it is not man
Made courage, or made order, or made grace,
      Pull down thy vanity, I say pull down.
Learn of the green world what can by thy place
In scaled invention or true artistry,
Pull down thy vanity,
               Paquin pull down!   [a Parisian courtier]
The green casque has outdone your elegance.
      Pull down thy vanity,
Rathe to destroy, niggard in charity,
Pull down thy vanity,
        I say pull down.

But to have done instead of not doing
          this is not vanity   [Wilfred Blunt, poet & diplomat
To have, with decency, knocked   [first Englishman to go to prison
That a Blunt should open   for defending home rule for Ireland]
      To have gathered from the air a live tradition
or from a fine old eye the unconquered flame   [ref to Henry James]
This is not vanity.
      Here error is all in the not done
all in the diffidence that faltered . . .

Nor can who has passed a month in the death cells
      believe in capital punishment
No man who has passed a month in the death cells
      believe in cages for beasts

There is fatigue deep as the grave.
The Kakemono grows in flat land out of mist
  sun rises lop-sided over the mountain
   so that I recalled the noise in the chimney
as it were the wind in the chimney
   but was in reality Uncle William   [i.e. William Butler Yeats]
downstairs composing   [Yeats' peacock poem was published
that he made a great Peeeeacock   [in *Poetry*, May 1914 based on luncheon
  in the proide ov his oiye   [in hommage to Blunt in January
   he had made a great Peeeeeeecock in the . . .
made a great peacock
  in the proide of his oyyee

at Stone Cottage in Sussex by the waste moor [Pound stayed with Yeats as his secretary
(or whatever) and the holly bush   [at Stone Cottage near Ashdown Forest
   who could not eat ham for dinner
because peasants eat ham for dinner
   despite the excellent quality
and the pleasure of having it hot

proide ov his oy-ee
as indeed he had, and perdurable

well those days are gone forever   [Pound read Wordsworth to Yeats
  and the traveling rug with the coon-skin tabs
and his hearing nearly all Wordsworth
   for the sake of his conscience but
preferring Ennemosor on Witches   [a book on *The History of Magic*]
               [the kind of stuff Yeats liked]

a fat moon rises lop-sided over the mountain
The eyes, this time my world,
   But pass and look from mine
    between my lids
     sea, sky, and pool
     alternate
     pool, sky, sea

morning moon against sunrise
like a bit of the best ancient greek coinage

and in my mother's time it was respectable,
it was social, apparently,
      to sit in the Senate gallery
or even in that of the House
   to hear the fire-works of the senators
(and possibly representatives)
as was still done in Westminster in my time
and a very poor show from the once I saw it

but if Senator Edwards cd/ speak
in short / the descent

```
has not been of advantage either
                to the Senate or to "society"
                            or to the people
        The States have passed thru a
                dam'd supercilious era
Down, Derry-Down /
        Oh let an old man rest.
```

```
ed ella: pocco.
        Poco, poco
ed io: peggio dei tedeshi?
        ed ella: uruale, thru the barbed wire
                you can, said Stef (Lincoln Steffens)
do nothing with revolutionaries
        until they are at the end of their tether
and that Vandenberg has read Stalin, or Stalin, John Adams
is, at the mildest, unproven.
```

```
If the hoar frost grip thy tent
Thou wilt give thanks when the night is spent.
```

Obviously, this is not the simple narrative structure of the *Iliad*. Pound's epic is a collage of high modernist fragmentation. The form of this 20th century epic imitates the modernist era's cubism, abstraction, abstract-expressionism, etc., and mirrors the fractured nature of a century characterized by wars, depressions, roaring prosperity, Bonnie & Clyde, the Charleston, Lindberg, and the Manhattan skyline. The above sampling from the "Pisan Cantos" can only suggest the symphonic nature of Pound's *Cantos*, but it can give an impression of the tonal changes characteristic of Homer's Greek that can easily be missed in an English translation, because it is not natural in our verse forms to attempt this kind of Homeric-Callimachian shift in tone and idiom. What modern poet would, in the middle of a contemporary sentence, suddenly shift to an Elizabethan diction:

```
What thou lovest best remains
                            the rest is dross
What thou lov'st well shall not be reft from thee
What thou lov'st well is thy true heritage
What thou lov'st well shall not be reft from thee.
```

Imagine this being translated into another language. Would the translator find an suitable archaic diction, or render it thusly:

```
What you love the most will stay
                    the rest is nothing but the scum
                    that forms on the surface of molten metal
What you love best will not be taken from you
What you love best will be your true property
What you love the most will remain
```

This is what they mean when they say something was lost in translation. For poets and writers working in the English language, the idioms of Shakespeare and the King James Bible are a treasure trove of riches. But this should not be confused with writers unconsciously using remnants of Elizabethan diction as filtered through 19th century Victorian prose and early 20th century "poetic" poetry. This is the diction that poets like William Carlos Williams and Ezra Pound fought against, and writers like Hemingway and Fitzgerald rejected. This is why Homer, when properly translated—and because language is constantly changing, he needs constant updating—this is why Homer, when properly translated, is still a modern writer. He was modern in his own time, and he remains modern today.

Where Agamemnon fumes, Achilles rages, then goes back to his tent to sulk for most of the rest of the story. But his prayer that the Greek's suffer reversals is answered. Without their greatest warrior, the Greeks falter and the Trojans, led by Hector, son of King Priam, gain the upper hand, breaking through the walls built by the Greeks to protect their vessels. Agamemnon, Odysseus, and an embassy of warriors appeal to Achilles to come to the rescue, and offer him restitution and abundant gifts in compensation for the insult to his honor. Agamemnon offers Achilles "gifts to match his insults," bars of gold, beautiful stallions, flawless women. But Achilles is obsessed with his grievance, and refuses to lead his own forces into battle.

> I hate that man like the very Gates of Death.
> Will Agamemnon win me over? Not for all the world. . . .
> Let him rack his brains with you and the other captains
> how to fight the raging fire off the ships. Look—
> what a mighty piece of work he's done without *me*!
> Why, he's erected a rampart, driven a trench around it,
> broad, enormous, and planted stakes to guard it. No use!
> He still can't block the power of man-killing Hector!
> My squadrons sail at dawn,
> fanning out on the Hellespont that swarms with fish, . . .
> That high and mighty King Agamemnon,
> that son of Atreus! . . .
>   Dog that he is
> he'd never dare to look me straight in the eyes again.
> No, I'll never set heads together with that man—
>   Die and be damned for all I care!
> Zeus who rules the world has ripped his wits away.
> His gifts, I loath his gifts . . .
> I wouldn't give you a splinter for that man!
> Not if he gave me ten times as much, twenty times over, all
> he possesses now, and all that could pour in from the world's

end—
not all the wealth that's freighted into Orchomenos, even
                                        into Thebes
Egyptian Thebes where the houses overflow with the greatest
                                        troves of treasure,
Thebes with the hundred gates and through each gate battallions,
two hundred fighters surge to war with teams and chariots—
no, not if his gifts outnumbered all the grains of sand
and dust in the earth—no, not even then.
                                        [Fagles]

After further battles, Achilles' friend and squire Patrocles tries to persuade Achilles to change his mind. When that fails, Patrocles asks to borrow his armour, hoping to inspire the Greeks in battle. Achilles consents, but warns Patrocles to turn back once the ships are saved, and not to engage Hector in combat. Patrocles takes no heed of Achilles' warning, and after a fierce struggle, is killed beneath the wall of Troy by Hector who then takes Achilles' armour as Patrocles' friends bear his body back to the Greek camp.

Achilles is plunged into a frenzy of grief, remorse, and rage. The anger he felt toward Agamemnon is forgotten, replaced by an even greater enmity toward Hector, the man who killed his friend. Achilles rouses his anger once again, vowing revenge for Patroclus' death, but his mother, the Goddess Thetis, warns him that it is fated that his own death shall follow soon after Hector's.

Achilles is given the news that the Greeks have suffered another defeat.

> "Why, why? Our long-haired Achaeans routed again,
> driven in terror off the plain to crowd the ships, but why?
> Dear god, don't bring to pass the grief that haunts my heart—
> the prophecy that mother revealed to me one time . . .
> she said the best of the Myrmidons—while I lived—
> would fall at Trojan hands and leave the light of day.
> And now he's dead, I know it. Menoetius' gallant son,
> my headstrong friend! And I told Patroclus clearly,
> 'Once you have beaten off the lethal fire, quick,
> come back to the ships—you must not battle Hector.!'"

Then he is told that Patroclus has fallen and that Hector has taken his armor.

> A black cloud of grief came shrouding over Achilles.
> Both hands clawing the ground for soot and filth,
> he poured it over his head, fouled his handsome face
> and black ashes settled onto his fresh clean war-shirt.
> Overpowered in all his power, sprawled in the dust,
> Achilles lay there, fallen . . .
> tearing his hair, defiling it with his own hands.

Achilles' mother, the goddess Thetis, hears his cries and asks the cause of his grief.

"Zeus has accomplished everything you wanted,
just as you raised your hands and prayed that day.
All the sons of Achaea are pinned against the ships
and all for want of you — they suffer shattering losses."

Achilles tells her of Patroclus' death at the hands of Hector.

"My spirit rebels — I've lost the will to live,
to take my stand in the world of men — unless,
before all else, Hector's battered down by my spear
and gasps away his life, the blood-price for Patroclus,
Menoetius' gallant son he's killed and stripped."

But Thetis answered, warning through her tears,
"You're doomed to a short life, my son, from all you say!
For hard on the heels of Hector's death your death
must come at once —"
                              "Then let me die at once —"
Achilles burst out, despairing — "since it was not my fate
to save my dearest comrade from his death! Look,
a world away from his home, he's perished,
lacking me, my fighting strength, to defend him.

No, no, here I sit by the ships . . .
a useless, dead weight on the good green earth —
I, no man my equal among the bronze-armed Achaeans,
not in battle, only in wars of words that others win.
If only strife could die from the lives of gods and men
and anger that drives the sanest man to flare in outrage —
bitter gall, sweeter than dripping streams of honey,
that swarms in people's chests and blinds like smoke —
just like the anger Agamemnon king of men
has roused within me now . . .
                              Enough.
Let bygones be bygones. Done is done.
Despite my anguish I will beat it donw,
the fury mounting inside me, down by force.
But now I'll go and meet that murderer head-on,
that Hector who destroyed the dearest life I know.
For my own death, I'll meet it freely — whenever Zeus
and the other deathless gods would like to bring it on!
. . . .
I'll lie in peace, once I've gone down to death.
But now, for the moment, let me seize great glory! —   [Dardanus was the forebear
and drive some woman of Troy or deep-breasted Dardan   of Priam and kings
to claw with both hands at her tender cheeks and wipe away   of Troy]
her burning tears as the sobs come choking from her throat —
they'll learn that I refrained from war a good long time!
Don't try to hold me back from the fighting, mother,
love me as you do. you can't persuade me now.

Because Achilles is without armor, Thetis goes to see Hephaestus, the god of fire, the great metalsmith, and asks him to make a special shield and armor for her son:

> But Thetis burst into tears, her voice welling:
> "Oh Hephaestus—who of all the goddesses on Olympus,
> who has borne such withering sorrows in her heart?
> Such pain as Zeus has given me, above all others!
> *Me* out of all the daughters of the sea he chose
> to yoke to a mortal man, Peleus, son of Aeacus,
> and I endured his bed, a mortal's bed, resisting
> with all my will. And now he lies in the halls,   [When Priam begs Achilles to release
> broken with grisly age, but now my griefs are worse.   his son's body, he reminds
> Remember? Zeus also gave me a son to bear and breed,   Achilles of his own father]
> the splendor of heroes, and he shot up like a young branch,
> like a fine tree I reared him—the orchard's crowning glory—
> but only to send him off in the beaked ships to Troy
> to battle Trojans! Never again will I embrace him
> striding home through the doors of Peleus' house.
> And long as I have him with me, still alive,
> looking into the sunlight, he is racked with anguish.
> I go to his side—nothing I do can help him. Nothing.
> That girl the sons of Achaea picked out for his prize—
> right from his grasp the mighty Agamemnon tore her,
> and grief for her has been gnawing at his heart.
> But then the Trojans pinned the Achaeans tight
> against their sterns, they gave them no way out,
> and the Argive warlords begged my son to help,
> they named in full the troves of glittering gifts
> they'd send his way. But at that point he refused
> to beat disaster off—refused himself, that is—
> but he buckled his own armour round Patroclus,
> sent him into battle with an army at his back.
> And all day long they fought at the Scaean Gates,
> that very day they would have stormed the city too,
> if Apollo had not killed Menoetius' gallant son
> as he laid the Trojans low—Apollo cut him down
> among the champions there and handed Hector glory.
> So now I come, I throw myself at your knees,
> please help me! Give my son—he won't live long—
> a shield and helmet and tooled greaves with ankle-straps
> and armor for his chest. All that he had was lost,
> lost when the Trojans killed his steadfast friend.
> Now he lies on the ground—his heart is breaking."

Hephaestus makes Achilles a new shield, richly engraved with many scenes of battle. Armed in new and splendid armour as a gift of a god, Achilles rides out in fury to find Hector and kill him, but even the horses warn Achilles that this is the last time they will bear him safely from the field. Now the Gods, who have been pulling strings from above, join the fray as well, with Athena, Hera, Poseidon, Hephaestus, and Hermes rooting for the Greeks, while Apollo, Ares, Artemis, Aphrodite, and Leto pull for the Trojans, who are eventually defeated. Hector is unwilling to give up the hope of a final victory, and decides not to retreat.

Where Homer presents Achilles as the lone warrior *par excellence*, he shows Hector as both warrior and family man. So much of the narrative is cinematic, but the scene between Hector and his wife, Andromache, is especially moving in its simplicity and attention to detail.

> Hector retraced his steps through the stone and tile streets
> Of the great city, until he came to the Western Gate. [The Scaean Gates,
> He was passing through it out onto the plain the main gate of Troy]
> When his wife came running up to meet him,
> His beautiful wife, Andromache,
> A gracious woman, daughter of great Eëtion,
> Eëtion, who lived in the forests of Plakos
> And ruled the Cilicians from Thebes-under-Plakos—
> His daughter was wed to bronze-helmeted Hector.
> She came up to him now, and the nurse with her
> held to her bosom their baby boy,
> Hector's beloved son, beautiful as starlight,
> Whom Hector had named Scamandrius,
> But everyone else called Astyanax, Lord of the City,
> For Hector alone could save Ilion now.
> he looked at his son and smiled in silence.
> Andromache stood close to him, shedding tears,
> Clinging to his arm as she spoke these words:
>
> "Possessed is what you are, Hector. Your courage
> Is going to kill you, and you have no feeling left
> For your little boy or for me, the luckless woman
> Who will soon be your widow. It won't be long
> Before the whole Greek army swarms and kills you.
> And when they do, it will be better for me
> To sink into the earth. When I lose you, Hector,
> There will be nothing left, no one to turn to,
> Only pain. My father and mother are dead.
> Achilles killed my father when he destroyed
> Out city, Thebes with its high gates,
> But had too much respect to despoil his body.
> He burned it instead with all his armor
> And heaped up a barrow. And the spirit women
> Came down from the mountain, daughters
> Of the storm god, and planted elm trees around it.
> I had seven brothers once in that great house.
> All seven went down to Hades on a single day,
> Cut down by Achilles in one blinding sprint
> Through their shambling cattle and silver sheep.

Mother, who was queen in the forests of Plakos,
He took back as prisoner, with all her possessions,
Then released her for a fortune in ransom.
She died in our house, shot by Artemis' arrows.
Hector, you are my father, you are my mother,
You are my brother and my blossoming husband.
But show some pity and stay here by the tower,
Don't make your child an orphan, your wife a widow.
Station your men here by the fig tree, where the city
is weakest because the wall can be scaled.
Three times their elite have tried an attack here
Rallying around Ajax or glorious Idomeneus
Or Atreus' sons or mighty Diomedes,
Whether someone in on the prophecy told them
or they are driven here by something in their heart."

And Great Hector, helmet shining, answered her.

"Yes, Andromache, I worry about all this myself,
But my shame before the Trojans and their wives,
With their long robes trailing, would be too terrible
If I hung back from battle like a coward.
And my heart won't let me. I have learned to be
One of the best, to fight in Troy's first ranks,
Defending my father's honor and my own.
Deep in my heart I know too well
There will come a day when holy Ilion will perish,
And Priam and the people under Priam's ash spear.
But the pain I will feel for the Trojan's then,
For Hecuba herself and for Priam king,
For my many fine brothers who will have by then
Fallen in the dust behind enemy lines —
All that pain is nothing to what I will feel
For you, when some bronze-armored Greek
Leads you away in tears, on your first day of slavery.
And you will work some other woman's loom
In Argos or carry water from a Spartan spring,
All against your will, under great duress.
And someone, seeing you crying, will say,
'That is the wife of Hector, the best of all
The Trojans when they found around Ilion.'
Someday someone will say that, renewing your pain
At having lost such a man to fight off the day
of your enslavement. But may I be dead
And the earth heaped up above me
Before I hear your cry as you are dragged away."

With these words, resplendent Hector
Reached for his child, who shrank back screaming
Into his nurse's bosom, terrified of his father's
Bronze-encased face and the horsehair plume
He saw nodding down from the helmet's crest.

This forced a laugh from his father and mother,
And Hector removed the helmet from his head
And set it on the ground all shimmering with light.
Then he kissed his dear son and swung him up gently
And said a prayer to Zeus and the other immortals:

"Zeus and all gods: grant that this my son
Become, as I am, foremost among Trojans,
Brave and strong, and ruling Ilion with might.
And may men say he is far better than his father
When he returns from war, bearing bloody spoils,
Having killed his man. And may his mother rejoice."

And he put his son in the arms of his wife,
And she enfolded him in her fragrant bosom
Laughing through her tears. Hector pitied her
And stroked her with his hand and said to her:

"You worry too much about me, Andromache.
No one is going to send me to Hades before my time,
And no man has ever escaped his fate, rich or poor,
Coward or hero, once born into this world.
Go back to the house now and take care of your work,
The loom and the shuttle, and tell the servants
To get one with their jobs. War is the work of men,
Of all the Trojan men, and mine especially."

With these words, Hector picked up
His plumed helmet, and his wife went back home,
Turning around often, her cheeks flowered with tears.
When she came to the house of man-slaying Hector,
She found a throng of servants inside,
And raised among these women the ritual lament.
And so they mourned for Hector in his house
Although he was still alive, for they did not think
He would ever again come back from the war,
Or escape the murderous hands of the Greeks.

                                        (Lombardo, VI: 408-527)

Hector waits alone for Achilles outside the walls of Troy, where they will fight mano a mano. Wearing Achilles' armor, Hector knows too that he is doomed, especially when his spear hits Achilles' shield and fails to pierce it

                    "My time has come!
At last the gods have called me down to death. . . .
And now death, grim death is looming up beside me,
no longer far away. No way to escape it now. This
this was their [the gods] pleasure after all, sealed long ago. . . .
So now I meet my doom. Well let me die —
but not without struggle, not without glory, no,
in some great clash of arms that even men to come

will hear of down the years!"
                                      And on that resolve
he drew the whetted sword that hung at his side,
tempered, massive, and gathering all his force
he swooped like a soaring eagle
launching down from the dark clouds to earth,
to snatch some helpless lamb or trembling hare.
So Hector swooped now, swinging his whetted sword
and Achilles charged too, bursting with rage, barbaric,
guarding his chest with the well-wrought blazoned shield,
head tossing his gleaming helmet, four horns strong
and the golden plumes shook that the god of fire
drove in bristling thick along its ridge.
Bright as that star amid the stars in the night sky,
star of the evening, brightest star that rides the heavens,
so fire flared from the sharp point of the spear Achilles
brandished high in his right hand, bent on Hector's death,
scanning his splendid body—where to pierce it best?
The rest of his flesh seemed all encased in armor,
burnished, brazen—*Achilles'* armor that Hector stripped
from strong Patroclus when he killed him—true,
but one spot lay exposed,
where the collarbones lift the neckbone off the shoulders,
the open throat, where the end of life comes quickest—*there*
as Hector charged in fury brilliant Achilles drove his spear
and the point went stabbing clean through the tender neck
but the heavy bronze weapon failed to slash the windpipe—
Hector could still gasp out some sounds, some last reply . . .
he crashed in the dust—
                              godlike Achilles gloried over him:
"Hector—surely you thought when you stipped Patroclus' armor
that you, you would be safe! Never a fear of me—
far from fighting as I was—you fool!
Left behind there, down by the beaked ships
his great avenger waited, a greater man by far—
that man was I, and I smashed your strength! And you—
the dogs and birds will maul you, shame your corpse
while Achaeans bury my dear friend in glory!"

   Struggling for breath, Hector, his helmet flashing,
said, "I beg you, beg by your life, your parents—
don't let the dogs devour me by the Argive ships!
Wait, take the princely ransom of bronze and gold,
the gifts my father and noble mother will give you—
but give my body to friends to carry home again,
so Trojan men and Trojan women can do me honor
with fitting rites of fire once I am dead."

   Staring grimly, the proud runner Achilles answered,
"Beg no more, you fawning dog—begging me by my parents!
Would to god my rage, my fury would drive me now
to hack your flesh away and eat you raw—

such agonies you have caused me! Ransom?
No man alive could keep the dog-packs off you,
not if they haul in ten, twenty times that ransom
and pile it here before me and promise fortunes more—
no, not even if Dardan Priam should offer to weigh out
your bulk in gold! Not even then will your noble mother
lay you on your deathbed, mourn the son she bore . . .
The dogs and birds will rend you—blood and bone!"

    At the point of death, Hector, his helmet flashing,
said, "I know you well—I see my fate before me.
Never a chance that I could win you over . . .
Iron inside your chest, that heart of yours." . . .

    Death cut him short. The end closed in around him.
Flying free of his limbs
his soul went winging down to the House of Death,
wailing his fate, leaving his manhood far behind,
his young and supple strength. But brilliant Achilles
taunted Hector's body, dead as he was, "Die, die!
For my own death, I'll meet it freely—whenever Zeus
and the other deathless gods would like to bring it on!"
[Fagles]

Noble Hector. Savage Achilles. Little has changed since the opening chapter. This is not a man prone to mercy. When Hector begs for an honorable dispatch, Achilles answers: "No, . . . not if they haul in ten, twenty times that ransom . . . . no, not even if Dardan Priam should offer to weigh out your bulk in gold! No, not even then!" At this point in the story, nearing its end, Achilles remains unchanged, a selfish, bull-headed, wrathful fighter driven by his arrogance and pride.

Achilles and Hector are the heroes of the poem, but it is Achilles who undertakes an inner journey from spiteful warrior, with a god-like image of himself, to one who has mastered his venomous wrath to attain inner peace. It would be too much to ask that Achilles' transformation be total. But in one of the closing scenes, he huddles in his tent with Priam, Hector's father, who's come to claim his son's body. Achilles and once proud Priam, King of Troy, weep together over the mystery of human life, how we are—in the words Aeschylus, the Greek dramatist—"made perfect by suffering." Though Achilles is in his prime and frail Priam knows he will witness the destruction of his kingdom, both men affirm the continuity of life. Achilles knows he will die in battle, but that his spirit will be subject to the supreme power of Fate, a destiny that lies beyond the control of Zeus and the other gods.

Achilles' matures before our eyes, his vengeful rage against Agamemnon and Hector softens to forgiveness, his fury against the Trojans resolves in a heartfelt scene with Priam. Achilles accepts his fate, as did Hector, both dying nobly in the cause of something greater than themselves.

Priam makes his way toward Achilles' tent, bringing ransom to claim his son's body. He meets up with Mytmidon, Achilles' aide.

And the old and noble Priam asked at once,
"If you really are the royal Achilles' aide,
please, tell me the whole truth, point by point.
My son—does he still lie by the beached ships,
or by now has the great Achilles hacked him
limb from limb and served him to his dogs?"

The guide and giant killer reassured him:
"So far, old man, no birds or dogs have eaten him.
No, there he lies—still there at Achilles' ships,
still intact in his shelters.
This is the twelfth day he's lain there, too,
but his body has not decayed, not in the least,
nor have the worms begun to gnaw his corpse,
the swarms that devour men who fall in battle.
True, dawn on fiery dawn, he drags him round
his beloved comrade's tomb, drags him ruthlessly
but he cannot mutiliate his body. It's marvelous—
go see for yourself how he lies there fresh as dew,
the blood washed away, and no sign of corruption.
All his wounds sealed shut, wherever they struck . . .
and many drove their bronze blades through his body.
Such pains the blissful gods are lavishing on your son,
dead man though he is—the gods love him dearly!"

                                                    [Fagles]

Priam is escorted to Achilles' tent, where several captains sit some way off, and two others are serving him.

                    He had just finished dinner,
eating, drinking, and the table still stood near.
The majestic king of Troy slipped past the rest
and kneeling down beside Achilles, clasped his knees
and kissed his hands, those terrible, man-killing hands
that had slaughtered Priam's many sons in battle.
Awesome—as when the grip of madness seizes one
who murders a man in his own fatherland and flees   [check this simile out:
abroad to foreign shores, to a wealthy, noble host,   notice Homer
and a sense of marvel runs through all who see him—   reverses the so
Achilles marveled, beholding majestic Priam.   parallel image]
His men marveled too, trading startled glances.
But Priam prayed his heart out to Achilles:
"Remember your own father, great god-like Achilles—
as old as *I* am, past the threshold of deadly old age!
No doubt the countrymen round about him plague him now,
with no one there to defend him, beat away disaster.
No one—but at least he heads you're still alive
and his old heart rejoices, hopes rising, day by day,
to see his beloved son come sailing home from Troy.
But I—dead god, my life so cursed by fate . . .

I fathered hero sons in the wide realm of Troy
and now not a single one is left, I tell you.
Fifty sons I had when the sons of Achaea came,
nineteen born to me from a single mother's womb
and the rest by other women in the palace. Many,
most of them violent Ares cut the knees from under.
But one, one was left me, to guard my walls, my people—
the one you killed the other day, defending his fatherland,
my Hector! It's all for him I've come to the ships now,
to win him back from you—I bring a priceless ransom.
Revere the gods, Achilles! Pity me in my own right,
remember your own father! I deserve more pity . . .
I have endured what no one on earth has ever done before—
I put to my lips the hands of the man who killed my son."

[Fagles]

Priam's appeal to Achilles' softens his wrathful heart and restores his humanity.

The war between Greece and Troy was not a civil war. But as a Greek, writing about Greece's victory over Troy, Homer treats its heroes and warriors the way one might treat the brave soldiers who fought on both sides in the American Civil War. There are no villiams, there is only human conflict, petty anger, and heroic action. The epic ends not with Achilles' triumph, or even with the triumph of the Greeks—which is still years ahead—but with the lamentations at Hector's funeral, as if the real hero, the tragic hero, if you will, of the *Iliad*, was not murderous and doomed Achilles, but man-killing Hector, tamer of horses.

Dawn spread her saffron light over the earth,
And they drove the horses into the city
With great lamentation. The mules pulled the corpse.
No one in Troy, man or woman, saw them before
Cassandra, who stood like golden Aphrodite
On Pergamon's height. Looking out she saw
Her dear father standing in the chariot
With the herald, and then she was Hector
Lying on the stretcher in the mule cart.
And her cry went out through all the city:

"Come look upon Hector, Trojan men and women,
If ever you rejoiced when he came home alive
From battle, a joy to the city and all its people."

She spoke. And there was not a man or woman
Left in the city, for an unbearable sorrow
Had come upon them. They met Priam by the gates
As he brought the body through, and in the front
Hector's dear wife and queenly mother threw themselves
On the rolling cart and pulled out their hair
As they clasped his head amid the grieving crowd.

they would have mounred Hector outside the gates
All the long day until the sun went down,
had not the old man spoken from his chariot:

"Let the mules come through. Later you will have
Your fill of grieving, after I have brought him home."

He spoke, and the crowd made way for the cart.
And they brought him home and laid him
On a corded bed, and set around him singers
To lead the dirge and chant the death song.
they chanted the dirge, and the women with them.
White-armed Andromache led the lamentation
As she cradled the head of her man-slaying Hector.

"You have died young, husband, and left me
A widow in the halls. Our son is still an infant,
Doomed when we bore him. I do not think
He will ever reaceh manhood. No, this city
Will topple and fall first. You were its savior,
And now you are lost. All the solemn wives
And the children you guarded will go off soon
In the hollow ships, and I will go with them.
And you, my son, you will either come with me
And do menial labor for a cruel master,
Or some Greek will lead you by the hand
And throw you ffrom the tower, a hideous death,
Angry because Hecktor killed his brother,
Or his father, or son. Many, many Greeks
Fell in battle under Hector's hands.
Your father was never gentle in combat.
And so all the townspeople mourn for him,
And you have caused your parents unspeakable
Sorrow, Hector, and left me endless pain.
You did not stretch your hand out to me
As you lay dying in bed, nor did you whisper
A final word I could remember as I weep
All the days and nights of my life."

The women's moans washed over her lament,
And from the sobbing came Hecuba's voice:

"Hector, my heart, dearest of all my children,
The gods loved you when you were alive for me,
And they have cared for you also in death.
My other children Achilles sold as slaves
When he captured them, shipped them overseas
To Samos, Imbros, and barren Lemnos.
After he took your life with tapered bronze
He dragged you around Patroclus' tomb, his friend
Whom you killed, but still could not bring him back.
And now you lie here for me as fresh as dew,

Although you have been slain, like one whom Apollo
Has killed softly with his silver arrows."

The third woman to lament was Helen.

"Oh, Hector, you were the dearest to me by far
Of all my husband's brothers. Yes, Paris
Is my husband, the godlike prince
Who led me to Troy. I should have died first.
This is not the twentieth year
Since I went away and left my home,
And I have never had an unkind word from you.
If anyone in the house ever taunted me,
Any of my husband's brothers or sisters,
Or his mother — my father-in-law was kind always —
You would draw them aside and calm them
With your gentle heart and gentle words.
And so I weep for you and for myself,
And my heart is heaby, because thereis no one left
In all wide Ttroy who will pity me
Or be my friend. Everyone shudders at me."

Then the old man, Priam, spoke to his people:

"Men of Troy, start bringing wood to the city,
And I have no fear of an Argive ambush.
When Achilles sent me from the black ships,
he gave his word he would not trouble us
Until the twelfth day should dawn."

He spoke, and they yoked oxen and mules
To wagons, and gathered outside the city.
For nine days they hauled in loads of timber.
When the tenth dawn showed her mortal light,
They brought out their brave Hector
And all in tears lifted the body high
Onto the bier, and threw on the fire.

Light blossomed like roses in eastern sky.

The people gathered around Hector's pyre,
And when all of Troy was assembled there
They drowned the last flames with glinting wine.
Hector's brothers and friends collected
His white bones, their cheeks flowered with tears.
They wrapped the bones in soft purple robes
And placed them in a golden casket, and laid it
In the hollow of the grave, and heaped above it
A mantle of stones. They built the tomb
Quickly, with lookouts posted all around
In case the Greeks should attack early.

When the tomb was built, they all returned
To the city and assembled for a glorious feast
In the house of Priam, Zeus' cherished king.

That was the funeral of Hector, breaker of horses.
(Stanley Lombardo, 1997)

☞ **The Odyssey**

"Book of the Dead, XI"
- A Gathering of Shades, lines 1-170,

After the Trojan war, Odysseus sets off from Troy over the wine-dark sea to his home back in Ithaca. Along the way he has many adventures. To see for yourself, rent the movie starring Kirk Douglas as Ulysses. See him undergo the wrath of the sea-god Poseidon, fight monsters, overcome sexual distractions and the loss of his crew. See him strapped to the mast of his ship, with no ear plugs, so he can hear the voice of the Siren. See them fight the Cylcops! See them sail to Circe's lands! As Book XI opens, they are about to embark with their boat laden with sheep, to sail toward Avernus, the gates of Hell. Odysseus hopes to speak to the dead, and hear Tiresias, the blind Theban prophet, tell them what lies ahead. [trans. by Robert Fitzgerald]

> We bore down on the ship at the sea's edge
> and launched her on the salt immortal sea,
> stepping our mast and spar in the black ship;
> embarked the ram and ewe and went aboard
> in tears, with bitter and sore dread upon us.
> But now a breeze came up for us astern —
> a canvas-bellying landbreeze, hale shipmate
> sent by the singing nymph with sun-bright hair;
> and with full sail made fast upon the fathomless unresting sea.

Into the Dreadful Night they sail, making their way along the banks of the River of Ocean until they reach the spot that Circe had described. As they prepare the trench of blood for Tiresias to drink, the dead begin to wander toward them—ghostly, thirsty shades right out of a scene from *The Night of the Living Dead*. There, Perimedes and Eurylochus

> pinioned the sacred beasts. With my drawn blade
> I spaded up the votive pit, and poured
> libations round it to the unnumbered dead:
> sweet milk and honey, then sweet wine, and last
> clear water; and I scattered barley down.
> Then I addressed the blurred and breathless dead,
> vowing to slaughter my best heifer for them
> before she calved, at home in Ithaka,
> and burn the choice bits on the altar fire;

as for Tiresias, I swore to sacrifice
a black lamb, handsomest of all our flock.
Thus to assuage the nations of the dead
I pledged these rites, then slashed the lamb and ewe,
letting their black blood stream into the wellpit.
Now the souls gathered, stirring out of Erebos,
brides and young men, and men grown old in pain,
and tender girls whose hearts were new to grief;
many were there, too, torn by brazen lanceheads,
battle-slain, bearing still their bloody gear.
From every side they came and sought the pit
with a moaning that was horrible to hear.
Panic drained the blood from my cheeks.
But presently I gave command to my officers
to flay those sheep the bronz cut down, and make
burnt offers of flesh to the gods below —
to sovereign Death, to pale Persephone.

Odysseus crouches beside the pit and has to fend off the dead who would drink their fill. Tiresias must be the first to drink. Suddenly Odysseus is approached by someone he recognizes, Elpenor, one of his own men who had failed to board the ship when they set sail from Circe's lands. [I switch here to a prose translation by E.V. Rieu in a Penguin Classic edition]

> The first soul that came up was that of my own man Elpenor. Tears started to my eyes and I was stirred with pity for him. I called across to him at once: "Elpenor! How did you come here, under the western gloom? You have been quicker on foot than I in my black ship?"
> I heard him sigh, and then his answer came: "My royal master, Odysseus of the nimble wits, it was the malice of some evil power that was my undoing, and all the wine I swilled before I went to sleep in Circe's palace."

Elpenor tells how he missed the ladder going down, fell from the roof, and broke his neck. He asks Odysseus to remember him and not leave him here unburied. Odysseus pledges to do so, "Nothing shall be forgotten." Next his mother Anticleia comes, but despite his compassion for her, he must keep her from the blood until Tiresias has a chance to speak.

Soon from the dark that prince of Thebes came forward
bearing a golden staff; and he addressed me:

"Royal son of Laertes and the gods of old,
Odysseus, of the nimble wits
master of land ways and sea ways,
why leave the blazing sun, O man of woe,
to see the cold dead and the joyless region?
Stand clear, put up your sword;
let me but taste of blood, I shall speak true."

At this I stepped aside, and in the scabbard
let my long sword ring home to the pommel silver,
as he bent down to the sombre blood. Then spoke
the prince of those with gift of speech:

"My Lord Odysseus,
you are looking for an easy way home.
But the powers above
are going to make your journey hard. . . .

"If you leave the fat sheep of the Sun-god
on the Isle of Thrinacie untouched
and fix your mind on getting home,
there is some chance that all of you
may yet reach Ithaca, though not in comfort.
But if you hurt them, then I warrant you
that your ship and company will be destroyed,
and if you yourself do manage to escape,
you will come home late, in evil plight,
upon a foreign ship, with all your comrades dead.

"Under strange sail shall you come home, to find
your own house filled with trouble: insolent men
eating your livestock as they court your lady.
Aye, you shall make those men atone in blood! . . .

"As for your own end, Death will come to you
out of the sea, Death in his gentlest guise.
When he takes you, you will be worn out
after an easy old age and surrounded by a prosperous people.
This is the truth that I have told you."

ॐ

[this section needs to be finished]

FOOD FOR THOUGHT

MEANWHILE, BACK AT THE RANCH:

While the oral tales of Odyseus and Achilles and the Trojan war were being told and retold, a small tribe of nomadic peoples handed dowqn their traditions by word of mouth, as well. Who knows how many other peoples of the Mediterranean world and the Near East recited tales of beginnings and endings, war and peace. For all we know, what we have today may just be the tip of a written iceberg of oral tales, poetry, and myth. What survives was eventually written down. What has been lost, is lost, unless another astonishing find like the Dead Sea Scrolls or the Sumerian tablets are discovered. In the early days of the Israelite nation, around the 12th century, the same time the Homeric tales were being passed down from generation to generation, the Isrealite tribes shared a common history which they celebrated in shrines associated with one of their patriarchs or significant events. Like the Homeric bards, tribes in the Canaanite highlands recited epic stories of the sacred past. Abraham and Moses were heroes, and their god, Yahweh guided them and gave them a distinctive religious vision. During the eighth century, influenced by the creation of the alphabet, their scribes began to write down these tales, their mythlogies, the story of their wanderings, their escape from Egypt to found a nation under King David, the founder of the Judaean dynasty. The literary revolution that swept across the Middle East and eastern Mediterranean resulted in the first five books of Moses, and eventually, over the course of the next 9 centuries, the Hebrew Bible. With the advent of Christianity and its acceptance as the religion of Constantine's empire, both the Hebrew Bible (the Old Testament) and the Christian Gospels (the New Testament) became *The Book* of Western Civilization, influencing art and literature for the next two millenia.

☛ **Hesiod (8th century B.C.)** *The Works and Days*

Second only to Homer in the affection of the classic Greeks, Hesiod's father was an impoverished farmer who took to the sea to make ends meet. As a shepherd boy and farm hand, Hesiod followed his flocks up and down the slopes of Mount Helicon and dreamed that the Muses breathed into his body the soul of poetry. *Works and Days* was addressed to Hesiod's brother, supposedly a wastral, who had cheated Hesiod of much of his share of the family property; the brother is so oddly rendered, there is some thought he may have been no more than a literary device. "Now I will speak to you with good intent, you exceedingly foolish Perseus," he begins.

> Look, you can choose vice easily,
> even in heaps;
> for the path is plain,
> and she dwells very near.
> But before excellence
> the immortal gods have placed
> the sweat of toil;
> long and steep is the road
> that leads to her,
> and rough it is at first;
> but when you reach the height
> then truly is it easy,
> though so hard before.

Hesiod goes on laying down rules for efficient husbandry, and the proper days for plowing, planting, and reaping. His style was rough, with lines plowing through stanzas that Virgil would later polish into perfect verse. About a wife, Hesiod can't quite make up his mind. Perhaps he was a bachelor, or a widower, for it's hard to imagine he would have written so acrimonously of women with a woman around. Hesiod claims Zeus gave women to men as an evil, but still Hesiod vacillates between choices: celibacy is as bad as marriage; a lonely old age is a miserable thing, and the property of a childless man reverts at his death to the clan. So, he concludes, a man had better marry—though not before thirty; and he had better have children—though not more than one, or his property will be divided.

> No better lot has Providence assigned
> Than a fair woman with a virtuous mind;
> Nor can a worse befall than when thy fate
> Allots a worthless, feast-continuing mate.
> She with no touch of mere material flame
> Shall burn to tinder thy care-wasted frame;
> Shall send a fire thy vigorous bones within
> And age unripe in bloom of years begin.

Hesiod goes on to explain how man's fall had been caused by the curiosity of the first woman Pandora, brought into the world to punish mankind for accepting the gift of fire from her father Promotheus. Like the author of The *Books of Job*, he was grappling with the problem of evil, and trying to explain why we have to suffer in a world controlled by a supposedly benevolent supreme deity.

The *Theogony* is quite different. It sets out to expound the devine creation and organization of the universe and the world—an early attempt to combine a mass of mythological material. Order is imposed by Zeus, and Dike (Justice) is his agent: she occupies the place that honour holds in Homer, as the central virtue of society. The work begins with an invocation to the Muse that is very personal: the first literary manifesto confirming Hesiod's title as pioneer of didactic poetry.

Hesiod wrote of the poverty and injustice of his time. He knew these first hand by sight and by feel; the past, which the poets had filled with heroes and gods, must surely have been nobler and lovelier than the life he was living. Homer was a poet who could comprehend how the touch of beauty redeems a heap of sins. Hesiod was a peasant who resented the cost of a wife and groused at the nerve of women who dared to sit at the same table with their husbands. He shows us the ugly basement of early Greek society, and he does it without lyric soothing. He gives us the hard poverty of the serfs and small farmers upon whose toil rested all the splendor and war sport of the aristocracy and kings. Homer sang of heroes and princes; Hesiod knew neither, but tuned his verse to the ways of the common man and plucked each note with a rough but steady hand.

GREEK ARCHAIC LYRIC, 7th TO 5th-CENTURY BC

T oward the beginning of the seventh century BC there was a flowering of "personal" poetry in the Greek world, poetry marked by a passion and a candor that are in striking contrast to the epic tradition. Until the late archaic age, poetry was the only form of Greek literature, and poets like Homer and Hesiod used but one rhythmic form. During the Archaic Age, a new form of poetry emerged, called lyric, that utilized a much greater rhythmic diversity. Unlike epic narratives or didactic poetry, lyric poems were shorter and encompassed numerous forms and subjects stressing personal expression. The Greek lyric, elegiac, and iambic poets of the two centuries from 650 to 450 BC produced some of the finest poetry of antiquity: perfect in form, spontaneous in expression, reflecting all the joys and anxieties of their personal lives and of the world in which they lived. The most personal of its topics was the passion of love, but poets like Alcaeus and Solon also wrote poems on contemporary politics, while others lamented the passing glory of youth and the brevity of life. Lyric poetry's focus on the individual's feelings represented a new stage in Greek literary sensibilities, one that continues to inspire poets to this day.

7th Century BC

☛ **Archilochus,**"the Father of Lyric Poetry," mid-7th Century

Ranked in antiquity as one of the greatest of poets, worthy to be named beside Homer and Hesoid, he was often called "the Second Poet of the West." Archilochus was both poet and mercenary (his name means First Sargeant).

> Sergeant to Enyalios,
> The great god War,
> I practice double labor.
> With poetry, that lover's gift,
> I serve the lady Muses.
>
> My ash spear is my barely bread,
> My ash spear is my Ismarian wine.
> I lean on my spear and drink.

Except for a few papyrus fragments, the only poetry we have of Archilochus is found in quotations of later writers. He was an innovator in metre, inventing iambic verse, and wrote in a variety of other metres, including elegiac and trochaic. His elegies are stronly influenced by Homeric diction.

Archilochus was a modern poet who expressed the sensibility of a new age in lyrics both tender and forceful, lyrical and blunt. His father was a nobleman; his mother, a slave. Hence, Archilochus was a bastard. Perhaps his ambigious social position made him ideally suited to speak for the high-brow as well as to the common man. We know little else of his life, except that he was born on the island of Paros, and took part in the colonization of Thasos, founding a town there.

> This island,
>   garlanded with wild woods,
> Lies in the sea

like the backbone of an ass.

Many of his poems give us vivid and moving glimpses of military conflict. He and was later killed in a battle between the land of his birth and Naxos.

> We walked backward under their javelins
> Until we reached the rampart of stones
> She, Zeus's daughter, led us toward.
> We attacked later, chanting hymns
> of Mytilenian Apollo, while they,
> Keeping their courage with harp and song
> Fell back to their hill, withered by arows.
> We crossed a harvest of our dead.
>
> Remember us, remember this earth,
> When with hearts against despair
> our javelins held Thasos from her enemy.

There's a ancient story that Archilochus fell in love with Neobule, the daughter of Lycambes. "O to touch Neobule's hand!' is perhaps the oldest surviving fragment of a love poem in lyric Greek. Marriage to Neobule would have made it possible for Achilochus to retire from military life, but her father reneged on the contract and cancelled the wedding. To get revenge, Archilochus wrote such biting satires that legend has both Lycambes and Neobule hanging themselves in shame.

> Papa Lycambes,
> What's this you've thought up?
> What's distracted the mind
> You once had?
> Mind? You're a laugh.
> You persist chattering like a cricket.
>
> You've gone back on your word,
> Given over the salt at table.
>
> May you lose your way on the cold sea
> And swim to the heathen Salmydessos,
> May the ungodly Thracians with their hair
> Done up in a fright on the top of their heads
> Grab you, that you know what it is to be alone
> Without friend or family. May you eat slave's bread
> And suffer the plague and freeze naked,
> laced about with the nasty trash of the sea.
> May your teeth knock the top on the bottom
> As you lies on your face, spitting brine,
> At the edge of the cold sea, like a dog.
> And all this it would be a privilege to watch,
> Giving me great satisfaction as it would,
> For you took back the word you gave in honor,
> over the salt and table at a friendly meal.

Lykames and Neobule probably did not commit suicide. other fragments of verse indicate that Neobule became a prostitute and was rejected by Archilochus years later when she came on to him.His poetic invective remained bitter.

> Now, she is a common woman for rent,
> but what sensuality and fat ankles.
> O fat whore for hire!

In one sense, we could call Archilochus the first confessional poet. He writes about leaving his shield behind in battle, mocking the heroic epigram. The poem was to have considerable influence on Alcaeus and Horace (see page _____), who wrote about similar experiences.

> Well, what if some barbaric Thracian glories
> in the perfect shield I left under a bush?
> I was sorry to leave it—but I saved my skin.
> Does it matter? Oh, hell, I'll buy a better one.

We can trace the delightful obscenities of Aristophanes and the erotic tone of Sappho and Anakreon to the frankly graphic poemof Archilochus that was discovered twenty-five years ago on a papyrus mummy wrapping. Peter Green has playfully titled it "The Last Tango in Paros." Any warrior-hero who writes about being so turned on during sexual intercourse that he has premature ejaculation must be forgiven the venom of his satires.

> There is a girl who watches you with foolish eyes,
> A slender, lovely, graceful girl,
> Just building into supple line,
> And you scare her and make her shy.
>
> O daughter of the highborn Amphimedo,
> I replied, of the widely remembered
> Amphimedo now in the rich earth dead,
>
> there are, do you know, so many pleasures
> For young men to choose from
> Among the skills of the delicious goddess
>
> It's green to think the holy one's the only.
> When the shadows go black and quiet,
> Let us, you and I alone, and the gods,
>
> Sort these matters out. Fear nothing:
> I shall be tame, I shall behave
> And reach, if I reach, with a civil hand.
>
> I shall climb the wall and come to the gate.
> You'll not say no, Sweetheart, to this?
> I shall come no farther than the garden grass.

Neobule I have forgotten, believe me, do.
Any man who wants her many have her.
Aiai! She's past her hday, ripening rotten.

The petals of her flower are all brown.
The grace that first she had is shot.
Don't you agree that she looks like a boy?

A woman like that would drive a man crazy.
She should get herself a job as a scarecrow.
I'd as soon hump her as [kiss a goat's butt].

A source of joy I'd be to the neighbors
With such a woman as her for a wife!
how could I ever prefer her to you?

You, O innocent, true heart and bold.
Each of her faces is as sharp as the other,
Which way she's turning you never can guess.

She'd welp like the proverb's luckless bitch
Were I to foster get upon her, throwing
Them blind, and all on the wrongest day.

I said no more, but took her hand,
Laid her down in a thousand flowers,
And put my soft wool cloak around her.

I slid my arm under her neck
To still the fear in her eyes,
For she was trembling like a fawn,

Touched her hot breasts with light fingers,
Against her fine, hard, bared crotch.

I caressed the beauty of all her body
And came in a sudden white spurt
While I was stroking her hair.

☞ Semonides (mid-7th century)

Very few fragments of his poetry survive. Unlike Archilochus, who was an activist and
resigned to the power of the gods, Semonides dual response to the experience of human
subjection to the will of the gods was a policy of live-and-let-live and
wine-women-and-song. Life was brief and should be lived to the fullest.

Later we will have a long time to lie dead
yet the few years we have now we live badly.

Loud-thundering Zeus controls the outcome, boys,

in everything, and makes it how he wants.
Men have no foresight, but from day to day
they live like cattle, knowing not at all
how God will bring each matter to its end;
yet everybody feeds on hope and trust
throughout his vain endeavors. Some wait
for the day to come, some the turning of the seasons;
there's no man does not think he'll reach next year
the Wealth-god's darling, and society's.
But one is overtaken by old age
before he makes his goal, others succumb
to grim diseases, others slain in war
Hades escorts below dark earth, while some
die out at sea, by tempests buffeted
and the salt purple deep's unending waves,
when they can make no living on the land;
others again fasten themselves a noose
and leave the sunlight by their own grim choice.
A thousand black spirits waylay man
with unending grief and suffering.
If I had my way,
we would not cling to sorrow, or so long
torment ourselves by dwelling on our woes.

Since life was brief, one must feed the soul as well as the body.

One verse by the blind poet of Chios is indelible:
"The Life of man is like a summer leaf."
Yet few who hear these words take them into their heart,
for hope is rooted in every youthful soul,
the lovely flower of youth grows tall with color,
life will have no end,
or there is no place for growing old, for death;
and while in health, no fear of foul disease.
Poor fools! in islands of illusion,
for men have but a day of youth and life.
You few who understand, know when death is near
the food you give your soul must be supreme.

The longest poem of his to survive describes various types of women by comparing them with animals, but was probably meant as a comic satire, much like a modern jokes about mothers-in-law. Writing in the ionic dialiect, his work is charactized by satircal humor and obscene narrative.

☛ **Callinus of Ephesus,** (first half of 7th century)

The first Greek poet known to have written in elegiac couplets. Only a few scraps survive, referring to the barbarian invasions of 'Cimmerians and Trerians" from south Russia. The only substantial fragment we have calls on his fellow countrymen to take up arms and defend their country. in that poem, Callinus combines a modern tone with Homeric style, similar to Patrick Henry's famous speech to the Virginia Congress, in which used the diction of Greek oratory and Old Testament prophets—"Give me liberty or give me death!"

> Boy, how long will you lie idle?
> When will the young show courage?
> How long will you lie back and do nothing
> While our land is bled by war?
> Throw your last spear before you die,
> for glory dazzles on our helmets when we fight
> defending our country, our children, our wives.
> Death will come only when the web of destiny is spun.
> So charge, hold your spear up high,
> grip your shield with a brave heart.
> There is no escape from death,
> all men face the same dark fate,
> even those whose blood be of immortal stock.
>
> Sometimes, men flee the carnage and the clash of spears
> only to return home to meet their doom.
> But these men are not loved or missed by their countrymen.
> But when a hero dies, his fate is mourned by all, the great and small alike shed tears.
> Alive, he is ranked with the demigods;
> as a marble pillar they look upon his strength
> for all alone he does the great deeds of an army.

FOOD FOR THOUGHT
America's Greek Revival of the early 19th Century

The American voice in poetry is small, inward, reserved. We speak from the hungry heart, sotto voce, one to one, the deep confessions and the dark testimonies of guilt and innocence. American poets are rather shy and reserved when it comes to raising their voice in rhetorical splendour—the speech-making power of persuasion and exhortation. Especially in this age, when our politicians are reduced to the "cool" voice of the television set. Yet there was a time when our public figures spoke with the voice of Greek and Roman poets who knew the power of the sung phrase to persuade and move an audience to action. Patrick Henry's speech to the Virginia Congress in St. John's Church on March 23, 1775 ignited the American Revolution. It was a fine spring day, and 122 of the colony's delegates were assembled in the Richmond church to vote on a series of resolutions. A crowd had gathered outside to listen to the deliberations. A resolution was on the floor that the colony prepare a plan of defense and armaments. When Patrick Henry rose to speak, he held no notes in his hands, his voice quiet and sincere, but soon the speech began to smoulder adn ended in a blaze of passion. A Baptist clergyman present wrote that "the tendons of his neck stood out white nad rigid, like whipcords. His voice rose louder and louder, until the walls of the building and all within them seemed to shake and rock in its tremendous vibrations."

The battle is not to the strong alone;
it is to the vigilant,
the active,
the brave. . . .
There is no retreat but in submission and slavery!
Our chains are forged!
Their clanking may be heard on the plains of Boston!
The war is inevitable—and let it come!
I repeat it, sir, let it come!
It is in vain, sir, to extenuate the matter.
Gentlemen may cry, "Peace! Peace!" but there is no peace.
The next gale that sweeps from the north
will bring to our ears
the clash of resounding arms!
Our brethren are already in the field!
Why stand we here idle?
What is it that gentlemen wish?
What would they have?
Is life so dear,
or peace so sweet,
as to be purchased at the price of chains and slavery?
Forbid it, almighty God!
I know not what course others may take;
but, as for me,
give me liberty, or give me death!

While the founders of the American Republic looked to Rome for a model of political structure, they also looked to Greece for their model of political oratory. For many, America was a second Athens. Modern Greece was beginning its struggle for freedom from the Turks, inspiring the Romantic movement just as Rome had inspired the Augustan age. Orators tightened their speeches to follow the patterns of classical rhetoric. Patrick Henry's revolutionary speech and Abraham Lincoln's Gettysburg Address are bookends exemplifying the demotic tone and style of Greek (and later Roman) oratory.

It is rather for us to be here dedicated
to the great task remaining before us,—
that from thse honored dead we take increased devotion
to that cause for which they here gave
the last full measure of devotion,—
that we here highly resolve
that these dead shall not have died in vain,
that this nation,
under God,
shall have a new birth of freedom,
and that government
of the people,
by the people,
and for the people,
shall not perish from the earth.

☛ **Tyrtaeus** of Sparta (

Elegiac poet who, like Callinus, exhorted his countrymen to defend their country, fight for glory, and avoid the shame of passivity and cowardice.

> For it is fine to die in the front line,
> a brave man fihting for his fatherland,
> and the most painful fate's to leave one's town
> and fertile farmlands for a beggar's life,
> roaming with mother dear and aged father,
> with little children and with wedded wife.
> He'll not be welcome anywhere he goes,
> bowing to need and horrid poverty,
> his line disgraced, his handsome face belied;
> every humiliation dogs his steps.
> This is the truth: the vagrant is ignored
> and slighted, and his children after him.
> So let us fight with spirit for our land,
> die for our sons, and spare our lives no more.
> You young men, keep together, hold the line,
> do not start panic or disgraceful rout.
> Keep grand and valiant spirits in your hearts,
> be not in love with life—the fight's with men!

[finish this later]

☛ **Mimnermus of Smyrna** (second half of 7th century)

He wrote chiefly love poems in elegiacs which were collected in two books, one of which was called *Nanno* after the flute-girl he is said to have loved. His most memorable poems are concerned with the pleasures of youth and love and the horrors of old age. Many of his poems speak to the decadence of Ionia, enervated by despair and by pleasure. He is admired for the musical qualities of his verse, and for the hedonism, tinged with melancholy, that he expresses. In his erotic elegies Momnermos is one of the ancestors of the later love-elegists of Alexandria and Rome.

CENSURE OF AGE

> What good is life when golden love is gone?
> Frankly, I would rather be dead than ignore
> a girl's warm surrender, her soft arms in bed
> at night: lovely flower of youth that all women
> and men desire!
>   When old age comes
> a man feels feeble and ugly and crawls under
> a crushing sorrow.

He loses the simple joy
of looking at the sun.
Children despise him.
He is repulsive to young women—in this sad
blind alley which God has made of old age.

TIME

When a man's good hour is past
though he once shone among mortals
he is neither honored nor loved.
Not even his own children favor him.

EXPECTATION

Like fragine shoots in the polyflowered spring
    growing quickly in amazing sun,
we love the blossom of youth for a brief season
    knowing from the gods nothing of evil
or good. Yet near us loom black Keres, and
    painful old age, or worse, death.
The fruit-tree of our life ripens swiftly like
    a morning sun. but our brilliance gone,
we are soon better dead than alive. Our heart
    is torn, our home is dark with poverty.
One man longs for a son and goes down childless
    into Hell; another shrivels in murderous
disease. No man on earth eludes the net
    of unending sorrows sent by Zeus.

☞ **Alcman** (last half of 7th century)

Alcman lived in Sparta. His poems were collected in six books, now all lost except for a few quotations in the work of others, and fragments found in 1855 on an Egyptian papyrus in the Louvre which was one of the first Greek literary papyri to be discovered. Most of the fragments defy classification, but are mainly choral lyrics composed for Spartan girls' to sing and dance to at certain religious festivals. One or two are love-songs, of which he was said to be the inventor. His work has a fresh and charming tone, written in the playful Laconian vernacular with some stylisitc Homerisms.

His longest choral ode is the *Hymn to Artemis of the Strict Observance*, "for a chorus of Spartan girls dressed as doves to sing at dawn on the feast of the plow," probably sung as part of the *agon*, or contest, which was part of a friendly city vs. city rivalry.

A wild heart must not crowd divinity
Nor rush upon Aphrodite not to marry.
. . . .
And there is the vengeance of the gods.

He is a happy man who can weave his days,
No trouble upon the loom.
And I, I sing of Agido,
Of her light. She is like the sun
To which she makes our prayers,
The witness of its radiance.
Yet I can neither praise her nor blame her
Till I have sung of another,
Sung of our choirmaster,
Who stands among us like a racehorse pawing the meadow,
One splendid stallion set among the sheep,
a thundering winner,
A horse that runs in dreams
as you doze in a cavern's shade..

Imagine her if you can. Her hair,
As gold as a Venetian mane,
Flowers around her silver eyes.
What can I say to make you see?
She is Hagesikhora and
Agido, almost, almost as beautiful.,
Is a Kolaxaian filly running behind her
In the races at Ibeno.
A Pleiades of doves that go up before daybreak
They are
Contending at dawn before the altar of Artemis
For the honor of offering the sacred plow
Which we have brought to the goddess.
They are the white star Sirius rising
In the honey and spice of a summer night.

Our purple finery is not the treasure that defends us with its glory,
Nor golden snakes engraved with eyes and scales,
Nor bonnets from Lydia and brooches,
Nor sweet violet eyes.
Nor Nanno's hair, no, nor nymphlike Areta,
nor Thulakis, nor Klesithera; nor
Will you go to Ainesimbrota's and say
"Oh please make Astaphis mine,"
Or "Make Philylla look my way,"
Damareta, or sweet Vianthemis.
No, she is own own,
It's Hagesichora, splendid-ankled Hagesikhora,
She is my heartache.

With Agido, by whose side she lingers,
She honors the rites with her beauty.
Gods, receive their prayers —
in the gods hands lies fulfillment.
Keep back defeat unless
Hagesikhora alone, our love,

Be our victory's shield.

. . . .

If she would just come up, take my young hand,
I'd soon be beggin her favour.
None, none shall bring us to our triump
Unless the lovely Hagesikhora lead the dance.

She leads, she and Agido; their ankles are the dance.
Listen, gods, to their hymn, for none is more beautiful.
Beside their singing my song is an owl's hoo!
I sing for them as they sing for the goddess,
And all for peace, till all at last is one harmony.
Dome, dawn, as to the trumpeting swans of Sparta,
As day finds the Sirens at their song.
Feed us, earth and heart and grace of peace;
Beauty, beauty, like that tossing yellow hair.

☛ **Sappho** (Late 7th - middle 6th Century B.C.)

Born on the Aeolian Isle of Lesbos about 612 B.C., Sappho was married at an early age to a rich man from the island of Andros, and spent some time in her youth as a political exile (probably because of the seditious activities of her husband & brothers). Though a small, delicate woman, with dark eyes, hair, and skin, she was a formidable presence: Her mind was sharp, and her words, said Plutarch, "were mingled with flames."

Alcaeus, a poet of scathing political poetry, was banished to Pyrrha along with Sappho for trying to overthrow Pittacus, the dictator. He sent her a vague note inviting her into an intimate relationship, but refrained from fully stating his desires "because shame disarms me." There was nothing vague about her reply: "If your wishes were fair and noble, and your tongue made not to utter what is vulgar, shame would not cloud your eyes, but you'd speak your just desires." Alcaeus wrote many poems praising her, but there's no record of any intimacy between them.

She was exiled a second time to Sicily when she was twenty-one and returned to Lesbos a young, rich widow and the leader of the island's aristocratic intelligentsia. She opened a school for young girls preparing for marriage and taught them poetry, music, and dancing, falling in love with one after another of her pupils.

To Atthis,

Once upon a time, I loved you, Atthis,
                              yes, long ago . . .
even when I thought of you as a small
                              and graceless girl . . .
All the good days we had together,
The wreathes you wore, of roses and violets
As we lay side by side, the necklaces
Woven from flowers to drape your soft shoulders,

The perfumes, precious, fit for royalty —

How much you used to anoint yourself!
As you leaned near my breasts on
The soft bed where you would satisfy . . . desire . . .

Her surviving poems deal with girlhood, marriage, and love; her themes the love of young women for each other, and the poignancy of separation. She writes of the tenderness of love, of passion and of jealousy.

Seizure

Like the very gods in my sight is he who
sits where he can look in your eyes, who listens
close to you, to hear the soft voice, its sweetness
    murmur in love and

laughter, all for him. But it breaks my spirit;
underneath my breast all the heart is shaken.
Let me only glance where you are, the voice dies,
    I can say nothing,

but my lips are stricken to silence, underneath my skin the tenous flame suffuses;
nothing shows in front of my eyes, my ears are
    muted in thunder.

And the sweat breaks running upon me, fever
shakes my body, paler I turn than grass is;
I can feel that I have been changed, I feel that
    death has come over me.

Sappho has given Greek—if not world—literature its most concentrated, vivid expression of sexual passion. Only fragments of her work survive. During her lifetime her poems were collected into nine books containing about twelve thousand lines. In 1073, a Bishop of the Church in Constantinople burnt what he considered vulgar pagan literature, including the poetry of Sappho and Alcaeus. Centuries later, in a tomb, coffins of papier-mâché were discovered which used scraps from old books, including the work of Sappho. Of her total output, only about 5% survives, but these extant works reveal an inimitable mastery of rhythm, of verbal melody, and a freshness of expression.

To Anaktoria, Now A Soldier's Wife in Lydia

Some there are who say that the fairest thing seen
on the black earth is an array of horsemen;
some, men marching; some would say ships; but I say
    she whom one loves best

is the loveliest. Light were the work to make this
plain to all, since she, who surpassed in beauty
all mortality, Helen, once forsaking
    her lordly husband,

fled away to Troy-land across the water.
Not the thought of child nor beloved parents
was remembered, after the Queen of Cyprus
    won her at first sight.

Since young brides have hearts that can be persuaded
easily, light things, palpitant to passion
as am I, remembering Anaktoria
    who has gone from me

and whose lovely walk and the shining pallor
of her face I would rather see before my
eyes than Lydia's chariots in all their glory
    armored for battle.

Eros Shakes Me

    Percussion, salt and honey,
    A quivering in the thighs;
    He shakes me all over again,
    Eros who cannot be thrown,
    Who stalks on all fours
    Like a beast.

Eros Comes Again

    Eros make me shiver again
    Strengthless in the knees,
    Eros gall and honey,
    Snake-sly, invincible.

Homage

    Our slender Adonis is dying,
    Kytherea, tell us what to do.
    Tear open your dresses, virgins,
    and batter your breasts?

Plato had such regard for her poetry that he added her name to his list of the Nine Muses, making Sappho the tenth. Legend has it she leapt from a cliff for love of Phaon, but this is probably more myth than fact. Late in life, Sappho replied to a marriage proposal thusly: "If my breasts were still capable of giving suck, and my womb were able to bear children, then to another marriage-bed I'd come, but this time not with trembling feet. But now on my skin age has brought many lines, and Love hastens not to me with his gift of pain." She suggested her suitor find a younger woman to marry.

☛ Alcaeus (b. born before 620 BC)

Alcaeus was a contemporary with Sappho, and lived in the same town of Mytilene on the island of Lesbos. Many of his lyric songs were later adapted to Latin poetry by Horace, who imitated and wrote variations upon Alcaic themes throughout the Odes. Probably, it was Alcaeus' directness and economy that appealed to Horace. Born into an established landowning family, Alcaeus became involved in the politics of the time, opposing a series of tyrants who ruled Mytilene, especially Pittacus. In some of his political poems he writes allegorically, using the image of the ship of state tossed by storm to describe political strife.

A NATION AT SEA

I can't tell you which way the gale has turned
for waves crash in from west and east, and we
are tossed and driven between, our black ship
        laboring under the giant storm.

The sea washes across the decks and maststep
and dark daylight already shows through long rents
in the sails. Even the halyards slacken as
        windward waves coil above the hull.

What sore labor to bale the water we've shipped!
Let us raise bulwarks and ride out the storm,
heeding my words: "Let each man now be famous."
        Yet base cowards betray the state.

ON THE TYRANT PITTACUS

        One and all,
y ou have proclaimed Pittacus, the lowborn,
to be tyrant of your lifeless and doomed
land. Moreover, you deafen him with praise.

ON PREMATURE POLITICAL ACTIVITY

It is late; for the harvest is in.
Before, we hoped that the full vines
would bring a plentitude of fine grapes,
but the clusters are slow
to ripen and the landlords
picked unripe bunches from the branch.
We have many grapes now — green and sour.

TO HIS FRIEND MELANIPPOS

Drink and be drunk with me, Melanippos.
Do you think when you have crossed the great fuming river,
you will ever return from Hell to see the clean
bright light of the sun?
Do not strive for wild hopes.
Even the son of Aiolos, King Sisyphus, wisest of men,

thought he had eluded death.
But for all his brains
Fate made him recorss the Acheron, and the son of Kronos
assigned him a terrible trial below the dark earth.
Come, I beg you not to brood about these hopless matters
while we are young.
We will suffer what must be suffered.
When the wind is waiting in the north,
a good captain will not swing into the open sea.

Pittacusevicted Alcaeus from his estates and as an exile, Alcaeus traveled widely, as far as Egypt. At some point, Pitticus forgave Alcaeus and he returned home. There was a closing of ranks when the Lesbians, Alcaeus among them, fought under Pittacus against the Athenians for the possession of Sigeum, a key stronghold on the Hellespont.

THINGS OF WAR

The great house glitters with bronze.
War has patterned the roof with shining helmets,
their horsehair plumes waving in wind,
headdress
of fighting men. And pegs
are concealed under bright greaves of brass which
block the iron-tipped arrows.
Many fresh-linen corslets are hanging and hollow shields
are heaped about the floor,
and standing in rows are swords of Chalkidian steel,
belt-knives and warriors' kilts.
We cannot forget our arms and armor
when soon our dreadful duties begin.

Athens held Sigeum and Alcaeus describes himsefl as abandoning his shield in the retreat, as the poet Archilochus did before him, and Horace was to imitate centuries later.

Give Melanippus the message at homne:
"Alcaeus is safe, but his fine armour and shield
the Athenians have hung up in the shrine
of the pale-eyed goddess."

Alcaeus wrote many love-poems, now almost totally lost, and lyric songs for drinking parties with male friends. Until recent years his poetry survived only in quotations made by later authors, but since the decipherment of certain Egyptian papryi, much more of his poetry has come to light, though the tattered fragments have yielded very few complete poems. Though all we have in many cases are fragments, from these we can glean the heart of a poet whose passion and imagery gave a reluctant nod to life's sad losses.

A WOMAN

Bad,
every misery and disaster I've known, a woman

with a home
of shameful feath,

incurable decrepitude coming on
and madness in the terrorized heart of the stag,

out of his mind
and ruined.

6th Century BC

☞ **Stesichoros** (first half of the 6th century)

Born in Sicily, his real name was Theisias. Stesichoros means "choir-setter," and he's known for his narrative lyric poetry, classified by the ancients as choral lyric because its structure was triadic (strophe, antistrophe, and epode), and he's even said to have been the inventor of this particular form, introducing full-fledged narrative into the choral lyric. Collected by Alexandrian scholars into twenty-six books, only fragments of his choral odes survive, and most of these have been recovered from papyrus in the 20th century.

The poems must have been extremely long, longer than many of Pindar's choral odes. The subjects were taken from a wide range of epic sources, from the "Epic Cycle" as well as from Homer. [The Epic Cylce is the name given to a collection of epics (including the *Iliad* and *Odyssey*), of which only some 120 lines now survive, written by various poets in the 7th and 6th centuries BC, which could be arranged so as to make a chronological narrative extending fromn the beginning of the world to the end of the heroic age. They formed the storehouse from which Greek dramatic and lyric poets drew many of their subjects. Among them were the Trojan cycle and the Theban cycle. Our knowledge of their contents derives in part from summaries made by Proclus (412-485 AD), the Neoplatonist philosopher, though some conjecture that this handbook may be the work of an earlier Proclus, of which we know nothing.]

Stesichorus' *Iliupersis*, "Sack of Troy," included an account of Epeus, who made the Wooden Horse; some believe that it may have been the source for the stories of Aeneas' wandering to Italy. Because of Stesichoros, Athena was shown fully armed at birth, Herakles got his club, lionskin and bow, and Geryon his wings. There's no way to fully calculate the effect he would have had on modern European literature if all of his work had survived intact. His influence on contemporary art was considerable, many of his subjects appearing on the vases of the day.

According to Ammianus Marcellinus, the great Roman historian, Socrates heard a song of Stesichoros' being sung by a prisoner in the next cell and asked him to teach it to him before he drank the hemlock. When the musician asked why, Socrates replied, "I want to die knowing one thing more."

According to Plate, in the Phaedros, when Stsichoros was blinded for having slandered Helen of Troy, he wrote a recantation and his sight was immediately restored.

RECANTATION TO HELEN

I spoke nonsense and I begin again:
The story is not true.
You never sailed on a benched ship.
You never entered the city of Troy.

Other fragments:

ON THE MARRIAGE OF HELEN AND MENELAOS

Many quince apples were cast upon the chariot of the king,
Many leaves of myrtle,
hundreds of roses and thousands of braided violets.

ON SONG AND LAMENT

Apollo loves happy play and cadenced singing
but he leaves groans and mourning to Hades.
Yet how futile even to weep for the dead —
for when dead, a man's glory dies among men.

☛ **Ibykos (**

Wrote love poems and choral lyrics, following Stesichoros' tradition of lyric narrative. In his early work, the brought together the eloquence of West Greek choral lyric and the East Greek confessional poetry as exemplified by Alcaeus and Sappho.

According to legend, Ibycus was attacked and killed by robbers. A flock of cranes was passing overhead and Ibycus exclaimed, "Those cranes will avenge me." Soon after, one of the robbers in a crowded theatre, seeing a flock of cranes hovering overhead, said to his companion, "There go the avengers of Ibycus." This was overheard, and the murderers were brought to justice. Hence the proverb: "The cranes of Ibykos, " and the other proverb by Diogenes, "As foolish as Ibykos." Friedrich von Schiller (1759-1805), whose *Ode to Joy* became the basis for the finale of a great symphony, wrote a ballad called "The Cranes by Ibykos."

Later in his life, Ibykos wrote more ornate poems based on erotic themes, noted for their vivid imagery.

ON FEMININE NATURE AND PUBLIC DECENCY

                              Spartain girls
are naked-thighed and man-crazy

LOVE'S SEASON

In spring the quince trees
ripen in the girls' holy orchard
with river waters;
and grapes turn vioet
under the shade of luxuriant leafage
and newborn shoots.

But for me, Eros
at no season is laid to rest,
and Like the North Wind of Thrace that comes
blazing with lightning,
the Cyprian goddess Kypris,
with withering frenzies,
 mutilates my heart with black
and baleful love.

☞ **Anakreon** (b. c. 570 BC)

Born of a noble family at Rhegium in the toe of Italy, he wrote in the Ionic Greek dialect. His love poems are tender and delicately sensous, often characterized by a self-depracating wit that give a nice touch of ambiguousness to the tone of some of them. [ech! rewrite this sentence later] After the Renaissance, his work became quite famous due in large measure to a body of short poems composed at various times in late antiquity modelled (not very accurately) on his style and subject matter and often ascribed to him. These "Anacreontea" have a certain charm but do not approach the exquisite craftsmenship of the originals. Anacreon is considered one of the very finest lyric poets. The man behind the poems tempers his passions with humor; the picture that emerges is the archetypal old soul who loves his wine and song, an old Eben Flood staggering home from the local pub with a twinkle in his eye, still in search of love.

In many ways, Anacreon was even more influential on later poetry than either Sappho or Alcaeus. Perhaps because his poetry has so many different tones and styles, and is difficult to categorize. His poetry is sometimes light and playful, sophisticated and witty, detached and ironic. In one of his lettters to the satirical Latin poet Lucilius, Seneca comments on the grammarian Didymos, who "wrote four thosand books . . . in which he discusses whether Anakreon was more of a rake than a drunk, whether Sappho was a prostitute, and other questions the answers to which you should forget it you knew them."

DICE

The dice of love
are shouting
and madness

THE VISION OF LOVE

On easy wings I glide to Olympus where
I seek my master Eros,
but he no longer lets me run down warm women
as in my doghood days:
he sees my graying beard and passes me by,
while I stand transfixed
in the win made by his wings of quivering gold.

ONA VIRGIN

My thracian foal, why do you glare with disdain
and then shun me absolutely as if I knew
nothing of this art?

I tell you I could bridle you with tight straps,
seize the reins and gallop you around the posts
of the pleasant course.

But you prefer to graze on the calm meadow,
or frisk and gambol gayly — having no manly
rider to break you in.

ON DEATH

My temples are white, my head largely bald.
graceful youth has deprted from my face,
and my teeth are the loose teeth of an old man.
            I have few years left of sweet life.

Therefore I tremble and fear the underworld,
for the lightness chasm of death is dreadful
and the descent appalling: once cast down
            into Hell, there is no return.

PREPARATIONS

For breakfast I broke off a bit of sweet sesame cake;
I've drunk a whole flagon of wine, and in luxurynow
I play my sweet harp, making merry beside my dear girl.
I pluck my twenty-stringed harp, striking an octave chord;
and you just are, young Leucaspis.

☛ **Lasus** (b. *c.* 548 BC)

An avant-garde poet in Hipparchus' circle who was interested in musical theory and may well have invented the word *mousike*, Lasus was the founder of the Athenian school of dithyrambic poetry and was Pindar's teacher.

☛ **Hipponax of Ephesus** (mid-6th century)

Writer of satirical, often scurrilous verses, he invented his own version of the iambic trimeter, making it end with a spondee, the so-called "limping iambic." His first person sexual narrative is not meant to be offensive, but funny. He is often credited with the invention of the parody. He comes off as a vulgar, low-class brawler who had quarrels with two sculptors named Boupalos and Athenis. Hipponax claims to have had a wild liason with Boupalos' mistress Arete.

> Hold my coat while I belt Boupalos in the eye.
> I am ambidextrous and never miss a punch.

> MISERIES
>
> In a Lydian voice she said, "Come quick,
> I will plug up your tight assole."
> And she beat my balls with a branch
> as though I were a scapegoat. I tripped
> and stuck on the gallows I suffered
> a double torture: a branch lashed
> my chest; someone wet me with cowshit
> and my ass stank. Beetles came, drawn
> by the stinking gook like summer flies.
> They fell on me, shoved, filing their teeth
> on my bones. The invasion complete,
> I ached more than from a Pygelian plague.

> MIDWIFE
>
> What navel-snipper wiped you, god-blasted one,
> and washed you as you kicked about the floor?

☛ **Ananius** (

☛ **Corinna**

Born in Boetia, she was probably a contemporary of Pindar, writing narrative choral lyrics intended for an audience of women. The Suda Lexicon claims she gained victory five times over Pindar in poetry competitions. Some claimed the judges were ignorant and had bad taste and that Pindar called her a pig.

6th to 5th Century BC

☛ **Anonymous Theognis**

☛ **Xenophanes**

☛ **Simonides** (556-468 BC)

A few years younger than Xenophanes, he was a professional poet who traveled widely in the Greek world, and is famous for his dirges and epigrams to be inscribed on dedications and tombstones, particularly for those refering to the dead of the Persian Wars, like that on the Spartan dead at Thermopylae.

> Tell them in Lacedaemon, passer-by,
> That here obedient to their words we lie.

Like Anacreon, he was one of the poets invited to Athens by Hipparchos as part of the program of cultural enrichment inaugurated under the Peisistratid tyranny. Simonides was widely known and had patrons in Euboa, Thessaly, Aegina, Sparta, Sicily, Italy, and Athens, and charged high fees for his services. His fondness for money became proverbial, to the point that he charged for writing a eulogy. The most famous story has him singing a lyric at a banquet glorifying his patron, Scopas of Thessaly. The poem included a lengthy digression in praise of Castor and Pollux (variously celebrated in Greek myth as brothers of Helen of Troy, sons of Zeus, and protectors of sailors), whereupon Scopas paid only half the agreed upon fee. When Simonides complained, Scopas suggested that he go to the two heroes mentioned in the poem and ask them to pay the other half, since he'd spent half the poem praising them.Awhile later, Simonides was summoned by a messenger who said two young men where asking to speak to him outside. When Simonides left the banguet hall, the two men were nowhere to be found, but while he was outside looking for them, the roof of the hall collapsed, killing the other guests. Simonides pattern of charging money for his poems was repeated by his nephew Bacchylides and by his rival, Pindar. By composing odes celebrating the famous battles of the Persian Wars, Simonides became the first poet to give expression to the new consciousness of Greek national identity.

Unlike Pindar, his style in chorla poctry was on the whole direct and harmonious, and often rather lighthearted. Compared to Pindar, Simonides was considered "modern." Aristotle tells a story of Simonides having a discussion about the relative merits of wisdom and wealth with Hieron's wife. When she asked him which was better, Simonides replied, "To become wealthy. For I see the wise sitting on the doorsteps of the rich."

For Those Who Died at Thermopylae

> Their tomb is an altar on which stand our bowls of remembrance
> and the wine of our praise.

Neither mold and worms, nor time
which destroys all things, will blacken their deaths.
The shrine of these brave men
has found its guardian
in the glory of Greece. Leonidas, the Spartan king,
lives in the great ornament he left behind
of unending fame and virtue.

Passage of Time

One thousand years, ten thousand years
are but a tiny dot,
the smallest segment of a point,
an invisible hair.

Accomplishments

Without the gods
a man or city can do nothing.
Only God knows everything, and man
suffers for what he does.

There is no evil
man may not expect, and soon
God wipes away the few things
he may have done.

☞ Pindar (518-after 446 BC)

Famous for his victory odes written in honor of the victors at the four great panhellenic games, very little is known about Pindar's life. He is most famous for his Epinician ("victory") Odes written in honour of the victors at the four great panhellenic games—the Olympian, Pythian, Nemean, and Isthmian, commonly abbreviated to O., P., N., and I. It's said that he studied composition with the Boeotian poet Corinna, and went to Athens to study music. He often competed with Simonides and Bacchylides, and was not always the winner. He can be difficult to read for the density of his style, blended from several dialects. But his work is also highly personal, expressing the conservative views of his aristocratic class. More than any other Greek lyric poet, Pindar's influence on European literature was the greatest. Bowra said, "He was capable at times, of a sublimity to which there is no parallel." Eustathios, in his Introduction to Pindar, lists nine major lyric poets: Alkman, Alcaios, Sappho, Stesichoros, Ibykos, Anacreaon, Simonides, Bacchylides, and Pindar. Quintillian later commented that "of the nine lyric poets Pindar is by far the greatest, in virtue of his inspired magnificence, the beauty of his thoughts and figures, the rich exuberance of his langauge and matter and his rolling flood of eloquence, characteristics which, as Horace rightly held, make him inimitable.

[more on Pindar]

☞ **Bacchylides** (b. end of 6th century)

Newphew of the poet Simonides, he was born on the island of Ceos. Like Pindar, who was his great rival, Bacchylides composed odes for at least two victories won in the great Games: the horse-race at the Olympian games of 476 BC, and the chariot-race at Delphi in 470 BC. Though he lacks Pindar's profundity and brilliant imaginative gifts, his narratives are quite dramatic and moving.

The poetry written by Pindar and Baccylides is generally described as *choral lyric*, or simply choral poetry, usually sung to music by a chorus specially trained in vocal performance and dance. Though the modern opera is our closest parallel, the Greek lyrics are much more complex and intricate than the usual operatic libretti. Greek choral poems are written in exact and intricate meters, the language is highly elaborate and rich, and unlike modern operatic texts, can stand on their own without the musical accompaniment.

Several of his Odes are unique in surviving choral lyric, especially Ode 18, sometimes called the Theseus poem, which is presented in the form of a dialogue between the leader of the chorusdressed as a legendary king and the rest of the chorus costumed as young soldiers of the past. The poem seems to have been heavily influenced by the theatre, and has no third-person narrative voice. It is also possible to speculate that this dithyramb's unparalleled dramatic style is a survival of an older form which Aristotle believed to be the precursor of Greek tragedy.

The performance probably began with a military trumpet call of some sort, followed by the entrance of the chorus from one side of the stage and the single performer from the opposite side. The soldier performers were the first to sing.

> King of our holy Athens,
>   lord of luxurious Ionians,
> why did the brazen-voiced trumpet
>   just now sing out the call to war?
> Has some enemy captain
>   broken across our borders
>   leading an army in?

Bacchylides combines both the Homeric and Doric language in a style that is more accessible than Pindar's, direct and forceful, yet characterized by the use of vivid and ornamental compounds, many of them newly coined.

PEACE

Only great peace
brings wealth to men
and a flowering of honey-throated song,
and to the gods
ox-thighs burning and long-haired sheep
flaming yellow on the sculpted altars,
and to the young
a love of wrestling and the flue
and Bacchic dance.

In the iron-covered shield
the brown spider hangs his web.
The sharpened spear and double-edged sword
are flaked with rust.
The noise of the brass trumpet is dead,
and the honey of our dawnsleep
is not dried from our eyelids.
Streets clamor with happy outdoor banquets,
and the lovely hyms sung by children
spring like fire up into the bright air.

In modern times, poets have tried to imitate his free-flowing, vigorous style with varying degress of success. [more on Bacchylides to come]

The Poets of Greek Tragedy

☛ **Sophocles** (d. 406 B.C.) *Oedipus Rex* and *Antigone*

I hesitate to begin including the Greek dramatists of the Golden Age of Pericles, because our focus should stay on poetry. But poetry and drama were closely linked, as in Shakespeare's day, and the greatest poets of this period in Greek hisotry wrote in verse drama. Furthermore, the plays of Aeschylus, Sophocles, Euripedes and Aristophanes profoundly influenced not only poetry for centuries to come, but all of literature. I can only suggest here that you read the great *Oresteia* trilogy by Aeschylus, and *Oedipus Rex* and *Antigone* by Sophocles. I can't stress enough how monumental these works are, and how directly and indirectly they have found their way into the work of so many modern poets. Nevertheless, I'd like to quote a few excerpts from *Oedipus The King* (produced around 441 B.C. when Sophocles was nearly seventy years old) and *Antigone*, probably written some fifteen years earlier.

☛ **Oedipus Rex**

King Laius and Queen Jocasta of Thebes are told by the Oracle that if their child is a boy, he will kill the father and lie with the mother. The King gives the infant to a shepard with instructions to kill the child. Deep in the forest that separates Thebes from Corinth, the Shepherd leaves the child in its swaddling clothes to die. He is later found by another shepherd:

> I loosed you;
> the tendons of your feet were pierced and fettered —

[Odeipus means swollen foot

[note the many references in the play to feet]

The child is taken to King Polybus and Queen Merope of Corinth, who raise the boy as their own. When Oedipus reaches manhood, he hears the Oracle's prophecy, that he will kill his father and lie with his mother. Attempting to escape his fate, Oedipus flees to Thebes, where he encounters King Laius on a fork in the road. Not knowing who he is, and after some altercation, in a fit of rage, Oedipus kills the old man. Later, he solves the riddle of the Sphinx ["What goes on four legs in the morning, two in the day, and three by evening?" Answer—"man."], releasing Thebes from its curse. Hailed as a hero and savior, he marries the widowed Queen Jocasta. They have four children—Antigone, Ismene, Polynices, and Eteocles. The play begins years later, in *medias res*, as the people come to Oedipus, their King, begging him to save their city once again in the grip of a curse.

> A blight is on the fruitful plants of the earth,
> A blight is on the cattle in the fields,
> a blight is on our women that no children
> are born to them; a God that carries fire,
> a deadly pestilence, is on our town,

strikes us and spares not, and the house of Cadmus
is emptied of its people while black Death
grows rich in groaning and in lamentation. . . .
You came and by your coming saved our city,
freed us from tribute which we paid of old
to the Sphinx, cruel singer. . . .
Now Oedipus, Greatest in all men's eyes,
here falling at your feet we all entreat you,
find us some strength for rescue.

Creon:

I will tell you, then,
what I heard from the God.
King Phoebus in plain words commanded us
to drive out a pollution from our land,
pollution grown so ingrained within the land;
drive it out, said the God, not cherish it,
till it's past cure.

They must find the man who murdered King Laius, and the city will be saved. Oedipus
calls in Tiresias, the blind prophet, to help them.

Oedipus:

Tiresias, you are versed in everything,
things teachable and things not to be spoken,
things of the heaven and earth-creeping things.
You have no eyes but in your mind you know
with what plague our city is afflicted. . . .
Do not begrudge us oracles from birds,
or any other way of prophecy
within your skill; save yourself and the city,
save me; redeem the debt of our pollution
that lies on us because of this dead man.

Tiresias:

Alas, how terrible is wisdom when
it brings no profit to the man that's wise!
This I knew well, but had forgotten it,
else I should have stayed home.

Tiresias refuses to tell Odeipus what he knows, until the King demands it of him:

Tiresias

Since you have taunted me with being blind,
here is my word for you.
You have your eyes but see not where you are
in sin, nor where you live, nor whom you live with.
Do you know who your parents are? Unknowing
you are an enemy to kith and kin
in death, beneath the earth, and in this life.
A deadly footed, double striking curse,
from father and mother both, shall drive you forth

out of this land, with darkness on your eyes,
that now have such straight vision. Shall there be
a place will not be harbour to your cries,
when you shall learn the secret of your marriage,
which steered you to a haven in this house, —
haven no haven, after lucky voyage?
And of the multitude of other evils
establishing a grim equality
between you and your children, you know nothing.
Misery shall grind no man as it will you.

As Oedipus investigates fruther into the prophecy, he is relieved to hear that Polybus, King of Corinth (whom he assumed is his father), has just died of natural causes.

Jocasta (to a servant)
Be quick and run to the King with the news!
O oracles of the Gods, where are you now?
It was from this man Oedipus fled,
lest he should be his murderer! And now he is dead,
in the course of nature, and not killed by Oedipus.

Oedipus
So he died of sickness, it seems, — poor old man!

Jocasta
                    That I told you before now.

Oedipus
You did, but I was misled by my fear. . . .
But surely I must fear my mother's bed?

Jocasta
Why should man fear since chance is all in all
for him, and he can clearly foreknow nothing?
Best to live lightly, as one can, unthinkingly.
As to your mother's marriage bed, — don't fear it.
Before this, in dreams too, as well as oracles,
many a man has lain with his own mother.
But he to whom such things are nothing bears
his life most easily.

Oedipus
All that you say would be said perfectly
if she were dead; but since she lives I must
still fear, although you talk so well, Jocasta.

Jocasta
Still in your father's death there's light of comfort?

Oedipus
Great light of comfort; but I fear the living. . . .
Once on a time the Oracle said
that I should lie with my own mother and
take on my hands the blood of my own father.
And so for these long years I've lived away
from Corinth; it has been to my great happiness;

Oedipus continues to press for the terrible truth. Jocasta is fearful of what may come out and wants him to stop searching.

Jocasta
> I beg you — do not hunt this out — I beg you,
> O be persuaded by me, I entreat you;
> do not do this.

Oedipus
> I will not be persuaded to let be
> the chance of finding out the whole thing clearly.
> Break out what will!

Break out it does. As Claudius says at the end of I Claudius by Robert Graves, "Let all the poisons that lurk in the mud hatch out." Oedipus finds out the true story, that he's killed his father and married his mother, and together they had children: Oedipus goes offstage and gouges out his eyes .

Oedipus
> O, O,
> where am I going? Where is my voice
> borne on the wind to and fro?
> Spirit, how far have you sprung?
> Darkness!
> Horror of darkness enfolding, resistless, unspeakable visitant sped
>   by an ill wind in haste!
> madness and stabbing pain and memory
> of evil deeds I have done!
> This darkness is my world.
> It was Apollo, friends, Apollo,
> that brought this bitter bitterness, my sorrows to completion.
> But the hand that struck me
> was none but my own.
> Why should I see
> whose vision showed me nothing sweet to see?
>
> What I have done here was best done — don't tell me
> otherwise, do not give me further counsel.
> I do not know with what eyes I could look
> upon my father when I die and go
> under the earth, nor yet my wretched mother —
> Would the sight of children, bred as mine are, gladden me?
> No, not these eyes, never.
> To this guilt I bore witness against myself
> No man but I can bear my evil doom.
> Yet I know this much:
> I would not have been saved from death if not
> for some strange evil fate. Well, let my fate
> go where it will.

Chorus

You that live in my ancestral Thebes, behold this Oedipus,—
him who knew the famous riddles and was a man most masterful;
not a citizen who did not look with envy on his lot—
see him now and see the breakers of misfortune swallow him!
Look upon that last day always. Count no mortal happy till
he has passed the final limit of his life secure from pain.

FOOD FOR THOUGHT

Did Oedipus Rex have an Oedipus Complex?
or just an "Appointment in Thebes"

While the play *Oedipus the King* is about Oedipus' tragic flaw—overweening pride and arrogance—its greater message seems to be that one cannot escape or change one's fate. This idea is an old one and has continued to be a theme in poetry and prose into modern times. In the 20th Century, it's one of the most popular plots found in science fiction and fantasy. A *Twilight Zone* episode involves a character going back in time trying to change the past in order to alter his future; or someone finds a fortune in a cookie and tries desperately to escape the prediction (a mellower word for prophecy), only to find that his very efforts make the prediction a reality. A famous fable that Somerset Maugham used in his play *Sheppey* was reprinted on the title page of John O'Hara's great novel, *Appointment in Samarra*.

DEATH SPEAKS:

"There was a merchant in Bagdad who sent his servant to market to buy provisions and in a little while the servant came back, white and trembling, and said, Master, just now when I was in the market-place I was jostled by a woman in the crowd and when I turned I saw it was Death that jostled me. She looked at me and made a threatening gesture; now, lend me your horse, and I will ride away from this city and avoid my fate. I will go to Samarra and there Death will not find me. The merchant lent him his horse, and the servant mounted it, and he dug his spurs in its flanks and as fast as the horse could gallop he went. Then the merchant went down to the market-place and he saw me standing in the crowd and he came to me and said, Why did you make a threatening gesture to my servant when you saw him this morning? That was not a threatening gesture, I said, it was only a start of surprise. I was astonished to see him in Bagdad, for I had an appointment with him tonight in Samarra."

There's an old adage that character is your fate. If that is true, could Oedipus have changed his fate if he had altered his character? If we interpret the Oracle's prophecy as being metaphorical, rather than literal, Jocasta herself says to Oedipus that men often have sexual dreams that involve their mothers. The subconscious desire to kill or overthrow the father are aspects of a developing child's normal urge to be separate and autonomous. A poem by actor and poet Macdonald Carey from his book *That Further Hill* gives us a humorous manifestation of that truth.

Growing

My boys are all 6'4"
And into their own lives now
We don't see each other much any more
I remember

We had a problem with one of them
He stammered
I kept trying to talk him out of it
(Speech is important to an actor)

The doctor said, "Your voice is very
Threatening to an eight year old. Tell him
You don't mean to sound that way."

I told him about my being an actor and all
And he never stammered again

One night after that
We were wrestling in the living room
After dinner
And I let him toss me over his shoulder

"There," he said
"I threw the whole father"

Given that Oedipus's fatal flaw was his overweening pride, arrogance, and quick temper, could Oedipus have changed his fate by modifying his character? Oedipus' encounter on the road with Laius might have turned out altogether differently. Or, even more to the point, if he'd taken the Oracle's prophecy as metaphorical, not literal, and processed the unconscious desire to kill the father and have sex with his mother, perhaps he'd never have fled Corinth in the first place. Thus, he would have avoided the encounter on the road with Liaus, and all that followed as a result of killing him.. The paradox seems to be that one meets one's fate by running away from it. Therefore, the question is—can one avoid one's worst fate by meeting it head on?

The answer seems to be yes. As for the question, "DId Oedipus Rex have an Oedipus complex?" the answer seems to be yes, as well. It was Oedipus' pride which prevented him from confronting his destiny and character, and it was his pride that led him to think he could escape his dreaded fate by running from it. Freud would have counseled Eddie to look at his desire for his mother, and the need to overthrow the father. It was Jung who focused more on the act of blindness at the end of the drama. Oedipus has not changed very much in all the years since his flight from Corinth, his marriage and fatherhood. At the end of the play, he's still in denial, and rather than face the truth of his own nature, and of everyone's nature, he fled once again into blindness, gouging out his own eyes. What if, upon finding out that Jocasta was not only his wife and mother of his children, but his own mother as well—what if he had shrugged his shoulders, accepted the truth and said, "Well, isn't life amazing! Here I got to do what many men only dream about. As far as my killing Liaus, it seems I have a debt to pay in that regard. I hope the court will be lenient, but in order to restore balance and harmony and health to the land, I'm ready to pay the price for my misdeeds." Ofcourse, then there's no drama, no tragedy.

Antigone (441 B.C.)

It has been said that Antigone was such a success when first produced, that it was responsible for Sophocles's election to the board of generals in 441 B.C. While this is probably an exaggeration, it suggests the impact the play had in its own day. The play has also affected modern writers. Two of the most famous adaptations are that of Jean Anouilh, produced in German-occupied Paris in 1944 (the same time that Marcel Carné was making his great film *Children of Paradise* under the noses of the Germans), and that of Bertolt Brecht, produced at Chur in Switzerland in 1948

George Steiner, in his overly dense critical study *Antigones*, profoundly analyzes the impact of the play on modern consciousness. He claims that it is the one literary text to express all five principle elements of human conflict: the conflict of men and women; of age and youth; of the state and the individual; of mortal beings and the gods; of the living and the dead. The scene that follows is one in which each of the five categories of conflict is exemplified. Oedipus's two sons war against each other, and are both killed, one fighting for the state, the other against it. Creon decrees that Eteocles' body is to be given a proper burial, while the body of Polynices will lay in the open, to decompose in sin for opposing the laws of Thebes. But Antigone, disobeying Creon's edict, invokes the higher law of the Gods and performs the proper ritual as she scatters sacred dirt on his body.

Creon

    [Wheeling on Antigone]   You,
    With your eyes fixed on the ground — speak up.
    Do you deny you did this, yes or no?

Antigone

    I did it. I don't deny a thing.

Creon

    You, tell me briefly, no long speeches —
    were you aware a decree had forbidden this?

Antigone

    Well aware. How could I avoid it? It was public.

Creon

    And still you had the gall to break this law?

Antigone

    Of course I did. It wasn't Zeus, not in the least,
    who made this proclamation — not to me.
    Nor did Justice, dwelling with the gods
    beneath the earth, ordain such laws for men.
    Nor did I think your edict had such force
    that you, a mere mortal, could override the gods,
    the great unwritten, unshakable traditions.
    They are alive, not just today or yesterday:
    they live forever, from the first of time,
    and no one knows when they first saw light.

    These laws — I was not about to break them,
    not out of fear of some man's wounded pride,
    and face the retribution of the gods.
    Die I must, I've known it all my life —

how could I keep from knowing? — even without
your death-sentence ringing in my ears.
And if I am to die before my time
I consider that a gain. Who on earth,
alive in the midst of so much grief as I,
could fail to find his death a rich reward?
So for me, at least, to meet this doom of yours
is precious little pain. But if I had allowed
my own mother's son to rot, an unburied corpse —
that would have been an agony! This is nothing.
And if my present actions strike you as foolish,
let's just say I've been accused of folly
by a fool.

Leader

Like father like daughter,
passionate, wild . . .
she hasn't learned to bend before adversity.

Creon

No? Believe me, the stiffest stubborn wills
fall the hardest; the toughest iron,
tempered strong in the white-hot fire,
you'll see it crack and shatter first of all.
And I've known spirited horses you can break
with a light bit — proud, rebellious horses.
There's no room for pride, not in a slave,
not with the lord and master standing by.

This girl was an old hand at insolence
when she overrode the edicts we made public.
But once she'd done it — the insolence,
twice over — to glory in it, laughing,
mocking us to our face with what she'd done.
I am not the man, not now: she is the man
if this victory goes to her and she goes free.

Never! Sister's child or closer in blood
than all my family clustered at my altar
worshipping Guardian Zeus — she'll never escape,
she and her blood sister, the most barbaric death.
Yes, I accuse her sister of an equal part
in scheming this, this burial.
    [to his attendants.]
                        Bring her here!
I just saw her inside, hysterical, gone to pieces.
It never fails: the mind convicts itself
in advance, when scoundrels are up to no good,
plotting in the dark. Oh but I hate it more
when a traitor, caught red-handed,
tries to glorify his crimes.

Antigone

Creon, what more do you want
than my arrest and execution?

Creon

Nothing. Then I have it all.

Antigone

Then why delay? Your moralizing repels me,
every word you say — pray god it always will.
So naturally all I say repels you too.
                                        Enough.
Give me glory! What greater glory could I win
than to give my own brother decent burial?
These citizens here would all agree,
they'd praise me too
if their lips weren't locked in fear.
            [*pointing to Creon.*]
Lucky tyrants — the perquisites of power!
Ruthless power to do and say whatever pleases *them.*

Creon

You alone, of all the people in Thebes,
see things that way.

Antigone

                        They see it just that way
but defer to you and keep their tongues in leash.

Creon

And you, aren't you ashamed to differ so from them?
So disloyal!

Antigone

Not ashamed for a moment,
not to honor my brother, my own flesh and blood.

Creon

Wasn't Eteocles a brother too — cut down, facing him?

Antigone

Brother, yes, by the same mother, the same father.

Creon

Then how can you render his enemy such honors,
such impieties in his eyes?

Antigone

He'll never testify to that,
Eteocles dead and buried.

Creon

                    He will —
if you honor the traitor just as much as him.

Antigone

But it was his brother, not some slave that died —

Creon

> Ravaging our country! —
> but Eteocles died fighting in our behalf.

Antigone

> No matter — Death longs for the same rites for all.

Creon

> Never the same for the patriot and the traitor.

Antigone

> Who, Creon, who on earth can say the ones below
> don't find this pure and uncorrupt?

Creon

> Never. Once an enemy, never a friend,
> not even after death.

Antigone

> I was born to join in love, not hate —
> that is my nature.

Creon

> Go down below and love,
> if love you must — love the dead! While I'm alive,
> no woman is going to lord it over me.

☛ **Plato** (427-341 B.C.) *The Dialogues & The Republic*

It is often said that all philosophy follows one of the two opposing views of the world contained in the work of Plato and Aristotle; after two thousand years of philosophy, it comes down to whether you're a Platonist or an Aristotelian. For Plato, the world we encounter on a daily basis is only a shadow of the world of Ideal Forms. Objects are only appearances, not the real thing. For Aristotle, it was the other way around. What we see and touch and feel contains the Real, the true Reality.

For the purposes of this study guide, our interest in Plato is not for his philosophical ideas, but for his literary account of Socrates. Plato came from an aristocratic family and envisioned a life of literary pursuit, until the influence of Socrates turned him in the direction of philosophy. But is there a greater literary portrait than Plato's portrait of Socrates, whose ideas are so effectively shown in the *Dialgoues* that it is easy to forget Socrates never wrote a thing down. It is only in the *Dialogues* of Plato (and the writings of Xenophon) that we receive the teachings of Socrates. In a series of dramatic dialogues written after Socrates' execution in 399 B.C., Plato recreated the personality of his beloved teacher and the "Socratic Method"—question and answer—that characterized his search for ethical definitions and truth. And while many of the dialogues are intricate philosophical debates between Socrates and someone who is taking an opposite view, many of them are vivid accounts of life in Greece. The characters in the *Dialogues* come to life as vividly as any characters in literature. Our picture of Socrates is so compelling, that anyone reading Plato's *Dialogues* comes away with a sense of having known him. It is as if Plato's memories of Socrates become our own: his disputations on the streets of Athens, of his trial, and his execution.

Despite the urgings of friends who could have helped him escape, Socrates accepted his death sentence and drank the hemlock, because to do otherwise would have disgraced the Laws by which he had lived his life.

"You die undeservedly," said one of his ardent followers.

"Would you, then," Socrates answered, "have me deserve death."

Socrates inquired into the nature of the Good, what the Good life is, and concluded that the pursuit of knowledge is one of the highest goals of a good life, and the greatest knowledge of all is the knowledge of the self. "Know thyself," he often reminded his students, refering to an inscription at the Oracle of Delphi. "The unexamined life is not worth living," was another of his famous admonitions. In person, Socrates was anything but pleasant: he annoyed citizen and friend alike by confronting them with question after question in search of truth, exposing the illogic of their behavior in hopes of getting them back on track toward the Good and proper life. Physically, he was rather unattractive—short, hefty, bearded with a broad nose and thick lips. He vowed several times to rid himself of his paunch by dancing more. Hounded by his wife Xanthippe, he walked the streets of Athens wearing the same shabby robe throughout the year, and preferred bare feet to shoes or sandals. As a young man, he fought in the war against Sparta and is said to have saved the life of Alcibiades, the Athenian general.

Aristophanes, the great comic playwright, poked fun at Socrates in *The Clouds*, portraying him as a buffoon, another Sophist fleecing the rich and the gullible. In the play, an old gentlemen hears that Socrates operates a Thinking Shop where one can learn to prove anything, even if it is false. When he gets to the "School of Very Hard Thinkers," he discovers Socrates hanging from the ceiling in a basket, deep in thought, while his students are bent over with their noses to the ground.

> "What are those people doing, stooping so oddly," asks the old man.
> One of the students says, "They are probing the secrets that lie deep as Hell."
> "But why—excuse me, but—their hind quarters—why are they stuck up so strangely in the air?" stammers the old man.
> "Their other ends are studying astronomy."

Plato's account of his life is the portrait of a gadfly that sits on the back end of a horse and is constantly being swatted away by the horse's tail. Such was Socrates, a gadfly on the conscience of Athens.

As literature, the *Dialogues* rival any novel for character and dialogue. For starters, read "The Symposium," an account of a racous party given by the poet Agathon to celebrate an award he'd won. The nature of love and beauty is discussed, with Socrates elucidating the different types of love from earthly passion to ideal beauty. The party grows more rowdy when Alcibiades comes crashing in, drunk and full of convivial spirits. Alcibiades was the personification of earthly love in all its splendor—the handsome, brilliant man who was the darling (and evil genius) of Athenian democracy.

. . . . Suddenly there was a loud knocking at the street door. It sounded like a party of drunks; one could hear a girl playing a flute.

"Go and see who it is," Agathon said to the servants, "and if it is any of our friends ask them in. Otherwise say that my party is over and that we are going to bed."

A moment later they heard the voice of Alcibiades in the courtyard, very tipsy and shouting, wanting to know where Agathon was and demanding to be taken to Agathon. He was helped by the flute-girl and some of his other companions; he stood in the doorway crowned with a thick wreath of ivy and violets, from which a number of ribands hung about his head, and said:

"Good evening, gentlemen. Will you welcome into your company a man who is already drunk, utterly drunk, or shall we just put a garland on Agathon, which is what we came for, and go away?" . . . .

There was a unanimous cry that he should come in, and Agathon joined in the invitation. He was trying to take off his wreath which was tilted over his eyes, and so he did not see Socrates, but sat down next to Agathon, with Socrates, who moved so as to make room for him, on the other side. As he took his place he embraced Agathon and crowned him.

"Take off Alcibiades' shoes," ordered Agathon, "so that he can put his feet up and make a third at this table."

"Splendid," said Alcibiades, "but who is our table companion?" With these words he twisted himself round and saw Socrates, then leapt to his feet, and said, "Good God, what have we here? Socrates? Lying there in wait for me again? How like you to make a sudden appearance just when I least expect to find you. What are you doing here? You ought to be next to Aristophanes or some other actual or would-be buffoon, and instead you've managed to get yourself next to the handsomest person in the room."

"Be ready to protect me, Agathon," said Socrates, "for I find that the love of this fellow has become no small burden. From the moment when I first fell in love with him, I haven't been able to exchange a glance or a word with a single good-looking person without his falling into a passion of jealousy and envy, which makes him behave outrageously and abuse me and practically lay violent hands on me. See to it that he doesn't commit some excess even here, or if he attempts to do anything violent protect me; I am really quite scared by his mad behaviour and the intensity of his affection."

"There can be no peace between you and me," said Alcibiades, "but I'll settle accounts with you for this presently. For the moment, Agathon, give me some of those ribands to make a wreath for his head too, for a truly wonderful head it is. Otherwise he might blame me for crowning you and leaving him uncrowned, whose words bring him victory over all men at all times, not merely on single occasions, like yours the day before yesterday." So saying he took some of the ribands, made a wreath for Socrates, and lay back.

When he was seventy, Socrates was accused of introducing new divinities, thereby corrupting the young by teaching them to worship gods not approved by the State. Though the charges were politically trumped-up, he was found guilty and sentenced to die by drinking hemlock, a poison.

In the "Apology," Socrates answers his accusers and makes his defense, discussing his life's mission as a philosopher who knows nothing, but pursues the truth. In the "Crito," Socrates and his friends are together in his cell before the execution. His disciples have arranged an escape, which probably would have been easy, and successful. Crito, a rich friend who had bribed some of the Athenian authorites, urges Socrates to take this last opportunity to escape death. But Socrates firmly refuses. He explains why he cannot escape, and dishonor the very Laws he has lived by: running away now would expose him as the ultimate hypocrite. The "Phaedo" is an account of his death. Socrates reminds his friends that his soul goes with peace because his life has been devoted to the pleasures, not of the flesh, but of acquiring knowledge. "Those who purify themselves sufficiently by philosophy live therafter altogether without bodies" in a paradisal state. And the philosopher is one who, "by decking his soul not with a borrowed beauty, but with its own—with self-control, and goodness, and courage, and liberality, and truth—has fitted himself to await his journey to the next world."

> "You Simmias and Cebes and the rest, will each make this journey some day in the future; but 'for me the fated hour' (as a tragic character might say) calls even now. In other words, it is about time that I took my bath. I prefer to have a bath before drinking the poison, rather than give the women the trouble of washing me when I am dead."
>
> When he had finsihed speaking, Crito said, "What can we do to please you best?"
>
> "Nothing new, Crito," said Socrates; "just what I am always telling you. If you look after yourself, whatever you do will please me and mine and you too, even if you don't agree with me now. On the other hand, if you neglect yourself and fail to follow the line of life as I have laid it down both now and in the past, however fervently you agree with me now, it will do no good at all."
>
> "We shall try our best to do as you say," said Crito. "But how shall we bury you?"
>
> "Anyway you like," replied Socrates, "that is, if you can catch me and I don't slip through your fingers." He laughed gently as he spoke. . . .
>
> Up until this time most of us had been fairly successful in keeping back our tears; but when we saw that he was drinking, that he had actually drunk it, we could do so no longer. Apollodorous, who had never stopped crying even before, now broke out into such a storm of passionate weeping that he made everyone in the room break down, except Socrates himself, who said:
>
> "Really, my friends, what a way to behave! Calm yourself and try to behave."
>
> Socrates walked about, and presently, saying that his legs were heavy, lay down on his back—that was what the man recommended. The man

(he was the same one who administered the poison) kept his hand upon Socrates, and after a little while examined his feet and legs; then pinched his foot hard and asked if he felt it. Socrates said no. Presently he felt him again and said that when it reached the heart, Socrates would be gone.

The coldness was spreading about as far as his waist when Socrates uncovered his face—for he had covered it up—and said (they were his last words): "Crito, I owe a cock to Asclepius; will you remember to pay the debt?"

"The debt shall be paid," said Crito. "Is there anything else?"

There was no answer to this question; but in a minute or two a movement was heard, and the attendants uncovered him; his eyes were fixed. When Crito saw this, he closed his eyes and mouth.

Such, Echecrates, was the end of our friend, who was, we may fairly say, of all those whom we knew in our time, the bravest and also the wisest and most upright man.

ಎ

☛ **Aristotle** (384-322 B.C.) *The Poetics*

As with Plato, we'll be looking at Aristotle's literary, rather than philosophical contribution; we are certainly not about to examine his works on Logic, Science, Metaphysics, Ethics or Politics. Unlike Plato, much of his writings deal with Science, not Metaphysics—perhaps it is a mistake even to think of him primarily as a philosopher. Never before had anyone built such an impressive monument of thought. His learning was so vast, and his extant works cover so much, that it's best to take him one step at a time, as the situation warrants. We'll look at his *Esthetics*, and that part of it called the *Poetics*. The same man who produced "Prior Analytics," "Posterior Analytics," "Sophist Reasonings," "Meteorology," "The Constitution of Athens," "Locomotion of Animals," "Nicomachean Ethics", "Eduemian Ethics", "Categories of Logic," "The Logic of Interpretation," "On the Soul," and his "Little Essays on Nature," also investigated the nature of poetry and literature and the nature of the creative process. Where Plato would have looked at Form (product), Aristotle examined the Function (process).

If there is a common denominator to his work, it's probably that his curious mind was interested in the process and technique of reasoning, even though he gave much space to defining terms. When he turned to the study of man, he became less of a scientist and more of a metaphysician. Where Plato considered how to make men Good, Aristotle, in his *Ethics*, proposed how to make men happy. When asked whether it was better to be wise or to be rich, Aristotle quotes the answer of Simonides to Hieron's wife: "Rich, for we see the wise spending their time at the doors of the rich." But for Aristotle, his principle of "The Golden Mean" between extremes defined his apporach to the happy life. Intelligence is necessary to understand the mean, and inner strength to make it practical. Virtue was the *habit* of doing the right thing. But like Socrates (or Plato), Aristotle concludes that the best life is the life of contemplation. "The most fortunate of men is he who combines a measure of prosperity with scholarship, research, or contemplation; such a man comes closest to the life of the gods," he writes in the *Ethics*.

He was not the first to write about art and poetry. Commentaries exist in the West as early as Homer and Hesiod, where poetry is seen as both entertainment and an instrument of education. The 5th century Sophists, attacked by Plato as deceivers, studied verbal effects extensively, though for a rhetorical end, persuasion. But Western poetic theory can be said to have begun with, and is still framed largely in the terms established by Plato and Aristotle.

Plato the Idealist saw all things in the world as merely the appearances of Reality, which manifested itself in the world of ideal Forms. Only the Ideal Form of the chair was Real; the actual chair was nothing more than a shadow, an appearance of reality. Poetry was therefore a "made object," that was consequently twice removed from reality. Plato went so far as to call this "making" dangerous. "All poets lie," he said, because their representation of life can only diminish Being, which is contained in Ideal Form. In *Republic* 10, Plato uses the concept of *mimesis* (imitation) to denote all artistic activity as an imitation of reality, and his doctrine of poetic inspiration by the Muses is a doctrine of "poetic madness." Poets, as mere mouthpieces of the gods, were superfluous. In his ideal state, he would have had them all banished.

Aristotle is the first Western writer known to have constructed a method for the systemic study of literature. We're probably more familiar with his comments in the *Poetics* that pertain to Tragic Drama. Tragedy was the portrayal of a superior and noble being who demonstrates great courage and perseverance while struggling against an eventual defeat that causes great pain and suffering. If the hero is not exalted to begin with, there can be no tragedy—just commonplace misfortune; thus the term "a tragic fall." Furthermore, the action of the tragedy must be generated by the tragic hero's fatal flaw, his *hubris*—an arrogance or overweening pride. The tragic hero can also be undone by the will of the Gods. The drama must show the tragic hero's *catharsis*—an insight that causes great pain and suffering, which also invokes in the audience sorrow and pity. (Max Ophuls' four-hour film/documentary masterpiece on the holocaust was titled *The Sorrow and The Pity*.) Finally, Aristotle expects the perfect tragic drama to include the three "unities" of time, place, and action; that is, it should all take place in continuous time (no flash-backs or jumps in time that are not the real time it takes on the stage), in one place (no scene changes), and there should be an organic unity to the action so that each incident follows logically from the one before. Many great Greek tragedies contained some of the "unities," but not all of them. The play that Aristotle praised the most for adhering to all three dramatic "unities" was *Oedipus Rex*. (Aristotle did not make the same claim for epic poetry, which had no limits in time.)

FOOR FOR THOUGHT

Brecht's Epic Theatre

To this day, Aristotle's concept of drama and how it best functions as theatre has been the dominant paradigm for over two thousand years. Shakespeare, Moliere, Ibsen, Tennessee Williams, etc., have all contrived a drama that is realistic and geared toward eliciting a sympathetic, emotional reaction from the audience, an audience which gets caught up in the action on stage and is able to "suspend its disbelief." The only attempt consciously to fashion a theatre that subverted the Aristotelian effect was made by **Bertold Brecht,** author of *Three-Penny Opera* and *Mother Courage.* Brecht was a German poet and dramatist who developed a radical staging technique as part of his theory of Epic Theatre. Brecht saw theatre as a means to agitate for political change. He borrowed some techniques from classical theatre such as the Chorus, and employed, variously, slides, music, film, and placards to alienate the audience and actors alike from traditional theatrical illusions. This "alienation effect" was used by Brecht to confound the audience's normal expectations and compel it to use its critical faculties—not *after* the emotional experience of the play—but during it. As a matter of fact, Brecht did not want the viewer to have such an emotional experience that they lost sight of the implications and intellectual ramifications of the text. Brecht distrusted Aristotle's concept of theatre as one which produced sorrow and pity in the viewer, who was drawn in by the seamless texture of a unified dramatic performance. Brecht's plays were often not held together by a narrative line, but instead consisted of a series of contrasting episodes, not necessarily connected in time. Brecht wanted to destroy the illusory nature of theatre and to instill in both actors and audience an awareness of the distinction between fantasy and reality. By causing the spectator to detach himself from the dramatic action rather than identifying with it, Brecht hoped that a play would become a vehicle for enlightening the public to new discoveries about their socio-political surroundings.

Trouble is, it is not easy managing such an effect. As an actor, I have been in several productions of Brecht's plays in which I felt the director did not completely understand the "alienation affect," or was unsuccesful in implementing it. In one production, we actors were to deliver our speeches in a menacing tone looking directly at the audience. The director wanted us to "alienate the audience." I don't think this was the point of the term "alienation effect." In another production of *Three-Penny Opera*, I experimented with ways to deliver my character's words so that the audience was aware that there was an actor behind him, commenting on the character—something that was strictly forbidden in the Aristotelian theatre of Stanislavky and Hollywood movies, since it could easily be mistaken for poor acting. I was not at all pleased with the outcome, especially since the other actors were all attempting to achieve the "alienation effect" in different ways. In the hands of a director lacking a strong overall vision, the play crumbled under the weight of so much self-consciouness. I don't regret what I learned in the experience, but to be honest, it's a thorny problem this epic theatre, and my experience has led me to believe that the success of Epic Theatre depends on a perfectly realized combination of elements—acting style, theatrical staging, music, etc.—that are under the control of a director that knows exactly how to achieve this effect. It's also possible that we are just not culturally suited for this type of theatrical experience. See pages 506-508 in this study guide where Augustine comments on the reactions of an audience that doesn't get it's money's worth of sorrow and pity.

Though most of the *Poetics* is taken up with critical theories of verse drama, Arisitotle also examines poetry in critical terms. Like Plato, his teacher for twenty years, Aristotle accepts the idea of *mimesis* as imitation, but he treats it as a natural, pleasurable, and productive human drive. Furthermore, he is not interested in how truthful the *mimesis* is, but in the skill with which the poet makes the poem. *Poietike* is not a class of objects but *techne*, i.e. "making." His concern is not with the *nature* of poetry, as much as it is with the *art* of poetry, the skill of making poetry that will succeed in moving its audience. The poem itself has Being; the ideas it "contains" or evokes are only of secondary reality. Here's one example of how Plato and Arisitotle in their overall philosophic theory differ. Form, for Aristotle, is not extrinsic to things, as it was for Plato, who saw behind every object (which could not be real, only a reflection of the Real) the greater reality of the Ideal Form. Aristotle felt that Form was intrinsic: the acorn contains the pattern for the oak, and the acorn is a primary reality. The poem contains a pattern found in life; the poem itself, as "a made thing," is Real.

Had Aristotle not confined much of his interest to the chief art form of his time—verse drama—he might have developed a broader view. He applied his theories mostly to the dramas of the Greek playwrights, especially Sophocles's *Oedipus Rex*, which he praised as a perfect model of the play that contains all of the "Unities." We see that extrinsic form is not of primary interest to Aristotle. Had he lived in our time, and read the correspondance between Robert Creeley and Charles Olson, he would have agreed with them that form and content were inseparable, that perhaps "form itself was only an extension of content," as they maintained.

Thus, Aristotle sees *poiesis* as a making, a process, and the point of the *Poetics* is the artful and successful carrying out of that process, not its ends, which will never emerge in precast or predictable forms. In this process, *mimesis* is a means, not an end.

We will see how Horace continues this mode of thought in his *Ars Poetica,* though Horace places a greater emphasis on craft and revision. Horace also stated that poetry was not merely an aesthetic object, but had a practical function to entertain and teach. This idea signaled a shift in critical thinking from poetry as a mimetic form, to poetry as a practical art. Aristotle's work was lost throughout most of the Middle Ages, and Horace was read and imitated throughout this period. Dante's work *On the Vulgar Tongue* argued that the range and power of poetry in the vernacular was equal to that in the Classical languages. He surveyed the various dialects of Italy and denied that any of them, including Tuscan, had the power and beauty of that "illustrious Italian vulgar tongue" in which the highest poetry should be composed by the best of writers. His decision to write the *Commedia* in Italian, not Latin, had a major influence on the spread of literature written in the vernacular speech of his country, and ranks as one of his greatest achievements. With the advent of Gutenberg's printing press, almost all the available classical works were published in Latin within a period of fifty years. By 1600, French, German, Italian and English literatures were establishing a new identity. Milton, who had considered writing *Paradise Lost* in Latin, switched to English, much to our benefit. It was not until the Renaissance that the recovery of texts of Classical times, including Plato and Aristotle, led to a further evolution of poetic theory. In the 19th century (The Romantic Period), a third conception of poetry arose as something neither mimetic nor practical, but Expressive. It didn't matter if the poem mirrored the world (*mimesis*), and it didn't matter that it served a practical purpose in entertaining and educating the reader. What counted was that it was an expression of the poet's feelings. The expression of the inner self was primary. By the end of the century Western poetry began to detach itself completely from Aristotelian and mimeticist premises. A fourth way of looking at the poetic art came with "The New Critics" in the mid-20th Century who studied poetry as an <u>Objective</u> art, something that could be analyzed not for its mimetic or practical aspects, and not at all as a representation of a particlar poet's expression of feelings. The poem was a <u>made object</u> that was looked at objectively, as a thing in itself, the same way you'd analyze a car or a particular tree. Who created it and why was unimportant, the so-called "intentional fallacy." The poem was a object to be studied apart from the who, when, where, how, and why of its making. "The Intentional Fallacy," a 20th century concept that proposes that a work of art's meaning is not tied to the intention of its creator, is one that has greatly shaped contemporary criticism. Does the meaning of a work of art and our estimation of its value even come from the artist's intentions? In the mid-20th century, in what would become both a philosophical and literary groundbreaking criticism, William K. Wimsatt Jr. and Monroe C. Beardsley published "The Intentional Fallacy." In it, they counter the contemporary assumption that the original creator's intention for a work was equal to the meaning and merit of the work. This raised serious questions in the critical realm about intentionality, autobiography, cultural context, and the fixed or unfixed nature of meaning. In the article, Wimsatt and Beardsley wrote, "The design or intention of the author is neither available nor desirable as a standard for judging the success of a work of literary art, and it seems to us that this is a principle which goes deep into some differences in the history of critical attitudes." They further argue that a criticism is largely shaped by the critic's definition and nuance of intentionality, how and why the mind purposes to do or create something.

Later, those critics who wanted to deconstruct the object of art, decided that it was *only* the who, when, where, and why that mattered; that the "reading" of a particular work of art was determined soley by the social, political, and economic agenda of the artist, and of the society of which he was a part. It made no difference what the poem said or meant, they contended, and that treating it as a made object outside of time and space was ludicrous. The conscious intention of the artist was only one part of the larger construction. What about the unconscious intentions, all part of the social, political, economic, class background. That is what was important, said the deconsctructionists. And to give Einstein the last laugh, other deconstructionists came along and said that the person doing the deconstructing of a work of art could not be wholly objective, that even the act of deconstruction was relative and had its unconscious intentions that were all part of the social, cultural and political background of the time. This gets very complicated, and makes eating a steak not what it used to be. But we'll pick up that thread later (not the steak; the other stuff).

For now, just keep in mind those four basic approaches to the making and understanding a work of art, and how those approaches have evolved over the centuries. First, art was seen as a <u>mirror of nature</u>; then, it was considered a <u>instructive</u> tool; in the 19th Century, with the advant of Romanticism and emotional expression, art was seen in the context of <u>expressionism,</u> how it grew out of the creator's emotional intention; in the 20th century, a fourth idea was advanced, that a work of art stood alone, and was detached from any intention of the artist, but rather seen in the context of itself, <u>an object </u>for study.

The Hellenistic Age:
(c. 323 BC-c. 133 BC)

T he Hellenistic age was that period of Greek culture which may be said to start from the death of Alexander the Great of Macedon in 323 BC. At the end of the 3rd century began the expansion of Rome into the Greek world, and Roman conquest was completed within the next two centuries. Thus, we may say the Hellenistic age ended with Rome's absorption of Greece and the Greek East in the latter parts of the first century BC. Created in the aftermath of the conquests of Alexander the Great, and under the umbrella of the Greek language, Hellenistic Greece fostered an astonishing degree of local cultural and political autonomy throughout the Mediterranean region and beyond. As a result, we still tend to look at classical Greece through Hellenistic glasses. We easily underestimate how great was the contribution of Hellenistic culture to the developments in the Roman Republic.

The term itself is problematic, and controversial. Hellenism could mean the benign transmission of Greek language and culture, but Hellenization has a connotation that is more active and agggressive, an imperialistic form of cultural domination. The spread of Greek culture was most intense in the years between Alexander the Great and the victory at Actium of Octavian (later Augustus Caesar), but 20th century historians have also stressed the Semetic contribution to Mediterranean countries. For convenience, we could say Hellenism is the general diffusion of Greek culture, and Hellenization or Hellenistic would be confined to the centuries 336-31 BC.

A vast amount of literature was produced during these two centuries, but only a small fraction has survived. Much of what we have today is largely verse. Only a few histories out of hundreds have come down to us, and almost nothing remains of the scores of tragic poets. Many of the poets influenced later Latin literature, but while some of the work of Callimachus and Theocritus survive, the poetry of Philetas of Cos and Euphorion have perished. Among the epic poets, the story of Jason and the voyage of the Argonauts by Apollonius of Rhodes survives.

The city that bore Alexander's name became the intellectual and cultural capital of the world, especially with the establishment of the great Alexandrian Library. It seems evident that in early Greece, even during the period of its highest literary development, there was no system for the production and distribution of books. The number of copies of any work of Greek literature available must have been exceedingly limited; it would probably be safe to say that before Alexandria became the centre of book-production, there simply was no reading public. Those manuscripts that were produced were maintained in royal archives or in a State collection such as the one in Athens. Some scholars gained fame as teachers due partly to the fact that they were owners of books.

The contemporary writers of the day were content to do their work without material compensation. Stranger still, they appear to have been unconcerned with the preservation and circulation of their work. Their only reward seems to have been fame with their own generation, and even for this to occur it would seem that some distribution of their compositions was essential. The thought of preserving one's work for future generations seems not to have been a major preoccupation.

The author appears to have been satisfied when his composition received the honor of dramatic presentation or of public recitation. If one's fellow citizens accorded the approbation of the laurel crown, the approval of the outer world or of future generations was of trifling importance. It's not known whether this lack of ambition stemmed from a lack of incentive on the part of authors, the non-existence of a reading public, or the absence of adequate machinery for the production and distribution of books; the fact remains that the knowledge of the "laurel-crowned" works diffused throughout the Greek community is evidence that public interest in dramatic performances and recitations made for an active-minded people. In Plato's "Symposium," an inebriated Alcibiades arrives at Agathon's house with several companions in a merry mood. They have just come from a poetry reading where Alcibiades has been awarded the "laurel-crown." He sees Socrates sitting on a sofa, staggers over to him, and attempts to place the crown on the grumpy philosopher's balding head. Poetry readings and the picking of a winner must have occured quite frequently, and was tantamount to publication. The poet who won many such laurel-crowns must have felt like someone winning the National Book Award today.

There's an interesting parallel here to our own time. In Rome, under Augustus, we shall see how poetry readings flourished just as they do now. Also under Augustus there existed a machinery for the production of books and a network for their distribution, just as we have now. Today, more poets are being published in journals and magazines and having their books distributed than ever before. Yet, paradoxically, much of the distribution is fragmented and local, either by geography, type, school or by some other pocket of identification. There are a great number of poets reading their work in public who receive the same kind of recognition that poets and writers in Greece received, and in many cases it functions as a substitute for publication, just as it did in Greece.

☞ **Menippus** (3rd century BC)

Cynic philosophy was so named because the founder of the sect, Antisthenes (c.445-c.360 BC) is said to have started teaching at a gymnasium called Cynosarges outside the city of Athens. The gymnasium was sacred to Heracles, the mythical hero who epitomized the ideal Cynic, living a life based on virtue, a virtue that consisted in action. Without virtuous action, they claimed, there is no virtuous life. Diogenes (*c*. 400-325 BC) is perhaps the most famous exponent of the Cynic philsophy, which stresses living a "natural life" renouncing all possessions, and satisfying one's barest natural needs in the cheapest and easiest way possible. Diogenes supposedly lived in a tub and was nicknamed "the dog," because of the life of self-sufficiency he led, losing the conventional sense of shame. His disciple, Crates (*c*.365-285 BC) came to Athens from Thebes, and was won over by Cynic doctrine, renouncing his large fortune and restricting himself to absolute necessities. Cynic philsophers developed no elaborate philosophical system, and its followers shared a variety of beliefs, though they all based their lives on virtuous action and finding happiness through the principal of self-sufficiency. Crates became a wandering begger, and was often mocked as he walked through the countryside carrying his stick and knapsack. Such beggars proliferated during the first and second centuries, and were satirically compared to those true Cynics who were not as extreme in their "self-sufficiency" but pursued nevertheless a life of simplicity and virtuous action. The double standards of many philosophers were thus easily mocked. A slave who later acquired his freedom, Menippus of Gadara in Syria was a Cynic philosopher who satirized the follies of men and philosophers in a serio-comic style, using a mixture of prose and verse. His writings are lost, but they were imitated in Latin by Varro "Reatinus" in his *Saturae Menippeae* and by Lucian in his dialogues. Menippus himself figures frequently in the latter's "Dialogues of the Dead," and one of Lucian's satires bears his name. Any work that combined poetry and prose came to be called menippean, and the form can be used in a variety of ways. Boethius' *Consolation of Philsophy*, written in the 6th century AD while he was awaiting execution, is a classic example of the menippean form.

☛ Theocritus (first half of the 3rd century BC)

Born probably at Syracuse in Sicily, he may have lived in south Italy before going to Alexandria during the reign of Ptolemy II Philadelphus. Theocritus is considered the originator of pastoral or *bucolic* poetry, an entirely new and fanciful genre. In fact, bucolic is derived from the Greek word for herdsmen, *boukoli*, and was first used to describe his poems. Many poets imitated Theocritus, writing in the pastoral genre, including Bion and Moschus, and most notably, the Roman poet Virgil in his *Eclogues,* which had a major influence on later European literature. There is no complete agreement on the criteria that define a bucolic poem, but in typical pastoral poems, the herdsmen-poets sing of themselves, their loves, and their music in a stylized Greek landscape with Pan and the nymphs. These scenes were later depicted by the great French landscapist Claude Lorrain (1600-1682), who brought out the poetic essence and idyllic aspects of the countryside filled with echoes of antiquity. His compositions are suffused with the hazy, luminous atmosphere of early morning or late afternoon; an air of nostalgia hangs over his vistas, of past experience gilded by memory. There's an artful simplicity to pastoral poems, appealing in their own right, but they were often used as a vehicle for veiled social comment. The simple shepherd or goatherd had long been used as a figure of analogy for characters of higher rank. Theocritus was the first poet to focus on the shepherd himself and bring the analogies down into the pastoral world. In turning the focus on the shepherd, Theocritus created a group of literary works with an inner structure so unique that later readers considered it a new genre.

Though Theocritus wrote in an artificial, literary Doric dialect for a sophisticated urban circle, the poems still convey an impression of the timeless pastoral life in the hills of Sicily and south Italy. His *Idyll #1* contains the beautiful lament for Daphnis, a dirge imitated in the "Adonis" of Bion and established the convention of the pastoral as a mask for grief, inspiring Milton's "Lycidas," Shelley's "Adonais," Matthew Arnold's "Thyrsis," and Yeats' "Shepherd and Goatherd."

Idyll 1—*Thyrsis*

Tityrus:

Sweet is the whispering of that pine tree, goatherd,
making music beside the spring, and sweet too
is the sound of your piping. After Pan you will take
the second prize. If he takes the norned goat,
you will get the she-goat. If he takes
the she-goat for his prize, the kid will fall to you.
The flesh of a kid is very nice before she's milked.

Goatherd:
More sweet, O shepherd, is your song than the water that rumbles
and splashes there from the rock above. If the Muses take
the ewe, you shall have the sall-fed lamb for your prize.
If they choose the lamb, you'll later get the ewe.

Tityrus:
Please, in the name of the nymphs, O goatherd, please sit here
beside this sloping knoll and shrubs of tamarisk
and pipe, and I shall meanwhile pasture your goats.

Goatherd:
O shepherd, we may not at noon, we may not pipe for fear
of Pan, for he is resting then and weary from
the hunt. His temper is bitter, and acrid wrath sits ever
at his nostril. But you, Thyrsis, often sing
the sorrows of Daphnis, and you have mastered the pastoral song.

Come let us sit beneath this elm, facing Priapus
and the springs, the shepherds' seat, and the oaks, and if you sing
as once you sang, contesting with Chromis of Libya,
I'll give you to milk three times a goat that has just borne twins,
who though she has two kids, gives two pails besides,
and a deep cup washed over to coat with sweet wax,
two-handles, freshly carved, and fragrant yet from the knife.
Ivy winds around above its lip, ivy
dusted with clusters of gold. Along it trails the tendril,
all aglow with its yellow fruit. Inside a woman
like a wondrous creation of gods is carved. She wears a headband
and cloak. Beside her two men with fair long hair
contend with one another from either side with words,
but this doesn't touch her heart, for now she looks at one
and smiles, and now she casts her thought to the other, while they,
long hollow-eyed from love, struggle to no avail.
Nest to them is carved an old fisherman
and a rugged rock upon which the ancient man
struggles to draw up a great net to make
a cast. He is like a man who labors mightily.
You would say that he was fishing with all the force
of his limbs. So do the sinews swell all about
his neck, though his hair is white; he has the strength of youth.
Not far from the ancient sea-worn man there is a vineyard,
beautifully weighted with darkening clusters. A little boy

sits on a dry-stone wall and guards it. Two foxes
skulk about. One roams up and down the rows
and plunders the vines of the ripe grapes. The other plots
against his purse and says she'll never let him go
until she's got his breakfast bread. But the boy plaits
a pretty cricket cage with rush and asphodel
and cares less for his pouch or for the vine rows
than he takes joy in his plaiting. Everywhere
about the cup the pliant acanthus spreads, a marvel
to goatherds and a wonder to strike your heart too.
I paid the ferryman of Calydna a goat for it
amd a big cheese of white milk, but never yet
has it touched my lips. It lies immaculate still. I'll give
you gladly the pleasure of it, my friend, if you will sing
that lovely song, nor do I mock you at all. Come,
my good man, for surely you nver can keep your song
down there in Hades that brings oblivion of all.

Thyrsis:
Begin, dear Muses, now begin the pastoral song.

Thyrsis of Aetna am I, and the voice of thyrsis is sweet.
Where were you when Daphnis was wasting, where were you, Nymphs?

[sings his song about Daphnis pining for the girl]

. . . . . .

Oh Muses, cease, come cease from the pastoral song.

So much he said and stopped, and Aphrodite wanted
to raise him up again, but all the thread from the Fates
was runm, and Daphnis went to the stream. The eddies washed over
him whom the Muses loved and the Nymphs did not dislike.

Oh Muses, cease, come cease from the pastoral song.

Now you must give me the goat and the bowl that I may milk her
and make libation to the Muses. Good-bye, Muses,
Good-bye. Another time i'll sing you a sweeter song.

Goatherd:
May your lovely mouth be filled with honey, Thyrsis, filled
with the honeycomb. May you eat the sweet figs of Aegilus,
for you surpass the cicada in song. Here is the cup.
See how sweetly it smells. You'll think that it's been washed
at the Springs of the hours. Come here, Cissaetha. now milk her. Nannies,
don't be so skittish — the billy goat will be aroused.

☛ **Leonidas of Tarentum** (first half of 3rd century BC)

Magna Graecia became the name for the Greek cities in southern Italy and Sicily, and before 300 BC had little to do with the Romans. The most important of these cities was Taras, later changed by the Romans to Tarentum, and now called Taranto, which lies on the gulf of that same name. One of the best poets in *The Greek Anthology*, Leonidas wrote highly polished epigrams, densely expressed and often melancholy, about the life of the poor, to which class he belonged. The Roman poets Virgil and Propertius admired his elaborate and artificial style, imitating some of its effects.

Fair Warning from Priapos

The season for sailing. Already the chattering swallow
returns with the slender west wind.
Meadows bloom, and the boiling waves of the sea,
whipped by gales, are smooth and silent.
Come then, sailor, haul in the anchors and loosen the hawsers
and sail with all the canvas flying.
It is Priapos, god of the harbor, who warns you now:
set out from this port for foreign cargoes.

Summer Thirst

Traveler, do not drink the warm water
from this pool,
all muddy from the quick mountain brook
and the intruding sheep.
go a little further up the hill
where the heifers are grazing,
and there by the shepherd's pine
                    you will find
bubbling up through the porous rock
a spring colder than northern snow.

Modern translators of his work catch his acerbic wit and the caustic tone of his verse. Kenneth Rexroth is responsible for the portrait of Teleso, translated in 1962, and Fleur Adcock rendered the poetic barb at Hipponax in 1973.

Teleso
For that goatfucker, goatfooted
Pan, Teleso stretched this hide
On a plane tree, and in front
Of it hung up his well cut
Crook, smiter of bloody-eyed wolves,
His curdling buckets, and the least
And collars of his keen-nosed pups.

Hipponax

Go softly past the graveyard where
Hipponax is asleep: take care!
Don't wake that spiteful wasp, who stung
Even his parents with his tongue.
In Hell itself, where now he lies,
His red-hot words can cauterize.

☛ **Apollonius of Rhodes** (c. 295-215 BC)

Though born in Alexandria, and tutor to Ptolemy III Euergetes and at some point head of the Alexandrian Library, he spent the later part of his life in Rhodes. Apollonius is best known for his epic poem on the story of Jason and the Argonauts, called the *Argonautica.* The 1963 film *Jason and the Argonauts,* featuring superb special effects and multiple mythological cretures, recounted the story of Jason, son of the King of Thessaly, who sails on the Argo to the land of Colchis, where the Golden Fleece is guarded by a seven-headed hydra. With Medea's aid, he brings back the Fleece and returns to Iolcus in Thessaly Theocritus' poem was the only epic before Virgil's *Aeneid* that could be compared with Homer in subject and extent, and the first epic to give a prominent place to love—Medea's for Jason. The structure of the work as a whole has been frequently criticized, beginning with his teacher, Callimachus, who quarrelled violently with him over his use of the epic genre, which he felt was outdated in its large scale. Callimachus was a leading spokesman for those who felt that short and highly polished poems were prefarable to long traditional epics. Though Callimachus was said to have won the theoretical battle, with Apollonius retiring to Rhodes in consequence, it was the long epic of Jason's voyage that continued in popularity. Apollonius was much admired in late antiquity and is one of the few Hellenistic poets whose work survived in medieval manuscripts.

In characteristic Hellenistic style, Apollonius combined poetry with scholarship and erudition, but the work also features many cleverly devised scenes noted for their delicate psychological characterizations.

In true epic fashion, the poem begins with an invocation to the muse and synopsis of the plot, the same way a writer might pitch the movie to a prospective producer. "Listen C.B., I got this great idea for an adventure story. There's this King see, who hears a prophecy that he'll be killed by a man wearing a single shoe. Close up of the shoe. Then Jason—we get Kennau Reeves or Brad Pitt to play our hero-warrior—when Jason meets this King, he's wearing only one shoe—see the other one got stuck in the mud. Now the King's no fool, see—Anthony Hopkins or Sean Connery could play the King. The King can't just whack Jason 'cause Jason is really popular with the people, so he has to think of someway of getting rid of this kid without it looking like he's the bad guy. So the King tells Jason to man his ship, the Argo, and he sends Jason on a long voyage down several great rivers—the Rhine, the Danube, the Po, the Rhone, then across the Mediterranean and North Africa, then through the Bosophorus and across the Black Sea—all to bring back the Golden Fleece. Now the King doesn't expect him to bring back the Fleece. He figures

Jason's gonna get lost at sea. But Jason meets this powerful broad—Sharon Stone or Jennnifer Lopez—who helps him win the Golden Fleece. Whaddaya think, C.B?" Here's how Theocritus begins his epic pitch:

Book I
Beginning from you, Phoebus, I shall tell the glory
of men born long ago who down the mouth of Pontus
between the Cyanean rocks at King Peleus' command
in search of the golden fleece sailed the well-benched Argo.
Such was the oracle Peleus heard, that a grim fate
awaited him to be slain at command of the man he should see
stepping forth from the people and wearing a single sandal.
And not long after in accord with that prophecy Jason,
crossing the streams of stormy Anaurus on foot, saved
one shoe from the mud; the other he left behind,
caught there below and held back by the floods. He came
to Peleus, face to face, to share the feast which he
prepared for Poseidon his father and all the other gods,
though he paid no heed to Pelasgian Hera. As soon as the king
saw him, he took thought and contrived for him the trial
of a troubled sailing so that he upon the sea
or among foreign men should lose his voyage home.
    The ship then, as bards who lived before make known,
Argus built with Athena's direction. But now I shall
relate the names and lineage of heroes, the paths
of the long salt sea, and all that in their wanderings
they did. May the Muses be inspiration for my song.

☛ **Callimachus** (b. *c.* 310-305 BC, d. *c.* 240 BC)

During the reign of Ptolemy II Philadelphus, King of Egypt (285-246 BC), Callimachus was commissioned to prepare a great catalogue of all the books in the Alexandrian Library. This was an enormous undertaking, to say the least, and when finished, Callimachus had compiled a list that required over 120 volumes to enumerate. He was an astonishingly prolific writer, having produced about 800 volumes of work, including numerous prose commentaries, though only a few of his poetical works have survived. [**INSERT TANSLATION OF CALLIMACHUS POEMS**]

Like many Hellenistic poets who combined poetry with scholarship, Callimachus' style was influenced by his work at Alexandria. Aristotle's contribution to an understanding of epic poetry has received the greatest press, but it was Callimachus who encouraged the writing of epic poetry that could encompass both the dramatic and the comic, the lyrical and the colloquial. His critical theories had a great impact on such Latin poets as Catullus, Virgil, Ovid, Lucan, and Statius, and through them on Dante, Shakespeare, and great epic novelists such as Tolstoy, Thomas Mann, and Thomas Pynchon, whose *Gravity's Rainbow* is an especially Callimachian epic.

Writing in the third century before Christ, Callimachus brought together the poetic possibilities in an age in which poetry tended toward the bombastic, and prose was becoming increasingly popular. According to Callimachus, great poetry did not have to confine itself to epic. While pointing out that Homer used colloquial passages to offset the more lofty tone of the epic hexameter, Callimachus also felt that the epic itself might be an obsolete form, and encouraged poets to write shorter, lyrical poems. Of all Greek epic poets, no one, with the single exception of Homer, enjoyed such posthumous fame as Callimachus.

Callimachus used Hesiod as a model, sanctioning a more personal tone. Instead of the lofty, often stilted poetic diction employed by Homer believed to be better suited to the epic, Callimachus called for a poetry that used direct speech and "unpoetic" turns of phrase. Furthermore, he urged poets to bring their personal lives to the work, or use the mask of persona to carry forth the poet's inner consciousness.

***[Callimachus section not finished, much more to come—a lot more; this cat was no slouch.]

Food for Thought

Hot Dogs and Cool Cats

It's a little known fact that Callimachus was a cat, but many poets of the late empire were cats. That fact had been surpressed in later history by the many Christian historians who rejected the pagan notion that animals as well as people could write poetry. The old Greek legend of the feline poeticai, or "the poetic cat," was a driving force in the creation of poetry in the Archaic Age. Of the great Latin poets, it is believed that Marcus Porcius Cato, Lucius Sergius Catilina, and Gaius Valerius Catullus were cats. Much of the epideictic poetry written during the 4th and 5th centuries BC was written by cats, and later imitated by the impressionable epheboi, those youths between the ages of 15 and 20 who attended the aphebia, the "colleges" that were founded following Athens' defeat by Macedon at Chaeronea in 338 BC. The ephebia gave these young men a compulsory and efficient poetic training, subject to the strict discipline by their trainers and teachers, many of whom were cats. In their characteristic dress of dark mantle and broad-brimmed hat they were during their existence a graceful feature of the Athenian scene. Eventually, the ephebia became a largely educational institution for the wealthy elite, and by the end of the second century it had been remodelled into a school especially devoted to philosophy and military tactics. Most of the cats were expelled or dismissed, and in the decades that followed, cats were no longer allowed to write poetry, and anyone writing like a cat was severely punished.

While cats were reduced to writing inscriptions on gravestones, dogs became increasingly popular as house pets, especially the small, white, long-haired Maltese dog: Publius' dog Issa was probably a Maltese dog. In time, dogs of the super rich were allowed to write, but their poetry was written more for the public festivals and sporting events. Their poetry showed no refinement whatsoever and was peppered by anamanapoetic sounds that resembled barks, growls, and yaps. Much was made of the myth of Icarus, in which his faithful dog Maera leads his daughter Erigone to his body. Some of the more famous dogs who wrote poetry were Laconian hunting dogs and Cretan hounds, also famous for their speed and tracking abilties. Umbrian and

Etruscan dogs also wrote poetry, but little of it has survived, except for a few words and phrases on tattered parchment, which many believed were shredded by the dogs themselves. Whether the shredding was done as a canine instinct or as a comment on the work itself is not known, but has been hotly debated by many historians and literary critics. Plutarch in his Life of Aratus tells how noisy little dogs belonging to a gardner proved a considerable hazard to Aratus in his attempt to write his history of Sicyon, either out of jealousy, or because the dogs believed that one should write as one talks, or barks, as the case may have been. Lucius Dokimasia was a famous hot dog of 5th century Parthia, as was Rebilus Caninius, the Roman senator and poet who achieved fame when Julius Caesar appointed him consul at noon on the last day of the year 45 BC for the remainder of the day (the consul of that year having died on his last day of office). This was the consulship in which, according to Cicero's joke, no one breakfasted and the consul never slept.

In time, all cats and dogs were forbidden to write poetry, though many continued to read it aloud in cafes and public fesitvals. During the Middle Ages, cats and dogs who wrote poetry were driven underground, and today, it is hard to tell whether the cat meowing on your front porch is yawning or reciting the 6th book of the Odyssey.

 Asklepiades of Samos (b. c. 320 BC, wrote during the 270s BC)

Also called Sicelidas, he was one of the earliest writers of the Greek literary epigram, and in particular of the love epigram, originating much of the tradtional imagery, including Cupid's arrow. He was a contemporary of Theocritus. Many of his poems survive in the Greek Anthology. He gave his name to the "asclepiad" metres, used earlier by Sappho and Alcaeus, because he revived them. Some of the earliest pick-up lines occur in poetry, as the opening of "Prudence" sets the type later used by Andrew Marvel and Pierre Ronsard in which the young maiden is encouraged to frolick in the hay because there's no sex in heaven or in hell. Or *carpe diem:* "Eat, drink, and be merry, for tomorrow we die."

Prudence

Save your maidenhead? What's the good?
My girl, down in Hades there are no lovers.
The pleasures of Kypris are for the living.
Once past Acheron, river of Death,
we shall lie as bones and dust.

Negress

Did my plunders me with her beauty.
When I look at her I am wax over fire.
If she's black, what of it? So are coals.
When kindled, they glow like blooming roses.

On a Man-Devouring Whore

Voracious Philainion bit me. The bite doesn't show
yet pain crawls in me, creeps to my very fingertips.
Love, I am drained, done in, dead! I fell half-dazed
on a viperous whore, and her embrace was death.

☛ **Moschos** (c. 150 BC)

Pastoral poet, to whom some half-dozen short pieces may be assigned.

Landlover

When wind dips calmly over the blue sea
my cowardly soul stirs. My love for land
becomes a craving for the vast salt waters.
but when the ocean bottom roars, and foam boils
spitting skyward on the wild crashing waves,
I gaze at the shore and its forests, and shun
the sea. Then I love black earth and shadowy
woods where even during a blasting gale
a pine tree sings. What a wretched life
the fisherman has — with his berth a home,
the sea his labor and fish his wandering prey!
I prefer to sleep under a leafy place
and hear the plashing of a bubbling spring
which soothes the sould and never
brings me pain.

☛ **Ariston** (lived in time to be included in Meleagros' anthology.)

We're not sure when he lives, except that it was within the time to be included in Meleagros' anthology.

A Poor Scholar's Warning

Mice, if you come for bread, go find another hole;
I live in a humble hut.
Go to some rich man's villa
where you can nibble on fat cheese and dried raisins
and make a feast out of scraps.

But if you come to sharpen your teeth on my books,
your supper will be a dull poison.

☛ **Meleagros** (c. 140-70 BC)

Of Gardara in Syria, he wrote short elegiac poems on love and death, about a hundred of which survive in the *Greek Anthology*. The word anthologia, literally "flower-gathering," has come to denote a collection of extracts from literary works, and particularly a collection of poems. Many such collections were made in Greece from the 4th century onwards, though all have been lost as separate entities. In 900 AD, Constantine Cephalas, an official of the Imperial Palace at Byzantium, published a collection of poems that he selected from three pincipal sources. The earliest source was the *Garland*, compiled by Meleagros in the early years of the first century BC. This anthology contains poems attributed to some fifty poets from Archilochus to Meleagros himself. The other two sources were anthologies compiled around 40 AD by Philip of Thessalonkika and in 560 AD by the Byzantine poet and scholar Agathias. All these various collections have perished as such, but two Byzantine compilations based on Cephalas' work became the basis for an anthology of sixteen books of epigrams, called the *Greek Anthology*. Two other well known anthologies are the *Palatine Anthology*, and the *Anthologia Latina*, which contains the famous *Pervigilium Veneris* which played an influential part in the development of medieval Latin poetry.

Meleagros' poems in the *Greek Anthology* are technically very accomplished and often moving, and his epigrams are mainly erotic, written in the florid and complex "Asian" style. His poem "Shining Foe" is also a precursor of the *alba*, or dawn song.

Shining Foe

O morning star, bright enemy of love,
how slowly you turn around the world
while Demos lies warm with another
           under his cloak.
but when my slender love lay on my chest,
how swiftly you came to stand above us,
drenching us with light that seemed to laugh
           at our loss.

Love's Wages

Heavy soul, now you bellow fire,
now recover your cool breathing.
But why cry? When you harbored Eros,
you knew he would rise against you.

So be resigned to fire and snow;
you sheltered him, and this is your pay.
you must suffer nor for being a fool,
as you sizzle in boiling honey.

The Wine Cup

The wine cup is happy. It rubbed against
warm Zenoophila's erotic mouth. O bliss!
I wish she would press her lips under my lips
and in one breathless gulp, drain down my soul.

Heliodora's Fingernail

Your fingernail, Heliodora, was grown by Eros
and sharpened by him. How else could
your mere scrtaching be a claw against my heart?

The Last Victory

I'm on the ground, cruel god, so bury your heel in my neck.
I feel, God knows! your ponderous weight
and arrows of fire. Yet you can't burn me any more.
Hurl your torches at my heart. All is ashes.

I, Meleagros

My nurse was the island of Tyros,
and Attic land of Syrian Gadara was
my birthplace. I was sired by Eukrates
—I, Meleagros, friend of the Muses
and first to waken to the Graces of
Menippos. A Syrian. What if I am?
Stranger, we all live in one country:
    the world.

Out of one Chaos were all men born.
in my old age I traced these letters
   on the slab before my grave,
knowing that old men are neighbors
   to death.
Passerby, wish me well, the talkative old man,
and you may also reach a loquacious old age.

☞ **Bion of Smyrna** (lived at end of 2nd century BC)

The last Greek pastoral poet known to us by name, though the pastorla element is not prominent in the seventeen fragments that have survived. He is generally linked with the pastoral poet Moschus. Virtually nothing is known of his life, except what we can glean from an anonymous poem called *Lament for Bion* written by a student of his, sometimes attributed to Moschus. According to tradtion he was poisoned by jealous rivals.

Lament for Bion

Nightengales mourning in the thickfoliage,
carry word to the Sicilian springs of Arethousa
that the cowherd Bion is dead.
And with him

song and Dorian poetry
have likewise perished.

He wrote in the literary Doric dialect. Since the Renaissance, he has been credited with the Lament for Adonis, perhaps intended for recitation at a festival. Besides the pastoral element, his poems are playfully erotic.

Hesperos

Evening Star, gold light of Aphrodite born in the foam,
Evening Star, holy diamond of the glassblue light,
you are dimmer than the moon, brighter than another star.
Hello, good friend!
                      i'm on my way to serenade
my shepherd love. Give me your rays in place of moonlight.
There was a new moon today, but quickly set.
I am no thief, no highwayman to plague a traveler at night.
A lover I am. And those in love must be helped.

Polyphemos

What will I do? I'll just go my way
across to that distant hill and down
again to the sandpits on teh shore.
And I'll sing quietly to myself
my prayer for Galateia, who doesn't care.
Yet till the shattering end of old age
I will never once abandon sweet hope.

In Greek myth, Adonis was a beautiful youth, son of Cinyras, King of Cyprus. There's a few versions, each basically explained as a vegetation myth, in which the god dies every year and is restored to life with the growth of new crops. The name could be oriental in origin, from the Semitic *Adon*, "Lord." His festival was marked by women mourning and lamenting his death, and by the setting on the house-tops of the "Gardens of Adonis," seedlings in shallow soil which withered as soon as they sprang up. One of the stories relate that Adonis, having been brought up by nymphs, was out hunting when Aphrodite met him abnd fell in love with him. He was killed by a wild boar, and from his blood sprang the rose, or from Aphrodite's tears the anemone.

Lament for Adonis

[it's a long poem, here's a part]

I weep for Adonis, "The lovely Adonis is dead."
"Dead the lovely Adonis," the Loves weep too.

No longer in crimson cover, Cypris, sleep.
Arise in dark robes, and beat your breasts

and say to all, "The lovely Adonis is dead."

I weep for Adonis. The Loves weep too.

The lovely Adonis lies in the hills, his thigh
struck with the tusk, white against white,
and Cypris grieves as he breathes his delicate last.
His black blood drips down his snowy flesh,
his eyes are numb beneath his brows, and the rose
flees from his lips. The kiss dies too. Cypris
will have it never again. The kiss of the dead
is enough, but Adonis knows not that she's kissed him dead.

I weep for Adonis. The Loves weep too.

Savage the wound that Adonis has in his thigh.
Cythereia bears a greater wound in her heart.   [Aphrodite, from the
His own hounds howl for that boy. The Oread   island Cythera]
nymphs bewail him too, and Aphrodite
unbraids her hair and through the oak woods
she wails, distraught, disheveled, unsandaled, and the wild
brambles tear and cull her sacred blood.
Shrilling through the long glens she goes,
calling her Assyrian lord, her child.
The black blood sprouted about his navel.
His chest was crimsoned from his thighs. His breasts,
white as snow before, were scarlet now.

Alas for Cythereia. The Loves wail too.

. . . .

Cease your grieving today, Cythereia, cease
beating your breasts. You must wail again,
weep again, come another year.

When we go from Greece to the Latin poets of Rome we see the same evolution of poetic forms, going from the Heroic to the vernacular of the contemporary world; In Greece we began with Homer—who wrote of gods and heroes in a highly polished form—and ended with a vernacular poetry of men and women at work in a contemporary setting. Now we go to the beginnings of literature and poetry in Rome with the Latin writers and poets of the Republic who prepared the way for the Empire's greatest poet, Virgil—who wrote of gods and heroes in a highly polished form. This so called "Golden Age" gave way to a "Silver Age," that ended with a vernacular poetry written in a contemporary idiom about men and women steering their way through the distractions of the city and the consolations of love.

map insert next two pages:

LATIN POETRY
The Period of the early Republic
(c. 500-287 BC)
The Period of the Classical Republic(287-133 BC)

Q. Fabius Pictor
Livius Andronicus
Cnaeus Naevius
Quintus Ennius
Plautus & Terence
Cato
Lucilius

The Late Roman Republic (133-30 BC)

Cicero
Lucretius
Catullus

THE EMPIRE 27 BC - 476 AD

The Augustan Age: The Golden Age of Poetry- 27 BC - 14 AD
Virgil
Horace
Sextus Propertius
Tibullus
Ovid

The Silver Age 54 AD - 138 AD

Lucan
Statius
Martial
Petronius
Persius
Juvenal

The Age of Iron and Rust 138-180
begins with reign of Hadrian in 138, ends with death of Marcus Aurelius,
who was Roman Emperor 161-180 AD
Hadrian
Apuleius
The poetae novelli
Marcus Aurelius
The Anthologia Latina (and it's most famous poem, the *Pervigilium Veneris*)

Poets of the Declining Empire, 3rd & 4th centuries
Nemesianus
Symmachus
Ausonius
Christian Poets:
Lactanius, Commodian, Juvencus, Claudian, Paulinus, Prudentius, Juvenus, Falconia Proba,
Dracontius, St. Hilary, St. Ambrose, St. Augustine,
Secular Poets:
Servasius, Avianus, Rutilius Namatianus, Sidonius Apolinaris
Cassiodorus, Boethius

ROME

Historical Overview

Ancient Rome stood on high ground overlooking the Tiber about 15 miles from the salt flats through which the river flowed to the sea. The Tibur was the peninsula's largest river (not counting the Po in northern Italy), and dominated its most substantial drainage area. Outlying swamps and small lakes were fed by the streams which ran down the slopes of the surrounding hills. Beyond the valleys lay a wide plain of woods and pasture, and from there one could see the Alban hills in the south, the Apennines that ran down central Italy to the east, and the empire of the Etruscans to the north. The only place for miles at which the Tibur could be crossed with ease was a bend in the river where an island lay like a stepping stone. Not only was this strategic junction the lowest of the Tibur's practical crossing places, but it was ideally situated so as to be close to the sea, yet far enough inland to provide advance warning of pirates. The lower part of the river led to rare salt-pan on its shore, while the upper part led into the central regions of the country. The crucial bridging point on the Tibur was situated along the principal north-south route that traveled through the western and more thickly populated flank of the peninsula, making this crossing point a vital commercial and communications link. It was above this bend in the river and along the hills that overlooked its southern bank that a small village became a city. No one could have predicted that this undistinguished settlement—merely one of several local centers gradually developing into cities during the 7th and 6th centuries BC—would evolve into a republic, and under the leadership of its ruling oligarchy, this republic would conquer the rest of Italy. Certainly, no one would have predicted that this republic would eventually become an empire that was to rule the entire Mediterranean world.

Italy's elongated peninsula, centrally positioned in the Mediterranean, had (second only to Greece) the most extensive coastline in Europe, linking the eastern and western reaches of the sea. Between hills and mountain ranges lay fertile plains promising agricultural benefits greater than any Mediterranean country had been able to produce. Whoever could organize the Italian peninsula and the island of Sicily into a common social, political and economic unit would certainly become a Mediterranean power. There were several early peoples other than the Romans who could have united Italy. From the middle of the second millennium BC, successive waves of Indo-European invaders, among them Celtic-speaking Gauls, crossed the Alps—despite their ruggedness, the Alps never presented an effective barrier against invasions. Many of these invading tribes settled in the Po Valley. The origin of the Etruscans is unknown, but like other Indo-European invaders, they penetrated the fertile valleys of central Italy sometime before the eighth century, later controlling much of the northern part of the peninsula, which possessed more iron than any other Mediterranean settlement. The Etruscans gave Rome writing (an alphabet they in turn had taken from the Greeks), public buildings (including the Temple of Jupiter on the Capitol) and a new political, social and military organization. It was the Etruscans who constructed the first major roads and bridges in central Italy, like the one that led north from the Etruscan city of Vulci, crossing the deep, narrow valley of the river Fiora on the Ponte della Badia. Their traditional symbols of power, the *fasces* (bundles of rods and axes, which have given their name to fascism) were also Etruscan in origin.

Where the Etruscans controlled the northern part of Italy, the southern coasts as far north as Naples, and the island of Sicily, were settled by Greek colonists. This fertile landscape was later called *Magna Graecia*, "Greater Greece." Sicily, the largest of all the Mediterranean islands, situated squarely at the crossroads of Europe and Africa, became part of *Magna Graecia* in the eighth century BC, and its largest city Syracuse, founded in 734 BC by Greek colonists from Corinth, soon grew to rival, and even surpass, Athens in splendor and power. It became the largest and wealthiest city-state in *Magna Graecia* and the bulwark of Greek civilization. Argigento, on Sicily's southern coast famous for its Valley of the Temples, was settled by the Greeks in 580 BC, and grew wealthy through trade with Carthage. The Greek poet Pindar called it "the most beautiful city built by mortal men." Along with the Temple of Hercules, the oldest temple built during the fifth century BC, is the Temple of Jupiter, considered the eighth wonder of the world. Until the fifth century BC, or even later, Etruscans and Greek colonists were more powerful and influential than the Latins living around Rome.

There were the Samnites, as tribe from the central highlands, who could have dominated the peninsula. Some believe that if the Samnites had conquered the whole of Italy, the resulting city-state would have been a federation of peoples instead of a dominion of Romans. But the future of Italy lay not with the Etruscans, the Samnites, the Greeks; it belonged to the Latin shepherds who came to live on the hills and valleys near a ford in the river Tibur. Sometime during the eighth century they gradually merged their villages, elected a king, built a wall around their "city," and called it Rome. Much of what we know about early Rome comes from the findings of archeology, and the traditional histories written by Livy and others centuries later. Little survives in literary or historical records of the people of the central highlands, the most prominent group being the Samnites. There are no surviving Etruscan, Samnite, Campanian, or Mamertine histories of Italy. The Celtic Gauls of the Po Valley were eventually exterminated. What we have, therefore, is a Romanocentric version of the history of the Roman Republic. But many of the cities of Italy had to choose between the overlordship of barbarian tribes and the rule of Rome. One reason the governing classes of those cities chose Rome had the power to protect them against their own lower orders—an arrangement Rome used to its advantage when acquiring future allies.

Like the Greeks and Israelites before them, the Romans turned to the stuff of legend when it came time to mythologize their history. Legend held that the Romans traced their ancestry back to Aeneas, the hero who escaped from the sack of Troy carrying his father Anchises on his back. Like Odyseus, Aeneas wanderered about the Mediterranean until he came to Carthage, where he met and fell in love with Dido before foresaking her and traveling northward to Latium where he founded the city of Alba Longa. It was from the kings of Alba Longa that Romulus and Remus, the founders of Rome, were directly descended.

Obviously, this is the stuff of invention. Archeological remains indicate that Troy was invaded in the 12th or 13th century BC, but Carthage was not founded until around the 8th or 9th. And It's highly improbable that those who fled the destruction of Troy would have gone as far as central Italy to find refuge. But there may be a kernal of truth in the myth of the founding of the city by Romulus and Remus, the twin children of the god Mars and Rhea Silvia, a Vestal Virgin (Vestal Virgins were priestesses who served Vesta, goddess of the hearth). The children were left to die in a bucket by the waters of the flooded Tibur, but somehow washed ashore where they were suckled by a she-wolf; later, they were rescued and raised by a local herdsman. Upon reaching manhood, the brothers overthrew the wicked king who had tried to kill them and founded a new settlement on the hills above the river where they had washed ashore. 753 BC is the generally accepted date for the founding of that settlement. The early Romans, borrowing from the Etruscans, incorporated divination into their religious practices to determine public or private decisions. To decide on who should be king, each brother ascended a hill and waited for the right omen. Six vultures circled above the hill where Remus stood, but Romulus counted twelve above the hill on which he was standing. The sign was interpreted that Romulus should rule as king. As the story goes, those who supported Remus took up arms, but when Remus scaled the walls that Romulus had built, he was killed. Romulus was now the undisputed king. To expand the city, he encouraged runaway slaves and even criminals to settle there. To secure wives for his men, he invited the neighboring Sabines to a feast while watching Rome's celebratory games, and during the festivities, the men carried off the Sabine women (c.f. "The Rape of the Sabines"). According to legend, Romulus disappeared from the earth enveloped in a cloud during a thunderstorm while reviewing his troops on the ground that lay beyond Rome's walls; today this ground is known as the *Campus Martius* (the Field of Mars). Some say Romulus was murdered by jealous senators who concealed his body. Others claimed that the gods had called him back from whence he came; eventually, Romulus was proclaimed divine.

Food for Thought

Seven Hills, Two Brothers, and a Wolf

In the territory of Latium, originally inhabited by a people called the Latini, Indo-European invaders fused their culture with that of the local natives. In the mid-eighth century BC, the settlement on the banks of the Tibur expanded to include its seven hills, and by the end of the seventh century the settlement became the city of Rome. The story of Romulus and Remus may have evolved from the fact that sometime during the 8th century, two existing settlements, one on the level summit of the Palatine Hill, the other on the Quirnal, coalesced to form a single village. It was on the Palatine Hill, a well-protected area overlooking the marshy valley below, that Evander (Book 8 of the *Aeneid*) showed Aeneas the cave of the Lupercal in which Romulus and Remus were supposed to have been suckled by a wolf.

"These woodland places
Once were homes of local fauns and nymphs

Together with a race of men that came
From tree trunks, from hard oak: they had no way
Of settled life, no arts of life, no skill
At yoking oxen, gathering provisions,
Practicing husbandry, but got their food
From oaken boughs and wild game hunted down.
In that first time, out of Olympian heaven,
Saturn came here in flight from Jove in arms,
An exile from a kingdom lost; he brought
these unschooled men together from the hills
Where they were scattered, gave them laws, and chose
The name of Latium, from his latency
Or safe concealment in this countryside.
In his reign were the golden centuries
Men tell of still, so peacefully he ruled,
Till gradually a meaner, tarnished age
Came on with fever of war and lust of gain."

. . . .

Then he showed the wood
That Romulus would make a place of refuge,
Then the grotto called the Lupercal
Under the cold crag, named in Arcadian fashion
After Lycaean Pan.

The Palatine was the chief of the seven hills of Rome (the other six are the Aventine, Caitoline, Caelian, Esquiline, Viminal, and Quirinal—in Latin the first five are termed *montës*, ("peaks" or "mountains,") and the last two *collës*, or "hills") . In later times, many famous Romans chose to build their houses on the Palatine hill, including the great orators Hortensius and Cicero, and Crassus of the "First Triumvirate" and Mark Antony of the "Second Triumvirate." The house of Hortensius was acquired by the emperor Augustus and became the nucleus of a group of buildings known as *palatia*, from which the English word "palace" is derived.

The festival of the *Lupercalia* was held every year on February 15. The *Lupercalia* was originally held in December, a shepherd-festival that honored Faunus, also worshipped under the name Lupercus (who had the power to drive away wolves, *lupi*, from the flocks). In Roman myth, Faunus was a pastoral god, the father of Latinus, king of the Latini, and as such was seen as a promoter of agriculture. Faunus also had the title Fatuus, "the speaker," and was regarded as an oracular god who revealed the future through dreams or supernatural voices. Because of the ghost-like appearances and terrifying sounds Faunus was believed to make in wooded places, he was often depicted as a monster with the legs and horn of a goat . Thus, he was often associated with the Arcadian god Pan.   The primary purpose of the festival of the Lupercalia was to secure fertility for fields, flocks, and people. Worshippers gathered at the mouth of the cave and two youths were smeared with sacrificial goats' blood. Then the *luperci* wrapped their naked bodies in goatskins and ran through the streets of the city striking people with thongs cut from the goatskin. The thongs were called *februa*, the "means of purification." Women especially stood in the way of the blows in order to be rendered fertile. Many of the city's magistrates took part in the festival, since the act of running was itself seen as a symbolic purification of the land. Mark Antony ran as one of the consuls of 44 BC and in his course mounted the Rostra and offered Julius Caesar a crown made of laurel leaves, which Caesar thrice refused (hence, refusing the title of king). The ceremony survived into Christian times, and was finally eradicated in 494 AD.

Further confirmation of Rome's founding in the 8th century comes from archeological discoveries on the Palatine, including oval hut foundations, and "hut-urns" used for cremations and ordinary burials in the Forum valley and on the Esquiline Hill. Some of the burial huts date back as far as the 10th century BC.

Other villagers settled atop the Esquiline on the eastern side of the city. The settlements on the Palatine and Esquiline hills eventually joined together for religious and political purposes and called themselves the Septimontium, or the Seven Mounts. Between 625 and 575 BC, a common area in the lower valley was drained and paved, becoming the central market and meeting place later called the Forum. Other hilltop settlements joined the Septimontium, including a Sabine community on the Quirinal and Viminal peaks, with the Capitoline Hill designated as the common acropolis and citidel, and the Aventine peak as a religious center.

The Early Republic

Among those who ruled Rome for the next few centuries were several Etruscan kings called the Tarquins, the first of whom was the grandson of an exile from Corinth who adopted the name of Lucius Tarquinius Priscus and began his rule around 610 BC. The Etruscans came to Italy from the Balkans and settled in the Po Valley and along the western coast in what was to become Tuscany. They were experts in metalwork and pottery, an energetic people who carried on trade with the Greek cities of southern Italy. Rome, which lay between the Etruscans in the north and the Greek cities to the south, was the nearest place to the sea at which the river Tibur could be crossed. Once the Etruscans were established in Rome, they influenced farming and trade, religious practices and fashion. When Lucius Tarquinius was murdered around 579 BC, a Latin king Servius Tullius assumed power and organized Roman society according to a fixed scale of rank, dividing the various classes according to their wealth. Servius helped develop for the Roman army the same military reforms that were being used in Greece. Influenced by Assyrian tactics and the innovations of central European metalworkers, Greece had developed a new kind of army manned by soldiers rich enough to afford heavy infantry equipment—round shield, body armor, and thrusting spear. Soldiers fought in a closely knit line or phalanx, calling themselves hoplites (from *hopla*, "arms"). The army was dominated by property owners so that it served to strengthen the monarchy, which they supported. Servius did the same for Roman. He was responsible for enlarging the reservoir of recruits who would someday, as Roman legions, conquer the world.

He also built a rampart around the northern part of the city, not to be confused with the erroneously named 4th century "Wall of Servius Tullius," which enclosed the entire city, making it a great hill-top fortress with the Capitoline hill equivalent to the Acropolis at Athens. There were numerous wars during this early regal period in which neighboring tribes were brought under Roman control. After capturing the town of Alba Longa on the slopes of the Alban Mount, Rome emerged as the leading power of north-western Latium, and many of the leading families of Alba Longa took up residence in Rome, thus aligning themselves with the Roman aristocracy. A temple to Diana ("the bright one"—Diou-piter, or Jupiter) was built upon the Aventine, thereafter, the Aventine became associated with the worship of Jupiter. On the Capitoline a shrine depicting Jupiter, Juno, and Minerva (called the "Capitoline Triad") was erected to correspond to the Greek deities Zeus, Hera, and Athena. Thus the Romans moved toward a conception of deity that was similar to the religious aspects of Hellenism.

When Servius distributed land captured in these wars to ordinary citizens, the Senators once again talked of overthrowing their king. This time they enlisted the support of the son of the murdered Lucius Tarquinius, and had Servius killed. Tarquin was encouraged by his wicked and ambitious wife, Tullia. She drove over Servius's corpse in her carriage, spattering her dress with his blood, and proclaimed her husband the new king. He was to be the last Etruscan king, *Tarquinius Superbus* (Tarquin the Proud), who was himself overthrown in 510 BC. (This date comes from Greek historians who may not have been able to resist making it the same date that the last tyrant of Athens was expelled from their own city.) The enterprising Etruscans last just long enough to bring writing and civilization to continental Europe. Virgil was descended from Etruscan forebears who had founded Mantua. After the Etruscans were driven out by the combined forces of the lower class and the disaffected aristocracy, monarchy was abolished and the Republican period of Roman history began. Judging from its later constitution, it was an aristocratic republic where the power of *imperium* formerly held by the king was transferred to two annually elected magistrates called consuls. Thus began an ingenious system of checks and balances. The consuls shared equal authority, but one could veto the decisions of the other. The senate reserved the right to appoint a dictator in times of crisis, who would serve until the crisis was over.

Times were not good following the expulsion of the Etruscan kings. Without the power of the monarchy, Rome was beset by Italian tribes striving to take advantage of the city's weakened position. Agriculture and trade suffered and plagues decimated the poor, who grew increasingly restive, seeing they had as little say in the Republic as they had under the monarchy. Senatorial representatives of the wealthy patricians helped oppress the plebians, many of whom suffered poverty and unemployment, while some were enslaved for debts. In 494 BC, a body of debt-laden plebians led a revolt by marching to the top of the Aventine, which had become a meeting place for those espousing democratic ideas. They organized a boycott and demanded that the government enact a law creating *tribuni plebis*, tribunal functionaries, to represent their interests. They refused to leave until they had been granted concessions and all laws were written down.

Many of their demands were met, but the first major step in the plebian drive for legal equality occured in 451 BC when Appius Claudius was appointed to head a board of ten magistrates called the *decemviri*, the Commission of Ten, and they drew up a new set of laws called the Twelve Tables, the first landmark in the history of Roman law. The rights and duties of Roman citizens were clearly defined in terse, gnomic sentences that, among other things, limited the amount of land any one person could own, and provided for the election of consuls and tribunes, a minimum number having to come from the plebian class. Enslavement for debt was still authorized, but the creditor now had to feed the debtor at least "one pound of grits a day." Plebs were allowed to marry foreigners, but not patricians, though eventually marriages between plebs and foreigners were legalized. Even robbery was classified according to whether or not the robber carried a weapon or used his bare hands. Though the Tables gave the citizens of Rome extensive rights and liberties, it did not alleviate the debt problem, nor did it bring the plebians any closer to sharing authority with the Senate, whose rich members still held the power to govern the city. These men became Consuls (high magistrates), Quaestors (financial administrators), Censors (tax collecting and military supervision), Praetors (judges), Pontiffs (high priests) Augurs (interpreters of the rules of divination), and the Aediles (overseers of streets, markets, games and festivals). From their ranks also came the Dictators when civil unrest or enemy invasion threatened the civil peace. It was assumed that dictators would serve for only six months, or until the emergency was over, whichever came first.

A measure of democratic rule was achieved, but the oligarchic system remained in place; tribunes, while supposedly representing the lower orders, acted more as agents of the Senate than as representatives of the people. Their efforts to pass laws that would lessen the debt or grant the plebs a fair share of public land were not prompted by a desire to transform the state into a socialist system, but to alleviate just enough of the stress to keep the ruling oligarchy in power. Radical reformers like the Gracchi brothers, and military leaders like Caesar may have claimed to represent the wishes of the people, but in actuality, they stood for one oligarchic faction over another.

Over the course of the next century, numerous Italian tribes went to war against Rome, but one by one they fell to Rome's military power. Each defeated town signed a bi-lateral treaty with Rome until the balance of power tilted in Rome's favor. Rome also began a policy of colonizing towns for the expressed purpose of setting up defensive bases against invading tribes from the north and hostile tribes from the unfertile hills, valleys, and glens of the Apennines. The Etruscans were finally subdued in 396 BC when Veii, its principal city, fell to a Roman force under the command of Marcus Furius Camillus, who may be said to be Rome's first, true historical figure. Veii was only twelve miles from Rome, and both cities competed for markets and available coastal salt. With her capture, Rome's territory doubled in size, and the other Etruscan cities fell in due time.

All Roads Lead to Rome: The Middle Republic

For nearly 360 years Rome's armies were undeafeated, but in 387 Italy was invaded by Celtic-speaking Gauls looking for land and plunder. They sacked Rome, destroying both the city and its records, though written records would not have been plentiful since literacy was uncommon until late in the 3rd century. Celtic peoples had spread out from central Europe reaching as far as Spain and Britain, and by the fifth century, had crossed the Alps and displaced the Etruscans from most of northern Italy, which thereafter was known as Cisalpine Gaul,or "Gaul this side of the Alps." The Gauls who spread into the Po Valley were a barbaric people, whose military organization included an innovation in ancient warfare—cavalry with iron horseshoes. Just eleven miles from the city of Rome, a force of 30,000 immigrants seeking land and plunder were met by a Roman force of 15,000, the largest army Rome had ever put into the field. The Roman army was crushed, its men slaughtered on the banks of the Tiber, or thrown into the Tiber and drowned, "overweighted by their armor," wrote the historian Livy. Some Romans escaped to the nearby town of Veii. Most of the patricians, some soldiers, the vestal virgins, and sacred religious objects were safely ensconced in the impregnable citadel on the Capitoline Hill, while the old men and the plebians were left to die in the city below. The Gauls entered a city that was virtually deserted. The old patricians left behind stood at attention in front of their homes, dressed in their best robes, as if receiving honored guests. The Gauls were perplexed at first. One walked up to Marcus Papirius, leaned in to look him closely in the face, and was promptly smacked by the old man on the head with an ivory scepter. The Gauls killed Papirius, then proceeded to plunder the city, slaughtering anyone unable to escape. The citadel held, but the city was burned. Today, you can still see a layer of burned debris, broken roof tiles, and carbonized wood and clay at the edge of the Forum. The Romans never forgot this devastation. It would be another 800 years before Rome would fall again to barbarian conquerors.

Out of their defeat a useful policy emerged. Rome rewarded Etruscan cities that came to her aid by granting them the *hospitium publicum,* which gave them the same rights enjoyed by Roman citizens, including tax privileges and legal equality. Rome used this unique formula again and again with other cities it deemed worthy. And shortly after the Gallic invasion, the Romans built the defensive rampart around the city that came to bear the erroneous, anachronistic name of the "Wall of Servius Tullius." Rome was now the largest city in Italy.

The two centuries of fighting were characterized by two main struggles: an internal class struggle between the ruling class of patricians who had inherited their land, and the plebians, the mass of peasants, workers, and traders who were not allowed to hold office. The second was external, Rome's struggle with surrounding warring tribes. But one by one, Rome conquered, assimilated, or gained as allies the Latin towns south of the Tiber. Rome's success in its three wars with the Samnites, warlike peasants and herdsmen who lived in unwalled villages throughout the landlocked valleys and gray limestone uplands of the Apennines, decided the fate of peninsular Italy. The Samnites possessed twice as much land and population as Rome. Rome lost a major battle in The Second Samnite War, but the Romans began construction of the Appian Way, 132 miles of paved road from Rome to Capua that gave them a great military and political advantage, and by 304 BC, they were victorious. During the succeeding decades, they constructed their famous roads which led from Rome directly to many dependent areas and permitted Roman armies to march speedily to the aid of any embattled local garrison. During the Third Samnite War (298-290), Roman armies penetrated into Samnite territory and ravaged it from one end to the other. In the process, Roman legions became more flexible and mobile than the Greek phalanx had been. It was a new kind of fighting machine, subdivided into smaller units that could maneuver and fight separately on its own, whatever the terrain, that became the key to Rome's ability to overpower any kind of military opposition. Beside the usual weapons, the legions carried a six-foot-long throwing javelin instead of the shorter thrusting spear.

Rome continued to progress toward a democratic republic. Plebs were eventually given the right to become consuls and priests, and in 287 BC, a law was passed allowing the tribunes, then ten in number, to attend Senate meetings and awarded the popular assembly the power to pass on all legislation proposed by the Senate. The senatorial class still retained firm control over the machinery of government, but this measure of internal political stability ensured Rome's ability to control the rest of the peninsula, then expand her influence to become a Mediterranean power. Once the Samnites of the central highlands and the Etruscans of the north were subdued, Rome turned its attention to the Greek cities of the southern coasts, *Magna Graecia*.

The Imperial Republic:
Rome Becomes a Mediterranean Power

The War against Tarentum (280-272 BC) was the first to bring Rome into conflict with a foreign power. The most important of those Greek cities on Italy's southern coast was Taras, the Roman Tarentum, now Taranto on the gulf of that name. Possessing an almost impregnable citadel and the safest and most spacious port on any Italian coast, they could also boast the largest fleet in Italy. After a dispute with Rome, the Tarentines sank the Roman fleet, killed its admiral, and jeered at the bad Greek spoken by Rome's envoys. Tarentum was soon joined by Epirus, another Greek colony just across the Adriatic led by King Pyrrus, who set sail for the south of Italy with a fleet carrying 25,000 mercenaries and twenty Indian war-elephants. Phyrrus won several victories, but the loss of men was so great that henceforth victories which did more damage to the victor than to the vanquished became known as "Pyrrhic." Eventually, King Pyrrus lost over two-thirds of his fighting force and retreated back to Argos in Greece, where two years later he was killed by a tile thrown accidentally by a woman from her rooftop.

It was clear that *Magna Graecia* could not stand up to the might of Rome's fighting legions. In the first war fought against a Greek army, Rome emerged victorious, and Tarentum accepted the alliance proposed to them. By 268 BC Rome controlled the entire peninsula south of the Po Valley and the northwestern Apennines, and had united its territories by a network of colonies.

Rome's early history was distinguished by two important characteristics—its willingness to grant citizenship to aliens—and thus easy access to its food supply—and its ability to bring other cities under its fold. Rome's ability to overpower the Hellenistic kingdoms to the south and east was due mainly to its superior manpower, but the granting of citizenship to all those it conquered gave Rome a political stability which carried it from the fifth century to the first without a revolution. It was a bit like a pyramid scheme. Once conquered by Rome, new citizens shared in the profits from the next victory over another city. Even slaves could become enfranchised and their children would reap the benefits of citizenship. Finally, Rome's oligarchy intermarried with the aristocrats of those they defeated, making the local ruling clans dependent on the Roman oligarchy for support. By the 3rd century BC, the city had become overcrowded and tenement houses were built, of which letter writers bitterly complained. Market places, temples, aqueducts, and buildings of every kind continued to be built in the centuries to come—Sulla, Pompey, and Julius Caesar all had their grandiose schemes.

The rise of Rome was due to its fertile soil, its position in the middle of Italy, and the fact that it possessed the most professional army in the world. By 266 BC, Rome was Italy's leading power, controlling a confederacy embracing all of Italy. Within two years, it was to begin its conquest of the rest of the Mediterranean world.

It is in this period of the early republic that we come across the works of the archaic Roman poets Livius **Andronicus**, Gnaeus **Naevius**, and Quintus **Ennius**, poets with whom we associate the birth of Latin literature. Though they mainly produced translations of Greek texts, their translations or adaptations were innovative, becoming the cornerstone of a new national poetry. They traced their influence more to the sophisticated refinements of Greek literature and Hellenic culture than to the impulses of their own primitive folklore. When the modern poets of the empire rejected the artificial constraints of the archaic Roman poets who imitated the lessons of Hellenism, they embraced instead the true Greek ancients, those distant poets who created a literature out of the dynamic speech of their time—Homer, Hesiod, Alcaeus, Archilochus, and Sappho, to name a few.

The Greeks had Homer to define their literary tradition. Like the early American poets who looked to the great English poets Chaucer, Shakespeare, and Milton as their models, the archaic Roman poets also had to constructed their literary beginnings from secondary texts, those translations of Greek and Hellenistic drama and poetry.

The earliest writing, of course, can be found in daily communications: inscriptions on wine cups and religious messages carved on gravestones. The earliest Romans wrote and spoke in Greek, Oscan, and Etruscan, with many Latin inscriptions written using the Greek alphabet. The famous Sibylline books supposedly composed during the time of Tarquin the Proud were written in Greek. But gradually, as is to be expected, the Latin alphabet emerged and was used not only for daily communication, but for literature as well. With the advant of the Roman Republic, literacy was common among both the middle and upper classes.

We've seen how Homeric poetry emerged from a tradition of epic songs performed by wandering bards. The same was true for the Romans poetry, though even in their earliest songs, a Greek influence was at work. As far back as the 6th century, Rome was a crossroads for trade and commerce. It was only natural for its poets to imitate Greek literary models, sometimes exaggerating the form or style to an overwrought degree. Ennius looked down upon his "primitive" predecessors, who spoke and wrote in an unrefined way, and championed poetic techniques derived from Hellenistic works. This tension between poetry that springs from the dynamics of natural speech and a poetry that mimics well-constructed literary forms has continued to this day. Some writers, like Naevius, who was brought up on Greek culture, made an effort to combine the most effective elements of both cultures.

We cannot fully understand the tensions that existed between those who wrote in an ornate, highly refined style and those who wrote in a simpler diction if we fail to account for the fact that writing itself was often set in opposition to speaking—the art of oratory—and the orator was accorded higher status than the writer. (Similar in our own time, where the screenwriter, whose written work is not meant to be read but heard, is often paid more than the writer of books).

Oratory

Before Roman culture came under the influence of Hellenic Greece after the war against Tarentum (280-272 BC), writing took second place to oratory. Oratorical ability was considered the key to success and power. We have only to look at Shakespeare's version of the speech Marc Antony made to rouse the masses against Brutus to see how effective powerful oratory can be (especially when a Shakespeare speaks through the mouth of Antony via Plutarch). Antony addresses a crowd clearly on the side of Brutus. He begins by assuring them that he intends no kind words for Caesar.

> Friends, Romans, countrymen, lend me your ears;
> I come to bury Caesar, not to praise him.
> The evil that men do lives after them,
> The good is oft interred with their bones;
> So let it be with Caesar.

By the time he's done, he's praised Caesar, shown them Caesar's bloody mantle, gained the sympathy of the crowd, and incited them to mutiny.

> *Antony.* Mark how the blood of Caesar follow'd it,
> As rushing out of doors, to be resolv'd
> If Brutus so unkindly knock'd or no;
> For Brutus, as you know, was Caesar's angel:
> Judge, O you gods, how dearly Caesar lov'd him.
> This was the most unkindest cut of all;
> For when the noble Caesar saw him stab,
> Ingratitude, more strong than traitors' arms,
> Quite vanquish'd him: then burst his mighty heart;
> And, in his mantle muffling up his face,
> Even at the base of Pompey's statue,
> Which all the while ran blood, great Caesar fell.
> O, what a fall was there, my countrymen!

Then I, and you, and all of us fell down,
Whilst bloody treason flourish's over us.
O now you weep, and I perceive you feel
The dint of pity; these are gracious drops.
Kind souls, what, weep you when you but behold
Our Caesar's vesture wounded? Look you here,
Here is himself, marr'd, as you see, with traitors.

    First Ple. O piteous spectacle!
    Second Ple. O noble Caesar!
    Third Ple. O woeful day!
    Fourth Ple. O traitors! Villains!
    First Ple. O most bloody sight!
    Second Ple. We will be revenged.
    [*All.*] Revenge! — About! — Seek! — Burn!
Fire! — Kill! — Slay! Let not a traitor live!
    Antony. . . . But were I Brutus,
And Brutus Antony, there were an Antony
Would ruffle up your spirits, and put a tongue
In every wound of Caesar, that should move
The stones of Rome to rise and mutiny.
    [*All.*] We'll mutiny.
    First Ple. We'll burn the house of Brutus.

Though Shakespeare was writing centuries after Caeser's death, we must assume that many a speech such as Antony's changed the course of an event and shifted power from one man to another. Thus, it is not surprising that when we study Latin literature, the first name we come across is a semi-legendary figure regarded as the founder of oratory.

☛ Appius Claudius Caecus (*c.* 355-275 BC)

The sons of nobility were regularly schooled in rhetoric and oratory, whereas poets like Accius and Lucilius were either freedmen or non-Roman Italians of the lower class. It was not teachers of poetry, but *rhetores*, Greek-trained "professors of eloquence," who were hired to teach their children to be first-class *oratores*. According to Cicero, Appius was the author of a collection of apothegms inspired by the philosophy of Pythagoras. Only a few lines attributed to him have come down to us.

> *Est unusquisque faber ipsae suae fortunae.*
> Every man is the artisan of his own fortune.

> *Tue animi compote es, ne quid fraudis stuprique ferocia pariat.*
> Be master of your soul, or your untamed nature will bring forth deceit
>   or disgrace.

Appius used his oratorical skills to attain office. Favoring the plebians, he became censor in 312 BC, consul in 307 BC, and finally dictator a few years later. He promoted numerous public works, and is best known today as the builder of the first aqueduct, named the *Aqua Claudia*, and the first great roads which linked Rome to Brundisium, the most important of which was named the *Via Appia,* or the Appian Way. In 200 BC, old and infirm, he was carried in a litter to the senate and spoke eloquently to persuade the Senate to reject Pyrrhus's peace proposals, enunciating the principle that Rome must never negotiate with an invader. His forceful oration was the first speech ever published in Rome. In that sense we may say he was a forerunner of the great orator Marcus Porcius Cato, "The Elder" or "the Censor" (234-149 BC), who is said to have found the poet Ennius in Sardinia and brought him to Rome.

Carmina

Though we can't call Appius a poet in the literal sense, the publication of his speeches contributed to the formation of a literary Latin. Afterall, a speech designed for a practical purpose, to move or rouse or persuade an audience, would naturally use alliteration, parallelism, similie, metaphor, and other formal devices. Even religious sayings and common prayers used formal devices to aid memory. The Romans used the word *carmen* (from *cano,* "to sing," "to sound") to mean poem, since a poem was often sung or declaimed. Yet a poet like Ennius wanted the reader to see his writing as text, not as a vehicle for oratory, and so he used the Greek word, *poema.*

During this time when the so-called archaic poets were writing, the difference between poetry and prose had a different connotation than it has today. The highest prose was used for oratory. Appius is not only considered the founder of oratory, but the father of prose as well. A good speech was highly stylized, it had a rhythmic texture, vivid repetitions, verbal parallelisms, and an emphasis on strong tonal dynamics, the kind of writing we normally associate with poetry. Archaic poetry, on the other hand, did not have a strong metrical structure, and unless the poet was clearly imitating Hellenistic formalities, was looser in its syntax and resembled everyday speech. A highly polished and metrically rigorous passage would be considered prose; a text that was loose and bantering might be called poetry.

This explains why Roman poets were so fond of the saturnian meter. Both Livius Andronicus's translation of the *Odyssey* and Naevius's *Bellum Poenicum* on the First Punic War are composed in Saturnian verse, perhaps the only classical meter not borrowed from the Greek. (It was so named to suggest its origin in a remote past, such as the Golden Age, when Saturn was king of the gods.) The Saturnian was ideal for the *carmina*, mostly because it was unpredictable and could be used for a wide range of effects, be they poetic or prosaic, oratorical or plain speaking. Thus the tradition of the *carmina* remained influential in all subsequent Latin poetry, allowing for a diction that could be both refined and informal, bridging the styles common to both prose and poetry. It was deeply ingrained in the Roman and other Italic peoples, so that when Catullus and Virgil echo this oldest literary style, it is not the Greek of the *Odyssey* and the *Illiad* we are hearing, but everyday speech, the rustic proverbs of the common people. Perhaps that's what Robinson Jeffers meant when he wrote in "Hellenistics,"

> Whatever it is catches my heart in its hands, whatever it is makes
> me shudder with love

And painful joy and the tears prickle . . . The Greeks were not its inventors.

Sacral Poetry

The first *carmina* were religious songs performed during the annual public rituals in which divine powers were invoked. They may have been sung while moving to a triple beat, chants that asked for aid and comfort, the triple rhythm similar to the repetition of magic words and incantations. The poet/songwriter worked in a folk tradition, with no concern for Greek formalities.

Popular Poetry

Before the written word, there was an oral tradition that probably included work songs, love songs, drinking songs and lullabies, maybe even parodies sung at weddings and other occasions. In the first three centuries of the Roman Republic, literate Romans read religious hymns and chants, crude cult songs, work songs and lullabies, and the popular lays (short narrative or lyric poems) of Rome's historic or legendary past. As the written forms of Latin in the Middle Ages resisted change, the language of literature diverged more and more from the speech of the people. The melodious Romance languages—Italian, Spanish, Portuguese, French, and Romanian—evolved from the crude popular Latin brought to the provinces by soldiers, merchants, and adventurers. This pattern is repeated throughout the history of literature as writers and poets in every age perceive the difference between the stultified literary language of aristocratic and academic formalists and common speech.

In every age there are poets who make a break with the past. They infuse their work with the melody of the spoken language, while preserving in some measure the nobility and character of the literary style. In their own time, they are called Moderns. *Corruptio pessimi optima*—the best comes from the worst.

Heroic Poetry

Epic poetry assumes a vast oral tradition of heroic songs and ballads. The same must have applied to the poetry of Rome, but there's no evidence in Latin literature for the kind of oral tradition that presaged Homer's epics . Cicero and Varro cite Cato, who referred to *carmina convivalia*, bardic tales of ancient deeds; Cato, however, does not claim to have heard these tales first hand. Later Latin writers may have wanted to believe they had an oral tradition as a way of making up for the fact that they had no Homer, but there's no trace of the singers and wandering Homeric-type bards in Roman literature. Latin poetry may have skipped a Homeric phase altogether and gone directly to its own Hellenistic age, mimicking the literary culture of Greece after the defeat of Tarentum. One would have heard poems influenced by the Hellenism in the literary circles of the aristocracy where poets and writers found their patrons. It was in the shadow of these great families that professional writers appeared, but from Andronicus onwards, they used literary forms modeled on the Greek counterparts of their time. Such poets were socially useful, writing in a proper style, distinguished in syntax and tone—a careful poetry modeled on their Greek contemporaries, just as early American poets copied the Elizabethan tones of their

British predecessors. The poetry of Andronicus, Naevius, and Ennius gave shape and stature to Roman literature at its beginning, and established a form of excellence against which later poets of the Republic would contend. This anxiety of influence is a common theme throughout the history of poetry. For instance, poets such as William Cullen Bryant, John Greenleaf Whittier, Oliver Wendell Holmes, and the other writers of the New England Renaissance represented a Victorian style that poets like Whitman and Emily Dickenson not only had to contend with, but overthrow, becoming influences themselves on the modern poets of the 20th century. [I'd make this idea a **food for thought**, but that's basically what this book is about—that, and the persistence of the modern, whatever the era.]

Nevertheless, categories are not always so neat. It's convenient to claim that writers of any era went from formal verse to spoken diction, or vice-versa; when seen from a distance this may be the case, but often the two impulses exist side by side, zig-zagging their way from one generation to the next until a new paradigm appears to emerge (the basic premise of Thomas Kuhn's *The Structure of Scientific Revolutions* may also apply to the structure of artistic revolutions). From its very beginnings, Roman literature showed both strains, a schooled, Hellenizing metric (borrowed from Greek epic poetry, as in the work of Ennius) and a more naturally cadenced verse used by the comic poets and dramatists (Plautus, Caeculius Statius, and Terrence). Just as Homer seemed to come out of the blue, Latin poetry seems to have jumped from an oral, regional tradition to the creation of a national literature by Andronicus, Naevius, and carried on by Ennius. What is undeniable is the absence of a counterpart to Homer in Roman literature; his masterpiece seemed to emerge full blown from the head of Zeus. What we see in Latin literature is a step-by-step evolution over the course of several centuries toward a great national epic—Virgil's *Aeneid*. Naevius was the first poet to incorporate into his epics subjects and characters that were drawn from Roman history. When he wrote the *Bellum Punicum*, parts of which dealt with the founding of Rome by Romulus, Naevius included descriptions of the departure of Aeneas from Troy, setting up the story of the founding of Rome linked to the stories in Homer's epics. It is fitting therefore that the first great work of Latin literature is a translation of Homer's *Odyssey*.

ııı➡

Food for Thought

The tendency for poets and writers to gravitate towards either a high-flown literary style or writing that flows from common speech is a pattern that will be repeated throughout history. While Latin remained the literary language for prose and poetry throughout the Middle Ages, spoken Latin gradually diverged more and more from Classical Latin, until the various dialects became separate languages: Spanish, Italian, French Provençal and Romanian. But the separate langauges themselves coalesced out of various dialects, and writers continued to "choose sides," as it were, favoring one dialect of the same language over another. Well into the Middle Ages, despite the rise of the Romance languages, any writing that was meant to be received as "literture," as opposed to ordinary communication, was written in Latin, not in the language or dialect commonly spoken. It was a significant choice when Dante, writing at the end of the 13th century, rejected Latin and chose

Italian—and more specifically, the Tuscan dialect—for the writing of his *Commedia*, the last great work of the middle ages, the first great work of the modern world.

📖

☞ **Livius Andronicus** (*ca.* 284-*ca.* 204 BC), translation of the *Odyssey*

One could say that Roman literature came into its own with the work of a former Greek prisoner of war from Tarentum, Livius Andronicus, who was later freed and wrote a series of tragedies and comedies based on Greek models. Ancients and moderns alike regard him as the originator of Latin literature. About 240 BC, when he came to Rome as a schoolteacher, there were no Latin books to teach from, so he undertook the Herculean task of turning the *Odyssey* into Latin. During this same period, other non-Hellenic peoples were turning to translation. The version of the *Pentateuch* known as the *Septaugint* was made at about this time (see Bible section, pgs 405-406), but the group of seventy-two Jewish scholars brought to Alexandria by Ptolemy II were translating into Greek, not Egyptian. The Romans borrowed almost everything from other cultures and civilizations—they copied Greek statues and imitated Greek literature—and they borrowed on a wholesale scale. The only thing Andronicus didn't borrow from the Greek was his meter. He turned to native Roman meter for that. His translation used the Latin *saturnian* verse, lines of loose irregular rhythms, scanned by accent rather than quantity, as was the Greek method. The use of dactylic hexameter was not introduced into Latin poetry until Ennius

---

Food for Thought

The saturnian meter became in time the vehicle through which the Greek quantitive meter gave way to the Latin accentual meter, though this took centuries to accomplish. Writers of epic and other formal verse still used the dacytalic hexameter and continued to write in a quantitative meter. But it was this stressed accentual verse, with its regular rhythmic beat, that was to evolve centuries later into rhyme with the Latin Church hymns. And the Latin hymns of the Middle Ages became the basis for a rhymed verse that flourished in the 12th Century poetry of the Troubadours of southern France who wrote—not in Latin—but in Provençal, a form of the French vernacular. Many poets in the 20th century looked back to the 12th century Provençal poets as the beginning of Modern poetry (our modern poetry!).

📖

The translation of Homer's *Odyssey* into Latin and the use of the Italic saturnian metre had immense historical importance. The schoolmaster Andronicus succeeded both in spreading Greek culture at Rome and in advancing literary culture in Latin. Cicero and Horace, among others, agreed that he was the originator of Latin literature.

The significance of his achievement rests on having created a translation that stands as a significant work alongside the original. This had never been done before. With no epic Latin tradition to speak of, Andronicus still managed to render an ancient Greek text into comparable Latin. In order to convey the flavor of Homer's archaic literary Greek, Livius chose an archaic Latin, which gave a loftiness and resonance to the text, but also established the conservative tendency that became so important in the history of Latin poetry.

> *Virum mihi, Camena, insece versutum* . . . .
> Tell me, O Muse, of the cunning hero . . . .

> *Namque nullum*
> *peius macerat humanum quamde mare saevum;*
> *vires cui sunt magnae topper confringent*
> *inportunae undae.*

> For there is no worse
> torment for a man than the cruel sea;
> even if he has great strength, it will soon be broken
> by the wild waves.

> *Cum socio nostros Ciclops impius mandisset* . . . .
> When the wicked Cyclops had crunched my comrades in his jaws . . . .

Andronicus's ability to dramatize the Homeric narrative characterized early Roman poetry, which strove for pathos, expressive force and dramatic tension. Where Homer has the swineherd Eumaios speak to the disguised Odysseus in the second person, saying, "Grief for Odysseus, who is no more, takes hold of me," Andronicus brings the irony and emotion of the situation to the fore: the swineheard blurts out in the first person, "Yet I have not forgotten you, dead son of Laërtes."

What remains of Andronicus's prolific output are quotations in the works of Republican authors and grammarians. Some sixty fragments survive, many just a single verse apiece. Despite his popularity in his own time, he soon fell out of favor, and was deemed primitive by Cicero and Horace; even Ennius was critical of his verse. Yet, all acknowledged his importance. He gave poets a respectability they had not had before, and because of him, writers and poets were allowed to meet and present votive offerings in the temple of Minerva on the Aventine, the most southerly of the seven hills of Rome; thus, through Livius Andronicus, poetry received official public recognition for the first time in Roman culture.

> *Mirum videtur quod sit factum iam diu?*
> Does it seem marvelous because it was done long ago?

●◆

The Punic Wars

Between 264 and 146 BC, Carthage fought three wars against Rome to decide who should rule the Mediterranean world. Rome's war against Tarentum and King Pyrrhus had brought them into closer contact with the leading Mediterranean power, Carthage, which lay only 130 miles across the sea from Sicily. It was now inevitable that these two city-states battle each other for control of the Mediterranean. Was that great body of water going to be a Roman or a Carthaginian lake? Polybius (*c.* 200-after 118 BC), the Greek historian of Rome's rise to power, called the conflict between Rome and Carthage the longest, most continuous and greatest war that had ever been fought. In the introduction to his *History*, Polybius declares that his aim in writing the book was to relate

> by what means and under what system of government the Romans succeeded in less than fifty-three years [from 220 BC, the start of the Second Punic War, to 168 BC, the end of the Third Macedonian War] in bringing under their rule almost the whole inhabited world.

The three Punic Wars (264-241, 218-201, 149-146 BC) were probably the most important undertaken by the Romans in their rise to a world power. Spectacular campaigns were fought in Italy, Spain, Sicily, and North Africa, directed by such military geniuses as the Carthaginian Hannibal and the Roman Scipio Africanus. Large-scale sea battles took place throughout the western Mediterranean, and states as far away as Macedonia and Pergamum in Asia Minor became involved in this prototype of a world war. As a result of her victory, Rome annexed Sicily, its first overseas province, and went on to acquire Sardinia and Corsica, as well as valuable parts of Spain, which they divided into two new provinces, Nearer and Further Spain.

The North African city of Carthage, founded in about 850 BC, had been a colony of Phoenicia (now Lebanon), before breaking away and becoming its own city-state. Sicily was the richest country between them and Rome was eager to lay hands on the abundant Sicilian grain. Control of Sicily would also be a strategic step in establishing control of the Mediterranean. The First Punic War (the Roman word for Phoenician was *Poeni*, thus the adjective becomes *Punic*) started over a town in Sicily and grew into a conflict lasting 23 years. Unlike the seafaring Carthaginians, Rome had no navy but quickly built up a fleet, craftily copying a storm-wrecked Carthaginian ship. The annexation of Sicily gave Rome its first overseas province, inaugurating an epoch of imperialism outside the mother country. A new stage in Roman history had begun, and its significant that forty years later, when Naevius chose to write an epic poem glorifying the power of Rome, he chose the Punic Wars as his subject.

During this period, Rome also had to face an invasion by the Celts in Gaul. After their defeat at the battle of Telemon in 225 BC, Cisalpine Gaul was pacified, but tensions between Gauls and Romans continued.

Rome eventually won control of the waters around Sicily, Corsica, and Sardinia. The Carthiginians were determined to get revenge. Their outstanding general, Hannibal, cleverly decided to avoid a battle at sea and led his men instead across the Alps toward Rome, starting the Second Punic War in 218 BC (often called the Hannibalic War). Many criticized Hannibal's seemingly impossible plan to transport an army of 50,000 men to

Spain, cross the Pyrennes, march northward through Gaul, and cross the Alps into Italy. Hannibal's initial success was electrifying, though many men were lost due to attacks by the barbarian hordes they encounterd along the way and the many soliders who drowned while trying to ford swollen rivers. After crosing the Pyrennes, he enlisted the Gauls as allies, increasing the size of his army. But his men were not prepared for a November Alpine crossing. Their clothing was insufficient to protect them from the cold, and many men and animals were lost as they led packhorses, mules, and three dozen elephants up treacherous paths that were iced over and narrow. Landslides caused the deaths of many. Finally, after fifteen days of gruelling work, his weary army successfully crossed the Alps. Over twenty thousand men had been lost. Of the 38 elephants that started the journey, only 12 survived.

Hannibal's army moved southward, overcoming all resistence as they continued southward from the Po valley down to Cannae in south-east Italy. There, in 216 BC, the Romans assembled an army of nearly a hundred thousand men and faced off against Hannibal's smaller force of fifty thousand. According to Plutarch, the night before the battle Hannibal said to his general Gisgo, "In all that great number of men opposite, there is not a single one whose name is Gisgo." The next morning, Hannibal's army skillfully outflanked, then surrounded the Romans, massacring between fifty and seventy thousand men in one of the worst defeats ever suffered by a Roman army. Hannibal lost one eye in the battle, but only six thousand troops. Gold rings taken from the fingers of the dead filled three bushel baskets, which were sent back to Carthage to mark the victory. After such a humiliating defeat at Cannae, the Romans changed their strategy, avoiding pitched battles whenever they could, and kept only a small force in the field to shadow Hannibal's army whever it went. Hannibal remained in Italy for twelve years, never once being defeated. He hoped to recruit disaffected members of the Italian populace who would rise in revolt against Rome. Though a few cities supported Hannibal's "liberation," most were not about to exchange a Roman for a Carthaginian master. Recalling Rome's leadership in the series of battles against Gallic raids, most of the cities remained loyal to the Roman cause. Hannibal's dream to ride in triumph through the streets of Rome and plant his flag in the Subara, as the center of the city was called, never came to pass. The Roman confederacy stayed together.

Finally, the Romans turned the tables on Hannibal. A Roman expeditionary force led by the brilliant general Cornelius Scipio set off to attack Carthage itself, encouraging the natives of North Africa to revolt against their Cathaginian masters. This forced Hannibal to return home, where he was defeated at Zama in a final battle in 202 BC. The defeat was humiliating, and the peace treaty worse. Carthage had to transfer Spain to Roman control. Thereafter, the Romans remained without rival in the western Meditarranean.

When Carthage was forced to compensate Rome for her loses, Hannibal upbraided the Carthaginian senate for weeping over the magnitude of war reparations.

> Apparently we are affected by public misfortunes only to the extent that they involve our private interests, and in these nothing hurts us more than loss of money. This is why no one groaned when the spoils of

defeated Carthage were being carted off; now that we must collect tribute money from private sources, you lament as at a public funeral.

Finally, Hannibal fled to Syria, then to Crete. When Rome demanded extradition, Hannibal committed suicide by drinking poison concealed in a small ring he was wearing for just such a purpose. Writing three hundred years later, the Roman poet Juvenal considered the transitory nature of glory.

> Put Hannibal in the scales: how many pounds will the dust of that peerless
> General weigh today? This is the man for whom Africa
> Was too small a continent . . . .
> Now Spain swells his empire, now he surmounts
> The Pyrenees. Nature throws in his path
> High Alpine passes, blizzards of snow; but he splits
> The very rocks asunder, moves mountains — with vinegar.
> Now Italy is his, yet still he forges on:
> "We have accomplished nothing," he cries, "till we have stormed
> The gates of Rome, till our Carthiginian standard
> Is set in the City's heart."
>   A fine sight it must have been,
> Fit subject for charicature, when the Gaetulian monster   [the elephant]
> Carried the one-eyed commander. Alas, alas for glory,
> What an end was here: the defeat, the ignominious
> flight into exile, everyone crowding to see
> The once-mighty Hannibal turned humble hanger-on,
> Sitting outside the door of a petty Eastern despot
> Till his Majesty deign to awake. No sword, no spear,
> No battle-flung stone was to snuff the fiery spirit
> That once had wrecked a world: but that punisher for
> Cannae and avenger for so much blood, a ring
> A little ring. Go, go you madman, run
> Over your savage Alps, to beomce the Schoolboy's favorite,
> To become a subject for speech-day declamations!
>   [see more on this poem on p. 394-395]

So this is what it comes down to, all one's grace and glory merely a fit subject of declamation by schoolboys studying Latin throughout the Middle Ages. Juvenal was not the first to write such set pieces on this age-old theme. We find a similar exposition by Hamlet in the graveyard scene as he lifts one, then another skull, as he laments the transitory nature of glory.

> There's another. Why may not that be the skull of a lawyer? Where be his
> quiddities now, his qualities, his cases, his tenures, and his tricks? Why does he
> suffer this mad knave now to knock him about the sconce with a dirty shovel,
> and will not tell him of his action of battery? Hum! This fellow might be in's time
> a great buyers of land, with his statutes, his recognizances, his fines, his double
> vouchers, his recoveries. Is this the fine of his fines, and the recovery of his
> recoveries to have his pate full of fine dirt? Will his vouchers vouch him no more
> of his purchases, and double ones too, than the length and breadth of a pair of

indentures? The very conveyances of his lands will scarcely lie in this box, and must th' inheritor himself have no more, ha?

On the other hand, the Roman general Scipio garnered his share of glory. He was hailed a hero, taking the surname Africanus. The emergence of Scipio Africanus as a charismatic leader of the people had unsettling implications for the rule of the oligarchy, who continued to fear their own usurpation by a powerful military commander. When Scipio Africanus reached Spain, he was hailed as king by the native Spanish troops. To avoid any political tension, Scipio created the title *imperator*, meaning military commander, so as not to be confused with emperor. (Julius Caesar later used the same title; when he did, there was no confusion—emperor it was.)

In the Third Punic War, which lasted from 149 to 146 BC, Carthage was completely destroyed by the Roman army, led by another Scipio, surnamed Aemilianus. The city was razed, and salt was spread over the ground, thereby preventing anything from growing—no grass to feed animals, no crops to feed the people of a rebuilt settlement. It was a mark of total annhilalation. As flames rose over the city, Scipio watched and wept, for, as he later told the Greek historian, friend, and former teacher, Polybius, he could foresee another conqueror some day issueing similar orders for the destruction of Rome—and to punctuate the prophecy, Scipio quoted several Homeric verses on the burning and destruction of Troy. The ruthless obliteration of Carthage and the later destruction of Corinth was a clear sign that Roman imperialism had made the Mediterranean theirs. Africa was declared a Roman republic, which it remained for another five centuries until it was conquered by Vandals in 451 AD.

Considered the first of the greater Roman historians, Sallust (86-35 BC) claimed to have become disgusted with the politics and morals of Rome, and turned to the intellectual pursuit of writing history. He felt that the destruction of Carthage was the beginning of the end of the Roman Republic and all its attendant virtues.

> Before the destruction of Carthage, the Roman people and senate together governed the commonwealth peacefully and moderately, nor was there rivalry among citizens for glory and power; fear of the enemy kept the state on the path of justice. But when the minds were freed from that fear, immorality and arrogance, which are encouraged by prosperity, entered them. Thus the peace which they had desired proved all the more cruel and harsh after they got it. For the nobles began to turn their dignity, and the people their liberty, into license, and every man took, robbed, and pillaged for himself.

Rome continued to expand in the 2nd century BC, and her economic and social life underwent profound changes. Industry and commerce grew, peasant husbandry gave way to capitalist farming of huge estates, and slavery increased both on the land and in households. The supply of cheap grain from Sicily and Spain almost destroyed the livelihood of the small peasant farmers. At the same time, government officials appointed to oversee the conquered areas found ample opportunities for becoming rich. As a result of Rome's new wealth from booty and tribute, there was a great increase in luxury of all kinds, and great public works were undertaken. In the span of a few generations, Rome was catapulted from a small, agricultural state into an imperialistic maritime power.

Significant for its influence on art and literature was the conquest of *Magna Graecia*—southern Italy and Sicily. This brought Romans into closer contact with Greek culture. The upper classes sought to imitate the high culture of the Greeks, and Hellenism in turn effected those poets writing for the upper classes. In all spheres—art and architecture, literature and religion—Hellenism held sway. The works of Ennius and most other poets reflected this Greek influence. One exception was the poet Cnaeus Naevius, whose work remained Roman in character.

☞ **Cnaeus Naevius** (*ca* 270-ca 201 BC), the *Bellum Poenicum* ("Punic War")

A younger contemporary of Andronicus, Naevius proved to be a more original poet. and gave Latin literature a nationalist direction. He was a plebian ex-soldier who shocked the conservatives by satirizing the political abuses of his day. For this he was jailed, and eventually banished. Later, in old age and still in exile, he wrote his principal work, the *Bellum Poenicum,* an epic poem on the First Punic War, in which he had fought. Here was an epic poem written in the national metre. The poem, written in four to five thousand saturnian verses, included the founding of Rome by Aeneas and other Trojan refugees. Virgil was later to pick up this theme, as well as a few of Naevius' scenes, when he composed his *Aeneid.*

The *Bellum Poenicum* is the first Latin epic with a Roman theme. One of its significant innovations was its fusion of myth and national history. The voyages of Aeneas were in some ways parallel to the wanderings of Odysseus; Naevius's account of the war against Carthage was especially meaningful to his readers, since Rome was again facing the same threat from across the sea.

Even more significant is the poem's stylistic features. The saturnian was a verse structure that formalists such as Ennius found "weak" and irregular, but it made elegant use of rich repetitions of sound. In many passages Naevius outdoes the lexical and formulaic richness of Homeric diction by inventing new compound words and syntactical combinations. He also took the long, unbroken narrative style found in prose historical writing and gave it dramatic tension with the poetic style, unheard of till then in Latin literature. Mundane subjects were treated with monumental flare and imagistic precision.

> *onerariae onustae   stabant in flustris*
> laden, the ships lay at anchor   upon the sluggish sea.

The language is direct and forceful, the word order linear. In the first half-verse, the words are linked by assonance and association of meaning; in the second half there's a striking image of the steadfast ship weighted down by the sea itself—*flustra* is a technical term that comes from sailor's language and is also in contrast to the more elegant words from classical poetry. Naevius does this often, using prosaic terms in conjunction with formal diction.

> *Seseque i perire mavolunt ibidem*

quam cum stupro redire ad suos popularis.

> They would rather perish on the spot
> than go back in disgrace to their countrymen

The *Bellum Poenicum* is a work of bold experimentation that gave Latin literature a nationalist direction. When the saturnian was eschewed in favor of the hexameter pioneered by Ennius, this epic poem was considered linguistically obsolete, overshadowed by Ennius' *Annals*. But as a writer of epic, Naevius continued to command respect, especially because of his influence on Ennius and Virgil.

Naevius also wrote comedies based on models from Greek "New Comedy," which were played in the vast Hellenistic theaters with their high stages and elaborate sets and backdrops. The Romans came into contact with the "New Comedy" as they extended their empire southwards into *Magnae Graecia*, and eventually Greece itself. The only Greek writer of note was Menander, whose plays were pleasantly humorous, politically inoffensive, though still bawdy, and noted for their fabricated plots. The "New Comedy" was easily understood and assimilated. Once imported into Italy, it underwent some significant changes, and gave rise to the works of Plautus and Terrence. Naevius set his comedies in Italy with comic situations of contemporary urban life. His outspokenness offended the powerful family of the Metelli: one line in particular became notorious (written in iambics, the metre of spoken drama, and so presumably delivered in a play).

> *Fato Metelli Romae fiunt consules*

In context, the word "fato" could mean either fate, or fatal. Which did Naevius mean?

> It is fate that the Metelli became consuls at Rome

or

> It is fatal that the Metelli became consuls at Rome

Metellus, consul in 206 BC, replied with a threat that became the most frequently quoted example of the saturnian metre. Metellus used an idiomatic expression that contained a double meaning.

> *Dabunt malum Metelli Naevio poetae.*

Literally, the sentence translates as "The Metelli will give the poet Naevius the apple," but *malum* can mean either "apple," which in those times had the same connotation as "the brass ring" and therefore meant "prize,"—Naevius will get the prize—or *malum* can mean "misfortune," "calamity," "punishment." As we might say today, Naevius didn't get the ring, he got the finger. Under an ancient law forbidding public criticism of officials, Naevius may have been imprisoned (according to Plautus) or sent into exile to Utica in North Africa, where in his last years he wrote his great epic, the *Bellum Poenicum*), and died shortly after its completion. Aulus Gellius preserved Naevius's proud epitaph, a rebuke to his countrymen in biting alliterative verse.

> *Immortales mortales si foret fas flere*
> *flerent divae Camenae Naevium poetam.*
> *itaque postquamst Orchi traditus thesauro,*

obliti sunt Romae loquier lingua latina.

Were it proper for the immortals to mourn for men,
the divine Muses would lament the poet Naevius.
And once death had taken him to her underground vaults,
Rome forgot how to speak Latin.

☞ Quintus Fabius Pictor

A senator who fought in the Second Punic War (218-202 BC), Pictor was the earliest Roman historian, he compiled a *History of Rome* in 202 BC, but in Greek; Latin was still considered unfit for literary prose, and would not be used by historians until Cato. Now that Rome had become a dominant power in the Mediterranean, historians tried to tie the origins of Rome to that of the ancient Greeks—a useful component of foreign policy. The Greeks held that Aeneas founded Rome, whereas the Romans traced their genealogy to Romulus and Remus. It was Fabius Pictor who reconciled these two views by having the twin brothers descend from Aeneas who founded Alba Longa in Italy.

Hellenism at Rome

By the middle of the 3rd century, the upper classes came under the influence of Hellenism—the Greek movement in art, literature, manners and morals which began sometime after the death of Alexander the Great in 323 BC, and ended with Rome's conquest of Greece and the Greek East in the latter part of the first century BC. The term itself is problematic, and controversial. Hellenism could mean the benign transmission of Greek language and culture, but Hellenization has a connotation that is more active and aggressive, an imperialistic form of cultural domination. The spread of Greek culture was most intense in the years between Alexander the Great and the beginnings of the Roman revolution in 133 BC which culminated a century later with Octavian's victory at Actium in 32 BC, but 20th century historians have also stressed the Semetic contribution to Mediterranean countries. For convenience, we could say Hellenism is the general diffusion of Greek culture, and the terms Hellenization or Hellenistics would be confined to the centuries between 336 BC and 31 BC.

Hellenistic literature had a profound impact on Roman poets and writers. The poetry of Callimachus, Euphorean, and Theocritus and the plays of Menander were imitated by scores of Roman authors—Greece was to Rome what Europe was to America in the 1920s. Eventually, it was not enough to be influenced by the Greeks, efforts were made to claim a historical connection. Scholars and poets tried to show that Romans were actually Greeks, descended from the Trojan warrior Aeneas, and that Latin was itself a Greek dialect.

The upper classes imitated even the most decadent of Greek practices, such as pederasty, and threw lavish parties with sumptuous banquets and loud music. Romans of the upper classes were the Great Gatsbys of their day. Some writers and orators condemned the moral decline of the Republic, while others celebrated the new Rome. Homes and public buildings were designed to reflect the architecture of Hellenistic Greece, especially theaters featuring performances by poets and the "artists of Dionysus." The porticoes and galleries of homes were often decorated with theatrical backdrops that served as stage sets for poetry readings and musical performances. Cato the Censor did his best to slow down the Republic's inexorable slide into corruption: he taxed everything Greek, from the importation of Greek food to the statues of Greek gods that adorned the estates of the rich. But despite its decadence, the culture of Greece was an enlightened one, and Rome was ready for its own awakening. The time was ripe for Latin to have a literature of its own. Naevius wrote several dramas on Roman history as well as numerous comic plays, but he was outshone by Plautus, who reworked the plays of Menander into something original and relevant to his audience. The comedies of Plautus, adapted from Greek models, had enormous impact on the poets and writers of his day. It is said that Latin literature began with the performance of a play by Livius Andronicus at Rome in 240 BC, but more likely it begins with Plautus, the poet-turned-playwright, who dazzled his audience with his boisterous and witty comedies.

☛ **Marcus Accius Plautus** (c. 250-184 BC)

Something familiar,
Something peculiar,
Something for everyone—
A comedy tonight!

Something that's gaudy,
Something that's bawdy,
Something for everyone—
A comedy tonight!

Nothing with kings,
Nothing with crowns,
Bring on the lovers, liars and clowns,
Old situations,
New complications,
Nothing portentous or polite—
Tragedy tomorrow,
Comedy tonight!

Stephen Sondheim, A Funny Thing Happened on the Way to the Forum
[Adapted from the comedies of Plautus]

The subtlety and refinement of the Greek comedies was not for Plautus. He transformed the sophisticated "New Comedy" into boisterous slapstick; even more impressive still, he took the cumbersome Latin tongue and combined it with the metrical refinements of the Greek language, creating a sleek but highly charged line that was truly original. Everyone came to see his plays, from the educated nobility to the shopkeepers and slaves who could just as easily have gone to see rival attractions—boxing matches, tight-rope walkers, exotic dancers, gladiatorial shows, and chariot races. But they came instead to the hard seats to see Plautus's irreverent and carnivalesque world of lovers, liars, and clowns; they came to laugh. His success and influence in the centuries to come, as well as in his own time, was enormous. Only 21of his comedies performed between 205 and 184 BC have come down to us intact.

Born in Sarsina, a backwater town in Umbria, Plautus spent part of his youth as a Roman soldier, then earned his keep as a stage carpenter and actor, knocking about Italy in the rustic farces played wherever a backdrop could be found. With the money he'd saved, he became a merchant, but lost everything when the ship carrying his goods was lost at sea. By the age of forty-five, he was an itinerant miller, grinding corn on a hand-mill which he wheeled about the city. It is unknown whether he was writing plays by night as he plied his trade by day, jostling shoulders with a Roman public eager for diversion. Surely as an actor he must have imagined he could improve upon the theatrical fare presented on the temporarily erected stages of the city.

The "New Comedies" of Menander were the basis for many of his plays, and like the Greek comedies, they were written in verse. Drama and poetry make different demands upon the writer, so it's not exactly accurate to call Plautus a poet, any more than we refer to Shakespeare as a poet. Of course, Shakespeare also wrote poetry, and much of what he wrote in his plays resonates as poetry, but we think of him as the playwright despite the fact that he is often referred to as The Bard.

With Plautus we come to the peak of Latin verse comedy. Like Shakespeare, Plautus was commercially successful in his own time and quite prolific. By the second century, critics were debating how many plays he had actually written—some speculated there may have been as many as 130. Varro compiled an edition of comedies by Plautus containing the twenty-one plays that have survived the centuries, the most popular of which were the *Menaechmi* ("The Brothers," in which twins separated at birth meet again as young men and share zany adventures due to the complications of mistaken identity), *Miles Gloriosus* (which also referred to the imprisonment of the poet Naevius for satirizing the aristocracy), *Pseudolus* (or "The Trickster"), *Amphituro, Bacchides* (a lively story about two courtesans), *Auluraria* ("The Crock of Gold"), *Captivi* (in which a father recovers his two sons), and *Mostellaria*. Later editors added production notes so that the metrical nature of the lines could be discerned.

Shakespeare used the *Menaechmi* (as well as one scene from the *Amphitruo*) as the basis for his only true farce, the *Comedy of Errors*, which later became the basis for the Broadway musical *The Boys from Syracuse. Miles Gloriosus* ("The Braggart Soldier") became the basis for the Elizabethan play *Ralph Roister Doister*. His gentle comedy *Amphituro* was adapted by thirty-six playwrights. The influence of *Pseudolus* and *Mostellaria* can be seen in the plays of Moliere. *The Crock of Gold* served as Moliere's model for *The Miser,* and *The School for Husbands* was based on Plautus's *Adelphi*. A favorite with teachers and anthologists because it's safe to print (nothing salacious in this one) is Plautus's *The Captives*. One of the prototypes for Shakespeare's Falstaff was the military bufoon found in *Miles Gloriosus*, or "The Braggart Soldier." His humble companion in that play is a character named Breadmuncher who is an early Sancho Panza.

The shady world of procurers, cheats, and courtesans in *The Persian Stranger* reappeared in *The Beggar's Opera*, which Bertold Brecht used as the basis for his *Threepenny Opera*. *Pseudolus* became the basis for the Stephen Sondheim stage musical *A Funny Thing Happened on the Way to the Forum,* which Richard Lester later adapted for the screen. *A Funny Thing* starred Zero Mostel as the wily poet-slave Pseudolus, who is a combination jester, rascal, trickster, con-artist, wise-guy/ wise-man philosopher/fool. Pseudolus gets into and out of any situation, always landing on his feet, unless he lands on his head, in which case he snaps out a witty rejoinder, does a backflip, and lands back on his feet. Unlike the tragic hero who must die to restore order to a world out-of-joint, the comic hero tricks the gods to set things back the way they were. The tragic hero is at the mercy of a flawed world and his own flawed character. The comic hero enters the action, directs the plot, and somehow escapes intact. He is the source, the springboard for the comedy. The Plautine comic hero is a poet as well as a fool, adept at verbal swordplay that ascends to a comic lyricism. Where the tragic hero is a king or prince, the comic hero is an underling, a slave, an imposter, an upstart who flies into the wings with a wink and flops on his noggin with a triumphant nod.

Boastful soldiers, pompous old men, miserly curmudgeons, and scheming servants have long been standard ingredients for comic writing. Of all the characters Plautus brought to life, perhaps his greatest creation was that of the irresistibly charming and conniving slave / trickster / con-artist. P.G. Wodehouse denied that he'd ever read Plautus, but Jeeves certainly falls within the tradition of the scheming servant. In our our time, we can best see him in the actors who have portrayed this type of character on the screen in various forms and incarnations: Charlie Chaplin, Harold Lloyd, Danny Kaye Phil Silvers, Jonathan Winters, Robin Williams, Eddie Murphy, Nathan Lane, and Roberto Bigninie (chk spelling) to name only a few.

In his comic hero, Plautus combined verbal alacrity and physical dexterity, as if Homer had joined the circus. Chaplin's tramp/clown has the heart of a poet, and Plautus's poet heroes have the agility of a clown. Here's Pseudolus addressing the audience.

> Just as the poet, when he has taken up his tablets,
> is looking for something that doesn't exist anywhere,
> and yet he finds it and makes a lie credible,
> I'll make myself a poet now:
> The twenty *minae*, which now don't exist anywhere —
> I'll find them anyhow.   [vv.401 ff.]

He lets the audience know that he knows what he's doing, even though it looks like he doesn't know what he's doing, a way of working that the actor turned playwright must have realized resembled the creative process itself. .

> I suspect that now you're suspecting
> that I promise these great projects to entertain you
> until I finish acting the play,
> and that I won't do what I'd said I would do.
> But I won't change a bit.

And yet surely, as far as I know,
I don't know how I'll do it.
Look, whoever comes on stage
ought to bring some new invention in a new way;
If he can't do that, let him give way to others who can.   [vv.562 ff.)

Plautus also may be said to have invented the musical comedy. Many passages were obviously meant to be accompanied by a reed-pipe, and some are musical set pieces (*canticas*), duets written in a variety of meters, as if today we were to see a musical in which some of the songs were classic ballads, others rock and roll, and still others done in the style of country, folk, or rhythm and blues. The *canticas* were not integral to the plot nor did they further the action. They were merely opportunities for the actor to perform, and there is nothing like them in Greek "New Comedy."

In contrast to the "Old Comedy" of Greece, which required men of great poetic talent, imagination, and political discernment to create fresh plots and unusual situations, the "New Comedy" employed stereotyped plots, the plays Menander wrote were domestic comedies of manners which after a time could become wearisome. At a time when Roman society was turning to Athens for its culture and art, with playwrights openly acknowledging they were translating or adapting from the Greek as if it were a badge of honor, Plautus went beyond adaptation of the type comedies created by Menander. He wrote plays that were Roman in character, not Greek; they possess a rowdiness that reminds us of burlesque and vaudeville, the kind of rollicking entertainment typical of Aristophanes. As in Shakespeare's day, there must have been the give and take between performer and groundling, the comic actor stepping downstage out of the action to deliver a series of one liners, sight-gags, and other topical jokes. His characters often remind us of stand-up comics delivering monologues on a variety of topics, with one liners as incisive as Shakespeare's. One of his scheming slaves is a character called Chrysalus, which means Goldfinger. Punning on the name, he jokes, "Goldfinger's got to get his hands on some gold!" Though Plautus used colloquial speech, he'd write a comic line using the alliterative style for added effect, such as "*Ut hoc utimur maxime more moro molestoque multum*," which was probably funnier because of the alliteration. "Twist the neck of wrongdoing" is a startling personification, one of many in a body of work that brought a literary eloquence to down-home farce. To paraphrase Shakespeare, his plays are skrimishes of wit. One of his characters notices a roof whose tiles have blown off in a storm. "That roof's more perforated than a percolator!" Imagine a borsht-belt comedian tapping ash off his cigar as he says it. In *Crock of Gold*, the young wise-guy says of the old skinflint, "He's so cheap that when he goes to sleep, he'll tie the bellows round his throat so he shouldn't waste his breath!" his wit and wisdom became commonplace schoolboy exercises.

Lupus est homo homini, non homo, quom qualis sit non novit.

To a stranger, man is no man, but a wolf.

Quem di diligunt

adulescens moritur, dum valet sentit sapit.

He whom the gods love
dies young, while he has strength and senses and wits.

Credo ego Amorem primum apud homines
carnificinam commentum.

I do believe it was Love that first devised here on earth
the torturer's profession.

Plautus seems to have enjoyed the success of his later years. He remained a man of the theater and a man of the people. Unlike Terrence, the comic playwright who followed him, he never became a polished gentleman or *litterateur*. He lived through one of the most momentus periods in Roman history; born in the middle of the First Punic War, he lived through the turmoil of the Second when Rome defeated Carthage. Hannibal died only three months after Plautus. Like other writers before him, he composed his own epitaph.

Postquam est mortem aptus Plautus, comoedia luget,
scaena est deserta, dein risus ludus iocusque
et numeri innumeri conlacrumarunt.

Since Plautus met death, comedy mourns,
and the stage is deserted, then laughter, frolic, wit
and countless numbers wept and wailed.

 Publius Terence Afer (b. 193 or 183 BC, -- 159 BC) Poet / Playwright

As his last name indicates, Terence was born at Carthage in North Africa. He was the son of a Libyan slave, and as a child became the slave of a Roman senator, Terentius Lucanus, who set him free after seeing to it that he received a liberal education. Talented and handome, he soon came to know many prominent Romans, and joined the circle of poets and writers under the patronage of Scipio Aemilianus; when it was alleged that Aemilianus composed some of Terence's plays, Terrance seemed proud to confirm the allegations, even if they were not true. Depending on which date you assigned his birth, he died when he was either 34 or 24 year old.

Only six of Terence's comedies have come down to us. Like Plautus, he wrote in verse, but followed the Greek originals more closely than Plautus did—so close, in fact, that he was often accused of plagarism. His diction is gentler as well, preserving the spirit and tone of the "New Comedy." Critics in his own time mistook his use of natural diction for feebleness of style, but in the centuries that followed, his even, eloquent voice and philosophical humaneness were greatly admired and left a strong imprint on the future theater of Europe. Cicero and Horace admired him for the urbanity and polish of his plays; Caesar noted that his style evolved out of his "pure speech." He was less interested in jokes than in the issues and situations confronting his characters, who are more realistic than those found in Plautus, and their monologues are more natural. Portraiture takes precedent over charicature; the farcical overtones found in Plautus are absent in Terence, whose plots are simpler and truer to life. Unfortunately, his plays were not as popular, but they were studied in the Middle Ages and influenced early English comedy and the Restoration comedy of manners perfected by Congreve and Sheridan. Wherever Latin is studied, Terence's plays hold a central place in the curriculum.

His greatest achievement may well have been the creation of a Latin literary style that was unique in its day, an elegance and clarity not found in other writers of the time. He was the first Latin writer to reproduce the elliptical style of natural conversation. Plautus mimicked the low colloquial speech of his characters, but his lines did not have a natural construction; they were more clipped and unrealistic, though good for the joke. Plautus was performed, but Terence was read and studied.

> *Ita vitast hominum quasi quom ludas tesseris:*
> *si illud quod maxume opus est iactu non cadit,*
> *illud quod cecidit forte, id arte ut corrigas.*
>
> Human life is like shooting dice.
> If the dice don't turn up as you hoped,
> you hav to make the most of how they did.

> *Sine Cerere et Libero friget Venus.*   [Ceres: goddess of agriculture, sister of Pluto]
> Without Ceres and Bacchus, Venus grows cold.   [Bacchus: the god of wine]

> *Facile omnes quom valemus recta consilia aegrotis damus.*
> When in health, we all have good advice for the sick.

Many of the lines, like those of Shakespeare, were taken out of context and studied for their wise sentiments. When Shakespeare has Ophelia's doddering father Polonius give his departing son advice—"Neither a borrower nor a lender be. . . . Above all, to thine own self be true, and it follows as the night the day, thou can'st be false to any man."—it's supposed to be funny. It's meant to parody the kind of moralistic advice an old man gives his son who is off to the big city. We laugh at the pomposity of the moral sentiments. In the classroom, it's another matter. Adolescents memorize the speech as the essence of wisdom.

The same was true for the moral sentiments espoused by Terence's characters when quoted out of context. Perhaps the most famous of all:

> *Homo sum:*
> *Humani nil*
> *A me alienum puto.*
>
> I am a man:
> I regard all that concerns men
> as concerning me.

The speaker is a nosy busybody who has been poking his nose into his neighbor's affairs. When caught, he defends himself with the above justification, which in context, makes him look even more ridiculous. Such is the irony of moral instruction and dramatic context.

Food for Thought

The Road Not Taken

The use of irony is a common feature of 20th century poetry, and few used it more effectively than Robert Frost. School kids memorize the last stanza of Frost's "The Road Not Taken," and it was featured as a "voice over" in a recent televison commercial: Be original, it seemed to say, dare to be unique, follow the less traveled road. Of course, that was not the point of those lines, as Frost himself admitted. The poem was a mocking parody of the bahavior of Frost's friend, the poet Edward Thomas (1878-1917) who used to choose a direction for their country walks, then, before they had finished, berate himself for not having chosen a diffferent, more interesting way. Oftimes, he'd look back to justify the path taken as a way to romanticize the walk. In the poem, in three separate places, Frost reminds us that both paths are the same, that the other path was "just as fair," that "the passing there had worn them really about the same, And both [paths] that morning equally lay in leaves no step had trodden black." Yet by the end of the poem, the speaker is *claiming* that the two paths were different, and that he had taken the one "less traveled by." How we glamorize our lives, how we make casual or arbitrary decisions, and later make them seem dramatic and portentious. Frost did not approve of "sighing over what might have been," but in "The Road Not Taken," he makes fun of our tendency to dramatize what was.

Frost's favorite was the Latin poet and satirist Horace. Frost was not trying to be obscure; he purposely seemed to say what he meant. But "we never say what we mean," he used to say. "We're all of us too much poets. We like to talk in parables and in hints and in indirections—whether from diffidence or some other instinct." He played his philosophy close to the vest. "Poetry," he said, "provides the one permissible way of saying one thing and meaning another." Frost used similiar irony in "Mending Wall," which ends with the llne "Good fences make good neighbors." Frost is making fun of that sentiment. He clues you in in the first line. "Something there is that doesn't love a wall." Try as you might, nature will defeat you at every turn. In time, walls between people will only come down. The walls of Jericho. The Berlin Wall. Yet, we memorize and quote out of context the last line of the poem, giving it a meaning Frost never intended.

In his own time, Terence was never a popular success. During one a performance of one of his plays, the audience heard of a boxing match taking place down the street and left the theatre in the middle of the show. Another time they walked out to see a gladitorial contest. In 160 BC, Terence traveled to Greece and wrote several plays that were sent back to Rome and lost at sea. It is said that when he returned from Greece, he died at sea.

Nallumst iam dictum quod non sit dictum prius.

Nothing is ever said that has not been said before.

☞ **Quintus Ennius (239-169 BC),**

The Roman tradition emerges full strength in the epic poetry of Quintus Ennius, who was born in Rudiae in southeast Italy and spoke Greek, Latin, and Oscan (an early Italic langauge), prompting him to claim he had three hearts. He served in the Roman army as a centurion during the Second Punic War, stationed in Sardinia. Cato brought him to Rome, and he became a Roman citizen in 184 BC. Ennius was about fifteen years younger than Plautus, and like Plautus managed to avoid offending the aristocracy, despite the moralizing tone of some of his work. Though a versatile writer of tragedies, comedies, epigrams, satires, a didactic poem on nature, a poem on mythology, a poem on Scipio's victory over Hannibal, it is his epic poem, the *Annals*, that represents his greatest contribution to Latin literature. Chronicling Roman history from the time of Aeneas down to the wars of the poet's own day, the *Annals* is made up of 18 books of more than 20,000 lines, only 600 lines of which have been preserved, many just single lines taken out of context and quoted by later authors. Judging from the space he gave to relatively unimportant events, the epic may have been longer than the *Iliad* or the *Aeneid*. For centuries Ennius remained Rome's national poet, eclipsed only by Virgil.

Food for Thought

To give you some idea of how popular Virgil's *Aeneid* was in the centuries following his death, one could reconstruct the entire *Aeneid* by piecing together the phrases, lines, and stanzas quoted by various authors throughout the Middle Ages and into the Renaissance.

●◆

In celebrating the history of Rome, the *Annals* conveys a view of the world that marks the triumph of the aristocratic ideology. Heroic deeds reside in the virtue and exploits of the warrior who also pursues peacetime values—a cultivated and humanistic wisdom, and the ability to think and speak with philosophical moderation. Their words, as much as their swords, create civilization. The shield does not always make the man; poetry does that.

Ennius set the tone for Latin hexameter, writing in the high style that was to be used and modified a century and a half later by Lucretius and Virgil. The hexameter was the traditional meter of Greek epic, but when Andronicus and Naevius wrote their epics in Latin, they wrote in the jerky *saturnian* meter. It was Ennius who showed how effective the more smoothly flowing hexameter could be in Latin, especially when joined with the poetic diction that became the mark of his style, a style that came to seem crude to later canons of taste, but was polished and eloquent for its time, yet not without a certain vigor and bold imagery, charming in its very awkwardness. Ovid, perhaps, put it best: *ingenio maximus, arte rudies*, "lofty in genius, crude in workmanship."

Vulturus in silvis miserum mandebat homonem.
Heu! Quam crudeli condebat membra sepulchro!

A vulture in the woods was eating the wretched man.
My God! into what a harsh grave were his limbs sinking!

Though his success as a playwright earned him the lofty position left vacant by Andronicus and Naevius, it was The *Annals* that made him the most prominent figure of early Latin literature. Until the age of Augustus the *Annals* was the most famous of all Roman epics, not displaced until Virgil's great epic. Virgil imitated some of his lines, and Lucretius, Cicero, Ovid, and Propertius all admired him.

In the *Annals*, Ennius celebrated the heroic deeds of the founders of Rome, following the paths taken by Homer and other writers of Hellenistic epic. In the "proem" introducing Book I, Ennius tells of a dream in which the ghost of Homer appears, promising that Homer would be reincarnated in him, the poet Ennius. With this stroke of imaginative *chutzpah*, Ennius dubbed himself the living replacement of the greatest Greek poet of all time. This scene of poetic initition remained famous for centuries. Many Latin authors referred to Greek models to legitimize their work, but Ennius' claim to be Homer reincarnate was an act of upsmanship that could never be topped.

In the proem to Book VII, Ennius criticizes the saturnian verse used by Naevius and Andronicus as a form suitable only for folk poetry and prophecy. Here, Ennius proclaims himself the first poet-philologist, or "cherisher of the word," one who could be classified in the great tradition of Alexandrian and contemporary Greek poetry. Since he was the first to adopt the dactylic hexameter, the regular meter of Greek poetry, for his national epic, he considered himself the first true Latin poet.

Food for Thought

Drugs, Sex, and Dactylic Hexameter

The iambic pentameter line was the most common line in English poetry. The term originates in ancient Greece where a girl named Iambe personified the obscene songs sung to relieve emotional tension. Iam—because the stress is short/long, as in "to dance," or "enjoy," and pentameter because there are five of those short/long (- /) units in the line.

When I see birches bend left to right
Across the line of straighter darker trees

A dactyl has one stressed syllable followed by two unstressed, / - -, as in Longfellow's

This is the forest primeval. The murmuring pines and the hemlocks

There are six units (or feet) to the line above, making it dactylic hexameter.

Why all the fuss over which meter to write in? If we read a line of poetry strictly according to the meter and not according to the natural inflections of the meaning, it's hard to get a feel for why one meter would be considered suitable for epic and another suitable for something rustic or folksy. Most Greek poems were accompanied by a musical instroement, and the elongation of the vowels could make a difference in the sound of the line. There's no way to get a feel for the effect Greek and Latin poetry had on the listener by comparing English written in various meters. Perhaps the best analogy can be found in the popular music of our own time. Chord structures and harmonic effects—what we might call "a basic riff"—best approximates the significance of metrical choice. If you were to write an opera prior to 1960, you'd hardly choose to use the popular ballad or rock and roll for the music. The American musical itself evolved in terms of the kind of music written for it. Today, composers of popular music and musical theater make choices based on the basic chord structure of their songs: ballad, popular, blues, rhythm & blues, rock, rock and roll, hard rock, heavy metal, country, folk, and all the hybrids they produce. Take the scene in the Whoopi Goldberg movie where she poses as a nun and teaches the sisters to sing rhythm and blues. When the Pope comes to visit, the nuns switch from singing typical choral chant to rhythm and blues. They start clapping and dancing to the Phil Spector song, "I Will Follow Him (whever he may go)." Everyone in the church is shocked at first, but the effect is delightful and comic. Considered in the religious context, the song is actually appropriate, and eventually even the Pope is moving his head and hands to the rhythm of the music. Poets in the Roman era would have achieved a similiar effect using the saturnian meter for epic subject matter. A contemporary poet gets the same effect mixing lofty diction and the spoken voice.

In his own day, Ennius was a "modern," a bold experimental poet. At times he composed in dactylic hexameter, sometimes using spondees, depending on the emotion. While the diction of the *Annals* is generally fresh and forceful, he also created verses that were heavily alliterative. The following translation pulsates with typical Enniusean vigor even though the alliteration is not as obvious in the English as it is in the Latin.

> Thus spoke the father, o sister, and disappeared at once,
> and did not present himself to my sight,
> even though I desired it in my heart, however often
> I stretched my hands towards the blue regions of the sky,
> weeping and calling him with tender voice.
> Only now has sleep left me, with my heart suffering.

Ennius brought the alliterative style common to the saturnian verse and worked it into the hexameter, thus applying a Roman device to Greek verse. This conjunction of the hexameter and alliteration came to be seen as the most archaic feature of his work. The rhythmic and repetitive sounds gave a regularity to the freer saturnian verse, but when applied to the hexameter, it sounded forced and monotonous. Later poets were selective in their use of alliteration, but it was a gradual process.

> *Qoumque caput caderet, carmen tuba sola peregit*
> *et pereunte viro raucus sonus aere cucurrit.*

> When his head was severed, the trumpet blared on,
> and as the warrior lay dying, a hoarse sound issued from the brass.

> *Oscitat in campis caput a cervice revulsum*
> *semianimesque micant oculi lucemque requirunt.*

> His head, severed at the neck, rolled down the field,
> the half-alive eyes twitching and longing for light.

Amicus certus in re incerta cernitur.

A friend in need is a friend indeed.

Despite his success, Ennius lived in modest style on the Aventine, teaching and writing. There are numerous anecdotes told about him and the other poets of his day. One, for instance, involves Scipio Amelianus, a patron and promoter of important figures of contemporary culture. Scipio gathered about him a circle of intellectuals interested in popularizing the works of ancient Greece. One day he went to see Ennius, who was busy writing and wished not to be disturbed, so he had his maid say he wasn't home. Later, when Ennius went to see Scipio, Scipio shouted out the window that he wasn't home. Ennius entered anyway, saying he recognized the voice. "Shame on you," said Scipio. "When I asked for you, I believed your maidservant when she said that you weren't home. Don't you believe me in person?" Horace made fun of him, writing, "Ennius never sallied forth to sing of arms unless he was drunk." But he was no ascetic.He enjoyed a social life of good food and strong liquor. According to Gellius, the passage quoted below from the Annals was actually a self-portrait.

> He sent for a man with whom he was often happy to share his table,
> and to talk about private affairs after a tiring day
> spent dealing with the most serious business of government. . . .
> To him he would speak frankly of matter great and small,
> tell jokes, and, if he so wished, speak well or ill of anything,
> confident of the other's distraction.
>   With this companion he spent many an agreeable, happy hour,
> both with others and alone. He had such disposition
> that he never deliberately perpetrated a misdeed nor lightly gave offense.

In one of his own satires, Ennius joked, "I never poeticize unless I have the gout." He died of gout at the age of seventy during the festival of *ludi Apollinares*, the public games in honor of Apollo that featured theatrical performances. His tragedy, *Thyestes*, was being performed at the time. He reputedly wrote his own epitaph:

> *Aspicite o civies senis Enni imaginis formam.*
>   *Hic vestrum pinxit maxima facta patrum.*
> *Nemo me lacrimis decoret nec funera fletus*
>   *faxit. Cur? Volito vivus per ora virum.*

> Look, O citizens, upon the features of Ennius in his old age.
>   It was he depicted your fathers' noblest deeds.
> Let no one honor me with tears or attend my funeral with
>   weeping. Why? I fly, still living, through the mouths of men.

☛ **Cato (234-149)** *De Agri Cultura, Carmen de Moribus*

Marcus Porcius Cato, known as "Cato the Censor," (or "Cato the Elder," to distinguish him from his son, Cato "the Younger) was born to a plebian family of prosperous farmers. He fought in the war against Hannibal and returned home to a political career. Cato was a rigid upholder of ancestral customs and champion of the ancient Roman virtues against moral degeneration. He was against the spread of Hellenistic culture which he felt was an evil influence pervading every aspect of Roman life. Hellenism, Cato said, encouraged individualism and undermined traditional ethics. The only reason he attended theatrical shows, it was said, was so he could be seen walking out of them. "How could two soothsayers," he wondered, "look one another in the face without laughing." He carried on a vindictive war of words with Scipio Aemilianus, the adopted grandson of Scipio Africanus, who gathered about him a circle of poets and writers sympathetic to Hellenism. Few escaped the sting of Cato's condemnation. With his red hair and piercing gray eyes, he was the epitome of puritanical repression. He advised his own son to resist the temptations of Greek literature, for, as Cato impressed upon him, the Greeks were a perverse and corrupting race. His biting wit, however, made him one of the most persuasive orators in Rome. After the second Punic War, he was concerned that Carthage might rebuild and called for a third Punic War with the destruction of Carthage as its chief aim. Almost as an afterthought, he ended every speech he made in the Senate—whatever the subject—with the words, *Ceterum censeo Carthaginem esse delendam,* "And I also think that Carthage must be destroyed."

Rome turned to Scipio Aemilianus to lead Rome in its last war against Carthage. A general less brilliant than his grandfather, Scipio was a great organizer with plenty of drive. Ironically, Cato died in 149 BC, three years before Rome's victory over Carthage. He did not live to see its destruction.

Like many senators and aristocrats, Cato was a large-scale farmer. In 160 BC, he wrote *De Agri Cultura*, a treatise on agriculture. It's the oldest extant complete prose work in Latin. While its organization is haphazard, it's full of frugal advice and stern warnings.

> What is good farming?
> Good plowing.
> What is the second thing?
> Plowing.
> What third?
> Manuring.

> This is how it is with farming: if you put off doing one thing, you will be late with everything.

> On a rainy day, see what can be done around the house. Rather than stand idle, tidy things up. Remember, though no work is done, the expenses never stop.

> Sell the oil, if it fetches a good price,

sell whatever excess there be of wine and grain;
Sell off the worn-out oxen, defective cattle, defective sheep,
wool, hides, the old wagon, old tools, the aged slave, the sickly slave,
and all else that is of no use. The proprietor of an estate
should be eager to sell, not to buy.

Cato is best known for his speeches, 150 of which were published. Only fragments have survived, but they show shrewdness and wit, honesty and simplicity. In his last years he was charged with a capital offense, and spoke to the jury on his own behalf, saying, "How hard it is for one whose life has been passed in a preceding generation to plead his cause before men of the present."

The *Carmen de Moribus* was a work written in prose, but the term *carmen* indicates that it was written in rhythmic prose. His seven volume history of Rome, *Origins* (now lost) was written in Latin, not Greek, and practically inaugurated Latin prose as a literary medium. He wrote with greater sophistication than is suggested by his precept, *rem tene: verba sequentur*, "stick to the meaning: the words will follow." A collection of Latin moral maxims in prose and verse, *Dicta Catonis*, "The Sayings of Cato," was a popular schoolbook in the Middle Ages, translated into several European languages.

> ☞ Human life nearly resembles iron. When you use it, it wears out; when you don't use it, it rusts. We see that men are worn out by work, but laziness and sluggishness do more damage.

> ☞ Those who steal from private individuals spend their lives in stocks and chains; those who steal from the public treasure go dressed in gold and purple.

Cato harbored some bitterness that he wasn't given his proper due. "After I'm dead," he wrote, "I'd rather have people ask why I have no monument than why I have one." In his history of Rome (based on Livy), Florus wrote that he preferred "a single Cato to three hundred Socrateses." In deference to Florus, it seems that in our own time, we have many Catos, but not a single Socrates.

☞ Marcus Pacuvius (c. 220- c. 130 BC)

Pacuvius was a tragic poet, nephew of Ennius, who lived in Rome and initially gained fame as a painter. The line below was supposedly sung at Julius Caesar's funeral.

Men servasse ut essent qui me perderent?
Did I save them that they might destroy me?

Pacuvius wrote fourteen plays and a satire, but all we have are a handful of fragments. He's hardly ever included in a book such as this, even as a minor poet. Pacuvius is not so much a minor poet, as a forgotten one. I recall the ghost of Hamlet's father saying, "Remember me! Remember me," and close with the epitaph Pacuvius wrote for himself, thinking that perhaps, in some future millenium, someone will do the same for me.

> *Adulescens, tam etsi properas te hoc saxum rogat*
> *Ut sese aspicias, deinde quod scriptum est legas.*
> *Hic sunt poetae Pacuvi Marci sita*
> *Ossa. Hoc volebam nescius ne esses. Vale.*

> Young man, though you hurry by, look at this tombstone
> and read what I have written here:
> Here lie the bones of the poet Marcus Pacuvius.
> Remember something of me. Farewell.

The Late Republic

In 146 BC, when the armies of the Republic razed Carthage to the ground at the end of the Third Punic War, it also sacked Corinth and stole most of its artistic treasures. Even historians of the time were dismayed by Rome's greed and cruelty, a perversion of the ancient ideals that had made the Republic great. While fighting Carthage, Rome also expanded northward and eastward, gaining control of the Po valley and Cisalpine Gaul. As a result of four wars with Macedonia, Greece passed under Roman control. By 133 BC, Rome had conquered the entire western coast of Asia Minor and seized control of the Dardanelles.

During the last century of the Roman republic, the social and political system grew more corrupt, with unscrupulous governors accumulating wealth and power, and army commanders becoming less obediant to the senate, which had become less democratic in its policies. The increase in the wealth of the oligarchy in the second century came mainly from Rome's wars, and since that wealth had to be invested, land was the way to go. Their large estates became devoted to pastures for livestock rather than grain production. It was also Rome's wars of the second century that provided slaves in almost unlimited numbers. This led to brigandage and local rebellions, and eventually the great slave wars from 135 BC to 70 BC that sent slaves and dispossessed peasants from farm to city, helping to make the Roman revolution possible.

☛ **Lucilius** (180-103 BC), The Personal Voice of the Satiric Genre

Ex praecordiis ecfero versum
"From my heart I bring forth my poetry"

It was an age of oratory and satire, with Gaius Lucilius writing outspoken criticism of other writers and men in public life. Lucilius, a member of Scipio Aemilianus' literary circle, was famous as the creator of the (poetical) satire, a purely Roman form of literature. His satires were read and enjoyed for centuries, and served as a model for later satirists, especially Horace.

The poems of Gaius Lucilius, even in the fragments that have survived, present us with savagely satirical vignettes of the aristocracy of the late 2nd century. Like Cato before him, Lucilius writes about the moral degeneration of the state and the duty of each citizen to enter public service, but Lucilius sees public service as part of the problem. Public service only leads to corrupt morals. Ambition itself is vulgar. As the first writer to come from the aristocracy, Lucilius's pen added taste and refinement to the acidic ink of satire.

The same qualities that made the Roman dramatists unsuccessful at comedy—their seriousness, their interest in moral questions, their unforgiving wit—led them to develop a form of literature unknown to the Greeks. Underlying Aristophanes' criticism of society was a real love of Athens. But when the Romans criticized their own society, they did it as moralists and realists, lacing their indignation with sarcasm. The most suitable form was satire, and Lucilius is the first Roman we know of to present scenes of life in verse. Ennius's moralizing verses were mildly satirical, but Lucilius mocked the social conventions of his day with a sharpness of wit that was fresh and irreverent.

Out of the medleys of prose and poetry called *saturae*—usually erotic banter or merry nonsense—Lucilius forged a new form that Horace and Juvenal would perfect a century or so later. Horace acknowledged himself as the follower of Lucilius, and extended the satire to include a genial character (based on himself, of course) who touched on the foibles and absurdities of mankind without bitterness. Horace's poems are vivid depictions of the Rome he knew; not only are they extremely funny, they are easy to translate into almost any language. Who can't relate to Horace's poem about the bore who tries to talk Horace into introducing him to his patron Maecenas, and Horace's attempts to get rid of him?

In the Silver Age that followed Horace, satire reached its height in the verses of Persius and Juvenal. Juvenal whipped himself into a fury at what he saw around him, though it's likely his portrait of Roman society, with its legacy hunters, gluttons, and its crooked contractors, was somewhat overdrawn. Juvenal was bitter and disillusioned, but that was the mood of his day. His portraits of people are vivid and convincing, and his depiction of the decadent society of the imperial capital has become the model for satirists ever since.

Lucilius was a member of the literary circle of Scipio Aemilianus, the military and political leader who urged the destruction of Carthage which resulted in the Third Punic War. It was Lucilius who established the hexameter as the standard meter for Roman satire. Perhaps his reliance on the dactylic hexameter was a self-imposed challenge: How to make everyday subject matter and colloquial diction adhere to the heroic meter used for lofty themes. From Horace onwards, the hexameter would become the sole verse prescribed for satire. We have no evidence that Lucilius used the term *satura*, calling his compositions *poemata* or *sermones*—actually *ludus ac sermones*, which means "joking chats" or "laughing sermons." The original title of his first work was actually Greek, *schedia*, or "improvisations."

Callimachus and the Mixed Stew

It's often written that the origin of the satiric genre called *satura* by the Romans was connected to the Greek word *satyros*, or "satyr." Recently, this notion has been discredited. Rather we should look to the Latin *satura lanx*, a "mixed dish" of offerings presented to the gods. The term probably ceased to be culinary and became solely literary.

Whether or not Lucilius used the term, his satiric impulse was specifically Roman, and can be understood as the search for a genre that would convey his voice. Latin literature from the period of Ennius on developed several standard poetic genres—epic, tragedy, comedy—but none provided the way for direct expression, in which the poet could muse, meditate, or grapple with his relationship to himself and the time in which he lived. Among the Greeks, only **Callimachus** (ca. 310 - 240 BC) demonstrated that one could go outside the canons of epic and narrative drama. His epigrams and hymns were complex compositions designed to be recited or read by a cultivated audience. He created a new literary genre that mixed traditional themes and events from daily life, a synthesis of polished verse and natural speech. This esthetic principle of variety (*poikilia*) avoided the high-sounding uniformity of epic narrative. In some of Ennius's satire, we find snatches of personal voice, the poet speaking in the first person about himself, what can be termed poetic self-consciousness; Ennius, however, did not train his sights on living people, thus not quite meeting the requirements for satire. Naevius was rumored to have lampooned a certain noble family in his verse, but there's no evidence of anyone specific in his compositions. Thus, we give credit to Lucilius for creating the genre we call poetic satire.

Lucilius wrote 30 books of satires of which only 1300 lines survive. His first book was published in 130 BC, and most of it comes down to us through the fragments quoted by grammarians, metricians, and commentators of the late Empire and the Middle Ages who were citing Lucilius because of the rare and unusual words used in his work.

SHOPPING TIP

Lady, you went to the market
and picked up hair, rouge, honey, wax and teeth.
For the same amount of money,
                    you could have bought a face.

GOSSIP

I heard some say that you dye your hair.
I told them, Nikilla, that they were wrong,
since in the open market
                    you bought it raven black.

LOVE OF LEARNING

Zenonis gives a place in her home to Menandros
                a bearded grammarian,
for she has delivered her son to his instruction;
and the bushy pedant even works long into the night,
                with the mother,
practicing their figures, her dangling participles
                and his copulative verb.

FIDELITY IN THE ARTS

Eutychos the portrait painter got twenty one sons,
but even among his children — never one likeness.

   This form of poetry, with its varied meter and subject matter, and use of personal voice and everyday realism, presented itself as an ideal means of expression. For Lucilius, the satire was not a minor genre to be practiced in the shadow of the epic, but aimed at a new audience, one interested in poetry that spoke to its own time, instead of to the heroic past. To this end, he even composed poems dedicated to his lover. One could say he was the precursor of personal love poetry, a genre used to greater effect in Catullus's epigrams and the Augustan elegy. Lucilius rejected the hollow conventionality of the traditional epic and mixed numerous styles—the elevated language of epic, often in a tone of parody, and the idioms of everyday language taken from various social classes, including Greek expressions. Perhaps because Lucilius belonged to the rich provincial aristocracy—Pompey the Great was his nephew—he could get away with the satirical barbs he leveled at some of the most distinguished men in contemporary Rome.

   Publicanus vero ut Asiae fiam, ut scripturarius
   pro Lucilio, id ego nolo et uno hoc muto omnia.

   To be a tax collector in Asia, to gather pasture duties for the government
   instead of being Lucilius — never! I would not trade being myself
                                               for the whole world.

He wasn't interested in running for public office, therefore he didn't care whom he offended, and he offended patricians and commoners alike.

   Yet nowadays from morning to night,
   whether it's a holiday or not,
   the plebs and the senate alike flock to the Forum,
   and never think of leaving.
   They are all up to the same tricks,
   engaged in the same business:
   cheating each other cleverly,
   battling treacherously,

outdoing one another in flattery,
posing as respectable citizens,
laying traps for each other — all of them
acting as though each were the other's mortal enemy.

Like Petronius, who authored the *Satyricon*, Lucilius comes as close to our notion of modern realism as Latin literature gets. His style rides a wave of disharmony and dissonance, an intentional blending of life and art.

Food For Thought

Lucilius in West Egg

The *Concilium Deorum*, one of the longer poems in his first book, presented an assembly of the gods meant to parody the councils held by the Senate to discuss esoteric elements of protocol. Lucilius made fun not only of the Senate, but of a certain writer disliked by the Scipionic circle. In their divine council, the gods decide to punish Lentulus Lupus by having him die of indigestion. Lucilius was mocking lofty literary texts, such as those by Homer and Ennius, whose portrayals of aristocratic and divine councils was a staple of epic poetry. In the same book he describes a rather sordid banquet, a motif we find in later writers such as Horace, who portrayed Nasidienus' banquet in the *Satires* (II.8), and Petronius, whose *Satyricon* presented Trimalchio's orgiastic feast. (The original manuscript title for F. Scott Fitzgerald's *The Great Gatsby* was "Trimalchio in East Egg," as a reference to the extravagant party thrown by the filthy-rich ex-slave in the notorious satire by Petronius, whose official title in Nero's court was Arbiter of Elegance.) Petronius, like Lucilius before him, mocked everything from the *Odyssey* to table manners. Trimalchio's literary ancestor was Lucilius's parvenu Granius, whose banquet gave Lucilius a chance to mock the gastronomic habits of the rich.

The *neoteric* poets of the next generation turned their backs on epic poetry and the declamatory style of Accius and other lofty poets. Thus, Lucilius is a link between Callimachus and the neoterics of the next generation. Almost a thousand lines of his work surivive, but no single substantial passage. Yet, even in the following eight line stanza, we catch a feeling for his cleverness and bite.

Doubly unfortunate are those who dwell in Hell —
    Eutychides the Lyric Poet,
out of breath at last, has had burned with him
    twelve lyres and twenty-five
crates of songs, which poor Charon will have to
    ferry over the charcoal waters.
Alas, where will music-lovers take refuge now that
    Eutychides will be singing for eternity?

An Age of Revolution

The poetry of Lucilius signaled a new era of luxury, depravity, corruption, moral degradation, and profound economic, social, and political change. It was an age of revolution, but one in which no revolution ever came. This era witnessed a major shift in Italian land ownership. Wealth became concentrated in fewer hands, many peasant proprietors sold out to the capitalist farmer, and larger holdings stimulated the growth of ranches and plantations, and cash crops like the olive and vine. Slave labor proved especially efficient. The small farmer had by no means vanished, but the trend was significant: a drop in the number of free peasants, heavier investment in cash-crop farming and in pasturage, and a major expansion of the servile work force. Even Cato supported a law to curb the ownership of excess public land by individual senators.

As the gulf between rich and poor widened, the well-assembled parts of the Roman Republic came unglued. The change in agrarian structure was possibly the most impactful. In the early republic, slavery was more of a domestic arrangement and the small number of slaves were usually absorbed into the family. But with the increase in the holdings of the big landlords, and the spread of the villa system, more slaves were needed to work large farms. The number of slaves in Italy increased to such an extent that modern estimates for the time of Augustus amount to some three million slaves out of seven and a half million inhabitants. Slaves were cheaper to exploit than the local peasantry, who were forced to migrate to the city to find work. The slaves who worked the large farms were brutally treated; this eventually led to the great slave uprisings called the Servile Wars.

Rome's internal problems essentially resulted from her aquisition of a vast overseas empire and her failure to alter her political forms from those of a city-state. The class structure had changed as well. Before, there had been two basic classes: the rich senatorial class, comprised of wealthy landholders, old patrician families, former consuls, provincial governors, and other office holders; and the vast masses of plebs, poor and often unemployed, flocking to the large cities—especially Rome—in ever greater numbers. Now there was a third class—not a middle class between plebs and patricians, but wealthy businessmen and rich financiers known as the *equites,* so-called because they had originally come from the ranks of those sufficiently well off to afford a horse and armor and provide the cavalry of the Roman army. Most of the *equites* were merchants, administrators, bankers, entrepreneurs, and *publicani,* i.e. private businessmen who bid for government contracts on public works and services, the most important of which was collecting taxes. Contracts for taxes owed were usually farmed out or sold by public contract to the highest bidder, who then recouped with as much profit as possible. The *publicani* set their own conditions and some of their number subsequently engaged in inventive fraud to turn a profit at the government's cost. They bought up contracts for the salt tax, harbor dues, and the *scriptura* or pasturage tax. The contractors continued to manage the organization of supplies for Rome's armies during the second century, a task that grew in magnitude as Rome's military conquests increased, and further augmented the *publicani*'s influence. More lucrative still was the operation of the Spanish mines, very probably in the hands of publicani since 194 *BC*. The *equites* were capable of exerting considerable political force, and were particularly influential in the time of Cicero, who, himself the son of an eques, tried to unite them with the senate in a *Concordia Ordinum*, "concord between the classes."

Those of the senatorial rank were not permitted to carry on trade or business, just as *equites* were not allowed to become senators, since that was reserved for large property holders.   One also had to own property to join the Roman legions, but as more soldiers were needed , that requirement was abolished. Military service was now extended to the landless proletariat whose main reason for joining the army was the expected reward of land upon retirement. Eventually, armies of proletarians, controlled by military governors and commanders, functioned almost as private armies that stood as a counterforce to the power of the Senate, the aristocracy, and the equestrian order. While most of the social agitation involved the poor against the rich, men like Caesar, Pompey, and Crassus who claimed to represent the people, were really aligned with one of the two higher orders, the senators or the *equites*, and in time many of the equestrian class shared the same social status as senators. When Cicero proposed his *Concordia Ordinum* to promote harmony between the different classes, it was really a proposed agreement between the two higher orders to fleece the rest of the Republic. When the final showdown came between Caesar, Pompey, and Crassus, it was a standoff between Caesar's claim to represent the people, Crassus' alignment with the *equites*, and Pompey's loyalty to the Senate. Of the three, it was Caesar who had the support of "the people," and controlled a powerful and efficient army as well.

A third pressure on social stabiltiy came from non-Roman Italians who wanted the same rights as Roman citizens, including entitlement to the corn dole and the right to a trial. The catch-22 was that most of those rights could only be exercised if one lived in Rome, and few of the peasants and farmers had that opportunity. It was the most influential members of the peninsula's aristocracy who stirred up their own people to fight Rome's ruling classes for greater participation in the government, which led to the civil unrest and bloodbaths called The Social War.

Each of these changes in the social and economic structure was further exacerbated by the increasing concentration of wealth within the governing class. The only way to maintain their fortunes was through political power, and many great families pursued political success as a way to hold onto the family fortune. Their political vision, however, was usually short-sighted, resulting in a resistance to changes that would in the long run have prevented the collapse of the republic. They moved to block the Gracchi brothers' proposed new agrarian law, for instance, for fear that their own estates would be diminished. But when Tiberius and Gaius Gracci proposed new land distributions, they did so in order to restore the class of small landholders, not to diminish the power of the aristocracy. They wanted to alleviate the widespread poverty and the shortage of men in various parts of Italy to work the farms. These were the men who migrated to the city, became landless proletarians, joined the army, and empowered the great military commanders destined to take control of the state; in the process, the constitutional basis of the Roman Republic was dismantled.

At the same time, through the influx of foreign wealth and new building, Rome was becoming the largest city in the Western world. The discovery of concrete made possible the construction of arches, arcades, aquaducts, basilicas, public halls and monuments. In many ways, of all the Roman's inventions, this mixture of lime and water with adhesives of sand, clay and volcanic cinder was the most revolutionary. But how were they going to keep men down on the farm once they had seen Rome. Half a centruy later, when Augustus proclaimed himself Emperor, the first thing his minister of propaganda did was encourage Virgil to write poems glorifying the countryside as a way to get young men to return to the farm.

The growth of the city attracted more and more people, especially dispossessed farmers and freed slaves who were forced to sleep in rickety shacks vulnerable to fires and floods. The growing discontent of slaves in both city and countryside led to social disruption. Initially, these slave revolts were confined to Sicily, which supplied Rome with more than half her grain. A major crisis erupted on that island in 135 BC (The First Servile War), and urban unrest continued well into the next century. In 104 BC, chain gangs of Greek slaves followed Titus, the mad young son of a Roman equestrian, who armed them with weapons he had purchased at a gladitorial auction. The revolt was put down, but another erupted a decade later when 60,000 slaves and 5,000 horsemen followed an Italian freedman and snake charmer called Salvius. Unable to charm the Roman army, Salvius was executed and his followers dispersed. In 74 BC, the last of the slave wars (The Third Servile War) shook the Roman world because it took place on the Italian peninsula itself. The principal rebels were professional gladiators led by a Thracian named Spartacus. During the initial phase of the insurrection, Spartacus and seventy of his followers climbed Mount Vesuvias, hiding out in the rugged wooded hollow on the summit. Trapped once their location was discovered, they spent the night braiding the wild grape vines that grew there and lowered themselves down the steep side of the mountain. The Romans camped below were caught unawares and were defeated in a skirmish before dawn. Before the revolt was over, Spartacus's seventy men had swelled to seventy thousand, including slaves of all kinds, creating a force strong enough to defeat four Roman armies. After several years of looting the rich Italian countryside, Spartacus and his men were finally defeated. He was crucified, along with six thousand of his slave followers, along the Appian Way outside of Rome. Thereafter, Rome looked fearfully upon their enormous slave population, which outnumbered them three to one.

The Gracchi brothers, Tiberius and Gaius, brothers-in-law of Scipio Aemilianus, proposed winning support of the people through radical reforms aimed at the alleviation of poverty, the protection of provincials from senatorial oppression, the limiting of senators' powers, and land resettlement for peasants. In 133 BC, conservative elements persuaded many of the people that Tiberius was really trying to seize autocratic control of the state. When the Assembly met to consider the agrarian land bill limiting the holding of public land and redistributing the surplus to the people, fighting broke out and a crowd of senators, with the help of their henchmen cornered Tiberius at the door of the Temple of Jupiter Capitolinus and clubbed him to death along with three hundred of his supporters.

> This was the first occasion in the city of Rome when the blood of Roman citizens was shed and recourse was had to the sword, in both cases without fear of punishment. Thereafter law was overwhelmed by force and greater respect was accorded to greater power, and civil strife which in the past had been resolved by agreement was settled by the sword.
>
> [Gaius Velleius (*c.* 19 BC-after 30 AD), Roman historian]

Tiberius's aim was not the disintegration of the Roman oligarchic system; his reforms were not that revolutionary, but his death foreshadowed a century of rebellion that ended in the fall of the Republic.

Ten years later, his more radical brother Gaius proposed laws that called for the provision of wheat at reasonable prices and new courts of law that would prevent illegal confiscation of land. Gaius infuriated senators when he proposed that all judges appointed to the lawcourts to investigate abuses by provincial governors should come from the *equites*, the rising body of knights whose interests naturally clashed with the men of property who comprised the Senate. The knights had made their fortunes as businessmen and *publicani*, private tax collectors. Perhaps the final provocation came when Gaius proposed extending Roman citizenship to all of Rome's Latin and Italian allies who fought against Hannibal. When Gaius tried to run for re-election as tribune, his opponent brought together a crowd of senators and their supporters to bring him down. When Gaius failed to win re-election, probably due to the senate's interference, violence broke out between the Senate and those who had voted for Gaius. The Senate declared a public emergency and Gaius was forced to flee for his life. When he reached the bridge that crossed the Tiber he was confronted by adversaries on both sides. At the point of capture, he committed suicide by ordering a slave to cut his throat. Subsequently, three thousand of his supporters were executed after perfunctory trials.

The attempted reforms of the Gracchi brothers helped bring about the two groupings that were to oppose each other over the course of the next century: a conservative faction called the *optimates* (best men) and the *populares* who were willing to bypass the Senate to work through the Assembly of the Roman People (*Populus Romanus*). While these groups seemed to function as opposing political parties, they were more like ideological labels. A politician of the *populares* worked through the popularly elected assemblies and the office of the tribune and probably supported economic measures such as land redistribution, debt cancellation, and subsidized corn; but once in power he was more likely to oppose anything that would jeopardize the power of the Senate. While the lower orders were continually demonstrating for greater rights and less economic oppression, the upper orders fought among themselves for a greater share of the pie. A politician might claim to represent the *populares,* but he was not about to champion a reform that would do ultimate harm to the large landowning class or the wealthy businessmen and *equites* that controlled the Senate. When and if tryanny were to come, the question was which oligarchic faction would the dictator represent. The two party system of *populares* and *optimates* was really two heads on the same aristocratic body. The old system of shifting alliances based on intermarriage and back door deals continued to function on down to the end of the Republic.

The unrest in Rome weakened its ability to deal with its territories in the east, especially those in Asia Minor and what is today Syria. Mithridates VI Eupator, ruler of the kingdom of Pontus along the Black Sea, took possession of these Roman territories, and in order to control them effectively, put to death all Romans living there. A hundred thousand men, women, and children were massacred, an early example of genocide, and one which Rome would not allow to go unavenged.

The failure of the reforms proposed by the Gracchi was disasterous for Rome and for the rest of Italy which was slowly being Romanized. A conservative reaction followed, leading to armed conflict between the senate and the people. In 91 BC, more slave revolts broke out. The building of Roman roads throughout Italy and the wealth that flowed in from the East created an efficient market economy and helped unify the whole peninsula. The rest of Italy wanted to benefit from Rome's prosperity, and the Italian demand for Roman citizenship exploded into the so-called Social War (from *socii Italici*—"Italian allies"—the 150 Italian communities who were allied with Rome but did not enjoy citizenship, and therefore the many privileges accorded the Latins) in which at least half of Italy rose in revolt. The rebels formed a government and even struck coins inscribed with the word "Italia" written in the Oscan letters of the old Oscan language. Among the towns that joined in the revolt were Pompeii and Herculaneum, which were quickly subdued by the Roman legions under the command of the ruthless general Sulla. Today, you can still see the marks made by Roman seige engines on the walls of Pompeii, and when Herculaneum is completely excavated, the signs of Roman battering will probably be found there, too.

Fighting for control of the city were two Roman generals, Lucius Cornelius Sulla (nicknamed Felix, Latin for "Lucky"), a fifty-year-old patrician and leader of the *optimates* in the civil war against the *populares,* and Gaius Marius, a crudely outspoken soldier who had become wealthy as a businessman and *publicani.* Because of the wealth it would bring him, Sulla wanted to command the army designated to fight Mithridates in the East. But the tribune Sulpicius Rufus relieved Sulla of his command, forcing him to leave Rome. Sulla assembled the six legions still loyal to him and marched on Rome, making it the first time in the Republic's history that a consul had entered the city at the head of his army. Known for his vindictive cruelty, Sulla took control of the city by force, killing Sulpicius and driving Marius from the city. Even Sulla's friends were shocked by his brutality. Sulla then took his army, crossed to Asia Minor, defeated Mithridates and amassed even more booty.

While Sulla was gone, Rome had fallen into the hands of his political enemies, the *populares,* led by Marius, who extorted taxes by recruiting a professional army from the proletariat—including volatile slaves he had freed from prison—who then got to share in the pickings. Marius increased their pay and gave them a laundry allowance and burial funds with enough left over to pay for a regimental dinner. He became one of the Republic's most popular generals. His new army of common citizens and former slaves carried a pack that weighed forty-five pounds, and each man carried a pike and dagger—to quote St. Paul, "the whole armour of God, the belt of truth, the breast-plate of righteousness, and the sword of the spirit." Clanking down the street with their heavy packs and armour, these slave-soldiers became known as "Marius's Mules." With the help of the patrician Cinna, Marius took revenge upon Sulla's supporters, instigating an orgy of violence, a series of bloody massacres that were the worst yet in Roman history. Marius ordered his bodyguards to kill any person whom he did not greet. For five days, the streets were filled with blood as thousands were killed. In its graphic depiction of carnage, Lucan's epic poem rivals modern films.

> With what speed death strode through the streets in his terrible progress!
> Noble and commoner died; not a breast was safe from the sword stroke.
> Unrestricted, the weapons of death ranged after its victims.
> Blood lay in pools in the temples, the pavement was red from the slaughter,
> Slippery, wet underfoot. Age counted for nothing. The killers
> Felt no qualms at all at anticipating the final
> Days of the elderly already near their departure,
> Nor at snapping the thread of life of a pitiful baby.
> Blood lust fed on itself, and by now the search for the guilty
> Showed an irresolute purpose. Some died for no better reason
> Than to make up a total, in other cases the butchers
> Sliced the heads from the shoulders of strangers simply to swing them
> While they walked—they felt ashamed to walk empty-handed.
> Time is too short to lament the death of the populace.
> Blood of tribunes soaked the wooden fixtures that grimly
> Caught the bodies thrown from the rock of Tarpeia. And Vesta
> Violated, failed to protect old Scaevola, slaughtered
> At the very shrine of his goddess, before her ever-
> Burning hearth; but his aged and weary body emitted
> Little blood from his throat, and he spared the life of the fire.

[Lucan, *Bellum Civile* ("The Civil War"), Book 2, 120-127]

Marius even refused to bury the bodies that littered the city. Once in power, he was elected consul five years in succession, but kept control of his loyal troops, becoming the first of a series of warlords who were to dominate the last century of the Republic. Shortly afterwards, Marius had a mental breakdown and died in 86 BC. But during his consulship, the Senate granted all Italians Roman citizenship.

Once again, the Senate tried to relieve Sulla of his command, but he refused to relinquish power. Returning from the East, he landed at Brundisium in 83 BC, and was joined by his protégé, a young man whose name has passed into English as Pompey. Gnaeus Pompeius Magnus, "The Great," was married to Sulla's step-daughter, Aemilia; Sulla advanced his career by giving him posts normally held only by consuls, and after Aemilia's death Pompey married Mucia of the well-connected Metelli family. Another of Sulla's lietenants was Marcus Licinius Crassus, who sought success through wealth and the influence that wealth could bring him. Their invasion of Italy ushered in another period of bloody civil war. Sulla seized Rome a year later and showed no mercy toward those who had sided with Marius. With the help of a bodyguard of ten thousand men known as "Cornelii"—composed of the freed slaves of his proscribed opponents—Sulla called for the immediate execution of his enemies, adding the device of proscription, the posting-up of the names of victims to be killed without trial and their property confiscated. Both Crassus and Pompey benefitted financially from the proscriptions, especially Crassus who enriched himself in a variety of ways—he was awarded ownership of silver mines and kept many slaves to rebuild houses damaged by fire, which he bought for next to nothing from distraught owners, often while the fire was raging. In time, he came to possess a large part of Rome.

The cities that had fought against Sulla were included in his vendetta and confiscated lands were distributed among his soldiers who squatted like colonists on the lands of dispossessed small farmers. The rights of citizenship these cities had been granted were revoked. After numerous proscriptions, in which over 40 senators and 1600 families of the equestrian class were listed as outlaws and their property confiscated, most of the accused were brutally executed in the bloodiest civilian massacre that Rome had ever experienced. During Sulla's reign of terror, nearly five thousand Roman citizens were killed, and hundreds of severed heads were prominently displayed around the city. Three thousand Samnite prisoners were slaughtered in voting pens (called *ovilia*, "sheep pens") on the Campus Martius, a military training ground outside the city walls where space had been set aside for horticulture, depots for wild animals, temples, and mausoleums.

> Bad indeed was the slaughter [of Marius], but worse the vengeance of Sulla.
> He proceeded to drain what blood remained in the city,
> Little enough by now.
> > The people who perished were guilty —
> Yes, but only the guilty by then could still be surviving.
> Then free rein was given to private feuding, and anger,
> Now untrammeled by law, went wild. No longer for one man
> Were all the crimes committed, but everyone did what he wanted.
> Servants ignobly drove their swords through their masters' bodies;
> Sons were bespattered with fathers blood — some even contended
> As to which had the right to sever the head of a parent.
> Brothers were killed to provide the blood-reward to their brothers;
> Fugitives crowded the tombs, the living jostled the corpses;
> No room even was left in the lairs of beasts of the forest.
> Heads of distinguished men were thrown on a heap piled up in the Forum.
> Anyone anywhere killed could there be identified.
> When the heads were decaying and time had erased from the features
> All distinguishing marks, the wretched parents (who knew them
> Still, in spite of it all) came trembling and furtively stole them.
> One man with the head of his brother in his hand toured the corpses
> Of Sulla's pacification in search of the neck that would fit the head he carried.
> [Lucan, *Bellum Civile*, 2, 139-173]

Once in control, Sulla revived the obsolete title of dicatator. The old republican constitution had provided for dictatorship in times of crisis, but it was assumed the holder of the title would remain in power no more than six months. Sulla declared that it would run for as long as the dictator deemed necessary. For the next two years this man, whose complexion was so pitted and blotched that one of the scurrilous jesters at Athens said it resembled a "mulberry sprinkled over with oatmeal" (hence the surname), personally controlled the government of Rome. He set about reforming the constitution, restoring the supremacy of the Roman Senate and pushing through several new laws, among them one forbidding provincial governors to make war outside the province they governed, or even to cross its borders with troops. If they did, it was treason. This was the law broken by Caesar three decades later when he crossed the Rubicon in 49 BC.

The state was still faced with serious social and economic problems. Sulla's inadequate solution was a series of vast building projects that included the construction of the Tabularium (the State Record Office) and the restoration of the ancient Senate House, the Curia, which was tradtionally founded by Tullius Hostilius, the third king of Rome. By the podium of the new Senate House stood a pedestal with a golden statue of the Goddess of Victory, which was removed four centuries later by a Christian emperor, replaced after a pagan protest, and finally taken out and destroyed two years later.

Sulla married his fifth wife, "a very beautiful woman of a most distinguished family." Plutarch tells us that he continued to see women who were ballet dancers or harpists, and kept company with "common people from the theatre."

> He drank with them on couches night and day. His chief favorites were Roscius the comedian, Sorex the arch mime, and Metrobius the female imnpersonator, for whom, though past his prime, he still professed a passionate fondness. By these courses he encouraged a disease which had begun from unimportant cause; and for a long time he failed to observe that his bowels were ulcerated, till at length the corrupted flesh broke out into lice and worms. Many people were employed day and night in destroying them, but the work so multiplied under their hands, that not only his clothes, baths, basins, but his very meat was polluted with that flux and contagion, they came swarming out in such numbers. He went frequently by day into the bath to scour and cleanse his body, but all in vain; the flesh changed into worms too rapidly and too abundantly for any ablutions to overcome it.
>
> [from Plutarch's account in the famous Drydan translation published
> at the end of the 17th century and revised in 1864 by Arthur Hugh Clough]

Finally, in 80 BC, he stepped down as dictator and became consul, then retired to private life in Campania, where he died a year later. The diseased body was brought back to Rome and laid upon a funeral pyre.

> The day being cloudy in the morning, they deferred carrying forth the corpse till about three in the afternoon, expecting it would rain. But a strong wind blowing full upon the funeral pile, and setting it all in a bright flame, the body was consuemd so exactly in good time, that the pyre had begun to smoulder, and the fire was upon the point of expiring, when a violent rain came down, which continued till night. His monument stands in the Campus Martius, with an epitaph of his own writing; the substance of it being, that he had not been outdone by any of his friends in doing good, nor by any of his foes in doing bad.

Poetry Between the Gracchi and Sulla:
"The Pre-Neoterics"

T he old-fashioned and respectable nobles looked about them and concluded that the Republic was already in decline. The old virtues and deep sense of responsibilty to the state were no longer as important as the great riches brought to the city from foreign plunder, the gold and silver that poured in from Spain, the luxurious furniture and art objects taken from the East. Victorious generals marched into Rome down the Via Sacra with their faces painted in the color of blood, holding aloft golden crowns too heavy to wear on their heads. Behind them walked their singing legions at the head of long lines of weary captives, many to become slaves, the rest to be executed in the cells beneath the spurs of the Capitoline Hill. Taking up the rear came the procession of chariots clattering over the cobblestones, leading the wagonloads of plunder that included jewels, gold vessels, tapestries and works of art. There was a time when these riches were meant for the city coffers and the honor of the gods. Now much of it was divided among the soldiers, with most going to their generals who became men of enormous wealth. The transference of the legions' loyalty to the state to loyalty to their commanders was to have profound consequences for the future of the Republic.

There were still poets imitating and copying the Greek epic, writing in traditional meters and touching on traditional subjects. But for the young, it was not an age that encouraged epic poetry steeped in the virtues of the nation. The influence of the Alexandrian school of Greek poets of the third and second centuries impacted the young Roman poets of the first century. The chief features of that school were a development of new, miniature genres, especially epyllion, elegy, and epigram. Their regard for form left a lasting impression on Latin literature. The greatest exponent of Alexandrianism was Catullus, the great lyric poet who was at the center of the radical social change that marked the end of the Republic. Catullus and his generation came of age in atime of great social unrest, not unlike the generation that came of age after World War I, calling themselves "moderns." In many ways they were also like the generation of the 1960s, hippies, artists, and intellectuals who rejected the academic school of verse and wrote highly charged, personal poetry. Likewise, the poets of the late Republic called themselves *neoterics* ("moderns"), and much of what they accomplished could be traced to the efforts of that generation who came before them, the first generatrion of Latin poets grown weary of the yoke of ancient tradition. These poets wrote in the period between the Gracchi and Sulla; they turned away from the epic poem glorifying the state and found that the only reponse to an age of turmoil and social dislocation was to focus on form and personal expression. Lucillus had paved the way with his satiric epigrams. The pre-neoterics turned inward and wrote polished poems that mocked the sloppy epics and tedious poetry of their day.

☛ **Quintus Latatius Catulus (150 BC - 87 BC)**

Quintus Catulus should not be confused with Gaius Valerius Catullus, the great lyric poet of the late Republic who was born three years after Quintus Catulus died. Where Catullus was the leading neoteric poet of his generation, we may consider Catulus the leader of the pre-neoterics. While these poets were influenced by the Alexandrian poets of Greece and were aware that they were breaking with traditional forms and metrics, they did not think of themselves as "moderns," as the neoterics did.

Catulus was known for his autobiographical *De Consulato et de Rebus Gestis*. He was an orator and writer of histories, but above all he was a poet, one of the first to write epigrammatic poems in the Hellenistic style. A group of poets who shared his penchant for light, entertaining poetry called themselves the "circle of Lutatius Catulus," probably meant to echo, tongue-in-cheek, the Scipionic circle. When Marius and Cornelius captured Rome in 87 BC, they put Catulus's name on the list of proscribed citizens, and he committed suicide. Only two of his epigrams survive.

☛ Valerius Aeditus (*fl.* beginning of 1st century BC)

Aeditus belonged to Catulus' circle, writing love epigrams that experiemnted with the new poetic form in the Alexandrian style.

☛ Porcius Licinus (*fl.* beginning of 1st century BC)

Licinus was another experimental poet who belonged to Catulus' circle. Only fragments in trochaic septenarii and one epigram survive.

☛ Volcacius Sedigitus (*fl.* beginning of 1st century BC)

Sedigitus was known for his *De Poetis*, a critical commentary in iambic senarii in which he lists the top Latin comic writers with Statius first, Plautus second, Naevius third, and Terence sixth.

☛ Laevius Melissus (*fl.* beginning of 1st century BC)

Laevius lived around 100 BC and wrote love poems in a great variety of meters called *Eroto-poegnia*, "The Diversions of Love." Known for his bold (and often morbid) sensuality, affected erudition, and odd juxtapositions of language, he was an important pioneer of the new poetics. Many of his poems were playful nuggets, in a style later called nugatory poetry (from *nugae*, "trifles"). His startling displays of linguistic imagination mark him as a direct forerunner of Catullus and the other neoteric poets. Sometimes Laevius playfully coined new words, like the sesquipedalian compound *subductisupercilicarptores*, which loosely translated, means "to persistently annoy someone by lifting one's eyebrows." He used the term to characterize those critical of his poetry, coining the word as an example of the linguistic trickery he was being criticized for—as if to say, "If you can't take a joke, *ambulatiuncula longus pontis brevis*," that is, " take a long walk on a short pier."

☛ Valerius Cato

Valerius was a poet who also enjoyed great prestige as a formidable critic, grammarian, and teacher. An epigram written by one of his circle, Furius Bibaculus, attests to his influence:

Cato grammaticus, Latina Siren,
qui solus legit ac facit poetas.

Cato the grammarian, the Latin Siren,
who alone reads talent, who alone can make a poets.

Nothing survives of Cato's work except his reputation for having been very influential as a poet and critic; he may well have been the originator of the neoteric movement.

The struggle of the *populares* against the entrenched nobles was the common theme of the Roman historian Gaius Sallust (86-35 BC). In his view, the moral collapse of Rome began when Sulla's troops marched on Rome. According to Sallust, once Carthage had been destroyed in 146 BC, Rome was left without an incentive to be self-disciplined. Greed and ambition became the motives of political service, not virtue and service to the state. Sallust was not the only historian who held this view. The notion of Rome's degeneracy as beginning with the elimination of her foreign foes in 146 BC became a commonplace in subsequent Latin literature, as well in the writings of Greek historians. Polybius (c. 200-after 118 BC) wrote a *pragmatike historia*, a factual history written in the *koine*, the "common dialect" of Greek, without the elegance of the Greek prose writers of the classical period. Polybius assessed the Hannibalic war as a central turning point for his universal history, and realized that the institutions and character of Rome's people had gained her a republic capable of becoming an empire, but once achieved, those very qualities and institutions would unravel and cause the empire to fall apart. The historian Posidonius (*c.* 135-*c.* 50 BC) lived through an age that witnessed the beginnings of Roman exploitation of the East on a systematic basis, the servile revolts in Sicily, the devastating conflict between Rome and her Italian *socii,* the eruption of the Mithridatic war, and the Roman brutality that followed it. Posidonius pointed to the destruction of Carthage and Corinth as marking a significant dividing line in Roman history. His fifty-two books of history were a continuation of the history of Polybius, from 146 BC to the dictatorship of Sulla. Very few fragments survive. Though biased in favour of the *optimates* and hence hostile to the Gracchi, he recognized the corruption that the *optimates* engendered. His book had a great impact on Cicero, Lucretius, and Virgil. The loss of his works is a particular misfortune for Latin literature. Where Polybius had witnessed Scipio's prophecy and had a foreboding himself of Rome's moral decline, Posidonius had seen it happen.

Sulla's methods and laws benefitted the politicians who supported him. As a reward for their loyalty, they received property confiscated during the proscription. Many of the new laws survived well into the late republic; even Cicero opposed changing them because he felt the cohesion of the state depended on them.

Cicero's reputation as an orator was so great that many speeches by other orators of the time have survived only in fragments. In this age of social unrest, oratory was the underpinning of political advancement. The written text was not as valued as the spoken word, though the principals of oratory had a significant effect on the writing of poetry. The age old conflict between eloquence and natural diction became part of the political agenda of those who taught and practiced speech-making. For centuries, the aristocracy brought in Greek teachers to educate their children; consequently the Asianic manner with its florid exuberance of style predominated in the speeches of politicians appealing to the members of the ruling oligarchy. When the school of rhetoric at Rome was closed by the censors, it was probably because it had a democratic, pro-Gracchan tendency, teaching children of the *populares* to speak in the natural diction and straightforward style known as Atticism. Those who believed in this type of oratory felt the speaker could appeal to a broader audience if his style were concise and to the point. The Atticists used the loose sentence structure that moved directly from subject to predicate, as opposed to the periodic sentences of Cicero which emphasized the building of meaning through appositive phrases that built dramatically toward a conclusion.

Food for Thought

"Lend Me Your Ears"

Marc Antony was an orator who used the Asianic style; among the outstanding Atticist orators were Julius Caesar and Marcus Brutus. Contrast Brutus's simple speech in Shakespeare's play to the more eloquent one delivered by Mark Antony. The eloquence of Brutus's speech is controlled and avoids grandiosity, unlike Mark Antony's, which uses the musicality of refined phrases and a series of colorful words. Shakespeare's genius as a writer can partly be attributed to his ability to blend both Asianism and Atticism in the speeches of many of his greatest characters, including Hamlet, Falstaff, and Macbeth. Many contemporary poets feel torn between the desire to write in a florid, dense academic style and the diction of natural speech. Contemporary confessional poets criticize academic poets for being too affected, writing in a style that's precious and overly controlled. Academic poets criticize the confessional poets for being whiners, writing in a discursive style that rambles on without musical coherence. This opposition can be traced back to the conflict between the Asianists and Atticists which first took shape in the political hothouse of Roman eloquence and oratory, and we see it become manifest in the writings of the two great poets of this period, Lucretius and Catallus.

Within the next few decades Italy became effectively Romanized. Numerous local cultures and languages were eradicated. Within Cicero's lifetime, Etruscan had virtually disappeared and Oscan inscriptions on tombstones were gradually replaced by inscriptions in Latin. Where religious practices and local customs had been diverse before the Social

---

War, rules governing marriage, inheritance, and religious observance became steadily more uniform. One of the most important changes in the social fabric was the resettlement of veterans on confiscated public land. As a result of Pompey's success in the eastern wars, thousands of veterans who had been uprooted from their homes were retired in places far from their place of birth, yet connected to Rome as a result of the new roads radiating out like spokes on a wheel from the great city. Imagine thousands of American veterans back from the war in the Pacific, settling into new housing tracts built throughout Southern California, creating an urban matrix unlike anything that existed before it, profoundly changing the fabric of American society. The golden age of Roman road-building linked the whole of Italy, both actually and symbolically. Returning from service with the armies of Rome, it was the soldiers who carried Roman coinage into the remote backwaters of the Apennines, and it was these same soldiers, after long decades spent in the Latin-speaking army, who facilitated the rise of Latin as the language of all Italy.

Of all the consequences of the Roman revolution, the spread of Romanization, and the social realignment of Italian communities, were the most significant and lasting. It made possible the cultural consenus necessary for a great national literature which finally emerged with the poems of Lucretius and Catullus, who wrote during the Classical Age of the Republic, and the poems of Virgil and Ovid, who wrote during the Golden Age of the Empire.

The Classical Age of the Republic

The last period of the republic (78-30 BC) is associated with the names Pompey, Caesar, Crassus, Catilene, Cicero, Verres, Lepidus, Clodius, and Cato "The Younger." Pompey was the most powerful Roman general of the 70s and 60s and chief architect of the downfall of Sulla's political system. He was elected consul several times, elimatede piracy from the Mediterranean and went on to conquer huge Asian territories. Julius Caesar, a politician of the left who achicvcd ultimatc triumph through brilliant gencralship, is considered "the sole creative genius ever produced by Rome," according to the Roman historian Mommsen. Marcus Crassus was a conservative politician noted for his avarice and political ambition, and a notorious profiteer in Sulla's proscriptions. Catiline was an impoverished patrician who benefitted from the corrupt Sullan era and headed a conspiracy to overthrow the state. Marcus Tullius Cicero was a great orator and prosecutor who exposed the Catiline conspiracy. Gaius Verres was prosecuted for gross dishonesty during his governship of Sicily. Marcus Lepidus amassed a fortune from Sulla's proscriptions and led a mass uprising of dispossessed Italians, dying shortly after his defeat at the Milvian Bridge. Publius Clodius Pulchur was a gangster politician notorious for his violence and profligacy whose control of street gangs facilitated political success. Marcus Porcius Cato, "the Younger," was a conservative senator who opposed Caesar. Any one of them might have emerged as sole ruler of the Republic, their political and personal lives intertwined in ways that made and broke alliances, a kind of musical chairs in which a political enemy one month became a political ally and an in-law the next.

Men like Pompey, Crassus, and Caesar rose from lawless beginnings to a preeminence in which they could discard the use of naked force. Money secured power, which required more money to maintain. Bribes had to be paid, and money made by corruption and fraud doled out to supporters. In order to finance those debts, more schemes were hatched. Commanders enjoyed control over loyal troops who understood that their own profit depended upon the success of their leaders. It was said of provincial governors that they needed to make three fortunes: one to recoup their election expenses, another to bribe the jury at their trials for misgovernment, and a third to live off of after the aquittal.

For the next two decades, these men danced a complicated round marked by political corruption and a series of shifting alliances, political deals, strong-armed tactics, resourceful marriages, and expedient divorces. By 70 BC, the consuls were Pompey, conqueror of Sertorius in Spain, and Crassus, who had suppressed the revolt of Spartacus in Italy, but Pompey, after crucifying many of the fugitives, claimed credit for the victory, deeply offending Crassus. Despite their personal differences, Crassus and Pompey joined forces against the Senate to repeal much of Sulla's legislation. Crassus had actually made a fortune in Sulla's proscriptions, and Sulla had spared the young Julius Caesar's life. Caesar was soon to marry Sulla's granddaughter Pompeia. But while Pompey was supressing revolt in the East, Crassus and Caesar became leaders of the popular party and plotted together in Rome against Pompey's return.

Caesar had covered many of his debts from the provincial spoils gained while governor of Further Spain (that part of Spain bordering the Pacific; Nearer Spain was roughly equivalent to the eastern half facing the Mediterranean). But now he "had to make a bigger profit in one year than Verres had in three." Neglecting his duties as praetor, he concentrated on attacking independent tribes. The booty enabled him to clear his debts and pay large sums into the treasury, ingratiating the Senate. But an incident, in which Publius Clodius Pulchur, an unsavory politician, profaned the mysteries of the Bona Dea, eventually led Caesar to divorce his wife, Pompeia. That year, in Caesar's absence, Clodius disguised himself as a woman and tried to seduce Pompeia at the rites of the Bona Dea, from which men were strictly excluded. She is supposed to have kicked him out, but Caesar felt Clodius had connections worth cultivating and a scandal could have damaged Caesar's chances for consulship. He maintained that Clodius did nothing immoral and divorced Pompeia to remove any taint of suspicion. He later married Calpurnia. Pompey also divorced his wife Mucia who allegedly committed adultery with Caesar. Pompey later married Caesar's daughter Julia, who died the year before Crassus died. Crassus failed to gain his own military command. In the end, he found that without military force, political power didn't count for much in the late republic. He died learning that lesson. His defeat by the Parthian army was one of the greatest military disasters in Roman history.

Meanwhile, Lucius Catiline, a patrician of disreputable character, failed in his attempt to overthrow the state. He was killed in 62 BC, and the other leaders of the conspiracy were arrested and executed. It was Cicero, the great orator and statesman, who was credited with foiling Catiline's attempt at revolution, and who called for a *concordia ordinum* (Concord

Between the Orders), a reconciliation of all moderate elements in the state, hoping to end the Republic's divisive factionalism—not with an eye toward mitigating the burdens of the poor, but to promote harmony among those of the upper classes so they could better exploit the lower orders. But it was not to be.

70-30 BC, The Ciceronian Age of Roman Literature: Cicero, Lucretius, Catullus,

☞ **Marcus Tullius Cicero (106-43 BC)***Brutus, Orator*

Much of what we know of the last years of the republic we know from the writings of Cicero, especially his speeches and letters. Atticus, a younger friend, said that one needs no organized history of the time, it is enough to read the 900 letters of Cicero. His letters cover personal and cultural matters and his official (and unofficial) views of the most significant political events of that era. If it weren't for Caesar's account of the Gallic Civil War, Varro's antiquarian and agricultural writings, and various Roman legal documents preserved on stone or bronze, we might easily think that the life of the late-Republic was all a figment of Cicero's imagination. The great quantity of his work survives because Cicero was considered the greatest prose writer of his day, and one of the most persuasive orators who ever lived. Schools of rhetoric used his texts as models of oratory; grammar schools used his letters as textbooks. Only his poetry was ignored. Justifiably so. Though he began writing poetry at an early age and continued writing it to the end of his life, he failed to impress his contemporaries or the generations that followed. Martial, the great Latin satiricist of the next century, mocked Cicero's pretentious verse, claiming he lacked the true heart of a poet and wrote "without inspiration from the Muses, without any assistance from Apollo." His self-aggrandizing and self-congratulatory verse was boring at best; later writers considered his pompous pat on the back the worse hexameter ever written:

> *O fortunatum, natam me consule Roman.*
>
> Oh, fortunate Rome, that dates its birth from my consulate.

Cicero's real literary impact came from the speeches he made before the Senate, Assembly, and the lawcourts. He developed a periodic style marked for its elaborately balanced clauses and persuasive rhythmic cadences, laying the foundations for modern prose.

He was born in a small village 70 miles south-east of Rome, the elder of two sons of a wealthy equestrian family. He studied law in Rome, and at the age of 17 saw military service in the Social War (90-88). He served under Pompeius Strabo, father of Pompey the Great, who was the same age as Cicero and whose acquaintance Cicero probably made at this time. Throughout his life Cicero was to remain a supporter of Pompey, seeing him as the one man who could save Rome from foreign enemies and internal revolution without destroying the constitutional fabric of the Republic. As a lawyer, Cicero became known for his great speeches, successfully defending, among others, Roscius of Ameria on a charge of parricide, the rich *eques* Cluentius on a charge of poisoning his step-father, and his friend the comic actor Roscius. Cicero was elected queastor (financial adminstrator) when he was 30 and served in the Senate until his death. While he made his fame with high-profile, tabloid-type cases, he made his fortune defending families of the equestrian class, who were to support him in his political career. His reputation was unshakably established in 70 BC with his brilliant prosecution of Gaius Verres, the governor of Sicily, who plundered the province for personal gain. Verres was represented by Hortensius, Cicero's great rival. Verres resorted to bribery, but the bribery didn't work, and Hortensius never got to plead his client's case. Cicero's first speech for the prosecution was so persuasive that Verres threw in the towel and retired into exile (keeping most of the plundered treasure). In Cicero's senatorial speeches, he made it clear that he supported Pompey and the cause of reform; he became the leading advocate and fearless opponent of corruption. But in the years that followed, he gradually moved away from his reformist position and allied himself more strongly with the conservative cause, while men like Crassus, Julius Caesar, and Catiline continued to speak out in favor of radical social reform.

Perhaps his most brilliant *tour de force* is his speech attacking the notorious Clodia, sister of Publius Clodius Pulchur, a talented, eccentric radical politician who led a group of urban gangsters. Clodia was the mistress of one of Cicero's friends who was charged with trying to poison her. She counted among her many lovers powerful politicans, artists and writers half her age, including the love-sick poet Catullus, who immortalized her as "Lesbia," the woman who broke his heart.

In 63 BC, Cicero was backed by conservative senators and won the consulship at the age of forty-three. He was opposed by the impoverished patrician Catiline who was still a prisoner on an embezzlement charge. The following year, Catiline, free once again, ran for office under a platform proposing sweeping land distribution and a general cancellation of debts. Defeated for the second time, Catiline saw that his only chance of success lay in the violent seizure of power. He hatched a plot to overthrow the government by marching on Rome with a rabble of discontented men from Etruria who planned to burn the city down. Cicero heard of the "conspiracy" and thwarted Catiline's attempt to have him assassinated. Two days later, at Catiline's trial for political violence, he addressed the Roman Senate in the first of four magnificent orations against Catiline, using facts gained from a scorned mistress.

The trial was a public spectacle, a theatrical performance held, like all trials in the Roman Republic, out in the open, surrounded by a crowd elbowing each other for a better view. The presiding magistrate was flanked by several dozen judges. The prosecution and defense sat on opposite benches, facing each other in a kind of mortal combat. Behind them sat friends, supporters, and the witnesses.

With a series of seven probing questions, Cicero began the denunciation, a dazzling display of oratorical virtuosity in which he repeatedly used parallel structure—"the enemies of good men, the foes of the Republic, the robbers of Italy." He used direct address to move back and forth between the accused and those he wished to persuade—"O conscript fathers." [I quote a small part of the oration and break the lines into verse units to emphasize its metrical and parallel structure.]

> *You are not, O Catiline,*
> *one whom either*
> *shame can recall from infamy,*
> *or fear from danger,*
> *or reason from madness.*

Do not the mighty guards placed on the Palatine Hill —
do not the watches posted throughout the city —
does not the alarm of the people, and the union of all good men —
does not the precaution taken of assembling the Senate
                 In this most defensible place —
do not the looks and countenances of this venerable body here present —
have any effect upon you?
Do you not feel that your plans are detected?
Do you not see that your conspiracy is already arrested and rendered
    powerless by the knowledge which everyone here possesses of it?
What is there that you did last night,
what the night before —
where is it that you were —
who was there that you summoned to meet you —
what design was there which was adopted by you,
with which you think that any one of us here is unacquainted?

O ye immortal gods,
Where on earth are we?
In what city are we living?
What constitution is ours?
There are here —
here in our body, O conscript fathers,
in this the most holy and dignified assembly of the whole world —
men who meditate my death,
and the death of all of us,
and the destruction of this city,
and of the whole world.
You are summoning to destruction and devastation
the temples of the immortal gods,
the houses of the city,
the lives of all the citizens;
in short, all Italy.

With these omens, O Catiline,
begone to your impious and nefarious war,
to the great safety of the Republic,
to your own misfortune and injury,
and to the destruction of those who have joined themselves to you
in every wickedness and atrocity.

The senate was convinced of the imminence of an uprising to be followed by a massacre at Rome. Catiline left the city, but Cicero spoke out strongly in favor of capital punishment. Caesar proposed life imprisonment; Cato the Younger (great grandson of "The Censor") voted in favor of the death penalty and carried the Senate with him. It was Cicero's responsibility to carry out the sentences. The leading conspirators were cut to pieces in battle a month later and several others were executed without a trial. Cicero never forgot, nor allowed anyone else to forget, how he had saved the state from grave danger, writing of the incident in both poetry and prose. But the execution was a violation of an arrested citizen's right to a trial, and Cicero was later exiled because of his involvment. During his exile, Clodius Pulcher's gangsters looted and burned his home.

While writing his poem *On The Nature of Things*, Lucretius complained that Latin was inadequate for rendering philosophical terminology of the Greeks. Before the writings of Cicero, Lucretius, and Catullus, Latin did not have the precision, the rhetorical flexibility or the muscle to express abstract thought. Cicero introduced new words into the language, and developed the periodic sentence, which contributed to the evolution of European prose. The Ciceronian period creates an expectant tension in the ear of the listener or reader. "Loose" sentences begin with the main clause; "periodic" sentences begin with dependent clauses or grammatical units, setting up an expectation that is not satisfied until the appearance, at the end of the sentence, of the main clause. When speaking, most people use a loose sentence structure. Periodic sentences are most often found in formal writing where structural variety and rhetorical emphasis is needed. Archaic Latin prose was characterized by a combination of awkward syntax and colloquial language. Cicero brought greater syntactical control, allowing for longer, complex grammatical units organized in lucid, dynamic sentences. The sentence you are reading now is a loose sentence. It's a simple subject-verb-object sequence. But a periodic sentence doesn't always begin with the main clause. Using parenthetical phrases, inflectional asides that take the reader's elbow and whisper in their ear, interlocking word order, and clausal digressions, which allow for a great structural variety, not to mention a kind of spoken chumminess, the periodic sentece not only delays the outcome of the meaning, keeping the reader attuned for the point that is being made, however tortuous the argument, it includes related information that doesn't become apparent until the "clausula"—that final part of the period for which the listener's ear has been waiting—like the sentence you just read.

Food For Thought

You Say Tomato,
I Say Deadly Nightshade *Lycopersicon Esculentum*

The periodic sentence can have a succession of rhythmic beats—for example, the dactyl and paeon for the steady tone, or the iambic sequence for the discursive familiar tone. In technical language, the periodic sentence replaces parataxis (syntactic coordination) with hypotaxis (syntactic subordination).

Loose sentences are common in speech and unstudied writing, where each sentence consists of two clauses, with the second introduced by a conjunction or a relative pronoun. Over the course of a paragraph, they can become tedious and trite in their mechanical symmetry and singsong tone.

> Julius Caesar came and saw and conquered and Mark Antony went and lost and died, and Rome was victorious and Egypt was not.

The interruption of meaning characteristic of a periodic sentence is often a deliberate device using balanced subordinate clauses to create rhetorical suspense. For all the delay and interruption of the main clause, the periodic sentence actually gives the main statement even greater emphasis. In *The Elements of Style*, Strunk and White give the following examples: [I have underlined the main clause of each sentence]

> With these hopes and in this belief <u>I would urge you</u>, laying aside all hindrance, thrusting away all private aims, <u>to devote yourself</u> unswervingly and unflinchingly <u>to the</u> vigorous and successful <u>prosecution of this war</u>.

> Four centuries ago, <u>Christopher Columbus</u>, one of the Italian mariners whom the decline of their own republics had put at the service of the world and of adventure, seeking for Spain a westward passage to the Indies to offset the ach.ievement of Portuguese discoverers, <u>lighted on America</u>.

In the following passage from Macaulay's *Essay on Milton*, <u>the first sentence is loose, the second periodic</u>. [The previous sentence is a simple periodic sentence, but the main clause, which I've underlined, is paratactic.]

> <u>They</u> [the Puritans] <u>rejected</u> with contempt <u>the</u> ceremonious <u>homage</u> which other sects substituted for the pure worship of the soul. <u>Instead</u> of catching occasional glimpses of the Deity through an obscuring veil, <u>they</u> <u>aspired to gaze</u> full <u>on his</u> intolerable <u>brightness</u>.

Milton's is the most notoriously Latinate style in English verse. Not only does the Latinate style give prominence to syntactic inversion, it uses words derived from Latin rather than those originating in Old English, e.g. *suspend* rather than *hang*. I offer the following—the opening sentence from Edward Gibbon's *Memoirs* (1796)—as a last example of a periodic sentence, because it brings us back, quite appropriately, to Rome.

> It was at Rome, on the 15th of October, 1764, as I sat musing amidst the ruins of the Capitol, while the barefoot friars were singing vespers in the Temple of Jupiter, that the idea of writing the decline and fall of the city first started to my mind.

Cicero also utilized a variety of tonal effects and degrees of style—simple, moderate, and sublime—from the rhythms of natural speech to passionate oratory. While Cicero's poetry was dismissed, even disdained, in his own time, his prose influenced those who wrote poetry because of his use of dactylic and iambic meter. He made fun of the "modern poets," calling them *neoteroi* or *poetae novi*, but his experiments in meter and adherence to the poetics of the Hellenist Callimachus, actually made him a precursor of the neoterics. He helped regularize the Latin hexameter, making it more elegant and flexible, useful for both poetry and prose. In the works of Lucretius, Virgil, Horace, and Ovid we hear echoes of Cicero.

Cicero created a stylistic model that made an impact, not just on the poets of his own day, but upon poets throughout the centuries, even those writing in our own time. We think of enjambment as a relatively modern device, but it can be traced back to Cicero's periodic sentences. In verse, the break of the line at crucial points in the phrase can push the reader forward or back, depending on which effect the poet is trying to achieve. Cicero's use of interlocking word order, in which two closely linked words are separated by the interposition of other words, can also be used by poets to create stylistic effects that open or close the grammatical unit, demanding greater or lesser breathing time. Modern poets like Whitman, Ginsberg, and Aimé Cesaire were influenced by poets and orators like Patrick Henry, William Shakespeare, and the translators of the King James Verson of the Bible, and they were influenced by Cicero.

As a lawyer and speech-maker, he was without peer. As a politician, he lacked the ruthlessness necessary for survival. He was unable to prevent the republic from crumbling, but he was willing to stand up against tyranny, and in the end, it cost him his life. But he will be remembered as the greatest writer of Latin prose, and as a founding father of the Western literary tradition.

THE NEW POETS:

Two outstanding poets completed much of their work during this period of political intrigue. The Hellenistic movement brought life and vigor to a tired literary culture, but except for the plays of Plautus and the epic of Ennius, Latin poetry remained primitive and parochial. Lucretius and Catullus were part of a movement called the "New Poets," and between them brought a technical perfection to Latin poetry that was modern. Lucretius's *On the Nature of Things* was a philosophical poem noted for its intellectual rigor and startling imagery. Though the miniature epics of Catullus were jewels of technical perfection, his short poems touched the reader with a heartbreaking intensity. In a time of war and revolution, Lucretius and Catullus elevated Latin literature with their timeless poems. Lucretius was only forty-three when he died; Catullus only thirty.

The Neoteric Revolution

The poets of this period departed from the traditions of early Roman literature. Like the moderns in our own century, Catullus, Lucretius, and the other "neoterics" proclaimed themselves "moderns," speaking to their contemporaries in a way that was immediate and direct. Neotericism was a version of Alexandrianism in that it worked on refining the Hellenistic epigram and incorporating the musicality of Greek lyric. They also achieved a modern tone through the use of direct speech . Like the Athenian poets of an earlier century, reading the poem aloud was tantamount to publication. Oral performance was the real thing. In the schools, poetry was taught to be read aloud. In the Hellenistic world of that time, poetry was often heard in the theater. Many of Catullus's poems take the form of personal correspondance, and if they were meant to be read aloud, it was probably not at a public reading, but at the private gatherings in the porticos and theatrically designed galleries of the rich and famous.

Sometimes these upstart young writers deliberately shocked their readers with unexpected colloquialisms and "unpoetic" turns of phrase. Even though Callimachus and the rest of the Hellenistic poets wrote a century before the neoterics, their poems and theories became the foundation of the neoteric movement. Callimachus was to the neoterics (and all the Latin poets who followed) what Whitman was to the Beats (and all the American poets who followed). Callimachus and his counterparts in Rome claimed to avoid the Homeric epic, but in many ways their real goal was to recover Homer from the cheap imitators of their own day. Virgil felt the influence of the neoteric movement, but their style lived on mainly in the works of the elegaic poets Tibullus, Propertius (who thought of himself as the Roman Callimachus), and Ovid.

In Greek, the word is *neoterikos*, in Latin, *poetae novi*. The terms were used to describe this new school of Roman poets who turned their backs on archaic diction and the epic poem. They freed themselves from the hexameters of Ennius and from most traditional Roman poetry that emulated the ancient Greeks. Instead, they modeled themselves after the Archaic Greek poets Sappho and Archolochus, and Hellenistic poets such as Euphorian, noted for his short dense poems. Their chief inspiration, however, came from that cool and ironic genius, Callimachus, known for his blend of elegance and sensitivity, dark humor and erudition, detachment and passion. The term *neoterics* was coined by

Cicero, who used it rather scornfully, calling them, in Greek, the *hoi neoteroi*, "the younger poets," or in Latin, the *novi poetae*, "the new poets." Cicero probably looked down upon them the way modern critics first dismissed the "beat" poets, who have since proven to be more traditional than was at first realized. Kerouac's first novel *The Town and the City* was in the tradition of Thomas Wolfe's *Of Time and the River*, and Allen Ginsberg's *Howl* was similar in rhythm and metrics to Whitman's *Song of Myself.*

As disciples of Callimachus, the neoterics tended to simplify some of his doctrines, particularly the suggestion that *only* the short poem mattered. The neoterics of the late Roman Republic aimed at perfecting the short poem and experimented with new meters, different kinds of language, new words (often Greek), new themes (romantic, erotic, exotic, bizarre), and often a mannered style. Ironically, this last effect was influenced by Cicero, despite his sarcastic dismissals of them, calling them *cantores Euphorionis*, "singers of Euphorion," and the *delicata iuventus*, "dainty juveniles,"—or as this term was later used by the French to put down the dandy poets of Baudelaire's day, the *juenesse dorée*.

Food for Thought

Neoteric Crocodile Piss

Frank O'Hara, a poet of our own time, comes to mind when describing the new poets of the late Republic. He's a classic Callimachian, writing neoteric verse that is both direct and simple, while also writing poetry that is dense, characterized by highly contrived syntax and wordplay. Below are the first few lines of his poem "A Step Away From Them." Note the off-hand, un-poetic language and enjambment.

> It's my lunch hour, so I go
> for a walk among the hum-colored
> cabs. First, down the sidewalk
> where laborers feed their dirty
> glistening torsos sandwiches
> and Coca-Cola, with yellow helmets
> on. They protect them from falling
> bricks, I guess.

The poem "Easter" is anything but simple, marked by linguistic density and obscure wordplay.

> When the world strips down and rouges up
> like a mattress's teeth brushed by love's bristling sun
> a marvelous heart tiresomely got up in brisk bold stares
> when those trappings fart at the feet of stars
> a self-coral serpent wrapped round an arm with no jujubes
> without swish
> without camp
> floods of crocodile piss and pleasures of driving

shadows of prairie pricks dancing
of the roses of Pennsylvania looking in eyes noses and ears
those windows at the head of science.

The neoterics of the late Republic would have felt right at home with the anti-academic American poets of the 1950s (variously called the Beats, the Open Form or Black Mountain poets, the San Francisco Renaissance, and the New York School). The neoterics disdained any verse that was not "new" and "hip." Perhaps one of them wrote a manifesto of their ideas, but none has survived, except in the comments and attitudes that run through their letters and poems written to each other. Take, for example, this poem by Catullus written to Calvus.

The other day we spent,
Calvus, at a loose end
flexing our poetics
and writing erotic poems.
Delectable twin poets,
swapping verses, testing
form and cadence, fishing
for images in wine
and wit. I left you late,
came home still burning with
your brilliance, your invention
your ironic humor,
restless, I could not eat,
nor think of sleep. Under
my eyelids you appeared
and talked. I twitched, feverishly,
looked for morning . . . at last,
debilitated, limbs
awry across the bed
I made this poem of
my ardour and for our
gaiety, Calvus . . . Forgive
this little measure
of my morning sorrow,
don't turn your back
on Nemesis, that ill-bred
bitch of a goddess.
Lure not her venom.

If ever there was a neoteric manifesto, it would be O'Hara's own tongue-in-cheek essay, "Personism: A Manifesto:"

I don't like rhythm, assonance, all that stuff. You just go on your nerve. If someone's chasing you down the street with a knife you just run, you don't turn around and shout, "Give it up! I was a track star for Mineola Prep."

For the neoterics of the late Republic, there was that same devil-may-care attitude; yet, like Frank O'Hara, they were acutely aware of what they were doing metrically, rhythmically, and stylistically. Like O'Hara, their work was experimental and avant-garde. They believed that poems should express the personality of the poet. No rehashed epics. Don't belabor form, yet, technique for its own sake can be invigorating. Sometimes you're fancy and write elaborate verses, other times they're simple and straightforward; why be straightjacketed by someone else's theory. Have the nerve, they might have said, to go on one's nerve. As O'Hara says in the following poem:

> My Heart
>
> I'm not going to cry all the time
> nor shall I laugh all the time,
> I don't prefer one "strain" to another.
> I'd have the immediacy of a bad movie,
> not just a sleeper, but also the big,
> overproduced first-run kind. I want to be
> at least as alive as the vulgar. And if
> some aficionado of my mess says "That's
> not like Frank!", all to the good! I
> don't wear brown and grey shirts all the time,
> do I? No. I wear workshirts to the opera,
> often. I want my feet to be bare,
> I want my face to be shaven, and my heart—
> you can't plan on the heart, but
> the better part of it, my poetry, is open.

The neoteric poets' appeal was to the young intellectuals born in the time of Sulla's dictatorship and who came of age during the turmoil of the late Republic. It was a time during which Pompey and Caesar were coming into prominence and Cicero's oratory was changing the poetics and literary tastes of a new generation, a time that marked a decisive turn in the history of Latin literature. They were the avant-garde, irreverently rejecting national tradition. In addtion to Catullus, the neoterics included Calvus, Cinna, Bibaculus, Philodemus of Gadera, and Cornificius Nepos.

☛ Gaius Licinius Calvus (82-*c*. 47 BC)

Calvus, one of the best of the new poets, was celebrated for the wide range of his poetry, especially his love poetry. He was also rather fussy about his health, writing an essay "On the Use of Cold Water," and was known to use lead plates as an antaphrodisiac. He became a successful lawyer, using the "Attic" style of oratory, which stressed speaking and writing in a clear, concise, and spare style, as opposed to the Ciceronian school, which used periodic sentences and interlocking word order for maximum rhetorical effect.

Calvus was a friend of Catullus, who wrote several poems addressed to him (#'s 14, 50, 53 & 96). In one poem Catullus called him, affectionately, *salaputium disertum*, "the eloquent dwarf." Catullus recounts a trial in which Calvus spoke against Vatinius, one of Caesar's gangster politicians. The speech Calvus made was so powerful that Vatinius supposedly wiped his brow and pleaded to the jury, "Judges, must I be condemned just becuase this man is so eloquent?" Calvus cooly replied, "It's not my eloquence that makes you perspire, Vatinius, but your guilt."

#53

I laughed, Calvus. I laughed today
when someone in the courtroom crowd, hearing
your quite brilliant exposé of
the Vatinian affair, lifted his hands up
in proper amazement, and cried suddenly:
"A cock that size . . . *and it spouts!*
I laughed, Calvus. I laughed.

Calvus was politically active and involved Catullus in a literary campaign against the triumvirs, including Julius Caesar, who later forgave Catullus for his ill-conceived, slanderous poems. Besides his love poems and epithalamia, Calvus wrote a grief-filled epicedion over the untimely death of his wife Quintilia. Catullus remembers the poem sadly and writes one of his own to comfort his friend.

#96

If those in their silent graves can receive any pleasure
or comfort at all, Calvus, from our lamenting,
from that desire with which we rekindle former affections
and weep for friendships we long ago surrendered,
then surely her premature death brings less grief than
joy to Quintilia, whom you continue to cherish.

Only fragments of the work of Calvus survive. We find an echo of Fragment #13 at the beginning of Virgil's eighth eclogue.

The Sun also remembers
to rest his everlasing courses

which became in Virgil's poem

The Muse of two shepherds, Damon and Alphesiboeus,
at whose contesting the wondering heifer forgot the grass,
at whose song the lynxes stood in astonishment,
and the rivers, altering their currents, stood still,
this Muse of Damon and Alphesiboeus we will sing.

Later poets such as Horace, Ovid, and Propertius ranked Calvus as equal to Catullus; unfortunately, all we have are a few meager fragments from his epic *Io* and the elegy on the death of his wife.

A! virgo infelix, herbis pasceris amaris!
Unfortunate maiden, you will have to graze on bitter herbs.

Cum iam fulva cinis fuero . . .
Will I be nothing but a heap of golden ashes . . .

Lilium, vaga candido
nympha quod secet ungui.

A lily that a wandering nymph
will cut with her shiny fingernail.

☛ Gaius Helvius Cinna (*d.* 44 BC)

Cinna, another friend of Catullus, was admired by his contemporaries for his erudition, his erotic poems, and his ability to write successfully in various meters and styles. He was lynched after Caesar's assassination by an angry mob that mistook him for Cornelius Cinna, the brother of Caesar's wife Cornelia. Cornelius Cinna was a supporter of the Republic and had spoken out against the dictator on the previous day. Shakespeare dramatizes the scene in *Julius Caesar*.

> *Third Citizen.* Your name, sir, truly.
> *Cinna.* Truly, my name is Cinna.
> *First Citizen.* Tear him to pieces; he's a conspirator.
> *Cinna.* I am Cinna the poet, I am Cinna the poet.
> *Fourth Citizen.* Tear him for his bad verses, tear him for his bad verses.
> *Cinna.* I am not Cinna the conspirator.
> *Fourth Citizen.* It is no matter, his name's Cinna; pluck but his name
> out of his heart, and turn him going.

Cinna, Calvus, and Catullus formed the core group of the modern poets. Cinna is said to have brought the poet Parthenius of Nicea to Rome, whose presence acted as a stimulus and point of reference for neoteric poetry. Cinna's most famous poem was the *Zmyrna*, most of which is lost. Poets who adhered to Callimachean poetics liked it for its obscurity. Like Eliot's *The Waste Land*, it required explanatory notes. The poem recounted the incestuous love of Myrrha for her father Cinyras. Catullus praised this poem for its brevity and erudition.

> #95
> Nine harvests and nine winters since its inception
> Cinna's *Zmyrna* is complete.
> Hortalus turns out 5,000 versicles yearly.
> Penetrating to the runnelled waves of Satrachus
> the remote regions of its setting.
> Cinna's *Zmyrna*
> shall be read by white-haired generations.
> The *Annals* of Volusius will wilt by the banks of the Padua,

pages of dactylics to wrap fish in.
Cinna's lapidary relics are to Catullus' taste:
let the dumb masses nod off for that old windbag Antimachus.

[Catullus, poem #95]

Zmyrna was the maiden of mythology whose incestuous love for her father Cinyras produced Adonis. Only three lines have survived. Here's one.

At scelus incesto Zmyrnae crescebat in alvo.
The heinous design was gaining strength in Zmyrna's incestuous bosom.

☛ Quintus Cornificius Nepos

Questor in 48 BC, he espoused the Senatorial cause and was killed in battle in 41 BC. Cornificius was one of the neoterics, friends with Cicero and Catullus. When Catullus was laid up with the flu, he wrote a poem to Cornificius complaining because Cornificius hadn't written him a consulatory poem.

38

Sick, Cornificius, sick at heart and sick in the head,   [Simonides was a 6th C
your Catullus gets worse by the day, nay, by the hour.   Greek elegiac poet
Do I get a word from you, some small consolation?   famous for his
I'm really pissed. Is this how you treat your buddy?   dirges and epigrams
Ah! Cornificius, just a word, a tiny word from you,   inscribed on tomb-
and I'm better, just a word of comfort   stones.
pathetic as Simonides' tears.   see pg 118]

☛ Cornelius Nepos (c. 100-c. 25 BC)

Like Catullus, a native of Cisalpine Gaul, Cornelius Nepos (not to be confused with Cornificius Nepos above) eschewed public office and devoted himself to writing. Like so many classical writers, all that survive of his work are fragments of light verse, a biography of Cicero's friend Atticus, and portions of a sixteen volume book of biographical sketches, *De Viris Illustribus* ("On Famous Men"). He is known to have also written a treatise on geography, a universal history in three volumes, a book of anecdotes, and lives of Cato the Elder and Cicero. Catullus dedicated his "little book" of poems to Nepos, begging his indulgence in deference to the "laborious and learned" tomes of Nepos. Surely, there was a touch of irony in Catullus' dedication. Nepos was not the most elegant of writers, but the fragments that have survived are clear and concise.

Matrem timidi flere non solere.
The mother of a careful man seldom has to weep.

Even though the surviving biographical sketches are marked by historical inaccuracies and omissions, their purpose seems to have been to eulogize their subjects and offer moral judgements, such as his comment on Alcibiades, the Greek politician and military leader, noted for his great personal magnetism, good looks, talent, vanity, dissolute life, and unscrupulous personal ambition who fomented revolt against Athens and betrayed the democracy.

Huic maxime putamus malo fuisse nimiam opinionem ingenii atque virtutis.
We think that what harmed him most was his excessive opinion
of his own gifts and merits.

In the centuries that followed, Nepos was a favorite of schoolmasters for his clearly written, edifying commentaries, an ideal writer for the young.

Sui cuique fingunt fortunam.
Character fashions fate.

I am far from holding that philsophy is a guide to life or that it furthers happiness; rather, I believe that no one is more in need of instruction in living than the majority of those engaged in teaching it. I have noticed that most of those who in schools formulate the subtlest precepts of moderation and self-mastery themselves indulge in every kind of unbridled passion.

☞ Marcus Furius Bibaculus

Marcus Furius Bibaculus was a neoteric poet with little money who had an affair with Juventius, the fourteen-year-old fickle-boy-lover of Catullus. In several poems, Catullus warned Juventius not to be lured away by Bibaculus's penniless charms.

O you who are the prefect budding flower
of all Juventians—not just of these now,
but those as well of past and future ages,
I'd rather have you give the riches of Midas
to that fellow who has no servant nor money-box
than have you give yourself to his embraces.
"Why not?" you ask me, "isn't he a darlingman?"
"Yes,
but Darling has no servant and no money.
Throw out my words, discount them if you want to,
but still he has no servant and no money.
[Catullus, poem #24]

Catullus may have complained at times that his purse was filled with cobwebs, but there was a certain bohemian feighning going on, since Catullus moved in wealthy circles and if cobwebs filled his purse, they were probably flecked with gold dust. But poor Bibaculus, he lived—according to Catullus in another poem—with his father and a stepmother, "whose teeth can grind the toughest stone to gravel!" There must have been something charming about Bibaculus, because Catullus wrote several poems dripping with sarcasm, making fun of Bibaculus, perhaps to make sure Juventius wasn't taken in by his charms.

Furius, you've got no servant, no money-box,
no bedbug, no spider spinning by—what!? no fire either.
It's beautiful, the life you lead with those two,
your father and your father's withered woman.
that dry stick whose teeth can chew even a flintstone.
No wonder, for the three of you are thriving,
your sound digestions undisturbed by worry:
no fear of fires, of collapsing buildings,
the knives of thieves, plots to poison you,
or any other routine urban perils.
Your constitutions are as dry as horn is,
or what (if anything) is ever drier,
thanks to your diet fasting and your outdoor lifestyle.
Remarkable, the way you go on living
with neither sweat nor slobber—thus, no hacking
coughs, no runny noses. To these *nice* touches,
add one last refinement: an assole gleaming
with all the radiance of a polished salt shaker!
You shit less than ten times a year, and then
a pellet harder than a bean or pebble—
and each of them so nicely inoffensive,
that if you crumble one between your fingers
it leaves no stain! O Furius, you prosper!
Don't throw away all this, don't say it's nothing!
You need a hundred thousand? No, stop asking:
you have your fortune—but it can't be counted!

[Catullus, poem #23]

He was also a friend of Aurelius. He is addressed in some poems of Catullus, including poems 11, 16, 23, 24, and 26. Bibaculus is mentioned along with Catullus by Tacitus (*Annals* lib. IV, 34) as having written invectives against Julius Caesar. Marcus Furius Bibaculus often wrote of his every day experiences in the Forum.

☛ Varro "Atacinus" (b. ca 82 BC) and Varro "Reatinus" (116-27 BC)

Publius Terentius Varro was often called "Atacinus" because he was from the valley of the river Atax in Narbonese Gaul, to distinguish him from Marcus Terentius Varro, who was called "Reatinus," because he was born at Reate in Sabine territory.

It is easily to confuse these two poets and writers because they are both often referred to simply as Varro. Atacinus continued the Ennian style of poetry, writing an epic poem on Julius Caesar's exploits in Gaul called *Bellum Sequanicum*, "The War against the Sequani," and a geographical poem called the *Chorographia*. Eventually, he fell under the influence of the neoterics and wrote one of the earliest erotic poems in Latin literature called *Leucadia*, from the name of his beloved. Varro also wrote satires in the manner of Lucilius. Perhaps his most significant work was the *Argonautae*, a free translation of the *Argonautica* by Apollonius of Rhodes. Varro was one of the last in that line of Roman poets who translated major Greek poems into Latin, and in so doing, he helped develop a new poetic language for Latin. Nothing is known of his life, and his work survives only in fragments.

Quintilian considered **Marcus Terentius Varro Reatinus** "the most learned of Romans." Varro Reatinus was opposed to Julius Caesar, and was later proscribed by Mark Antony, escaping with his life, though losing his property and books. His output was enormous, writing over 600 volumes on just about everything from philosphy to farming, poetry to science, education to geography. Little of his work survives, and most of it in fragments. Only his *De Re Rustica* ("On Farming") survives complete. We also have six books of of the twenty-five of his *De Linguia Latina* ("On the Latin Language"), and some 600 fragments of his *Saturae Menippeae* ("Menippean Satires"). Like the Greek satirist Menippus, who combined poetry and prose in making fun of philosophers and their double standards, Varro's criticial sketches of Roman life were written in a variety of forms—some were dialogues, others semi-dramatic, some in verse and others in prose. His language was forceful and earthy, humorous barbs directed at the pretentious Romans of his day who pursued a life of greed and luxury while espousing higher philsoophical ideals. Varro looked back nostaligically upon the time of the classical Republic when citizens led a life of moderation and civic virtue.

Equally influential was his historical encyclopedia, *Antiquitates rerum Humanarum et Divinarum* ("Human and Divine Antiquities"), which dealt with the history of Rome, religion, and the liberal arts. For the purposes of study, he divided the liberal arts into nine categories: grammar, dialectic, rhetoric, geometry, arthimetic, astonomy, music, medicine, and architecture. Using all but the last two, Martianus Capella (5th century AD) divided those remaining seven liberal arts into the *trivium*—grammar (i.e. literature), rhetoric, and dialectic—and the *quadrivium*—geometry, arthimetic, astronomy, and music.[see page 516] We can trace this idea of an educational curriculum to Aristotle who in the "Politics" talks of *eleutherai epistemai*, "the branches of knowledge worthy of free men." Since there was no organized form of higher education in 5th century Athens, itinerant teachers went from city to city expounding on the new geographical and scientific ideas. Hippias, a contemporary of Socrates vividly depicted in two of Plato's dialogues, was one of these traveling sophists. He lectured on geometry, arithimetic, astronomy and music, which were listed by Plato as essential to an educational program. In the 6th century AD, Boethius gave these four liberal arts the name *quadrivium*. An opponent of Plato was Isocrates, who taught rhetoric as the culmination of philosophy; Plato was opposed to rhetoric and literature on moral grounds, but it was the program devised by Isocrates which ultimately became the norm throughout the ancient world and was later called the *trivium*—rhetoric, dialectic, and grammar (i.e. literature). Early in the 5th century AD, Martianus Capella wrote *De Nuptiis Mercuri et Philogiae* ("On the Marriage of Mercury and Philologia"), an elaborate allegory in nine books, in Latin prose and verse (in the manner of the Menippean satire which Varro "Reatinus" popularized in Rome). The Middle Ages accepted Capella's work as an authoritative description of the seven liberal arts.

Virgil later based some of his *Georgics* on Varro's *De Re Rustica*, not just for its agricultural information, but some of the scenes themselves, especially in Book I where

Varro shows characters looking at a map of Italy (see Georgics, 2.235ff), and the end of that book which depicts one of the characters being murdered in the street, the kind of lawlessness and violence Virgil was lamenting. Virgil's famous image of the bees also can be traced to Varro's section on bee-keeping.

After Varro was reconciled to Caesar, he was to have been the head of the public library whose creation Caesar was contemplating. Later, Augustus Caesar appointed him to the post. Below are a few of the fragments of Varro's verse that survive.

> *Divina natura dedit agros, ars humana aedificavit urbes.*
> Divine nature gave us the contry, human art built our cities.

> *Convivarum numerum incipere*
> *oportere a Cratiarum numero*
> *et progredi ad Musarum,*
> *id est proficisci a tribus et consistere in novem.*
>
> The number of guests at dinner should not be less
> than the number of the Graces
> nor exceed that of the Muses,
> i.e., it should begin with three and stop at nine.

> *Et rex et misellus ille pauper amat,*
> *habetque intus ignem acrem.*
>
> Both king and poor man love,
> each carries the consuming fire within his heart.

> *Ergo tum Romae parce pureque pudentes*
> *vixere in patria; nunc sumus in rutuba.*
>
> And so, in the Rome of those days, people were thrifty and modest.
> Theirs was a homeland; today we live in chaos.

☞ Philodemus of Gadara (fl. 75-35 BC)

The Syrian poet and critic Philodemus was probably not a member of Catullus' group of poets, but he would have shared their ideas on neoteric writing. He came from Gadara near the Sea of Galilee, where Hellenistic culture and Alexandrian literature would have made a great impact on him. In Rome, he became one of the circle of poets led by the wealthy aristocrat and patron of poets Lucius Calpurnius Piso Caesobinus. Piso's daughter Calpurnia was married to Julius Caesar. In one of his poems, Catullus called them "Rome's topmost tycoons, father- and son-in-law, playing billiards with our world." Catullus thinks all poets who flock to Piso's palatial estate a bunch of punks. In another poem, Catullus calls Piso a mobster with poets for henchmen. In translating Catullus, how do we do justice to his forceful and witty imagery? In poem #47, he describes Piso as *verpus praeposuit Priapus ille*, where *verpus* means "the penis with foreskin drawn back," *praeporto* means "to carry in front of one," and *Priapus* is the name of the phallic god of fertility? To say Piso is a "dickhead" comes close, but Catullus' Latin is more graphic and comic. In the poem, Catullus puts down two poets in Piso's entourage, while feeling sorry for his friends Veranius and Fabullus who were not invited to one of Piso's *dolce vita* parties.

> *Porci et Socration, duae sinistrae*
> *Pisonis, scabies famesque mundi,*
> *vos Veraniolo meo et Fabullo*
> *verpus praeposuit Priapus ille?*
> *Vos convivia lauta sumptuose*
> *de die facitis, mei sodales*
> *quaerunt in trivio vocationes?*

> Porcius and little Socrates, Piso's sinister
> hoods, scabs on the ass of the world,
> has that prickfaced Priapus picked you two
> over my dear pals, Veranius and Fabullus?
> Are you lapping up the luxury from dawn to dusk
> while my good buddies have to beg for a handout?   *[Catullus, poem #47]*

Piso was an Epicurean and may have invited Philodemus, a noted teacher of Epicurean philosophy, to live in his magnificent villa at Herculaneum, a wealthy residential town built on a spur projecting westward from the lower slopes of Mount Vesuvius about five miles from Naples. Much of the town of Resina sits atop the rock-hardened mud of Herculaneum, which was destroyed along with Pompeii when Vesuvius erupted in 79 AD. Over centuries that followed its destruction, looters were discouraged by volcanic gas that seeped up from the rock. More recent excavations have uncovered Piso's luxurious villa, now known as the "Villa de Papyri," so named because a library of charred papyrus rolls was found there containing works on Epicurean philosophy, including the collected works of Philodemus, much of which remains undeciphered.

Food for Thought

The Villa de Papyrii

Herculaneum was a choice suburb of Rome, one of the most fashionable centers on the Bay of Naples and home to about five thousand members of the aristocracy and the new rich. After the aborted revolt in the Third Servile War, peace and prosperity brought about the construction of new and even more elaborate homes and villas. The charm of the coast attracted many of the rich looking for a weekend getaway. To the west lay the Bay of Naples; to the south was the Phlegraean Fields with its smoking caverns and steaming geysers. Sybyl, the famed prophetess, dwelt in a grotto at Cumae, not far from the infernal Lake Avernus, whose waters were said to be black as hell. It was here that Odysseus and Aeneas entered the underworld through its poisonous mephitic gases. Yet, Romans built

---

luxurious baths there that were fed by the celebrated spa at Baiae, where hot mineral waters bubbled up from the earth.

A few Romans were aware of Mount Vesuvius's volcanic shape. The Sicilian Greek historian Diodorus Siculus said as much in his forty-volume world history that centered on Rome. The Greek geographer Strabo (64 BC—after 24 AD) who came to Rome in 44 BC and developed a profound admiration for the Romans, whom he believed were creating an earthly world-state comparable with the heavenly one, climbed to the top of Vesuvius in his old age and noted that it was a "spent" volcano. The idea that it was extinct was also proferred by Vitruvius Pollio (1st century BC), engineer and architect, whose treatise on architecture was highly regarded during the time of the Renaissance (the term "Vitruvian man" refers to his theory of human proportion, in which the human figure is shown to fit into a square circumscribed by a circle—famously illustrated by Leonardo da Vinci). No one had ever seen so much as a puff of smoke issue from its wooded cone. The last time Vesuvius had erupted was during the Bronze Age, about 1200 BC.

On August 24, 79 AD, the top of Mount Vesuvius was blown off during a volcanic eruption, its force ten times that of Mt. St. Helens in 1980. Vesuvius rained down six inches of pumice per hour, followed by a burning avalanche of sulfurous gases, rocks, and pumice that poured down the mountainside and completely buried Pompeii and Herculaneum under a layer of ash some fifteen to twenty feet deep. Because of the prevailing winds, Pompeii received the mass of ash and pumice stone while Herculaneum was submerged by the torrential flow of pyroclastic matter, a mix of ash, pumice stones, cinders, and gases that virtually sealed everything as if in plastic. Many escaped, but sixteen thousand people living near the base of the volcano were killed.

When the Roman historian Tacitus was researching his later histories, he asked Pliny the Younger to recount the death of his uncle and adoptive father, Pliny the Elder, who had sailed from Misenum across the bay from Pompeii to rescue those he could and, being a man of scientific bent, to take notes on the natural phenomenon. The young Pliny was invited to accompany his uncle, but stayed behind to attend to his studies. The elder Pliny set sail across the bay as ashes, pumice stones, and cinders fell on the ships. Pliny noted all the changing conditions of the eruption as they approached shore and dictated his observations to his secretary. Landing at Stabiae, just south of Pompeii, he instructed people to gather what moveables they could and place them shipboard. Pliny the Younger's account continues:

> To calm fears by an appearance of unconcern, he asked for a bath. Then after bathing, he sat down to eat with gusto, or at least (no less admirable) making a pretense of gusto. From Mount Vesuvius, meanwhile, great sheets of flame and extensive fires were flashing out in more and more places. My uncle, to relieve his companions' fears, declared that these were merely fires in villas deserted by their peasants. Then he lay down and slept. His sleep was unmistakable, for his breathing, heavy and stentorious because of his bulk, was heard by those who listened at the door. But the courtyard on which his room opened was being choked by a rising layer of cinders and ash, so that if he delayed any longer it would have become impossible to escape. The walls of the house were swaying with repeated violent shocks, but they dreaded the rain of pumice stones, though small and light, in the open air. After deliberation they chose the latter of the two dangers—my uncle moved by the stronger reasons and his companions by the stronger fears. With strips of linen they tied pillows to their heads and went out.

Elsewhere day had come, but there it was night, blacker and thicker than any ordinary night, though relieved by torches and flares of many kinds. Once on the shore, my uncle lay down on a sailcloth which had been cast ashore, and called repeatedly for water, which he drank. Then the approaching flames, and the smell of sulphur which heralded the flames, put the others to flight. Aroused, my uncle struggled to his feet, leaning between two slaves; but immediately he fell down again. I assume that his breathing was impeded by the dense vapors, and his windpipe blocked—for constitutionally it was narrow and weak, and often inflamed. When daylight returned (on the second day after my uncle had last seen it), his body was found intact, without injury, and clad as in life. He looked more like a sleeper than a dead man.

In a second letter to Tacitus, the Younger Pliny recounts his own experience from Misenum, twenty miles distant from Vesuvius.

A curious brightness revealed itself to us not as daylight but as approaching fire; but it stopped some distance from us. Once more, darkness and ashes, thick and heavy. From time to time we had to get up and shake them off for fear of being actually buried and crushed under their weight. I believed that one and all of us would perish—a wretched but strong consolation in my dying. But the darkness lightened, and then like smoke or cloud dissolved away. Finally, a genuine daylight came; the sun shone, but pallidly, as in an eclipse. And then, before our terror stricken gaze everything appeared changed—covered by a thick layer of ashes like an abundant snowfall.

Pliny's letter recounted the progress of the eruption so well, that his description has proved of great scientific value to modern volcanologists, who have named the first phase of a volcanic eruption the "Plinian phase." Over the course of the next millenium, Pompeii and Herculaneum were largely forgotten. During the desolation of the Middle Ages, many old Roman cities were torn apart stone by stone, either by barbarian invaders, or by locals intent on smashing pagan buildings, burning marble statues for lime, or using stones and marble to build other structures. Though weeds and vines grew wild amid the wrecked temples and buildings, ancient towns like Pompeii and Herculaneum lay untouched beneath the earth, waiting the archaeologist's spade.

With the Renaissance's interest in classical learning and ancient manuscripts came a fever for Greek and Roman relics. Bronze and marble statues dug from the earth were worth their weight in gold. Rumors began to circulate about the lost cities of Pompeii and Herculaneum, but their exact location remained a mystery until 1709, when an Austrian prince named Maurice de Lorraine, Prince d'Elbeuf, decided to build a luxurious villa for his Italian bride. Digging a well on the site of a monastery in the town of Resina, a workman uncovered rare marble that was part of an upper tier of seats in Herculaneum's Theater. Sinking several tunnels into the earth, Prince d'Elbeuf plundered the site for over a decade until his villa was finished, then abandoned the tunnels without realizing what he had uncovered. Not until 1738 was the Theater identified as belonging to the ancient town of Herculaneum. When Charles III assumed the throne of Naples, he appointed Rocco Gioacchino de Alcubierre, a colonol of engineers, to excavate the site, which he proceeded to do, digging tunnels in all directions, damaging important relics and haphazardly destroying important archaeological evidence, until they reached the core of the now legendary city. There's no telling how many significant artworks and artifacts were lost due to Alcubierre's stupidity—what wasn't smashed was snatched, what wasn't mapped was scattered to the winds.

It wasn't until 1748 that systematic excavations of the two cities began. In 1750, the Swiss archaeologist Karl Weber accidentally discovered Piso's villa, the "Villa de Papyrii," with its covered walkways, sculpture-filled courtyards, terraced gardens, bronze marble, mosaic fountains, small and large fish ponds, atriums, the Grand Peristyle and entrance portico. Jealous of his methods and success, Alcubierre tried to sabatoge Weber's work, knocking down support timbers and allowing water to flood the tunnels. After several years of excavation, carbonic gases began escaping from underground shafts and Weber was forced to shut down operations, uncovering only a small portion of this vast estate, which was buried under 65 feet of hardened volcanic matter. Nevertheless, through systematic tunneling and a disciplined archaeological approach, Weber uncovered the greatest single collection of ancient bronze statuary ever found. But what made this site unique was the retrieval of the first complete ancient library, consisting of 1,787 papyrus scrolls, including the almost complete collection of the works of Philodemus of Gadara. In time, other suburban villas were uncovered, including "The Villa of the Mysteries," "The House of the Wooden Partition," "The House of the Relief of Telephus," but none were as significant or as opulent as the "Villa de Papyrii," the richest and most valuable villa of the ancient world yet to be discovered, with a front more than eight hundred feet long, according to Weber's unfinished measurements.

Piso's villa was built along an embankment above the Bay of Naples; a beach equipped with private docks, and boathouses lay below. Imagine Piso leaving the hustle and bustle of Rome to relax in his country house, the afternoons spent sitting on the grass, reading poems, as he looked across the waters to the Isles of Capri and Ischia, hazy in the distance, or as he glanced behind him at the serene majesty of Mount Vesuvius, green with olive groves and vineyards. Imagine Piso and his son-in-law, Julius Caesar, warming their hands at the ithyphallic brazier, delighting in one of Philodemus' racy epigrams. Perhaps they strolled along the colonnades surrounded by gardens, fountains, palms and cypress trees that stretched the length of a football field, and read aloud several of Philodemus's lascivious poems—Caesar was known to enjoy salacious songs and jokes.

Among the pieces of sculpture recovered from the dig was a bronze bust of the Roman hero Scipio Africanus, the conqueror of Hannibal. But the recovery of the papyrus scrolls of Philodemus is what established the villa as one of the most important finds in the history of archeology. During the third year of excavation, a tunnel was found that led into a small room with an elegant marble floor, a reading room of some sort, and next to that was another small room with carbonized wooden shelves. Lying atop the shelves were cylindrical briquettes of charcoal, and more of those briquettes were found stacked on a wooden stand in the center of the room. When carefully examined, it became apparent that the briquettes were rolls of papyrus badly scorched by the pyroclastic flow (also called ignimbrites). A painter was called in to find a way to unroll the scrolls—eighteen hundred of them. Today, we've discovered enzymes and freeze-dying techniques that aid in such an endeavor, but back then no such scientific methods were available. The best the painter could do was decipher a few words. The Vatican sent over a specialist, Father Antonio Piaggio, who devised a machine similar to one used to make wigs, and he was able to unravel a scroll at the rate of about one centimeter an hour. After four years, and the destruction of many scrolls, they were able at last to read a fragment of the *Treatise on Music* by Philodemus. Piaggio worked on the scrolls for another 40 years, and by 1806 nearly a hundred rolls had been deciphered.

Within a decade of Weber's excavations, tunneling opened up fissures of poisonous sulfurous gas, forcing the closure or refilling of many of the tunnels. Excavation shifted to the town of Pompeii, where sensational new finds were announced. Pompeii became famous throughout the world, and Herculaneum became a gravesite once again. Serious excavations of the site did not begin again until 1927, when the charred scrolls became the focus of the recovery. This lost literature of antiquity fired the imagination of scholars and writers throughout the world. Specialists and emissaries were sent from England and Russia to see the papyrii, which narrowly escaped destruction in this century when the German army burned major portions of the city's ancient archives. Today, you can see the scrolls in the Biblioteca Nazionale of Naples, though eight hundred have still to be deciphered. The town of Resina has also reclaimed it's original name, Ercolano.

Among Philodemus' surviving poems was one addressed to his patron Piso.

> To Piso from his pet friend—
> I send you this letter, Sir,
> And beg you graciously to come
> Tomorrow to my humble home.
>
> Please arrive around four o'clock
> To celebrate our annual rite;
> A feast of friendship while we read
> poems sweeter than even Homer could write.
>
> I admit I've no vintage wine
> or fatted paunch whereon to dine.
> But if you'll approve my poems,
> what banquet could be more sumptuous.

Today, most of this greatest of all villas has yet to be completely excavated. J. Paul Getty had considered a proposal to fund the rest of the excavation at an estimated cost of 150 million dollars. But such an undertaking would have taken years, and he was already in his seventies. Instead, using the incomplete floor plans drawn up by Karl Weber, he decided to construct a recreation of the original villa, not in Italy, but on the California coast. Instead of overlooking the Isle of Capri, Getty's reconstruction would overlook the Isle of Catalina. The practical difficulties were enormous. Master craftspeople had to be found who could make intricate marble inlays, gold-leaf rosettes, hand-molded roof tiles, not to mention perfect copies of bronze masterpieces. No groin vaults had been built in California in almost fifty years, and such rare types of marble could only be found in ancient quarries that had not been worked in almost fifteen hundred years. Working from carbonized wooden prototypes, furniture was precisely copied. The inner peristyle looks exactly as it did at the time of Julius Caesar, and the five so-called "Dancing Maidens" flank the long, narrow fishpond in the center of the peristyle, surrounded by a colonnade of Ionic columns. The project cost over 70 million dollars, but within a few years the recreated "Villa de Papyrii" was open to the public, who were awe-struck by the flamboyance of this Roman country estate. Critics were shocked; at first, those who went beyond their initial stammering called it "bizarre." In time, though, the faithfulness of the reconstruction became apparent. Giuseppe Maggi, Director of the Excavations at Herculaneum, saw it and judged the Getty Museum, a reconstruction of the famous Piso Villa, to be essentially the same as the original. Unfortunately, Getty did not live to see its completion.

❦

Philodemus wrote numerous love poems, often erotic or playfully sexual. They were also marked by neoteric wit and brevity. His critical writing espoused the neoteric notion—swiped from Callimachus—that poems need not be didactic epics, but could be charming and short, the subject matter trivial. No need for weighty tomes recounting the deeds of ancient heroes; poems could be, as Catullus called them, "trifling nuggets," a freewheeling kind discourse between friends. One could write about anything. What counted was the sophistication of technique and the use of a contemporary idiom.

Though they shared similar ideas on poetry, the neoterics were not a brotherhood; like the modernists in this century, they often took pot shots at each other for minor differences. In one poem, Catullus obliquely refers to the year he spent in Asia Minor while on the staff of Gaius Memmius, Roman praetor of Bithynia, who failed to provide Catullus with adequate opportunities to profiteer. Catullus seems jealous that his two buddies, Fabullus and Veranius, whom he defended in another poem, are now rubbing shoulders with "moneybags" Piso and his group.

> So you've joined Piso's caravan,
> carrying your pauper's baggage;
> my excellent Varanius and you,
> my Fabullus, how goes things these days?
> Still enduring famine and frostbite
> with that wind-bag old governor
> you thought would cover you with gold.
> I'll bet your account books are in the red
> just like mine. Truth is, when I followed
> in my praetor's caravan, all I got was
> the shaft, so much for profit! Memmius,
> you gave it to me good, on my back, stuffed
> me with the whole length of your beam!
> Listen guys, you're going to get poked
> for sure, just like me. Leave your friend and
> go chasing after noble ol' moneybags,
> and you'll get what you deserve:
> curses on you both from the gods
> and goddesses, you're a blemish on the names
> of Romulus and Remus.
> *[Catullus, poem #28]*

Like Catullus, Philodemus was expert at concision and slang effects. One short poem is a snappy dialogue between a street-walker and her pick-up. Philodemus does twenty changes of voice compressed into three elegiac couplets, which goes something like this.

> Hey, babe. Me? Busy? Does it look it?
> Dinner? If you're buying. Then what?

Whatcha got? What's your price?
Put out now and pay later, when you're laid out.

My kinda lay, but when? You name it.
How 'bout now? Your place or mine?

Much of Philodemus's work remains unread. There are those who believe that some of the
poems found on the charred rolls and attributed to Philodemus were actually written by his
patron, the owner of the "Villa de Papryii," old dickhead himself, Lucius Calpurnius Piso.

☞ Laberius Decimus (c. 105-43 BC)

Decimus Laberius and his younger contemporary Publilius Syruswere not actually
neoterics, but participated in the literary ferment of the time. Technically speaking, they
wrote "mimes," or dramatic sketches. The word mime in the Greek and Latin sense should
not be confused with "mime" in the modern sense, the pantomime. The word originally
was Greek and meant mimic, one who presented a scene from daily life centering upon a
stock character such as the "quack doctor" or the "faithless wife," or a scene from myth,
like Dionysus and Ariadne. Mimes were usually written in rhythmic prose, which today we
would take for poetry. The comic sketches we see on TVshows like *Saturday Night Life*
and *Mad TV* are modern examples of what the Romans called mimes, though a mime could
last as long as a standard play. After the conquest of *Magna Graecia*, the mime was
introduced into Roman literature through dramatic performances and short farcical
sketches that followed the playing of tragedies. There was a tradition In the Greek cities of
Southern Italy, mimes riduled social life and mocked the fashions of the well-to-do and
other public figures. Domestic squabbles were charicatured using ribald language and
profane gestures. In Rome, the actors included both men and women in bare feet and
without masks playing out scenes from everyday life, tales of romance, or mythological
subjects. Many of these sketches were performed as part of the *Ludi Florales,* festivals
noted for their wild celebrations and lack of restraint. A popular feature of the *ludi* was the
appearance of actresses, *mimae*, naked. Audiences liked the free-wheeling style of mimes
and reveled in their liscentious shows. The mime took a literary form in the first century BC
with writers such as Publilius and Decimas who included elements of social and political
criticism. Mimes became extremely popular during the empire and contributed to the
decline of tragedy and high drama. They were finally suppressed in the Roman world in
502 AD.

Laberius Decimus was a Roman knight who was the first to give written form to mimes,
and there was some controversy as to their literary merit. Cicero called them boring and
was unable to sit through an entire performance, much as he tried. Horace felt they were
vulgar and unpoetic. Laberius is said to have written over 40 mimes; judging from the
hundred or so lines that survive, his style was forceful and he displayed a keen wit.
According to Macrobius, in the year 45 BC, when Laberius was over sixty, his outspoken
criticism of Julius Caesar brought upon him the humiliation of being required to appear on
stage in his own mimes in competition with the younger Publilius Syrus who had thrown

down a dramatic challenge to all comers. The mere act of appearing on stage was enough to have his knighthood status revoked. Caesar was out not just to humiliate Laberius, but to assert his own control over the equestrian order. It is said that at one point, all eyes turned towards Caesar when a character said *necesse est multos timeat quem multi timent*, "he must fear the man whom many others fear." The prologue itself was written in the lofty six-foot iambic senarius meter, and Laberius made his command appearance by addressing the audience, condemning tyranny and celebrating the ideals of the Republic.

> When I was young, though I never offered bribes,
> I flattered the gods of Necessity, who stood firm
> and wavered little from their course, though many
> have tried to escape from the dictates of Fortune.
> Look at me, an old man who now staggers his way
> to the edge of the stage, commanded by the complacency
> of our most excellent Roman, to give this submissive,
> fawning, groveling speech.
>
> How could the gods, who denied not this conqueror of Gaul,
> allow but one calm and complaisant man to say no to him.
> And so here I am, I, who have lived these sixty years without stain,
> A Roman Equestrian who must journey from his paternal gods
> to the foot of this stage, a mime. For me, this day marks the day
> one day beyond the day I should have died.
> Fortune—who holds back nothing in time of plenty or time of ill,
> Fortune—who took pleasure, lured by the praise of letters,
> to shatter the pinnacle of my good name,
> Fortune—who watched me prosper when my limbs were green with youth,
> when I could make an audience, even that noble Roman, laugh,
> Fortune—who bent my abilities to the will of the theatre,
> Fortune, why now, do you spit on me?
> Why now, do you cast me out?
> Where would you have me go?
> What have I done that you bring me here, to this stage.
> Was I but an ornament of beauty,
> Was it the dignity of my flesh,
> Was it the free fire of my free spirit,
> the musicality of my youthful voice?
> As ivy wraps clutches the stout heart of the tree,
> so has senility in time's heartfelt hug crushed me,
> and like a tombstone, all you have left to read
> is my good name.

Upon completion of the two mimes, Caesar declared Publilius the winner, but out of embarassment and with ostantatious condescension, he returned the ring to Laberius that outwardly confirmed his Knighthood. After the show, Clodius Pulcher, a notorious demagogue, made Laberius an offer he couldn't refuse, asking him to write a mime for him. Amazingly, Laberius refused, and lived to tell about it. With this dramatic contest, the crown for mime was officially placed on the head of Laberius rival, Publilius. A year later,

Caesar was assassinated, and Laberius, who had retired to Luteoli, died peacefully in his sleep.

Food for Thought

"There's No Business Like Show Business"

One of the stock characters familiar in the mimes of Laberius and Syrus was the wealthy matron with the morals of a whore (see Cicero's speech aimed at Clodia Pulchur). But not all mimes were crude and farcical. Many shared the same literary style and tone found in elegiac love poetry. One mime-actress was Eucharis, a freed slave who achievedgreat renown, and had it not been for her untimely death, she might have become a wealthy woman. She probably performed on the mimic stage—because of the Hellenistic influence, often called the "Greek stage"—during the votive games and various annual festivals such as *Ludi Florales* (April 28-May 2), *Ludi Cereales* (April 12-19), *Ludi Apollinares*, the *Ludi Romani* which had featured the plays of Andronicus and other playwrights, and the expensive funerals called *Ludi Nobilium* that celebrated the families of the noble deceased. Eucharis' patroness mentioned in the funerary inscription may have been Licinia, related to Licinius Calvus, the poet-lawyer, or the powerful politician Licinius Crassus. We can only speculate. She was probably a woman of nobility and wealth, much like Clodia Pulchur, sister of Clodius Pulchur and Catullus' mistress, with the same tastes and noble background. Who could she have hired to write the poem that graced her tombstone? Again, we can only speculate. If Licinia were related to Calvus, she would have rubbed elbows with many of the poets of the neoteric circle. Perhaps Catullus or Cinna or Calvus himself wrote the words that honor the popular mime-actress.

> Eucharis, freedwoman of Licinia.
> She lived fourteen years, a maid skilled and learned in all the arts.
> Ah, you who with casual eye look on the house of death,
> halt your step and read my epitaph to the end.
> My father's love gave it to his daughter
> where the remains of my body where to be laid down.
> Here, when my fresh youth was flowering in the arts
> and attaining glory as my age increased,
> the gloomy day of my fate came in haste
> and denied any further breath to my life.
> Skilled and taught almost by the Muses' hand,
> I who recently graced with my dancing the games of the nobles,
> who was first to appear to the people on the Greek stage—
> see how in the tomb the ashes of my body
> the cruel Fates have laid down with a dirge.
> The encouragement of my patroness, care, love, applause
>   and honour
> are mute at the body's cremation, are silent in death.
> A daughter, I left grief to my father;
> born later, I went before him to the day of death.

Twice seven birthdays are with me here,
held fast in the darkness
in the eternal house of Dis.   [Dis: ruler of the underworld]
As you leave, please pray
that the earth my be light on me.

Before Laberius, the mime was mainly crude farce with stock characters—the faithless wife, the lover, etc. Laberius transformed it into a literary genre and a vehicle of social criticism.

Ut hedera serpens vires arboreas necat,
ita me vetustas amplexu annorum enecat.
Sepulcri similis niil nisi nomen retineo.

As ivy chokes the life of the tree it enlaces,
so is old age killing me with the embrace of years.
Like a tomb, I have been left with nothing but my name.

Non possunt primi esse omnes omni in tempore.
Summum ad gradum cum claritatis veneris,
consistes aegre et citius quam escendas cades;
ceci ego, cadet qui sequitur; laus est publica.

Not all can occupy the first rank forever.
Once you have reached the highest pitch of fame, it is hard to holdonto it,
and you fall down faster than you climbed.
He who follows me will fall in turn; it is the public that confers renown.

Porro, Quirites, libertatem perdimus.

From now on, Romans, it's all over with our freedom.

☛ Publilius Syrus (first century BC)

When Caesar proclaimed Publilius the winner in the competition against Laberius, Publilius capitalized on the opportunity and caught the attention of the public with his inventive mimes. The Elder Pliny called him "the founder of the mimc stage." Of Syrian origin, Publilius was brought to Rome as a slave and eventually freed. Only two of Publilius' titles have come down to us in uncertain form—*The Pruners* and *The Murmidon*. By the time of Nero, the mime had lost its pupularity, and it's possible that many of Pulilius' mimes were improvisational performances with little to preserve for posterity in the way of an official text. What did survive, perhaps due to the didactic element in some of Publilius' work, were lines and couplets noted for their quotability.

Seneca the Elder felt he outdid all other dramatists, Greek and Roman, in his pithy sayings. They were perfect for the classroom, and Roman educators used them for their lessons in grammar and rhetoric. Publilius' lines found their way into numerous anthologies and textbooks. When he was a young boy, St. Jerome memorized *aegre reprendas quod sinas consuescere*, "reproof comes ill for a habit you countenance." Publilius is best known by a collection of moral maxims made for school use which purport to have been selected from his plays. One of his maxims,—*iudex damnatur cum nocens absolvitur*, "when the guilty man is let off, the judge stands convicted,"—was adopted by the *Edinburgh Review* in 1802 to express its stern attitude in literary criticism. Some believe that the collection of moral maxims contained the sayings of others, many composed after his death. Despite the number of sayings and proverbs that can only problematically be attributed to Publilius, there is general acceptance of over 700 lines as genuine survivals of what was once a considerably larger selection. It is often difficult to know exactly what Publilius meant to convey by some of his lines since the original dramatic context is unknown. Some of Publilius' lines appear in variant form meaning two different things. For instance:

> *Deliberando discitur sapientia*
> Deliberation teaches wisdom

has often been quoted as

> *Deliberando saepe perit occasio*
> Deliberation often loses a good chance.

Some of the proverbs are profound, others comic, some mere platitudes.

> *Aperte mala cum est mulier, tum demum est bona.*
> Only when a woman is openly bad is she really good.

> *Cum ames non sapias aut cum sapias non ames.*
> When you are in love you are not wise, or rather,
> when you are wise, you don't fall in love.

> *De inimico non loquaris male sed cogites.*
> Don't *speak* ill of your enemy: plot it.

> *Inopiae desunt mulota, avaritiae omnia.*
> Poverty is a lack of many things; avarice of everyting.

> *Irritare est calamitatem cum te felicem voces.*
> Knock wood!

> *Etiam in peccato recte praestatyr fides.*
> There is honor among thieves
> (literally: Even in crime, loyalty is rightly displayed)

> *Honesta turpitudo est procausa bona.*

The end justifies the means.

Amori finem tempus, non animus, facit.
It's time, not the mind, that puts an end to love.

Semper iratus plus se posse putat quam possit.
Anger always thinks it has power beyond its power.

Malivolus animus abditos dentes habet.
The spiteful mind has hidden teeth.

☛ **Lucretius** (*c.* 98 –*c.* 55 B.C.)
De Rerum Natura (*On the Nature of Things*)

The stylistic revolution of the *poetae novi*, the "new poets" who sought a less archaic style and used modern diction, flourished amid a decline in the political system which brought corresponding changes in religious tradition. State cults were neglected or degenerated into mere forms largely devoted to divination. Some temples fell into ruins and priesthods were often left vacant. New religions and mystery cults sprang up all over the eastern Mediterranean, stressing the theme of death and resurrection. Senators and the upper classes generally objected to these new cults because their emotional ceremonies and vegetation myths seemed un-Roman and might lead to immoral behavior. Instead, Hellenistic philosophies—Stoicism and Epicureanism—became favored by the upper classes. Thus Cicero worked out a modified Stoicism in *Scipio's Dream*, with its emphasis on man's duty to the state and the promise of future fame in the form of an afterlife in heaven rather than reputation among men. The poet Lucretius expounded a form of Epicureanism in his poem *On The Nature of Things* in which the universe was shown as an agglomeration of atoms. Lucretius was an adherent of the Athenian philosopher, Epicurus (341-270 BC). Epicurus based some of his ideas on the philosophy of Democritus (460-370 BC), who was called, because of his cheerful disposition, "the Laughing Philosopher."

Democritus believed that the universe was composed of atoms, which are eternal, move about in space, and form themselves into bodies. The soul is a form of fire, which animates the human body. Democritus felt that pleasure, along with self-control, was the goal of life. It is said that he put out his eyes so that he might think without distraction.

Only fragments of the work of Epicurus remain, but some of his teachings were transcribed by his biographer, Diogenes Laertius, who tells us that Epicurus advocated reliance on the senses; he sought to prove that the universe was completely material, consisting of nothing but atoms and the space in which they move. He tried to eliminate superstition and the dread of death. Epicurus taught that pleasure was actually the freedom from pain, which was often caused by abusing activities of pleasure. Serenity, the harmony of mind and body, is best achieved, he said, through virtue and simple living. The current usage of the term *epicure,* to describe one devoted to sensual pleasures, reflects a misunderstanding of his teachings.

The Epicureans were an austere, unpretentious, and unambitious sect who gained a certain amount of support in Italy, and by Lucretius' time had adherents in Rome. But

Lucretius transformed the philosopher's undistinguished Greek prose into an ingongruously, impassioned Latin poem on the nature of the universe, variously translated as *About Reality, How Things Are,* or the more commonly accepted title, *On The Nature of Things*. It is the only philosophical poem of antiquity written in dactylic hexameter to come down to us in its complete form.

Lucretius may have considered the poem's philosophy of prime importance, but we read it today for its brilliant visual imagery. In presenting his philosophical and scientific concepts, he proved himself the most original, adventurous, imaginative, and dedicated thinker of his day, and perhaps the most formidable intellectual ever to write in the Latin tongue. Lucretius declares, as Epicurus did before him, that a materialistic interpretation of the universe makes the fear of the gods, and death itself, pointless.

Sing, Goddess, the wrath of Achilles . . .

So begins Homer's epic poem, the *Illiad*. Milton, at the beginning of *Paradise Lost*, invokes the Muse and asks for her aid "to my adventurous song." Poets often began their epic poems with an invocation to the Muse. Lucretius begins his with one of the most memorable invocations of them all, a hymn to the goddess Venus; but why is his so unusual? *On The Nature of Things* is a poem that rejects religion, and posits that if there are gods, they do not bother with the doings of humankind, nor do they listen to our foolish supplications. Yet Lucretius asks the goddess Venus for help in guiding him through the difficult job ahead.

> Mother of Romans, joy of gods and men,
> Venus, life-giver, who under planet and star
> visits the ship-clad sea, the grain-clothed land
> always, for through you all that's born and breathes
> is gotten, created, brought forth to see the sun,
> Lady, the storms and clouds of heaven shun you,
> You and your advent; Earth, sweet magic-maker,
> sends up her flowers for you, broad Ocean smiles,
> and peace glows in the light that fills the sky.
> For soon as the year has bared her springtime face,
> and bars are down for the breeze of growth and birth,
> in heaven the birds first mark your passage, Lady,
> and you; your power pulses in their hearts.
> Then wild beasts, too, leap over rich, lush lands
> and swim swift streams; so prisoned by your charms
> they follow lustily where you lead them on.
> Last, over sea and hill and greedy river,
> through leaf-clad homes of birds, through fresh green fields,
> in every creature you sink love's tingling dart,
> luring them lustily to create their kind.
> Since you, and you only, rule the world of nature,
> and nothing, without you, comes forth to the coasts
> of holy light, or makes for joy and love,
> I pray you be with me as I write these verses

that I compose about the world of nature.
Grant then to my words, Lady, a deathless charm.

Lucretius uses Venus symbolically because she personifies the creative force, as well as *uoluptas* or pleasure, the prime impulse and supreme good according to the Epicurean moral system. He reminds the reader that Venus represents the forces of inventive earth, thus suiting a philosophy that sees man as part of nature. He calls upon Venus to grant his words "a deathless charm" (*aeternum da dictis, diua, leporem*). Here the archaic alliteration suits the solemnities of old Roman poetry, but his use of "charm" (ironically combined with the request that it be everlasting), indicates that Lucretius had one ear atuned to the old diction, and the other to the modern; this strategy is used throughout the poem, juxtaposing religious or archaic diction with the more modern diction of the "New Poets" of his own day. Along with Catullus, he was associated with the neoteric movement in the late Republic, a group of poets who took the profession of poetry with utmost seriousness. Some emphasized natural language, while others showed interest in a more aesthetic language and form (technique for technique's sake). Lucretius skillfully combined the two. In the opening of the poem, when he suggests that Venus bring peace by seducing Mars, the God of War, he surprises us by blending romantic eloquence with imagery that is sensuous, colloquial, and modern.

> Cause meanwhile that all savage works of war
> by land and sea drop off to sleep and rest.
> For you alone can bless our mortal race
> with peace and calm: though Mars the War Lord rules
> war's savage works, yet often he throws himself
> into your arms, faint with love's deathless wound,
> and there, with arching neck bent back, looks up
> and sighs, and feeds a lustful eye on you
> and, pillowed, dangles his life's breath from your lips.
> Then, as he falls back on your sacred body,
> Lady, lean over and let sweet utterance pour
> from your holy lips — a plea of peace for Rome.

> [note how he repeats certain words in different or
> recurring combinations:
> charms, deathless charm, deathless wound.]

In this passage, Lucretius applies a Homeric touch to his own juicy story, combining melodrama with the erotic and sophisticated reminder that from this union of Mars and Venus will come their daughter, Harmonia, whom the gods changed into a serpent destined to live in the woods avoiding the presence of men but precluded from doing them harm. Written at a time when Caesar was already subverting the Republic, the passage continues to have relevance for anyone living through times of societal chaos. And it doesn't take Lucretius long to get to the crux of the problem, the fear of death.

> Will you hang back, indignant that you must die:
> Alive and awake, you live next-door to death;
> you waste the greater part of life in sleep,

and, even waking, you snore, and dream, dream on;
you wear a heart confounded by empty fears
yet rarely can tell what caused them, when oppressed
and drunk and wretched with unremitting cares
you wander, waver, and wonder where to turn.   alliteration]
    If men, who clearly sense the weight that rests
upon their souls and drags them weary down,
could also know what causes this, and whence
this pain that lies like lead upon their hearts,
they would not live as commonly now we see them,
not knowing what they want, seeking always to change
their place, as if they could just drop their burdens.
Here is one who leaves his palace,
bored sick with home, yet comes right back again
because he finds no better world outside.
He drives his nags top-speed out to his country house
as if it were burning, and he to put out the fire;
he's yawning before his foot has passed the door;
in weary search for oblivion, he sleeps,
or turns and gallops away to town again.
Thus each man runs from himself—the self, of course,
he can't escape but must hold close; he hates it
because, being sick, he can't know why he's sick.
If he could see this clearly, he'd cast aside his business
and before all else would seek to understand the nature of things.

We know very little about the poet who lived through the terrifying years that marked the end of the Roman republic. Lucretius witnessed half a century of Roman revolution: through the Social War, Marian massacres, and Sullan proscriptions; through Catiline's conspiracy and Julius Caesar's ascendancy after defeating Pompey. Lucretius came from the aristocratic class and lived through its obvious decay and the demoralizing breakdown that accompanied the dissolution of the old ways. The small city-state was giving way to larger institutions more suited to the governing of a world empire. No fortune was secure. Lucretius' philosophic poem is thus a yearning for social stability and inner peace.

    The turbulence of the times transformed not only the economy and government, but morals and religion as well. Perhaps as a youth he was moved by the mystery and pageantry of religion, only to find the ancient faith corrupted by superstition and hypocracy. Many flocked to the bloodstained shrines of the Phrygian Great Mother, or the Cappadocian goddess Ma, or some of the Oriental deities that had entered Italy with soldiers or captives from the East. Chaldean fortune tellers and astrologers were thriving in Italy, casting horoscopes for paupers and millionaires alike, predicting wealth and future events, interpreting omens and dreams with profitable flattery. It was this proliferation of pseudo-religious superstition and ritualism against which Lucretius rebelled.

    But in the writings of Epicurus he seemed to find solutions to his internal dilemmas. Here was a philosophical outlook that exalted the omnipresence of natural law, the integrity of nature, and the forgivable naturalness of death. Lucretius set himself the task of transforming the abstract Greek prose of Epicurus into Latin hexameters at a time when

Latin had no philosophic vocabulary. The result was a philosophic poem that has never been equaled.

Lucretius was ten years younger than Cicero and perhaps ten years older than Catullus, but apart from a few references, the poet remains a shadowy figure. Cicero writes a letter to his younger brother and mentions that "Lucretius' poetry is just as you say—flashes of brilliant genius, but also signs of great literary art." The most extensive biographical notice comes from St. Jerome, writing centuries later in his translation of Eusebius' *Chronicles* of various Latin writers. Under the date 94 B.C. he writes: "The poet Titus Lucretius is born. Subsequently driven to madness by a love-philtre, after having written several books in the intervals of lucidity that his madness allowed him; he died by his own hand at the age of 43." Perhaps Jerome had trouble believing that Lucretius, a rational sceptic, could dismiss the notion of the eternal soul, of a life after death. After all, *On The Nature of Things* was written to free men's minds from religious fears. If we accept Lucretius' conception of the structure of the soul and his rejection of religion, we free our minds of the fears of suffering in another world. As one of the early Church fathers, St. Jerome may have concluded that Lucretius was driven mad by such beliefs.

On The Nature of Things is an epic-didactic poem composed of six books of some twelve hundred lines each. It stands with Virgil's *Aeneid* as one of the most ambitious undertakings and monumental achievements of Latin literature. While Lucretius speaks of his poetry as mere "honey on the rim of the cup to sweeten the bitter medicine" of philosophy, the poem's superb imagery, its epic-heroic tone, and the persuasiveness of its language make it a work of unusual force and power. It's the fullest exposition we have of the physical system of Epicurus, whose aim was to inspire the wise conduct of life and to teach men how to face life's disasters with serenity.

According to Epicurus, death is nothing once we realize that when we lose die, we lose all sensation of desire. While we live, death does not exist; and once it does, we cease to experience it. So what is there to fear? In the very nature of things, life and death cannot exist together. The Gods go about their business of serence contemplation and give us hardly a thought; therefore, we need not fear them, nor is there any point in praying to them, because there is no after life. Yet even if the world is merely a chance pileup of atoms in a meaningless void, according to Luctretius, they do not move in a predetermined fashion; on the contrary, they show independence of movement and sometimes "swerve" unpredictably. This means, he concludes, that individuals are not slaves to fate. We are free agents. His description of the triumphs of the human brain and will, which together have created civilization, is one of the supreme expositions of what individuals are capable of achieving. We can shape our lives without dread of punishment by capricious gods. And the wisest choice we can make is to live a life of pleasure, and to avoid pain. Excess in bodily pleasures and over-indulgence leads to pain; therefore it is a life of moderation, of serenity, we should seek. When we learn "what can come to pass and what cannot," we attain *ataraxia*, the tranquility of soul, or absence of mental pain.

Happiness comes from having the right kind of knowledge and living a life free from disturbance. Lucretius must not have thought Caesar and Pompey possessed this knowledge, otherwise it's likely he would have referred to them in his poem. He expressed a poor view of all politicians, whose rat race was dragging the Roman Republic to its extinction:

> Men lost,
> Confused, in hectic search for the right road,
> The strife of wits, the wars for precedence,
> The everlasting struggle, night and day,
> To win towards heights of wealth and power.

Where Lucretius stood in relation to the intellectual ferment of the times is hard to say. Compared to the lively, unrestrained, and imaginative poetry of the *neoterics* ("the moderns") led by Catullus, Lucretius seemed conservative. The "modern poets" irreverently rejected national tradition in order to pursue an avant-garde poetic ideal. Lucretius was no less venturesome. His selection of a philosophic topic was certainly a bold move; but to shape that subject into an epic with all nature as its heroine, to marry philosophy and poetry, was an even bolder stroke.

Lucretius wrote in the standard hexameter and used words and expressions provided for him by the archaic tradition, especially compound adjectives such as "sweet-speaking" (*suaviloquens*), "high-flying" (*altivolans*), "ship-carrying" (*navigerum*), and "fruit-bearing" *frugiferens*). He also coined novel adverbs—"thread by thread" (*filatim*), and "with anticipatory fear" (*praemetuenter*). From the elevated Roman poetry of archaic tradition he used alliteration, assonance, solemn and common words blended into convenient archaic constructions and, in general, sound effects that belong to Rome's earliest poets. He was especially influenced by Ennius, one of the most versatile of the early Roman poets, regarded by the Romans as the father of their literature. Lucretius also imitated or echoed Homer, the dramatists Aeschylus and Euripides, the poet Callimachus, the historian Thucydides, and the physician Hippocrates. Yet, Lucretius' tone is modern, evidenced in his use of enjambment and concreteness of expression. His descriptions were vivid and to the point, plain and lively, sometimes rough and colloquial. Lucretius himself declared that he was forced to use vivid imagery to express abstract thoughts because there was no pre-existing language in Latin to give form to his discourse. The irony is obvious. The images he presents are meant to convey abstract ideas; the ideas pertain to moderation and rational thought; yet the images themselves elicit a visceral response; the poetry helps clarify philosophic thought, and the logic of the ideas becomes beautiful. Speaking of physics, Einstein said that when written in its highest form, it evolves into poetry. The same could be said of Lucretius' philosophical writing. His work combines colloquial language and epic-tragic diction. No one thought to do so before him. At least, not in Latin. His style is capable of harshness and elegance, yet each passage is filled with exceptional ardor. No matter how you slice it, this was a modern poet.

The book that perhaps more than any other demonstrates his skill at imagery and argumentation is the third, which is devoted to dispelling the fear of death. There is no after-life. The only hell is the one we make for ourselves in this life, on this earth.

> Away with your tears, you rascal, and muzzle your moans . . .
> Because you always long for what you don't have

and disregard what you have, your life
has slipped away from you unfulfilled and unenjoyed . . .
Now give up things unsuited to your years
and make way for younger men; for there is no escape. . .
For in this world the new drives out the old
always; one thing must die to build another.
Nothing goes down to darkness and the Pit;
there must be matter that worlds to come may grow;
they too will run their course and follow you.
Before your day, men died, and men will die;
there's never an end; one thing grows from another.
Life is no grant in freehold: Life's a loan . . . .
    And all those things men tell of down in hell,
far under the earth, are right here in our lives. . . .
Hell is right here, the work of foolish men!

Earlier in the poem, Lucretius denounces the cruelties of traditional religion by portraying the famous scene of Agamemnon sacrificing his daughter Iphigenia at Diana's temple at Aulis so that a favorable wind might enable the Greek fleet to depart for Troy (the story is told by Euripedes in his play *Iphigenia at Aulis*).

               More commonly
religion has prompted vile and vicious acts.
Remember Aulis? How Diana's altar
was shamed and fouled by Iphigenia's blood
spilled by the Lords of Greece — great heroes, they!
They coiffed the poor girl for her wedding day;
a ribbon, long braids to hang each side of her face.
But there by the altar she saw her father standing
grief-stricken, and near him acolytes hiding knives,
and people staring at her with tear-stained faces.
Voiceless with terror she crumpled to her knees.
Poor thing, no help to her in such an hour
that she'd been first to call the king "my father."
Men led her to the altar, raised her up
all trembling, not to say their sacred office
and carry her home with nuptial shout and song,
but that her innocence at the bridal hour
fall criminal victim by a father's blow,
that ships might have clear sailing and fair winds.
So much evil could religion prompt.

The Epicurians' quest was for a life of pleasure, but that meant avoiding pain, and any overindulgence in pleasure that led to pain. In other words: "moderation in all things." The following passage from Book IV, admonishes those who would throw sexual caution to the winds and expresses a cynicism that counters the growing romanticism of the poets. Here, Epicurean rejection of over-indulgence is an echo of the contemporary view of compulsion. The imbibing of the substance—be it flesh or drugs or alcohol—does not satiate; rather, indulgence leads to greater hunger (anxiety) which can lead to further impulsive action, which leads to a loss of control of one's overall functioning, of one's fate.

So Venus deludes fond lovers with simulacra.
They view bare bodies but get no fill of viewing;
hands chafe but win no substance from young flesh,
though they roam wildly over all the body.
Besides, when two lie tasting, limb by limb,
life's bloom, when flesh gives foretaste of delight,
and Venus is ready to sow the female field,
they hungrily seize each other, mouth to mouth
the pittle flows, they pant, press tooth to lip —
vainly, for they can chafe no substance off
nor pierce and be gone, one body in the other.   c.f. Milton
Yet, when impounded lust has burst from sinew,   8. 618-29
hot passion, just for a moment, makes a pause.
Then men go mad again, wild lust returns,
while even the passionate wonder what they want,
and find no artifice to assuage the pain,
so helpless, weak, and blind the world has left them.
    Add that they waste their strength, they strain, they die;
add that the will of a woman rules their life.
Fortunes go first, for Oriental robes,
then honor and reputation totter and fall.
Perfumes, fine slippers for her pretty feet,
of course, and flashing emeralds, huge and green,
set in pure gold; blue gowns for everyday,
to be rumpled and sweat-soaked in the act of love.
Fathers' hard-won earnings turn into ribbons and head-scarves, . . .
yet from the very fountain of enchantment a bitterness wells up
to bring anguish amid the blossoms, when the lover's mind
is gnawed by the awareness that he is passing his life
in idleness and going to ruin in brothels,
or because she has left unclarified a word she has let fly
that sticks fast in his passionate heart and ignites like a flame,
or because he thinks she flaunts her eyes too freely
or gazes at another, and he sees in her face a trace of mockery.

Some scholars consider this poem, with its abrupt ending, unfinished. One reason why many consider this poem unfinished is its abrupt ending. Book VI eulogizes Epicurus and Athenian civilization, then goes on to describe natural phenomena such as thunder and lightning, waterspouts and rain, earthquakes and volcanoes. Finally he turns to epidemics with a translation of Thucydides' description of the plague that occurred at Athens in the second year of the Peloponnesian War four centuries earlier. His treatment is less objective than the Greek historian's; Lucretius emphasizes the horror, to make a point. It's a gruesome account, with mourners struggling to find a place for their departed loved ones on other people's pyres. Perhaps Lucretius planned all along to end his long poem with an unsettling description of the plague, as if to shock the reader into facing death. He opens his poem with a depiction of spring and rebirth in the hymn to Venus, a celebration of life and the procreative force of nature. He closes it with a somber picture of life's inevitable end. In this vivid and disturbing ending, he repeats what are by now familiar themes: the mechanical causation of calamity, the terror of death, and the uselessness of religion.

> Their sufferings knew no rest; their bodies lay
> exhausted. Doctors muttered, shook, fell dumb,
> as over and over those staring eyes turned toward them,
> infected, burning with fever, never asleep.
> Men showed many other fatal symptoms, too:
> a mind deranged by agony and by fear,
> a grim expression, the madman's piercing stare,
> the hearing impaired, ears full of roaring sound,
> the breathing rapid, or slow to come, and labored,
> the neck all wet and shiny with streaming sweat,
> the spittle in tiny droplets, saffron-colored,
> and salty, hawked from the throat with hard, hoarse coughs.
> Then as the final moment came,
> the nose was pinched, the tip of the nose was sharp,
> eyes hollow, temples sunk, skin cold and taut,
> lips in a snarling grin, brow tight and swollen.
> It was not long before they died and stiffened;
> As dawn began to break on the eighth day
> Or perhaps the ninth, they parted with their lives.

If we are not explicitly offered the consolations of philosophy, it is because Lucretius believed there is solace in clear-sightedness, in seeing the world as it is, and to accept, with sublime objectivity, the nature of things.

> No therapy was proposed that worked for all.
> For what gave one the right to roll the air
> of life on his lips, and gaze on heavenly zones,
> to others was fatal and brought a prompt demise.
> Pathetic here, and bound to rouse profound
> compassion, was this: when anyone observed
> himself infected, as though condemned to die,
> he lost his courage and, full of grief, lay down
> to wait for death: right there, he lost his life.
> You see, the infection never flagged: contagious,
> greedy, it passed from one man to another,
> as if twixt wool-clad flocks and cow-horned kind.
> And this above all else piled death on death.
> Yes, all who shrank from visiting their sick
> from too great lust for life and fear of death
> were later punished: they died disgraced, forgotten,
> with none to help them, victims of neglect.
> But those who stayed on hand died by contagion
> and of the labors forced on them by conscience
> and the sufferers' wistful and heart-rending pleas.
> This way all truly good men met their death.

Such were the times, no man could be discovered
untroubled by death or sorrow or disease.
   Further, every shepherd and herdsman now,
likewise the brawny hand, guide of the plow,
fell sick, and in dark huts their bodies lay
huddled, ragged, diseased, consigned to death.
Over dead babies one might well have seen
the lifeless bodies of parents, and again
on mother and father the child yielded up his life.
And everywhere through the public parks and street
people lay sick and dying; one could see
their tattered, rotting flesh, bandaged with rags,
wasting away, their bodies skin and bones,
already half-buried in pus-filled sores and filth.
And death besides had filled each holy shrine
of the gods with lifeless bodies; the sacred precincts
were everywhere loaded with corpses unremoved
where temple guards had packed the grounds with strangers.
For now, to scruple and fear of god, men paid
small heed; their present agonies prevailed.

In the *Georgics*, Virgil wrote: *felix qui potuit rerum cognoscere causas*, "happy the man who was able to understand the causes of things." It's clear Virgil was referring to Lucretius, whose influence on him was unmistakable. Virgil, like Horace, never mentioned Lucretius by name for fear of being labeled subversive. Pagan Rome looked upon the Epicurean philosophy with suspicion, and in Christian Rome, "Epicurean" became synonymous with "infidel." Virgil and Horace did, however, attempt to honor Lucretius with veiled allusions. Not only did Lucretius' achievement elevate the Latin hexameter for Virgil's use, but the substance and spirit of *De Rerum Natura* profoundly influenced Virgil, the greatest poet in all classical literature. A Roman poet of the time remarked that "Virgil not only adopted single words of Lucretius but also closely followed very many verses and passages almost in their entirety." Modern scholars have pointed to hundreds of individual passages in Virgil which show Lucretius' influence. A generation later Statius praised the *docti furor ardus Lucreti*, "the towering frenzy of the learned Lucretius." But the Epicurean philosophy was unsuited to a Roman government that exalted mystic power over natural law. They wanted an ethic that promoted Rome's imperial mastery, rather than serenity and peace. They wanted a political philosophy that, like the philosophies of Virgil and Horace, would justify such a course.

By the Middle Ages, Lucretius seemed all but forgotten. Not until Poggio Bracciolini discovered a manuscript of Lucretius' in 1417 did the Renaissance once again embrace his reasoned poetry and his powerfully imagined philosophy. Molière translated part of book IV when dwelling upon the defects of women in the *Misanthrope*. Lucretius remained a source of inspiration for many didactically-minded Romantic poets, including Wordsworth, Shelley, and Goethe. Tennyson's dramatic monologue "Lucretius" (1869) repeats the legend that the poet committed suicide in a fit of insanity induced by a love potion given him by his wife. Voltaire read *De Rerum Natura* devotedly, and agreed with

Ovid that its rebel verses would last as long as the earth. In Lucretius, as in Catullus and Cicero, Latin literature came of age; at last, the leadership in letters passed from Greece to Rome.

☛ Caius Valerius Catullus (c. 84—c. 54 B.C.),

It was an age of war and revolution, a time when writers sought refuge in scholarship, historical research, critical monographs, commentaries, grammars on morals, political tracts, and a new kind of poetry that brushed aside stale, historical subjects. The *poetae novi* were avante-garde for their time, reforming literary tastes during the ascension of Roman power when the archaic society of peasant-soldiers began to revolt against the upper classes. At the same time, Rome was becoming civilized. Like the Americans who discovered avant-garde European art movements after the First World War, Roman intellectuals, artists, and writers looked to Greece for their models.

The older Roman aristocracy, however, guarded its traditions jealously, especially in the fields of epic and drama, which were reflective—politically and morally—of their way of life. The historical epic was the link between literature and propaganda, between literature and those in power. But new sensibilities of urban taste demanded new literary genres. Scipio and his circle encouraged the importation of Greek culture and new literary forms, typified by poets such as Lucilius (180-102 BC), the first man of letters from a good family to lead the life of a writer by deliberately removing himself from public life. Like the lost generation of the roaring twenties who reveled in their own hipness from the far side of paradise, the so-called neoterics (the "moderns"), flouted their break with tradition. They performed their poems on the Aventine, snubbing the old generation with their direct and forceful lyrics, as if to say, "Take this, you old farts!" Here was an opportunity for poets to grind a personal axe or reflect on the nature of the self in relation to the contemporary world. This poetic impulse was a reaction to Ennius' lofty verse, yet Lucretius and Virgil were able to use Ennius' alliterative style to give certain verses a traditional ring, especially those that involved a grand event or personage. But the leading *poetae novi* of that time, the one who best captures the amoral and amorous lifestyles of Roman high society, the one who speaks most directly to us twenty centuries later, is Valerius Catullus, who was born in the dreadful time of Marius and Sulla, and fell in love with Clodia Metelli, the *mulier nobilisa* with dark eyes and secret fires, fourteen years his senior. Catullus died at the age of twenty-nine, ten years before the assassination of Julius Caesar.

While still in his early twenties, Catullus left Veronna for Rome, the year following the Catilinarian conspiracy. Apparently well-off (his father was quite wealthy and knew Julius Caesar), Catullus nevertheless complained constantly of his poverty. He wrote of the villas near Tibur and on Lake Carda and his elegant house in Rome as being choked with mortgages. From his poems we get a picture of a sophisticated man of the world who, upon his arrival in Rome, joined the fashionable literary circle and dallied among the young and restless intellectuals who opposed Caesar with their pithy epigrams (if not their knives). Of this group of clever orators, politicians, lawyers, poets and men of letters was **Valerius Cato**, a Veronese freedman who many scholars believe to have been the originator of the neoteric movement. Another poet, also known for his biographical sketches *The Lives of Famous Men,* was **Cornelius Nepos,** to whom Catullus dedicated his "so carefully polished little book" of poems. Catullus called his own book "little" with a touch of irony, an acknowledgment of Cornelius' "laborious and learned" three-volume history of the world, the *Chronica* (which has not survived). Another poet was **Gaius Helvius Cinna**, mistakenly taken for Cinna the conspirator and beaten to death by an angry mob provoked by Anthony when Caesar was assassinated. Cinna was a friend of Catullus and a fellow New Poet. Shakespeare was to make him famous with the touching image of Cinna fending off the mob, shouting as they are clubbing him to death, "I am Cinna the poet! I am Cinna the poet!" Lucretius dedicated his poem *De Rerum Natura* to Catullus's patron, **Gaius Memmius Gemellus,** poet and politician, who was married to Sulla's daughter, and took Catullus and Cinna with him to Bithynia where he was praetor in 57 BC. Also part of the *neoteric* circle were **Quintus Cornificius**, a patrician who supported the senatorial cause and was killed in battle in 41 BC, and **Marcus Caelius Rufus**, a poet who became a communist, siding with Catiline and later prosecuted for "political violence." Though Catullus was not fond of his verse, we should also mention another neoteric, **Hortensius Hortalus**, "that nuisance from Hatria," the distinguished lawyer and orator, rival to Cicero, and author of the "5,000 versicles yearly" that Catullus claimed would "penetrate to the runnelled waves of Satrachus." Another *poetae novi* was the "eloquent dwarf," **Gaius Licinius Calvus,** another of Clodia's lovers. Calvus encouraged Catullus to write political invectives directed at reactionary military commanders. In one poem, Catullus took on Julius Caesar and Mamurra, Caesar's chief engineer in Spain and Gaul (who was the first to cover the front of his mansion with marble). Catullus called them

a couple of queers, both identical	[Catullus here combines two verbs
two *cognoscenti* in one snug sofa,	*cognosco,* "to know" &
both of them fucked out and used up,	*cogo,* "to bring up the rear."
you'd think they were twins,	*cognoscenti* can be rendered as
partners in competing	" ass-fucking
with the girlies of the town.	know-it-alls"]

In several others poems Catullus referred to Mammura as "dick-face" and "penis-brain," and said of Caesar, "Caesar who?" As Cicero put it, Rome was a *maledica civitas*, a city in which slander and personal smears were common political ploys. When the poet Naevius offended the powerful Metelli famliy, he was jailed for *maledicentia,* "non-stop bad-mouthing," then exiled for life. Lucilius got away with his satirical jests, probably because he came from an aristocratic family and was a member of Scipio Aemilianus's literary circle. Naevius was not so well-born, and that seems to have been the difference. Catullus was a *Transpadanus*, coming from a well-to-do Veronese family; his grandfather built a large homestead on the peninsula of Sirmio. When he dedicated his book of *nugas*, "trifles," to his fellow-Transpadane Cornelius Nepos, he addressed him as *unus Italorum.*

Still, calling the man who had conquered Gaul and Britain "Miss Julius Caesar," and in another poem a *cineade Romule* (variously translated as "Pansy Romulus," "faggot Romulus," and "Noble Pederast") would probably not have gone unpunished. Catullus wisely sent an apology, and Caesar invited him to dinner.

What these keen wits and impecunious aristocrats shared was a desire to overthrow the old forms of literature (typified by Naevius and Ennius) and to celebrate the wild sentiments of youth in bold metrics and lyric songs. They were after a modern tone filled with the vigor of speech, yet executed in a way that honored the literary style of Callimachus, the Greek poet who served as their model. Down with the old morals preached by those exhausted elders! Up with spontaneity, instinct, the glories of sex and song, the passions of love, the grand thrall of dissipation.

> The time to live, the time to love, is now. What our
>   parents think about it means nothing to us.
> It can't wait. Every morning the sun returns to life —
> our light as brief as day.

Different as they were from each other, the poetry of Catullus and Lucretius rang with the "new" that every age proclaiming itself modern seeks. It was a time when poets reacted to the demands of contemporary life with a call to overthrow the archaic traditions of the past. These new poets, the *poetae novi*, were innovators of a style that marked a decisive turn in the history of Latin literature. Cicero had no use for them, dismissing them as *cantores Euphorionis*, "singers of Euphorian." Celebrated for the density of his lyrics, Euphorion was a 3rd century BC poet who was a symbol of the notorious Alexandrian poetic ideal later picked up by Callimachus.

Another type of "modern poetry" popular among the Roman elite was epigrammatic verse, often playful in tone, called *nugae*, "trifles." Influenced somewhat by Lucilius' short satiric poems, nugatory poetry expressed personal sentiment in a jesting manner (the Greek term for them was *paignia*, "jests" or "diversions"—see Laevius Melissus's *Erotopoegnia*, "The Diversions of Love"), and they functioned as prelude to the neoteric revolution. Neoteric poetry was sweeping and modern in its rejection of the Latin tradition of poetry exemplified by Ennius. Poets were no longer interested in serving the state with epics glorifying the founding of the Roman Republic—hardly foreseeing that within a half-century Virgil would write an epic masterpiece celebrating the founding of the Roman Empire.

These poets celebrated the ideals of love and *otium*, the time spent among friends in pursuit of personal needs, intelligent conversation, and literary interests. Thus, we see how the Epicurean philosophy espoused by Lucretius and the values of neoteric poetry converged to create a modernist revolution in verse. Except for Lucretius, who withdrew from the pain of extreme sensation, the neoterics, especially Catullus, celebrated eros and all its resulting pain and anxiety. Love was the central emotion of life, the reason for existence. Twenty-five of Catullus' poems, written under the influence of Hellenistic Greek poetry in racy, often erudite language, chronicle his love affair with Lesbia from an idyllic beginning to hopeless passion and final disillusionment, making his affair one of the most memorable in literary history.

These poets were not a "school" exactly, nor did they define their ideas in a manifesto. They met together often, held meetings on the Aventine, attended each other's readings, and discussed the changing metrics in Roman verse. They compared notes on the Callimachean ideal: a concern for form while keeping the content topical and lively. They often mocked the ancient epics, just as Callimachus had attacked the followers of Homeric epic, for their careless form, sloppy lyrics, and pompous rhetoric:

> I despise neo-epic sagas: I cannot
> Welcome trends which drag the populace
> This way and that. Peripatetic sex-partners
> Turn me off: I do not drink from the mains,
> Can't stomach anything public.

The neoterics championed the short, personal poem, a crisp style, a contemporary tone. Catullus was the leading figure among them, and while most sought to mix modern diction with traditional meter, the blend of colloquial speech with complex literary forms is Catullus' own. He displayed a facility with language previously unknown in Roman literature.

B ased on the one manuscript copy of his works that contains unfinished poems, and some that look like rejected first drafts, our supposition is that Catullus carried on a passionate, and in the end unhappy, love affair with a married woman he called "Lesbia."

> #2
> Lesbia's sparrow!
> Lesbia's plaything!
> in her lap or at her breast.
> She's the bright center, the glowing light
> of my life.
> It pleases Lesbia to toy with you.
> When love has ebbed,
> you are invited to nip her finger
> you are coaxed into pecking sharply,
> the love bites that help her forget her pain.
> Ah, If only I could lift this dark sorrow
> I feel inside,
> and play with you as she does
> her sparrow.

In a book containing over a hundred poems, Catullus devotes twenty poems to his Lesbia. Some of the poems are touching and tender, like the "kiss" poem, which begins with the lyrical plea that every lover utters—*Vivamus, mea Lesbia, atque amemus*, "Let's live, my Lesbia, and love."

#5

Let's live, my Lesbia, and love,
and count the loose-lipped gossiping
old men barely worth a penny.
Suns may set and rise again.
But For us, when our short light
has finally set,
only the sleep of one unbroken night
will remain. So my love,
make this night last forever,
give me a thousand kisses,
then a hundred,
then another thousand,
then a second hundred,
then yet another thousand,
then a hundred more.
Then, when we have lost count,
a hundred thousand kisses
gone between us and more to come,
we'll tear up the account books
and start again, miscount
the kisses so that any malicious person
casting the evil eye upon us
will lose track of all the kisses
there'll be so many,
so many kisses there'll be
my love, between us.

The sentiments are those of a love-sick teenager, but they're expressed with a tender lyricism that reaches out to anyone who has been in love. At the same time, the poem is written with a technical virtuosity that almost defies translation. For example, the first lyrical line is followed by three lines—alliterative whispers of kisses that no one reading the lines aloud could fail to miss.

Vivamus, mea Lesbia, atque amemus,
rumoresque senum severiorum
omnes unius aestimemus assis.
Soles, occidere et redire possunt:

Lesbia was the proverbial older woman, and judging by the poems and other historical clues, the relationship seemed one-sided, with Catullus the love-sick puppy tagging along beside his more sophisticated and worldly mistress. Scholars suspect that the name Lesbia was a metrical substitute for Clodia Pulcher Metelli, descendant of a noble family that traced its lineage back to Appius Claudius who tore up the proposed peace with King Pyrrus, and built the first Roman aqueduct and the first portion of the Via Appia. Her husband was Caecilius Quintus Marcus Metellus Celer, from the noble Metelli family.

Metellus was an arrogant, cold-blooded politician who once told an opponent in the Senate that he would kill him with his bare hands. Metellus easily could have, having been a soldier, like Caesar, fighting in the Mediterranean campaigns with his brother-in-law Pompey. In recognition for his service, Metellus was given the governship of Transalpine Gaul by senatorial decree. Had he not died suddenly in 59 BC, he might have eclipsed Caesar. Clodia was also the sister of Publius Clodius Pulcher—a gangster politician in the service of Julius Caesar and a violent enemy of Cicero. Without the existence of a police force to protect its citizens, Rome's politicians and men of wealth were forced to walk the streets with armed bodyguards. One November day in 57 BC, while walking down the Sacra Via, Cicero and his men were attacked by Clodius and his thugs; Cicero wrote later that his escort carried swords and cudgels, and could have killed Clodius if necessary. When Cicero called Clodia a *mulier nobilis*, it was an understatement; *nobilis* means "renowned," but it can also mean "infamous," or "powerful." Clodia was a member of one of Rome's oldest and most distinguished families, at the heart of the ruling class of the Roman Republic. Clodia and her siblings were connected by marriage to many powerful Romans, including Lucullus, Sulla, Pompey, Cato, Brutus, and Octavian. Though married, she was notorious for her love affairs and penchant for picking up soldiers and students in taverns, some of which were also brothels. We get a fictionalized portrait of her in Thornton Wilder's *Ides of March*, a historical drama in which Clodia is a central character. In one of the scenes, Caesar characterizes her as "one of those innumerable persons who trail behind them a shipwrecked life, . . . who lives only to impress the chaos of her soul on all that surrounds her." In one of his speeches, Cicero called her "Lady-Ox-Eyes," a reference to Homer's characterization of Hera (βοῶπιζ), who was both sister and wife to Zeus. Clodia lived in a villa north of Rome, had a vacation home in Baiae, the fashionable resort on the Bay of Naples, and owned homes, townhouses, and apartments on the Palatine, renting them out to some of her lovers. In his defense of Caelius, Cicero refered to a line in Ennius' *Medea*—"sick in spirit, wounded by cruel love"—and coined an epiteph for Clodia, calling her the "Palatine Medea." Caelius himself gave her a nickname that became quite popular, "the penny Clytemnestra," in reference to the admission fee to the public baths being the same as the cheap rate for which Clodia allegedly sold her favors. In another of his speeches, Cicero characterized her as having "strange desires" and "ravishing secrets." He condemned her life style and the life style of all like her.

> Look at the smart and fashionable—people with the best chefs and confectioners, the choicest fish, fowl, game and all that. They avoid overeating, they have their wine, as Lucilius puts it, "decanted from a full cask, with nothing caught in the strainer." They go in for shows, and what follows shows, the things without which Epicurus announces he doesn't know what the Good is. Throw in beautiful boys to wait on them, and clothes, silver, Corinthian bronzes, the dining places itself and the house, all in keeping. Well, I would never admit that profligates like that live a good or happy life.

It was rumoured that her brother Clodius Pulcher had incestuous relations with Clodia and her two sisters. She married Quintus Metellus Celer when she was only fifteen, and was widowed while still in her early thirties. Soon after, she was a prosecution witness in the trial of Marcus Caelius Rufus, who was charged with *vis* (political, as opposed to personal, violence) under the *Lex Lutatia de vis*. Caelius was prosecuted for inciting a riot in Naples, for murdering several political rivals, and for poisoning the Alexandrian ambassador, Dio, a distinguished philosopher of the Academic school. As a corollary charge, Caelius was accused of trying to poison Clodia herself, thus prompting Cicero's rebuke that the trial was "financed by a whore." Caelius had been a friend and pupil of Cicero, but they had a falling out when Caelius supported Catiline, the conspirator Cicero exposed and had executed. After a reconciliation in which Caelius assured Cicero that he was no longer a radical, Cicero agreed to defend him. In his famous opening speech, he undercut the prosecution's case by characterizing it as an attack on the younger generation for their scandalous parties and life-styles. He then went after Clodia, implying that she was nothing more than a fashionable whore. "I never thought I should have to be unfriendly towards a woman, especially one with the reputation of being friendly with everyone."

> I shall show that it was this Palatine Medea, and Caelius' change of lodging that caused all the young man's troubles—or rather, all the talk. . . . Now there are two charges, one relating to gold, and the other to poison, and the very same indivual is involved in both. It is said that the gold was taken from Clodia, and the poison procured so that Clodia should drink it. All the other matters are not charges but slanders, more for a shouting-match than a court of justice. . . . Gentlemen, the whole case revolves round Clodia. She is a woman of noble birth; but she also has a notorious reputation. . . . Indeed, my arguement would be more forceful if I did not feel so inhibited by the fact that the woman's husband—sorry, I mean brother, I always make that slip—is my personal enemy.

Cicero then uses a clever strategy, pretending to be the venerable Appius Claudius himself, come back to chastise her.

> He would say, "Woman, what business have you with Caelius, who is little more than a boy? . . . . Why did you let the vices of your brother influence you more than the virtues of your father and your ancestors? Did I tear up that bargain with Pyrrhus just so every day you could drive some disgusting sexual bargain. Did I bring water to Rome only for you to have something to wash yourself with after your impure copulations? Was the sole purpose of my Road that you should parade up and down it escorted by a crowd of other women's husbands?"
> As for you, madam—for now I speak to you in person, with no imaginary character in between—if you intend to justify your fabrications, intrigues, allegations, plots, charges, then you will have to give an account and explanation in full for this intimacy, this familiarity, this whole relationship. The prosecutors go on about orgies, love-affairs, adulteries, trips to Baiae, banquets and beach parties, songs and music, revelry on shipboard—and they also suggest that they have

your approval for everything they say. And since in some uncontrolled and reckless mood you have decided to bring all this into the Forum and the court, you must either disprove it and show it to be false, or else admit that neither your charge nor your testimony is to be believed.

Cicero went on to minimize Caelius' involvment with Clodia, while portraying her as the real culprit.

I am saying nothing now against that woman. But if there were someone now like her, who made herself available to every man, who had a calendar of different lovers for every day, owned gardens, a town house and a villa at Baiae where every lecherous riff-raff could come and go as they pleased, kept young men and subsidized their pocket money at her own expense—if there were a widowed lady living permissively, a shameless widow living wantonly, a wealthy lady living extravagantly, a lascivious widow living like a whore—should I call it adultery if some man were a little free in his attentions to her?

And if a woman who has no husband throws upon her home to every debauchee and publicly leads the life of a whore; if she makes a habit of being entertained by men who are total strangers; if she pursues this mode of existence in teh city, in her own gardens, among all the crowds at Baiae; if, in fact, she behaves in such a way that not only her general demeanour but also her dress and associates, her hot eyes and uninhibited language, her embraces and kisses, her beach parties and water parties and dinner parties, all show that she is not only a prostitute but a lewd and depraved prostitue at that; if a young man should happen to be found in the company of such a woman, then surely, you would agree that this was not so much adultery as just plain sex—not an outrage to chastity, but mere satisfaction of appetite. . . .

Either, then, Caelius told you the truth, you unspeakable woman, and you knowingly let him have the gold for a criminal purpose; or he did not bring himself to tell you, in which case you can never have given it to him at all!

Cicero charges that Clodia's testimony was prompted by revenge, to get back at Caelius, who did what her other lovers dared not do—*he* left *her*.

The whole accusation emanates from a house that is malevolent, disreputable, merciless, crime-stained and vicious. . . . You are invited to say whether you do not agree that the parties who confront one another are, on the one side, an unstable, evil-tempered nymphomaniac, who has completely fabricated the charge, or a serious, sensible and moderate man who has given his evidence conscientiously.

Before he closed his argument, dropping the bombshell that shocked everyone in the Forum crowd, he dismisses her credibility with a comment that must have deeply wounded Catullus, assuming he was there to hear it.

What's the fuss about? You pick up some good-looking boy, you give him presents to keep him, but now he wants to get away. So pick up another—after all, that's why you've got your gardens just where the boys go to swim.

In one last stroke of oratorical virtuosity, Cicero confessed that he'd been there when Metelles died. Caelius tried to poison no one, he says; rather, it was Clodia herself who poisoned her own husband.

You immortal gods! Why do you sometimes close your eyes to the worst crimes of men, or put off until tomorrow the punishment of today's wrong-doings? . . . . I personally participated in the scene which casued me as profound a feeling of sorrow as anything else in my life, for I saw it—I saw it, when Quintus Metellus when Quintus Metellus was being snatched away from the bosom and embrace of his native land . . . While he was still in the prime of life, enjoying excellent health and full bodily vigour, only two days after he had been seen at the height of his powers in the Senate, the law courts, and all the political affairs of our city, his life was snatched away from our midst, to the most grievous loss of every loyal citizen and the entire commonwealth of Rome. At that moment, when death was already approaching and his mind in all other respects had begun to fail, he devoted his last thoughts to his country, and fixing his gaze upon me as I wept, he endeavored in broken, dying words to warn me of the grim storm that hung over my head, and the tempest that menaced the state. [The impending disasters were Cicero's banishment and the civil unrest to come.] He pounded his hand upon the wall again and again, calling out my name abd the name of Rome itself.

And will *that* woman, coming from *this* house [meaning that she still lived in the house in which Metellus was murdered], dare to speak of quick-acting poison? Will she not be terrified that the house itself will find a voice, will she not shudder at the walls that know her secret, and tremble at the memory of that night of grief and death?

Cicero made a last appeal, that Caelius's youthful reputation, it was true, had suffered a temporary set-back by his association with Clodia, but that he was ready now to lead an exemplary career.

What I do want to stress, on the other hand, is his drive, and his keened to win, and his burning ambition to do well. In men who have reached our time of life these passions ought to have become somewhat less ardent than they were, but in youths, as in plants, they give promise of what future ripeness and the rewards of industry are going to bring. Very clever young men, in their pursuit of glory, always need the rein more than the spur; the intellectual exuberance of early years requires pruning more than grafting. As for his energy, spirit, the flamboyant glamour of his personality, you will find that in due course such things will settle down. Age, and events, and the passage of time, will mellow them all.

Caelius was found innocent of all charges, and Clodia's reputation cemented. Through innuendo and rhetoric, Cicero painted images of her sexual escapades that lingered for years. Obscene songs about the wealthy matron with the morals of a whore must have reached her ears, but she may not have cared. Maybe they pleased her—details of her conquests, several lovers at once hiding in the bathtub, for instance, as she engaged several others in the bedroom, certainly added to her allure. Cicero's allegations included a reference to one of the witnesses who was her brother's friend: "Go and look for him, you'll find him hiding at your sister's house—with his head down."

Food for Thought

"You'll Find Him With His Head Down."
Tis Better to Give than to Receive

There was more to Cicero's jibe than the innuendo that the witness was having sex with Clodia. Everyone knew that Clodia was a promiscuous woman. Cicero's comment was meant to insult the witness. But how great an insult could that have been—having sex with Clodia? One needs to understand the nature of Roman sexual *mores* to understand the meaning of the insult. In so doing, we also shed some light on Catullus's sexual allusions, especially those that involve homosexual references. This is one of the reasons why Victorian readers found Catullus so offensive, and why some critics asked whether or not Catullus was homosexual.

Romans didn't make much of a distinction between homosexual and heterosexual sex. Their interest was more in the area of penetration—oral (*irrumare*), anal (*pedicare*), or vaginal (*futuere*)—and whether one was the penetrator or the penetrated, the submissive or the dominant partner. There was no disgrace in having sex with another man or boy. Slaves and catamites (young boys kept for the purpose of anal sex) did their duty, and a common joke was to tell someone *non facis mihi officium*, "you aren't doing your duty." The question was which one was willing to "submit to the woman's role" (*muliebria pati*).

Catullus's poems went unread during the Middle Ages because they were considered too graphic and obscene, despite their lyricism. They might have appealed to a more enlightened upper class, but would not have bothered the monks whose job it was to preserve only the classical literature that rose above pagan licentiousness. Modern critics and scholars who wonder whether or not Catullus was homosexual miss the point of his references. In almost every case, Catullus is the penetrator, the aggressor; he is never the one being penetrated.

> #56
> A matter for mirth, Cato, and a smile
> worth your attention, you'll laugh
> you'll laugh as you love your Catullus, Cato
> listen—a matter for more than a smile!
> Just now in the alley I came upon a young boy
>   doing the in-n-out with his girl.
> I rose, naturally, and
>   (with a wink to Venus)

pulled out my cane and beat his ass,
giving him a few in-n-outs,
                    and a tit-for-tat
for good measure.

In other words, it was better to give than to receive. Poem #16 begins with a clear distinction: Aurelius is the *pedicabo*, taking on the role of the catamite (a young boy who submits to anal sex), and Furius (probably Marcus Furius Bibaculus) was the *irrumabo*, the one having oral sex performed on him. Both characters, therefore, are shown in the submissive role. (The poem is a response to something Bibaculus wrote in which he made fun of the famous "kiss" poem, in which Catullus appears tender, loving, and submissive.)

#16

Pedicabo ego vos et irrumabo,   [my underlines for emphasis]
Aureli pathice et cinaede Furi,
qui me ex versiculis meis putastis,
quod sunt molliculi, parum pudicum.

.   .   .   .

vos, quod milia multa basiorum
legistis, male me marem putatis?
pedicabo ego vos et irrumabo.

To the modern reader, without the historical context, such distinctions are meaningless.

#16

I'll bugger you and stuff you,
you catamite Aurelius and you pervert Furius,
who have supposed me to be immodest,
on account of my verses,
because these are rather naughty.
For the sacred poet ought to be chaste himself,
though his poems need not be so.
Why, they only acquire wit and spice
if they are rather naughty and immodest,
and can rouse with their ticklings,
I don't mean boys, but those hairy old 'uns
unable to stir their arthritic loins.
Because you've read of my many thousand kisses,
do you think I'm less virile on that account?
Yes, I'll bugger you and stuff you all right!
                    [trans. Francis Warre Cornish, Loeb Edition]

#16

I fuck your asses, I feed you my dick,
Aurelius (you love it) and cocksucking Furius.
You said that I lack modesty, basing your charge on a few   [note
    little verses about a boy?   how
Of course a god-fearing poet   the
has to lead an upright life—   translator

that's no reason his poems shouldn't live it up
—poems which are witty, elegant compositions, even if
    they are a bit unbuttoned,
even if they do scratch you where it always itches, even if
    they do get people steamed up—
—I don't mean just school boys, no, even big hairy studs,
real animals, guys who need both hands to lift their dicks.
You thought I was naughty for writing the poem about
    wanting a million kisses!
Well, fuck you.

gets a double
meaning on
"upright life"]

                    [trans. Jacob Rabinowitz]

#16

Oral Aurelius, anal Furius,
I'll fuck you both, you
who read my verses but misread their author:
you think that *I'm* effeminate, since *they* are!
Purity's proper in the godly poet,
but it's unnecessary in his verses,
which really should be saucy & seductive,
even salacious in a girlish manner
and capable of generating passion
not just in boys, but in old men who've noticed
getting a hard-on has been getting harder!
But you, because my poems beg for kisses,
thousands of kisses, you think I'm a fairy!
I'll fuck the pair of you as you prefer it.
                    [trans. Charles Martin]

Peter Whigham doesn't even translate the terms; he keeps the original Latin (though simplifies the syntax).

#16

Pedicabo et irrumabo
Furius and Aurelius
           twin sodomites,
you have dared deduce me from my poems
which are lascivious
           which lack pudicity . . . .
The devoted poet remains in his own fashion chaste;
his poems not necessarily so:
           they may well be
lascivious
           lacking in pudicity
stimulants (indeed) to prurience
           and not solely in boys
but those whose hirsute genitalia are not easily moved.

You read of those thousand kisses.

you deduced an effeminacy there.
You were wrong. Sodomites. Furius and Aurelius.
Pedicabo et irrumabo vos.

In another poem he calls Memmius an *irrumator*. The insult could only have been greater if he had used *fellator*—or *fellatrix*—to perform oral sex on a woman. In time, the words came to designate someone who was gotten the best of by someone else. For Cicero to say that the witness was "going down on Clodia" was the greatest of insults.

This may seem to be an archaic distinction, and a literary one at that. But a recent episode of an HBO television series, *The Sopranos,* proves otherwise. A cross between *The Godfather* and *The Patridge Family,* the series tracks the lives of a suburban gangster family. In one episode, an elderly don is having a relationship with a woman he has true feelings for. One day, under the hairdryer in a beauty salon, she makes the mistake of confiding in the woman next to her that her man "goes down on her." Word spreads, and his buddies begin to make fun of him. He denies it vehemently, seething because his power is being questioned. He's a boss; associating him with *irramure* is an insult and weakens him in the eyes of his men. In the last scene, reminiscent of the scene in William Wellman's 1931 film *Public Enemy* in which James Cagney squashes a grapefruit into Mae Clark's face, the mob boss picks up the cream pie his girlfriend has baked for him and does the same to her. If he had not loved her so much, he'd have killed her.

Clodia was also a *mulier potens*, a woman with power that made her *peroculosa potentia*, a "dangerous woman with political connections." Beside the nicknames "Palatine Media" and "Penny Clytemnestra," she got another one, "Quadrantaria," when a young man she had dallied with, then cast off, sent her a bag of quarters for revenge. Clodia got two of her "bully boys" to beat and sodomize him. This is the woman young Catullus fell madly in love with. Like the pet sparrow Lesbia holds in her hand, stroking its neck with her thumb, the naive poet sticks his own neck out—and into the hands of a woman seemingly without conscience. When Catullus submits to Lesbia's affections, he submits to her power. When she tosses him out, he doesn't send her a sack of quarters or a bag of pennies for revenge. He immortalizes her, instead, composing the most beautiful lyrics in the Latin tongue.

In paying homage to Sappho, whose poems he occasionally translated and often imitated, Catullus matches her description of a lover's frenzy. In one poem, which became the prototype of Roman elegy, he relates the sorrows of his life to his meeting with Lesbia, an omen of doom.

My radiant goddess entered with dainty steps,
and planting her gleaming foot on the worn threshold,
halted there with a click of her slipper.

He combines the sensitive rhythms of Sappho with the harsh satire of Juvenal. Unfortunately, no one has yet rendered Catullus' poems into equivalent English verse. Translating slang and idiomatic expressions is especially difficult. Catullus combines Latin obscenities and figures of speech—some of which, even in his own day, were archaic, some only slightly out-of-fashion, and others very contemporary—with startling imagery that conveys several meanings at once. Take, for example, the last few lines of poem #58, addressed to his friend, the politically ambitious Marcus Caelius Rufus, who rented a house in the desirable Palatine quarter near Clodia, supplanting Catullus in her affections. We can't be sure if this was written before or after the trial, but the poem may have been a warning to Caelius that, just as Clodia had tossed Catullus off, the same fate awaited Caelius.

> #58
> Caeli, Lesbia nostra, Lesbia illa,
> illa Lesbia, quam Catullus unam
> plus quam se atque suos amavit omnes,
> nunc in quadriviis et angiportis
> glubit magnanimi Remi nepotes.

> O, Caelius, our Lesbia, that Lesbia,
> that Lesbia whom Catullus alone
> loved more than himself and all his own,
> now in the cross-roads and alleys
> serves the filthy lusts of the descendants of lordly-minded Remus.
> [trans. Francis Warre Cornish, Loeb edition]

Catullus mourns not only the loss of Lesbia's love—"loving her more than himself,"—but the fact that her lust has driven her to the "crossroads" (*quadriviis*) and "back-alleys" (*angiportis*) of Rome where she

> serves the filthy lusts of the descendants of lordly-minded Remus.
> (*glubit magnanimi Remi nepotes*)

That last line contains a complex metaphor, and translators are driven to extreme lengths to include all the associations—hence the length of the translated line far outruns the original Latin which contains only four words. The translation quoted above doesn't do the original justice. The word that begins the line, *glubit*, does not mean "to serve one's filthy lusts." (Cornish was a Victorian translator; he probably couldn't help inserting the adjective "filthy." Catullus was skewering Clodia, not the boys she was defiling. One can lust for power or fame. Lust is an overwhelming desire, but is not necessarily "filthy." But I digress.) Catullus is harsh in his imagery, but avoids obscentity. The Latin word *magnanimi* implies high-mindedness, a greatness of soul, so Cornish's "lordly-minded" is accurate, but it adds unduly to the metrical length of the line. *Remi nepotes* means "grandsons of Remus" or "descendants of Remus" (Remus and Romulus, you'll recall, were raised by wolves and founded the city of Rome). One could translate the phrase as "scions of Rome's founders," but that is also metrically long-winded. So just what is Lesbia doing to the magnanimous grandsons of Remus (or is it the grandsons of magnanimous Remus? It has been translated both ways. Logic tells me it's the grandsons who are magnanimous, not Remus, who was the brother "not chosen.") The Latin verb is *glubit*. She's "glubitting" them. Does *glubit* mean to "serve their filthy lusts?" Obviously, *glubit* is the key word, meaning to rub the husk off an ear of corn, to shuck or peel. Peter Whigham, a modern translator, has Lesbia "tossing them off."

> Lesbia, our Lesbia, the same old Lesbia,
> Caelius, she whom Catullus loved once
> more than himself and more than all his own,
> loiters at the cross-roads
> > and in the backstreets
> ready to toss-off the 'magnanimous' sons of Rome.

But Whigham's choice of words doesn't convey the sexual innuendo. The reader is led to think that she will toss the men aside, just as she did to Catullus. That meaning conveys only one of the poet's double *entendres*. We miss the sexual entendre, which makes all the difference in the point of the poem. Charles Martin's version also misses the sexual innuendo.

> Lesbia, Caelius—yes, our darling,
> yes, Lesbia, the Lesbia Catullus
> once loved uniquely, more than any other!
> —now on streetcorners & in wretched alleys
> she shucks the offspring of greathearted Remus.

But we still miss the sexual connotation. Perhaps if Martin had said "she shucks them off," the association would be clearer. At least the Loeb version correctly indicates that someone's lusts are being serviced. It just doesn't say how, and that's why Catullus chose a word that called up the image of an ear of corn—an obvious phallic reference—and simultaneously contains an echo of farm life, the opposite of fashionable urbanity called up by the phrase that followed, *magnanimi Remi nepotes*.

Catullus chooses the word *glubit* to show that Lesbia is masturbating her pick-ups, not engaging in sexual intercourse. To say she "tossed" them off (which is close to the verb's literal meaning) misses the distinction between masturbation and copulation. There's another consideration: in the middle of the phrase, Catullus inserts the adjective *magnanimi*. This unlikely juxtaposition is like saying one "chuggalugged the King's finest cognac, then pissed in the deep blue sea." When combined with *nepotes*, the image gives the impression that these aristocrats are involved in a sexual encounter that might take place on a farm. The line is a savage indictment of Lesbia, but is rendered with a lyric flair that satirizes the encounter. To translate the line effectively, both meanings have to come across, but in keeping with Catullus's Latin, it would have to be done without the use of graphic expressions such as "jerk off" or "blow job." Is it enough for a translator to say that Lesbia waits at the crossroads of Rome, "rubbing the husks off ears of corn before the high-minded descendants of Rome's founders?" Should one strive for something less literal, but closer to the spirit of the line? Jacob Rabinowitz has Lesbia in Rome's back alleys

> sliding back the foreskins of great-souled Remus's descendants.

Trouble is, Rabinowitz's translation is too graphic, the image too direct and the last part of the line—"great-souled Remus's descendants"—too clunky. This is not the way people speak, and Catullus's lyrical gift stems partly from his use of natural speech. He is also adept at using euphemisms. In two other poems, Catullus mocks Caesar's chief of staff, Mammura, calling him Mentula, "the Tool," and puns on his name at the end of the poem by saying that he has a *mentula magna minax*, a big, overhanging mentula. Cornish translates *mentula* as "cock."

> #114
> Mentula habet iuxta triginta iugera prati,
> quadraginta arvi: cetera sunt maria.
> Cur non divitiis Croesum superare potis sit,
> uno qui in saltu tot bona possideat,
> prata, arva, ingentes silvas vastasque paludes
> usque ad Hyperboreos et mare ad Oceanum?
> Omnia magna haec sunt; tamen ipsest maximus ultro,
> non homo, sed vero <u>mentula magna minax</u>.   [note alliteration]

> Cock has something like thirty acres of grazing land,
> forty of plough-land: the rest is salt water.
> how can he fail to surpass Croesus in wealth,
> who occupies so many good things in one estate,
> pasture, arable, enormous woods and vast lakes
> as far as the Hyperboreans and the Great Sea?
> All this is wonderful: but he himself is the greatest wonder of all,
> not a man like the rest of us, but a monstrous menacing cock.
> > [Cornish, Loeb edition]

In Latin, an iron tool is a *ferramentum*, hence *mentula* is a play on the word *mentum*, tool; the sexual connotation is obvious. The Latin *minax* can mean "projecting," "overhanging," or "threatening." Cornish does a good job in getting the alliteration in the last three words, "a monstrous menacing cock" for *mentula magna minax*, but in English, "cock" is not necessarily a pejorative, whereas calling someone a "big prick" is, and Catullus certainly meant the latter. Peter Whigham gives the man the name "O'Toole," thereby solving the problem of the euphemism for the word "tool."

> O'Toole is the proud master of
> 20 acres of pasture
> > & 27 acres of arable land
> the rest is unfortunately swamp.
> Where is our latter-day Croesus
> the man loaded with such an estate,
> grass plough wood moor & marsh land

> stretching away to the Hyperborean North
> and down to the shores of the Adriatic?
> Everything here's on a grand scale
> including the owner,
>   and he's not a man either,
> but a tool larger than life,
>   upreared & rampant at the gates!

Though he preserves the alliteration in "upreared & rampant," there's scant indication of the pun on "penis," except for "upreared," which is forced and doesn't provide the parallel association with the name—Mentula is a mentula, that is, a big prick. Rabinowitz is more direct and uses the name Catullus was avoiding.

> Mamurra the Penis actually owns about
> thirty acres of meadow, ...
> .   .   .   .
> Well, that's a tall tale to be sure. But he himself is far
>   more amazing
> —the very idea of a Penis owning real estate!

This strays too far afield from Catullus 's intent to avoid words that are obscene or vulgar; hence his use of euphemism to make a point. His Latin is lyrical, yet the effect is ribald.

Going back to Lesbia's encounter with the great descendants of Rome, one can imagine this aristocratic woman at her villa at Solonium forty miles south of Rome, throwing sophisticated dinner parties—Cicero called them *delicatum convivium*—now, in Catullus's poem, kneeling in a damp alleyway, masturbating a young stud whose father was probably a senator or magistrate. That's the scene Catullus calls up, but it's all done indirectly. Rabinowitz's translation—that she's "sliding back the foreskins" is also vague about the nature of the encounter. Are they having intercourse, is Lesbia performing oral sex, or giving them, to use common slang, a "hand-job?" But the Latin verb *glubit* makes it clear—it's a "hand-job." The translation misses the artful way Catullus turns the metaphor, juxtaposing the image of an ear of corn with the "aristocratic sons of Remus." In 1979, translator Humphrey Clucas found an almost perfect solution to rendering the original Latin of poem #58 into English. He discards the corn metaphor completely, using another image that is also rural, graphic, and lyrically captivating all at once. For the word *magnanami*, he uses a phrase that conveys both the sense of nobility and the sexual connotation.

> My Lesbia, Caelius, that same Lesbia
> Whom once Catullus loved more than himself
> And all his own, now in the alleyways
> And at street corners milks with a practised hand
> The upright members of magnanimus Rome.

There's a great depth of feeling in the poet's shorter poems. Catullus adores his Lesbia, even as he rails against her betrayal of him. He wants done with the pain, but never regrets the experience.

> Wretched Catullus! You have to stop this nonsense,
> admit that what you see has ended is over!
> Once the sun shown bright upon you,
> when you would follow wherever your lady led you,
> she who was loved as no other will ever be loved;
> there was no end in those days to our pleasures,
> when what you wished for was what she also wanted.
> Yes, once the sun shown bright upon you.
> Now she no longer wishes; you mustn't want it,
> you've got to stop chasing her now—cut your losses,
> harden your heart & hold out firmly against her.
> Goodbye now, lady. Catullus' heart is hardened,
> he will not look to you nor call against your wishes—
> how you'll regret it when nobody comes calling!
> So much for you, bitch—your life is all behind you!
> *Now* who will come to see you, thinking you lovely?
> Whom will you love now, and whom will you belong to?
> Whom will you kiss? And whose lips will you nibble?
> But, *you*, Catullus! *You* must hold out now, firmly!

He tried to forget her by traveling to distant cities, and at the grave of his brother he composed tender lines that gave the world a famous phrase.

> Driven across many nations, across many oceans,
>   I am here, my brother, for this final parting,
> to offer at last those gifts which the dead are given
>   and to speak in vain to your unspeaking ashes,
> since bitter fortune forbids you to hear me or answer,
>   O my wretched brother, so abruptly taken!
> But now I must celebrate grief with funeral tributes
>   offered the dead in the ancient way of the fathers;
> Accept these presents, wet with my brotherly tears, and
>   now and forever, my brother, hail & farewell.

Mixing popular speech into his poetry, Catullus once wrote of the efforts he made to produce poetry that sounded natural; It took much art to conceal his art. His is witty and humorous even when lyrical and eloquent.

> 13
> You will dine well with me, my dear Fabullus,
> in a few days or so, the gods permitting.
> —provided you provide the many-splendored
> feast, and invite your fair-complected lady,
> your wine, and your salt & all the entertainment!
> Which is to say, my dear, if you bring dinner
> you will dine well, for these days your Catullus
> finds that his purse is only full of cobwebs.

But in return, you'll have from me Love's Essence,
—or what (if anything) is more delicious:
I'll let you sniff a certain charming fragrance
which Venuses & Cupids gave my lady;
one whiff of it, Fabullus, and you'll beg the
gods to transform you into one big nose!

49

Silver-tongued among the sons of Rome
the dead, the living & the yet unborn,
Catullus, least of poets, sends
Marcus Tullius his warmest thanks:

—as much the least of poets
as he a prince of lawyers.

84

"Hadvantageous" breathes Arrius heavily
                              when he means
        "advantageous,"
intending "artificial" he labours "hartificial,"
convinced he is speaking impeccably while
he blows his h's about most "hartificially."
One understands that his mother—his uncle—
his family, in fact, on the distaff side
spoke so.
              Fortunately he was posted to Syria
and our ears grew accustomed to normal speech again,
unapprehensive for a while of such words
until suddenly the grotesque news reaches us
that the Ionian Sea has become
                              since the advent of Arrius
no longer Ionian

            but (inevitably) Hionian.

11

Friends, prepared for all of these far off lands, whatever
Province the celestial ones may wish me,
Take a little bulletin to my girl friend,
    Brief but not dulcet:
Let her go and get on with her fucketeers,   [*moechis*: debauched adulterers]
Opening her legs to them all,
all three hundred of them (simultaneously),
With no true love for any, dragging the guts
out of each of them each time she does it.
She need not look, the tart, as once she did, for my love.
By her own fault it died, like a tumbling flower
At the field's edge when touched by a passing ploughshare.

85

I hate and I love. And if you ask me how,
I do not know: I only feel it, and I'm torn in two.
We have heard of Quintia's beauty. To me she is tall, slender
and of a white "beauty." Such things I freely admit,
but such things do not constitute beauty.
               In her there is nothing of Venus,
not a pinch of love spice in her long body.
She's just a big body, compared to Lesbia.
It's as if when Lesbia was perfected, there wasn't enough charm
left over to adorn the rest of mankind.

There is something quite modern about Catullus, perhaps because he shares so much of himself; we feel we know him more intimately than we do other Roman poets.

And all the mumbling of harsh old men
We shall reckon as a pennyworth.
Suns may sink and return;
For us, when once our brief sun has set,
There comes the long sleep of everlasting night.
Give me a thousand kisses, then a hundred, . . .

It's easy to sympathize with his love-sick celebrations of love, and of love's end.

You once said that only Catullus really knew you, Lesbia
     that you'd rather have me than Jupiter —
I loved you, not as an ordinary man loves a woman,
but as a father loves his sons, with patient selflessness.
Now I really *do* know you. While I'm even more ruinously
in love with you, I've learned how worthless you are.
Why do I still love you?
The way you hurt me makes me love you more,
even if it makes me like you less.

His ecstacies of adoration and spite reveal a child-like spirit, capable of generous lyricism as well as boyish obscenities. Yet his poetry leaps off the page with a naturalness and spontaneity that seems effortlessly modern.

83

Lesbia cursed me out — her husband was there — that jerk
     was overjoyed to hear it.
Asshole, you don't understand a thing. If she was silent, it
     would mean she didn't care
about me. If she growls and bitches,
spitting out my name as she bares her white teeth,
not only am I on her mind, but
She burns for me, scratching the wound
ripening herself while she talks..

70

My woman says she'd rather marry me than anyone, than
     Jove himself.
What a woman says to an eager lover

is fit to be inscribed on air, or running water.

Sophisticated readers during Catullus' lifetime read his poems avidly. His work had a significant impact on most of the poets of Virgil's day, especially poets of the Augustan Golden Age who used a refined literary style to convey sensual content, often jumping from natural speech to ornate diction. But it was the erotic content of Catullus' poems that Christian writers of the Middle Ages found distasteful, and he is hardly ever mentioned until 966 when a Bishop from Catullus' own home town of Verona noted that he had discovered a manuscript of Catullus' poems; he expressed guilt that the poems had consumed him day and night. Bishop Rather's manuscript promptly vanished and was not rediscovered until 1300. The story goes that the rolled-up manuscript was used to cork a wine barrel in Verona, and some of the text was lost when the wine eroded the parchment. From this single manuscript comes all surviving copies, and had it not been found, we'd know only the one poem that was preserved in a ninth-century French anthology of verse.

The Verona manuscript does not contain all of Catullus' work, but the 116 poems we do have confirm the magnitude of his achievement, making him one of the great lyric poets of all time. No other Latin poet appeals to modern readers the way he does. His short *nugae*, "bagatelles" or "diversions," are light, witty, and sensuous on the surface; imagery and metaphor are often discarded in favor of direct language. The longer poems are all in elegiacs, using a complex variety of styles and meters, including iambic trimeters and the metre which Catullus made peculiarly his own, the Phalaecian hendecasyllable. In these longer poems, he draws on several traditions: the Roman epic and tragedy, and the Roman comedy and satire. He combines the grandeur of tragic language with the colloquialism of comedy, blended into the form of the love elegy. His expression of tender emotion using colloquial language and the elevated manner of epic rendered in contemporary slang, had never before been done in Latin verse.

As the leading exponent of the neoteric revolution, Catullus used his poems to transform not only literary taste, but the accepted ethical content of poetry as well. He chose as his canvas not the ideals of the state but the small universe of the individual. If there is epic, it is in the private joys and pains of love; if there is drama, it is in the enactment of private events and the recovery of intimate space, lost in literature during the medieval period, not to be recovered again until the 12th century in the work of Peter Abelard and the Troubadour poets of Provence. A poet's greatness often rests on his or her ability to synthesize previous traditions while creating something original in the process. If his poems appear to be spontaneous expressions, it was their outer appearance that was revolutionary. Tucked within the casual banter of Catullus' elegiac poems are associative references to traditional literary forms and subjects, but it was their outer appearance that was revolutionary.Their immediacy and accessibility, their expression of tender emotion using colloquial language and slang, combined with the elevated manner of epic and a sophistication of form created a poetry wholly new in Latin verse.

In the well-known "kiss poem" (#5), images play off of one another to convey the urgency of his passion. Where Marvel was to say to his lover seventeen centuries later, "had we but world enough and time" to dally a thousand years in admiration of a cheek,

Catullus reminds his lover that their night together can fend off the approach of that everlasting sleep which is death.

Vivamus, mea Lesbia, atque amemus	Let us live my Lesbia, and let us love
rumoresque senum severiorum	and let us value at one penny all
omnes unius aestimemus assis.	the talk of censorious old men.
Soles occidere et redire possunt:	Suns can set and rise again:
nobis, cum semel occideit *brevis* <u>lux</u>,	but once for us has set that brief light
<u>nox</u> est *perpetua* una dormienda.	we must sleep one long perpetual night
Da mi basia mille, deinde centum,	Give me a thousand kisses,
	then a hundred
dein mille altera, dein secunda centum,	then a second thousand,
	then a second hundred
deinde usque altera mille, deinde centum.	then still another thousand,
	then a hundred more.
Dein, cum milia multa fecerimus,	Then, when we have made up many thousands
conturbabimus, illa, ne sciamus,	we will confuse the counting
	so that we do not know it
aut ne quis malus invidere possit,	and so that no wicked person be able
	to cast an evil eye upon us
cum tantum sciat esse basiorum.	when he knows the number
	of our kisses.

(my underlines and italics)

Translating a poet like Catullus is not as easy or as straight-forward as it looks. The pitch of his jargon, the tone of his personality, and the sound of his words, can all be lost with a clumsy translation. But since poetry is often said to be "what gets lost in translation," any translation of Catullus is bound to be clumsy. Poem #5 is especially susceptible to innacurate translation because the poem achieves its effect by the manipulation of sounds, especially vowel sounds. These are carefully arranged in such a way as to reinforce the structural organization. But the poet is also capable of creating sound effects with consonants, using both hard *t*'s and *k*'s, and soft *s*'s and *m*'s. Add to that the problem of literal meaning, and any translator would be tearing their hair out to convey the effect of this poem. For instance: How do we render *senum severiorum*, which literally means severe old men? One might be tempted to translate *severiorum* as severe, but the better connotation is strict, not severe. One translator turned the adjective into the noun, rendering the phrase as "old men's strictures." I'm not faulting the translation, merely pointing out the difficulty of finding the right equivalence for a two-word phrase, trying to catch the literal meaning, the tone, the sound, and the image all at the same time. It's not easy. I've compared a number of different translations of that one phrase:

    crabbed old men,
    senile busybodies,
    grumbling old men,

muttering coots,
gossip-mongering elders,
sour-faced strictures of the wise,
old prudes,
and rabinowitz's "parents."

While Catullus's short poems can be lyrical and touching, there's also a good amount of vulgarity and slang. Perhaps for this reason, his work did not become better known in English poetry until the early 17th century, Shakespeare's time, even though there were a few allusions to his made-up words in Malmesbury's *History of the Kings of England*, and John Skelton's *Phyllyp Sparowe* written in 1508. Sir Walter Raleigh, in his *History of the World* cribed a very delicate translation of the famous poem #5 about the kisses:

The Sunne may set and rise:
But we contrariwise
Sleepe after our short light
One everlasting night.

After that, numerous English poets discovered Catullus and translated him, including Ben Jonson, Robert Herrick, Richard Lovelace, Lord Byron, Samuel Taylor Coleridge, and even Ezra Pound. Thomas Campion turned the kiss poem into a song written around 1614:

When timely death my life and fortune ends,
Let not my hearse be vext with mourning friends,
But let all lovers, rich in triumph come,
And with sweet pastimes grace my happie tombe;
And, Lesbia, close up thou little light,
And crowne with love my ever-during night.

In *Catullus in English* (2001), Julia Haig Gaisser edited many poems and translations, with eight translations of #3, about the death of Lesbia's sparrow, probably the most famous of Catullus's poems, followed by seven versions of #5, about the number of kisses. Those two poems, #3, and #5, are the most popular, and I think in Latin, #5 is the most often quoted and memorized, if only because of the way it starts:

Vivamus, mea Lesbia, atque amenus,
rumoresque senum seuerorum
omnes unius aestimemus assis!

and of course the wonderful repitions in Latin further along in the poem:

da mi basia mille, deinde centum,
dein mille altera, dein secunda centum,
deinde usque altera mille, deinde centum,
dein, cum milia multa fecerius,
conturbabimus illa, ne sciamus,
aut ne quis malus inuidere possit,
cum tantum scait esse basiorum.

One could do worse than memorize that poem and rattle it off at a party in Latin. It's only 13 lines. One way of looking at it is to see it as two parts, the first six lines and the last seven. First he's saying let's love as much as we can, and then, in line seven, he shifts into a game of numbers, the poem's second theme. But even that is hinted at in line three with *assis*, suggesting the language of the account book, to calculate or portion out. And *ne sciamus* is such a great Latin sound, and when he follows *facerius* at the end of one line with the explosive *conturbabimus* at the begining of the next line, he not only gets a neat sound effect, but the meaning of not keeping score, or of puposefully shuffling the figures like an accountant, making it so confusing that someone checking the books would not be able to tally the total, in case they were to file for bankruptancy of kisses. It's so clever how he uses accounting figures of speech, and the cleverness that they will use so many kisses they'll go bankrupt, that even the IRS won't be able to track them down. It's masterful, playful, touching, plaintive, sad, and poetically brilliant in terms of Catullus's technique hidden amid the contemporary and hip Latin, all in 13 lines.

Remember, Catullus came from a rather wealthy and well-placed family. His father was one of the wealthiest, most prominent citizens of Verona, hosting Caesar often when he was governor of the province. They had a palatial villa at Sirmio. Their wealth probably came from tax-farming and exporting, and such business transactions would have probably required the counting of money and coins, with fingers flicking beads across an abacus. Read the last 7 lines of the poem in Latin aloud, and you can almost hear the clicking.

In poem #7 he picks up the same theme of counting, this time comparing the number of their kisses to grains of sand. In that poem, #7, he's also making fun of the poetry, all that about the resinous weeds of Cyrene, from the sweltering oasis of Jupiter-Ammon's temple, to the tomb of ancient Battus, this is all meant to be a little over the top, kinda funny. Catullus didn't use the usual Latin word for kiss, *osculum*, but a word then almost unknown, *basia*, which is a rather soft Celtic word from his native tongue. It was a novelty that became so pleasant and intimate, that over the centuries, as Latin broke into the Romance languages, it became, in Italian, "il bacio," in French, "le baiser (which today almost means to fuck), and in English some time ago we had "buss," but that meaning has been almost forgotten. To buss someone on the lips, like to give them a smack on the lips. Shakespeare used it in King John when he wrote: "Come, grin on me; and I will thinke thou smil'st and busse thee as thy wife." In French it has taken on a more vulgar intimation, if you kiss someone it's "embrasser" (embrace) but if you "baiser" them, it can have the connotation of sexual intercourse. We see it already shifting in the 18th century with Robert Herrick's poems in which he says:

> Kissing and bussing differ both in this,
> We busse our wantons, but our wives we kisse.

By the 19th century, the meaning of the word had taken on that more graphic image with Browning and Meredith using is in their poems, and Tennyson writing: "nor buss'd the milking maid."Notice how in the Latin he balances the contrasting images of *brevis* and *perpetua* with the assonant monosyllables *lux* and *nox*. The insistent repetition of *deinde*, *dein, dein, deinde, deinde, dein,* creates a sense of urgency that comes, not just from the demands of passion, but the use of passion to avoid thoughts of death. What might appear to be emotional gushing is really a tightly structured poem balanced by sound and image, and rhythmic beat.

In the famous sparrow poem, #3, Catullus uses a well-modulated sense of voice layered over carefully constructed patterns of sound.

Passer, deliciae meae puellae,	Sparrow, pet of my darling,
quicum ludere, quem in sinnu tenere,	with whom she often plays
	whom she holds in her lap,
cui primum digitum dare appetenti,	and whom she provokes to sharp bites
et acris solet incitare morsus,	whenever she, the shining object
	of my desires
cum desiderio meo nitenti	wants to enjoy some pretty play
carum nescioquid libet iocari,	in order that,
credo, ut, cum gravis acquiescet ardor	as I think, when her fierce passion
	abates
sit solaciolum sui doloris:	it may be a small relief from her pain
tecum ludere sicut ipsa possem	if only I could play with you as she does
et tristis animi levare curas!	and lift the gloomy cares from my heart!

For all its lyrical sentiment, it is a dark and troubling poem. Delicate images of the sparrow lay as uneasily in the poem as the sparrow itself in the lap of his mistress, easily crushed by her hands, should she wish to. One dares to imagine Lesbia calling Catullus "her little sparrow."

Catullus and the other neoteric poets thought of themselves as scholar-poets. Some of Catullus' longer poems are complex in allusion and oblique in meaning. This penchant for complexity can be traced back to their Greek model, Callimachus, who worked and taught at the great library Ptolemy had built in Alexandria. Founded in 332 BC, it became the principal center of the world's knowledge and culture. The "new poets" of Catullus' time had great respect for technique, form and structure. While they championed the use of direct speech in their lyric verse, they also admired the dense, sometimes obscure poem laden with mythological references and arcane allusions, like Cinna's *Zmyrna*, whose verses Catullus called "lapidary relics." Thus, it's no accident that some of Catullus' intricate and highly wrought longer poems read a little like *The Waste Land*. Here Catullus writes of the legend of Theseus in the Minoan age, using myth and dense imagery to depict the passing of a time that had once seemed like Eden.

> No man tills the field,
> the bullock's neck grows soft.
> No bull pulled the goughing plough downfield,
> tearing up the soil in clods
> nor the pruning hook lessen

the olive tree's deep shade.
        Oxen do not turn the lumps of loam
        Red rust flakes the neglected plough.
But in the royal halls
        wherever you look
as room unfolds into room
        silver & gold gleam
an effulgence of ivory,
        carved thrones,
flittering cups on the long tables
the whole building thrums with the spendour of royal goods,
and there, in the middle,
        inlaid with Indian tooth
and quilted with arras,
        the divan of the small goddess
        the arras ochred with rock-lichen &
        tinctured with stain of rose shell-fish.

A blight lay over the narrow streets of Athens . . . .
You could see Ariadne on the shore of Naxos,
in the tideline's watery noise,
staring out after Theseus, who falls away
into a vanish, ferried out of sight
by no slow boat. She stands there, madness
building up inside her.

" — waste words shredded now on wind.
as long as they itch for it
they will say anything
        do anything,
but with lust slaked
        the soft words are forgotten
        the promises null.
I caught you from the back-coil of your fate. . . .
You are flint
        where the bitch-cat whelps under the desert rock,
or spume
        when brine-water sickens with sea-spawn,
you are the kindless issue of the twin gulfs
            — storm-ridden Syrtes —
of the octopus & the maelstrom,
        epitomes of ruin.
Did a lioness in labor drop you in the desert?
Did the sea spit you up? Did you swim up into existence
from a pool of quicksand? This is how you pay back
the rescue of your life.
If you did not want to marry me
you could have taken me home with you
and I should have tended you
got your bath ready for you,
each day smoothing the colored bedspread in your room.

But why should I give my tears
to this wind? In this state?
Wind is deaf as well as dumb.
And he's wind-driven in the middle distance.
There's nothing here but rocks & seaweed.
In the hubris of indifference Fate
deprives me even of an ear to listen.
If only the Athenian sloop
had never entered the bay
at Knossos, with its grim cargo
for the bull, fixed hawsers to the quay,
captained by an attractive sailor . . .
with a soul like a trap-door
whom we took in out of pity —

                     his name was Theseus."

It's hard to imagine that the poet who wrote the above lines also wrote the personal epigrams for which Catullus is best known, but it is just this ability to broaden the topicality of the Roman epigram, using a wide variety of meters, and making it hauntingly personal, that makes his voice so indelible. And his early death so tragic. By the age of thirty, Catullus describes himself as bankrupt, both emotionally and financially.

#76

.   .   .   .

Why protract this pain? why not resist
yourself in mind; from this point inclining
yourself back, breaking this fallen love
counter to what the gods desire of men?
Hard suddenly to lose love of long use,
hard precondition of your sanity
regained. Possible or not, this last
conquest is for you to make, Catullus.
May the pitying gods who bring
help to the needy at the point of death
look towards me and, if my life were clean,
tear this malign pest from my body
where, a paralysis, it creeps from limb to limb
driving all former laughter from the heart.
I do not now expect — or want — my love returned,
nor cry to the moon for Lesbia to be chaste:
only that the gods cure me of this disease
and, as I once was whole, make me now whole again.

He died a few years later. Because biographers have had only his poems with which to assemble the details of his life, the "facts" must be taken with a grain of salt. Did he not reproach his friends "for daring to deduce *me* from my work." He was, above all, constructing poems, using his craft to express deeply felt experience. What does it matter what is true, what is exaggerated, and what is totally fabricated. There is mundane truth and there is the beauty of the poetic lie. The truth affirms what we know is there; the lie, in poetry, can show us worlds we've sensed but never quite grasped. If the poet is good enough to open our eyes to such a world, we are forever changed by it. Made larger. More compassionate. Maybe even more alive. But what is certain is that we are more tangibly linked to the rest of humanity. Imagine—a poem can do all that. If the poet's good enough. And the "facts" of his life have nothing to do with it.

#3

Lesbia's plaything
                Lesbia's sparrow
                                is dead
dearer to her than her two eyes
sweeter than honey
                closer (even) than the young girl to her mother,
in her lap or at her breast
hopping from one shoulder to another
now here now there
cheeping continually
                to its mistress alone

. . . Now he goes along the dark road,
down that dark alleyway of no return
evil shadows of the underworld
                        Orcus
who swallows up all beautiful things.
Such a pretty sparrow you have taken away.
Needless act! a small bird!
to close in on Lesbia's sparrow,

and swelling my girl's veiled eyes
                which redden with tears.

He was romantic in a modern age, and modern in an age of classical restraint. In his mastery of language, he is without peer in extant Latin literature. His genius lies in his lyric, in the way he penetrates an emotion and surrenders to its truth. For him, love was everything. Where Virgil will have Aeneus give up Dido for Rome, Catullus would lose the world rather than give up his Lesbia.

87

No woman can say truly
that she has been loved
as much as you
Lesbia mine
have been loved by me.

Catullus died in 54 BC, Lucretius a year earlier. Many of the neroteric poets did not live to witness the assassination of Caesar in 44 BC, the subsequent civil war, and the triumph of Octavian that effectively ended the Republic. Calvus died in 47 BC, and Cinna was killed within days of Caesar's assassination. After the trial against Clodia, Caelius Rufus continued his political career and was elected tribune, aedile, and praetor, but when he failed to win reelection, he instigated a riot in the Forum and was forced to leave the city. Shortly after, he was killed trying to bribe Caesar's centurions posted in Thuurii in southern Italy.

And Clodia? We hear very little of her after the trial in which Cicero exposed her to public ridicule. Except for Catullus' tender and vindictive poems, and Cicero's speeches and letters, we know little else about her. Two years after Catullus died, Clodia's brother was murdered on the Appian Way by an armed escort of a political rival. To make his funeral pyre, the Roman people burned down the Senate house. Clodia made no appearance at the killer's trial. She rarely visited her townhouse on the Palatine. Perhaps she settled comfortably in one of her villas at Baiae or Solonium, spending time in the lush gardens that overlooked the river. Her daughter Caecilia Metella was living in Rome, taking up where her mother had left off.

And Cicero? In 45 BC, when Clodia was fifty-two, Cicero's good friend Atticus asked her if she was interested in selling her riverside gardens to an elderly politician looking for a place to retire. The garden, Atticus told her, was the perfect place to build a shrine to the politician's beloved daughter. "Who's the politician?" she asked. It was her old nemesis, Cicero. Atticus went back to Cicero and told him she didn't want to sell. "She really likes the place," he said, "and she's got all the money she needs." Cicero found another villa in Caieta, and devoted the last two years of his life writing dozens of literary and philosophical works; among them: *Brutus*, a history of Roman oratory; the *Consolatio*, on the deaths of great men, occasioned by the death of his daughter Tullia; the *Hortensius*, a plea for the study of philosophy, which greatly moved St. Augustine; the *Tusculanae Disputationes,* on the conditions of happiness, the most intensely felt and expressed of all his philosophical works; two charming essays, *De Senecture* (of Old Age) and *De Amicitia* (of Friendship); an examination of Stoic belief concerning fate and the possibility of prediction, *De Divinatione*, published soon after Caesar's assassination; and his last work on moral philsophy, *De Officiis*, which he wrote for the edification of his son then studying philosophy at Athens. Written in the form of a letter, it was illustrated throughout with examples from Greek and Roman history. In it, Cicero condemned the Stoic precept to withdraw from public life, and encouraged his son to devote himself both to the public good, and to his fellow human beings, a duty that goes beyond patriotism.

After the assassination of Caesar, Antony and Octavian went after Brutus and Cassius, financing the civil war by exacting widespread proscriptions. Antony wrote Cicero's name on the first list sent to Rome. On December 7, 43 BC, soldiers in Antony's army caught Cicero trying to escape and killed him, bringing his head and hands back to Rome and displaying them on the Rostra, the platform in the Forum from which great orators like Cicero himself addressed the people.

When Catullus sent Cornelius Nepos his "little book of poems," Nepos must have chuckled at the humor, but how could he have imagined that Catullus' little book would outlive his own three-volume universal history, the *Chronica*, or his series of *Lives of Famous Men*. Nepos wrote his history for the ages; Catullus's poems were "trifles," tasty biscuits meant for nibbling over tea. It's no stretch to mention Lucretius and Catullus in the same breath. Both were endowed with a sublime gift of language, and the urgency to make art that marks the greatest writers. Above all, they spoke the truth—Lucretius without the obfuscation of philosophic wordplay, and Catullus, without the veil of poetic rhetoric. Even those 19th century translations that force Catullus' metrics into rhymed verse cannot deaden his intensity, nor soften his candor.

> I loathe her and I love her. "Can I show
> > How both should be?"
> I loathe and love, and nothing else I know
> > But agony.

Despite the heartbreak and agony, his love for Lesbia—"my lady, my light"—remained, and he infuses those poems with a range of emotion that elevates his readers to a sublime understanding of human nature.

> And the light of Catullus's own life
> when she looked for his embrace
> > > gave little
> in the matter of passion.

> Cupid was clothed in saffron
> > > and shone and played
> in her love-movements . . .
> > > who looks (it is true)
> elsewhere
> > > for other love.
> And though she is not content
> > with Catullus alone
> > > I will bear the faults,
> > for few they are,
> > > of my modest mistress,
> lest we become as tiresome as jealous fools.

> No father's hand gave me this daughter,
> > who came to my house
> fragrant with Assyrian odors,
> > > her husband unaware
> of the wondrous night sweet stolen gifts
> > she brought, marking the days
> in the calendar of my love
> > > with a whiter stone.

But far above all,
　　　　　always she
who is dearer to me than my own self,
my light and my eyes,
　　　　　who, living,
invests life for Catullus
　　　　　　with its sweet reason.

He ranks with Sappho and Shelley as one of the world's great lyric poets.

The Fall of the Republic

W hile Pompey was subduing the East, Caesar and Crassus became leaders of the popular party and plotted together in Rome against Pompey's return. But in 60 BC, Caesar, Pompey, and Crassus were each in turn rebuffed by the senate who feared their growing power .

Julius Caesar had been serving as governor of Further Spain. Pompey had defeated pirates in the Mediterranean and when he returned home he disbanded his army as proof that he had no ambitions to become dictator. But he made two requests of the Senate: that he be granted enough land to settle his veteran soldiers, and that they ratify the financial arrangements he'd made with the eastern provinces. The Senate refused to ratify the treaty and were not disposed to distribute land to his army. Increasing disorder in the capital intensified the Senate's fear of dictatorship, the terrors of the Sullan proscriptions still vivid in their minds. The deeper question was, which oligarchic faction would a dictator favor? Quite simply, the Senate did not feel the civil disorder was great enough for them to risk losing their power.

When Caesar returned from Spain, he made similiar demands on the Senate that were also rejected. Crassus backed a group of equestrian tax gatherers but had his financial proposal turned down. The three men decided to bury their differences and join forces against those Senators and members of the ruling oligarchy who had snubbed them. Their coalition was an informal one, and secret at that, but it wasn't long before it was publicly known. Modern historians have labeled this compact between Pompey, Crassus, and Caesar, "The First Triumvirate." "The Second Triumvirate," composed of Marcus Aemilius Lepidus, Marc Antony, and Gaius Octavian (Caesar's newphew, whom he adopted as his son), was formed the year after Caesar's assination in 44 BC. Like the members of "The First Triumvirate," they divided the world among themselves, until Lepidus was forced into retirement and Antony and Octavian were left to fight it out. (Octavian, later known as Augustus, the first of the Roman emperors, emerged the victor when he defeated Mark Anthony at the Battle of Actium in 31 BC, one of history's great turning points.)

After the failure of the Catiline conspiracy, neither political intrigue nor attempted revolution secured the *populares'* control of Rome. Cicero's *Concordia Ordinum* was aimed at reconciliation of all moderate elements. But Caesar, Pompey, and Crassus had built their fortunes on conquests made as military commanders and they kept their troops loyal by dividing the plunder among them. With the populace demanding relief from debt and social unrest, and a new military coalition ready to subvert constitutional rule, the Senate's position grew increasingly tenuous.

Caesar asked Cicero to join the triumvirate; Cicero bravely, but unwisely, refused. This was not the reconciliation Cicero envisioned. He believed that the Senate's authority would be weakened by an alliance between the military power of Pompey, the great wealth of Crassus, and Caesar's loyal following. Caesar invited Cicero to join the Triumvarite again, and again Cicero refused. Caesar then supported a bill prosecuting anyone who had put Roman citizens to death without a trial. Cicero was exiled the following year, and his home was razed to the ground. A few years later, Cicero was called home in triumph. In a period of violent civil unrest, it was politically expedient for Cicero to make peace with Caesar, who always behaved with generosity toward him. Rome was fast approaching civil war. The Triumvirate further consolidated their power and the Senate was reduced to being just another political group. When civil war did break out, Cicero left the city along with many of the senatorial party. In 45 BC, his beloved daughter Tullia died, and Cicero was devastated by the loss. He realized that Caesar would never restore the republican constitution, so he took what consolation he could in literary composition. In 44 BC, after the murder of Caeser, Cicero returned to political life and at the end of that summer began his fight against Marc Antony; but when Octavian withdrew his support from the Senate and joined Antony and Lepidus in the "Second Triumvarite," Cicero's name was added to the proscriptions. On December 7, 43 BC, Cicero was tracked down by Antony's assassins who executed him on the grounds of his Villa at Caieta. The civil war began again. It was to last another twelve years until Octavian gained sole power with the defeat of Marc Antony at the Battle of Actium on September 2, 31 BC. A year later, Antony would commit suicide, dying in Cleopatra's arms.

☛ Gaius Asinius Pollio (76 BC-4 AD)

Pollio's erotic poems have not survived. As one of the younger neoterics, he hung out with Catullus and the other *poetae novi*, writing tragedies, poems, and historical narratives, and winning a reputation as an orator. A sharp critic as well, he ventured to correct Cicero, Caesar, and Sallust, and to criticize Livy for his provincialism (which he called *patavinitas*). Catullus mentions him in the humorous poem about the stolen napkin (#12). When dining out, Romans usually brought their own napkins. Many were expensive pieces of linen; others cherished as gifts from friends. Much like our present-day practice of taking towels from motels, napkin-snatching was quite common. In Catullus's poem, his napkin was snatched away by Pollio's brother, Asinius Marrucinus.

Asinius Marrucinus, when we are laughing
 and drinking, I see you extend
that left claw of yours,
snatching our napkins for your own use.
Do you think this is funny?
Maybe you think it clever,
but it's a shabby piece of tomfoolery,
in bad taste and bad-mannered.
You don't believe me?
Believe your brother, Pollio,
a boy crackling with wit
who'd give a tidy sum
in exchange for the embarrassment
you cause him.
You've got two choices, Asinius.
Either expect 300 hendecasyllabic verses
from me to bombard your doorstep,
or give me back my napkin—
it's not the napkin I care about,
but it's keepsake value, having
been given to me by my old friends
Veranius and Fabullus,
who sent that fine piece of Saetaban linen
all the way from Spain.
Catullus cherishes that napkin,
for it reminds him always
of his cherished friends,
Veranius and Fabullus.

With Catullus, Cinna, Calvus, and Cicero gone, and the excitement of neotericism lost in the social unrest of the civil wars, Pollio became a supporter of Julius Caesar in the civil war against Pompey. His greatest recognition came after Catullus's death. first, for his history of the civil wars from the consulship of Metellus in 60 BC (when Caesar and Pompey made their original pact) to the battle of Philippi in 42 BC (when Brutus and Cassius were defeated by Antony and Octavian); second, for his military triumph in 39 BC over the Parthini in Illyria; and third, because it was Pollio who first recognized the genius of Virgil, and who came to his assistance when Virgil's farm was confiscated after the battle of Philippi. Virgil celebrated him in his fourth and eighth Eclogues.

But you who now sail past the rocks of great Timavus
Or coast the Illyrian sea—say, will there ever come
The day when I may be allowed to tell your deeds?   [a *corthurnus* was
May be allowed to cite your songs throughout the world   the high thick-soled
As rivalling alone the Sophoclean cothurnus?   boot worn by ancient
You were the starting-point, for you I'll end: accept   Greek & Roman
The songs begun at your command, and let this ivy   tragedians]
Entwine among the victor's bays around your brow.   [VIII, 6-12]

Pollio was elected consul in 40 BC, the year of the signing of the treaty of Brundisium between the contending commanders Octavian, Antony, and Lepidus—"The Second Triumvirate." He refused to fight against Antony at Actium, but became a supporter of the Augustan settlement. Pollio also founded the first public library in Rome, and is said by the Elder Seneca to have introduced the practice of reciting his own works to an audience.

Historians see the emergence of "The First Triumvirate" as the symbolic end of the Roman Republic, even though free elections continued for another decade. Though the Triumvirs'control was not absolute, the oligarchy never recovered its power again.

Over a hundred years later, in the epic masterpiece *the Bellum Civile, or* The Civil War (also known by the name of the battle that ended that war, the *Pharsalia*) the Latin poet Marcus Annaeus Lucan (39-65 AD) bitterly criticized the First Triumvirate as the cause of the war that destroyed the republic.

> Greatness falls by its very greatness: . . .
> Rome was her own downfall, allowing to rule her
> Three despots, a triad, a concentration of power
> Fatal and never before bestowed on a gang of masters.
> What a disastrous accord, what ambition-engendered blindness!
> What induced them to pool their resources and share the world out
> Jointly? So long as the sea is supported by earth, and the earth lies
> Poised on the air, and the Titan sun continues his weary,
> Arduous circuits, and night follows day through the signs of the zodiac—
> Never will trust exist between tyrannical partners.
> Every exercising power resents a sharer.
> No need to look abroad or afar for examples: there lies one
> All too close at hand—the earliest walls of our city
> Reeked with a brother's blood shed by the hand of his brother.
> Nor was the prize for such madness the rule over land and ocean:
> What provided the source of dispute was no more than a village.   [1, 90-108].

Food for Thought

Lucan's Civil War, or the "Pharsalia"

Until the end of the 19th century, Lucan's poem recounting the civil war between Caesar and Pompey was considered one of the great masterpieces of Latin literature, ranking second only to Virgil's *Aeneid*.

> War, civil war and worse,
> fought out on the plains of Thessalia,
> Times when injustice reigned,
> and a crime was legally sanctioned,

Times when a powerful race,
whose prowess had won it an empire,
Turned its swords on itself,
with opposing armies of kinsmen—
This is my theme.

In the *Commedia*, Dante encounter's Lucan when he comes to the first circle of Hell, after being ferried across the river Acheron. Here, souls live in an honorable Limbo, suffering grief without torment as they live in desire for God but without hope of ever being with him in Paradise. They are not in Hell for any grievous, unrepented sin, but for lack of baptism; they are souls born before the time of Christ. As Virgil and Dante walk along, they arrive at a great dome of light occupied by the world's great pagan poets, the *bella scola*—Homer, Horace, Ovid, and appearing as the final member, Marcus Annaeus Lucan, "L'ultimo Lucano."

When the voice had ceased and was silent,
I saw four great shades coming toward us:
their expression was neither sad nor happy.

My good master began to speak: "Behold the one
with that sword in his hand, coming in front
of the other three as if their lord:

that is Homer, the supreme poet;
the next is Horace the satirist;
Ovid is the third, and the last, Lucan.

So I saw come together the lovely school
of that lord of highest song, who soars   [Virgil]
above the others like an eagle.

(Inferno, Canto 4, lines 82-96)

Joined by Virgil and Dante, these six poets walk together, "talking of matters that were fitting for this place, but of which it is well to keep silent now." The only major Latin epic poet omitted in this section of the *Commedia* was Statius (45-c.96 AD), a contemporary of Lucan's, whom Dante eventually meets in Purgatory. Statius and Lucan were poets of Rome's Silver Age, which followed on the heel's of Rome's Golden Age—the age of Virgil, Horace, Propertius, and Ovid, an age of poetry said to have ended with the deaths of Augustus in 14 AD amd Ovid in 17 AD. Though Statius and Lucan were highly regarded throughout the Middle Ages, the Renaissance, and well into the 19th century, their critical esteem has drastically fallen in the last century.

Both poets will be covered more extensively in a later section; for now, I'll quote several stanzas of Lucan's epic that cover the events relating to the war between Caesar and Pompey. Content-wise, those stanzas are more relevant in this section. In the section devoted specifically to Lucan, I'll focus more on the poem's stylistic elements, and why it was so highly regarded for nearly two millennia, and why it seems to have fallen out of favor in our own time. Pompey was eventually defeated at Pharsalus in 48 BC, and so Lucan's epic, the *Bellum Civile*, is often referred to as the *Pharsalia*, to distinguish it from Caesar's account of the war, *De Bello Civili*.

●◇

The civil war between Pompey and Caesar was precipitated when Crassus was killed on June 9, 53 BC fighting the Parthians in Mesopotamia in which a Roman army of forty-thousand was destroyed. Crassus' head was used as a stage-prop in a scene from the *Bacchae* performed at a banquet for the Parthian king. Now Caesar and Pompey (like Antony and Ocatavian after the departure of Lepidus), with their rival ambitions, stood alone in direct confrontation.

Caesar needed to extend his power and amass enough money to oppose Pompey and the Roman oligarchy. He found his first opportunity in Gaul A movement by the Helvetti (a Celtic people who in about 100 BC had migrated to an area in modern Switzerland) gave Caesar an opportunity to start a major war. After nearly a decade, Caesar had conquered the whole of Gaul. Booty from this conquest was breathtaking. Young Roman aristocrats flocked to him to make their fortunes, and vast sums flowed into the pockets of the upper-class Romans. Plutarch, calculating from Caeasr's own figures, reported that a million Gauls were killed and another million enslaved. Reprisals and requisitions of food produced a human, economic, and ecological disaster probably unequalled until the conquest of the Americas.

One event caught the imagination of the Roman populace: Caesar built a bridge across the Rhine into barbarian territory where no Roman commander had ever set foot before. This feat of engineering became a symbol of Rome's ability to extend its frontier anywhere.

His next move was against Britain, a rich country, particularly in metals. Many Celtic Gauls had escaped Rome's attacks by migrating to Britain and forming tribal to support their kinsmen in Gaul. This induced Caeasr to launch a military expedition against Britain. Perhaps his hope was to eclipse Pompey as a miltiary leader. Building a bridge across the Rhine was daring enough; but launching an amphibious assault across the English Channel seemed lunacy. Pompey tried to diminish the scope of Caesar's plan, claiming the Channel was just an insignificant mud flat. In 54 BC, Caesar crossed the Channel, bringing five legions and two thousand cavalry on eight hundred ships with him—the largest fleet to ever cross the Channel, not to be surpassed until the Allied Invasion of Normandy in 1944.

After Caesar's conquest of Britain, Cicero and most of the senate grew increasingly afraid of his power, and so aligned itself with Pompey, who claimed to represent constitutional republican government. The stage was set for a civil war that would determine the future of Rome. While Caesar's forces in Gaul were disciplined and hardened from their recent conquests, Pompey's army had grown soft from easy living.

Once again, Caesar needed a pretext to make his move. During Caesar's Gallic camplaign, Caesar's agents in Rome kept him informed of the increasing civil unrest that plagued the capital, which seemed on the verge of chaos. Rioting ensued, and Pompey backed a resolution to have Caesar resign from his post as consul. Following its acceptance, the senate called upon Pompey to take command of all the forces of the Republic and assume the role of sole consulship. Caesar had no choice but to step down or confront Pompey and the Roman Senate. "Rivalry spurred them forward," wrote Lucan in the *Pharsalia*.

> Pompey feared that his triumphs, now old, would be overshadowed,
> Conquest of Gaul outshining his victory over the pirates:
> Caesar, exhilarated by years of successful campaigning,
> Put his faith in fortune, loath to be second in order.
> Caesar, to sum it up, could no longer brook a superior,
> Pompey not even an equal. Impossible to determine
> Which had the juster cause, for both had impeccable sanction:
> Gods on the conquering side, but Cato choosing the conquered.
>
> > [*Victrix causa deis placuit, sed victa Catoni*]
> > [Best known epigram in the poem]

> Equally matched they were not. For Pompey was growing older,
> Tamer from years of ease, of peacefully wearing the toga,
> Unused to taking the field. What he coveted now was status,
> Happy to meet their applause when he entered his own theater,
> Adding nothing, though, to his real power, but trusting
> Far too much in his past; a shadow of his old greatness;
> Like a towering oak that dominates a wheat field,
> Carrying on its branches the ancient spoils of a people,
> Sacred gifts of their chieftans, a tree whose roots are no longer
> Firmly fixed in the ground: it supports itself by its own weight,
> Spreading with its trunk alone instead of verdure and leafage,
> Yet, although it totters and may not weather the next storm,
> Even though other trees of healthy timber around it,
> This one alone is worshipped.

> > Quite other the case with Caesar.
> He had not just the name, not only the fame of a marshal:
> He had restless courage; the only thing that would shame him
> Would be to win without war. [I, 134-160]

While Lucan blames the two protagonists for the conflict, he says the real cause of the war was the corruption of Roman morals by luxury, the results of Rome's conquests.

> Wealth was the root of the trouble. For when we Romans established
> Mastery over the world and fortune spoiled us with riches,
> When prosperity ruined our moral fiber, and booty
> Grabbed from our enemies led to extravagance and excesses, . . .
> Clothes were worn by men that would hardly be decent for women;
> Poverty was shunned, that traditional mother of manhood;
> All the wrold was ransakced to pick from each nation the special,
> Signal vice that destroyed it. [I, 176-185]

With the capital veering toward anarchy, Caesar claimed to defend the rights of tribunes who had been forced to flee to him for protection. An emergency decree was passed to stop

Caesar. If he returned to Rome, stripped of his consulship, it would mean a return to private life, leaving him open to prosecution on trumped up civil charges, and certain exile. One of Sulla's laws forbade a governor to lead his troops outside his province. To do so was an act of treason. But Caesar believed he had no choice. He led a single legion across the Alps, and on the night of January 10, 49 BC, reached the small river Rubicon, which formed the border between Cisalpine Gaul and eastern Italy. He reminded his troops that Pompey had been corrupted by enemies jealous of his reputation, while Caesar had always been loyal, respecting the reputation and *dignitas* of Pompey. He harangued his soldiers, reminding them of the wrongs done to him by his enemies over the years. "A revolutionary change has taken place in the government of the state! Will you defend me from my enemies the reputation and *dignitas* of someone under whose leadership as a general you've had success for nine years serving the *res publica* with outstanding success and won numerous victories, and had conquered the whole of Gaul and Germany?" The soldiers of the thirteenth legion shouted in reply that they were ready to defend him and save the Republic.

As Caesar was about to lead his men across the river, he has a vision of the figure of Rome, with whom he conducts a dialogue.

> When, however, he reached the Rubicon's modest waters,
> (Night it was) there appeared the enormous figure of Roma
> trembling in distress, quite clear in spite of the darkness,
> Wearing on her face an expression of utter sadness.
> On her head was a crown in the shape of a turreted tower;
> Down from it hung white hair, dishevelled and torn. Bare-shouldered,
> Sobbing, with broken speech, she stood and addressed the army:
> "Where are you bound for, soldiers? Where are you taking my standards?
> Mine they are, and if you are coming with lawful purpose,
> If as citizens, this is your limit." The marshal's body
> Trembled with awe, his hair stood on end, and lassitude held him,
> Slowing down his steps at the very edge of the river.
> After a while he spoke: "O Juppiter, Thunderer, gazing
> Down from the Parpaeian rock at the walls of our might city;
> household gods, once rescued from Troy, of the house of Iulus;
> Romulus, spirited up to beomce Quirinus in heaven;
> Latian Juppiter, whose shrine is on towering Alba;
> Vestal fires; and Rome, with godhead as great as the greatest—
> Be on my side. O Rome, I am not here to attack you,
> Not as an enemy: no, but as your all-conquering captain,
> Everywhere yours, your soldier, and now too, if you accept me."
>
> [206-226]

Under a full moon, Caesar moved his troops across the bridge and effectively declared war on the Senatorial army.

> Standing on forbidden terrain, on Italian soil, Caesar cried out
> "Here I abandon peace and the laws that the others have flouted.
> Fortune, I follow you. Away with pacts and agreements—

Those I have trusted enough. Let war be the judge of our causes."

A series of bloody battles across the length and breadth of the Mediterranean world followed Caesar's crossing of the Rubicon. The nation was plunged into an empire-wide civil war for which neither side was ready. The horrors of the Sullan proscriptions still made Cicero shudder. In his *ad Atticum* (IX, 10, 2-3) Cicero wrote:

> . . . I was horrified at the sort of war which Pompey envisaged, cruel and all-embracing, of a kind which men do not yet comprehend. What threats against the townships of Italy, against men of repute by name, in fact against everyone who had not followed him! How often he said, "Sulla could do it, shall I not be able to do it?"! . . . Sulla or Marius or Cinna have been regarded as having been in the right; on the side of the law, perhaps; but what have we ever witnessed more cruel or more devastating than their victories?

Caesar was soon joined by Marc Antony, and with no reliable veteran legions to oppose him, Caesar rapidly overran Italy, meeting little resistance as one town after another welcomed him with open arms. Pompey's veterans were languishing in Spain, and the rest of his troops stationed at home were no match for Caesar's army. Pompey and his allies in the Senate fled Rome in such haste they left the reserve treasury back in the city. After several minor defeats, Pompey decided not to fight in Italy where Caesar had command of greater forces. In Greece and Macedonia, Pompey had huge resources upon which to draw, so he sailed from Brundisum harbor, evading Caesar's attempt to blockade him, and set out across the Adriatic to Greece, where loyal forces awaited. At first, Cicero refused to join Pompey, believing that leaving Italy was a mistake. But in the end, Cicero decided that if Pompey emerged victorious, he'd probably preserve the republic, whereas Caesar would take dictatorial powers. Cicero followed Pompey, joining him at Thessalonica in Macedonia.

Using the coasts of Greece as a base for their naval operations, Pompey's forces could encircle Italy by sea, depriving them of their much needed-grain supply. First Caesar defeated Pompey's forces in Spain and Sicily, then he quelled a mutiny in Gaul where soldiers refused to follow Caesar's policy of clemency because it deprived them of their booty. Then Caesar entered Rome, assumed the post of dictator, and set in motion numerous administrative arrangements to deal with social unrest. After a short time, he gathered his army and went after his opponents in the Balkans. Antony joined him with reinforcements, and they attempted to blockade Pompey's key base in Dyrachium (present day Albania). Caesar's strategy was a disastrous failure. But this tactical defeat turned into a *de facto* strategic victory. For some unknown reason Pompey panicked and retreated inland into the Thessalian plain where both sides received more reinforcements. Lucan recounts a dream Pompey has on the eve of the battle.

> Pompey's sleep that night was troubled, but gave him his final
> Hour of pleasure by sending a dream of happy illusion.
> Rome was the scene, in his own Pompeian theatre.   [Caesar was assassinated

He sat there, watching the swarming crowd   in the Senate, Of
the Roman people, and heard them   on the steps
Raising his name to the skies with joyful cheers,   of Pompey's Theater.]
And applauding, each tier eager to drown the next.

    .   .   .   .

                    It may be that,
Now when Pompey had come to the end of his greatness and splendor,
Anxious about the future, his sleeping mind had returned to
happier days; or perhaps it operated by contrast,
As can happen with dreams, and presaged a future directly
Opposite to his vision—an omen of fatal disaster;

    .   .   .   .

Nothing but sadness and fighting, nothing but death and disaster.

By morning his troops are ready for battle, chomping at the bit.

                              They demanded
Battle, for destiny was dragging the world to destruction.
Most of the wretched fellows would not be alive on the morrow;
Now they crowded round and vociferously protested
Outside their general's tent, undisciplined and excited,
Thereby advancing the hour that was hastening on to destroy them

    .   .   .   .

All over Pompey's camp the cry was, "On to Pharsalia!"

Cicero was ill at the time and stayed behind at the camp near Dyrhachium. He had tried to
persuade Pompey to delay the confrontation, but his soldiers and staff all urged immediate
action. Lucan was unable to resist using Cicero at this point in his narrative, having
Rome's most persuasive orator join in the chorus of those advocating immediate attack.

        If this war is for us, who have chosen you as our leader,
        Why prevent the world from lunging its swords into Caesar?
        Hands are ready on weapons; the soldiers hardly can stand it,
        This unbearable waiting. To action, then! It is either
        That, or be left behind by the trumpets that you should be sounding.
        We, the senators, ask: are we following you as your soldiers
        Or as your retinue?"   [7: 94-101]

At dawn, Pompey led his troops down from the hills toward the river Enipeus, the sunrise
hitting them full in their faces. By chance, Caeser had abandoned his static position,
intending to forage for grain, when he noticed Pompey's forces coming down from the
hills to the flat ground. The chance had come for one conclusive encounter that would
decide everything once and for all. Bringing his troops to the ready, he spoke to them.

        "Conquerors of the world, my sourcfe of destiny, soldiers!
        Here is the chance of battle that you have prayed for so often.
        No more prayers: it is time to summon fate with your swords now.
        This is the day, I remember well, that you promised to give me
        By the Rubicon, in the hope of which we invaded

Italy, and to which we deferred our legitimate Triumph,
banned by teh Senate. This day will decide, with fate as the witness,
Which side took up arms with greater justice; . . . .
                                   Our aim is not my advancement,
No, but to make you free, with dominion over the whole world.
Anxious although I am to return to the life of a private
Citizen, unpretentious and dressed like the rest of the people,
Still, to give up the scope that you deserve, there is nothing,
Nothing that I would refuse to be. Let yours be the power,
Mine the discredit involved.
                                   "And your hopes of winning the world will
Cost you little in lives. Your opponents are hardly impressive —
Greeks gymnasium-trained, devotees of effeminate wrestling,
Barely tough enough to carry their load of equipment;
That, or a motley crew of assorted foreigners, speaking
Gibberish to each other, who wilt at the sound of the trumpet,
Terrified to hear, when their line of battle advances,
Even their own war cries. Very few of you will be fighting
Truly Civil War; your major task in the battle
Will be to rid the world of the enemies of the Romans.
Mow your way right through those cowardly peoples and vicious
Kingdoms, and with one stroke of the sword dispose of the whole mass.

.   .   .   .
                                   I see in my mind's eye
Rivers of blood, the trampled bodies of kings, the mangled
Corpses of senators, and whole nations drowned in the carnage.
                                   We are only
One small strip of land away from all we have prayed for.
I am the one who will have the power to grant and distribute,
Once the fighting is done, the possession of kings andof nations.

"Thessaly! Gods, what change in the great celestial order
Gave that place the honor of being the stage of the battle?
Picture the chains, and Caesar's head stuck up on the rostrum,
Picture his body unburied. Think back to the crime of the sheep pens,
When they cordoned the Campus for that magnificent battle.
Sulla was guilty of that, and we are fighting another
Civil war with a general who learned his business from Sulla.

.   .   .   .
                                   I offer a prayer for the victory:
May it go to the one who does not feel bound to be cruel,
Drawing his ruthless sword against his defeated opponents,
But considers the fellow citizens who oppose him
Innocent of crime. . . . I want no enemy soldiers
Struck in the back; if they run, you will count them as comrades and Romans.
Till that point, no mercy.   [7: 279-354]

In the largest battle ever fought between Romans, Pompey's army was utterly defeated
at Pharsalus in 48 BC.

Magnus by now was in angusih, aware that the gods and the Roman

Destiny had deserted his side; he despaired of his fortune
Even before the disaster was total. He stood on a hillock
Giving a widespread view, from which he could see the destruction
Spread all over the landscape of thessaly, hard to determine
During the haze of battle. He saw the tragedy clearly —
Everywhere missiles aimed at his life and everywhere corpses,
he and his cause expiring in one great welter of blood.   [7: 709-716]

Toward the end of his epic, Lucan meditated on the accursed land of Thessaly.

Thessaly, luckless land, you must have offended the high gods
Grievously, far beyond others, for them to make you the scene of
Such a display of evil and death. No passage of time will
Let generations to come forgive you, and leave in oblivion
These calamitous losses. When will the drops in the wheat fields
Sprout untinged with red? And when will the countryman's ploughshare
Cease to disturb the bones and affront the spirits of Romans?
Armies will clash, before that,   [a reference to Philippi, 42 BC
in a second murderous battle,   where Brutus & Cassius
Staining with Roman blood   were defeated by
this soil still wet from the first one.   by Antony & Octavian]
Myriads of bones lie there.

. . . . . .

Still you would not collect as many bones as the farmer
Strikes in Thessaly while he ploughs and rakes for a living.
         But the gods have spread the crime through the whole world
Making it equally guilty, or equally innocent; Munda,
Sicily, Mutina, Actium — all this chain of disasters
Shares in the obloquy and lifts the blame from Pharsala.   [7: 935-940]

Pompey escaped and fled to Egypt to get help from Ptolemy's son, the boy-king Ptolemy VII. But Egyptian politicians there knew that Caesar was in hot pursuit, and wanted no part of an invading army. When Pompey landed on the coast of Egypt, he was stabbed in the back by a renegade centurion; his head was embalmed and presented to Caesar when he arrived shortly afterwards. The Egyptian hoped that would end the matter, and that Caesar would have no excuse to stay. But Caesar had other plans; and then there was the unexpected affair with Cleopatra.

At first, Caesar planned only to claim tribute from the wealthy country on the northern coast of Africa. As a pretext for staying, though, Caesar claimed he was there to help Ptolemy VII reconcile with his exiled half-sister, the twenty-one-year-old Cleopatra. One night, Cleopatra secretly entered Caesar's lodgings and charmed him into supporting her cause. She was thirty years younger than Caesar, resourceful, and politically astute. Likenesses of her on various coins indicate she was not beautiful, but contemporary historical accounts indicate that men were attracted to her because of her intelligence and personality. She persuaded Caesar to support her cause, and when Caesar's army finally landed in Egypt, they defeated Ptolemy's royal forces in a battle south of the Nile delta. Cleopatra became queen and Egypt a client state of Rome. Caesar returned to Italy, then left for Spain to defeat the last of the opposing armies led by one of Pompey's sons. By 45 BC there were no more armies in the field against Caesar, and it seemed the war was over.

Unlike his enemies, Caesar made a point of showing mercy to the defeated; there were to be no proscriptions. Caesar even pardoned Cicero for siding with Pompey. *Clementia* (or clemency) was the characteristic virtue of the monarch. Caesar gave himself the title *Imperator*. The word "emperor" derived from "imperator," but not until later. Caesar used it to designate himself supreme military commander. We don't know whether Caesar wanted to be called king. He was certainly a *de facto* monarch. As Shakespeare had Marc Antony say,

> You all did see that on the Lupercal
> I thrice presented him a kingly crown,
> Which he did thrice refuse: was this ambition?

Caesar had one more year to live. He showed himself to be a man of great administrative talents. To reward his ex-soldiers and retired legionaries, he established colonies from Corinth in Greece to Carthage in Africa. To alleviate poverty, he resettled another eighty thousand civilians in the newly established colonies. His handling of the debt crisis was a brilliant compromise. Cicero had warned that wholesale cancelation of the debt would destroy private property, and he was probably right. But Caesar made hoarding against the law, which helped put more money into circulation. Creditors were forced to accept land or other fixed assets in repayment of loans, and any interest that had accrued since the beginning of the Civil War was canceled, wiping out at least one-quarter of all debts. It wasn't a perfect solution for anyone; as a compromise, though, it helped bring a measure of stability.

Caesar also introduced the Julian Calendar in 46 BC. The Gregorian calendar we use today evolved from it. He added a month to the year (July, named after him) and designated January 1st—instead of March 1st—as the beginning of a new year. (Later, Augustus was to add a twelfth month.)

Despite his efforts at reform, Caesar appeared to have no overall plan for basic social, economic, or constitutional reforms. Opinion is divided on what kind of ruler Caesar really was. As a military leader, he brought the provinces of Italy under control, defeated Pompey, and effectively did away with the oligarchy that had ruled Rome. In so doing, he ended the disorder that had plagued the Republic for decades and laid the groundwork for the formation of the empire under his grandnephew Augustus in 27 BC. Caesar was a distinguished orator in the "Attic" manner, believing in "analogy" (on which he wrote a treatise, *De Analogia*), and in the use of ordinary words. He wrote a total of ten books on his battles in Gaul (58-50 BC), and *De Bello Civili*, his account of the civil war between Caesar and Pompey. Though written to ensure that his view would survive for posterity, these commentaries are still considered masterpieces of military history. (One reason why Lucan's poem *Bellum Civile* was referred to as *The Pharsalia* was to avoid confusion with Caesar's *De Bello Cicili*.)

Perhaps the republic could not be saved by anything other than a dictator, and this is what the nobles feared. The constitution provided for the appointment of a dictator in times of crisis, and like Sulla before him, Caesar chose that title as a temporary measure in

49 BC and again in 46 BC. Finally, in February of 44 BC, he became dictator for the rest of his life—the coins that bore his portrait (the first portraits of any living man or woman ever to appear on a Roman coin) also had the word *Perpetvo* (meaning, in perpetuity) written on them. Senators and other nobles became alarmed at this symbol of an institutionalized autocracy.

Caesar had no intention of sitting idly on his throne and counting out his money. As a youth, he had supposedly wept when he realized that Alexander the Great was his age when he had conquered the world. It was Caesar's ambition to take those territories in the east that Alexander had conquered. He was fifty-six and no longer fit. And the abyss between him and his fellow aristocrats created political tension that Caesar was not adept at handling; a simpler approach was to wage war and escape from the political intrigues of Rome. Legions were dispatched to eastern Europe to prepare for an attack on the kingdom of Dacia as a prelude to the conquest of the Orient. His departure was set for March 18, 44 BC. Everyone remembered the disruption caused by his absences during the Civil Wars; the prospect of being ruled by an absent divine monarch for years ahead proved intolerable even to his friends who began to view him as an ambitious tyrant and a threat to the Roman Republic. Prominent noblemen complained of Caesar's growing arrogance and ambition. Those defenders of the republic who had contemplated assassination realized that time was of the essence. A widespread conspiracy was stitched together. Gaius Cassius was the ring-leader, recruiting sixty other senators and nobles who wanted to prevent Caesar from taking total power, among them Publius Servilius Casca, Lucius Tillius Cimber, and Marcus Junius Brutus, rumored to be Caesar's illegitimate son. On February 15 of that year, at the festival of the Lupercalia to ensure fertility, Mark Antony had attempted to place on Caesar's head a diadem, or headband worn as a symbol of royalty. Caesar refused it, and Antony offered it twice more. Each time Caesar refused it, to the great cheers of the multitude. But what if at a later date, he should accept it? In Shakespeare's *The Tragedy of Julius Caesar*, Brutus considers the words of Cassius, the leading intriguer against Caesar, who convinced the high-minded Brutus that Caesar was only mortal, and that his plan to become king had to be stopped. Brutus finally agrees.

> It must be by his death: and, for my part,
> I know no personal cause to spurn at him,
> But for the general. He would be crown'd:
> How that might change his nature, there's the question:
> It is the bright day that brings forth the adder;   [a snake]
> And that craves wary walking. Crown him? — that; —
> And then, I grant, we put a sting in him,
> That at his will he may do danger with.
> The abuse of greatness is when it disjoins
> Remorse from power: and, to speak truth of Caesar,
> I have not known when his affections sway'd
> More than his reason. But 'tis a common proof,
> That lowliness is young ambition's ladder,
> Whereto the climber-upward turn his face;
> But when he once attains the upmost round,
> He then unto the ladder turns his back,

Looks in the clouds, scorning the base degrees
By which he did ascend: so Caesar may;
Then, lest he may, prevent. And, since the quarrel
Will bear no colour for the thing he is,
Fashion it thus; that what he is, augmented,　　　　　　　　[crowned]
Would run to these and these extremeties:
And therefore think him as a serpent's egg
Which hatch'd would as his kind grow mischievous,
And kill him in the shell.

Three days before Caesar was scheduled to leave for the East, the conspirators met in Pompey's Theatre of the Senate house, ostensibly to vote on legislation. Caesar came without his usual bodyguards, unwilling to believe that anyone wanted him out of the way. Afterall, he had brought peace to the Republic and solved pressing problems. At the Lupercalia, every senator had sworn allegiance to the father of their country, as Caesar had now come to be called. Despite omens and warnings to "beware the ideas of March," Caesar made his way to the Senate house. It was not unusual for passersby to ask him to consider petitions, so when a friend put into his hand a scroll revealing the plot, Caesar made no attempt to read it. He carried the unopened parchment to his death. When Caesar entered the Senate chamber around noon, he took his seat in a recessed area below the statue of Pompey. Senators loyal to Caesar had been prevented from attending the meeting, and at that moment, Mark Antony was called away on some pretext. Cimber made a show of petitioning Caesar for the return of his brother from exile. Armed with daggers in their stylus cases, the conspirators began to move toward himas though to second the petition. Casca managed to come around behind Caeasr and jabbed him with his dagger. Caesar used his stylus to strike back at Casca, but the other senators closed in with their daggers and riddled his body with thirty-five stab wounds. The attack was so frenzied, that they wounded each other in the process. Then the senators fled, leaving his bleeding body at the foot of Pompey's statue.

Word spread rapidly of the assassination. Those who had opposed him declared it a triumph of liberty over tyranny. But the city was in an uproar. Mark Antony took charge, promising to carry out Caesar's programs and taking control of his money. Days later Caesar's body was laid atop a pyre built in the Forum. His body was burnt in a frenzy of mourning and lamentation never before seen in Rome.

Shakespeare based his play on Sir Thomas North's translation of Plutarch's *Lives of the Noble Grecians and Romans*, a large portion of the play consisting merely of North's text, couched in blank verse. The speeches of Brutus and Antony may have derived from the English translation of Appian's *History of the Roman Wars*. Mark Antony's career and personality has been overlaid by legend—he was first presented as a villian, then romantic biographers transformed him into a figure of tragic self-destruction. Shakespeare is even-handed in his depiction of both Brutus and Mark Antony—Plutarch's portrayal must have been convincing.

At the funeral, Brutus justifies the actions of the conspirators. (Notice that Shakespeare has Brutus speaking in prose, whereas Antony speaks in blank verse.)

Romans, countrymen, and lovers! Hear me for my cause, and be silent, that you may hear: believe me for mine honour, and have respect to mine honour, that you may believe: censure me in your wisdom, and awake your senses, that you may the better judge. If there be any in this assembly, any dear friend of Caesar's, to him I say that Brutus' love to Caesar was no less than his. If then that friend demand why Brutus rose against Caesar, this is my answer: not that I loved Caesar less, but that I loved Rome more. Had you rather Caesar were living, and die all slaves, than that Caesar were dead, to live all freemen? As Caesar loved me, I weep for him; as he was fortunate, I rejoice at it; as he was valiant, I honour him; but as he was ambitious, I slew him. There is tears for his love; joy for his fortune; honour for his valour; and death for his ambition.. . .

Enter ANTONY *and others, with* CAESAR'S *body*

With this I depart,—that, as I slew my best lover for the good of Rome, I have the same dagger for myself, when it shall please my country to need my death.

Antony then turns Brutus' speech on its head and incites the crowd. He reminds them that Caesar refused the crown three times. "Ambition should be made of sterner stuff," he says. After Antony's speech, the people began to riot, and Brutus, Cassius, Cicero, and the other conspirators fled the city. Cleopatra, sill in Rome, sailed home to Egypt .

This was Antony's moment. After a wild youth spent drinking and womanizing—he fathered a son and two daughters by three different wives—he distinguished himself as a cavalry commander with Caesar in Gaul, defending Caesar's interests in the Senate, and served in Greece where he commanded Caesar's left wing at the battle of Pharsalus. Now almost forty, he had become a charismatic leader, handsome and vigorous. Plutarch wrote of him:

> There was a noble dignity about Antony's appearance. His forehead broad, his nose aquiline, and these gave him a certain bold and masculine look . . . This swaggering air, his ribald talk, his taking of his food while standing at the common mess-table . . . made his troops delight in his company.

But when Caesar's will was read in public, his vast wealth was left to his adopted son, his great-nephew Octavian, who was nineteen and studying in Apollonia, a small town on the Illyrian shore in Dalmatia. Taking Caesar's name, he was called Gaius Julius Caesar Octavian. Antony disdainfully called him "the youth who owed everything to his name." In the weeks that followed Caesar's death, Antony went about consolidating his power base in Rome, and had no intention of turning over the government to this delicate boy of nineteen.

Octavian had last seen Caesar in December, before leaving to resume his studies in Apollonia. In late March, he received a letter from his mother, dated March 15, detailing the events in Rome. "The time has come when you must play the man," she wrote. "Decide, and act, for no one can tell the things that may come froth." Octavian acted with decisiveness and alacrity, leaving for Rome and letting his beard grow as a sign of mourning. Over the next few months Octavian wooed Caesar's veteran troops by paying them more money, a course of action that brought him into conflict with Antony.

Octavian began to cooperate with the republicans in the Senate and received their backing, including that of Cicero. The Caesarians were now divided into two parties, Antony's and Octavian's. In 42 BC, their combined forces defeated the armies of Brutus and Cassius at Philippi. Cassius committed suicide after his forces were crushed by Antony's troops, and after Brutus was completely routed by Octavians army, Brutus committed suicide.

[do "noblest Roman of them all speech]

The next years were marked by retribution and violence. Antony's brother and his were murdered at Perusia, veterans settled on confiscated lands, and Octavian was as ruthless as Sulla had been in proscriptions in which certain citizens were decalred outlaws and their goods were confiscated. Their names were published throughout Italy, and the proscribed were hunted down and executed by squads of soldiers.

☛ Virgil (70- 17 BC), *The Eclogues*

Publius Vergilius Maro began writing the ten unconnected pastoral poems in the *Eclogues* when he was twenty-eight years old. They were composed between 42 BC and 35 BC, during the troubled times that followed the assassination of Julius Caesar, when Italy was torn by civil war and the Mediterranean world was split between the contending Roman factions led by Octavian and Antony. Virgil was born at Andes near Mantua in Cisalpine Gaul where his parents owned a farm. His father came from humble origins, but became quite wealthy; his mother was supposedly well-connected. In his twenties, he went to Rome and studied rhetoric and philosophy. He must have been influenced by the work of Lucretius, since he soon joined an Epicurean colony on the Gulf of Naples where he became a pupil of the Epicurean philsopher Siro. After Philippi, Antony and Octavian began confiscating land in the proscriptions, and Virgil's family estate was turned over to returning veterans. Virgil was fortunate that the three commissioners appointed by Octavian to confiscate land in north Italy were all former poets and writers who were friends of his. **Gaius Asinius Pollio** had been one of the neoterics, friends with Catullus, and one of the first to recognize Virgil's talent. P. Alfenus Varus (not to be confused with Quintilius Varus, the Roman general who committed suicide) was a Cremonese mentioned by Horace in his first satire as having given up a cobbler's shop for a career in the law courts. Catullus addressed two of his poems to him. Varus became the first Cisalpine to attain the consulate. Gallus Gaius Cornelius was a soldier and poet and friend to Virgil. Gallus's love-elegies centered upon the poet's mistress, the famous actress Cytheris (also loved by Mark Antony). His poetry was influenced by the Hellenistic Greek poets Callimachus and Euphorion, and the neoterics. In his tenth Eclogue, Virgil worked in some of Gallus' own lines. These men helped Virgil get a piece of property in Naples, where he was based for the rest of his life. The ninth eclogue may have been an appeal to Varus to restore his father's farm.Much of the tone of sadness emanates not so much from the loss of the land, but from the loss of inspiration for his poetry.

L. Moeris, where do you go? Is it to town perhaps?

M. O Lycidas, that we have lived to come to this: that
    a stranger (whom we never feared), should grab our little farm
    and say, "The fields are mine now. Get off, tenants of old!"
    Beaten down, sad that Fortune's wheel turns again, reversing all,
    We drive these kids for him (let's hope it does him no good!).

L. Did I hear right, that where the hills slope down
    and move out from beyond the ridge right up to the water
    and to the ancient beeches, their tops broken —
    that all this Manalcas saved with his songs?   [Manalcas could be Virgil]

M. Yes, and the song (still unfinished) he sang to Varus:
    "Varus, your name, if only our Mantua be spared,   [towns supporting
    Mantua, ah so near, alas to wretched Cremona,   the losing side]
    singing swans will carry your name to the stars."

L. Start over with what you have. The Pierians have made   [The Muses'
    me a poet, too. I have my songs. Even the shepherds   [early home
    call me poet, but what do they know.   was Pieria]
    I'm not saying I sings as well as Varius or Cinna,
    my song's a goose's gabble next to the high-pitched swans.

[They each sing a song by Theocritus, a pastoral lament that if performed in the theater would strike the audience as both funny and sad, something like two Irishmen singing sad songs on their way home from the pub, endearing us to both, while we laugh at their off-key yodeling. Afterwards, Moeris and Lycidas would remain silent, thinking of their own sad losses, moved by the words of the song.

M. The years take everything away; the mind as well. I remember
    as a boy singing all day under the summer sun.
    So many songs I've forgotten; even Moeris loses
    his voice now, the wolves come close, they see me before
    I see them. But Menalcaswill sing them for you often enough.

L. You try our love too long with these apologies.
    And now the sea has calmed, a hush just for you, and look
    how the leaves dip, no wind whispering them to attention.
    And look, you can see Bianor's Tomb in the distance,
    we're halfway there. Here where the farmers strip
    the thickly-grown leaves, here, Moeris, let's do a few songs.
    Let the kids rest, We'll get to town no matter what, why rush.
    Or, if you think the rains going to come before nightfall,

> We can always walk, singing as we go.

> M. Let's no more of that, my boy. We've got work to do.
>   When Menalcas comes, we'll sing his songs, and sing them better.

The *Eclogues* was Virgil's first published work. It celebrated a love for the countryside and the bucolic concerns of shepherds and small farmers. The longing for a simpler time must have been deeply felt by all Romans who suffered through the severe political and social tensions of the time because Virgil's poems were an immediate and popular success. They were read in the theater where the poet was publicly acclaimed.

Though Virgil later came under the patronage of Maecenas, Augustus's chief minister of propaganda, it was Pollio, his first literary patron, who suggested he write a series of pastoral poems, perhaps using Theocritus as a model. **Theocritus**, the Hellenistic Greek, was the model for all pastoral poetry, and, in the opionion of many critics, has never been surpassed. Virgil composed a number of poems in this style, collectively called the *Eclogues*, though not all concerned with shepherds and shepherdesses and the usual subjects of the pastoral poem. Several of them are charming, though obviously imitative. The fourth eclogue, however, is of a different sort, containing a prophecy of the birth of a child who was to usher in a Golden Age. Christians, of course, took this to be a prophecy of the birth of Jesus, and this was probably the chief reason they looked upon Virgil as inspired. In one sense, the *Eclogues* clearly express Virgil's semi-mystical temperament, and the hopes aroused in him by the era of peace inaugurated by Augustus, who would become his patron at the urging of Maecaneas.

The term "eclogue" means "short selected poem." The book—ten short pieces, professedly fiction about imagined goatherds and other country people—was published a few years later and became an instant hit. On the surface, the poems appear to celebrate the peace of rustic life. The herdsmen are not just part of the idyll, but are themselves poets and singers of song. Several eclogues feature contests or duels between two shepherds to see who can create the best poem or song. Virgil opens the first eclogue identifying the point of contrast between the countryside and the city. Tityrus is helped by a divine young man in Rome and is able to return to his farm with a new appreciation for his tranquil life. Meliboeus, dispossessed of farm and house, will wander far and wide in search of purpose.

> I am not envious, more amazed: the countryside's
> All in such turmoil. Sick myslf, look, Tityrus,
> I drive goats forward; this one I can hardly lead.
> For here in the hazel thicket just now dropping twins,
> Ah, the flock's hope, on naked flint, she abandoned them.
> I keep remembering how the oak-trees touched of heaven,
> If we had been right-minded, foretold this evil time.

He asks why Tityrus went to Rome in the first place, and Tityrus tells his story.

> I used to think, Meliboeus, fool that I was,
> that the city men call Rome was like our market-town

where on market days we bring our lambs and kids to sell.
I had it all figured out. Puppies grow up to be hunting dogs,
so small things grow to be large. But Rome,Rome is different.
She has raised her head among the other cities
high as a cypress, standing tall
among the drooping shrubs and guelder-rose.
There was no hope of liberty nor thought of thrift.
Though many a sacrificial victim left my pens,
and much cream cheese was pressed for the ungrateful city,
my right hand never came back home heavy with bronze.

But beneath the lyric song and magical tales is a reminder of the forcible transfer of land into soldiers' hands, a ruthless re-location that even poetry was unable to reverse. Virgil's shepherds realize that poetry is often powerless in a world ruled by the War God, Mars. The first eclogue ends with Meliboeus lamenting his fate and the future of Rome.

You lucky old man, Tityrus, the land will remain your own,
and large enough for you, although bare rock and bog
with muddy rushes covers all the pasturage. . . .
Lucky old man, among familiar rivers here
and sacred springs you'll angle for the cooling shade;
the hedge this side, along your neighbor's boundary,
its willow flowers as ever feeding Hybla bees,
will often whisper you persuasively to sleep.
Then sooner will light-footed stags feed in the sky,
sooner in exile, wandering through each other's land,
will Parthian drink the Arar, or Germany the Tigris,
than from our memory will face ever fade.
But some must leave here, some for thirsty Africa,
Others for Scythia and Oäxes' chalky flood
and the Brittani quite cut off from the whole world.
Look, shall I ever, seeing after a long while
My father's bounds and my poor cabin's turf-heaped roof,
hereafter marvel at my kingdom—a few corn-ears?
Some godless veteran will own this fallow tilth,
these cornfields a barbarian. Look where strife has led
Rome's wretched citizens: we have sown fields for these!
Graft pear trees, Meliboeus, now set vines in rows.
Go, little she-goats, go, once happy flock of mine.
Not I hereafter, stretched full length in some green cave,
Shall watch you far off hanging on a thorny crag;
I'll sing no songs; not in my keeping, little goats,
You'll crop the flowering lucerne and bitter willow.

Tityrus consoles Meliboeus, offers him a place for the night, and closes the first eclogue with a haunting image, couched in Virgil's sonorous hexameters, a disquieting reminder that beneath the tranquil idylls lay the truths of how things are and portents of things to come.

I can offer you ripe fruit

and mealy chestnuts and abundance of milk cheese.
Far off the roof-tops of the farms already smoke
and down from the high mountains taller shadows fall.

Virgil provides no last comment from Meliboeus. The silence that follows is a stark, unsettling moment. Virgil was the poet Augustus chose to sing his praises, but this image is an odd way to say thank you to the young Octavian. Though told through the gauze of pastoral poetry, Virgil shows us the results of Octavian's victory—the disruption of the countryside, the evictions, the human loss. In poem after poem, he sets up a gentle reverie, as if we were one of the shepherds in those tranquil landscapes painted by Claude Lorraine in the 17th century, paintings modeled on the mood of the *Eclogues*, shepherds playing their flutes under a tree while cows and goats graze nearby. The first and last eclogue, as well as others inbetween, end with the image of evening shadows falling across the landscape—Virgil's way of reminding us that even nature cannot protect us from the flames of a world burning down.

It is often pointed out that Virgil lacked originality. His poems, they say, were mere imitations or distillations of the work of his predecessors. The overall structure and format of the *Eclogues* is almost a direct imitation of Theocritus' *Idylls*, ten short pieces that pictured a simpler time: Shepherds were the protagonists of the action, and everything seemed suspended in the tranquil world of nature brightened by the poetry of the shepherds' songs. The *Eclogues* were clearly written in the tradition of Greek pastoral poetry, and Theocritus' *Idylls* was that genre's finest example. The opening of the sixth eclogue shows the influence of Callimachus. Virgil invokes Lucretius in one eclogue, and Catullus in another. Part of Virgil's genius was his ability to use another poet's work for his own ends, appropriating its structure and content, then setting it within a different time and context, transforming in the process a simpler view into his own complex modern vision. Virgil had grown up in Theocritus' rural world. In the *Idylls* he found a motif through which the reader could perceive deeper implications. What Virgil did is without precedent in Roman literature, and in some ways, has hardly been attempted since. Virgil's is no simple process of imitation. While many paralellisms exist between Virgil's and Theocritus' poems, no single Virgilian eclogue stands in a one-to-one relations with a single Theocritean idyll. Out of the fabric of Theocritus' world, Virgil has woven a complex tapestry out of the fabric of Theocritus' world, characterized by neoteric learning, stylization, and a devotion to the poetic ideal. In this sense, the *Eclogues* is truly the first text of Augustan literature, which tended toward a reworking of Greek texts while treating them as classics. We know of no other ancient book of poetry that shows the same level of architectural complexity and unity. This first of Virgil's three literary works was but a dress rehearsal for his masterpiece, in which he took both the *Iliad* and the *Odyssey*, and reassembled story and structure into an epic poem that celebrated how things were, and at the same time, warned of things to come.

After defeating Brutus and Cassius in 42 BC at Philippi, Antony was asked by Octavian to reorganize the eastern half of the empire. In 41 BC, he met Cleopatra at Tarsus and spent the following winter with her in Egypt. Their twins, Alexander Helios and Cleopatra Selene were born a year later. When Antony returned to Italy, he renewed his alliance with Octavian by marrying Octavian's sister Octavia, and gave up his control of Gaul, thereby solidifying the division of the empire into east and west. Three years later, when he left for the east, he renewed his relationship with Cleopatra. Their third child Ptolemy Philadelphus was born.

At the outset, this liason did not bode well for Octavian, who knew that Antony's hand would be strengthened. A political partnership with Egypt gave Antony valuable economic resources and strategic advantage for control of the Mediterranean. Antony soon realized that he would eventually clash with Octavian. The following spring, Antony and Cleopatra hosted a ceremony (regarded by some as sacrilegious) where their children were paraded in the national costumes of the various countries they might inherit were Antony to become king of Egypt and/or Emperor of Rome. One of the children was Caesarion, whom Antony provocatively declared to be Caesar's acknowledged son.

The war between Antony and Octavian began with a propaganda campaign in Italy, orchestrated by Maceanas and won by Octavian. Coins depicting Octavian as heroic and wise were distributed throughout the empire, and graffiti critical of Antony turned up all over Rome. were struck that showed Octavian as a wise hero, while graffiti critical of Antony turned up all over Rome. Antony was portrayed as immoral and treacherous, and a formal oath was drafed by Maecenas in which all Italians swore loyalty to Octavian's cause. When Antony divorced Octavia to marry Cleopatra, Octavian published Antony's will, which left bequests to his children by Cleopatra and stipulated he wanted to be buried in Alexandria, not in Rome. Whatever support Antony had once had in Rome was gradually eroded. Spectacular games were held in public stadiums and crowds were whipped into a frenzy, demanding that Octavian declare war on Egypt. Octavian did, and the people waited to see what Antony would do—come back to Rome and fight for his country, or remain in Egypt and fight with Cleopatra. Antony sided with Cleopatra, an act which was perceived as treason.

The Battle of Actium, September 2, 31 BC.

Octavian and Agrippa built a special harbor on the bay of Naples for the purpose of assembling the greatest naval armada Rome would ever have. Their 400 ships were light and fast. Ground troops were organized totalling 80,000 infantry and 12,000 cavalry. Octavian sent messages to Antony that he would allow him safe passage to Italy, ports for his fleet to dock, and ground for his army to pitch their camp, where they could then do battle. Even though he was older than Octavian, Antony wrote back and challenged him to single combat. When that was refused, Antony proposed to meet Octavian in the Pharsalian fields, where Caesar and Pompey had fought. That was refused as well. While Antony waited with his fleet near Actium, Octavian left Maecenas in charge of Rome, and went to war in Greece, crossing the Ionian sea and landing at a place in Epirus called "the Ladle." Upon hearing of this, Cleopatra supposedly said, "We may well be frightened if

Octavian has got hold of the Ladle." But the inevitable clash finally came at Actium, where Antony had been forced to retreat.

Actium was a flat sandy promontory at the entrance to the Ambracian Gulf on the western coast of Macdeonia—about 50 miles north of Ithaca, Odysseus' homeland. A cult of Apollo was located at Actium. The cape was the site of Mark Antony's camp and gave its name to the naval battle fought just outside the gulf. There Antony and Cleopatra had assembled both their army and their fleet—500 ships, 75,000 legionaries, 25,000 light infantry and 12,000 cavalry. Across the Mediterranean to the southeast was Egypt; across the Adriatic to the west lay Rome. Octavian instructed Agrippa to attack Antony's supply lines at Methone on the western edge of the Peloponnese. Thus, Antony's vast and hungry land army could not rely on seaborne supplies from the south. In August, Agrippa's fleet sailed into view.

According to Plutarch's version, written a century after the event, Antony saw the enemy ships sail to the mouth of the bay and realized that Octavian would see that most of Antony's fleet was undermanned and unprepared for battle. Below is Plutarch's account of the battle in the famous Drydan translation published at the end of the 17th century (revised in 1864 by Arthur Hugh Clough).

> Antony armed all the rowers, and made a show upon the decks of being in readiness to fight; the oars were mounted as if waiting to be put in motion, and the vessels themselves drawn up to face the enemy on either side of the channel of Actium, as though they were properly manned and ready for an engagement. And Octavian, deceived by this strategem, retired.

In time, Agrippa's skillful naval attacks whittled away Antony's initial numerical superiority. In one action just off Actium, Antony lost nearly a quarter of his fleet to Agrippa.

Antony lost men daily, due not only to Agrippa's attacks, but to malaria, starvation, disease, and desertion. Rome's ships were now blockading the bay. Facing their 400 ships at the mouth of the bay were Cleopatra's 60 vessels and Antony's 170, all that remained after months of fighting. Cleopatra and her naval commanders wanted to take the fight to Rome's navy, using their larger ships to burst through the blockade—if successful they could continue on to Rome; if not, they could flee to Egypt and regroup. But Antony's land commanders were skeptical. They were strongest on land, that's where the showdown should occur, they counseled. Here's Plutarch's account is followed by Shakespeare's version in *Antony and Cleopatra*, based on Sir Thomas North's translation of Plutarch.

> Antony's fleet at that point was so unready on every occasion, that Antony was driven again to put his confidence in the land forces. Canidius, too, who commanded the legions, . . . was now of the advice that Cleopatra should be sent back, and that after, retiring into Thrace or Macdeonia, the quarrel should be decided in a land fight. For Dicomes, also, the King of the Gatae, promised to come and join him with a great army, and it would not be any kind of disparagment to Antony to yield the sea to Octavian, who, in the Sicilian wars, had had such long practice

in shipfighting; on the contrary, it would be simply ridiculous for Antony, who was by land the most experienced commander living, to make no use of his well-disciplined and numerous infantry, scattering and wasting his forces by parcelling them out in ships. But Cleopatra had an eye to flight, and ordering all her affairs, not as to assist in gaining a victory, but to escape with the greatest safety from the first commencement of a defeat.

When it was resolved to stand to a fight at sea, they set fire to all the Egyptian ships except sixty; and of these the best and largest, from ten banks down to three, he manned with twenty thousand full-armed men and two thousand archers. Here it is related that a foot captain, one that had fought often under Antony, and had his body all mangled with wounds, exclaimed, "O my general, what have our wounds and swords done to displease you, that you should give your confidence to rotten timbers? Let Egyptians and Phoenicians content the sea, give us land, where we know well how to die upon the spot or gain the victory."

Shakespeare, as usual, cuts to the bone of the dramatic moment.

> *Enobarus*
> Wage this battle at Pharsalia,
> Where Caesar fought with Pompey . . . .
> Your ships are not well mann'd,
> Your mariners are muleters, reapers, people
> Ingrossed by swift impress; in Octavian's fleet   [ingrossed=gathered]
> Are those ships that often   [impressed=conscription]
> have 'gainst Pmpey fought.
> Their ships are yare, yours heavy: No disgrace   [yare=light,
> Shall fall you for refusing him at sea,   easy to handle]
> Being prepared for land.

> *Antony*
>   By sea, by sea.

> *Enobarus*
> Most worthy sir, you therein throw away
> The absolute soldiership you have by land,
> Distract your army, which doth most consist
> Of war-marked footmen, leave unexecuted
> Your own renowned knowledge, quite forego
> The way which promises assurance, and
> Give up yourself merely to chance and hazard
> From firm security.

> *Antony*
>   I'll fight at sea.

> *Soldier*
> O noble emperor, do not fight by sea:
> Trust not to rotten planks. Do you misdoubt
> This sword and these my wounds? Let the Egyptians

And the Phoenicians go a-ducking: we
Have used to conquer standing on the earth
And fighting foot to foot.   [III,vii]

The truth is, Octavian wanted to avoid a sea battle as well. It was Agrippa who persuaded him that there was nothing to lose. If Antony and Cleopatra escaped and turn ed back to Egypt, it would only help their own campaign and demoralize Antony's land troops. Best to wait until the Egyptians made a run for it.

The weather was bad for days, but on September 2, the clouds lifted, the sky cleared, and the waters were calm.

> And they fought. Antony commanding with Publicola the right, and Coelius the left squadron, Marcus Octavius and Marcus Insteius the centre. Octavian gave the charge of the left to Agrippa, commanding in person on the right. As for the land forces, Canidius was general for Antony, Taurus for Octavian; both armies remaining drawn up in order along the shore. Antony in a small boat went from one ship to another, encouraging his soldiers, and bidding them stand firm and fight as steadily on their large ships as if they were on land. Of Octavian, they relate that, leaving his tent and going round, while it was yet dark, to visit theships, he met a man driving an ass, and asked him his name. He answered him that his own name was "Fortunate, and my ass," says he, "is called Conqueror." And afterwards, when he disposed the beaks of the ships in that place in token of his victory, the statue of this man and his ass in bronze were placed amongst them. After examining the rest of his fleet, he went in a boat to the right wing, and looked with much admiration at the enemy lying perfectly still in the straits, in all appearance as if they had been at anchor. For some considerable length of time he actually thought they were so, and kept his own ships at rest, at a distance of about eight furlongs from them. But about noon a breeze spung up from the sea, and Antony's men, weary of expecting the enemy so long, and trusting to their large tall vessels, as if they had been invincible, began to advance the left squadron.
>
> When they engaged, there was no charging or striking of one ship by another, because Antony's, by reason of their great bulk, were incapable of the rapidity required to make the stroke effectual, and on the other side, Octavian's did not charge head to head on Antony's, which were all armed with solid masses and spikes of brass; nor did they like even to run in on their sides, which were so strongly built with great squared pieces of timber, fastened together with iron bolts, that their vessels' beaks would easily have been shattered upon them. So that the engagement resembled a land fight, or, to speak yet more properly, the attack and defence of a fortified place. . . . with spears, javelins, poles, and several inventions of fire, which they flung among them, Antony's men using catapults also, to pur down missiles from wooden towers.

By afternoon, the wind shifted and pushed Agrippa's fleet northward. Cleopatra took advantage of this sudden breeze.

Cleopatra's sixty ships were seen hoisting sail and making out to sea in full flight, right through the ships that were engaged. The enemy was astonished to see them sailing off with a fair wind towards Peloponnesus. Here it was that Antony showed to all the world that he was no longer actuated by the thoughts and motives of a commander or a man, or indeed by his own judgment at all, and what was once said as a jest, that the soul of a lover lives in some one else's body, he proved to be a serious truth. For, as if he had been born part of her, and must move with her wheresoever she went, as soon as he saw her ship sailing away, he abandoned all that were fighting and spending their lives for him, and put himself aboard a galley of five banks of oars to follow her that had so well begun his ruin and would hereafter accomplish it.

She, perceiving him to follow, gave the signal to come aboard. So, as soon as he came up with them, he was taking into the ship. But without seeing her or letting himself be seen by her, he went forward by himself, and sat alone, without a word, in the ship's prow, covering his face with his two hands. . . . And thus he remained for three days, either in anger with Cleopatra, or wishing not to upbraid her, at the end of which they touched at Taenarus. Here the women of their company succeeded first in bringing them to speak, and afterwards to eat and sleep together. And, by this time, several of the ships of burden and some of his friends began to come in to him from the rout, bringing news of his fleet's being quite destroyed, but that the land forces, they thought, still stood firm.

Cleopatra's escape was not promted by panic; she had planned it in advance, but Antony's was a surprise to everyone—his enemies, his troops, and even, it seems, to himself. Perhaps only Cleopatra could have predicted it. Anton's retreat left his land army to fend for itself. At first his men couldn't believe that he had fled. As word spread, there was sporadic fighting that lasted a few more days. Finally, realizing that realized that Antony was gone, the remaining troops surrendered to Octavian.

When it became clear to Antony that his campaign was lost, he sent a new challenge to Octavian to fight him hand-to-hand, but as before Octavian declined, saying that he could not die more honorably than in battle, and that he would endeavor to do so on land and sea. Antony knew that by the next day, Octavian's forces would arrive, and he made preparations. Cleopatra, fearing that Antony might come to repay her for her betrayal, locked herself in her monument and sent word to Antony that she had killed herself. Antony berated himself for not having the courage to do the same, then called his faithful servant, whose name was Eros, to run him through with his sword. Eros drew the sword, but suddenly turning round, slew himself. "It is well done, Eros," said Antony, "you show your master how to do what you had not the heart to do yourself." Then he removed the sword from Eros and ran it through his own belly. Later, Antony's body was hoised up to her monument. Seeing his body, Cleopatra took her own life.

The romantic view of Antony, as portrayed by Plutarch, shows him to be a great general with unusual powers of leadership and personal charm, who was destroyed by his own weaknesses. The faults which characterized his youth came back to haunt him in the end. But he was also a great orator and astute politician who lost the war of propaganda to Octavian and the military campaign to Agrippa, Octavian's chief general. It's tempting to speculate on what would have happened had he defeated Octavian and led the empire in the decades ahead. Until late in the war, Antony had the support of many old republicans who preferred him to Caesar's heir, Octavian. Most of Antony's administrative arrangements in the east were clear-sighted and continued by Octavian. All of Antony's chidlren were killed by Octavian, except for the two daughters born to Octavian's sister, both named Antonia—"the Elder" and "the Younger"—whose children Gaius, Claudius, and Nero each became Roman Emperors.

Saving the Republic had seemed impossible, but Octavian did what Caesar was unable to do, he proclaimed himself emperor Augustus Caesar and transformed the Roman Republic into the Roman Empire.

ROME: The Empire

The literature of Rome is a good example of how a clean break in political history does not always correspond to a clean break in the history of literature. Lucilius, who died in 102 BC, is still considered pre-classical, yet in his satires we encounter a decidedly subjective character, which was also to mark the later development of Roman poetry. This development reached its first peak with Lucretius and Catullus .

The Republican system in Rome broke down in the first century BC when the aristocracy tried to use it to govern a world empire. Following the assassination of Caesar in 44 BC, a period of civil war ensued. Five years after Octavian—Caesar's adopted son—put down the rebels by defeating Mark Anthony at the Battle of Actium in 32 BC, he became Emperor and took the name Augustus Caesar, marking the transition from the period of the Roman revolution to the beginnings of Empire. There is no question that Augustus's use of Virgil, Horace, Ovid and other poets to propagandize the needs of the new state coincided with the beginning of Rome's **Golden Age** of Poetry. The poets and the state needed one another; indeed, each made the other possible. Augustus died in 14 AD, Ovid in 17 AD, and Virgil in 19 AD. In this case, there's a clear connection between political and literary ages. The poets of the Augustan age embodied the Latin humanistic tradition, which remained fundamental to the literature and intellectual life of Europe until early modern times.

The age of Nero (made emperor after the death of Claudius in 54 AD) marked the beginning of a second flowering of Roman literature known as the Silver period of Latin verse. Many of the epic poets of this age, such as Lucan and Statius, looked to Virgil as their model, and satiric poets such as Martial, Persius, and Juvenal took up the tone and line pioneered by Horace. **The Silver Age** lasted close to a century. The Roman Emperor Hadrian died in 138; Juvenal died two years later. The Silver Age ends and **the period of Iron and Rust** begins when Latin literature becomes saturated with rhetoric.

Rome began its history about the year 500 BC as a city-state republic, with a few square miles of territory on the southern bank of the Tiber. It was as a republic that Rome spread her conquests over nearly the whole civilized world during the following five centuries, a period of almost continuous warfare with unparalleled success. Ancient empires and barbarian tribes were reduced to the position of subject peoples. There was a vast territory to exploit, and the prizes of power were enormous. The leading aristocractic families could no longer work out an equitable division of power and dissension led to revolution. The history of first century BC Rome is the story of struggles for power within the republican oligarchy. Each family tried to eliminate its competitors, each family tried to gain control of the Senate and the military, not to mention imperial office. After Caesar's assassination in 44 BC, anarchy was followed by civil war, and eventually one family succeeded in attaining supremacy—the family of Augustus Caesar, the Julio-Claudian line. It was Caesar's grandnephew, Octavian, adoped by Julius as his own son, who finally brought order with the final defeat of Mark Anthony and the rebels at the Battle of Actium in 31 BC. City and provinces alike welcomed the firm rule of Octavian. Rome discovered that an empire needed an emperor and Octavian proclaimed himself Emperor of Rome, taking the name Augustus Caesar. To Augustus and his successors over the next two centuries was left the task of transforming Rome from a city-state to a world-state with universal citizenship and political unity.

It was in Augustan times that Roman poetry reached its summit. The influence of the Greeks was for a long time paramount, the epic being the consumate form of poetic enterprise, but three new genres were developed by the Romans—satire, the satirical epigram, and letter writing. The great Roman poets combined precise expression with a perfection of form in various genres—epic, ode, satire, and love. The result was a measured balance of metrics and poetic rhythm, a perfect congruence of form and content. Poets of this age, with the exception of Ovid, labored to write a polished verse that was stylistically and intellectually challenging; they did not dash off one epistle after another for quick consumption. The Greeks had also composed epigrams, but the Romans extended the form from short panegyrics praising famous people and events to pointed, witty and often biting thumbnail sketches, such as those written by Martial. The Romans may well have invented the novel, of which the earliest example known to us is the *Satyricon* of Petronius.

These poets also helped to consolidate a new political system. The Augustan ideology used propaganda to justify and legitimize its own claims. The Roman ruling class had always used art, literature, coins, architecture and public games to support their social prestige and to remind all citizens of the achievements of their respective families, but never before had it been done on such a scale. What was unique in Augustan propaganda was the size of the "tool kit," the massive manipulation of public views, the molding of opinion to identify one man and his family with the sovereignty of the state. In Octavian's fight against Pompey and Mark Anthony, slogans and mottos—"revenge for Caesar"—were launched under an all-Italian banner. The lessons of Caesar's murder and the decades of civil war that followed were not lost on Octavian. His apparent respect for republican tradition was used to cloak his own power. When Octavian proclaimed himself Emperor Augustus, he brought into his fold the writers and poets of his day to glorify his imperial control, using the best and the brightest to mask the contradictions between façade and reality.

Virgil and Horace were the foremost contributors to the atmosphere in which the political system of Augustus became stabilized. The uniqueness of their achievement was due in no small measure to the very aloofness and discretion they were able to maintain. We would certainly not consider them "court poets." Only with Ovid, a generation later, do we find the exaggerated veneration of the Emperor, which became customary thereafter in the panygeric. Though Ovid did this for personal reasons, it was most ironic that of them all, he alone became a victim of the new regime. Despite his attempts to write the "unobjectionable" long major poem such as his masterpiece, the *Metamorphoses*, he was unable to alter his fate—exiled by Augustus to die in a small village on the coast of the Black Sea.

♣

☞ **Virgil** (70-19 BC), *The Aeneid*,

Homer's *Odyssey* was about a Greek hero, the "nimble-witted" Odysseus, who returned to his home in Greece after defeating the Trojans and burning the city of Troy. Virgil's *Aeneid*, written 750 years later, was about a Trojan warrior, "pious and dutiful" Aeneas, who survived the fall of Troy, and after long wanderings, founded a Trojan settlement, Lavinium, named after his Italian bride Lavinia. This settlement was in the part of Italy called Latium. His son Ancanius became the first King and from that settlement came Alba Longa, and eventually the city of Rome. Thus, Aeneas became through his (Trojan) son the founder of Rome, and ultimately, the founder of the Roman empire. Link Augustus to Aeneas, and the Emperor becomes the culmination of a thousand years of history, the crowning moment of Roman destiny.

Virgil began writing the poem two years after Octavian defeated Mark Anthony at the Battle of Actium in 31 BC. After Octavian proclaimed himself Augustus Caesar, he looked to several prominent poets to write the great epic that would ordain and glorify the new imperial state. Most poets shied away from such a monumental task, including Horace, Propertius, and Ovid. Not so Virgil. In his first book of poems, the *Eclogues*, he wrote that he looked forward to the day when he'd be able to compose Rome's great epic poem.

> Now the last age of Cumae's prophecy has come;
> The great succession of centuries is born afresh.
> Now too returns the Virgin; Saturn's rule returns;
> A new begetting now descends from heaven's height.
> O chaste Lucina, look with blessing on the boy
> Whose birth will end the iron race at last and raise
> a Golden through the world: now your Apollo rules.
> With you to guide, if traces of our sin remain,

They, nullified, will free the lands from lasting fear.
He will receive the life divine, and see the gods
Mingling with heroes, and himself be seen of them
And rule a world made peaceful by his father's virtues.

This famous passage from Eclogue IV was later interpreted by Christians as Virgil's prophecy of the coming of Christ. To the Romans, it could have referred to the child that might have been borne from the marriage of Anthony and Octavia (Octavian's sister), which temporarily averted war between the two men. But to most Roman's, the child was Octavian himself, the adopted son of Julius Caesar, the beloved Emperor of a Golden Age. As Augustus Caesar, Octavian would spark a return to order, prosperity, agriculture and commerce, as well as art and literature.

Look at the cosmos trembling in its massive round,
Lands and the expanse of ocean and the sky profound;
Look how they all are full of joy at the age to come!
O then for me may long life's latest part remain
And spirit great enough to celebrate your deeds!
Linus will not defeat me in song, nor Thracian Orpheus,
Though one should have his father's aid and one his mother's,
Orpheus Callíope and Linus fair Apollo.
If Pan challenged me, with Arcady as judge,
Pan too, with Arcady as judge, would own defeat.

Virgil was not afaid of this challenge. How much more confidence can a poet have than to assume that no one could match his song, not Orpheus, the greatest singer and musician of Greek mythology, nor the ancient and mournful Linus, a music teacher killed with his own lyre by Heracles. Virgil hoped that one day he'd have the chance to prove what he could do.

But you who now sail past the rocks of great Timavus
Or coast the Illyrian sea — say, will there ever come
The day when I may be allowed to tell your deeds?

Most of the other poets who felt the pressure to write "the Great Roman Epic" made it clear that they were artistically ill-equipped to do so, or would not do so even if they could. Perhaps they sensed the difficulty of such a task. The conceptual problems alone were complex. Does one make Augustus the hero of such a poem, glorifying the Republic, its subversion and the civil wars which were brought to an end by Octavian's victory? Or would it be better to use a mythical hero and set the story in a historical . . . . or maybe mythical past. But what was Rome's mythical past? Most Romans assumed their city was founded eight centuries earlier by Romulus and Remus, the twin sons of Rhea Silvia, whose father Numitor, was the rightful King of Alba Longa. Numitor was overthrown by his brother, Amulius, who made Rhea a Vestal Virgin to ensure that she did not marry and produce an heir. But Rhea was impregnated by Mars, the God of War. She was then imprisoned by Amulius, and her twins thrown into the Tiber. Luckily they were washed ashore, suckled by a she-wolf, and eventually founded the settlement that would someday become the city of Rome.

Virgil realized at some point that Augustus could not be his hero, mythical or otherwise but he also knew that the whole point of the epic was to glorify Augustus. Such an epic in the Homeric tradition must call upon the writers who came before Virgil—such as Ennius and Naevius—then reach back to the cultural ideas Rome had inherited from Greece, a civilization Rome had conquered. The story should evoke the same heroic grandeur contained in the *Iliad* and the *Odyssey*. Virgil later confessed to a friend that he must have been mad to attempt it. Furthermore, the story of Romulus and Remus was not suitable for an epic, and had no direct link with Augustus.

There were other legends to consider. Some wanted Romans to link their history with that of Greece, or with legendary Troy, defeated by Greece in 1184 BC (which became the subject of Homer's *Iliad*). But Romulus and Remus were supposed to have founded Rome in the 8th century. To reconcile these distant origins a story was proposed that Rhea's twins were descendants of Aeneas (a character mentioned briefly at the end of Homer's *Iliad*), whose son, Ancanius becomes the first of a series of Alban kings. The last king in Aeneas's line of descent was Amulius, responsible for throwing his twin nephews into the Tiber. By the 3rd century BC, Aeneas's wanderings from the shores of his homeland to Italy was familiar to everyone. In the 2nd century BC, the Julian family, Julius Caesar above all, exploited his family's supposed descent from Aeneas and the mother of Aeneas, the goddes Venus, for political aggrandizement. By using Aeneas as his hero, Virgil could present the triumphs of a thousand years of Roman history as the overture to the Golden Age of Augustus. Part of Virgil's vision was the conception of Italy as a single nation, and of Roman history as a continuum from the founding of a settlement that would become the city of Rome to the fulfilled promise of the city that would become the Roman Empire. The traits that Virgil gave to Aeneas were models for every Roman boy: dutiful and obedient to the will of the gods, a responsible leader to his people, and a devoted father and son. In the *Aeneid*, Virgil escapes from Troy and eventually lands in Italy, where he defeats the Rutulians, an Italian people whose leader was Turnus. The Romans knew this history when they read the *Aeneid*, but just to make sure, Jupiter, in Book I, reminds the reader of Aeneas' destiny:

> In Italy he will fight a massive war,
> Beat down fierce armies, then for the people there
> Establish city walls and a way of life.
> When the Rutulians are subdued he'll pass
> Three summer of command in Latium,
> Three years of winter quarters. But the boy,
> Ascanius, to whom the name of Iulus
> Now is added—Iulus while Ilium stood—
> Will hold the power for all of thirty years,
> Great rings of wheeling months. He will transfer
> His capital from Lavinium and make
> A fortress, Alba Longa. Three full centuries   [Hector,
> That kingdom will be ruled by Hector's race,   the Trojan warrior
> Until the queen and priestess, Rhea Silvia   slain by Achilles
> Pregnant by Mars, will bear twin sons to him.   in the *Iliad*]
> Afterward, happy in the tawny pelt
> His nurse, the she-wolf, wears, young Romulus

Will take the leadership, build walls of Mars,
And call by his own name his people Romans.
For these I set no limits, world or time,
But make the gift of empire without end.
.... From that comely line
The Trojan Caesar comes, to circumscribe
Empire with Ocean, fame with heaven's stars.
Julian his name, from Iulus handed down:
All tranquil shall you take him heavenward
In time, laden with plunder of the East,
And he with you shall be invoked in prayer.
Wars at an end, harsh centuries then will soften, . . .
And grim with iron frames, the Gate of War
Will then be shut: inside, unholy Furor,
Squatting on cruel weapons, hands enchained
Behind him by a hundred links of bronze,
Will grind his teeth and howl with bloodied mouth.

Though unholy Furor waits in the wings, Augustus brings to the world a period of peace and stability, an optimistic time of hope that inspired Rome's greatest poets. The epic of the *Aeneid* was its crowning achievement, a masterpiece of such stunning complexity, that even today critics are unsure what to make of it. In those few lines above, Virgil depicts the coming of Augustus as a miracle of history, but embedded in the poem are reminders of the price paid for empire, the toll exacted from its hero. Augustus must have realized that the poem's stark ending suggests that Dido's curse and prophecy were yet to be fulfilled: as Aeneas had lost his humanity to found the Republic, Augustus will lose his soul to rule the Empire. Virgil's poem is not just a simple heroic epic, but a cautionary tale that must have been disturbing to Romans who could read between the lines and chose to. It remains a cautionary tale for us as well.

The dutiful son of a fairly prosperous farmer, Virgil was born October 15 near Mantua in the Roman province of Cisalpine Gaul, as the north of Italy was then called. After schooling in Cremona and Milan, he was sent to Rome to study rhetoric and the physical sciences, but didn't stand up well in the competitive city of Rome: one story has it that he appeared once as an attorney and thereafter gave up the idea of practicing law. He joined an Epicurean group at Naples to study their philosophy, which he probably first encountered through reading *On the Nature of Things* by Lucretius. Eventually, he returned to his father's farm, where he continued to study Greek philosophy and poetry.

Despite his education, amd rugged good looks, he was slow spoken and shy; many took him for an illiterate peasant. Donatus, the fourth-century poet, scholar, and author of the *Life of Virgil*, wrote that Virgil shunned publicity, was bisexual, of weak health, and abstemious. He was twenty-five when Caesar was assassinated, plunging all the Roman world, even the small villages, into political chaos and civil war. A quarter of Italy's land changed hands in the proscriptions, evictions, and bloody reprisals that followed. Vast areas of Italy were devasted by fighting and famine, and Rome's very survival in doubt.

His father's farm lay within the territory confiscated by the ruling Triumvirs for the purpose of bestowing grants of land upon their soldiers. Forced to desert his heritage upon peril of death, Virgil escaped by swimming the river Mincio, working his way south, and finally settling again in Rome. There he began to write the *Eclogues*, a collection of "Pastoral Poems" also called the *Bucolics,* or "cowherds songs." [see discussion of the Eclogues on page 317]

THE AENEID

Though modeled on Homer, the *Aeneid* is not the simple celebration of heroic adventures it purports to be. It conveys a certain ambivalence toward the origins of the empire. Virgil wrote about war with a harsh clarity still unsurpassed by more realistic mediums—paintings, photographs, newsreels, television and movies. Slow motion scenes from *Platoon* or *The Wild Bunch* that show bloody bodies flying through the air or a soldier waving his arms at a rescuing helicopter as he is riddled in the back by bullets—the gory display of death presented in filmic ballet—approach the effect Virgil creates when he renders such scenes in phrases one might use to describe birds resting on a tree at sunset.

> The onward rush of men and horses neighing
> Blazed in the sunlight. When they came within
> Spear-throw of one another, Trojan and Latin
> Pulled up in a halt; then, all at once,
> With shouts they spurred their furious mounts and flung
> Their javelins in showers from both sides
> As thick as snow-flakes, making a daytime dusk.
> Now shaft to shaft, Tyrrhenus and the savage
> Latin horseman, Aconteus, met head-on
> With a mighty crash that caused the first downfall
> From shock of horses, breast to bursting breast:
> Aconteus, pitched off like a thunderbolt
> Or stone out of a catapult, came down
> Far off, his life dispersed into the air. . . .
> Now, when they came together a third time,
> The two formations mingled, man to man,
> And then indeed groans of the dying rose,
> Then arms and bodies in a mire of blood
> Went down, and dying horses, with their riders
> Butchered, as the bitter fight surged on.
> Orsilochus, in dread of meeting Remulus,
> Hurled his javelin at the other's mount
> And left the steel point under it's ear; at this
> The war-horse reared in fury, forelegs high,
> To shake the wound away, with towering chest,
> And Remulus was thrown to earth. Catillus
> Brought down Iollas, then Herminius,
> Great-souled, great bodied warrior, his bare head
> Flowing with tawny locks, his shoulders bare.
> Wounds held no terrors for him, great as he was,

Fighting uncovered — but the driven lance
A-quiver passed clean through his shoulder's breadth
And made him double up in agony.
Dark blood spilt everywhere. Men dealt out death
By cold steel as they fought and strove by wounds
To win the beauty of courageous death.

Or this scene at the end of the *Aeneid* in which Turnus is finally struck down by a spear, then raises his hand to plead for his life.

Just as in dreams when the night-swoon of sleep
Weighs on our eyes, it seems we try in vain
To keep on running, try with all our might,
But in the midst of effort faint and fail; . . . .
                      just so with Turnus now:
However bravely he made shift to fight
The immortal fiend blocked and frustrated him.
Flurrying images passed through his mind.
He gazed at the Rutulians, and beyond them,
Gazed at the city, hesitant, in dread.
He trembled now before the poised spear-shaft
And saw no way to escape; he had no force
With which to close, or reach his foe, no chariot
And no sign of the charioteer, his sister.
At a dead loss he stood. Aeneas made
His deadly spear flash in the sun and aimed it,
Narrowing his eyes for a lucky hit.
Then, distant still, he put his body's might
Into the throw. Never a stone that soared
From a wall-battering catapult went humming
Loud as this, nor with so great a crack
Burst ever a bolt of lightening. It flew on
Like a black whirlwind bringing devastation,
Pierced with a crash the rim of sevenfold shield,
Cleared the cuirass' edge, and passed clean through
THe middle of Turnus' thigh. Force of the blow
Brought the huge man to earth, his knees buckling,
And a groan swept the Rutulians as they rose,
A groan heard eachoing on all sides from all
The mountain range, and echoed by the forests.
The man brought down, brought down low, lifted his eyes
And held his right hand out to make his plea:

This is a classic moment; we've seen this in movies time after time. Whether it's John Wayne or Mel Gibson, the hero does not kill the bad guy when he's defenseless and down. How Virgil resolves this moment that closes the *Aeneid* is nothing short of brilliant, yet expected, if one has followed the tragedy of the hero instead of the success of his heroic efforts to found a new nation. One suspects that Virgil's real purpose was to hint at the human cost of political and military triumph: Aeneas' life was ruled by his sense of duty to his gods, his people, and his family. Can a heroic civilization recover what its heroic founder had to lose? Writing this epic was not just a display of genius, it was an act of courage: while fulfilling the emperor's desire for a glorification of his methods and divine status, Virgil hinted at the madness of those methods, war's waste and ugliness, and how it makes us—gods and mortals alike—ugly as well.

Virgil soon got to know Horace, and through Horace he met Caius Maecenas, a wealthy businessman and minister of culture under Augustus. Maecenas generously patronized literature and art, and was himself the center of the literary society of the day. Upon reading the *Eclogues*, Maecenas encouraged the young emperor to return the farm to Virgil, which he did.

In the period that followed, Augustus brought security and prosperity, and that surplus wealth trickled down to literature and art. Augustus believed it was better to have the populace taken up by literature than by politics and insurrection. He was so generous to poets that they flocked around him wherever he went. After one persistent Greek continued to push poems into his hands as he left his palace, Augustus stopped in his tracks, wrote a few stanzas, and handed them to the supplicant. The poet read them, scraped up a few coins and put them in the Emperor's palm, to which Augustus, rewarding this poet's humor if not his poetry, had an attendant give him what amounted then to $25,000. An instant NEA Fellowship.

More books were published during Augustus's reign than ever before. Everyone from the foolish to the wise wrote poetry. Literary readings were held all over Rome, in cafés, open squares, and the gardens of the rich. Most Roman literature borrowed models from Attic Greece, but the satire was wholly Roman. **Juvenal**, the last of the Roman satirists, focused on the dark, lurid, and frequently revolting vices of a decadent Rome: the decay of the great noble houses and the contempt for morality, shown by all in the pursuit of wealth. He combined a street-talk idiom with flowing hexameters and a lusty style. In his witty and acerbic *Satires*, he decided to get back at all the poets who had bored him at readings of epic poetry by writing—not the epic, but satires, like Horace wrote. After all, he said, Rome being what it is, it is difficult *not* to write satire. "*Difficile est saturam non scribere.*"

> Must I always be stuck back in the audience at these poetry-readings, never
> Up on the platform myself, taking it out on Cordus
> For the times he's bored me to death with ranting speeches
> From that *Theseid* of his? Is X to get off scot-free
> After inflicting his farces on me, or Y his elegies? Is there
> No recompense for whole days wasted on prolix
> Versions of *Telephus*? And what about that *Orestes*—
> Each margin of the roll crammed solid, top and bottom,
> More on the back, and *still* it wasn't finished.
> The stale themes are bellowed daily
> In rich patrons' colonnades, till their marble pillars
> Crack with a surfeit of rhetoric. The plane-trees echo
> Every old trope—what the winds are up to, whose ghost
> Aeacus has on his hellish rack, from what far country
> The other fellow is sneaking off with that golden sheepskin.

You get the same stuff from them all, established poet
And raw beginner alike. When you find
Hordes of poets on each street-corner, it's misplaced kindness
To refrain from writing. The paper will still be wasted.
Don't you want to cram whole notebooks with scribbled invective
When you stand at the corner and see some forger carried past
On the necks of six porters, lounging back, like Maecenas
In the open litter?

Despite the wrench of parting, I applaud my old friend's
Decision to make his home in lonely Cumae—the poor
Sibyl will get at least one fellow-citizen now! Myself, I would value
A barren offshore island more than Rome's urban heart:
Squalor and isolation are minor evils compared
To this endless nightmare of fires and collapsing houses,
The cruel city's myriad perils—and poets reciting
Their work in *August!*

Poets crowded into the many bookstores along the Argiletum to compare writers. Those who couldn't afford to buy the books, read them standing among the bookstalls. Placards on the walls advertised the latest titles. Chapbooks sold for a few coins; the average volume cost what amounts to five-dollars today. For a beautiful edition, illustrated with portraits of the author, you might have to pay $15. Rome was to rival Alexandria as the literary center of the world.

In Rome, during the Augustan period, we find evidence of a publishing boom. A well-organized body of publishers utilized connections with Athens, Asia Minor, and Alexandria, importing Greek manuscripts and distributing books as far afield as Spain, and Gaul (present day France), and the far off Roman towns in Great Britain. We find numerous references in the literature of this period to the relations of authors with their publishers and to the business interests retained by authors in the sale of their books. The Augustan age gives us the first example of a culture disseminating its literature for posterity. Writers marketed and distributed their work to reach an extensive reading public. Some Roman gentleman in his villa in Gaul, Germany, or far off Britain was able to order copies of the latest ode of Horace or satire of Juvenal—the beginnings of an effective publishing organization.

It's not certain how those early authors were compensated. Records are scanty or confusing. Apart from the aid granted by wealthy patrons like Maecenas, it seemed the rewards of literary production were often meagre and precarious. Where the Romans had Augustus and Maecaneas, we now have the NEA and the Lannan Foundation. Now, as in Virgil's day, most poets either have a second profession, or struggle to survive day to day.

Maecenas, seen above in Juvenal's satire being carried through the streets of Rome, was one of many wealthy patrons who supported literature by giving poets and artists land, estates, and money to finance their literary endeavors. He took a liking to Virgil, who was ill at ease in the fashionable literary marketplace. A shortage of grain threatened another revolution and Maecenas encouraged Virgil to write poems that would glorify agricultural life in order to attract young men crowding the city to return to the farms.

The *Georgics*, or "Poems of Farm Life," was based on Hesiod's *Works and Days*, but like the *Bucolics*, it evokes sense of the past and imbues the present with an aura of hopefulness that Rome, under Augustus, will enter an era of peace. Many consider it the most original didactic poem in the Latin language, and, considering its purpose, more effective than the *Aeneid*, which contained much of the poet's best work. The *Georgics* established Virgil's position as the chief poet of his age. Though it successfully depicts the atmosphere of the Italian farm life in which the poet was reared, all of the scenes, no matter how detailed, are presented with a halo of romance upon them. The *Georgics* was not regarded as a handbook of agriculture, even in Virgil's time; the rural ecstasies were written more to please an urban taste. After reading the book, no city dweller exchanged his tunic for a sheepskin, nor did any homeowner packed his bags only to swap the Forum for a farm.

With Virgil's subsequent fame came an invitation to live on the minister's estate in Naples and begin work on a more ambitious project, which Virgil had already outlined. The civil wars now over, the victorious Augustus began laying the foundations of imperial government. It was at this time that Virgil began the poem which was to be the supreme expression of national life, a story about the imagined origin of the Roman nation in times long before the foundation of Rome itself. He chose to work in the most exalted genre of classical literature, the epic. Epic poems form a large class, beginning with the Babylonian epic of *Gilgamesh* over four thousand years ago and Homer's *Iliad* and *Odyssey* more than a thousand years after it. After much consideration, he decided on the story of the Trojan prince Aeneas, the son of Venus, the Goddess of Love, and of a mortal father, Anchises. It was Aeneas' descendants who founded Rome. Again Virgil used an ancient model, this time the *Iliad* and *Odyssey* of Homer. The *Iliad* dealt with the Greek side of the war against Troy, or Ilium; the war was fought over Helen of Troy, "the face that launched a thousand ships." According to the Greek myth, Helen and Clytemnestra were sisters, the latter fathered by Zeus. Her mother was Leda, who, in the form of a swan, laid an egg and from this Helen was hatched. In the literary tradition, she is the entirely human wife of King Menelaus of Sparta, the younger brother of Agamemnon, King of Mycenae and leader of the Greek forces in the Trojan war. The *Odyssey* tells how Agamemnon, on his return from Troy, was feasted in the palace of his wife's lover, and there murdered by them both, together with his captive lover, Cassandra. Famous for her outstanding beauty, Helen bore Menelaus a daughter, but while he was absent in Crete, Paris arrived in Sparta, and either persuaded Helen to flee with him or carried her off by force to Troy. When Menelaus returned and discovered what had happened, he and his brother Agaamemnon raised an expedition of a thousand ships against Troy to seek vengeance. In the *Iliad,* Helen was a tragic figure, aware that her wrong-doing has caused suffering for everyone. In writing the *Iliad*, Homer focuses on the the tenth and final year of the seige of Troy, and the theme is the "wrath of Achilles," arising from an affront to his honor given by Agamemnon, the leader of the Greek army, yet its action encapsulates the whole war, with the final death of the Trojan hero, Hector symbolizing the fall of Troy that will soon follow. The *Odyssey* traced the homeward voyage of the Greek hero Odysseus after the burning of Troy. Virgil begins his narrative where the *Iliad* ended and the *Odyssey* began, but instead of following

Odysseus, we accompany Aeneas and his Trojan warriors who are not returning home, but trying to find a new one for their people and their gods.

As Homer's *Iliad* closes, Priam, Hector's father, hears that Achilles will return the body of his son if he pays sufficient ransom. The messenger of Zeus speaks to him "in a small voice, and yet the shivers took hold of his body:"

> "Take heart, Priam, son of Dardanos, do not be frightened.
> I come to you not eyeing you with evil intention
> but with the purpose of good toward you. I am a messenger
> of Zeus, who far away cares much for you and is pitiful.
> The Olympian orders you to ransom Hector the brilliant,
> to bring gifts to Achilles which may soften his anger:
> along, let no other man of the Trojans go with you, but only
> let one elder herald attend you, one who can manage
> the mules and the easily running wagon, so he can carry
> the dead man, whom great Achilles slew, back to the city."

Priam's wife fears that the Greeks will kill Priam once he is in their camp. She counsels that they

> sit apart in our palace
> now, and weep for Hektor, and the way at the first strong Destiny
> spun with his life line when he was born, when I gave birth to him,
> that the dogs with their shifting feet should feed on him, far from his
> parents
> gone down before a stronger man; I wish I could set teeth
> in the middle of his liver and eat it. That would be vengeance
> for what he did to my son; for he slew him when he was no coward
> but standing before the men of Troy and the deep-girdled women
> of Troy, with no thought in his mind of flight or withdrawal."

Priam tells her he plans to go, that if it is his destiny to die by the ships of the "bronze-armoured Achaians," he will accept it. "Achilleus can slay me at once, with my own son caught in my arms, once I have my fill of mouring above him." Then Priam lashes out in anger at the Trojan warriors assembled in his halls.

> "Get out, you failures, you disgraces. Have you not also
> mourning of your own at home that you come to me with your sorrows?
> Is it not enough that Zeus, son of Kronos, has given me sorrow
> in losing the best of my sons.? You also shall be aware of this
> since you will be all the easier for the Achaians to slaughter
> now he is dead. But, for myself, before my eyes look
> upon this city as it is destroyed and its people are slaughtered,
> my wish is to go sooner down to the house of the death god."

Then, after chasing the men out with a stick, he scolds his own sons "cursing Helenos, and Paris, Agathon the brilliant, Pammon and Antiphones, Polites of the great war cry, Deïphobos and Hippothoös and proud Dios. There were nine sons to whom now the old man gave orders and spoke to them roughly."

"Make haste, wicked children, my disgraces. I wish all of you
had been killed beside the running ships in the place of Hector.
Ah me, for my evil destiny. I have had the noblest
of sons in Troy, but I say not one of them is left to me,
Mestor like a god and Troiles whose delight was in horses,
and Hector, who was a god among men, for he did not seem like
one who was child of a mortal man, but of a god. All these
Ares has killed, and all that are left me are the disgraces,
the liars and the dancers, champions of the chorus, the plunderers
of their own people in their land of lambs and kids. Well then,
will you not get my wagon ready and be quick about it,
and put all these things on it, so we can get on with our journey?"

Priam is told that the Trojans will be given five days to bury Hector and mourn their loss, then the city will be burned. The *Iliad* ends with the Trojans taking several days just to assemble a towering pyre for burning. While the fire is still raging, brothers and companions of Hector gather his bones up, lay them in a golden casket wrapped in purple robes, and set it down into the hollow of a grave. "Such their burial of Hector, the breaker of horses." Though Homer ends the poem with this line, focusing on Hector's heroic end, readers knew that what was to follow was the burning and destruction of Troy.

This is where Virgil's *Aeneid* begins. In the first half of the *Aeneid,* Virgil follows the familiar structure of the *Odyssey*. In flashback, Aeneas tells the story of the fall of Troy and his escape, the same way *Odysseus* did in Homer's epic. But it is how Virgil changes his models that marks his genius. The second half of the *Aeneid* invokes the structure of the *Iliad*. In so doing, Virgil seems to defy the laws of dramatic action. He goes from a dazzling opening—the first four books about the fall of Troy and Aeneas' escape, then his affair with Dido and her suicide as he sails off for Italy—to Book Six where he descends into the underworld. Romans knew this episode from the *Odyssey*, when Tireseas, the blind seer, tells Odysseus what is to come of his journey. In Virgil's poem, Aeneas speaks to Dido, who curses him and his people. The second half of the *Aeneid* hardly matches the human drama of the first half, despite the scenes of battle and bloody death. The epic ends abruptly, almost shockingly, with Turnus and Aeneas in mortal combat. If the average Roman was expecting a victorious ending, what they got was a complex tragedy, in which the Roman people triumphed, but the humanity of their hero was lost—the exact opposite of the ending of the *Iliad*, in which Hector, in death, is exalted, though Troy is destroyed. From the *Eclogues* to the *Aeneid*, Virgil kept his sight on the cost of empire in human terms.

As David Slavit has pointed out in his book, *Virgil*, the *Aeneid* was supposed to have been written to honor Augustus and his government. After years of uncertainty, warfare, slaughter, and anarchy, Augustus Caesar imposed upon the empire a moment of order and peace, of stability and even a fair measure of justice. Rome now stood in all its grandeur, a marble city on seven hills. A lesser poet and thinker would have produced a cheerier work, something akin to *Semper Fidelis* in hexameters. What is extraordinary about the *Aeneid* is that, while celebrating such a moment and such a ruler, it leaves no scene without a sense of sadness. It is predominately a tragedy; it portrays the world's grief, the cost of military victory. Even in the moment of triumph, the impact of lost lives, and lost innocence and lost humanity tugs us into the tragic sweep of history, the sad state of human affairs. Few works of literature are as profoundly moving.

It is not an easy poem to appreciate in any language but the original, and translating the *Aeneid* is a difficult and complicated task. It's almost a cliché now to remind readers that no translation can do a poem complete justice. The truth is, despite most common and obvious problems, translating a poem or a story from one language into another is not always that complex. With the supreme works of art, it is. There are those who say we are not really reading Dante, or a translation of Dante, but Dante-in-translation. While we might think they're splitting hairs, there's a deep truth in that. It's almost impossible to get Rilke in any language but the original German. Perhaps with four or five translations before us, and someone to tell us what certain specific words mean, can we begin to get an idea of the complexity of his work. Then, once you've memorized the meaning of the verse, and integrated the complex layers of thought that one word carries, the final effect must come from listening to the poem in its original language. It's poetry, and the sound of the words, the music of the phrases and tonal changes from one verse to another convey something beyond the simple *meaning* of the words. With Dante the biggest obstacle, I think, is not so much the ideas or the words, but the exquisite effect of his lyric song, and the way the rhyme is so crucial to that effect. I've never found an English translation of Dante in rhymed verse to be satisfying. With Rilke, the problem is not just the music, but the complex meanings behind key words, the way an idea is rendered in an image that deepens the meaning, reveals the idea in all its glorious complexity, which Rilke somehow manages to compress into one or two words—something that German is ideally suited to do.

With Virgil, we have the difficulties mentioned above, plus others. The *Aeneid* is written is strict dactylic hexameter, which means that each line contains precisely six metrical stresses, and not five in one line and maybe six in the next. Most translations, if they render strictly every Virgilian line, will sacrifice the perfect Latin synatax a sentence has used to convey a beautiful image expressed with striking musicality. That's why many English translations use the iambic, not the dactylic, and follow the Alexandrine, which uses a twelve syllable iambic line, feeling that this best represents English verse.

But much of Virgil's language is removed from ordinary Latin speech. Sometimes he combines the written, literary sentence with the natural syntax of speech. Occasionally Virgil uses an archaism. Some are hard to represent in English. Where Virgil's line might have a certain strangeness, even an awkwardness abou it, the translator may be tempted to avoid the difficulty of rendering it correctly, and make the line sound natural and contemporary. Whatever subtle effect Virgil was going for, which was not lost on the Romans of his day, would be lost for the contemporary reader, and more important, for the contemporary poet, whose work it is to use his own langauge in unique ways—sometimes simple, sometimes written, and sometimes archaic, depending on the effect the poet wants to have on the reader. I know, there's a tendency in modern translations to make the English sound very contemporary. And in many cases this is correct, since the original was probably in a contemporary idiom as well. When I think of all the 16th to mid-20th century translations of Latin poetry that I read in college that made me think Horace and Juvenal and Ovid and Cattulus were old fashioned and quaint, and how that turned me away from these great poets, a sadness wells up in me. And when I think of how so many of us are turned away from the power and force of great poetry, it's a cultural loss I take personally. So if a modern translation in a contemporary idiom can bring someone closer to the heart of the original, I'm consoled, even if the translation is inaccurate. Maybe poetry will not die, I think, afterall. But as a poet, writing this book mainly for poets, it would be a disservice not to remind you of the great poets of the past whose verse functioned on multiple levels and in various tonal ways. As poets, we look for more than just the correct word when we read a translation. We're asking ourselves, What were those poets doing with the language of their day, and what can I learn from that, and how can I do the same using the English that is available to me in my own time. That even now the English language—changing as we speak (the pun is intended)—glows with possibilities; its words and figures of speech are but embers that can burst into flame should some poet make the effort to blow on them.

Manuscript copies of the *Aeneid* circulated extensively in central Italy after Virgil's death, but the earliest surviving manuscripts date from the 4th and 5th centuries. His popularity continued into the Middle Ages. Dante considered him the wisest and most closely Christian of the ancient pagan poets, taking him as guide not only through hell and purgatory, but in the art of flowing narrative and beautiful speech. Milton kept him in mind as he wrote *Paradise Lost*, with its pompous orations of devils and men. After the invention of printing, there were innumerable Latin editions of Virgil's works, one of which, printed in Birmingham, England, in 1750-52, was the first production of John Baskerville's press. John Dryden, the 17th century English poet and dramatist and literary dictator of his age, was a master of English versification; his verse translation of the *Aeneid*, which appeared in 1697, was the first important English version, and stood, until modern times, as the only version to become an English classic. Dryden renders the opening in rhymed couplets:

> Arms and the man I sing, who forc'd by fate,
> And haughty Juno's unrelenting hate,
> Expell'd and exil'd, left the Trojan shore.
> Long labors, both by sea and land, he bore,
> And in the doubtful war, before he won
> The Latin realm, and built the destin'd town;
> His banish'd gods restor'd to rites divine,
> And settled sure succession in his line,
> From whenc ethe race of Alban fathers come,
> And the long glories of majestic Rome.
> . . . .
> And sev'n long years th' unhappy wand'ring train

Were tosse'd by storms, and scatter'd thro' the main.
Such time, such toil, requir'd the Roman name,
Such length of labor for so vast a frame.

Other significant verse translations into English are those of the poets Rolfe Humphries (1950) and C. Day Lewis [father of Daniel Day Lewis, the actor] (1953). Allen Mandelbraun's 1963 version was considered the only one since Dryden which read like English verse and conveyed the majesty and pathos of the original. Book One begins:

I sing of arms and of a man: his fate
had made him fugitive; he was the first
to journey from the coasts of Troy as far
as Italy and the Lavinian shores.
Across the lands and waters he was battered
beneath the violence of High Ones, for
the savage Juno's unforgetting anger;
and many sufferings were his in war—
until he brought a city into being
and carried in his gods to Latium;
from this have come the Latin race, the lords
of Alba, and the ramparts of high Rome.
. . . .
For long years they were cast across all waters,
fate-driven, wandering from sea to sea.
It was so hard to found the race of Rome.

Having translated the *Illiad* and the *Odyssey* to great acclaim, Robert Fitzgerald's version of the *Aeneid* (1983) was a long-awaited literary event. This poetic rendering speaks directly to the modern reader, revealing at once why Virgil's *Aeneid* has remained a centerpiece of Western civilization through the centuries. In Fitzgerald's hands, the tale of Aeneas & Dido, Pallas, Camilla, and Turnus, becomes an exciting new adventure and a profound poetic experience.

I sing of warfare and a man at war.
From the sea-coast of Troy in early days
He came to Italy by destiny,
To our Lavinian western shore,
A fugitive, this captain, buffeted
Cruelly on land as on sea
By blows from powers of the air—behind them
Baleful Juno in her sleepless rage.
And cruel losses were his lot in war,
Till he could found a city and bring home
His gods to Latium, land of the Latin race.
. . . .
For years they wandered as their destiny drove them on
From one sea to the next: so hard and huge
A task it was to found the Roman people.

The first book of the *Aeneid* begins in the seventh year of the Trojans' wanderings. They've reached Sicily, but the goddess Juno, enemy of Troy and guardian of Carthage (which she knows is fated to be destroyed by a race of Trojan descent), has the wind-god Aeolus let loose a storm on the Trojan fleet. Aeneas and the surviving ships reach the Libyan coast, where they are well received by Dido, queen of the newly founded Carthage. The goddess Venus, mother of Aeneas, arranges that Dido should fall in love with the Darden warrior. Book II contains the flashback sequence, a brilliant poetic narrative.

Dido asks Aeneas to tell how he reached her shores, and Aeneas begins the tale:

> "Sorrow too deep to tell, your majesty,
> You order me to feel and tell once more:
> How the Greeks leveled in the dust
> The splendor of our mourned-forever kingdom —
> Heartbreaking things I saw with my own eyes
> And was a part of. Who could tell them,
> Even a Myrmidon or Dolopian
> Or ruffian of Ulysses, without tears?
> Now, too, the night is well along, with dewfall
> Out of heaven, and setting stars weight down
> Our heads toward sleep. But if so great desire
> Moves you to hear the tale of our disasters,
> Briefly recalled, the final throes of Troy,
> However I may shudder at the memory
> And shrink again in grief, let me begin."

Aeneas relates the story of Troy's demise: the building of the Trojan horse and the cunning of Sinon, the burning of the city, the desperate but unavailing resistance by the Trojans, Priam's death and Aeneas' own flight at the bidding of Venus. He tells how he carried his father Anchises on his shoulders and took his son Iulus (Ascanius) by the hand, how his wife Creusa, who followed, was lost, and his destiny revealed to him by her ghost.

While the epic is usually a long tale full of action, it also tells us something about human life. It's protagonist is a "hero," someone stronger than the ordinary mortal, but who must contend not only with mortal enemies, but with those on a divine level, the gods and goddesses who support or oppose them. Juno, the Queen of the Gods and wife of the supreme god Jupiter, had been the enemy of Troy and she opposed Aeneas fiercely. Jupiter, on the other hand, endorsed the Trojans destiny, and worked to help them. Other gods and goddesses take sides and participate in the action below. From the reader's point of view, these divine beings move across the chess board of the Mediterranean heroic and tragic figures like Aeneas and Queen Dido, fiercely and passionately commiting their souls to action. For Juno and Jupiter, it's a marital spat. Virgil had no doubt that the affairs of men were influenced by the powers of the gods, and this belief is one of core motifs of the poem.

They finally get as far as Sicily only to be driven by a storm to the north African coast, where Dido, queen of Carthage, gives shelter to the men and falls in love with Aeneas. Already we see the similarity in plot between the *Odyssey* and the *Aeneid*: where Odysseus loved Calypso, Aeneas, blown into the Carthegian port by one storm, is then driven into Dido's arms by another; Odysseus tells Calypso, as in a flashback, of his wanderings since leaving Troy—Aeneas does the same: He recounts the ten years siege of Troy, the stratagem of the wooden horse ("Beware of Greeks bearing gifts!") and the burning of the city. We learn how he fled, carrying his father on his shoulders, leading his little son by the hand, and his wife following behind until she becomes lost in the confusion. Suddenly, he comes upon her ghost who tells him he must settle his household gods in another country. She tells him of the land he is destined to found and bids him on his way. His father dies when they get to Sicily, from which a tempest blew them across the sea to Carthage. At this point, Dido realizes her love for Aeneas, a love engineered by Juno, that meddling Goddess, to prevent Aeneas from reaching Italy. Juno also rasies a storm during a hunting match, and they seek the same cave for refuge. Rumor proclaims the marriage, but Aeneas is determined to get to Italy, despite Dido's passion to keep him. When nothing works, she contrives her own death. After more adventures, Aeneas encounters the Sybyl who shows him the way into Hell. There he speaks to his father, Anchises, who reminds him of his destiny. Again, another obvious parallel to the *Odyssey*, where Odysseus descends into Hell to speak to Tiresias. Finally Aeneas reaches Italy, where King Latinus promises him his only daughter, Lavinia, the heiress of his crown. But Turnus, being in love with Lavinia, is stirred to anger by Juno and war breaks out between the Trojan forces of Aeneas, and the Rululians, led by Turnus. After much intrigue and war, Aeneas finally meets Turnus on the battlefield, forces him to a duel, and kills him.

In this great twelve-book myth, Virgil's countrymen were to see not only a symbolic summation of their history, but a statement of their noblest aspirations. It was also intended as a tribute to Augustus, the adopted son of Julius Caesar, who claimed he was the last descendant of the founder of Rome, the legendary Trojan prince Aeneas. The *Aeneid* was at once accepted as the supreme epic of the Roman world. Some of the scenes in the poem are direct imitations of Homer, but this was part of Virgil's intention—to remind the reader that the *Aeneid* was an extension of that great epic tradition. The first sex books imitate the *Odyssey*, the last six follow the structure of the *Iliad*. Taken as a whole, though, the work is original, and most of its best episodes are not even paralleled in the *Odyssey*. Unfinished and uneven, there is grandeur in the work, showing Virgil as the great literary artist who was master of the Latin langauge.

The medievals, with their special feeling for Rome, regarded Virgil as the greatest of the pagans, a prophet as well as a poet, and in Rome itself the book was a classic as soon as he was dead, to be studied by every Roman schoolboy. His influence until the present century was probably greater than that of any writer of the ancient world. Generations ago, many a school boy had to memorize the famous opening lines (from a translation by Delabère-May):

> **Arms and the man I sing,** who earliest came
> Fate-bound for refuge from the coasts of Troy
> To Italy, and her Lavinian shore,
> Much tossed about was he alike by land
> And on the deep, by violence of gods,
> Through savage Juno's unrelenting wrath,
> And many hurts endured in war beside,
> Till he could found a city, and bring in
> His gods to Latium, whence the Latin race,
> And Alban sires and walls of lofty Rome.
>
> (continuing with Mandelbaum translation:]
>
> Tell me the reason, Muse: what was the wound
> to her divinity, so hurting her
> that she, the queen of gods, compelled a man
> remarkable for goodness to endure
> so many crises, meet so many trials?
> Can such resentment hold the minds of gods?
>
> There was an ancient city they called Carthage —
> a city facing Italy, but afar
> away from Tiber's mouth: extremely rich
> and, when it came to waging war, most fierce.
> This land was Juno's favorite — it is said — and her hope
> and tender plan: for Carthage to become the capital
> of nations, if the Fates would just consent.
> But she had heard that, from the blood of Troy,
> a race had come that some day would destroy
> the citadels of Tyre; from it, a people
> would spring, wide-ruling kings, men proud in battle
> and destined to annihilate her Libya.
>
> The Fates had so decreed. And Saturn's daughter —
> in fear of this, remembered the old war
> that she had long since carried on at Troy
> for her beloved Argos . . .
> was angered even more; for this she kept
> far off from Latium the Trojan remnant
> left by the Greeks and pitiless Achilles.
>
> [back to the Delabère-May version]
>
> And many a year driven by the fates
> They roamed all seas around,
> So huge the toil to found the Roman race.

As noted above, Virgil patterned the sixth book on Homer's "Book of the Dead." [see pages 23-25] At the edge of the underworld, Aeneas seeks out the Sybil for prophesy just as Odysseus sought Tiresius: Aeneas asks if he can descend into the underworld. She tells him that the gates of hell are always open:

> "Easy
> the way that leads into Hell: day
> and night the door of Darkest Dis is open.
> But to recall your steps, to rise again
> into the upper air: that is the labor;
> that is the task"

But first he must pass through the sacred grove and find the Golden Bough:

> "Hid in the leafy darkness of a tree,
> There is a **golden bough**, the leaves and stem
> Also of gold, and sacred to the Queen
> Of the enfernal realm. The grove around
> Hides it from view; the shades of valleys dim
> Close in and darken all the place. Only he
> may pass beneath earth's secret spaces who
> first plucks the golden-leaved fruit of that tree. . . .
> And if the Fates have summoned you,
> the bough will break off freely, easily."

FOOD FOR THOUGHT

Sir James Frazer's *The Golden Bough*

The Golden Bough was the first work to trace the evolution of human behavior from savage to civilized man. What Freud did for the individual, Frazer did for civilization as a whole; his study of primitive magic, taboos, sexual practices, superstition, and wizardry is one of the richest achievements of the human imagination, and a mine of information on folklore, ancient fertility rites, dying and resurrected gods, and ritual human sacrifice.

First published in England in 1890, many of the ideas and assumptions in this twelve-volume anthropological study have been outmoded and superseded, even impeached by modern scholarship. But the book had a profound influence on modern literature, and Eliot cites this work as one of two books (Jessie Weston's from Ritual to Romance being the other) upon which much of The Waste Land was based, especially the volume on "Dying and Reviving Gods."

The priest of the sacred grove of Diana at Aricia was called the King of the Wood. His function was to control and regulate fertility and vegetation. The king serves also as the bridegroom of a female spirit and has to mate with her annually to produce fecundity for the people. Such "sacred marriages" are common in both ancient and primitive usage. They are formal expressions of the idea that sexual intercourse can promote vegetation—an idea which likewise inspires the orgiastic practices characteristic of primitive seasonal festivals.

As the embodiment of the spirit of fertility, the priestly king is a human god, and special care has to be taken to prevent any impairment of his "soul" or vital essence. If, despite all precautions, the priestly king does show signs of debility, he has to be put to death or deposed, and his power passes to his successor. Moreover, to forestall the natural infirmity of old age and the decay of the land, it is often the custom among primitive peoples to slay or depose the king after a fixed term.

There are also non-human embodiments of the spirit of fertility, e.g., trees, which have to be felled periodically or at the first signs of decay (Maypole and Yule log beginning of summer and midwinter). Sometimes the spirit of fertility is a corn-god or corn-spirit. The body of the corn god buried in the winter sprouts again in the spring and assures that out of the decay of winter comes the great renewal of spring.

There were many mythic embodiments of fertility: The Mother Goddess, The Burned God, The Hanged God, Dionysus and Bacchus, Demeter and Persephone, The Hyacinth son of Attis and Adonis, and The Egyptian God Osiris whose death and resurrection were annually celebrated with alternate sorrow and joy because it gave them hope of a life eternal beyond the grave. Taken all together, these legends point to a widespread practice of dismembering the body of a king, magician, or goddess and burying the pieces in different parts of the country in order to ensure the fertility of the ground and probably also the fecundity of man and beast. Many were naturally conceived as gods of creative energy in general.

Every aspirant to the office of King of the Wood at Aricia had first to pluck a golden bough or sprig which grew high up on a sacred tree.

In one of the many prophecies, his father Anchises reveals to Aeneas the names of the first lands destined to fall to Roman domination—words that Lucan will invert a century later in the *Pharsalia*, his anti-*Aeneid*, not to glorify Rome, but to foretell of its eventual destruction: [see page 125]:

> What warriors! . . . These shall build for you
> Nomentum, Gabii, and Fidenae's town,
> These on the mountains set Collatia's towers,
> Bola and Cora. These shall be their names
> Then,—for they now are lands without a name.

Virgil worked for ten years on the epic. He wrote slowly, with great devotion and attention to each verse, dictating a few lines in the morning and rewriting them in the afternoon. Augustus Caesar was anxious for the poem's completion, and like a producer wanting a film finished for the holiday season, kept tabs on the project, ordering each finished fragment to be brought to his attention. Virgil stalled as long as he could, then finally went to the Emperor's estate and read to the assembled family the second, fourth, and sixth books. Octavia, Anthony's widow, fainted at the passage describing her son Marcellus, who had just died.

Virgil's gentle spirit adorns each page; we feel his sympathies spread from his own country to all men, to all of life. He touches on the sufferings of the poor and ignoble as he does on the pagentry of the rich and great; the obscene ghastliness of war finds amplification in his terse versification; his words hold from consonant to vowel the mortality that stalks our days, the grief and pain, the *lacrimae rerum*—"tears in things"—that bruise and shape our days. It was not in vain he stroked every line, "licking it into shape as the she-bear does her cubs," wrote Seutonius, the Roman biographer and historian. Only one who has written can imagine the work that made his tale so smooth, the passages so sweet. Every second page cries out for quotation and urges us to read aloud. Some lines, like the following which tell of Dido being tricked into falling in love with Aeneas, will be later stolen by Eliot for use in "The Waste Land."

> Trenchers were taken off, they put out wine bowls,
> Grand and garlanded. A festive din
> Now rose and echoed through the palace halls.
> **Lighted lamps hung from the coffered ceiling**   [golden ceiling]
> Rich with gold leaf, and torches with high flames
> Prevailed over the night.
> (Book I, lines 720-730)

Juno wants to keep Aeneas from Italy, so she sends a storm and tricks Aeneas & Dido into spending a night in a cave, whereupon the rumor is spread that they are married.

> That day
> First was the cause of death to her, and first
> The cause of ills; for Dido is not moved
> By look of what she does or what men say,
> Nor love in secret does she now desire;
> She calls it wedlock, and she cloaks her fault
> Beneath the name.
> Through Libya's great towns
> Rumor goes forth at once, Rumor than whom
> No other speedier evil thing exists;
> She thrives by rapid movement, and acquires
> Strength as she goes; small at the first from fear,
> She presently uplifts herself aloft,
> And stalks upon the ground and hides her head
> Among the clouds.
> . . . Marvel to be told,
> Bears just so many watchful eyes beneath,
> So many tongues, so many babbling mouths,
> And just so many ears she pricks to hear.
> (Book IV, 172-186)

For awhile they live as man and wife, but The Trojan chief—Venus's Darden grandson—tells her he must continue on his way, that he is the helpless instrument of his divine mission. Dido dismisses him with scorn, then persuades her sister Anna to build a pyre, ostensibly for magic use. The Queen mounts the pyre, upon which she has placed all her momentoes of Aeneas.

> But Dido, desperate, beside herself
> with awful undertakings, eyes bloodshot
> and rolling, and her quivering cheeks flecked
> with stains and pale with coming death, now bursts
> across the inner courtyards of her palace.

She mounts in madness that high pyre, unsheathes
the Darden sword, a gift not sought for such
an end. And when she saw the Trojan's clothes
and her familiar bed, she checked her thought
and tears a little, lay upon the couch
and spoke her final words: "O relics, dear
while fate and god allowed, receive my spirit
and free me from these cares; for I have lived
and journeyd through the course assigned by fortune.
And now my Shade will pass, illustrious,
beneath the earth; I have built a handsome city,
have seen my walls rise up, avenged a husband,
won satisfaction from a hostile brother:
o fortunate, too fortunate — if only
the ships of Troy had never touched our coasts."
She spoke and pressed her face into the couch.
"I shall die unavenged, but I shall die,"
she says. "Thus, thus, I gladly go below
to shadows. May the savage Darden drink
with his own eyes this fire from the deep
and take with him the omen of my death."

Virgil felt it was going to take three more years to polish the work and make final changes. In the summer of 19 BC to set out for Athens. His intention was to spend those three years in Greece and Asia perfecting the poem while abroad. In Athens he met Augustus, who persuaded the poet to return with him to Italy. On the way home, Virgil stopped at the Greek seaport of Megara and fell ill with sunstroke. Stubbornly, he continued his voyage, rapidly growing worse. On September 21, a few days after landing at the Italian port of Brundisum, he died. On his deathbed, he begged his friends to destroy the manuscript, saying it would take another three years to give it finished form. Augustus forbade them to do so. For centuries after, the epic story was one schoolchildren learned the same way our kids remember the movies of their youth. I lifted the following description from the back of my paperback copy (a translation by Allen Mandelbaum published in 1961. It could easily be a movie poster from the 1950s advertising an epic film:

A sweeping epic of arms and heroism!
The searching portrait of a man caught between
love and duty,
human feeling and the force of fate!
Filled with drama, passion,
and the universal pathos
that only a masterpiece can express!

[Remember Frankie Laine singing the theme song to *High Noon*?

"Oh to be torn twixt love and duty,
supposin' I lose my fair-haired beauty,
I'm not afraid of death but ohoh,
what will I do if you leave me."

Aeneas might have meant the first two lines, but Dido would have sung the last two before she killed herself.]

In Book XI, Latinus calls a council to propose offers of peace to Aeneas, which only inflames Turnus. In the meantime, the Trojan and Latine troops clash in a bloody battle, and Camilla charges into the fray.

> Now, when they came together a third time
> The two formations mingled, man to man,
> And then indeed groans of the dying rose,
> Then arms and bodies in a mire of blood
> Went down, and dying horses, with their riders
> Butchered, as the bitter fight surged on.
>
> Dark blood spilt everywhere. Men dealt out death
> By cold ssteel as they fought and strove by wounds
> To win the beauty of courageous death.
>
> Amid the carnage, like an Amazon,
> Camilla rode exultant, one breast bared
> For fighting ease, her quiver at her back.
> At times she flung slim javelins thick and fast,
> At times, tireless, caught up her two-edged axe.
> At her side rode chosen comrades, virgins all: Larina,
> Tulla, Tarpeis shaking her bronze axe.
> So ride the hardened Amazons of Thrace.
>
> Savage girl, whom did your lance unhorse,
> What victims, first and last,
> How many thrown down on the battlefield,
> Torn bodies dying? Eunaeus, Clytius' son,
> Came first: he faced her with her unarmored breast,
> And with her shaft of pine she ran him through. He tumbled, coughing streams
> of blood, took bites
> Of bloody earth, and dying writhed on his wound.

After several encounters, Camilla is killed but the Latine troops are entirely defeated. In the final book, Turnus challenges Aeneas to a single combat. They agree on weapons, but before the fight begins Aeneas is struck from behind by Rululians, whose leader was Turnus, and is critically wounded. But his mother, Venus (or Aphrodite) miraculously cures him, whereupon Aeneas forces Turnus to the duel. After fierce fighting, Aeneas casts his spear with such force that it pierces the shield Turnus holds before him and passes clean through the middle of his thigh. The force of the blow buckles his knees; the huge warrior is brought to earth.

> And a groan swept the Rutulians as they rose,
> A groan heard echoing on all sides from all

The mountain range, adn schoed by the forests.
The man brought down, brought low, lifted his eyes
And held his right hand out to make a plea:

"Clearly I earned this, and I ask no quarter.
Make the most of your good fortune here.
You have defeated me. The Ausonians
Have seen me in defeat, dpreading my hands.
Lavinia is your bride. But go no further
Out of hatred."
    Fierce, clad in arms, Aenaes stood and rolled
His eyes, and stayed his right hand from the stroke.
And more and more the other's speech began
To sway him as he hesitated — until
high on the Latin's shoulder he made out
the luckless belt of Pallas, of the boy
whom Turnus had defeated, wounded, stretched
upon the battlefield, from whom he took
this fatal sign to wear upon his back,
this girdle glittering with familiar studs.
And when his eyes drank in this plunder, this
memorial of brutal grief, Aeneas,
aflame with rage — his wrath was terrible —
cried: How can you who wear the spoils of my
dear comrade now escape me? It is Pallas
who strikes, who sacrifices you, who takes
this payment from your shameless blood." Relentless,
he sinks his sword into the chest of Turnus.
His limbs fell slack with chill; and with a moan
his life, resentful, fled to Shades below.

(The End)

Virgil had arranged with Varius, before he left Italy, to burn the incomplete manuscript if anything should happen to him. Varius emphatically declared that he'd do no such thing. On his death-bed, Virgil constantly asked for his book boxes, intending to burn the poem himself, if no one else would do so. But no one would bring the manuscripts to him. The *Aeneid* was published with only a few slight corrections made by Varius; incomplete lines were left just as they were.

Virgil's ashes were taken to Naples and laid to rest on the via Puteolana less than two miles from the city, in a tomb for which he himself composed this couplet:

Mantua gave me the light, Calabria slew me:
   now holds me
  Parthenope. I have sung shepherds, the country,
and wars.

[There's more to do on Virgil, but for now this will have to do]

☛ **Horace** (Quintus Horatius Flaccus: 65-8 B.C.)

His father started life as a slave. Upon gaining his freedom, he worked as a tax collector (some say he was a fishmonger), and scrimped and saved to provide his son with the best possible education. He took Horace to Rome to study grammar and rhetoric, then to the University of Athens for philosophy. It was here the youth heard the news that Julius Caesar had been assasinated. He joined the revolution, and fought in Brutus's army as commander of a legion. Years later, he wrote of this experience in his famous *Odes:*

> Let the healthy boy learn to suffer
> strait poverty gladly in hard campaigns;
> and lead a fresh air life amid perilous
> undertakings. From enemy ramparts
> a queen and her daughter shall groan
> for some struggling tyrant:
>
> It is sweet and honorable to die for one's country . . .
> *(Dulce et decorum pro patria mori!)*

Of course, Horace was fighting against Octavian (later to become Augustus Caesar); it must have been especially ironic when he admitted in the *Odes* that he had dropped his shield and run, invoking an ancient form of valorous discretion.

> and death harries even the man who flees
> nor spares the hamstrings or cowardly
> backs of battle-shy youths.
>
> Manhood reveals their heaven to those
> who deserve not to die, attempts the narrow pass,
> and spurns with its soaring wings
> the common crowd, the muddy ground.
>
> Safe the recompense likewise of loyal
> tact: who broadcasts the mysteries of Ceres
> shall be forbidden to lie beneath
> the same timbers or sail the same dinghy
>
> as me — slighted, the Ancient of Days is apt
> to confuse the innocent with the guilty:
> though lame in one foot, Retribution
> rarely abandons the Sinner's trail.

Brutus and the rebels, Mark Anthony & Cleopatra were finally defeated and Augustus restored peace to the ravaged Empire. Returning to Rome penniless, Horace paid the rent working as a clerk, but writes later that "barefoot poverty drove me to writing verses."

Horace was twenty-five when he met Virgil, who so admired his poetry that he introduced him to his patron Maecenas, famous for his palace with its heated swimming pool. He gave Horace a mansion and an income-producing farm tended by a dozen slaves in the Sabine valley forty-five miles from Rome. (In 1932 this estate was unearthed; it was a spacious mansion with twenty-four rooms, three bathing pools, and a large formal garden surrouned by an enclosed portico.) Horace was now free to live and write as he pleased, with homes in the city and the country. He first made his reputation as a writer of poems known as *Satires*, a genre that owed little to Greek models, and one that Romans claimed entirely as their own. As a matter of fact, Horace became one of the Western world's first literary critics, suggesting in his *Ars Poetica* that writers should employ a more conversational style, simple and clear diction, and avoid words that are new, obsolete, or "sesquipedalian"—foot-and-a-half-words. Virgil was the master of a sonorous hexameter, whereas Horace used his meters in a deliberately unmajestic way, filled with everyday slang, giving his verses the feel of elegant, musical prose.

> This is what I prayed for. A piece of land, not so very big,
> with a garden and, near the house, a spring that never fails,
> and a bit of wood to round it off. All this and more
> the gods have granted. So be it. I ask for nothing else,
> O son of Maia, except that you make these blessings last.
>
> I wish my little farm could take in that corner of my neighbor's,
> which at present spoils its shape;
> I wish I could stumble on a pot of silver and be like the fellow
> who on finding some treasure bought and ploughed the very field
> in which he had worked as a hired hand; this is my prayer:
> make fat the flocks I own and everything else
> except my head, and remain as ever my chief protector.
>
> Well then, now that I've left town for my castle in the hills
> what can I better celebrate in the satires of my lowland muse?
> Here I am not worried by the rat-race or the leaden sirocco,
> which in the unhealthy autumn makes a grim profit for the undertaker.
>
> O father of the dawn, or Janus if you would rather have that name,
> I must go to Rome on business.
> Later, after saying something loud and clear to my own disadvantage,
> I have to barge through the crowd, injuring the slow movers.
> "What do you want, you idiot, and what are you doing?" says a lout,
> cursing angrily. "Do you think you can kick everything aside
> just because you're dashing back to keep an appointment with Maecenas?"
>
> I like that, I admit, and it's sweet music to my ears.
> But as soon as I reach the grim Esquiline, a hundred items
> of other people's business start buzzing through my head and jumping round
>   my legs.
> "Roscius would like you to meet him at the Wall by eight tomorrow."
>   "The Department said be sure to come in today, Quintus;
>   an important matter of common concern has just cropped up."
>   "Get Maecenas' signature on these documents."
>   "I'll try,"
> you say.
>   "You can if you want to," he replies, refusing to be put off.

Time flies. It's now seven, in fact almost eight
years since Maecenas came to regard me as one of his friends—
or at least he was willing to go so far as to take me with him
when making a journey in his carriage and to risk casual remarks
like "What time do you make it?" "Is the Thracian Chick a match
    for the Arab?"
All this time, every day and hour, yours truly has become
a more frequent target for jealous comment.
If a chilling rumour runs through the streets
from the city centre, everyone I meet asks me for details.
"Excuse me, sir, but you must know, for you're so close
to the supreme power—you haven't by any chance heard some news
about the Dacians?"
              "No, none at all."
                         "Teasing as usual!"
"I swear it; I don't know a thing."

That's how the day is wasted. In exasperation I murmur:
"When shall I see that place in the country, when shall I be free
to browse among my old books or laze in sleep and idleness,
drinking in a blissful oblivion of life's troubles?
When shall I sit down to a plate of beans, those relatives of Pythagoras,
and cabbage with just some fat bacon to make it tasty?"

Doesn't some of this remind you of Frank O'Hara's or Kenneth Koch's poems about New York? (see pgs. 502 & 508) Where Virgil gave us heroes, farm-boys and peasants, Horace shows us the living men and women of Rome, the Imperial capital. Where Ovid paraded before us legendary lechers and wanton courtesans beguiling sophisticated men, Horace gives us the public square: statesman and streetwalker, pompous lecturer and jabbering bore, the conceited poet and the wily slave, the stingy philosopher and the shrewd businessman—all rub elbows, all turn their faces and tell their stories. Here at last was Rome! He satirizes the restless go-getters who long for the peace of the country, and once there, long for the rush of the city again; those who never enjoy what they have because someone else has more. He pokes fun at those who lament the passing of the "good-old-days": "if some god were for taking you back to those days you would refuse every time." The trouble with Rome, as with modern cities, is the mad pursuit of wealth, the gluttony for gold, for the easy life:

Why do you laugh at Tantalus,
from whose thirsty lips the water
always moves away?
Change the name, and the story
is about you.

He even makes fun of himself, having his slave tell him to his face that he spouts all these morals and is himself the greatest hypocrite of all, a slave to his passions like everyone else. In beginning his second series of *Satires*, Horace complains that the first group was criticized as either too tough or lacking bite.

"What should I do?" he asks.
"Take a rest," he's told.
"What?" the poet says, "not write verses at all?"
"Of course."
"But I can't sleep."

Despite the success of his *Satires*, Horace realized there was greater work to be done. The distractions of the city fed his urban commentaries, but if he was going to write something for the ages, he'd need the peace of his estate. He leaves the city and his friends to begin the *Odes* that would assure his reputation forever. With "painstaking felicity," he discarded the classical hexameter and wrote in a bolder Roman lyric form, expressing his thoughts on numerous topics in stanzas that were fresh and direct, yet musically and philosophically complex. He celebrated the fire of youth, and counseled the enjoyment of life's simplest pleasures.

> Do not inquire, we may not know, what end
> the Gods will give, Leuconoe, do not attempt
> Babylonian calculations. The better course
> is to bear whatever will be, whether Jove allot
> more winters or this is the last which exhausts
> the Tuscan sea with pumice rocks opposed.
> Be wise, decant the wine, prune back
> your long-term hopes. Life ebbs as I speak—
> so *seize the day*, and grant the next no credit.   [*carpe diem*]

This idea of seizing the day, *carpe diem*, was to echo throughout literature for centuries (see page Marvell, p. 212 & pgs 223-226, Pierre Ronsard, p. _____, and Herrick, p. _____)
Here, from the12th Century *Rubaiyat of Omar Khayyam*, is another way of saying it:

> Some for the Glories of This World; and some
> Sigh for the Prophet's Paradise to come;
> Ah, take the Cash, and let the Credit go,
> Nor heed the rumble of a distant Drum!

And then there were the ladies Horace loved who grew tired of his attentions:

> O lovelier daughter of a lovely mother,
> make what end you prefer
> of my hurtful lines—on the fire,
> in the sea, as you will.

> It is said that Prometheus, obliged to add
> to our primal substance particles drawn
> from wherever, put in our stomachs
> the urge of the ravening lion.

> Govern your spirit: in sweet youth
> heart's passion tried me too
> and set me to raving

in rash lampoons. Now I would change
those acid lines for sweet, if only (since I take
back all my taunts) you'll be my friend
And give me back my heart.

It's thought that Horace was rather shy about love and fabricated tales of conquest and loss. In the spirit of the time, these literary exercises were almost compulsory. He could show pain, but swaggered as well.

You avoid me, Chloe, like the fawn
seeking mother on the pathless
mountain and starting with groundless
fears at the woods and winds.

Am I a tiger or fierce Gaetulian lion
to hunt you down and maul you?
It is time to get loose from Mamma:
you are ripe for a man.

He bemoaned the new luxury and frivolity that flourished in the Augustan peace, the lust and avarice and jaded attitudes.

Alas, the shame of our scars and crimes,
and of brothers slain.
What have we of this hard generation
shrunk from, what iniquity have we left
untouched? From what have our youth
refrained through fear of the Gods?
What altars spared?

Where in the world's literature do we find poems like this, that combine such craft with an ease of expression and natural diction. Poems that are at one moment tender and another harsh, intricate in their learned references yet powerfully evocative. Horace blends the various metrics in the service of common diction. If any criticism be leveled, one could fault the *Odes* for their lack of passion, but he makes up for it with grandeur of thought.

Horace had always wanted to be a philosopher, and turned eventually to literary criticism. One of the letters of his *Epistles*, later named "The Art of Poetry," is recognized as one of the first works of literary theory, written as a bit of friendly advice to fellow poets. The *Ars Poetica* was later adapted as a handbook on style by the neoclassicists of the 17th and 18th centuries, and its words of wisdom apply equally well today.

Pick a subject you know, he says. Beware of working on an elephant and producing a mouse. As Shakespeare was to say nearly 16 centuries later, brevity is the soul of wit. Get to the point, don't wear your reader's patience thin with tedious scene-setting exposition—begin the action right in the middle—in *medias res*. Emotion is not everything; true, you must feel something if you wish your reader to feel, but the art is not the feeling, the art is in the form ("Write *from* the feeling, not *about* it," said another poet, who shall here remain nameless). Beware of your friends and mates; they'll see the wrong things and make the wrong suggestions. Let the action tell the story. The goal is to entertain and educate: "he who has mingled the useful with the pleasant wins every vote"—*omne tulit punctum qui miscuit utile dulce.* Study life and philosophy, for without observation and understanding, even the truest voice can be an empty thing. *Sapere aude*: Dare to know.

Toward the end of his life, Horace suffered the breakdown of his body with stoic simplicity, grateful for the full glass he'd drunk. "You have played enough, eaten enough, drunk enough; it is time to go." A few months after his patron Maecenas died, Horace died too. He gave his property to Augustus, and his body to the earth near Maecenas' tomb.

❁

The Elegy: Tibullus, Gallus, and Propertius

The word elegy comes from the Greek word elegeia, "lament." In Greek and Roman literature, any poem using the elegiac couplet was considered an elegy. The lament could be on such subjects as love, war, death, etc. For classical poets, the elegy could be one of lamentation, but any poem that was written in alternating hexameters and pentameters was considered an elegy. So mood or content was secondary to the chosen meter.

☛ **Sextus Propertius** (c. 50 B.C. - after 16 B.C.), *Elegies*

Augustus used imperial need as an excuse when requesting epic poems on war, nature, religion, history, and conduct. What the state was unable to commission or outlaw was the poetry of love. The amorous revolt that followed the great period of epic poetry flourished with a joy and reckless abandon unmindful of its own tragic end.

Albius Tibullus, deprived of his family lands during the revolution, was rescued from poverty and set free to write genderless love poems. He polished his elegiac verse in the manner of the Alexandrian Greeks. Sextus Propertius sang similar lyrical verses of lechery and lust in the decadent atmosphere of the languid rich. While his poems were often overburdened with learned ornamentation and pedantic aphorisisms, those that found the mark did so with a haunting beauty. Pale, thin, delicate and obsessively overemotional, he devoted his elegies to depicting the ups and downs of his love affair with "Cynthia." Propertius veered rapidly, in accordance with her whims, from high ecstasy to wild, self-pitying depression.

Like Virgil and Horace, Sextus was a protégé of Maecenas, but brought a more cynical eye to the celebrations of love and a jaded view to the victories of war. Perhaps it was this skeptial, war-weary voice that attracted Pound and Lowell to his work—Pound critical of The First World War, and Lowell of the Vietnam Conflict. Pound wrote his *Homage to Sextus Propertius* which included renderings into English of many of his poems, and Lowell also translated his work into a very syllabic, metered American English.

Sextus turned down a chance to travel on official business to the East to enjoy "Athens' sophistications and glance at costly Asian antiques when their price is Cynthia saying her kisses will belong to the wind that comes against me, and nothing is harder to bear than betrayal." He criticized a friend whose "love has always been the business of the nation's wars," and admitted that he was "born unfit for action" because he prefered dying "in the extremity of length of love." His Elegies contain many poems which offer a disquieting view of intimate relationships.

Elegies, from Book IV

> Ghosts do exist. Death does not finish all.
> The colourless shade escapes the burnt-out pyre.
> Though lately buried beside the rumbling road,
> Yet Cynthia seemed to lean above my bed
> When after love's last rites my sleep hung back

And I grieved that my bed was now a chilly realm.
She had the selfsame hair and eyes as on
Her bier, her shroud was burned into her side,
The fire had gnawed at her favourite beryl ring,
And Lethe's water had wasted away her lips.
She breathed out living passion, and spoke,
Yet her brittle hands rattled their thumb-bones.
"Can sleep already possess your faculties?
Had walking Suburan secrets, the window-sill worn
By nightly intrigue, already slipped your mind? —
From which for you I've often hung on a rope
And descended hand over hand to your arms!
Often our love was joined in the very street,
Heart to heart: our cloaks warmed up the path.

"Why, no one cried out at my glazing eyes:
Your calling me back would have gained one day!
No watchman rattled split reeds on my account,
My head was bruised by the intervening tile.
In short, who saw you stooping by my corpse,
Your mourning-toga grow warm with tears?
Why didn't you pray for a breeze to fan my pyre,
Ingrate, why weren't my flames perfumed with nard?
Was it too much to strew cheap hyacinths,
Propitiate my tomb by breaking a jar?

"However, I'll not carp, though you deserve it,
Propertius: my reign in your books was long.
By the irreversible chant of the Fates I swear
I have kept faith. If I prove false, may vipers
Hiss on my grave and couch above my bones.
With tears in death we ratify life's loves —
But I conceal your myriad perfidies.

"Whatever poems you made in my name, burn them;
For me: cease to enjoy my reputation.
Indite on a column these verses worthy of me,
But brief, that travelers from the town may read:
'Here golden Cynthia lies in Tibur's soil."

"For now, let others possess you: soon I alone
Shall have you: you shall be with me,
And I shall grind down bone entwined with bones."

Having brought to a close her complaint and suit,
Her shadow fell away from my embrace.

☞ **Albius Tibullus** (*c.* 55-19 BC)

Tibullus came from a well-to-do family of the equestrian class, though his work is
peppered with complaints of economic hard-time and poverty, a motif he has in common

with the other elegiac poets, Gallus, Propertius and Ovid. He secured the patronage of Messalla Corvinus, a republican nobleman and politician who led several victorious military expeditions, some in which Tibullus took part. Tibullus was also friends with Horace and Ovid, and wrote two books of elegies, mainly concerned with love. In his elegies, full of sentiment, Tibullus places himself at the mercy of his two loves, Delia and Nemesis, and writes of the rejections with weary despair. In his last years, he withdrew to the countryside, and judging from Horace's epistle (I.4), he must have been a melancholy retiree.

> Tibullus, who reads, and enjoys, and understands my Satires,
> How shall I say what you're doing, now, off in the countryside?
> That you're writing something to outdo old Cassius
> Of Parma? Walking peaceful, silent, in those healthful
> Woods, meditating as a good man, a wise man, meditates?
> You were never mere flesh, always soul embodied: the gods gave you
> Beauty, and wealth, and the gift of relishing both.
> What more could a nursemaid want for her ward — that he thought,
> And said what he thought, and said it well; that fame came to him,
> And a good name, a good health — all in abundance — and that
> He lived as well as he needed to, and wrote as well, and as much, as he could.
>   Live with hope and with fear, with worry and with angry passion,
> But expect every hour to be your last:
> Days come even more delightful, unexpected.
> And when it's laughter you're looking for, come this way: you'll find me
> Fat and happy, like a hog from Epicurus' herd!

have brooded He can seem like two different poets, depending on the translation. First a piece of a poem translated by James Grainger in 1759, and then another translated by Michael Longley in 1979.

> She's mine. Be blind, ye Ramblers of the Night,
> Lest angry Venus snatch your guilty Sight:
> The Goddess bids her Votaries Joys to be
> From every casual Interruption free:
> With prying Steps alarm us not, retire,
> Nor glare your Torches, nor our Names inquire:
> Or if ye know, deny, by Heaven above,
> Nor dare divulge the Privacies of Love.
> From Blood and Seas vindictive Venus sprung,
> And sure Destruction waits the blabbing Tongue!

Peace
> Who was responsible for the very first arms deal —
> The man of iron who thought of marketing the sword?
> Or did he intend to use it against wild animals
> Rather than ourselves? Even if he's not guilty
> Murder got into the bloodstream as gene or virus
> So that now we give birth to wars, short vuts to death.

Blame the affluent society: no killings when
The cup on the table was made of beechwood,
And no barricades or ghettos when the shepherd
Snoozed among sheep that weren't even thoroughbreds.

I wouldlike to have been alive in the good old days
Before the horrors of modern warfare and warcries
Stepping up my pulse rate. Alas, as things turn out
I've been press-ganged into service, and for all I know
Someone's polishing a spear with my number on it.
God of my Father's, look after me like a child!
And don't be embarrassed by this handmade statue
Carved out of bog oak by my great-great-grandfather
Before the mass-production of religious art
When a wooden god stood simply in a narrow shrine.

A man could worship there with bunches of early grapes,
A wreath of whiskery wheat-ears, and then say Thank you
With a wholemeal loaf delivered by him in person,
His daughter carrying the unbroken honeycomb.
If the good Lord keeps me out of the firing line
I'll pick a porker from the steamy sty and dress
In my Sunday best, a country cousin's sacrifice.
Someone else can slaughter enemy commanders
And, over a drink, rehearse with me his memoirs,
Mapping the camp in wine upon the table top.

It's crazy to beg black death to join the ranks
Who dogs our footsteps anyhow with silent feet—
No cornfields in Hell, nor cultivated vineyards,
Only yapping Cerberus and the unattractive
Oarsman of the Styx: there an anaemic crew
Sleepwalks with smoky hair and empty eye-sockets.
How much nicer to have a family and let
Lazy old age catch up on you in your retirement,
You keeping track of the sleep, your son of the lambs,
While the woman of the house puts on the kettle.

I want to live until the white hairs shine above
A pensioner's memories of better days. Meanwhile
I would like peace to be my partner on the farm,
Peace personified: oxen under the curved yoke;
Compost for the vines, grape-juice turning into wine,
Vintage ears handed down from father to son;
Rust keeps the soldier's grisly weapons in their place;
The labourer steering his wife and children home
In a hay cart from the fields, a trifle sozzled.

Then, if there are skirmishes, guerilla tactics,
It's only lovers quarrelling, the bedroom door
Wrenched off its hinges, a woman in hysterics,

Hair torn out, cheeks swollen with bruises and tears—
Until the bully-boy starts snivelling as well
In a pang of conscience for his battered wife:
Then sexual neurosis works them up again
And the row escalates into a war of words.
He's hard as nails, made of sticks and stones, the chap
Who beats his girlfriend up. A crime against nature.

Enough, surely, to rip from her skin the flimsiest
Of negligees, ruffle that elaborate hair-do,
Enough to be the involuntary cause of tears—
Though upsetting a sensitive girl when you sulk
Is a peculiar satisfaction. But punch-ups,
Physical violence, are out: you might as well
Pack your kit-bag, goose-step a thousand miles away
From the female sex. As for me, I want a woman
To come and fondle my ears of wheat and let apples
Overflow between her breasts. I shall call her Peace.

☞ **7) Ovid** (Publius Naso, 43 B.C. - 17 A.D.), *Amores*, *The Metamorphoses*, *The Black Sea Letters*

If there is a poet laureate of the school of passionate verse, it is Publius Ovidius Naso. He was born a year after the assassination of Julius Caesar, on March 20, 43 BC, in Sulmo, a district in central Italy ninety miles east of Rome. His father came from a prosperous if not wealthy equestrian family. Their estate lay in the shadow of the Apennines, in a lush valley of vineyards, olive groves, cornfields, and sparkling streams that he would one day dearly miss during the barren exile of his later years. One of Ovid's ancestors was given the surname Naso, apparently in recognition of an unusually prominent nose. As was typical of members of the knightly class, Ovid was instructed by his parents in reading, writing, and arithmetic, but his father was aghast to learn that at the age of 12 the boy wished to be a poet. "Consider the awful fate of Homer," he instructed, "who died blind and poor."

Ovid agreed to a classical education in the Greek tradition which prepared him for an honorable and financially rewarding career in public service or the law. Obeying his father's wishes, Ovid went to Rome at the age of thirteen and took advanced courses in rhetoric from the virtuoso orator Arellius Fuscus, who made a lasting impression on Ovid with his imaginative presentations. The Elder Pliny later wrote that Ovid applied himself to the emotional rather than the argumentative side of rhetoric. Whatever the reason, the poet within him was aroused but in deference to his father's wishes, he went on to study law and eventually was elected judge. Much to the dismay of his father, however, he joined a group of writers under the patronage of the aristocratic consul M. Valerius Messalla Corvinus, who had commanded the fleet at the battle of Actium in 31 BC, helping Augustus to defeat Mark Anthony's forces. Messalla was one of several patrons (Maecenas was another) who took part in the emperor's plan to encourage artists to celebrate the return of peace and the flowering of the new empire. Among those in Messalla's circle were

Propertius, Horace, and Tibullus. Ovid even met Virgil during one of the reclusive poet's infrequent visits to Rome. Before he turned eighteen, Ovid was attending readings, where he heard Horace recite from his *Odes*, "the ink still wet," and soon began to read his own poems in public. They were the most erotic love poems of his day. Horace enjoyed his seductive wit, but felt that Ovid was a bit heavy-handed at times, going beyond propriety. "He cannot leave well enough alone," he said.

Eventually Ovid wore the tunic of a politician, mostly to please his parents, and married the girl chosen by his father, but he continued to write love poems, and to read them in public. Then, on the eve of his run for the Senate, Ovid walked away from the life of politics, divorced his wife, and devoted himself completely to the poet's life. In doing so, he captured the imagination of an upper-class Roman society disillusioned by the failure of the old Roman ideals to maintain the republic. He soon gained the reputation of being the most brilliant poet of his generation with a series of light, sophisticated love elegies. By the time he was forty, Ovid was a success, renowned throughout the empire. "I lisped in lyrics and the lyrics came."

His first collection of poems was published in five volumes, perhaps in 20 BC, when Ovid was 23 years old. The title, *Corinna*, is believed to be the woman who figures prominently in them. Most of the poems are studies or sketches of love, nearly always of sophisticated love, in the context of a pleasure-seeking, leisured society. They are polished, contrived, and amusing, the product of wit rather than of passion. These five books were later edited down to three, and published about 20 years later as a second edition, under the simple title *Amores*, or Love Poems, and this is the collection that has come down to us—49 poems in three books.

About the same time the second edition of *Love Poems* was published, Ovid also brought out the first two books of his *Ars Amatoria*, the Art of Love, and a year later (about 1 AD) the third volume appeared under the title *Remedia Amoris*, The Cure for Love. That was quickly followed by *Medicamina Faciei Femineae*, Facial Treatment for Ladies. These "how-to-books" were immensely popular, much to the displeasure of Augustus, who felt the tone of sexual lasciviousness and the encouragement of casual sex ran counter to his program of family values and traditional moral codes. Within a few years, Augustus found reason to punish Ovid, who was unaware that he would become the scapegoat for a generation of sexual dilettantes. Ovid was planning his next book, and it was to be an epic in stately hexameters—the *Metamorphoses*, his masterpiece. No sooner was it finished than Ovid was "struck by Jove's own lightning." Augustus's granddaughter Julia was notorious for her sexual escapades, even sleeping with men whom Augustus feared might be plotting against him. When he found out that Ovid had been witness to and perhaps took part in one of Julia's scandalous episodes, Ovid was "relegated" to Tomis, a barbarian outpost on the western shore of the Black Sea. *Relegato* was a milder form of exile in which one was not deprived of citizenship or property. Initially, Ovid hoped for a pardon, but as time went by and his supplicant letters in verse failed to move Augustus, he begged at least to be sent to a more congenial spot. When that plea went unanswered, the poet was willing to settle for burial in beloved Rome. His last poems, written during his exile, were titled the *Tristia*, or Sorrows, and poems in verse, *Epistulae ex Ponto*, the Black Sea

Letters. Ovid spent ten years among the barbarians, and died at Tomis in 17 or 18 AD, at the age of 60.

Food for Thought

Compare Ovid's poems of exile (the Sorrows, or Lamentations, and the Black Sea Letters) with the Consolations of Philosophy, a work of prose & verse, written by Boethius, while awaiting execution in the 6th century AD. Ovid's work had a practical purpose, to persuade Augustus, and eventually his successor, Tiberius, to grant him a pardon, or at least a more comfortable banishment. Boethius expected no reprieve. What made Ovid's poems at the end so tragic was the his refusal to give up hope. What gave Boethius' work its majesty was his anguish at facing death, and his attempt to find consolation in the eternal truths of philosophy.

Reading the work of poets who wrote during the time of Augustus, one is struck by the volume of work written by Ovid—over 33 thousand lines of verse, more than Propertius, Horace, and Virgil combined! He also worked in many different genres, another testament to his genius. The love elegy was not a life's work for Ovid, but one of several forms he mastered. Over the course of two millennia, each of his works (except perhaps the poems written during his exile) were at one time or another considered his greatest. One common form was the *recusatio*, where the poet begins by claiming he lacks the skill to write about a certain subject, or to write in an epic form, and then proceeds to do just that. It was in that spirit that Ovid experimented with several genres without identifying himself with any one of them. If anything, the theme that ran through all his poems was his stated intention to achieve immortality through his verses, be they elegiac couplets, epic hexameters, or elegiac lamentations (which he practically invented).

Like the *neoteric* poets of an earlier age, who proclaimed themselves "modern," Ovid was a modern poet, mirroring the spirit of a new Rome. It was an era of abandon, comparable to our own "Roaring Twenties," a post-war boom dominated by the young. Ovid was the F. Scott Fitzgerald of his day, celebrating the hedonism of youth and the sophisticated *amores* of the fashionably rich. In poetry, the archaic models were thrown off, the epic was set aside (except by Virgil, who attempted what no one else was willing to try), and a rigid moral standard was replaced by a relaxed refinement and a youthful zest. Ovid's work has a tone of innovation, a snappy wit that swept away the cobwebs of classical tradition. Listen to his use of language, especially in his love poems, and you can hear the literary modernity of Latin poetry that began with Catullus and continued for another century after Ovid through Martial, Petronius, and culminated with Juvenal.

In the *Metamorphoses*, he changes course and crafts the diction toward a more elegant line, and uses the hexameter of epic poetry to elevate the subject matter. Ovid perfected the terse and elegant style of the elegiac couplet, but when writing his *Tristia*, he gave elegy a tone of lamentation toward which imitators in later centuries would strive. Any age that thinks of itself as "modern" will hold Ovid's work up as fresh, and it was that contemporary tone that assured it a universality in its own day and in the centuries that followed.

☞ **The Amores**, *Love Poems* (1st edition. 20 BC, 2nd edition. around 1 BC)

Written before Ovid was twenty, these 49 poems seem as casual and hip as a comedian's monologue, yet are filled with erudite references to mythology and legend and to the great poets who wrote before him, as well as his own contemporaries. Quite often he models a poem, or part of one, on a poem by Propertius or Virgil, either parodying the poem or extending its form. Many of Ovid's poems would make good subject matter for a TV sit-com. "The Amorous Adventures of Publius Ovidius Naso"—Episodes of secret rendezvous, midnight serenades, lovers' spats, jealous encounters, impotence, anger and betrayal. We laugh at these escapades, partly because they're so unlike the dramas of Catullus, Propertius, or Tibullus, each of whom were obsessed with a single great love (Clodia, Cynthia, and Delia, respectively). Ovid's monologues are most often ironic and rendered with a grain of detachment. Though Corinna is the only named lover, Ovid tells us in the second poem that he's in love with love, not with any one woman. As a matter of fact, he wants to "love them all." One begins to wonder if this is really true, or the masked response of the lover betrayed, pretending he's beyond being hurt by anyone.

The first line of the *Amores*, the first word itself, parallels the opening of Virgil's *Aeneid*—"Arms and the man I sing." Ovid's work begins: "Arms, warfare, violence . . . " The reader is prepared for a Virgilian-style epic in hexameters, but Ovid lets us know before the first line is done that this is a mock-heroic tale told in a sly, comic tone that celebrates the arms of love and the violence of sexual conquest. What is fair in war, is also fair in love. Ovid discarded the grand epic style in favor of elegiac couplets—a hexameter line alternating with a pentameter line, the latter using two groups of two-and-a-half feet each. The epic's tone (a dactylic six-foot line used since the days of Homer) is high-minded, more serious than the ironic tone of the elegy. Ovid's erotic poems are by turns sensuous, comic, defiant, apologetic, and mocking. Even when serious, he's careful to avoid pretention, and if he doesn't, he soon deflates it with parody. In the opening poems of the *Amores*, Ovid admits he's in love with love, then in love with an unnamed girl; finally, by the fifth poem, we meet Corinna, the woman who steals his heart. We are never sure whether Corinna is fictional or his actual mistress.

Even in these early poems, Ovid's knowledge of mythology is impressive. In the first poem he refers to Minerva—the Roman counterpart to the Greek goddess Athena—who presided over intellectual and academic activity. "Our Lady of the Wheatfields" is Ceres (Demeter in Greek), the goddess of grain, of agriculture. Demeter and her daughter, Persephone (whose father is Zeus) were known as the Goddesses. Persephone's uncle, Hades (Pluto), fell in love with her, and while she was picking a narcissus, or a lily, the ground opened, Hades appeared, and dragged her down into the Underworld. Demeter wandered the world, a lighted torch in either hand, looking for her, forsaking her divine role until her daughter was returned to her. This self-imposed exile made the earth sterile, so Zeus ordered Hades to return Persephone. But having eaten seven pomegranate seeds while in the Underworld, Persephone became bound to Hades, so a compromise had to be reached: Demeter would return to Mount Olympus, and Persephone would divide the year between the Underworld and her mother (seven months in the underworld, one month for each seed eaten). Each spring, when the first shoots appear in furrows, Persephone makes her way toward the sky, only to return to the shades at seed-time. During her annual separation from Demeter, the ground remains sterile as winter grips the land. The cults of Dionysus and Demeter were established at the same time, in 496 BC. The "Virgin Huntress" is Diana (Artemis), associated with the moon. Besides being the Virgin, she was a ferocious goddess of woods and mountains who kept company with wild beasts. The "War God" is Mars (Ares). Ovid's readers were as familiar with these mythological characters as we are with comic book heroes. Where Virgil might invoke them for a serious, high-minded tone, Ovid uses them for purposes of parody. Imagine the first five lines of the opening poem being delivered by a borscht-belt comedian.

1

Arms, warfare, violence—I was winding up to produce a
Regular epic, with verse-form to match—
Hexameters, naturally. But Cupid (they say) with a snicker
Lopped off one foot from each alternate line.
``Nasty young brat," I told him, "who made you Inspector of metres?
We poets come under the Muses, we're not in your mob.
What if Venus took over the weapons of blonde Minerva,
While blonde Minerva began fanning passion's flame?
Who'd stand for Our Lady of Wheatfields looking after rides and forests?
Who'd trust the Virgin Huntress to safeguard crops?
Imagine long-haired Apollo on parade with a pikestaff
While the War-God fumbled tunes from Apollo's lyre?
Look, boy, you've got your own empire, and a sight too much influence
As it is. Don't get ambitious, quit playing for more.
Or is your fief universal? Is Helicon yours? Can't even
Apollo call his lyre his own these days?
I'd got off to a flying start, clean paper, one magnificent
Opening line. Number two brought me down
With a bump. I haven't the theme to suit your frivolous metre:
No boyfriend, no girl with a mane of coiffured hair—"
When I'd got so far, presto, he opened his quiver, selected
An arrow to lay me low,
Then bent the springy bow in a crescent against his knee, and
Let fly. "Hey, poet!" he called, "you want a theme? Take *that!*"
His shafts—worse luck for me—never miss their target:
I'm on fire now, Love owns the freehold of my heart.
So let my verse rise with six stresses, drop to five on the downbeat—
Goodbye to martial epic, and epic metre too!

Come on then, my Muse, bind your blonde hair with a wreath of
Sea-myrtle, and lead me off in the six-five groove!

The tone clues us in to Ovid's real desire—to get into her pants. Every line in the book, including a variation of the *carpe diem* approach (*seize the day!* Live for today and forget about tomorrow!), designed to seduce the object of his desire. This gambit was used in later centuries by poets such as Pierre Ronsard and Francois Villon who added another wrinkle: make love to me and I'll immortalize you in poetry!

3

Fair's fair now, Venus. This girl's got me hooked. All I'm asking from her
Is love—or at least some future hope for my own
Eternal devotion. No, even that's too much—hell, just let me love her!
(*Listen*, Venus: I've asked you so often now.)
Say yes, pet. I'd be your slave for years, for a lifetime.
Say yes—unswerving fidelity's my strong suit.
I may not have top-drawer connections, I can't produce blue-blooded
Ancestors to impress you, my father's plain middle-class,
And there aren't any squads of ploughmen to deal with *my* broad acres—
My parents are both pretty thrifty, and need to be.
What *have* I got on my side, then? Poetic genius, sweetheart,
Divine inspiration. And love. I'm yours to command—
Unswerving faithfulness, morals above suspicion,
Naked simplicity, a born-to-the-purple blush.
I don't chase thousands of girls, I'm no sexual circus-rider;
Honestly, all I want is to look after you
Till death do us part, have the two of us living together
All my time, and know you'll cry for me when I'm gone.
Besides, when you give me yourself, what you'll be providing
Is creative material. My art will rise to the theme
And immortalize *you*. Look, why do you think we remember
The swan-upping of Leda, or Io's life as a cow,
Or poor virgin Europa whisked off overseas, clutching
That so-called bull by the—horn? Through poems, of course.
So you and I, love, will enjoy the same world-wide publicity,
And our names will be linked, for ever, with the gods.

So much depends upon translation. It's clear Ovid is trying to get the girl to put out; passion, not ideal love, is the engine here. Following is a translation by F.A. Wright (1869-1946), of the same poem, not only taken out of context, but given a tone of sincerity that changes Ovid's original intent. Ovid did not rhyme, either, but since rhyme was the English convention for poetry, Wright turned Ovid's elegiac couplets into rhyming quatraines, rendering the work less offensive. That would be like translating Frank O'Hara's self-mocking irreverent lines into sentimental verse.

Myself
Take me, and I your slave will be
    As long as life endure:
Constant in my fidelity

And in your service sure.

Mine is no name of ancient might
    Nor have I lands untold;
My father's but a simple knight
    And careful with his gold.

But Phoebus and the Muses nine
    Come ever to my call,
And Bacchus, finder of the vine,
    And love, who gives me all.

My life is pure and free from strain,
    My heart is sound and true.
No gallant I, of conquests vain,
    But faithful still to you.

The above example is how the ancient and classical poets were translated into bland English verse. Since Shakespeare's day, translators and publishers felt it their duty to render such sassy verse into politically correct sentiments for their day, giving students of English literature a distorted view of the work and the poet's relevance. Great poets have always been "modern," their diction alive and natural, whether it is the diction of the more formal epic, or the everyday banter we associate today with poets like Frank O'Hara and Charles Bukowski. Modern poetry was a revolution that urged poets to write the way the classic poets wrote, in the living speech of their own day. The modern had to appear to discard the phony diction of the classical poets, when what they were really doing was discarding the *translations* of classical poetry, and the stilted 19th century English verse upon which those translations were based.

In another poem, Ovid exploits the dinner party theme. Lovers secretly give each other clandestine signals to convey thoughts and feelings, a stock theme for Augustan elegists. It's clear in this poem that Ovid is referring to married women of his own class, thumbing his nose at the Augustan legislation that made the seduction of a married woman cause for banishment. Later, Ovid said that he wrote only with courtesans and freedwomen in mind, but this and other poems seem to contradict this claim, even though the ambiguous Latin word *vir* could mean both "husband" and "lover." In this, the translator uses the term "man."

4

"So your man's going to be present at this dinner-party?
I hope he drops down dead before the dessert!
Does this mean no hands, just eyes (any chance guest's privilege) —
Just to *look* at my darling, while he
Lies there with you beside him, in licensed embracement
and paws your bosom or neck as he feels inclined?
I'm no longer surprised at those Centaurs for horsing around over
Some cute little filly when they were full of wine —
I may not live in the forest, or be semi-equipped as a stallion,
But still I can hardly keep my hands to myself

When you're around. Now listen, I've got some instructions for you,
And don't let the first breeze blow them out of your head!
Arrive before your escort. I don't see what can be managed
If you do—but anyway, get there first.
When he pats the couch, put on your Respectable Wife expression,
And take your place beside him—but nudge my foot
As you're passing by. Watch out for my nods and eye-talk,
Pick up my stealthy messages, send replies.
I shall speak whole silent volumes with one raised eyebrow,
words will spring from my fingers, words traced in wine.
When you're thinking about the last time we made love together,
Touch your rosy cheek with one elegant thumb.
If you're cross with me, and can't say so, then pinch the bottom
Of your earlobe. But when I do or say
Something that gives you especial pleasure, my darling,
Keep turning the ring on your finger to and fro.
When you yearn for your man to suffer some well-merited misfortune
Place your hands on the table as though in prayer.
If he mixes wine specially for you, watch out, make him drink it
Himself. Ask the waiter for what *you* want
As you hand back the goblet. I'll be the first to seize it
And drink from the place your lips have touched.
If *he* offers you tid-bits out of some dish he's tasted,
Refuse what's been near his mouth.
Don't let him put his arms round your neck, and oh, don't lay that
Darling head of yours on *his* coarse breast.
Don't let his fingers roam down your dress to touch up
Those responsive nipples. Above all, don't you dare
Kiss him, not once. If you do, I'll proclaim myself your lover,
Lay hand upon you, claim those kisses as mine.
So much for what I can see. But there's plenty goes on under
A long evening wrap. The mere thought worries me stiff.
Don't start rubbing your thigh against his, don't go playing
Footsy under the table, keep smooth from rough."
(I'm scared all right, and no wonder—I've been too successful
An operator myself, it's my own
Example I find so unnerving. I've often petted to climax
With my darling at a party, hand hidden under her cloak—)
"—Well, you won't do that. But still, to avoid the least suspicion,
Remove such natural protection when you sit down.
Keep pressing fresh drinks—but no kisses—on your husband,
Slip neat wine in his glass if you get the chance.
If he passes out comfortably, drowned in sleep and liquor,
We must improvise as occasion dictates.
When we all (you too) get up and leave, remember
To stick in the middle of the crowd—
That's where you'll find me, or I you: whenever
There's a chance to touch me, please do!"
(Yet the most I can win myself is a few hours respite:
At nightfall my mistress and I must part.)

"At nightfall he'll lock you inside, and I'll be left weeping
On that cold front doorstep—the nearest I can come
To your longed-for-embrace, while *he's* enjoying, under licence,
The kisses, and more, that you give me on the sly.
What you *can* do is show unwilling, behave as though you're frigid
Begrudge him endearments, make sex a dead loss."
(Grant my prayer, Venus,. Don't let either of them get pleasure
Out of the act—*and certainly not her!*)
"But whatever the outcome tonight, when you see me tomorrow
Just swear, through thick and thin, that you told him No."

Finally, in the fifth poem of Book I, we meet his mistress in person, and discover her name. This charming poem has no ironic barbs or political parody. There's a sweetness to the love-making, an unpretentious, and straightforward account of a meeting of lovers that was absent from Latin poetry, until Ovid. He comes home to his afternoon siesta, common among Mediterranean cultures for centuries. As he drifts off to sleep, he associates the afternoon light with the image of a young girl, bashful and modest, and . . . . suddenly, there she is, stealing her way into his room in her summer skirt, ready for love. Is this a dream, or is there a real Corinna haunting these poems?

5

A hot afternoon: siesta-time. Exhausted,
I lay sprawled across my bed.
One window-shutter was closed, the other stood half-open,
and the light came sifting through
As it does in a wood. It recalled that crepuscular glow at sunset
Or the trembling moment between darkness and dawn,
Just right for a modest girl whose delicate bashfulness
Needs some camouflage. And then—
In stole Corinna, long hair tumbled about her
Soft white throat, a rustle of summer skirts,
Like some fabulous Eastern queen *en route* to her bridal-chamber—
Or a top-line city call girl, out on the job.
I tore the dress off her   not that it really hid much,
But all the same she struggled to keep it on:
Yet her efforts were unconvincing, she seemed half-hearted—
Inner self-betrayal made her give up.
When at last she stood naked before me, not a stitch of clothing
I couldn't fault her body at any point.
Smooth shoulders, delectable arms (I saw, I touched them),
Nipples inviting caresses, the flat
Belly outlined beneath that flawless bosom,
Exquisite curve of a hip, firm youthful thighs.
But why catalogue details? Nothing came short of perfection,
And I clasped her naked body close to mine.
Fill in the rest for yourselves! Tired at last, we lay sleeping.
May my siestas often turn out that way!

Whether or not Corinna is real has some bearing upon the persona Ovid employs in his writing. After his exile, he protested that he wasn't the rakish playboy of his poems, but a faithful husband. "Who was this *I* you read, this trifler in tender passions?" he asks in his *Poems from Exile*. "The fact that my poetry's more wanton than my life, that my fun is free of real offence does me no good." Of course, he may well have been pleading his case to Augustus, hoping for a reprieve. But there might have been some truth to his claims. "My morals, believe me, are quite distinct from my verses—a respectable life-style, a flirtatious Muse—and the larger part of my writings is mendacious, fictive, assumes the license its author denies himself." Why the fiction then, why the mask? Perhaps, like a comedian wearing the persona of a hip lover, a rogue driving in the fast lane, Ovid wanted to speak to the new generation who were quick to laugh at such licentious behavior. How fashionable would it have been for Ovid to admit that, in reality, he was a one-woman man, a faithful puppy dog? Then who was this Corinna? Another man's wife, a figment of his imagination?

   She's introduced in the above poem ambiguously. Was she just a dream, and are we meant to assume that her presence in the *Amores* is a fantasy. There's another possibility. Ovid must be in his own house, since it's unlikely that he'd arrange a siesta in Corinna's home. But where did Corinna come from when she suddenly glided through the open window? It's not likely that she walked through the streets alone, but where is the maid if she came escorted? If Ovid was the habitual Casanova he claimed to be, an experienced porter would know how to sneak his lovers in, but what about Ovid's wife? Would he have been that daring? In the *Tristia* letters from exile, he tells us

> When first I recited my earliest poems in public
> my beard had only been shaved once or twice:
> she fired my genius, who now is a Roman byword
> because of those verses, the girl to whom I gave
> the pseudonym of "Corinna." My writing was prolific, ...
> > My heart was soft, no stronghold
> against Cupid's assaults, prey to the lightest pang.

Unless we assume that Ovid used a friend's house, like Catullus had done, or made up the whole relationship based on common Hellenistic themes, we are left to wonder how Ovid and his lover were able to meet so easily. Perhaps Corinna was not his mistress, but his first wife, who stole, then broke, his heart.

   Ovid was also charged with being a slacker for not participating in military service; instead he indulged in sexual escapades. Poem #9 goes to the heart of that criticism by claiming that love, not war, is the best cure for idleness. Going a step further, Ovid declared that love and war were much the same, and seduction itself the battle.

9

> Every lover's on active service, my friend, active service, believe me
> And Cupid has his headquarters in the field.
> Fighting and love-making belong to the same age-group—
> In bed as in war, old men are out of place.
> A commander looks to his troops for gallant conduct,
> A mistress expects no less.

Soldier and lover both keep night-long vigil,
Lying rough outside their captain's (or lady's) door.
The military life brings long route-marches — but just let his mistress
Be somewhere ahead, and the lover too
Will trudge on for ever, scale mountains, ford swollen rivers,
Thrust his way through deep snow.
Come embarkation-time *he* won't talk of "strong north-easters,"
Or say it's "too late in the season" to put to sea.
Who but a soldier or lover would put up with freezing
Night — rain, snow, sleet? The first
Goes out on patrol to observe the enemy's movements,
The other watches his rival, an equal foe.
A solder lays seige to cities, a lover to girls' houses,
The one assaults city gates, the other front doors.
Night attacks are a great thing.
Catch your opponents sleeping
And unarmed. Just slaughter them where they lie.
That's how the Greeks dealt with Rhesus
and his wild Thracians
While rustling those famous mares.
Lovers, too, will take advantage of slumber (her husband's),
Strike home while the enemy sleeps: getting past
Night patrols and eluding sentries are games both soldiers
And lovers need to learn.
Love, like war, is a toss-up. The defeated can recover,
While some you might think invincible collapse;
So if you've got love written off as an easy option
You'd better think twice. Love calls
For guts and initiative. Great Achilles sulks for Briseis —
Quick, Trojans, smash through the Argive wall!
Hector went into battle from Androchmache's embraces
At the sight of Cassandra's tumbled hair;
Even Mars was caught on the job, felt the blacksmith's meshes —
Heaven's best scandal in years. Then take
My own case. I was idle, born to leisure *en déshabillé*
Mind softened by lazy scribbling in the shade.
But love for a pretty girl soon drove the sluggard
To action, made him join up.
And just look at me now — fighting fit, dead keen on night exercises:
If you want a cure for slackness, fall in love!

[Rhesus, King of Thrace, famous aid the Trojans, and was killed by Odysseus. Notice, Ovid lists examples of Homeric heroes who were great fighters & lovers, implying that sex does not impede military valor. Furthermore, he puts himself in pretty good company.]

In the beginning of the poem Ovid states that just as he was searching for an appropriate epic theme, Cupid came along, and he was impelled to write the erotic elegy. Along with the success of his poems came critics who resented his idler status, that he didn't have to work. The image of the poet sitting under a tree and scribbling verse was something of a cliché by Ovid's time. An upper-class Roman could practice *otium*—read fine literature or history at one's *ease* or *leisure* (as Cicero wrote: *otium suum consumere in historia scribenda*), especially after a hard day of *negotium*—work. (Again, quoting Cicero: *negotium alicui exhibere*, to cause someone trouble.) If one were to practice *otium*, the leisure had to conform to socially acceptable norms. For an adult to sit under a tree and scribble poetry was not considered socially responsible. Ovid makes it clear in the above poem that though he had been idle and lazy, love changed all that. He was now tough as a soldier.

There are, however, inconsistencies in Ovid's case for his industriousness as a soldier in the wars of love. Three poems later he presents the poet as idler, angling for a few more hours with his lover and sleep after a night of love.

Food for Thought

Holding Back the Dawn

A common scene; Ovid's readers had read such set-pieces before. In the 12th century, this was a common motif among the troubadour poets of the south of France, who called it a dawn song, or *alba*. (see chapter on Troubadour Poets, page ____) Here Bernard de Ventadorn celebrates lying side by side with his lover (notice the repetition of the word "joy," which was a euphemism for sex, combining in its meaning the provençal word for "sport" and "ecstacy.")

> When the new grass and the leaves come forth
> and the flower burgeons on the branch,
> and the nightingale lifts its high
> pure voice and begins its song,
> I have joy in it, and joy in the flower,
> and joy in myself, and in my lady most of all:
> on every side I am enclosed and girded with joy,
> and a joy that overwhelms all other joys.

But the dawn song had a note of anguish in it, since the song of the nightingale was replaced by the sound of the lark, signaling daybreak—time for the lover to leave before he's discovered. We find a famous dawn song in Shakespeare, where Juliet spends her first (and last) night with her new husband before his banishment.

> Juliet
> Wilt thou be gone? it is not yet near day:
> It was the nightengale, and not the lark,
> That pierced the fearful hollow of thine ear;
> Nightly she sings on yond pomegranate-tree:
> Believe me, love, it was the nightengale.

> Romeo
> It was the lark, the herald of the morn,
> No nightengale: look, love, what envious streaks
> Do lace the evering clouds in yonder east:
> Night's candles are burnt out, and jocund day
> Stands tiptoe on the misty mountain tops:
> I must be gone and live, or stay and die.

> Juliet

Yon light is not day-light, I know it, I:
It is some meteor that the sun exhales,
To be to thee this night a torch-bearer,
And light thee on thy way to Manua:
Therefore stay yet; thou need'st not to be gone.

Romeo

Let me be ta'en, let me be put to death;
I am content, so thou wilt have it so.
I'll say yon grey is not the morning's eye,
'Tis but the pale reflect of Cynthia's brow;
Nor that is not the lark, whose notes do beat
The vaulty heaven so high above our heads:
I have more care to stay than will to go:
Come, death, and welcome! Juliet will it so.
How is 't, my soul? let's talk: it is not day.

Juliet

It is, it is: hie hence, be gone, away!
It is the lark that sings so out of tune,
Straining harsh discords and unpleasing sharps.
Some say the lark makes sweet division;
This doth not so, for she divideth us:
Some say the lark and loathed toad change eyes:
O, now I would they had changed voices too!
Since arm from arm that voice doth us affray,
Hunting thee hence with hunts-up to the day.
O, now be gone; more light and light it grows.

Romeo

More light and light; more dark and dark our woes!

Like all great writers, Shakespeare gives added poignancy to a common, set-piece, lovers having to part before daybreak, wishing to hold back Aurora (or Eos, its Greek parallel). Aurora was depicted as a goddess whose rosy fingers opened the gates of heaven to the chariot of the Sun—the wish to hold back the personified dawn.

Hold Back the Dawn was a 1941 film where gigolo Charles Boyer marries spinsterish Olivia de Havilland to get into the United States. Another pair of contrasting lovers, each with their own reason for wishing dawn wouldn't hurry so. In that film, we get a film within a film, where the director of *Hold Back the Dawn*, Mitchell Leisen, plays himself on a Hollywood sound stage directing Veronica Lake and Ray Milland in *I Wanted Wings*, which was released the same year. In that one, Milland, Brian Donlevy, and William Holden undergo air force training and chastise dawn for being in such a hurry to send them off to war.

Like Shakespeare after him, Ovid takes the set piece and adds to it the *suasoria*, a rhetorical exercise in persuasion. With his characteristic wit, Ovid makes a case for why dawn should (in Christopher Marlowe's 16th century translation) "hold in thy rosy horses that they move not," or (in Peter Green's contemporary translation), "What's the hurry! Exert those rosy fingers, rein in awhile!" Persuasively, he gives examples where she is often too hasty in sending soldiers, farmers, sailors, schoolboys and housewives off to their day.

13

She's on her way over the sea from her doddering husband,
The blond day-bringer, wheels all aglint with frost—
What's the hurry, Aurora? Take it easy, let Memnon's spirit
Enjoy the yearly sacrifice by his birds!
Now, if ever, I love to lie in my mistress's tender
Embrace, feel her close by my side,
At this cool hour of deep sleep, with liquid bird-song
Tremulous in the air.
What's the hurry? All lovers, men and girls, resent your coming:
Exert those rosy fingers, rein in awhile!
Seamen out in deep water, eyes fixed on the constellations,
Steer closer before your rising, don't yaw off course.
Even the weariest traveller's out to greet you,
Every soldier's armed and ready by the time you arrive.
You're always up first. You challenge the weary peasant, trudging
Along with his mattock. You call
The ploughman to yoke up his weary oxen. You rob young
Children of sleep, drive them out to school
And the cruel cane. You send cultured guarantors crowding
Down to the courts, where a one-
Word pledge may lose them a fortune. Pleaders and advocates
Resent your summons, forcing them to resume
The daily legal grind. When a woman might still be resting
You jerk her back to dull domestic chores.
I could put up with everything else—but only a crusty
Misogynist, surely, would stand
For girls getting up at dawn? The times I've prayed that darkness
Might stand fast against you, and the stars
Not vanish before your countenance, that a hurricane
Would crack your axle, or your horses fall
Headlong through blinding cloud! Why hurry, spoilsport?
How I wish Tithonus could spill the truth about you—no distaff
Reputation in heaven would drop so low.
You hurry away from him because he's so much older,
To mount the chariot he weakly hates—
But if it was your love, your Cephalus, you were embracing,
You'd cry: "Run slowly, horses of the night!"
Why should I suffer in love just because your husband's senile?
Did you marry the old buffer on my advice.
Just think how long a sleep the Moon allowed her beloved
Endymion—and she's as beautiful as you!
The father of Gods himself was so averse to seeing you,
Once, that he ran two nights of love into one.
Ah: that last crack must have gone home—I saw her blushing.
But the sun still (as usual) rose on time.

Compare the translation above, with Christopher Marlowe's.

The air is cold, and sleep is sweetest now,
And birds send forth shrill notes from every bough.
Wither run'st thou, that men and women love not?
Hold in thy rosy horses that they move not.
Ere thou rise, stars teach seamen where to sail,
But when thou comest, they of their courses fail.
Poor travellers, though tired, rise at thy sight,
And soldiers make them ready for the fight.
The painful hind by thee to field is sent;
Slow oxen early in the yoke are pent.
Thou cozenest boys of sleep, and dost betray them
To pendants that with cruel lashes pay them.
Thou mak'st the surety to the lawyer run
That with one word hath nigh himself undone.
The lawyer and the client hate thy view,
Both whom thou raisest up to toil anew.
By thy means women of their rest are barred;
Thou det'st their labouring hands to spin and card,
All could I bear; but that the wench should rise,
Who can endure, save him with whom none lies?

Christopher Marlowe was not the only Elizabethan poet to translate Ovid. Caxton translated him into English from the French in 1480; the most influential 16th century version was Arthur Golding's *Metamorphoses* published in 1567. English poetry took on a markedly Ovidian colouring, and, as Francis Meres wrote in 1598, "the sweet witty soul of Ovid lives in mellifluous and honey-tongued Shakespeare, witness his *Venus and Adonis*, his *Lucrece*, his sugared sonnets among his private friends." Shakespeare's Latin was not up to Spenser's, evidenced by the numerous references Spenser made in his *Fairy Queene*; but it was sufficient to allow him to make occasional references to the original.

The recurring theme—that Ovid's sexual escapades will make the women famous because he will write about her—reappears in the next poem, which deals with the gifts the lover is expected to give his mistress.

> Let courtesy, trust, devotion
> Be the poor man's tribute. From each
> Lover his all—but according to his resources. *My* gift
> Is poetry, the praise
> Of beautiful girls. I can make them immortal. Fine dresses,
> Jewellery, gold, all perish. But the fame
> Bestowed by my verse is perennial.

Ovid ends Book I with a reply to his critics, who claimed that writing poetry was not a fit occupation. Ovid makes it clear that he's got his eye on a bigger prize than gold. And he doesn't mince words when it comes to dismissing the work and waste of talent in practising law, which he equates with the prostitution of one's rhetorical skills. Ironic, especially since many Latin poets—Virgil, Martial, Juvenal, etc.—), were trained for the legal profession , which they abandoned to write poetry.

15

Why, gnawing Envy, impute an idler's existence to me?
Why dismiss the poet as a drone?
What's your complaint? That' I've failed (though young and healthy) to
        follow
 Tradition, or chase the dusty rewards
Of a soldier's career? That I haven't mugged up dull lawsuits,
Or sold my eloquence like a whore
In the courts and Forum? Such labours are soon forgotten.
What *I* seek is perennial fame,
Undying world-wide remembrance. While Ida and Tenedos
Still stand, while Simois still runs swift to the sea,
Old Homer will live. While clustering grapes still ripen
And wheat still falls to the scythe
Hesiod's works will be studied. The verse of Callimachus—
Weak in imagination, strong on technique—
Has a worldwide readership. Sophoclean tragedy
Is safe from Time's ravages. . . . What age
Will not cherish great Varro's epic of Argo's voyage,
Jason's quest for the Golden Fleece?
The work of sublime Lucretius will prove immortal
While the world itself endures;
And so long as Rome's empire holds sway over the nations,
Virgil's country poems, his *Aeneid,* will be read.
While Cupid's armoury still consists of torch and arrows
Tibullus' elegant verse
Will always be quoted. . . .

Though time, in time, can consume the enduring ploughshare,
Though flint itself will perish, poetry lives—
Deathless, unfading, triumphant over kings and their triumphs,
Richer than Spanish river-gold. Let the crowd
Gape after baubles. To me may golden Apollo proffer
A cup, brimming over, from the Castalian spring
And a wreath of sun-loving myrtle. May my audience always
Consist of star-crossed lovers. Never forget
It's the living that Envy feeds on. After death the pressure
Is taken off. All men get their due in the end.
So when the final flames have devoured my body, I shall
Strive, and my better part live on.

Book II anticipates the *Art of Love* as a practical guide to winning a woman. The first poem is a companion piece to the first poem of Book I, a statement of Ovid's literary intentions. In the first one he tells us that he was beginning to write an epic but Cupid hit his heart and the epic was abandoned for the elegy. Here, his current mistress (presumably Corinna) stages "a lock-out," and Ovid has no choice but to resume the elegy.

Book II,

1

A second batch of verses by that naughty provincial poet,
Naso, the chronicler of his own
Wanton frivolities; another of Love's commissions (warning
To puritans: *This volume is not for you*).
I want my works to be read by the far-from-frigid virgin
On fire for her sweetheart, by the boy
In love for the very first time. May some fellow-sufferer,
Perusing my anatomy of desire,
See his own passion reflect there, cry in amazement:
"Who told this scribbler about my private affairs?"
One time, I recall, I got started on an inflated epic
About War in Heaven, ... but while I was setting up
My mistress staged a lock-out. I dropped Jupiter and his lightnings
That instant, didn't give him another thought.
Forgive me, good Lord, if I found your armoury useless —
Her shut door ran to larger bolts
Than any *you* wielded. I went back to verses and compliments,
My natural weapons. Soft words
Remove harsh door-chains. There's magic in poetry, its power
Can pull down the bloody moon,
Turn back the sun, make serpents burst asunder
Or rivers flow upstream.
But epics are a dead loss for me. I'll get nowhere with swift-footed
Achilles, or with either of Atreus' sons.   [Agamemnon & Menelaus]
Old what's-his-name   [Odysseus]
wasting away 20 years on war and travel,
Poor Hector dragged in the dust —
No good. But lavish fine words on some young girl's profile
And sooner or later she'll tender herself as the fee,
An ample reward for your labours. So farewell, heroic
Figures of legend — the *quid*
Pro quo you offer won't tempt me. A bevy of beauties
All swooning over my love-songs — that's what *I* want.

4

I wouldn't attempt to defend my spotty morals, or whitewash
My flaws with aggressive lies.
If it's any help, I confess. Admission of guilt. Then why not
Go the whole hog, indict
My faults myself? I hate what I am, yet (try as I may) can't
Not be the thing that revolts me. It's hell
Being stuck with what you can't kick. I lack all firmness
And strength to control my moods, get whirled away
Like a skiff in a current. There's no one type of beauty
That calls my passion forth: there are a hundred causes
To keep me always in love — blame my wide-ranging interests.
If it is some fair one with modest eyes downcast upon her lap
I am aflame. I'm hooked, her innocence my unsnaring.
But it's just the same if she's a saucy jade; I'm smitten because

She is not rustic simple, but gives me hope of enjoying her embrace
On the soft couch. Sophistication promises well in bed.
A primly old-fashioned appearance, then? I always suspect that's
 Mere camouflage for unacknowledged desire.
A prudish bluestocking turns me on with her intellectual powers,
A featherbrain ditto just by being naïve.
Then there's the girl who tells me
Callimachus is a bungler   [305-240 BC,
Compared to me—I always go for my fans—   [the most popular
Or the critical termagent who slates   poet in Roman times;
both poems and author: only Homer is quoted
How I long to be laid by her as well!   more often
One's got a slinky walk: *that* gets me. Another's uptight—
She can be softened out with a little sex.
Another dances before the mirror, swaying arms and curving her sides
—Put Hippolytus in my place and even *he'd* go priapic!
My sex-life runs the entire mythological gamut. So my tastes.
Young girls have the looks—but when it comes to technique
Give me an older woman. In short, there's a vast cross-section
Of desirable beauties in Rome—*and I want them all!*

Compare this poem to the fourth poem of Book 3, and you'll be juggling two, apparently contradictory statements of Ovid's position. Unless we remember that the literary persona that Ovid hides behind shifts and changes, and he can never be taken too seriously. In this poem, he tells the husband of a mistress that unless the husband guard his wife more closely, Ovid will become bored and lose all interest. In poem #4 of Book 3, he tells the husband that keeping tabs on his wife will do no good, since only her natural desires to stay faithful (or chaste) will determine her actions. While this may seem contradictory, from Ovid's point of view, it makes perfect sense, each piece of advice is sound. Beneath both propisitions is the notion that one put on a show of restraint, or a show of trust. Love is a game, and what counts is that each participant play their role accordingly.

   If one were to assume that Corinna was based on Ovid's first wife, poems 13 & 14 give one reason to assume it may have been so. He expresses anger that she got an abortion, and admits the child may have been his. If she were his mistress, certainly it would complicate matters if she got pregnant and had a child. Yet, Ovid is upset that she got an abortion.

13

Corinna got pregnant—and rashly tried an abortion
Now she's lying in danger of her life.
She said not a word. That risk, and she never told me!
I ought to be furious, but I'm only scared.
It was me by whom she conceived—or at least, I assume so.
I often jump to conclusions. . . . .

Ilithyria, Goddess of Childbirth, hear my entreaties, save her—
She's worth it, truly. Just say the world,
And I'll robe myself in white, burn incense on your smoking
Altar, lay at your feet the gifts I vowede,

With a label reading "From Ovid, ingrateful thanks for Corinna's
Recovery'—ah please make it all come true!
Look, sweetheart, I know how you're feeling, I know it's no time for
Recriminations—but never try that again!

The following poem lends itself to speculation: was Ovid the father of Corinna's unborn
child? Ovid's objections to abortion are not based on moral grounds. His reasoning
focuses on practical and historical considerations. What would have happened if the
parents of Achilles, Romulus, Aeneas and Caesar practiced abortion? Or is Ovid, as he was
wont to do, mocking the moral legislation of Augustus?

14

What's the point of a girl being exempt from active service—
No shield-drill, no column-of-route
marching away to the wars—as if she uses weapons against her
Self, suffers hurt from her own hand?
The woman who first ripped foetus from placenta should have
Died by such butchery herself.
Would you *really* chance your arm in that bloody arena
Just to keep your belly unwrinkled? Suppose
Mothers in olden times had caught on to such practices,
Mankind would be quite extinct,
And we'd need a new-style stone-throwing demiurge
to repeople our empty world.
Who would have cracked Priam's might   [King of Troy]
if the sea-goddess Thetis
Had refused to carry her load?
Had Ilia ripped those twins from her swollen belly
Our City's Founder would hav been lost.
Had Venus aborted the unborn Aeneas, no Caesars today would
Exist in the world. You too
Would have perished, your beauty still embryonic, had your
Mother attempted the same game.
Take my own case—I'd rather die from a surfeit of loving
Than find myself mother-scuppered before birth.
Why cheat the laden vine when grapes are ripening
Or strip an apple-tree while the fruit's still green?
Let all things mature in season, come forth, develop—
have patience. Life is a prize
Well worth the waiting. Why probe your entrails with lethal
Instruments? Why poison what's still unborn?
Child-blood on Medea's hands excites our horror, dismembered
Itys brings tears to the eye:
Parental savagery rampant. yet both these women had bitter
Cause to destroy their own dear flesh—
Revenge on a husband. But *you*—what Tereus or Jason
Drives *you* to commit this deadly self-abuse?
No Armenian tigress would foul her den iwth such actions:
No lioness would destroy her own cubs.
Yet tender young firls do this—though not with impunity: often
The uterine murderess dies herself,
Dies, and is carried out for cremation, hair all dishevelled,

To cries of "Serve her right!" from the passers-by.
May these utterances of mine be scattered down the wind, and
No weight attach to such ill-omened words!
Be merciful, Gods. Let her first offence go unpunished,
That's all I ask. If she errs again—then strike!

19

You may not feel any need (and more fool you) to guard that
Girl of yours—but it sharpens my desire,
So would you oblige? What's allowed is a bore, it's what isn't
That turns me on. What cold clod
Could woo with his rival's approval? We lovers need hope and
despair in alternate doses. An intermittent rebuff
Makes us promise the earth. Who wants a beautiful woman
When she never deceives him?
If you're after what's lawful and easy, then why not gather
Leaves from the trees, or drink
Water out of the Tiber? To prolong your dominion over
Your lover calls for deception. (I hope I won't
Have cause to regret that statement.) Yet come what may, indulgence
Irks me. I flee the eager, pursue the coy.

And as for *you*, man, so careless of your good lady,
Why not start locking up at night?
Why not ask who it is comes tapping, ever so softly,
On your front door—or why it is the dogs
Start barking at midnight? What about all those to-and-fro missives
The maid delivers? How come your wife now sleeps
Alone so often? Why can't you get really worried just
Once in a while, allow me to display
My skill at deception? To covet the wife of a dummy
Is like stealing sand off the beach.
I'm warning you: put your foot down, play the heavy husband,
Or I'll start going cold on your wife!
I've stood it quite long enough, always hoping you'd lock her
Away out of sight, so that I
Could outwit you. But no. You clod, you put up with things no husband
Should stand for a moment. Let me have the girl
And there's an end to my passion. Won't you *ever* deny me
Entry, won't you beat me up one night?
Can't I ever feel scared? have insomnia? sigh in frustration?
Won't you give me some good excuse
To wish you dead? I've no time for complaisant, pimping
 husbands—Their kindness spoils my fun.
Find someone else, who *likes* your easy-going habits, or if you
Must have me as a rival, then *get tough!*

Book 3

Because the following poems appears to contradict the poem above, many readers and critics have supposed that Ovid was inconsistent and dishonest because he used various literary poses, or personas. He's simply saying that to keep too close an eye on the lady will stimulate both the husband and the lover; best to give her free reign. Ovid switches masks merely to make the same point, from different points of view.

4

Being tough's no good, man. Guarding your girl won't help you.
Try exploiting her feminine instincts. Remove
All restraints. If she's still chaste, that's genuine chastity. If she
Only holds back from compulsion, then the first
Chance that she gets, she'll do it. With body mewed up, her urges
Are whorish as ever. No watchdog can stopper desire—
Or even sequester the person. Bolt each door, bar every lover,
Adultery still will lurk within.
But give her free scope, she'll get bored—will full endorsement
The itch for illicit affairs
Very quickly subsides. Believe me, your prohibitions
Exacerbate vice. Why not try a permissive regime?

In the next poem, Ovid recounts a dream, to a "dream interpreter." After the above poem, in which Ovid is so cavalier about advising the husband to trust his wife, it's more than ironic that he would follow up with a poem that turns the tables. Since dream-interpretation was a common pastime throughout antiquity, Ovid is clearly spelling out the truth of his relationship with Corinna (and if she was truly based on his first wife, the deteriorating marriage, and the ultimate irony, that Ovid is the husband being cuckolded. The poem opens with a stock pastoral description, the "sunlit hillside, ... a grassy meadow beyond." Suddenly, a white heifer appears with her "privileged mate," a bull. They settle on the grass and the bull nods off to sleep.

"Then a carrion-crow swooped down on the widespread pinions
And sat cawing there in the grass:
Three times, with mischievous beak, it pecked at the heifer's
Breast, and tore out a snow-
White tuft. The heifer at last abandoned bull and meadow,
A livid bruise on her throat,
And seeing other bulls at pasture in the distance,
Bulls in the distance, and fine
Pasturage to be had, moved over and joined them,
In quest of more fertile fields,
A richer diet. So tell me, my unseen expounder
Of dreams (if such dreams do have significance), what
Does mine portend?"
              The interpreter pondered on all I'd told him
Then answered: "That heat you tired
To escape from by sheltering under the breeze-stirred branches,
Yet in vain, was the heat of desire.

The heifer stood for your girl—white, a most appropriate color—
The bull, her companion, was you.
The sharp-beaked crowthat pecked at her breast was some elderly
Bawd fast-talking her into another affair.
Just as theheifer, at last, after long hesitation,
Left her bull, so you too will be left
Alone in your own cold bed. The bruise on her breast bears witness
To the stain of adultery."
                                    There
His interpretation ended. At those words the blood ran freezing
from my face, and the world went black before my eyes.

In the next poem, the longest in the *Amores*, Ovid tries to persuade a river to let him cross so he cankeep a date with his lover. But no matter what rhetorical and poetic arguements Ovid produces, the river runs higher and higher. Ovid becomes angry and curses the river, and ultimately realizes that poetry is not magic, and the world is often deaf to the music of poetic genius. We do not know what poems Ovid cut from the first edition, but it is clear that Ovid deliberately placed this poem between one advising marital trust and one about sexual impotence.

6

Reed-choked and muddy river, would you please mind stopping
Your flow for a moment? I'm late
For a date with my girl. There's no bridge, no cable-ferry
To get me across without oars.
I remember you as a shallow stream, easily fordable, only
Just deep enough to wet
My ankles—but look at you now, all swollen with melted
Mountain snow, turbid, whirling down in spate!
If only I had winged sandals, ... or that airborne chariot
From which the first seed-corn fell
On earth's virgin soil! (All lies, old poetic nonsense
That never really happened—and never will.)
Look, river, your banks are capacious enough—why don't you
Stay within them? . . . Believe me, if it gets known that you held up Me, a poet in love, then your name
Will stink to high heaven. Why, rivers should help young lovers—
Rivers know all about love themselves. . . .

[Ovid goes on to catalogue eight examples.]

Has some girl warmed *you* up, too? I suppose it's just credible—
This woodland greenery would make a fine
Camouflage for such crimes.
                                    Your stream (I declare) has widened
While I've been talking! Those banks
Aren't deep enough to contain it. What's the grudge against *me*, though?
    Why interrupt my journey, postpone the joys

Of a lovers' meeting? If only you were a proper river,
Well-known internationally, on the map,
And not this anonymous product of *ad hoc* drainage,
With no settled source or route,
Dependent instead upon flash floods and melting snows, the
Largesse that dull winter bestows!
I must have been crazy, telling you tales of rivers
That fell in love, dropping names
Of Inachus, Acheloüsm Nile adn the rest of them
To a no0-name dribble like you!
May you get what you deserve, you fouled-up torrent—
Heatwave all summer, and in winter, drought!

7

I can't fault the girl on looks, or style, or sophistication—
And I'd tried for her often enough. But
There we lay, in bed, embracing, and all to no purpose:
I was limp, disgusting, dead.
Heaven knows I wanted it badly, and so did my partner,
But still I failed to measure up.
She tried every trick—wound her arms (whiter than snow or
Ivory) around me, pressed
her thighs up snug under mine, plied me with sexy kisses,
Tongue exploring like mad,
Whispered endearments, called me her master, tried me
With nice four-letter words—they often help.
No good. My member hung slack, as though frozen by hemlock,
A dead loss for the sort of game I'd planned.
There I lay, a sham, a deadweight, a trunk of inert matter,
Not even sure if I was alive, or a ghost.
What sort of old age shall I have (if I ever reach it)
When I can't make out as a youth?
I'm ashamed, at my age. Little good in being young and virile
If as far as *she* could tell
I was neither. She left my bed with sisterly decorum,
Pure as a Vestal off to tend
The sacred flame. But it's not all that long since I made it
Twice with that smark Greek blonde, three times
With a couple of other beauties—and as for Corinna,
In one short night, I remember, she made me perform
Nine times, no less. Perhaps some witch is busy transfixing
My image, and name, in red wax,
Sticking pins through my liver. Magic spells can transform wheatfields
Into barren tares, can dry up springs at source,
Charm acorns off oaks, grapes from vines, strip orchards bare of
Their fruit without human aid—so what's to stop
Some magician giving my member a local anaesthetic?
Maybe *that* was the trouble, made worse
By embarrassment when I couldn't, the final humiliating
Blow to my masculine pride.

Such a marvelous girl—her own dress couldn't cling closer
Than I did to her: I eyed her, touched her, but that
Was as far as it went. . . .
I'm sure the Gods must regret the gift with which they endowed me—
Just look at the way I've messed it up! I got
Everything that I hoped for, an enthusiastic welcome,
Kisses, the girl on her own: yet where
Did all my good fortune take me? What's ownership minus
Possession? To leave such a wealth intact
Was a trick fit for misers. I lay there like Tantalus, parching
Because if his indiscretion, eyes on the fruit
That always hung just out of reach. I mean, one just *doesn't*
Get up simon-pure after a night with a girl—
And it's not that she wasn't seductive, just think of those marvelous
Kisses she wasted on me, the tricks she tried!
She could have shifted an oak-tree, broken hard adamant,
Worked up unfeeling stones:
A living, virile partner, for her, was a pushover—but just then
I lacked both virility and life.
What joy can a blind man get from a painted picture?
What's the use of a singer performing for the deaf?
I imagined every variety of erotic pleasure, invented
No end of positions—in my head—
But still my member lay there, an embarrassing case of
Premature death, and limper than yesterday's rose.
Yet *now*—what perverse timing!—just look at it, stiff and urgent,
Eager to go campaigning, get on the job.
(Oh why can't you lie down? I'm ashamed of you, you bastard—
I've been caught by your promises before.
You let me down, it was *your* fault I landed weaponless
In this embarrassing adn expensive fix.)
My girl tried everything, even some gentle massage
Of the offending part—
Yet *still* it wouldn't come up. All her varied resources
(She saw) left it quite unmoved.
Then she really got mad. "You're sick" she told me. "Stop wasting
My time. Who sent you along
To gatecrash my bed? Look, either some witch has hexed you
Or you've just been making love with another girl."
That did it. She jumped out of bed, her nightdress flying, with a
Delectable flash of bare feet,
And to stop her maids from guessing nothing had happened
Splashed around with some water—as though it had.

#8, he laments the loss of his mistress, who's taken another lover. His poems are useless to
win her back.

Does anyone nowadays look up with admiration
At the liberal arts, or believe
Love-elegies rate a dowry? Time was when poetic talent
Came dearer than gold, but today

To lack cash is plain vulgar. When my poems please my mistress
They can go in where *I* can't.
A few pretty compliemnts, and the front door slams behind me —
Me, genius, out in the cold,
Traipsing round like a fool, replaced by some new-rich soldier,
A bloody oaf who slashed his way to the cash
And a knighthood.

#9 - a touching lament for the death of the poet Tibullus, who, like Virgil, suffered some loss of property in the confiscations after the civil wars. Tibullus's two books of elegies celebrated his love for Delia (pseudonym for Plania).

In the last six poems of the *Amores*, Ovid swings back and forth between wanting to hold onto Corinna, and using his anger and pain to let her go. We also witness the shift of persona, the pretense of emancipation from the chains of love, and finally the sad sailing away toward grief. These emotional shifts, and the switching of masks often confuse those who expect a consistent response to what is happening. In one poem, or one part of a poem, Ovid's tone is flippant, in another angry and hateful. But love is a serious business, to use a typical Ovidian oxymoron. How else to show the truth of the experience than by complex irony. Ovid may have been the romantic classicist, but unlike the romanticism of the 19th century poets, Ovid could joke about such serious stuff, knowing that the flippant persona failed to completely hide the mask of tragedy beneath. The irony of the verse allows us to feel the conflict and pain, the shifting emotions of love and hate.

Poem #11 is thought to be two separate poems because of the change in tone, and thus called 11a and 11b.

11

I've stood enough, for too long. Heart and patience are both exhausted
By this fickle obsession. So — *out!*
That's right, I've slipped the chain, achieved emancipation
Can blush — now — for what I once
Bore so unblushingly. Triumph: passion spurned and trodden
Under my feet. A tardy access of horn-
Stiff will. Keep it up, stand firm. Such suffering's bound to
Pay off in the end. Nasty medicine does you good.
How *could* I have swallowed such insults?

. . . .

Why remind you of all your sordid lies, those broken
Promises, worthless oaths
You swore to my undoing, the young men who gave you private
Signals at parties, coded exchanges? "She's sick,"
They told me: at once I hurried back like a madman, found you
The picture of health — and in my rival's arms.
Such incidents (there were others I'd sooner omit) have hardened
My heart at long last. So go find
Some other more willing victim. My vessel lies safe in harbor,
Garlanded, indifferent to the swelling storm outside.

Leave off your blandishments. The old line's lost its magic
Hold on my senses. I'm not the fool I was.

11b

My capricious heart's a cockpit for conflicting emotions,
Love versus hate—but love, I think, will win.

More literally, his struggling, fickle heart beats from love to hate, but love conquers.

Lactantur pectusque leve in contraria tendunt
hac amor hac odium, sed, puto, vincit amor.

The phrase at the end of the line, "vincit amor," calls to mind Virgil's famous line from the *Eclogues*, "Omnia vincit amor, et nos cedamus amori." The line has often been rendered, "Love conquers all, let us too yield to love." Another, more fatalistic translation is "All-conquering is Love—no use to fight against it." There's a complex irony here. Love conquers, love defeats one. Ovid takes an even subtler approach.

I'll hate if I can. If not, I'll play the reluctant lover:
No ox loves the yoke—he's just stuck with what he hates.
A fugitive from your vices, I'm lured back by your beauty:
Your morals turn me off, your body on.
So I can live neither with nor without you, I don't seem
To know my own mind. I wish you were
Either less beautiful or more faithful.

It's hard to tell which is the greater irony. We expect a wife to be "faithful," not a mistress. If Corinna is his mistress, not his wife, there's irony there, too, that he wants her to be "faithful."

Poem #13 seems out of place, almost violating the structural unity of the *Amores*. If Corinna were his mistress, this poem is about his wife, thus breaking a cardinal rule of Roman erotic elegy: don't mention the wife. If Corinna really was his wife, he's finally brought the real and the fictional portrait together. Whatever the case, this poem has nothing to do with any erotic motiff; it seems out of place. But Ovid deliberately places this poem between painful entreaties to his "mistress." This is a lyric poem celebrating the festivals of the Roman countryside during, a visit to his in-laws on an important feast-day. The poem closes with a touching, hearfelt plea.

We had come to Falerii—good orchard land: once captured by Camillus:
And (the why of our visit) my wife's home town.
Priestesses were busy with Juno's chaste festiveal—sacrifice
Of a local heifer: crowded games.
Despite an exhausing journey over mountain roads, to witness
This ritual more than made up for the delay.
There stood the goddess's grove, dark-shadowed, immemorial—
One step inside, and you know
That some spirit haunts the place.

Ovid describes the yearly procession, a show-wite heifer sacrificed on the alter, the children throwing little spears at the bleating goat—whoever scores first wins "a nannygoat prize."

> Ahead of the goddess walks youths and shy maidens,
> Skirts sweeping the broad street.
>   Then the crowd hushes in reverence
> As Juno herself goes past on a gilded float
> Drawn by her priestesses. The ritual came from Argos:
> On Agamemnon's murder Helaesus fled
> The scene of the crime, fled his heritage: after long wanderings
> By land and sea, he founded these city-walls
> And taught his prosperous burghers the worship of Juno.
> Lady, look kindly always on me, on them.

If wife and mistress are one and the same, the following poem is even more ironic.

14

> I don't ask that you should be faithful, you're far too attractive:
> i'd just prefer *not* to know about your affairs—
> So depressing. My principles aren't based on exclusive possession,
> But they do require some attempt
> To cover one's tracks. Any girl who can swear she didn't,
> Didn't. Only admission ruins her name. . . .
> Show a little more decency (or at least pretend to): then I
> Can think you faithful even when you're not.
> Keep on with your present life, *just don't admit it*. A moderst
> Persona, in public, shouldn't prove too bad
> An embarrassment. . . . Keep your misconduct for bed.
>
> . . . . Lay them all, but allay my suspicions, leave me
> In ignornace, let me cling
> To my foolish sillusions. All those to-and-fro notes—need I see them?
> Couldn't you even smooth out the bed
> Or tidy your hair? (That degree of dishevelment takes more
> Than sleeping alone.) *Must* you flaunt the bites
> On your neck? All you draw the line at is doing it in my presence—
> If you don't care for your good name, please think of me!
> Each time you confess a liason it kills me by inches, my reason
> Blanks out, I'm covered in a cold sweat.
> Then love's overlaid by vain hatred for what I can't help loving,
> Then I wish I were dead—with you.
> I'll make no inquiries, won't probe into your secrets:
> Self-deception will be my official line.
> But if ever you're caught in the act, if I actually witness
> Your shameful conduct with my own eyes,
> Make sure you contradict the evidence of my senses,
> And then I'll accept your word

Against what I saw. No trouble inj defeating a would-be-loser —
Just let your tongue
Remember that phrase "Not guilty." Two words will free you,
    Your case may
Be weak — but then so is your judge!

No other series of erotic elegies show such dramatic movement from free-wheeling confidence and humor to ironic detachment and self-delusion. If Corinna was taken as a mistress, we can imagine Ovid reading these poems in public getting quite a laugh, even from the above poem, where anyone guilty of adulterous escapades could see and laugh at themselves caught in the double-bind of love and/or marriage. If we laugh at that last line, we pity the poet who has sunk this low, who has truly been conquered, not only by the lover, but by love itself, who struck him with the arrow in the first place. Where else can Ovid go, but to pull the arrow out, hand it back to Venus, and say good-bye forever to true love, to the heart worn so precariosly on the sleeve of verse.

15

Mother of tender loves, you must find another poet:
My elegies are homing on their final lap.
Postscript concerning the author: of Paelignian extraction,
A man whose delights have never let him down,
Heir — for what it's worth — to an ancient family,
No brand-new knight jujped up
Through the maelstrom fortunes of war. Mantua boasts her Virgil,
The Veronese their Catullus. I shall become the pride
Of my fellow-Paelignians — a race who fought for freedom,
Freedom with honour, in the Italian wars
That scared Rome witless. I can see some visitor to Sulmona
Taking it its tiny scale, the streams and walls,
And saying: "Any township, however small, that could breed so
Splendid a poet, I call great." Boy-god
And you, Cyprian goddess, his mother, remove your golden
Standards from my terrain —
Horned Bacchus is goading me on to weightier efforts, bigger
Horses, a really ambitious trip.
So farewell, congenial Muse, unheroic elegiacs —
Work born to live on when its maker's dead.

Any reader or critic wishing to strip away Ovid's numerous masks, or *personae*, and capture Ovid's elusive personality must begin with the *Amores*, the poems of his youth. Even before he turned to poetry, his rheotircal speeches written and declaimed as part of his education were, as Seneca believed, nothing but poetry masquerading as prose. If we accept the premise that Corinna was his first wife, then we follow Ovid's developement from passionate adolescent to cynical rogue, entertained and touched by the masks Ovid wore to hide his inner pain. The *Amores* begins with the notion that true love flames with irrationality, knows no moderation, and that to plan and plot a seduction is the mark of elderly caution. As he said in Book I, figuring the odds and measuring one's words—*sic senes amant*, thus do old men love. He was seventeen when he wrote this, but behind the mask was the deathless passion between husband and wife, later hidden from the reader; by the end of the *Amores*, he's a cynic exploiting love for sex, cavalierly hiding that innocent martial devotion that was willing to give up the world for love, willing to give up a promising legal and political career for the difficult life of the poet. The poems in the *Amores* begin in happy innocence, chronicle the wounds and betrayals, and conclude, not with the end of an affair, but the breakup of his marriage.

The development continued from bon-vivant to literary seducer to love's instructor—*praeceptor amoris*. The persona Ovid adopted for his love poems was replaced in his cycle of didactic poems that begin with the *Art of Love* by the calculating Casanova, the cynical *praeceptor amoris*, the seducer's friend. We catch a glimpse of this persona in elegy I.8 of the *Amores*, where Ovid shows us the cunning, experienced procuress who advises a young woman on the best ways to get a man.

> She's a witch, mutters magical contrips, can make rivers
> Run uphill, knows the best aphrodisiacs —
> When to use herbal brews, or the whirring bullroarer,
> How to extract that stuff from a mare i nheat.
> She can control the weather, make a day overcast with
> Cloud at will, or brilliant an clear;
> I've known times (believe it or not) when the moon turned bloody,
> And blood dripped from the stars.
> It wouldn't surprise me if the old botch grew feathers at nightfall
> And went flapping round like an owl —

He imagines her giving flirtatious Corinna instructions.

> Well: this old hag undertook to suborn our relationship,
> And a glibly poisonous tongue she had for the job.
> By pure chance I overheard her. The big double doors stood up.
> Here, then, is what she said: "You know,
> Dearie, you made a great hit with that rich young gentleman
> Yesterday. He'd got eyes for nbody else.
>   .... but Nature's method
> Is so unpredictable. Safer to stick to Art.

How ironic—the procuress is telling Corinna not to rely on chance, better to follow the methods of her art. But we can't help hearing it as Ovid's advice to himself: A woman can betray you, but your verses won't. And then, of course, the greatest irony of all, that eventually, he was betrayed, not onlly by a woman, but by his own poems, as well.

Ovid was invited to the homes of the rich and the famous, great senatorial families spicing their social gatherings with the presence of the erotic poet. Flushed with success, Ovid published a manual of seduction called *Ars Amatoria*, The Art of Love, which established him finally as the poetic mouthpiece for a new generation of impious, rebellious youth who grew up decades after the civil wars and flouted the prudish morality of Augustus' reign. The *Ars* was written in a deadpan style, similar to a "how-to manual" on farming or building a house (c.f. Hesiod's *Works and Days*). It's subject, though, was how and where to pick up eager, unmarried women, hinting to his readers that his artful precepts should only be used on courtesans and slaves. Try the temples of various oriental or libertine dieties such as Venus Genetrix, suggested Ovid, or the marble colonnades of the Forum whose frescoes and unclad statues were suggestive of *amatoria*. The Circus Maximus was considered a good place to find women who might be looking for love, (or maybe, married women looking for a fling). Best of all, though, was the theater, with its comedic and bawdy displays, not only on stage, but in the audience, where a fashionable crowd came to see and be seen. The next section of the book was titled "How to Win Her," which included tactics and strategy, a tongue-in-cheek tone that likened seduction to seige-warfare and night-exercises of a military conquest. Finally, Ovid offered advice on "How to Keep Her" ("By my art she's been caught, by my art she must be held"). At the conclusion, Ovid playfully boasted, "I have armed you. But whoever overcomes the Amazon with my sword, let him inscribe on his spoils, 'Naso was my teacher.'"

Augustus may have tolerated the sexual innuendoes of the *Love Poems*, but he resented the *Ars* for thumbing its nose at family values. Despite Ovid's later claim that it was written for single people, it was clear that extra-marital affairs were hinted at. This clearly ran counter to Augustus's moralalistic legislation.

For those who followed his lessons too dearly, he followed up with another how-to book, *Remedia amoris*, On Curing Love. "Best to work hard, go hunting, or if that fails, leave town." I've tried all three and think only love mends the heart that love itself has broken. Ovid asserted that it was not only possible to free oneself from love, but obligatory, especially if it brings suffering. Finally, his success was crowned by a little volume called *De medicamina faciei feminineae*, "On Facial Treatment for Ladies," a manual of cosmetics that sold all over the Roman world.

☛ The *Heroides*

At this point, Ovid entered a new, more mature phase of his work. The use of mythological allusion in the *Love Poems* anticipates the other great source of his poetry. The *Heroides* was a series of letters written by famous women, heroines of Greek myth such as Penelope, Dido, Phaedra, etc, to their absent lovers or husbands. Once again he creates a new literary genre. Propertius had written an elegy in which Arethusa writes to her husband Lycotas, and this may have given him the idea of an extended composition, drawing upon the Greek epic tradition, in which letters written in verse form could be used to bring together the narrative material of epic, tragedy, and myth. We find subtle, and not so subtle references to Callimachus, Catullus, and Virgil. But Ovid once again extends the scope of his previous models by layering the tone of lamentation with the unifying theme of love. Thus, the *Heroides* use of myth serves as a bridge to his masterpeice, the *Metamorphoses*, and the tone of lamentation sets the stage for the cries of the heart we will find in his Letters from Exile, the *Tristia*.

☛ The *Metamorphoses*

After two failed marriages, Ovid married for the third and last time at the age of forty-six to Fabia, who was from one of the most distinguished families in Rome. He then set about writing what was to become his greatest work, the Book of Transformations, or *Metamorphoses,* which links all the Greek myths, before and after Homer, to the Roman myths of Ovid's day into a cohesive whole. These fifteen "books," in compelling hexameters, conveyed the renowned transformations of inanimate objects, animals, mortals, and gods—almost everything in Greek and Roman legend that changed its form. The structure is also chronological, going from the beginning of the world down to the Augustan age.

Even though he began the *Metamorphoses* twenty years after Virgil completed the *Aeneid*, Ovid must have felt that no matter how great his success as a poet, it wouldn't be until he composed something of Virgilian epic porportions that he could claim literary immortality. But Ovid's sensibility was decidedly different from Virgil's. Where Virgil was gloomy, Ovid was funny; where Virgil's tone was grave and sacred, Ovid's was self-depracating, often mocking himself and his own generation' vanities; where Virgil was grand and historical, Ovid was intimate and personal. In order to match Virgil's accomplishment, Ovid had to transform epic structure and the way it could work. Thus, he structured the *Metemorphoses* in such a way that one event and character did not expand into another event and character, but instead, one tale was followed by another tale, with stories imbedded within stories. Speakers quote other speakers, who quote another story told by someone else. Stylistically, Ovid uses a more formal Latin than he had used in the *Love Poems* and works against the grain of that stately verse by allowing for rhetorical flexibility of the speaker's voice when appropriate. It's clear we're not anymore in the Kansas of the comedic monologues of his love poems, but the Cecil B. DeMille cast of thousands and Hollywood's epic sets (mocked in Nathanial West's *Day of the Locust*).

Where Virgil's epic traced Augustus's lineage to Aeneas and the founding of Rome, Ovid's treatment made the Golden Age the culmination of world history. The opening six line proem states the theme: (First a translation by Allen Mandelbaum, who chose to rhyme, then the same six lines inventively rendered by David Slavitt.)

> My soul would sing of metamorphoses.
> But since, o gods, you were the source of these
> bodies becoming other bodies, breathe
> your breath into my book of changes: may
> the song I sing be seamless as its way
> weaves from the world's beginning to our day.   [trans. Allen Mandelbaum]

> Bodies, I have in mind, and how they can change to assume
> new shapes—I ask the help of the gods, who know the trick:
> inspire me now, change me, let me glimpse the secret
> and sing, better than I know how, of the world's birthing,
> the creation of all things from first to the very last.   [trans. David Slavitt]

Thus, Ovid was able to touch upon the entire realm of classical mythology—a history of the world from chaos to the deification of Julius Caesar. Whereas Virgil wrote of the destiny of Rome, and Livy of the decline of Roman virtue, Ovid tells a shifting story of the world, of the instability of nature's form, of new being out of old. A woman is transformed into a bird, rocks metamorphosize into human beings, a young girl becomes a laurel tree. Phaethon falls to earth with the chariot of the sun and sets the world on fire. Diana changes Actaeon into a stag and his own dogs tear his body to pieces. Pentheus is punished by Bacchus, while jealous Minerva exacts revenge on Arachne, turning her into a spider. Daedalus and Icarus fly, the lattar into the sun and to his death. Embedded within the story of Orpheus and Eurydice are other tales of love: Cyparissus, Hyaninthus, Pygmalion, Myrrha, Venus and Adonis, etc.

In the Middle Ages, Ovid's poetry was one of the major sources of Western man's knowledge of his own past. Once again, he had become the arbiter of elegance—this time for the 12th century trobadour poets of courtly love. Next to the Bible, the *Metamorphoses* exerted the greatest influence on English literature. Myrrha's indulgent nurse became the model for Shakespeare's marvelous creation of Juliet's nurse in *Romeo and Juliet*. Through the Renaissance and up to modern times, Ovid's poetry has been regarded as a treasure of mythic themes, the suggestiveness and psychological content of which have inspired the imagination of writers from Dante to Ezra Pound. The *Metamophoses* became the inspiration for thousands of poems and paintings and statues down through the ages: Pyramus and Thisbe (parts of which are comically acted out by Quince, Bottom and the rest in Shakespeare's *Midsummer's Night Dream*), Perseus and Andromeda, Jason and Medea, Galatea and Polyphemus. There is no better way to learn the old myths than by reading this cosmos of men and gods.

Bacchus, the God of vine, wine and mystic ecstasy and inspiration, was the son of Zeus and Semele. When Semele, six months preganant, asked Zeus to show himself to her in all his majesty, he clothed himself in his splendors, not putting on all his terrors, as when he overthrew the giants, but wearing what is known among the gods as his lesser panoply. Her mortal frame could not endure his immortal radiance; she was struck dead by lightning and consumed to ashes. Their unborn child was taken from her womb and sewn up inside Zeus's thigh, to be born alive and perfectly formed three months later. This was Dionysus, or Bacchus, the "twice-born" god. In order to deceive Hera, who wanted to destroy the child as the fruit of her husband's adultery, Bacchus was dressed as a girl, then later transformed into a kid. After discovering the vine and its uses, Bacchus was driven mad by Hera, wandered throughout Europe until Cybele initiated him into the rites of her orgiastic cult. Returning to Thebes, where Pentheus reigned, Bacchus introduced his revels in which the whole populace—and especially the women—were seized with mystical ecstasy and went out of the city into the wild countryside. Pentheus tried to prevent the spread of this subversive cult by imprisoning Bacchus in chains, calling him a charlatan magician and an imposter, and vowed to cut his head off. Bacchus freed himself, set the royal palace on fire, and persuaded Pentheus to climb the mountain to spy on the women and witness the excesses in which they indulged.

> Pentheus went out
> To holy Cithaeron, loud with the cries
> Of Bacchanalian songs; and as a stallion

Whinnies when he has heard brass horns of war
And is all heat to enter in the battle,
So now the air, filled with the songs of Bacchus,
Spurred Pentheus and fired his rage white-hot.

Half up the mountain, edged with a dense forest
Was a plateau, open on every side.
As Pentheus, narrow-eyed, came near the altar,
The first to know him was his mother, first
To clutch at him, to curse him madly, lash
Out at him with an ivy wand and cry,
"Come, sisters, come to see the wild pig plough
Our peaceful meadows! Look at him, I'll tear
Arms, legs, all hanging parts from that rough body."
The riot came from everywhere upon him,
And as he crawled, came after him; in terror
His voice grew soft, admitting faults, mistakes.
Then from his bleeding body Pentheus cried,
"Pity for me, O my aunt, Autonoe!
Remember the poor shakes of Actaeon!"
But she had never heard of him; she twisted
Pentheus' right arm from his body, then
Ino, maddened, ripped the left away, nor had
He arms to reach in prayer toward mother, yet he
Showed where they should have been, and dying, cried,
"O Mother, gaze at me!" She screamed at him
And shook her flying hair. Then Agave ripped
His head from fallen shoulders, raised it up
So others saw her prize in blood-red hands;
She cried, "Here is my work, my victory."
Quickly as leaves touched by an autumn's frost

Tremble, half clinging, then are swept away,
Even from the tops of trees, so Pentheus' limbs
Were scattered by mad hands to wind and earth.
Aware of his odd fate, his grave example,
Thebans in crowds came to a new god's altar.

This myth was very well known in classical art and literature, having been cast in threatical form by both Aeschylus and Euripides. The latter's account in the *Bacchae* is even more graphic.

She was foaming at the mouth, and her crazed eyes
rolling with frenzy. She was mad, stark mad,
possessed by Bacchus. Ignoring his cries of pity,
she seized his left arm at the wrist. Then, planting
her foot upon his chest, she pulled, wrenching away
the arm at the shoulder—not by her own strength, for the god had put inhuman
power in her hands.
Ino, meanwhile, on the other side, was scrathcing off
his flesh. Then Autonoe and the whole horde

of Bacchae swarmed upon him. Shouts everywhere,
he screaming with what little breath was left,
they shreiking in triumph. One tore off an arms,
another a foot still warm in its shoe. His ribs
were clawed clean of flesh, and every hand
was smeared with blood as they played ball with scraps
of Pentheus' body.

Ovid ended his account at this point, but in Euripides' *Bacchus*, Agave impaled his head on a thyrsus and marched into Thebes, daubed with her sons blood, carrying what she claimed was the head of a wild lion. When she came to her senses, she realized that she had killed her own son. Then Dionysus appears, justifies the death of Pentheus, but orders his mother exiled.

The tales—some are fables, some legends, some case histories—are told with insight, perception, and a savage, sophisticated wit. Ovid's desire to show life's ridiculous futility is rendered with a perceptiveness that only a poet of Ovid's literary gifts and life experience could understand. The outer form was epic, but Ovid's model was not Virgil (whose model was Homer), but Hesiod, whose *Theogony* was a collection of independent stories linked by a single theme. Hellenistic literature included several examples of this genre, notably the *Aitia* of Callimachus, which was a series of aetiological tales in elegiac meter. But whereas Callimachean poetics had disdained the long epic poem, Ovid clearly revealed his intention to rival the *Aeneid*, and create a poem of Homeric-style, a national epic for Roman culture. His grand ambition, boldly stated in the first six lines of the opening proem, was to create a synthesis of universal history, which had hitherto only been sketched out in Latin culture. Virgil's sixth eclogue may well have served as inspiration.

Ovid's lyrical, dramatic monologues foreshadow the melodramatic monologues of Seneca's tragedies, and through them, the soliloquies of Shakespeare. While Shakespeare's soliloquies provide a model for the modern, meditative poem, one could say that Ovid invented the passionate "aside," the "internal" monolgue of drama and fiction, which do not necessarily advance plot or philosophies, but reveal the conflicts of emotional situations. Ovid's contemporary readers, as well as those who read him today, saw the projection of their own desires and weaknesses in these internal monologues. Today we realize that we are often overpowered by forces greater than our conscious will.

In the terror of Narcissus' all-conquering self-love, the play of emotional extremes, the forces of illogical and conflicting impulses, Ovid offers a richness of psychological detail to the modern reader.

Tiresias

While these events had taken place on earth
By will of Fate and twice-born Bacchus safe
Within his crib, it came about that Jove,
Wine in his veins, grew cheerful and dismissed
Affairs of state to joke awhile with Juno:
"And I insist you women have more joy
In making love than men; we do the work,

While you have all the fun." But she denied it,
So they agreed to settle their dispute
By calling wise Tiresias to court
To be their judge—he who knew well enough
The two extremes of Venus' subtle arts:
One day while walking through a green-grown wood
He thrust his stick between two monstrously
Large and love-joined serpents (and then, O mir-
Acle!) was changed into a woman, and as
A woman lived for seven autumns. Then,
As he came to the eighth autumn he saw
The same two creatures in the act of love,
And stopped to say, "If miracles are done
To those who strike at you and sex is changed,
I strike again—" And so he did; at once
His gender shifted to his sex at birth.
Therefore when asked to settle this light quarrel
Of gods, he took the part of Jove,
And Saturn's daughter (who was offended
More deeply than she had a right to be)
Damned judge Tiresias to eternal blindness;
Then (since no god has power to unmake
What other gods may do) Jove, the kind father
Of them all, gave to Tiresias for loss
Of sight the gift of prophecy, an honour
That made the darkness of his doom much lighter.

Echo and Narcissus

Throughout the cities of Boetia
Tiresias had become a famous man;
The first test of his power to tell truth
came from Liriope, a water-lady
Whom Cephisus raped within a winding brook
And nearly drowned her. Then in her due time
The pretty girl gave birth to a sweet child,
A son so charming even as a baby,
That he inspired girls with thoughts of love—
She called the boy Narcissus. When she asked
Tiresias how long her child would live—
To great old age? the prophet answered, "Only
If never he comes to know himself." Then for
A long time after this his prophecy
Seemed vain, and yet what finally happened
Proved it true: Narcissus' death, the way he died,
And his odd love.
[Narcissus grows up to be a a beautiful boy, loved by both girls and boys, yet he
has little feeling for either]

One day
A girl with a queer voice stood gazing at him—

Echo, who could not check her tongue while talking,
nor could she speak till someone spoke to her.

[While Jove was out making love to young girls on mountainsides]
Echo kept Juno in long conversations
until the girls had run away. When Juno
discovered this, she said, "That tongue which has
Deceived me shall make nothing but the poor
Brief noises of the last words."

[The day that Echo saw Narcissus stroll through the forest,
she followed, so entranced by his beauty. She could not call to him,
but had to wait for him to speak, which he did finally, having strayed so far from
his friends. He shouted, "Is anybody here?"]

"Here," Echo answered, and the wondering boy
Looked far around him and cried louder, "Come."
"Come," she called after him. He glanced behind
Saw no one there, then shouted, "Why do you run from me?"
And only heard the same words follow him.
Then he stood still, held by deceptive sounds;
"Here we shall meet," he said, and Echo never
Replied more eagerly — "Here we shall meet."
To make those words come true, she slipped beyond
The shelter of the trees to throw her arms
Around the boy she would embrace. Yet he
Ran from her, crying, "No, you must not touch —
Go, take your hands away, may I be dead
Before you throw your fearful chains around me."
"O fearful chains around me," Echo said,
And then no more. So she was turned away
To hide her face, her lips, her guilt among the trees,
Even their leaves, to haunt caves of the forest,
To feed her love on melancholy sorrow
Which, sleepless, turned her body to a shade, . . .
And last her voice remained. Vanished in forest,
Far from her usual walks on hills and valleys,
She's heard by all who call; her voice has life.

The way Narcissus had betrayed frail Echo,
Now swift, now shy, so he had played with all:
Girls of the rivers, women of the mountains,
With boys and men. Until one boy, love-sick
And left behind, raised prayers to highest heaven:
"O may he love himself alone," he cried,
"And yet fail in that great love." The curse was heard
By wakeful Nemesis. Deep in the forest
Was a pool, well-deep and silver-clear, where
Never a shepherd came, nor goats, nor cattle; He bent
to drink, to dissipate his thirst, yet as he
Drank another thirst rose up: enraptured

Beauty caught his eyes that trapped him;
He loved the image that he thought was shadow,
And looked amazed at what he saw — his face.
He sought himself and was pursued, wooed, fired
By his own heat of love. Again, again
He tried to kiss the image in the well;
Again, again, his arms embraced the silver
Elusive waters where his image shone.
    Neither desire of food or sleep could lure
Him from the well; "O trees, O forest, has anyone been cursed
With love like mine? I am entranced, enchanted
By what I see, yet it eludes me, error
Or hope becomes the thing I love. Nothing can
Keep us apart. Only this veil of water.
O lovely boy, why do you glide from me,
Where do you vanish when I come to meet you?

Look! I am he; I've loved within the shadow
Of what I am, and in that love I burn,
I light the flames and feel their fires within;
Then what am I to do? Am I the lover
Or the beloved? Then why make love? Since I
Am what I long for, then my riches are
So great they make me poor. O may I fall
Away from my own body — and this is odd
From any lover's lips — would my love
Would go away from me. And now love drains
My life, look! I am dying at life's prime."

Then in his agony he tore his dress
And beat his naked breast with his pale hands. So did Narcissus
Wear away with love, drained, fading in the heat
Of secret fires. Echo, still resentful,
Felt a touch of pity at the sight.
Then with his last "Goodbye," "Goodbye," said Echo.
At this he placed his head deep in cool grasses
While death shut fast the eyes that shone with light
At their own lustre. As he crossed the narrows
Of darkest hell he saw the floating image
Of his lost shade within the Stygian waters.

Sometimes, the portraits are less classical and more violently baroque. After all, the very theme of metamorphosis depends on rapid transformations and distortions of the normal law of subtle literary action. As Ovid moved from the chronology of myth to the events of history, the characters of the Trojan War come to the fore with tales of Odysseus and Ovid's "little Aeneid." The cycle of miraculous changes begins to turn in the direction of pro-Roman interpretations of the fall of Troy, though Ovid's approach is different from Virgil's. In Book X11, Caenis is transformed from a woman to a man, whose name becomes Caeneus, not for love, but for hardiness in battle in which she becomes a supernatural warrior, before being finally transformed into a golden bird. Her desire to be a man could be traced to her rape by Nepture. Afterwards, she prayed never to fall by any sword held by a man. Considering Ovid's popularity among Elizabethan poets, we might find an analogy to Caenis in the legend of Elizabeth I, who as a child of thirteen, fended off the advances of Admiral Lord Seymour of Sudely, her Neptune, figuratively if not literally. Her fears were said to have made her a virgin Queen and through Essex and Leichester she became a warrior. Ovid's insightful psychology and his ability to flex his creative imagination seemed to act as a preview of behaviour in historical biography. It's also interesting that Ovid conjures an old man whose memory is failing to recount the story.

Before we get to the Caesars, Ovid brings in Pythagoras, who gives us the philosophical basis for the entire poem, that constant change and transformation is the law of the universe.

> Because he hated tyrants and their habits
> A man of Samos left his island home
> and Came to Croton for his place of exile. . . .
> Whatever nature would not let him see
> He saw with clarity of mind and heart.
> The intellectual vision of his spirit
> Showed him the universe, all things in order.
> And when he felt that what he was was true
> He entertained the public with his knowledge,
> And silent crowds were captured in his spell
> Of what he had to say: first came first causes,
> How the great world began, what is Divine,
> The source of all things, whether of snow or lightning,
> Or was Jupiter's fire in the thunderbotl —
> Or was that tearing noise and flash of light
> The storm of winds within the roaring clouds?
> What unknown power shakes and splits the earth?
> These mysteries of all things dark to man —
> And he the first vegetarians,
> Dispraising meat as diet: . . . .
>
> "Your are the gifts of earth who spends her riches
> Without the taint of butchery and blood,
> As some wild creatures tear at flesh for dinner. . . .
> Unnatural flesh that feeds on flesh, on blood
> Fior its own blood, body in body
> So like its own, swells its own fat, its bowels
> With living breathing creatures of its kind!
> Here where the best of mothers, our dear Earth
> Surrounds you with her riches to each taste,
> Men eat the sad flesh of the murdered beast
> That's tamed for killing, and their mad teeth tearing
> At flesh the way a Cyclops has of eating!
> Life eating life to feed the devouring belly
> That never eats enough of flesh that dies!
> . . . .

"Men who seem born to die, and chilled by death,
Why tremble when the river Styx is mentioned,
Or names that foolish poets have in mind,
All nightmares of a world that never was? . . . .
Our souls survive this death; as they depart
Their local habitations in the flesh,
They enter new-found bodies that preserve them. . . .
Which proves that all things change, yet never die!
Or here or there, the spirit takes its way
To different kinds of being as it chooses,
From beast to man, from man to beast; however,
Or far or near or strange, it travels on.
As wax might take new shapes in many figures,
None quite the same, the same wax lives within it —
So does the soul pass through its transformations.

"And so I ride (which is my metaphor)
A full-sailed ship upon an endless sea,
A universe where nothing stays the same,
Sea, sky, wind, earth, and time forever changing —
Time like a river in its ceaseless motion;
The flying moment gone, what once seemed never
Is now, which vanishes before we say it,
Each disappearing moment in a cycle,
Each loss replaced with the living hour.
     "One day — and that was very long ago —
We lived within the womb of our first mother,
And we were scarcely more than hopes of men,
Seeds of the first beginning, till Nature's hands
(How artfully she worked to suit her purpose!)
Gave us our destiny to live beyond
Distending walls which held us coiled ind arkness,
So from that home we fell to worldly being.
Yet without strength the child first knew the light,
Rearing itself to creep, four-legged, slowly,
Like any littered beast, then slower still,
Unsteady at the knees, it stands, falls, rises,
Grasping at anything to step upright.
From there it walks, and with increasing ardour
Runs through boyhood to man to middle age,
To slip, then downward, toward senility. . . .
— the flesh gone slack and saggin from the bone.
And Helen, no less desolate than he,
Weeps at the old bitch staring from her mirror.
And who would dare rape her once or twice or now?
Time and Old Age eat all the world away —
Black-toothed and slow, they seem to feast forever
As all things disappear in time, in death.

"Even the so-called elements are shifting.
I know their transformations; . . . .

"Nothing retains the shape of what it was,
And Nature, always making old things new,
Proves nothing dies within the universe,
But takes another being in new forms.
What is called birth is change from what we were,
And death the shape of being left behind.
Though all things melt or grow from here to there,
Yet the same balance of the world remains.

"Nothing, no nothing keeps its outward show,
For golden ages turn to years of iron; . . .
And where a swamp once flowed beneath the willows,
Is now a strip of land, and where a desert was,
A little lake sways under growing reeds. . . .

"Yet, some things have been proved: or have you seen
The dead? I mean those bodies black with heat
In their decay, fluid in rot and bursting —
And in that place small creatures come to life?
It is well known that many a buried bull,
Tossed in a trench after he's served the altar,
Breeds flower-loving bees from his torn sides —   [c.f. Virgil's
Who, following ancient habits of their kind   *Eclogues*]
People the meadow with their hours of labour. . . .

"How many creatures walking on this earth
Have their first being in another form?
Yet one exists that is itself forever,
Revbron in ageless likeness through the years.
It is that bird Assyrians call the Phoenix.

"Yet, if these miracles seem marvelous,
Think how the wild hyena shifts her sex. . . .
[and] When vine-haired Bacchus took his India
They gave him wildcat chariots to ride,
And when the beasts made water as they ran,
Pink piss turned into amethysts and rubies,
And, like the pliant coral, weak in water,
Yet hard as polished stones in open air.

"If I would list the many changes seen,
The day would fall behind us in the sea.
Great Troy, the greater for her men and riches,
Poured blood as water in a ten-year war,
Now shows earth-fallen ruins to the sky,
Her riches ancient names in broken tombs. . . .
But what of Oedipus and Thebes today?
Or Pandion's Athens rising to the sky?
Names that are heard in halls of memory,
Names, names, names, and nothing more!
Now there is news that Trojan Rome is here,

That city built on stone where Tiber winds,
Whose sources are the Apenninean snows.
Each day she changes to a greater city
To rule the great unmeasureable world
From oracles that guide us to the future,
From lips that speak our destiny on earth. . . .

"But I must not digress, nor let my hroses
(A metaphor of what I wish to say)
Run wild, forgetting what my speech should be,
To let you know how all things are mutations —
Heaven or Earth and all that grows within it,
And we among the changes in creation.
Beyond the very natures of our bodies,
Our spirits take to wing through other creatures."

The last poem brings the "history of the world" up to the apotheosis of Caesar, the last of
Aeneas's descendants, and the celebration of Augustus. Then, matching the proem that
launched this epic, Ovid closes with a firm declaration that with this work he will achieve
the immortality he sought—not of the body, but through the work.

Caesar is our god of native birth.
Nor war nor peace gave him divinity —
A flaming comet lifted him to the skies —
But more than these, his children gave him glory,
Greater than battles and their victories,
For he had made our emperor his son. . . .
               go to that body
That falls beneath its wounds in Caesar's dress,
Gather the spirit from its dying lips,
To make that soul a star that burns forever
Above the Forum and the gates of Rome. . . .
So Caesar burns as an eternal star.
Though here on earth bright Caesar's son denies
A glory that outshines his father's light,
Fame calls him much too modest, and ignores
His will to be far less than she desires:
So Saturn shines with lesser light than Jove.
Our triple world of heaven, earth, and sea,
Has Jupiter as father of us all,
And earth is ruled by Emperor Augustus,
Both masters of their kind, or earth or Heaven.
And now the poet speaks to all his gods, —
To these, all these, the poet sends his prayer:
Long life to our Augustus here on earth,
And may he live beyond my transient hour,
And when at last he takes his throne in heaven,
Then he may hear a Roman poet's song.

EPILOGUE
And now the measure of my song is done:

The work has reached its end; the book is mine,
None shall unwrite these words: nor angry Jove,
Nor war, nor fire, nor flood,
Nor venomous time that eats our lives away.
Then let that morning come, as come it will,
When this disguise I carry shall be no more,
And all the treacherous years of life undone,
And yet my name shall rise to heavnly music,
The deathless music of the circling stars.
As long as Rome is the Eternal City
These lines shall echo from the lips of men,
As long as poetry speaks truth on earth,
That immortality is mine to wear.

I've been using the Horace Gregory translation (1958), but because the last word of the *Metamorphoses* is *vivam*—I shall live" or "I shall have life"—here are two more recent versions of that ending by David Slavit (1994) and Allen Mandelbaum (1993), respectively.

My work, my fame, will continue, ascending as high as the sky,
and among the stars the name of Ovid shall never die
but twinkle on forever—wherever the eagle has spread
its wings and as long as the Latin language is written and read.
If the words of poets have any truth or worth, they give
this hope to me, who wrote them—that I shall become them,
        and live.

But, with the better part of me, I'll gain
a place that's higher than the stars: my name,
indelible, eternal, will remain.
And everywhere that Roman power has sway,
in all domains the Latins gain, my lines
will be on people's lips; and through all time—
if poets' prophecies are ever right—
my name and fame are sure: I shall have life.

Ovid himself was doomed to suffer a severe "metamophosis"—from the witty cosmopolitan, whom Rome had hailed as the fit successor to Virgil, to a tired, lonely old man living out the last ten years of his life among fur-clad barbarians.

Despite the grander, epic theme of the *Metamorphoses*, the continued popularity of Ovid's love poems and manuels of seduction continued to anger and frustrate Augustus. Though written in an eminently good-natured way, anyone with a sense of humour would have taken it all with a grain of salt. Augustus's granddaughter Julia probably read the *Amores* and the *Ars*, as did most of her generation. It's doubtful that her notorious delinquencies were prompted by the poems. But Augustus was sure she had been ruined by a book, and may have been looking for a scapegoat to blame for the corruption of his own granddaughter. He could well have looked to his own misconduct, which was often the main source of gossip among the populace in his younger days. His daughter's sexual escapades proved embarrassing, especially because of her affair with the son of Augustus' old enemy, Marc Anthony. Julia was punished and sent away, while Augustus tried to stem the tide of moral decay and the rising divorce rate which made a mockery of marriage. Augustus instituted pro-family legislation, which made adultery a public crime punishable by banishment for life and confiscation of at least a third of both guilty parties' property. Those from aristocratic families were forbidden to marry into the lower classes, especially to actors and prostitutes. Poets and playwrights who mocked and made fun of this puritanical legislation soon found out how deadly serious Augustus was, especially after his granddaughter, Julia, was found guilty of sexual intrigues with men who allegedly were plotting to oust Augustus and steal the succession from Tiberius. Julia was banished, and so was Ovid.

Beneath the tone of sexual playfulness was a political innuendo that poked fun at Augustus personally—suggestions that the Augustan Forum was a good place to pick up women reminded readers of the emperor's own highly questionable personal morality, and his constant cheating on Livia which became part of common street gossip. Augustus dismissed his escapades by saying he only took these women to bed so he could find out what their husbands were plotting. Perhaps Ovid didn't realize how dangerous his flippant criticisms were becoming. Augustus claimed first century Rome was a golden age of virtue and simplicity, but Ovid stuck a needle in that balloon. "Golden, truly, is the present age," he mocked, "for gold most honors are sold, by gold love is won."

The last story of the *Metamorphoses* was barely finished when information concerning some serious indiscretion on Ovid's part came to the attention of Augustus. At the time, Ovid was staying in Elba, and received word from his friend and patron Cotta Maximus who was upset with what Ovid had done (or "seen"), but thought Augustus could be placated. Ovid left immediately to see Cotta, and when asked if the report was true, Ovid admitted (in his *Black Sea Letters*)

> I stuck
> between half-hearted confession, half-hearted denial,
> choking with classic fright,
> and like snow melted by a damp south wind, the tears welled
> up in distress, flowed free.

Then a summons arrived and Ovid was ordered back to Rome to meet privately with Augustus. Augustus was outraged. After a severe tongue-lashing, Augustus decided to forego a trial to ensure secrecy, but banished Ovid, in perpetuity, to Tomi, a bleak fishing village on the northwest coast of the Black Sea near the mouth of the Danube estuary, a barbaric unsettled province. Ovid was not stripped of his property or rights of citizenship, so it was not an official exile, but a type of banishment known as *relagatio*. Ovid had just turned fifty, and the news was a shock to him. He was probably the most popular and famous poet in the empire. Why, in one of the last stories, he had even penned a lyrical tribute to the Emperor! Augustus gave no reason for the banishment, but at the same time he banished his own granddaughter, Julia, and ordered that Ovid's works should be taken from the public libraries. Did Ovid write something that prompted Julia's indiscretion? Was Ovid an accomplice in her misconduct? Or did he actually participate in one of her lustful escapades? From Ovid, all we get is his admission that he had made "an error," that his only crime was something he had "seen." Generations of scholars have searched in vain for evidence of Ovid's "crime." Many suggest that what he "saw" was the greed and liscentiousness of Rome, the flagrant decline of moral standards and civic responsibility, and that he was speaking as a poet, not a political adversary. Some believe that the incident involved a politcal intrigue to overthrow Augustus. In the letters/poems written during his exile, he wrote:

> . . . emphasize I only
> survive by courtesy of a god.
> For the rest, keep silent. If people demand more details
> take care not to blab out
> any state secrets:

Ovid denied any wrongdoing, and pleaded with Augustus to reconsider. He refused to change his mind. On the last evening he was to spend in Rome, his household was filled with weeping. His wife pleaded with him to let her go, too. "I will be but a small additional burden to the ship of exile," she said. Perhaps Ovid believed he would get a pardon, that his exile—or his *relagato*, to be more exact—would be a short one. Relagated so far away, he still did not suffer the confiscation of his property and citizenship, as he would have were he officially exiled. Ovid comforted his wife and said no.

> I was dazed, like someone struck by Jove's own lightning (had I not been?), who
> survives, yet remains unsure
> Whether he's dead or alive. Sheer force of grief unclouded my mind in the end.
> When my poor wife revived
> I had one last word with my friends before departure—
> those few friends, out of many, who stood firm.
> My wife, my lover, embraced me, outwept my weeping,
> her undeserving cheeks
> rivered with tears. Far away in north Africa, my daughter
> could know nothing of my fate. From every side,
> wherever you looked, came the sounds of grief and lamentation,
> just like a noisy funeral. The whole house
> mourned at my obsequies—men, women, even children,
> every nook and corner had its tears.

After everyone had gone to bed, Ovid walked out into the night and looked up at the marble temples on Capitol hill.

> By now all was still, no voices, no barking watchdogs,
> just the Moon, on her course aloft in the night sky.
> Gazing at her, and the Capitol—clear now by moonlight,
> close (but what use?) to my home.

While preparing to leave home, he burned his manuscripts of the *Metamorphoses,* but some readers had made copies and preserved them. Shortly after dawn, he sailed with what belongings he could carry from Brindisi, a port on the southeastern tip of Italy. It was November of the year 8, and a fierce wind and stormy sea nearly blew the ship back to the mainland, but the crew managed to hold steady, and Ovid watched from the stern till he could barely see his homeland. Across the Ionian Sea to Greece, then island-hopping across the Aegean via the Cyclades, they arrived at the Hellespont. The sea voyage had been rough, with waves nearly swallowing the boat, but not rough enough for Ovid. He regretted surviving and embraced his grief on land the way one would use a life-preserver to stay afloat on the heavy sea.

Next, Ovid traveled overland through Thrace, a land teeming with bandits and highwaymen. Another ship took him across the Black Sea, setting him down finally at the town of Tomis (Constanta in modern Romania). It was a barren wasteland, wild and barbaric. Through the dark, long winters Ovid watched the forceful waters of the Danube freeze solid. Shards of ice collected on men's beards, and wild horsemen from the north and east swept down upon the cities and farms destroying dwellings and taking what they could. Ovid was to spend the last years of his life on what seemed the wild edge of the world, never to see his wife, family, or friends again. Even his beloved muse seemed to desert him. "Here I am, bereft of country, home and family, everything that could be taken from me. . . . Words often fail me when I try to say something (I'm ashamed to confess), and I've forgotten how to talk . . . . I am the barbarian here, understood by no one; and the stupid Getans laugh at Latin words." For Ovid, there was nothing left but "to wander forever, a foreigner among the Sarmatian shades." When it was apparent that no reprieve was to come, he hoped only that he would be buried back in his homeland, not the barbarian earth where he'd die, and that his verses would

> What pleasure do you get from stabbing this dead body?
> There is no space in me now for another would.

He poured his grief into those last verses known as the *Tristia,* or "Sorrows." He declared that the letters contained "no instructions on love, not one page, not a syllable. . . . You'll find nothing here but lamentation." These last poems are sublime, filled with remorse, lamenation, and a longing for home.

> Nagging reminders: the black ghost-melancholy vision
> of my final night in Rome,
> the night I abandoned so much I dearly treasured —
> to think of it, even now, starts tears.
> I was dazed, like someone struck by Jove's own lightning
> (had I not been?), who survives, yet remains unsure
> whether he's dead or alive. Sheer force of grief unclouded
> my mind in the end.

Until recently, the *Tristia* was not very highly regarded. In this century, writers who have been banished, exiled, or fleeing their own native land have given their lamentations epic resonance. When we read Ovid's supplications, we imagine ourselves, torn from family and friends, living in some remote place where even our native tongue is not spoken. Ovid's gay and lusty persona had to be changed. In order to get sympathy from Augustus and those in high places who might influence him, Ovid had to recast his persona, and in his desperation, constructed a voice that finally reached tragic dimensions

> Books, my unlucky obsession, why do I stay with you
> when it was my own talent brought me down?
> Why go back to those fresh-condemned Muses, my nemesis? Isn't
> one well-earned punishment enough?
> Poetry made men and women eager to know me —
> that was my bad luck;
> poetry made Caesar condemn my and my life-style
> because of my *Art*, put out   the *Art of Love*
> years before: take away my pursuit, you remove my offences —
> I credit my guilt to my verses. Here's the reward
> I've had for my care and all my sleepless labour:
> a penalty set on talent.
> Why didn't I rather churn out yet another epic poem
> on how Troy fell to the Greeks?

He answers the charge that his life-style was decadent and immoral.

> Ah, why did I ever study? Why did my parents
> give me an education? Why did I learn
> so much as the ABC's? It was my *Art*'s wantonnes turned you
> against me, because you were convinced
> it encouraged illicit sex. But no brides have become intriguers
> through me: no one can teach what he doesn't know.
> Yes, I've written frivolous verses, erotic poems — but never
> has a breath of scandal touched my name. There's no
> husband, even among the lower classes, who questions
> his paternity through any fault of mine!
> My morals, believe me, are quite distinct from my verses —
> a respectable life-style, a flirtatious Muse —
> and the larger part of my writings is mendacious, fictive,
> assumes the licence its author denies himself.
> 　　　　　　　　　　　　Lastly, it's not
> as though *I* were the only composer of erotic verses —
> yet I, and I alone, have paid the price
> for producing such things.

> Yet even the fortunate author of your own *Aeneid* brought his
> Arms-and-the-Man into a Tyrian bed —   [
> Indeed, no part of the whole work's read more often
> than this union of illicit love. . . .
> 　　　　　　　　　The fact that my poetry's more wanton
> than my life, that my fun is free of real offence
> does me no good. . . . Show mercy to the dying, let me
> at least be buried in my native soil? [or] see that my bones
> are brought home in a little urn: then I'll not remain exiled
> even in death. This nobody forbids —

Theban Antigone buried her slaughtered brother
against a king's commands.
So mingle my ashes with sweet dried herbs and spikenard,
bury them close to the City, and inscribe
these lines in gold letters on my marble-headstone
for travellers to glance at as they hurry by:
I who lie here, sweet Ovid, poet of tender passions,
fell victim to my own sharp wit.
Passer-by, if you've ever been in love, don't grudge me
the traditional prayer: "May Ovid's bones lie soft!"
So much for an epitaph. My books make a more enduring
and greater monument.

In one of the poems/letters addressed to a friend, he offers this advice: "Live for yourself, keep far from all great names," especially that "illustrious citadel" from which "a savage bolt descends. Only potentates can protect us, yet what use is that if they prefer to obstruct?"

Book IV is noted for the famous poem #10, written in 11 AD, three years after his departure from Rome. The poem passes for autobiography, but since Ovid had slid from one persona to another throughout his poems, even this must be taken with a grain of salt, at least as far as those parts that offer a defense of his "mistake," "blunder," "indiscretion," "error"—words Ovid is adamant about substituing for "crime." In the poems that precede #10, he celebrates those who have not deserted him, his wife, a few friends, and above all, the Muse.

Steadfast companion I had then, she alone feared no ambush,
no barbarous swordsman, neither sea nor wind.
She knows what error it was undid me at my downfall—
that there was fault in my case, but *no crime.*
That surely, is why she's fair to me now—the damage
she did me before, co-indicted on a joint charge.
If I'd know the harm I'd suffer from her and her sisters
I'd never have set my hand to their holy game—
but what to do now? I'm hooked. Creative inspiration
had got me. Though verse-ruined, I'm mad enough
to love verse still. When Ulysses' companions savoured
the exotic lotus, their palates relished the taste
that undid them. Often a lover recognizes his own destruction
yet clings to it, hunts down
the stuff of his doom. So I relish the books that have hurt me,
love the weapon that inflicted my wounds.

Ovid's irreconcilable masks have tempted many critics to dig for the the poet's elusive personality. There was always an element of masquerade, even where Seneca wrote that Ovid's rhetorical speeches while studying law were nothing but poetry masquerading as prose. Ovid's *Metamorphoses* was not just a strategy to solve the problem of the epic. Transformation and change were part of his own life experience, having had to transforma himself from a passionate lover and husband who was cuckolded more than once, to the *praeceptor amoris*, the professor of love. Earlier he'd thrown off the purple cloak of senatorial aristocracy and chose to wear the poet's toga. If Ovid is a modern poet, part of that comes from his elusiveness, his ability to work from several levels of awareness,and his concern with the aspects of the public and private self, as well as with the self divided. In his poems, transformation becomes a metaphor for the human condition, not to mention the very nature of the creative act itself.

Ovid is one of the first poets in history to use the mask of the persona so skillfully, so artfully, that the reader is apt to lose sight of the trick behind the magic. In Ovid's case, it may well have been the cause of his downfall. Just what was the realtionship between the witty, ironic womanizer we meet in the *Amores* and the didactic poems of the *Ars Amatoria*, and the real, historical poet. What creative inventions, what imaginative constructs lie between the poet who was married three times and rejected a public career as lawyer and senator, and the literary hedonist, the poet who absorbed the tradition of elegy that went back to Callimachus, and then treated it both seriously and as the object of parody.

We live in a time in which self-portraiture is a common theme of contemporary poetry. Few critics are able to deal with the complex problem posed by so-called "confessional" poetry. That goes for the poets as well. We're discovering that T.S. Eliot's poems were more autobiographical than was first apparent, and the same is true for other modern poets who used persona as a literary device to either hide or reveal a multiplicity of selves: Frost, Pound, Sylvia PLath, Anne Sexton, John Berryamn, Charles Bukowski, to name only a few. There's no simple formula to characterize the persona, and no critic that I'm aware of has written extensively of this poetic strategy. But any analysis would have to begin with Ovid, who reveled in the use of literary masks, and seemed at times obsessed with the phenomenon of metamorphoses. And he knew what he was doing; it was not an accident of whimsy or imagination. The tenth poem in Book IV, that has ben held up as an autobiographical source, begins with his admission that his various personae have often hid behind a literary smokescreen. His other weapon, irony, was also used, even here, when he finally appears to be coming clean with the facts, when in fact, it may well be another smokescreen. While a pure biographical portrait or fictional portrait can ever truly be presented, Ovid can't help but use the guise of self-disclosure for imaginative construction. Even to the end, his concern was with his art, and with poetic immortality. The boast at the conclusion of the *Metamorphoses* may come off a bit self-serving and self-indulgent, but two thousand years later, we who are here are reading it, not because the boast is interesting, or because the boast has come true. We are reading it because it's part of a literary masterpiece that continues to fascinate and entertain us.

☛ Book IV, #10.

> Who was this I you read, this trifler in tender passions?
> You want to know, posterity? Then attend:—
> Sulmo is my homeland, where ice-cold mountain torrents
> make lush our pastures, and Rome is ninety miles off. . . .
> . . . . but I, even in boyhood, held out for higher matters,
> and the Muse was seducing me subtly to her work.

My father kept saying: "Why study such useless subjects?
Even Homer left no inheritance." . . .,
[as for the law or politics], I lacked both endurance and inclination:
the stress of ambition left me cold,
while the Muse, the creative spirit , was forever urging on me
that haven of leisure to which I'd always leaned.
The poets of those days I cultivated and cherished:
for me, bards were so many gods.
. . . . aging Macer would read me what he'd written
on birds or poisonous snakes or healing herbs;
often Propertius, by virtue of that close-binding
comradeship between us, would recite
his burning verses. Ponticus, noted for epic, and Bassus,
pre-eminent in iambics, both belonged
to my circle; Horace, that metrical wizard, held us
spellbound with songs to the lyre.
Virgil I only saw, while greedy fate left Tibullus
scant time for our friendship.

When I was scarce past boyhood I was briefly married
to a wife both worthless and useless; next
came a bride you could not find fault with, yet not destined
to warm my bed for long; third and last
there's the partner who's grown old with me, who's learnt to shoulder
the burden of living as an exile's wife.
My daughter, twice pregnant (but by different husbands) made me
a grandfather early on, while she was still
just a slip of a girl. By then my father had completed
 his lifespan of ninety years. For himI wept
just as he would have done had I been the one taken.
Then, next, I saw my mother to her grave.
Ah, lucky the pair of them, so timely dead and buried,
Before the black day of my disgrace!
And lucky for me, that they are not still living
To witness my misery, that they felt no grief
on my account. Yet if there survives from a life's extinction
something more than a name, if an unsubstantial wraith
does escape the pyre, if some word, my parental spirits,
has reached you about me, if charges stand to my name
in the Stygian court, then understand, I implore you
—and you I may not deceive—that my exile's cause
was not a crime, but an error. So much for the dead. I return now
to you, my devoted readers, who would know
the events of my life. Already my best years were behind me—
age had brindled my hair, and ten times since my birth,
head wreathed with Pisan olive, the victorious Olympic
charioteer had carried off the prize
when the wrath of an injured Prince compelled me to make my way to
Tomis, on the left shore of the Black Sea.
The cause (though too familiar to everyone) of my ruin
must not be revealed through testimony of mine.

Why rake up associates' meannesses, harm done me by house-slaves,
and much further suffering, not a whit less harsh
than the exile itself. Yet my mind disdained to yield to trouble,
showed itself invincible, drew on its strength,
till I, forgetting myself and my old leisured existence,
took arms on occasion with unpractised hand;
by sea and land I suffered as many misfortunes
as the stars between the unseen and the visible poles.
Through long wanderings driven, I at length made landfall
on this coast, where native bowman roam; and here,
though the din of neighboring arms surrounds me, I still lighten
my sad fate as best I can
with the composition of verse: though there is none to listen
this is how I spend, and beguile, my days.
So the fact that I live still to grapple with such grim hardships,
unwearied, yet, of the light and all it brigns,
I owe, my Muse, to you: it's you who afford me solace,
who come as rest, as medicine to my cares;
you my guide and comrade, who sprit me from the Danube
to an honoured seat on Helicon; who have
offered me that rare benefit, fame while still living,
a title rarely granted till after death. . . .
There are many I'd rank above me: yet I am no less quoted
than they are, and most read throughout the world.
So if there's any truth in poetic predicitions, even
should I die tomorrow, I'll not be wholly earth's.
Which I was it triumphed? True poet or fashion's pander?
Either way, generous reader, it is you I must thank.

Behind his petitions lay his great hope for a pardon. None came. Six years later, his spirit broken, realizing he would never return to the city he loved, he lay in his bed, welcoming the end.

Born in the year after the murder of Julius Caesar, Ovid grew to maturity without having had to experience the horrors of civil war, and like most of his generation, found the policies of the Augustan regime repressive and strait-laced. While there was tremendous opportunity for financial and political advancement, Ovid was single-minded in his devotion to poetry. He refined the rules of composition for the elegiac couplet through his virtuostic metrical and linguistic displays. He lacked Virgil's tragic vision and human insight, and was often frivolous and irresponsible, over-exuberant in tone—like Horace said, he didn't let well enough alone. But his wit and inventiveness made him the most consistently entertaining of the Roman poets. When his imaginative sympathy was aroused, he could write movingly and simply, without rhetorical strain or artificial eloquence. Like Virgil, he was a good story-teller and knew how to let the significant moment in a scene speak for itself, and was sensitive to the real beauty of love in a way that was rare in classical literature. The Elder Seneca tells a story concerning Ovid's tendency toward verbal extravagance. His friends approached him one time and wanted to cut three lines from his poems. Ovid agreed, but only if he could select three lines that could *not* be removed. It turned out that each side picked the same three lines.

The *Metamorphoses* was one of the most often read and quoted books during the Middle Ages, and Ovid was the favorite Latin poet of the Renaissance. Numerous translation of his works were made into English, and Chaucer referenced many of his lines, as did Spenser in his *Faerie Queen*, and Marlowe in his *Doctor Faustus*. Shakespeare knew the *Metamorphoses* in Golding's translation, and we find references to Ovid in many of his plays, including *As You Like It* and *Taming of the Shrew*. The line in Romeo and Juliet—"At lovers' perjuries they say Jove laughs."—is a direct translation from the *Ars Amatoria*.

The greatest Roman poet of the age died on a bleak rim of the empire. With Ovid's death came the passing of the greatness of the Latin langauge as a poetic medium, a subtle and compact language that with Virgil and Ovid had reached a zenith. Virgil was the classical classicist; Ovid, the classical romanticist. The *Amores,* the *Ars Amatoria*, the *Metamorphoses*, and his *Poems of Exile*, written at the beginning of the Christian Era, were the last major works of a great age in Latin poetry.

Food for Thought

Meanwhile, Back at the Ranch . . .

. . . a child is born in Bethlehem in a manger because there was no room at the inn. His parents were from Galilee in Nazareth, but they came to Bethlehem to be counted in the census directed by Augustus Caesar. Thus, Jesus of Nazareth was born in an obscure corner of the ancient world somewhere between seven and two years before the birth of Jesus Christ. How is that possible? Well, let's do the math.

There is no contemporary historical evidence demonstrating the date of Jesus' birth. In Roman times, dates were counted from the reign of an emperor or king or the date of the founding of the Roman Republic. Two centuries after the birth of Jesus, Julius Africanus, one of the first great scholars of the ancient world to be a Christian, tried to piece together a coherent chronology for Christian events. The common Gregorian calendar method for numbering years is based on an early medieval attempt to count the years from a point of reference—namely, Jesus' birth. Julius placed the Saviour's birth in a year which he reckoned as the 5,500 from Creation. This calculation became embedded in the work of later historians, such as the sixth century monk, Dionysius Exiguus (Dionysius the Humble, or the Short) who placed, either mistakenly or intentionally, Jesus' birth as occuring sometime between 2 BC/BCE and 1 AD/BCE. Thus, Dionysius gets the credit for fixing the first Year of the Lord, *anno Domini,* and is best known as the inventor of the *Anno Domini* era, which is used to number the years of both the Gregorian calendar and the Julian calendar. When Dionysius devised his table of dates, he himself stated that the "present year" was "the consulship of Probus Junior [Flavius Probus],"which he also stated was 525 years "since the incarnation of our Lord Jesus Christ." How he arrived at that exact number is unknown. He invented a new system of numbering years to replace the Diocletian years that had been used in an old Easter table because he did not wish to continue the memory of a tyrant who persecuted Christians. The *Anno Domini* era became dominant in Western Europe only after it was used by the Venerable Bede to date the events in his *Ecclesiastical History of the English People*, completed in 731.

The Gospel of Matthew states that Jesus' birth occurred during the reign of Herod the Great who died in 4 BC/BCE, but also with the intimation that Jesus may have been as much as two years old when Herod ordered the Massacre of the Innocents, and therefore that Jesus may have been even older at the time of Herod's death. *The Gospel of Luke* similarly points to Jesus' birth as having occurred during the reign of Herod the Great, but the author of Luke also describes the birth as taking place during the first census of the Roman provinces of Syria and Judaea, which is generally believed to have occurred in 6 AD/CE. Most scholars assume a date of birth between 6 and 4 BC. Thus, Jesus of Nazareth was born several years before the date assigned to the birth of Jesus Christ.

As to where Jesus was born, Matthew says only that he "was born in Bethlehem of Judea," before relating how Jesus came to live in Nazareth in Galilee, starting with the story of three wise men (magi) who follow the star to the newborn Jesus. On their way, these wise men visit King Herod, who fears that the child will be the king-Messiah prophesied in scripture, so he orders the slaughter of all the infants of Bethlehem. The holy family flees to Egypt and after Herod's death they return, not to Judea, now ruled by Herod's despotic son Archelaus, but to Nazareth in Galilee, where Jesus spent his childhood.

In the context of the Golden Age of Roman poetry, it is doubtful that anyone reading the work of Virgil, Ovid, and Horace would have taken note of the birth of this child in far away Palestine. Yet, within a few centuries, Christianity was to become the official religion of the Roman Empire, and after the fall of Rome, it was Christian poets and writers who were to dominate the literature of the Middle Ages. Edward Gibbon, in his *Decline and Fall of the Roman Empire,* blamed Christianty for Rome's demise, but even if that were not so (and it's not), how is one to imagine medieval culture without Christianity. Whatever literature existed and flourished, it was mainly due to the medieval monks who both read classical literature and preserved it, and the majority of poets and writers of that age received their education in the monasteries or ecclesiatical schools. Had Christianity not filled the vacuum left by Rome's fall, what would the culture of the Dark Ages and the medieval world have been like? Catholic Christianity was so pervasive in the Middle Ages, they are almost synonymous. Believer or not, anyone living during the Dark and Middle Ages could hardly have experienced daily life without the culture of Christianity. For the moment, we'll set aside the question as to why God picked the reigns of Augustus and Tiberius to have Jesus born and then die for our sins. (What if Jesus had been "born," sacrificed, and risen a few centuries earlier, or a few centuries later? Had mankind reached a peak of sinfullness in the Glory days of Rome? Why not the Grandeur days of Greece?) Whatever the case, there is almost no way to imagine the Middle Ages without the culture of Christianity.

There is no question that the major influence on English and European literature was the Bible, and when we say the Bible, we mean both the Old and New Testaments, or put another way, the Hebrew Bible and the books of the New Testament. Without Christianity, it is doubtful that the literature of the Hebrew Bible would have been as ubiquitous in

Western literature and art, not to mention science and philosophy. Without Christianty, Judaism would have probably remained a fringe mono-theistic cult. The gods of the classical world did not play the same central role in the universe as did the one God of the Christians and Jews. For the Greeks and Romans, the universe was eternal and uncreated. Where there was chaos, Plato introduced the "Demiurge" (*demiourgos*), a kind of cosmic architect or engineer, who brings order to the material universe. The traditional gods of the Greek world were often portrayed as children with superpowers who often lacked moral predicatability. Human beings on earth were mere playthings for sport. The Greeks did their best to placate these gods and goddesses with temples and shrines and offerered up ritual ceremonies in their homes. But in the *Timaeus*, Plato conceives a God far removed from the fickle and quarrelsome gods of the Greek Pantheon. Adhering to his theory of ultimate Forms, Plato envisions a true deity as possessing not just the attribute of goodness, but oneness as well, a oneness that implies perfection. And being perfect, such a supreme God must be without passion, since passions involve changes from one mood to another. A perfect being cannot change. The God of the Jews, on the contrary, displays no passionless perfection. He is angry and compassionate, stern and loving. Satan challenges Him to a bet that Job will renounce Him once He takes away his good fortune. God can't resist and takes away, one by one, Job's material gifts and family. Both Platonic and Hebrew views of God stress transcendence, but Plato has trouble imagining a God who creates a world filled with impermanence and death.

Plato's famous pupil, Aristotle, followed a different path toward the conception of a supreme being. God is a "prime mover," which explains motion and change, but He is not a personal God who hears us and guides our lives. The Judeo-Christian philosophy of the Middle Ages and the Renaissance was finally challenged by the scientific revolution of the 17th century, the Enlightenment of the 18th century, the evolutionary materialism of the 19th century, and the rise of analytic and existentialist philosophies of the 20th century. Even today, as we move into the 21st century, philosophers, scientists, poets and writers assume a rather naturalistic outlook that attempts to replace theological with rational explanations for the nature of the universe, and often at the risk of what Voltaire called "the logic of the sword."

The poets writing during the Golden Age of Rome could have had no inkling of what was portended by the birth in a remote part of the Empire of a child who would come to be regarded variously as a charistmatic teacher and healer, the leader of an apocalyptic movement, an itinerant sage, or the Messiah as foretold in the Hebrew Scriptures who came to provide humankind with salvation and reconciliation with God by his suffering and death. The great poets of Rome's Golden Age—Virgil, Ovid and Horace—all died a few years before Jesus was born. All we know of Jesus' life before his public ministry and crucifixion come from the Gospels of Matthew and Luke. As mentioned earlier, Matthew implied that Mary and Joseph lived in Bethlehem and moved to Nazareth later, whereas Luke writes that they lived in Nazareth but moved to Bethlehem for the census, then returned to Galilee—the point being that even though Jesus spent most of his life and ministry in the northern district of Galilee, in order to conform to the predictions in "scripture," the Old Testament, Jesus had to be born in Bethlehem.

Many of the people therefore, when they heard this saying, said, Of a truth this is the Prophet. Others said, This is the Christ. But some said, Shall Christ come out of Galilee? Hath not the scripture said, That Christ cometh of the seed of David, and out of the town of Bethlehem, where David was? [John 7.40-42]

The part of scripture John was referring to was the book of the Prophet Micah:

But thou, Beth-lehem Ephratah, though thou be little among the thousands of Judah, yet out of thee shall he come forth unto me that is to be ruler in Israel; whose goings forth have been from of old, from everlasting. . . . And he shall stand and feed in the strength of the Lord, in the majesty of the name of the Lord his God; and they shall abide: for now shall he be great unto the ends of the earth. [Micah 5.2-4]

When it comes to the birth narratives, both Matthew and Luke agree on several facts, and there is speculation that both drew from a gospel written earlier that has since been lost, called the *Q Gospel*: Joseph and Mary are named as parents and were betrothed (in Judaism, the first stage of marriage, meaning Mary was still a virgin); Jesus is said to have descended from King David; an angel's annunciation of the birth of a son (to Mary in Luke, to Joseph in Matthew); the angels' message that Mary has conceived by the Holy Spirit and that the child should be named Jesus (Yeshu or Yeshua, Joshua, which means "God saves." It is Luke who gives the familiar details of Jesus' birth in the stable of an inn that had no spare room, and describes the shepherds who come to visit the new-born Messiah. Jesus is circumcised, named, and presented in the Temple.

And when eight days were accomplished for the circumcising of the child, his name was called Jesus, which was so named of the angel before he was conceived in the womb. And when the day of her purification according to the law of Moses were accomplished, they brought him to Jerusalem, to present him to the Lord; (As it is written in the law of the Lord, Every male that openeth the womb shall be called holy to the Lord;) And to offer a sacrifice according to that which is said in the law of the Lord, A pair of turtledoves, or two young pigeons. . . . [and Jesus was blessed, saying] Behold, this child is set for the fall and rising again of many in Israel; and for a sign which shall be spoken againt; (Yea, a sword shall pierce through thy own soul also,) that the thoughts of many hearts may be revealed. [Luke 2.21-35]

Afterwards, the family returns to Nazareth, where Jesus grows up with God's favor and "filled with wisdom."

From the Gospels, there is only one mention of Jesus' childhood and young adulthood, the episode recounted in Luke, when, aged 12, he goes missing during a visit to Jerusalem for Passover. His parents find him in the Temple—in the precincts, where rabbis would teach, rather than the sanctuary—debating with religious teachers, who are "amazed at his understanding." Jesus' age may be significant because 13 is the usual age of religious maturity in Judaism. Jesus remains in Galilee until 29AD when he begins his ministry, returning a year or two later to Jerusalem where he is arrested, tortured, and executed.

Outside the New Testament, there are only a few references to Jesus. Flavius Josephus, the Jewish historian, in his *Antiquities of the Jews*, written around 90 AD, says that:

At this time lived Jesus, a wise man (if one may rightly call him a man), a worker of miracles and a teacher of people who receive the truth with pleasure; as followers he gained many Jews and many Greeks. He was the Christ, and when by the accusation of our chief men Pilate condemned him to the cross, those who first loved him did not cease from doing so; for he appeared to them, alive again, on the third day, since the divine prophets [Isaiah, Jeremiah] had foretold this as well as countless other marvels about him. Up to the present the tribe of Christians, named after him, has not disappeared.

[*Ant.* 18.63-64]

Most biblical scholars question the authenticity of the above passage. Doubtless, it was copied many times by a Christian scribe, who couldn't help but touch it up and make a few additions, a common practice. Josephus, a devout Jew, could hardly have written the most overtly Christian parts of that passage, though Josephus does mention John the Baptist and James, brother of Jesus. The Roman historian Tacitus (ca. 55-ca. 120AD) mentions Christianity as a "mischievous superstition" that was spreading to Rome from Judea and that Nero blamed the great fire of Rome in 64 on the "Christians, who were named for Christus." Seutonius (ca.69-ca. 140AD) refers to the emperor Claudius expelling "Jews" from Rome in 49AD, but he's unclear whether he means Jews, or followers of "Chrestus." A few other sources outside the Gospels mention Jesus, probably representing an oral tradition, some authentic, and some fabrications and imaginative tales.

Not long after Jesus' crucifixion, other stories of Jesus as a youth were soon in circulation. Behind many of these legends lay a fundamental question: If Jesus was a miracle-working Son of God as an adult, what was he like as a child? Did he possess superpowers, was he prophetic, etc.? Not to belittle the sacredness of these stories, but it's somewhat like the comic book editions that focused on the stories of Superman when he was just a boy. Most of these non-canonical gospels have probably been lost, but among the trove of early Christian writings found at Nag Hammadi in 1946 was the so-called "Infancy Gospel of Thomas" (called "the Israelite," not to be confused with the writer of the Coptic Gospel of Thomas). It is not clear whether the author intended his readers to recognize him as Judas Thomas, thought by some early Christians to have been Jesus' own brother. If he did, then his accounts of Jesus as a youth, needless to say, would have been based on a reliable source, assuming they were true. We see Jesus perform simple miracles such as turning sparrows he had fashioned out of mud into real birds who fly off, while in other stories he is able to heal other children.

Now Joseph sent his son James to bundle some wood and bring it to the house. The child Jesus also followed him. While James was gathering the firewood, a snake bit his hand. When he was stretched out on the ground dying, Jesus came up to him and breathed on the bite. The pain immediately stopped, the animal burst, and straight away James was returned to health. [The Infancy Gospel of Thomas, 16: 1-2]

Jesus often challenges his teachers, bettering them in discussions of scripture, revealing their ignorance, much to their annoyance. While working with his father in his workshop, he often fixes his father's mistakes, as when he miraculously makes a beam meant for the bed of a rich man the same length as the longer beam, which had been cut correctly. "His father Joseph saw what he had done and was amazed. He embraced the child and gave him a kiss, saying, 'I am blessed that God has given me this child.' " Working with his father in the field, he sows a single grain of wheat which produces a hundred large bushels. But some of the stories show a mischievous boy who often harms his playmates with his divine power, and in other tales Jesus is portrayed as vindictive and vengeful, capable of turning someone into a cripple, or causing them to die for no other reason than his own annoyance at being reprimanded or contradicted.

> Now the son of Annas the scribe was standing there with Joseph, and he took a willow branch and scattered the water that Jesus had gathered. Jesus was irritated when he saw what had happened, and he said to him: "You unrighteous, irreverent idiot! What did the pools of water do to harm you? See, now you also will be withered like a tree, and you will never bear leaves or root or fruit." Immediately that child was completely withered. Jesus left and returned to Joseph's house. But the parents of the withered child carried him away, mourning his lost youth. They brought him to Joseph and began to accuse him, "What kind of child do you have who does such things?"
>
> [*Infancy Gospel of Thomas*, 3.1-3]

> Somewhat later he was going through the village, and a child ran up and banged into his shoulder. Jesus was aggravated and said unto him, "You will go no further on your way." And right away the child fell down and died. Some of those who saw what happened said, "Where was this child born? For everything he says is a deed accomplished." The parents of the dead child came to Joseph and blamed him, saying, "Since you have such a child you cannot live with us in the village. Or teach him to bless and not to curse—for he has killed our children. Joseph called to the child and admonished him privately, "Why are you doing such things? These people are suffering, they hate us and are persecuting us!" But Jesus replied, "I know these are not your words, and so I also will keep silent for your sake. But those others will bear their punishment." And immediately those who were accusing him were blinded. [*Infancy Gospel of Thomas*, 4.1-2]

One is reminded of the Rod Serling teleplay in which a child with special powers can banish to the pumpkin patch anyone he becomes annoyed with. The author of this Gospel says he is relating these stories "so that you may know the magnificent childhood activities of our Lord Jesus Christ." It is understandable why the Church excluded this gospel from the final canon, but puzzling why the author thought some of these stories were exemplary.

In the Synoptic Gospels, Jesus does not return to the Temple in Jerusalem untl the last week of his life, around the same time that three of the great poets of Rome's Silver Age—Lucan, Martial, and Persius—were born. Paul composed his letters two decades after the Crucifixion, around the same time that the other great poets of the Silver Age—Statius, Petronius, and Juvenal—were born. The major works of these poets of the Silver Age were written in the same period in which Paul was writing his letters, in which Matthew, Mark, Luke and John were writing the Gospels, in which the Acts and other books of the New Testament were being written. Juvenal, the last great poet of Rome's Silver Age, died just a few years after the composition of the *Book of Revelation*, written in the second decade of the 2nd Century AD.

But all of that was happening off-stage, as it were, "back at the ranch." Except for the writings that made it into the New Testament, and the writings that didn't, there is no specifically Christian literature (poems, etc.) until the end of the 3rd Century, and it doesn't really begin to flourish until well into the 4th Century after Constantine accepts Christianity as the state religion, the religion of the Empire. Of course, there were still a few variants to be worked out, heresies, if you will, most of which were taken care of at the Council of Nicea in 325. But as you read the next chapter on Rome's Silver Age, keep in mind what was going on in Palestine, "back at the ranch": Jesus' ministry and crucifixion, and in the half century that followed, the letters and writings, most of which were lost until recent discoveries, and those writings that survivied to become the Four Gospels, the Pauline Epistles, The Acts of the Apostles, the Revelation of John the Divine—the twenty-seven books that were eventually canonized as *The New Testament.*

- **Lucan** (39-65 A.D.), the *Pharsalia*—also called the *Civil Wars*
- **Statius** (c. 61-96 A.D.), the *Thebaid*
- **Martial** (c. 40-102 A.D.), *Epigrams*
- **Persius** (34-62 AD)
- **Petronius** (? - 66 A.D.), the *Satyricon*
- **Juvenal** (c. 60-c. 140 A.D.), *Satires*

The Silver Age of Latin letters, generally said to have begun around 14 A.D. with the death of Augustus (Ovid died in 17 A.D.), lasted for a century, and in contrast to the Age of Augustus, this was a period of decline and decay. The speech of the comman man re-entered poetry and the Latin tongue itself began to change, as if preparing to give birth a millenium later to Italian, Spanish, and French.

When we trace the evolution of great poets, we jump from Homer to Virgil, and from the great poets of the Augustan Age (Virgil & Ovid), directly to Dante. There's no one of comparable stature between Virgil and Dante (with the possible exception of St. Augustine, whose *Confessions* can be considered a strictly literary work). The work of Petronius and Juvenal continue to delight us today, but the most celebrated works of that era were the epic poem *Pharsalia* by **Lucan** (39-65 A.D.), called by many an anti-*Aeneid.*, and the *Thebaid* by **Statius**.

In contrast to Virgil's optimistic view of Augustan ideology, Lucan denounced fratricidal war and the imperial regime that was born out of the ashes of the *libera res publica*. Lucan did not glorify the civil wars between Pompey and Caesar, but presented them in all their brutality. He foreshadowed the inexorable decline and collapse of Rome, "ruins covered in dust." When Marcus Annaeus Lucan came to Rome, he entered Nero's court and became one of Nero's intimate friends. Some think Nero became jealous of Lucan's poetic gifts, because Lucan fell suddenly into disgrace with the Emperor and was banished from court favor. Forbidden to publish because of Nero's jealousy, Lucan took part in Piso's conspiracy against Nero. When his role in it was discovered, he was forced to commit suicide.

The other great Roman epic poet was Publius Papinius **Statius** (c.45-c.96 A.D.), who wrote an epic, the *Thebiad*, describing the war between the two sons of Oedipus, Eteocles and Polyneices, for the overlordship of Thebes. He concludes the poem with an expression of the most profound respect for the "divine *Aeneid*," which he can but imitate from afar and whose footprints he worships. Though little read today, Statius was the most eminent poet of his time and popular throughout the Middle Ages. Dante gives him an honored place in Purgatory, where he takes over for Virgil and leads Dante into Paradise. And Chaucer puts Statius with Virgil, Ovid, Homer and Lucan as one of the world's great poets.

The change in attitude toward the high classical poetry of Virgil's day was already evident in the poetry of Ovid and Propertius. As we move into the Silver Age, the poets of the Early Empire reflect its disintegration. After Maecenas died, there was no one else to mediate between the political powers and the artistic elite. With the end of patronage came poetry that was sharper and more criticial of the Julio-Claudian dynasty. Rhetoric replaced eloquence, grammar deteriorated at the expense of poetry; and the mania for rhetoric, previously applied to oratory and performance, invaded poetry, while prose became more poetic. Everyone was writing poetry. Pithy epigrams and pills of wisdom became the rage—reading it aloud wherever friends and fellow poets could be assembled, even in the bath. There was a renewed passion for poetry among the general populace, amateur and professional alike celebrating the darker age of the city with its sexual freedom and gradual breakdown of order.

Surprising to modern readers is the fact that Nero made great efforts to reestablish patronage and encourage poets to continue the classicism of Augustan literature. A poet himself, Nero created a public poetic competition in 60 A.D. in order to hasten what he hoped would be a cultural renewal. These public contests continued even after his death, with festivals and readings, often bordering on spectacular theatrical performances. Many poets composed classical and anti-classical epics in the quiet of their rooms, and in order to earn board and bread, wrote for paying clients or composed librettoes for dramatic spectacles. Poets turned increasingly to the theatre to make their way, just as many poets today try their hands at the novel, or the screenplay which promises bigger bucks than poetry can ever supply. Statius wrote a libretto for a pantomime, a genre received with unbridled enthusiasm by the populace, making the actors immensely popular. In order to compete with the bread and circuses (*panem et circenses*—Juvenal's phrase), these theatrical representations increased in popularity as they became more and more elaborate with special effects created by ever more ingenious stage machinery and actors going to greater and greater lengths to astonish and amaze their audience: some vomited blood on stage, others recreated realistic crucifixions. The parallels to our own time seem obvious. Popular film is filled with sex, violence, and special effects. Stage productions and rock concerts compete for spectacular effects such as falling chandeliers and smoke. Television news transmits horrific pictures that cater to our fixation for "realistic crucifixions." And as in Roman times when the Empire declined even in its Silver Age, our poetry has become more rhetorical and our poets more theatrical in their presentation.

In the new atmosphere of Rome's Silver Age, it was only natural that poetry took on theatrical traits and moved toward a more vernacular idiom and away from high classical epic. The custom of public readings had the effect of introducing oratory and rhetorical aspects to the writing of poetry. As the practice of recitation became increasingly common, poems tended toward a baroque style, and poets worked to astonish the audience with bold and unusual metaphors, luxurious images, and astonishing subjects. Most celebrated or parodied the moral decay of the Empire. While Juvnal's satires were written for public declamation—*recitatio*—he directed some of his most biting invective at the widespread mania for readings in public halls and theaters [see page 53-54]. Juvenal mocked this notion of literature as performance, the vulgarization of the literary product, the writing of tour-de-force poems meant to elicit applause from the audience.

☞ **Lucan** ((39-65 A.D.), the *Pharsalia*—also called the *Civil Wars*

The hand of Fortune is just as fickle as the hand of Fate. After Lucan's death, his *Pharsalia* (also called the *Civil War*) became one of the great successes of world literature. It was enormously popular in antiquity and throughout the Middle Ages, and Lucan became a central medieval school author. This epic of the civil war between Caesar and Pompey was admired and studied for various reasons: its historical account, its rich grandiose rhetoric and epigrammatic wit, and its tragic style and horrific expressionism.

When Appius came to consult the Oracle, intent on learning
the secrets of Rome's destiny, no priestess had occupied the sacred tripod
for many years, and silence therefore reigned on the towering crag.
Phemonoe was strolling idly from the Castalian Spring towards
the laurel grove when he caught hold of her, dragged her to the shrine,
and pushed her inside.
She approached the lip of the great chasm and seated herself on the tripod.
Then for the first time she experienced the divine afflatus,
still active after so many centuries, and Appolo finally possessed her.
He forced his way into her heart, masterful as ever,
driving out her private thoughts and draining her body of all that was mortal.
She went blundering frantically about the shrine,
with the God mounted on the nape of her neck, knocking over the tripods
that stood in her path. The hair rose on her scalp,
and when she tossed her head the wreaths went flying across the bare floor.
Apollo's fury was so fierce that fire seemed to boil from her mouth.
He whipped her, goaded her, darted flames into her intestines;
but at the same time kept her on the curb and prevented her from disclosing
all that she knew. Countless centuries crowded tormentingly in her breasts;
rival secrets contended within her for utterance. She understood all that was
or would be, from the beginning of the world to its very end.
She chose that of Rome for sole revelation.
As soon as she recognized it, her mouth foamed frenziedly; she groaned,
gasped, uttered weird sounds, and made the huge cave re-echo
with her dismal shrieks. In the end Apollo forced her to intelligible speech,
and here is the response she gave:

> Appius, you shall avoid the tremendous perils of warfare,
> Taking your solitary ease in Euboea, that haven of refuge.

I wonder why the divine oracles, capable of universal truth,
were disinclined to reveal the closing chapter in this fatal history—
the fall of generals, the death of emperors, the ruin of so many nations,
which Rome's civil war implied.
Or was it that the Gods themselves had not yet decided on this catastrophe,
that the stars were equally doubtful whether or not Pompey should be killed?

Many writers of the Renaissance borrowed its language and style. After a short period of obscurity, Lucan was rediscovered by the poets of the Enlightenment, and embraced by the Romantics who saw themselves reflected in this poet of irrational genius. They especially related to the impassioned urgency of his verse, which was marked by frequent enjambment and a flexible syntax that gave an unusual expressive tension by escaping the bonds of the expected hexameter. Shelley thought the *Parsalia* "a poem of wonderful genius and transcending Virgil." By the middle of the 19th century, however, he was hardly read, and since then has ceased to be a vital presence in world literature.

Nevertheless, in the opinion of Robert Graves, who supplied the above translation, this failure may prove to be only temporary since Lucan's "modernist" traits—impatience with craftsmanship, digressive irrelevances, emphasis on the macabre, lack of religious conviction, turgid hyperbole, inconsistency, appeal to violence—have been rediscovered by this new, disagreeable world."

Like the *Aeneid*, the *Pharsalia* is structured around a series of prophecies. But instead of calling forth the future glories of Rome, these prophecies expose the ruin that awaits it. Where Virgil invoked the myths of Rome's founding, Lucan touched upon its darker fate, the anti-myth of Rome's decline and fall. Throughout this epic account of the civil war between Caesar and Pompey, Lucan contrasts the liberty of the ancient republic with an explicit condemnation of the imperial regime, and he does this by including Virgil's heroic epic in the condemnation. There's a tone of indignant reflection, as if Virgil's glowing hexameters were partly to blame for the transformation of the Republic into a tyranny. The *Pharsalia* is almost a mirror image of the *Aeneid*, with chapters and passages and allusions set up for parody or disdain. Lucan places the *nekyomanteia*, "necromany," in book 6, just as Virgil introduced the chapter on the Underworld in book 6, where Aeneas makes his descent to the dead to receive the prophecies. And Virgil had mirrored this chapter on Homer's sending Odysseus descending into the Underworld to speak to Tiresias. Lucan inverts the famous passage where Aeneas' father lists the lands that will come under Roman rule [see page 98] :

> Then the Latin name
> will be known only by hearsay: ruins
> covered in dust will scarcely be able to indicate
> Gabii, Veii, and Cora."

In Lucan and Statius we have representations of both aspects of the Silver Age—Lucan's inversion of Virgil's nationalistic epic, and Statius' grand attempt to revive classical poetry with his *Thebaid*. Statius was perhaps the purest poet in the history of imperial Rome. Crowds gathered to hear him read his epic in a Naples theater, but the sensitive eloquence of his verses read rather badly today, and the action of the poem is weighed down by references to gods we no longer care about.

☛ **Lucillius** (fl. 60s AD)

Lucillius was the author of one hundred twenty three epigrams in Greek preserved in the Greek Anthology (*Anthologia Palatina*). He lived under the emperor Nero, who gave a strong stimulus to the arts, and was connected to the poestic circles of the Neronian period. Many of Lucillius's poems describe stereotyped people, such as doctors or thin people; as such his works are in the tradition of the Characters of Theophrastus. He influenced the Latin epigrammatist Martial. Sometimes his name is (incorrectly) spelled "Lucilius", creating confusion with the Roman Satirist Lucilius.

☞ **Martial** (c. 40-102 A.D.), *Epigrams*

Had Statius been as obscene as Marcus Valerius Martialis, he might have struck a more contemporary chord. But where Statius opted to court rich friends to stave off penury, Martial refused to cater to aristocratic clients or to practice law (the profession he was trained in), choosing instead to starve on poetry. In time, Statius ran up against the fickle tastes of the Roman public. When his popularity waned, and other poets were crowned in the various contests, he returned to his boyhood home in Naples. There, with his wife who longed for the fading splendor that was Rome, Statius began another epic that celebrated the forgotten glory that was Greece, and died suddenly at the age of 35.

When Martial's friends Lucan and Petronius were implicated in the conspiracy against Nero and forced to commit suicide, Martial turned to rich men who traded dinner for an epigram written in their names. The Latin language was eminently suitable for epigram, and in Martial it found its master. Most of his epigrams are extremely witty and pointed, and defy translation with the same condensation in any other language. In English it's especially disappointing, more so when forced into rhyme, where the orginal didn't. What we often end up with is an emphasis on the rhyme itself, giving the epigram a greeting card mentality.

Martial continued to live in a third-floor garret, cheated out of royalties by an unscrupulous publisher who enriched himself from the sale of Martial's books of epigrammatic poems which were being read throughout the Empire. Martial sharpened the form into a barb with satiric sting. In his skillful hands, the epigram became a recognized genre of literature. There was no need for the mythological scraps that littered the literature of the age. Martial laced his poems with an obscene wit fashionable for the times. Even the Goths read his books. His picture of the decadent society of Rome coincides in all essentails with that of Juvenal, and all classes of Roman society came within range of his biting wit. While his verses are metrically correct, he avoided epic subjects and wrote instead of living people in contemporary Rome: barbers, cobblers, perverts, and prostitutes: "My pages," he wrote, "taste of men."

The most recent translation I have of Martial's poems is a Penguin Classic papaerback published in 1973, translated by James Michie who taught at Oxford. All of his translations rhyme. Keeping that in mind, we can still find the nugget of wit that made Martial the model for later generations of poets working in the satiric epigram.

Book III, #12

Last night, Fabullus, I admit
You gave your guests some exquisite
Perfume—but not one slice of meat.
Ironic contrast: to smell sweet
And yet be desperate to eat.
To be embalmed without being fed
Makes a man feel distinctly dead.

Book II, 38

You ask me what I get
Out of my country place.
The profit, gross or not,
Is never seeing your face.

Rhymed translations can sometimes be a tip-off that the translations have been cleaned up a bit. Aside from his wit, Martial was also known for the crudeness of his verse. In his 6th book he even brings it up, though the greater motive seemed to be getting Rufus to pay him enough money to get a new cloak.

82

The other day, Rufus, somebody gave
Me the once-over, as though I were a slave
Or a gladiator open to inspection
At a sale. A thumb was jerked in my direction
Together with a surreptitious glance,
Then up he came: "Are you by any chance
Martial, whose wicked empigrams are famous,
Whom everyone but a deaf Dutch ignoramus
Has heard of?" With a slight nod of the head
And a modest smile I bowed. "Then why," he said,
"Do you walk around wearing that terrible cloak?"
"Because I'm a terrible poet." Terrible joke!
Rufus, to save me making it again,
Send me a cloak that keeps out the rain.

A high proportion of Martial's epigrams is obscene, and there's a cheerful way he goes about titillating his readers. Martial didn't clean his cloak, and thankfully Michie avoids cleaning up much of Martial's vulgarity. Reading over translations made in 19th century Victorian England is a laugh in itself, as are the translations of Catullus. Martial was one of the first poets to celebrate, with mixed feelings, the modern megalopolis, and he does it with all the acerbic wit and crude language of a contemporary comedian in a smoke-filled comedy club.

Book Nine, #4

We all know Galla's services as a whore
Cost two gold bits; throw in a couple more

And you get the fancy extras too. Why, then,
Does your bill, Aeschylus, amount to ten?
She sucks off for far less than that. What is it
You pay her for? Silence after your visit.

Book Nine, #33

If from the baths you hear a round of applause,
Maron's giant prick is bound to be the cause.

Book Ten, #90

Why poke the ash of a dead fire?
Why pluck the hairs from your grey fanny?
That's a chic touch which men admire
In girls, not in a flagrant granny;
Something, believe me, which might suit
Andromache but looks far from cute
In Hecuba. Ligeia, you err
If you think sex could rear its head
To burrow in your mangy fur.
Remember what the wise man said:
"Don't pluck the lion's beard when he's dead."

Book Eleven, #19

Why won't I marry you? You're a blue-stocking,
And my cock's educated something shocking.

Many available translations are over a century old, with archaic English phrases. One has
him mentioning Milton and Bacon, an obvious anachronism. Since the translators seem to
have been British bluenoses, it becomes comic seeing how they conceal the vulgarisms.

The Result

Rome's quoting, praising, singing out my verses,
In every hand and pocket there's my book:
A chap there blushes, blenches, coughs, and curses —
That's how I want my verses to make 'em look!

There was something endearing about his use of obscenity, for comman man and
highbrow maidens laughed at his wit. Martial himself blushes at times, asking us to
remember that his life didn't necessarily imitate his art. His poems of mourning for
children who died young are filled with sympathy and tenderness, and in the poems written
to friends, we catch a glimpse of his kind and genial spirit. In this a poem on the death of
Erotion in childhood, he achieves pathos without losing his epigrammatic turn-of-phrase;
the poem could well have slipped into maudlin sentimentality. Even the convention of
asking his deceased parents to watch over her gives the poem a charming poignancy. [the
translation below combines Goldwin Smith's rhymed version from the 19th century with the last four
lines from a recent translation by Richard Jenkyns.]

Erotion

Dear father and ear mother: Let me crave
Your loving kindness there beyond the grave
For my Erotion, the pretty maid
Who bears these lines. Don't let her be afraid!
She's such a little lassie — only six —
To toddle down that pathway to the Styx
All by herself! Black shadows haunt those steps
And Cerberus the Dread who never sleeps.
May she be comforted, and may she play
About you merry as the livelong day,
And in her childish prattle often tell
Of that old master whom she loved so well.
Let the turf be not hard
that covers her soft bones;
earth, be not heavy upon her;
she was not heavy upon you.

Marriage

Why not marry money? 'Tis more in my way
To love and to cherish than love and obey.
For a match to be equal, in person and purse
A man's better half should be rather the worse.

To An Unfriendly Critic

Sour critic, who can here no merit find,
May you, unenvied, envy all mankind!

Scale

Your few quatrains are not amiss,
Your couplets too are neat; for this
    You earn a mild regard,
But little fame, for many men
Can write good verses now and then —
    To make a book is hard.

If He Writes Poetry, Disinherit Him

For ages you've been agonizing,
bothering me with the problem:
to which schoolmaster should you entrust your son?
Right, them. The boy should avoid anyone who teaches
Grammar or rhetoric;
let him steer clear of Virgil,
skip Cicero's speeches and leave Tutilius
to stew in his own fame.
If he writes poetry,

for the sake of the family honor,
disinherit him.
If it's money he wants to earn,
he can easily learn to twang the harp in the chorus,
or toot the accompanist's flute.
If he seems short on brains,
Make him an auctioneer or an architect.

He continued to earn a meagre living by writing epigrammatic verse. In one, as we've seen, he complains of needing a new toga, and gets one, though in another epigram, he complains that it is cheaply made. By the age of fifty-seven, Martial became fed up with Rome and longed to return to his native Spain to live a more tranquil life. He dedicated a series of poems to Pliny the Younger, who then paid for his voyage home. The provincial town of Bilbilis welcomed him, celebrated his fame and overlooked the impropriety of his naughty verse. He spent his few remaining years in a small villa given to him by a generous lady who, perhaps, secretly blushed at his verses when she was younger. Martial longed for the quiet, wholesome life, but once settled, found himself unable to tolerate the pettiness of a small town. He died within a few years, disappointed and still unhappy, missing the turbulent life of the great and decadent city of Rome.

☛ **Marcus Manilius**, *Astronomica* (fl. 1st century AD)

So little is known of Manilius that he is somewhat of an enigma. In all 4,200 verses of his didactic poem in five books, the *Astronomica*, there is not one autobiographical clue as to who he was. Furthermore, he is neither quoted nor mentioned by any ancient writer. Even his name is uncertain, but it was probably Marcus Manilius. The best we can surmise from the poem itself is that the writer lived under Augustus or Tiberius, and that he was a citizen of and resident in Rome, though some scholars think he was . an Asiatic Greek, and others that he was an African. His work is one of great learning; he had studied his subject in the best writers, and generally represents the most advanced views of the ancients on astronomy (or rather astrology).The poem attempts to treat with some dignity the cultural fascination with astrology. He models much of the poem on Lucretius, insofar as he attempts a rational explanation of nature from the point of view of zodiacal signs and the determination of a horoscope. Manilius was a stoic, whereas Lucretius was a realist. Lucretius espoused an atomistic materialism in his great poem, *On The Nature of Things,* while Manilius went beyond mere description in emulating Lucretius in the structure of its exposition and the disposition of its material, taking the dry, technical bones of his subject and making it come alive with his poetry. You might say he was Lucretian in his didactic enthusiasm. Nevertheless, he was in all other respects the first real exponent of the "Silver Age" of Latin poetry, and in terms of the fluidity of his hexameter and the regularity of the poem's structure, we can see the dominant influence of Ovid. Manilius is also one of the most difficult of Latin poets to translate, partly because there are numerous instances of deliberate obscurity, a pecularity of diction (though the style is metrically correct), and a tendency toward *brevitas*, not to mention the basic difficulty of the subject he treated. The astrological systems of houses, linking human affairs with the circuit of the zodiac, has evolved over the centuries, but they make their first appearance in the *Astronomicon*. The earliest datable surviving horoscope that uses houses in its interpretation is slightly earlier, around 20 BC. Claudius Ptolemy (c. AD 130 - 170), the father of classical astrology, almost completely ignored houses (templa, as Manlius calls them) in his astrological text, *Tetrabiblos*.

The latest event referred to in the poem is the great defeat of Varus by Arminius in the Battle of the Teutoburg Forest (AD 9), one of the great military defeats in history. The fifth book was not written until the reign of Tiberius; the work appears to be incomplete, and was probably never published, for it was never quoted by any subsequent writer.

Two manuscripts of the *Astronomicon* made in the 10th and 11th centuries lay hidden in monasteries, one at Gembloux in Brabant (now in Brussels) and another that has come to rest in the library at Leipzig. The unknown text was rediscovered by the humanist Poggio Bracciolini somewhere not very far from Constance, during a break in the sessions of the Council of Constance that he was attending, in 1416 or 1417. The editio princeps of Astronomicon was prepared by the astronomer Regiomontanus, using very corrupted manuscripts, and published in Nuremberg about 1473. The text was critically edited by Joseph Justus Scaliger, whose edition appeared at Paris in 1579 and a second edition, collated with much better manuscripts, at Leiden in 1600. A greatly improved edition was published by Richard Bentley [1] in 1739. The edition of A.E. Housman, published in five volumes from 1903 to 1930, is considered the authoritative edition, although some may find G.P. Goold's edition for the Loeb Classical Library (Harvard, 1977) less intimidating. The first full length monograph in English on Manilius appeared in 2009 [2].

☛ **Phaedrus** (c. 15 BC - c. 50 AD) *Romulus* (verse fables)

Phaedrus was probably a Thracian slave, born in Pydna of Macedonia (Roman province) and lived in the reigns of Augustus, Tiberius, Caligula and Claudius. He is recognized as the first writer to Latinize entire books of fables, retelling in iambic metre the Greek prose fables of Aesop. This was no mean feat. His work doesn't fall in the same class as even the minor poets of the "Silver Age," who appeared more learned and came from the higher literary circles. Phaedrus, by contrast, represents a completely isolated voice, a marginal author who practiced a minor literary genre, which was itself marginal to the great literary currents of the early empire. But considered in a different light, his work is one of the greatest glories of Latin literature. While others were writing historical epics, social satire, pastoral verse, and mythological poetry, Phaedrus was the first author in Greco-Roman culture to assemble a collection of over ninety fables, divided into five books, as an independent poetic work. He draws primarily from the Aesopic tradition, and one can hardly call his verse original. His writing introduces a mannerist style, rendered in iambic trimeters, interspersed with anecdotes drawn from daily life, history and mythology.But he was committed to giving the fable a dignity within the poetic genre. Often, he elevated the point of view to social criticism, often bordering on satire. In his prologues, he shows himself quite conscious of the literary nature of the work. His use of Latin is typified by a particular use of abstract concepts that belies an awareness of the literary canon, especially Augustan works.

According to his own statement in one of the prologues, he was born on the Pierian Mountain in Macedonia, but he seems to have been brought to Italy at an early age, since he mentions reading a verse of Ennius as a boy in school. According to the heading of the chief manuscript he was a slave and was freed by Augustus. He incurred the wrath of Sejanus, the powerful minister of Tiberius, by some supposed allusions in his fables, and was brought to trial and punished. We learn this from the prologue to the third book, which is dedicated to Eutychus, who has been identified with the famous charioteer and favorite of Gaius. But Phaedrus was not very popular with the educated public; at best, because of their simple style and moral content, the fables were used mostly for teaching Latin in the schools where thoughout the Middle Ages he exercised a considerable influence through the prose versions of his fables, where the original verse versions and even his name were apparently forgotten. His own writings were rediscovered in the 15th century, when they proved to be quite influential, especially on the famous French fabulist, La Fontaine. Of the prose versions, the oldest existing one seems to be that known as the *Anonymus Nilanti*, so called because it was first edited by Nilant at Leiden in 1709 from a manuscript of the 13th century. It follows the text of Phaedrus so closely that it was probably made directly from it. Of the sixty-seven fables which it contains, thirty are derived from lost fables of Phaedrus. The largest, oldest known and most influential of the prose versions of Phaedrus is that which bears the name of *Romulus*. A version of the first three books of Romulus in elegiac verse, possibly made in around the 12th century, was one of the most highly influential texts in medieval Europe. Referred to variously (among other titles) as the *Verse Romulus* or *Elegaic Romulus*, it was a common teaching text for Latin and enjoyed a wide popularity well into the Renaissance. It contains eighty-three fables, is as old as the 10th century, and seems to have been based on a still earlier prose version, which, under the name of "Aesop," and addressed to one Rufus, may have been made in the Carolingian period (8th century) or even earlier. About this Romulus nothing is known. Some scholars have tried to restore these lost fables by versifying the prose versions. Interpretive vernacular "translations" of the elegaic *Romulus* were very common in Europe in the Middle Ages. Among the collections partly derived from it, one of the most well-known is probably that in French verse by Marie de France, who influenced Provençal poetry in the 12th century. A collection of fables in Latin prose based partly on *Romulus* and given a strong medieval and clerical tinge was made at the beginning of the 13th century by the Cistercian monk Odo of Cheriton. In 1370 Gerard of Minden wrote a poetical version of *Romulus* in Middle Low German. However, the most developed poetic derivation from the elegaic Romulus text, combined with other genres, was made in Dunfermline in the late 15th century by Robert Henryson. His version, composed in Middle Scots, is the only surviving example known to have made high art of the genre.

☛ **Gaius Petronius Arbiter** (ca. 27–66 AD), *Satyricon*

During the Middle Ages and into the Renaissance both Lucan and Statius were mentioned in the same breath with Homer, Virgil, Ovid and Dante. Today, Statius and Lucan are read only by literary scholars. In the case of Petronius's *Satyricon*, we have a work that was hardly known in the centuries that followed its composition. The text itself was purposefully mutilated and because of its obscenity and ammorality, was seldom read as a medieval school author. Portions of the work were rediscovered in the 9th and again in the 15th centuries. A combined manuscript was copied, then that version disappeared, not to be rediscovered for another century. Since the 17th century, Petronius has become one of the most popular of all ancient authors, notwithstanding, or because of, his fascination with erotic matters and sexual license.

Piso's conspiracy against Nero also snared Petronius, famous in his day not so much as a literary figure, but as an intimate friend of Nero himself, who felt a kinship with this hedonistic literary genius. But when the plot to assassinate Nero was discovered, Petronius, along with Lucan and others, was also forced to commit suicide. This master of literary parody carried out his own death in the manner that parodied the theatrical suicides typical of opponents of the regime. Perhaps he went so far as to imitate a scene from the most famous chapter of his own novel, "The Banquet of Trimalchio." Petronius cut his veins just enough to bleed slowly to death, as he supped his last hours, reading poetry aloud, disdaining philosophical epitaphs, and compiling a list of Nero's crimes in a testamentary letter that was sent to Nero and later published. Just before Petronius dropped, he destroyed his signet ring to prevent its use in some act of counterfeiting, or political intrigue.

Food for Thought

Quo Vadis?

The incident provided the inspiration for the famous novel *Quo Vadis?* by nobel laureate Henryk Sienkiewicz. His novel was used as the basis for several spectular motion pictures. *Quo Vadis?* was made five times, the first one by Ferdinand Zecca for Charles Pathé in 1901. In 1912 a nine-reel version directed by Eurico Guazzon ran two hours fifteen minutes, where the spectacle of Rome burning (mostly smoke screens) and crowds filling the arena was relieved by witty impersonations of Nero and Petronius. At the time, it was the longest and most expensive film ever made and established the conventions of the super-scpectacle, capturing the world market for the Italian cinema. The film featured lavish special effects: an enormous three-dimensional set, crowd scenes with 5,000 extras, a real chariot race, a feal fire representing the burning of Rome, and a Coliseum full of real lions to devour the Christians. The news of its exciting opening in New York (at $1.50 a seat, compared to fifteen cents standard admission fare at the time) reached D. W. Griffith, but Biograph refused to let him go east to see it. The Italian film industry went brankrupt after a 1924 version. The 1951 Hollywood technicolor production was long, full of action and spectacle, starring Robert Taylor and Deborah Kerr, with Peter Ustinov playing Nero. Finally, another Italian version came out in 1985, a ponderous and overblown rendition of the classic story, starring Klaus Maria Brandauer, Antony Quinn's son Francesco, and Max von Sydow. The film is so bad it's almost comic, especially Brandauer's exaggerated portrayal of Nero, and the tw0-dimensional sets which looked cardboard, and probably were.

In 1969, Federico Fellini's film version of Petronius' work, *Fellini Satyricon*, was a lavish costume extravaganza that created a nightmarish portrait of the decadence of ancient Rome, a feast for the eye every bit as decadent and grotesque as its subject matter. The film outraged some classicists who felt it lacked a human point of view, while supporters of the movie felt Fellini had created a unique audiovisual language that transcended traditional narrative to suggest the continuity of depravity throughout human history. The film certainly won Petronius many new admirers who, having seen the movie and read the novel, may have been surprised by the book's literary merit. With a little less luck, Petronius's great work, the *Satyricon*, that bawdy, erotic, immoral, scandalous, satircal tale of debauchery and homosexuality could easily have vanished forever.

Petronius may have titled this work *Satyrica*, or even *Saturae*. *Satyricon* is an inexact title that combines both the Greek derivation—from *satyr*—and the Latin derivation—from *satura*. Satyrs were the half-man, half-goat followers of Dionysus, a god of wine, also called Bacchus. In Greece, the satyr-play developed from phallic celebrations in honor of Dionysus and from these developed Greek tragedy and comedy. The satyr-play was a grotesque form of burlesque, comically obscene. The Latin *satura* refers to a literary work that combined verse (usually accented verse rather than syllabic verse) with sections of prose. Thus the *Satyricon* is a long narrative in prose with many and varied poetic inserts: Not only was this combination of prose and poetry unique in its time, but it anticipates the modern novel, and may well be considered the first picaresque novel.

The Spanish tale *Lazarillo de Tormes* (c. 1554) is usually cited as the earliest example of the picaresque novel, perhaps because it gave the genre its name. Other novels in that tradition are Defoe's *Moll Flanders*, "the history of a female rogue," about a third of *Tom Jones*, Mark Twain's *Huckelberry Finn*, and Thomas Mann's *Confessions of Felix Krull, Confidence Man*, to name just a few. *Picaro* is Spanish for rogue, and the picaresque novel follows the adventures of a clever, amusing rascal, usually of low social class, who makes his way in the world by trickery and deceit rather than by honorable industry. The loose plot is often held together by a particular journey, with a lovable adventurer traveling from one destination to another, exposing and satirizing the corruption and hypocrisy, folly and injustice, immorality and brutality of the world. Thus, the rediscovery of the *Satyricon* in the late 17th century coincided with the initial development of the European novel. Flaubert and James Joyce have clearly acknowledged their debt to this singular and impressive experiment of ancient narrative.

It might be hard to believe that a man of such aristocratic tastes, a lord of luxury, should have written a tale so vulgar. All its major characters are slaves, ex-slaves, and plebians, engaged in episodes of lower class carousing. Our sly, naughty narrator Encolpius assumes that all men are as unethical and immoral as he—an adulterer, a liar, and a thief.

He meets Ascyltos in a brothel, and from there, the adventure begins; they pick up a young boy and embark on a series of escapades that eventually lead to one of the most astonishing dinner parties in all literature, hosted by the egotistical and ex-slave Trimalchio. Silver dishes fall to the floor and are thrown into the garbage along with left over stuffed capons, sows' bellies, succulent pieces of wild boar whose tusks were hung with baskets loaded with dates, and little suckling pigs made of pastry. "When the carver plunged his knife into the boar's side, thrushes flew out, one for each guest." Between courses, hands are washed, not in water, but wine. Trimalchio proclaims to his guests, "If the wine doesn't please you, I'll change it."

More courses follow. Into the room, three white hogs are paraded about so the guests can take their pick. As they go through several more courses, the chosen hog is roasted; when carved, sausages and meat puddings fall from its belly. The savageness of the satire reaches a peak when Trimalchio's wife catches him making love to a young boy. Trimalchio throws a goblet at her head and says,

> "This Syrian dancing whore has a poor memory. I took her off the auction block and made her a woman, and now she puffs herself up like a frog. . . . But that's the way it is: if you're born in an attic you can't sleep in a palace. Please, keep her statue off my tomb, else I'll be nagged even after I'm dead."

Only a few chapters of the *Satyricon* have survived, but judging from those we have, it appears the work was quite a hefty tale. For all we know, it might have been as long as *War and Peace*. The novel is also one of the only sources we have of the popular, spoken language of the time, which is different from literary Latin, thus giving us our only real knowledge of how Latin was spoken among the people of Rome and Italy in the early empire. What is striking is that Petronius combines the various types of Latin and subliterary Latin in a way that implies conscious artistry. His mixing of prose and verse was also avant-garde: characters suddenly begin reciting poetry to other characters in the novel, and at other times there are poetic inserts written by Petronius-as-narrator to create an ironic counterpoint. Another modern effect is the fragmentary and discontinous nature of the text itself, not to mention scenes and descriptions so realistic they foreshadow the realistic novel of the 19th century. All together, these strategies suggest a deliberate literary intent and formalistic vision.

☞ **Calpurnius,** *The Laus Pisonis* (around time of Nero)

Titus Calpurnius Siculus was a Roman bucolic poet. Eleven eclogues have been handed down to us under his name, of which the last four, from metrical considerations and express manuscript testimony, are now generally attributed to Nemesianus, who lived in the time of the emperor Carus and his sons (latter half of the 3rd century).

Hardly anything is known of the life of Calpurnius; we gather from the poems themselves (in which he is obviously represented by Corydon) that he was in poor circumstances and was on the point of emigrating to Spain, when Meliboeus came to his aid. Through his influence Calpurnius apparently secured a post at Rome. The time at which Calpurnius lived has been much discussed, but all the indications seem to point to the time of Nero. He described the emperor as a handsome youth, like Mars and Apollo, whose accession marks the beginning of a new golden age, prognosticated by the appearance of a comet, doubtless the same that appeared some time before the death of Claudius.

Meliboeus, the poet's patron, has been variously identified with Columella, Seneca the philosopher, and Gaius Calpurnius Piso. Although the sphere of Meliboeus's literary activity suits none of these, what is known of Calpurnius Piso fits in well with what is said of Meliboeus by the poet, who speaks of his generosity, his intimacy with the emperor, and his interest in tragic poetry. His claim is further supported by the poem *De Laude Pisonis* which has come down to us without the name of the author, but which there is considerable reason for attributing to Calpurnius, the other main contender being Lucan. Whoever he was, the author says in the concluding verses of his poem that he was not yet twenty years old.

The Laus Pisonis (Praise of Piso) is a Latin verse panegyric of the 1st century AD in praise of a man of the Piso family. The exact identity of the subject is not completely certain, but current scholarly consensus identifies him with Gaius Calpurnius Piso, consul in AD 57. The Latinity is straightforward; the subject is praised for his oratorical ability as an advocate in law cases, for the kindness with which he maintains his house open to poor men of talent, but also for his skill at playing ball and especially the board game of *latrunculi*, for which the poem is one of our main sources.

The poem exhibits a striking similarity with Virgil's *Eclogues* in metre, language and subject-matter. The author of the *Laus* is young, of respectable family and desirous of gaining the favour of Piso as his Maecenas. Further, the similarity between the two names can hardly be accidental; it is suggested that the poet may have been adopted by the courtier, or that he was the son of a freedman of Piso. The attitude of the author of the *Laus* towards the subject of the panegyric seems to show less intimacy than the relations between Corydon and Meliboeus in the *Eclogues,* and there is internal evidence that the *Laus* was written during the reign of Claudius.

Mention may here be made of the fragments of two short hexameter poems in an Einsiedeln manuscript, obviously belonging to the time of Nero, which if not written by Calpurnius, were imitated from him.

Although there is nothing original in Calpurnius, he is a skilful literary craftsman. Of his models the chief is Virgil, of whom (under the name of Tityrus) he speaks with great enthusiasm; he is also indebted to Ovid and Theocritus. Calpurnius is a fair scholar, and an apt courtier, and not devoid of real poetical feeling. The bastard style of pastoral cultivated by him, in which the description of nature is made the writer's pretext, while ingenious flattery is his real purpose, nevertheless excludes genuine pleasure, and consequently genuine poetical achievement.

The work, comprising 261 dactylic hexameters, has come down to us via a single manuscript once preserved in the monastery of Lorsch, and now lost; although sizable portions were also preserved in several medieval *florilegia*, the manuscripts of which are still extant.Calpurnius was first printed in 1471, together with Silius Italicus and has been frequently republished, generally with Gratius Faliscus and Nemesianus.

Gather ye Rosebuds While ye May

In medieval Latin a *florilegium* (plural *florilegia*) was a compilation of excerpts from other writings. The word is formed the Latin *flos* (flower) and *legere* (to gather): literally a gathering of flowers, or collection of fine extracts from the body of a larger work. It was adapted from the Greek *Anthologia,* "anthology", with the same etymological meaning. Medieval florilegia were systematic collections of extracts taken mainly from the writings of the Church Fathers from early Christian authors, also pagan philosophers such as Aristotle, and sometimes classical writings. A prime example is the *Manipulus Florum* of Thomas of Ireland, which was completed at the beginning of the fourteenth century. The purpose was to take passages that illustrated certain topics, doctrines or themes. It is also applied literally to a treatise on flowers or medieval books that are dedicated to ornamental rather than medicinal or utilitarian plants. After the medieval period, the term was extended to apply to any miscellany or compilation of literary or scientific character.

☛ Abronius Silo

Abronius Silo lived in the latter part of the Augustan age. He was a pupil of the rhetorician Marcus Porcius Latro. His son was also a poet, but degraded himself by writing plays for pantomimes. Only two hexameters of his work survive today.

☛ Tiberius Catius Asconius Silius Italicus (ca.28–ca. 103), the *Punica*

Silius Italicus was a Roman consul, orator, and Latin epic poet. His only surviving work is the 17-book *Punica*, an epic poem about the Second Punic War and the longest surviving poem in Latin at over 12,000 lines. The sources for the life of Silius Italicus are primarily letter 3.7 of Pliny the Younger, which is a description of the poet's life written on the occasion of his suicide, some inscriptions,and several epigrams by the poet Martial. Silius is believed to have been born between 23 and 35 AD, but his birthplace has not been securely identified. Italica, in the Roman province of Hispania i.e., Spain (a city established by Sciptio Africannus) was once considered the prime candidate, based on his cognomen Italicus, but if that were the case Latin usage would have demanded the form Italicensis, and it is highly improbable that Martial would have failed to name him among the literary celebrities of Spain in the latter half of the 1st century. The city of Patavium,

Padua has been suggested by J. D. Campbell based on a seeming bias in favor of the region in the Punica and the prevalence of the name Asconius in inscriptions from the region.

In early life Silius was a renowned forensic orator, later a safe and cautious politician. Silius was generally believed to have voluntarily and enthusiastically become an informer under Nero, prosecuting in court those whom the emperor wished condemned. He was consul in the year of Nero's death (68 AD), and afterward became a close friend and ally of the emperor Vitellius, whom he served, according to Pliny "*sapienter et comiter,*" wisely and amicably. He is mentioned by Tacitus as having been one of two witnesses who were present at the conferences between Vitellius and Flavius Sabinus, the elder brother of Vespasian, when the legions from the East were marching rapidly on the capital. Silius became proconsul of Asia ca. 77 AD as attested in an inscription from Aphrodisias which describes his activities in maintaining the institutions of the city. According to Pliny, he performed his duties well and earned himself a place of importance in the empire.After his proconsulship in Asia, Silius seems to have left politics in favor of a leisurely life; despite his wealth and importance in the state, he seems to have exercised little power and avoided offense.Thus, he outlived the Flavian dynasty without incident.

Pliny depicts him spending time in learned conversation at his villas, writing, passionately collecting books and sculpture, and giving recitations of his works. Silius was evidently writing poems as early as 88 AD. It is firmly believed that the Punica was written during this retirement period of Silius' life. Martial (7.63) indicates that some of the *Punica* had been published by 92 AD and that Silius was no longer making speeches in court. Book 14 has been dated tentatively to after 96 AD based on the poet's treatment of Domitian. His poem contains several passages relating to the Flavians, and Domitian is eulogized as a warrior and as a singer whose lyre is sweeter than that of Orpheus himself. The poem mentions primarily Domitian but later seems to discuss the emperor Nerva, although Domitian may be meant by the latter reference. The poet's attitude to Domitian tends to be laudatory and friendly, employing the full spectrum of Virgillian panegyrical language and imagery.

Silius was considered highly educated by contemporaries. The philosopher Epictetus judged him to be the most philosophic spirit among the Romans of his time, and Cornutus, the Stoic, rhetorician and grammarian, dedicated to Silius a commentary upon Virgil. He had two sons, one of whom, Severus, died young. The other, Decianus, went on to become consul.As he aged, he moved permanently to his villas in Campania, not even leaving to attend the accession ceremony of Trajan, which ordinarily would have gotten him into trouble, but it appears Trajan was forgiving. Silius idealized and almost worshipped two great Romans of the past, Cicero and Virgil. He purchased Cicero's estate at Tusculum and the tomb of Virgil in Naples, which he restored. There's a wonderful painting by Joseph Wright of Derby depicting Silius Italicus at Virgil's tomb. Pliny records that Silius especially revered Virgil, celebrating Virgil's birthday more lavishly than his own and treating the poet's tomb as a shrine.His dual interests in composing epic poetry and discussing philosophical questions have been compared to the intellectual efforts of his heroes, Virgil and Cicero respectively.

Silius was one of the numerous Romans of the early empire who had the courage of their opinions, and carried into perfect practice the theory of suicide developed in Stoicism; *Punica* 11.186-88 contains a praise of suicide. Stricken by an incurable tumour after the age of 75, he starved himself to death around 103 CE, keeping a cheerful countenance to the end. Pliny remarks that Silius was the last person to die who was consul under Nero.

Whether Silius committed his philosophic dialogues and speeches to writing or not, we cannot say. His only preserved work is his epic poem entitled *Punica*, about the Second Punic War (218–201 BC) in seventeen books, comprising some twelve thousand lines, making it the longest preserved poem in Latin literature. The dating of the *Punica* has been a difficult issue for classical scholars, but two passages, 3.594 and 14.680ff, along with several poems of Martial cited above indicate that it was composed sometime between 83 and 103, with Book 3 being dated to 84 AD and Book 14 around 96 AD. Other books cannot be dated with any precision. The poem is divided into 17 books and is composed in dactylic hexameter. It has been thought that the poem was initially planned in hexads and that the original intent was to round off the composition in 18 books. Another wonderful painting by Raphael, *The Vision of a Knight,* is based on an episode in Book 15 of the *Punica*, Scipio's favorite episode.

The poem takes Virgil as its primary stylistic and dramatic inspiration throughout the poem; from its opening, the Punica is configured as the continuation of Juno's grudge against Rome developed in the *Aeneid.* Livy and Ennius are important sources for historical and poetic information, and Homer specifically is declared an important model by Silius who says of him, (12.788-9), "his poetry embraced the earth, sea, stars, and shades and he rivaled the Muses in song and Phoebus in glory." Lucan is also an important model for the writing of historical epic, geographical excursus, and Stoic tone, although Silius' approach toward the gods is much more traditional.

The poem opens with a discussion of Juno's wrath against Rome on account of Aeneas' treatment of Dido and of Hannibal's character and upbringing. Hannibal attacks Saguntum and receives a Roman embassy. In Book 2, the Roman legation is heard at Carthage, but Hannibal takes the city after the defenders heroically commit suicide. The Carthaginians are catalogued, Hannibal crosses the Alps, and Jupiter reveals that the Punic War is a test of Roman manliness in Book 3. In 4 and 5 the Romans suffer defeat at Ticinius, Trebia, and Lake Trasimene. Book 6 looks back to the exploits of Atilius Regulus in the First Punic War, while Book 7 describes Quintus Fabius Maximus' delaying strategy. Books 8-10 describe in vivid detail the battle of Cannae; Juno prevents Hannibal from marching on Rome. In Book 11, Hannibal's army winters in Capua, where Venus enfeebles them with luxury. Hannibal is defeated at Nola in 12, emboldening the Romans. He makes an attempt on the city, but Juno stops him, revealing that the gods are against him. Book 13 reports the Roman's invasion of Capua and the death of two Scipios, which leads to Scipio Africanus' journey to the underworld (*nekyia*), his meeting with famous dead heroes, and a prophecy by the Sybil of Hannibal's defeat. In 14 Marcellus' successful Sicilian campaign and the siegecraft of Archimedes are described. In 15, Scipio, choosing Virtue over Vice, has a successful campaign in Spain, while at the Battle of the Metaurus, Hannibal's brother is killed. 16 describes the alliance between Rome and Masinissa and the Scipio's crossing into Africa, while 17 describes the bringing of the statue of Cybele to Rome, Hannibal's stormy crossing into Africa, Juno's appeal to Jupiter for the life of Hannibal, and the Battle of Zama. The poem ends with Scipio's triumphal return to Rome.

Silius' style is unlike Virgil in that he does not focus on a few central characters but divides his action up between many significant heroes. This allows him to describe important events from the Roman past as a reflection on the characters and their actions in the poem's present, echoing the Roman tradition of using *exempla*. While many important set pieces of epic are included, such as elaborated similes, ekphrases of objects, such as Hannibal's shield in 2.391-456, a *nekyia*, and divine participation in and prophecy of events, there are also important elements of historiography such as paired contrasting speeches and detailed geographical description. Allegory is particularly important in Silius, and he includes such figures as Fides (faith) in Book 2, Italia in 15, and Virtus and Voluptas also in Book 15, continuing a trend towards allegory which was significant in Statius, Silius' contemporary.Silius' metrics and language can be closely compared to Virgilian usage, especially his use of spondees.Stoicism and stoic ethical thought are significant themes in the *Punica*. The war is configured as a trial of Roman *virtus* which must be overcome with hard work, akin to the Stoic ideal of overcoming adversity with inner courage and trial. The "choice of Hercules", a favorite Stoic parable, is given to Scipio in Book 15, and everywhere the war brings out moral lessons and discussions of Stoic concepts like emotion, reason, and destiny.

His influence on later poets seems minimal, if non existsent. The only ancient authors to reference Silius are Martial, Pliny, and Sidonius Apollinaris. Pliny's judgment that Silius wrote poetry *maiore cura quam ingenio*, "with more eagerness than genius," has encouraged the view that Silius was a talented but mediocre and uninspired poet. The poem seems to have been mostly unknown in the Middle Ages, with any copies of the work being lost. Petrarch's *Africa* was composed independently of the *Punica*. A manuscript was finally discovered by Poggio Bracciolini in 1417 at St. Gall during the Council of Constance, but Julius Caesar Scaliger's harsh opinion of Silius damaged his reputation. Nevertheless, many authors became familiar with Silius' work, such as Montaigne, Milton, Dryden (who considered him better than Lucan), Gibbon, and Alexander Pope. Joseph Addison particularly includes many quotations of Silius in his *Dialogue on Medals* as does Thomas Macaulay in his works. By the 19th century, Interest in Silius mostly vanished, though there are references to him in several painters, such as Raphael's *Vision of the Knight* mentioned earlier. Despite Silius' poor reputation, classical scholars with their renewed interest in later Imperial epic seem to be finally turning their attentions to Silius' poetry.

☛ **Persius** (AD 34-62)

The exalted genres of the epic and the lyric ode could become a burden to poets wishing to leap more easily into the vitality of satire. In a disrespectful allusion to the fountain Hippocrene, a classic symbol of poetic insiration, Persius declared, "I have not drenched my lips in the nag's spring." This Latin satirical poet belonged to an equestrian family, was educated at Rome, and along with fellow student Lucan, studied with the stoic Corrnutus, who exercised a strong influence on his work. His satires are probably among the most difficult pieces of Latin we know, written in an often precious and artificial style modeled on the satires of Lucilius. He describes himself as "clever at the pungent combining of words." Thick with literary allusion, his poems are a blend of a compressed, clotted style and a contorted moral seriousness, which can make for difficult reading. The satirists of the English renaissance admired and imitated his work, and those reading Donne's satires will catch something of his odd, intriguing style.

The ideas and values he expressed had already been voiced by Horace. Often Persius used an incongrous mixture of styles. Sometimes the language was obscure, but the unforced, moral sincerity of this modest and gentle man came through. He was only 28 when he died, bequeathing his books and part of his large fortune to Cornutus, who took the books but not the money. To the world Persius left six satires that preach an uncompromising Stoic philsophy that could be applied to private life. Unlike other satirists, Persius hardly touched on the public life of Nero's Rome. He criticised the poet's of Nero's court and the contemporary fashion for elegant, unrealistic poetry that only masked the essential corruption of the Roman virtues. Many of these poems are homilies rather than satires. In one, he diagnoses the damage done to sick souls by sloth and vice. In another he expresses concern for the right use of prayer, mocking those who ask for external goods rather than virtue.

> Souls bent to earth with nothing heavenly in you,
> what's the good of giving our temples the modern touch
> or guessing what the gods like from this sinful flesh,
> which for its use ruins good oil by dissolving spices in it,
> or boils up white Calabrian wool with spoiling purple
> or makes us tear the pearl from its shell
> and separate the veins glowing metal from crude ore?
> It too sins, it sins yet gains by sinning — but you,
> tell me, priests, what good is gold in a holy place?
> No more than what maidens dedicate to Venus — dolls!
> Why don't we give the gods what great Messalla's
> blear-eyed son could not give from his abundance,
> justice and right blended in the soul,
> purity in the shrine of the intellect
> and a heart steeped in generous honesty?
> Grant me to bring these to the temples,
> and a pinch of meal will do the rest.

ði.

☛ **Gaius Valerius Flaccus** (died ca AD 90), *The Argonautica*, ca. 70AD

Flaccus flourished under the emperors Vespasian and Titus and wrote a Latin *Argonautica* that owed a great deal to Apollonius of Rhodes' more famous epic. He has been identified on insufficient grounds with poet and friend of Martial (1.61.76), a native of Padua, and in needy circumstances; but as he was a member of the College of Fifteen, who had charge of the Sibylline books (1.5), he must have been well off. The subscription of the Vatican manuscript, which adds the name Setinus Balbus, points to his having been a native of

Setia in Latium. The only ancient writer who mentions him is Quintilian (10.1.90), who laments his recent death as a great loss; as Quintilian's work was finished about 90 AD, this gives a limit for the death of Flaccus.

His only surviving work, the *Argonautica*, dedicated to Vespasian on his setting out for Britain, was written during the siege, or shortly after the capture, of Jerusalem by Titus in 70 AD. As the eruption of Vesuvius in 79 AD is alluded to, its composition must have occupied him a long time. The *Argonautica* is an epic poem probably intended to be in eight books (though intended totals of ten and twelve books, the latter corresponding to Virgil's Aeneid, an important poetic model, have also been proposed) written in traditional dactylic hexameters, which recounts Jason's quest for the Golden Fleece. The poem's text, as it has survived, is in a very corrupt state; it ends so abruptly with the request of Medea to accompany Jason on his homeward voyage, that it is assumed by most modern scholars that it was never finished. It is a free imitation and in parts a translation of the *Argonautica* of Apollonius of Rhodes, "to whom he is superior in arrangement, vividness, and description of character" (Loeb Classical Library). The familiar subject had already been treated in Latin verse in the popular version of Varro Atacinus. The object of the work has been described as the glorification of Vespasian's achievements in securing Roman rule in Britain and opening up the ocean to navigation (as the Euxine was opened up by the Argo).

In 1911, the compilers of Encyclopaedia Britannica remarked, "Various estimates have been formed of the genius of Flaccus, and some critics have ranked him above his original, to whom he certainly is superior in liveliness of description and delineation of character. His diction is pure, his style correct, his versification smooth though monotonous. On the other hand, he is wholly without originality, and his poetry, though free from glaring defects, is artificial and elaborately dull. His model in language was Virgil, to whom he is far inferior in taste and lucidity. His tiresome display of learning, rhetorical exaggeration and ornamentations make him difficult to read, which no doubt accounts for his unpopularity in ancient times."

The first printed edition was in 1474. Increased interest in the last decades has resulted in a full-length general introduction, two new editions, in 1997 (Liberman) and 2003, and commentaries by H.J.W. Wijsman, 1996 (Book V) and 2000 (Book VI), F. Spaltenstein, 2002 (Books I and II), and Adrianus Jan Kleywegt, 2005 (Book I)[3] which attempts to amend the faulty text.

Flaccus also appears as a recurring character in Caroline Lawrence's Roman Mysteries series of children's novels. In the television adaptations he is played by British actor Ben Lloyd-Hughes.

☛ **Juvenal** (AD 60-140)

The epic poets of the Silver Age were most successful when they flavored their work with the spice of satire, as Lucan did. Martial and Persius threw off the mantle of epic seriousness completely and chose to fling their poisonous barbs untipped with the antidote of grandeur. But the greatest poet of the Silver Age fused a rhetorical magnificence with epigrammatic harshness, and brought the satire to a perfection of form hardly equalled in any age.

Juvenal, born during the reign of Nero, was one of the supreme masters of the Latin tongue. We know little of his life. His date of birth is a close guess, and he probably died a year or two before, or a year or two after the Emperor Hadrian died. When Juvenal came to Rome as a young man, he apparently practiced law but failed to achieve financial success. When he turned to the writing of poetry he was already in his late thirties, and throughout the remainder of his long life wrote of the frustrations of poverty in a style that was dense, muscular, and declamatory.

Because his satiric voice seems closest to us in a modern sense, we forget that he departed decisively from the traditions of Roman *satura*. Both Lucilius and Horace used a discursive, informal manner, showing us the poet, as it were, on his lunch hour tossing off a few unedited lines filled with the quirks of their personality and an easy-going manner. Juvenal's voice is quite distinctive, but we get very little of the man behind that voice. It is Lucretius that Juvenal most resembles, using a dynamic blend of the grand tone with the acidic sharpness of satire. Yet, the poet who had the most influence on Juvenal was Virgil. When Juvenal points up the ironic contrast between the fantasy world of pastoral heroic myth and the ugly realities of his own time, he is echoing the poetic imagination and complex literary tones of Virgil.

Juvenal's 16 satires were published at irregular intervals with the last published in his seventies. Throughout all of them, he spits out savage condemnation of the evils of the contemporary Roman scene. He viewed the Empire as a sick, maladjusted organism, overflowing with corrupt men and vicious women. In furious disgust, colloquial hexameters move with a strong lusty style and supply a kind of grim humor with their street-corner vocabulary and satiric wit. In the end, Juvenal spared no one. As he wrote in Satire I:

> When the mincing eunuch takes to matrimony,
> when Mevia goes pigsticking in Tuscany
> and bare-breasted wields her hunting spear,
> when the one-time barber who shaved me in my youth
> now risen to riches challenges all the patricians,
> when the guttersnipe from the Nile, Crispinus,
> slave-born in Canopus, now with a toss of his purple
> cloak brandishes the thin gold ring on sweaty fingers
> and can't bear the weight of a heavier gem—
> well, then it's difficult *not* to write satire.

In Satire VI, his longest and most famous, he finds not one woman in Rome worthy of praise. His friend Postumus is thinking of marriage; Juvenal advises against it, warning him that the women of Rome are selfish, shrewish, vain, litigious, unfaithful, and contentious. A good wife is a rare bird (*rara avis*), stranger than a white crow. Ah, Juvenal laments, "the last time Chastity still lingered on earth was when caves were the only homes men had."

> when no one
> Feared thieves in the cabbage-patch and orchard, when

kitchen gardens
Were still unwalled. Thereafter, by slow degrees,
Justice withdrew to heaven, and Chastity went with her,
Two sisters together, beating a common retreat.

    To bounce your neighbor's bed, my friend, to outrage
Matrimonial sanctity is now an ancient and long-
Established tradition. All other crimes came later,
With the Age of Iron; but our first adulterers
Appeared in the Silver Era. And here you are in *this*
Day and age, getting yourself engaged,
Fixing up marriage-convenant, dowry, bethrothal-party;
Any time now some high-class barber will start
Coifeuring you for the wedding, before you know it the ring
Will be on her finger. Postumus, are you *really*
Taking a wife?You used to be sane enough—what
Fury's got into you, what snake has stung you up?
Why endure such bitch-tyranny when rope's available
By the fathom, when all those dizzying top-floor windows
Are open for you, when there are bridges handy
To jump from? Supposing none of these exits catches
Your fancy, isn't it better to sleep with a pretty boy?
Boys don't quarrel all night, or nag you for little presents
While they're on the job, or complain that you don't come
Up to their expectations, or demand more gasping passion.
    But no: you staunchly uphold the Family Encouragement
        Act,   [special privileges went to those with 3 or more children]
A sweet little heir's your aim, though it means foregoing
All those pickings—fat pigeons, bearded mullet, the bait
Of the legacy-hunter's market. Really, if *you* take a wife, I'll
Credit anything, friend. You were once the randiest
cocksman about town, you hid in more bedroom cupboards
Than a comedy juvenile lead. Can this be the man now
Sticking his silly neck out for the matimonial halter?
And as to your insistence on a wife with old-fashioned
Moral virtues—man, you need your blood-pressure checked,
    you're
Crazy, you're aiming over the moon.
Marry a wife, and she'll make some flute-player
Or guitarist a father, not you.

Satire VII deplores the genral decline in study and the wretched condition in which the writers of the day are forced to live; by contrast, he longs for the patronage that nourished Augustan literature.

    All hopes for the arts today, all inducement to study, depend
    Upon Caesar alone. Who else spares a glance for the wretched
    Muses in these hard times, when establishment poets lease
    An out-of-town bath-concession or a city bakery
    To make their living, when hungry historians are quitting
    Helicon's vales and springs for the auction-rooms? No
        comedown,

They feel no disgrace; if you can't turn an honest penny
In the shady grove of the Muses, you might as well
Accept the title—and income—of an auctioneer, join in
The saleroom battles, flog lots under the hammer
To a crowd of bidders—winejars, three-legged stools,
Bookcases, cupboards, remaindered plays by nonentities
On stale mythological themes.
                    But if you had thoughts of obtaining
Patronage for your art from some other benefactor,
And it's in this hope that you continue to scribble
On your nice buff parchment, you might as well give up—
Order a bundle of firewood, make a burnt sacrifice
Of your works to Vulcan; or else just lock them away
And let the bookworms riddle them full of holes.
Break your pen, poor wretch, destroy all those battle-pieces
That kept you awake so late, the high-flown compositions
Hammered out in that cramped garret, the dreams of a laureate's
    wreath
On your gaunt and sculptured brow!
So the prime of life slips by, the years when you might
Have been a sailor, soldier, farmer, until the spirit
Grows weary, until old age creeps up on your penniless
Gift of the gab, and you hate yourself and your art.

            But the outstanding poet,
Whose inspiration is rare and unique, who makes
Nothing from common stock, strikes no debased
Poetic currency, minted with platitudes—though
I can't think of one just now, still I'm sure they exist—

            Of course, it comes cheaper
To feed a lion than a poet: poets have bigger bellies.
    Fame may satisfy Lucan, lying at rest now
In his park with its statuary; but for epic poets
Less well endowed, poor starvelings, glory alone,
However great, must remain eternally insufficient.
The City is all agog when Statius agrees
To fix a recital-date. He's a sell-out, no one
Can resist that mellifluous voice, that ever-popular
Theban epic of his: the audience sits there spellbound
By such fabulous charm. Yet despite the cheers and the stamping
Statius will starve, unless he can sell a libretto
To Paris, Director-in-Chief of Imperial Opera and Ballet.
                Yet you need not begrudge the living
A poet makes from the stage. Today the age
Of the private patron is over; Maecenas and Co.
Have no successors. Genius got its reward
In those days; many a poet found it worthwhile to sweat
At his desk, on the wagon, right through the Decemmber vacation.

Though he mocks and satirizes the times in which he lives, Juvenal is above all a social observer. Any pretense of wisdom must come from the reader. He has no need to comment on the waste and absurdity of war. He merely presents the images, which function as social comment. In Satire X, he holds up to ridicule the transitory nature of wealth and glory, giving example after example. Look at the glory of war, he says. *Look* at it. Look, and you will have your answer.

> Consider the spoils of war, a corslet fastened to a stump as a
>   trophy—
> A breastplate, a cheek-piece hanging from a broken helmet,
> A yoke shorn of its pole, the flagstaff of a captured trireme
> And a sad prisoner on a triumphal arch . . . . These are the prizes
> For which every commander, Greek, barbarian, Roman,
> Has always striven. . . .

He then considers the Carthaginian general, Hannibal, famous for his crushing defeat of the Romans in the battle of Cunnae, and also for using elephants (those "Gaetulian beasts") to cross the alps. Hannibal had even lost one eye in battle, but wanted to ride in triumph through the streets of Rome and plant his flag in the Subara, a shabby and crowded part of the city.

> Put Hannibal in the scales: how many pounds will the dust
>   of that peerless
> General weigh today? This is the man for whom Africa
> Was too small a continent . . . .
> Now Spain swells his empire, now he surmounts
> The Pyrenees. Nature throws in his path
> High Alpine passes, blizzards of snow: but he splits
> The very rocks asunder, moves mountains—with vinegar.
> Now Italy is his, yet still he forges on:
> "We have accomplished nothing," he cries, "till we have stormed
> The gates of Rome, till our Carthaginian standard
> Is set in the City's heart."
>   A fine sight it must have been,
> Fit subject for caricature, when the Gaetulian monster
> Carried the one-eyed commander. Alas, alas for glory . . . .

But Hannibal was finally defeated at Zama in 202 BC by Scipio Africanus. Later, Hannibal fled to Syria when his right-wing political enemies convinced Rome that he was intriguing with another country, and from Syria he went first to Crete, then sought refuge with a petty Eastern despot, King Prusias of Bithynia. When Roman authorities demanded his extradition, Hannibal drank the poison that was concealed in a small ring he was wearing for just such a purpose. Worse than ending up as dust, Hannibal becomes the topic of schoolboys' declamations, recited by rote before a dreary class. In Satire VII, Juvenal mocked these shows of oratorial eloquence, saving a dash of pity for the schoolteacher who must hear them recited by every kid in the class.

> Or do you teach declamation? You must possess iron nerves

To sit through a whole large class's attack on "The Tyrant."
       Each boy
Stands up in turn, and delivers by rote what he's just
Learnt at his desk: all gabble off the same
Stale old couplets and catchphrases — bubble-and-squeak
Rehashed without end, sheer death for the poor master,
[Who responds to parents complaints:]
                   "Of course, it's the teachers
   fault
If some bompkin pupil isn't thrilled to the marrow
Week after week, while dinning / his awful Hannibal speech
Into my wretched head, whatever the set theme
Up for discussion — should Hannibal march on Rome
From Cunnae? And after that / torrential thunderstorms,
                 should he
Play safe, and withdraw his rain-sodden, dripping troops?
What wouldn't I give — just name your fiture, I'll pay it,
Cash on the barrel — for any boy's father to hear him
As often as I do!"

In this tenth satire, Juvenal brilliantly sums up Hannibal's path to glory that lead to the poison in a "little" ring, and the boring declamations of schoolboys. The final irony here, Juvenal's joke on himself, is that after mocking the declamation in an early satire, he finishes his piece on Hannibal with the kind of epigrammatic couplet that usually concludes such set speeches.

                 Alas, alas for glory,
What an end was here: the defeat, the ignominious
Flight into exile, everyone crowding to see
The once-mighty Hannibal turned humble hanger-on,
Sitting outside the door of a petty Eastern despot
Till His Majesty deign to awake. No sword, no spear,
No battle-flung stone was to snuff the fiery spirit
That once had wrecked a world: but that punisher for
Cannae and avenger for so much blood, a ring
A little ring. Go, go you madman, run
Over your savage Alps, to become the Schoolboy's favorite,
To become a subject for speech-day declamations!

As a declamatory piece, the rhetoric is simply magnificent. In the original Latin, we can see how carefully Juvenal breaks the last six lines and gets the maximum effect from enjambment and tonal dynamic.

    finem animae, quae res humanas miscuit olim,
    non gladii, non saxa dabunt nec tela, sed ille
    Cannarum uindex et tanti sanguinis ultor
    anulus. i, demens, et saeuas curre per Alpes
    ut pueris placeas et declamatio fias.

The word "anulus," isolated at the beginning of a line but the end of the long sentence which leads up to it, holds its place with a slender, scornful sound, set against the slow massive rhythm of the line before. "Anulus" is a diminutive: it is not just a ring, but a *little* ring, worn on his pinky, in which Hannibal kept his poison. Juvenal's metrical technique works not just in the shift in tone, but provides a visual effect as well. Such a small object to bring so great a life to an inglorious end.

We admire Juvenal for his biting satire, but credit must also be given for his imagistic power that shows us how great a poet he really was. His imagery is vivid and suggestive. In Satire XIV, he ridicules the avarice of the wealthy, who cram so much money into their purses, they "swell like mouths stuffed full of food." The rich are so bent on getting richer that they starve not only their slaves, but themselves as well, "living in squalor just to die a millionaire." The greedy man's passion for gain is so insatiable that

> He'll pinch his slaves' meagre bellies
> By chiselling on their rations — but he starves himself too,
> > those crusts
> Of stale bread, blue with mould, are something even *he*
> > baulks at.
> He'll rehash yesterday's mince in mid-September's heat and
> Keep all the left-overs — beans, a tail-end of mackerel,
> Half a catfish, already stinking — under lock and key; he'll even
> Count up the chopped spring onions. Professional beggars
> Would turn down an invitation to this kind of feast.

The poems are replete with examples of his superb imagistic touch. Spotlighting the intrigues of the powerful, he compares Crispinus, "a monster of wickedness," to the ruthless Pompeius

> more savage than he at slitting men's throats
> with his thin whisper. . . .

The image is sinister, but it's matched in the Latin by the sound of the words. "Thin whisper" conveys the image of the thin edge of a razor being drawn across the neck of an informer, whose breath expires through the slit in his throat.

> saevior illo Pompeius tenui iugulos aperire susurro

Juvenal took the fashion for rhetorical eloquence and elevated it to true poetic heights, even when he satirized the fashion. His bitter, grating voice and the selectivity of his themes only add to the power of his work.

Juvenal's *Satires* drop out of sight completely for about a century after his death, but were rediscovered by a generation of Christian writers who enjoyed his righteous indignation and condemnations of pagan Rome. Since that time, they haven't been out of favor with readers. His poems were read and praised throughout the Middle Ages where he was popular mainly as a moralist and thus had a secure place in medieval school curriculm. During the Renaissance, the *Satires* suffered a small decline, but since then, has regained its dominant influence, especially during times of imperial breakdown and ethical and moral decline—times like our own.

Tiberius (14-37 AD) succeeded Augustus, and Caligula (37-41 AD) followed him as Emperor of the Roman Empire. In his abuse of power, Caligula became the prototype of "Caesar madness." Within a century, poets like Juvenal were seeing signs of imperial decay everywhere, but it was Claudius, a clownish antiquarian, dragged to the throne by the Praetorian Guard to succeed Caligula, who best prophesied the coming decline, if not the fall, of the Roman Empire. Claudius was taken for a fool, a muttering stutterer who nevertheless attempted to achieve genuine authority in order to reform the government.

At the end of his book *I, Claudius*, Robert Graves shows Claudius a broken old man, sitting alone on his throne, everything he'd tried to do having drifted toward decay and decadence, including his beloved wife, lost to lust and sexual depravity. In a PBS production of Graves's book, Derek Jacoby plays the part of Claudius with unforgettable humanity, humour, wisdom, and ultimately, with a sad and tragic grace as he sits alone at the end after hearing of his wife's unfaithfulness. So drunk that he barely notices the empty wine cup slide from his hand onto the palace floor, Claudius slurs in despair as fine a poetic prophesy as any poet could write.

Let all   the p-p-p-poisons

that luuurrrrk

in the mud

h-h-h-h-hatch out.

When Claudius died (some say he might have been poisoned by his wife), the throne was given over to his successor, Nero (37-68 AD), the pyromaniacial fiddler. Nero possessed considerable talent. He drew, painted, made models, sang, and composed poetry. His patronage of the arts and encouragement of musical and dramatic contests (in which he himself sometimes performed) scandalized the senatorial classes and were responsible for much of his unpopularity. The disastrous fire which destroyed one half of Rome in 64 was probably not started on his orders but he made the Christians scapegoats for the misfortune. His last words, before his suicide, are reputed to have been *qualis artifex pereo!* (What an artist dies in me!")

Within a century, another poet-Emperor brought this period to a close. Hadrian (117-138 AD) died about the same time Juvenal did. One of his legacies is the defensive wall that bears his name built across northern Britain. He also built the Pantheon, the temple of Venus and Rome, and an extensive villa at Tibur (Tivoli), which has been a rich source of art treasures. One of the most intellectual and cultivated of all the emperors, Hadrian was well versed in the literary and artistic culture of Greece, and a fine poet as well. Only a few of his poems survive. A famous apostrophe to his soul written just before his death and reputedly whispered on his deathbed (*"animula, vagula, blandula . . ."*) is remarkable for its neoteric musical grace. Not as bitter as Claudius's utterance, it can still be seen as a harbinger of decadence.

> Little soul,
> wandering soul,
> sweet soul,
> guest and companion of my body,
> now you will leave for places
> Pale,
> Harsh,
> and barren,
> and you will not
> play games
> as before.

Meanwhile, Back at the Ranch . . . .

. . . . while the poets of the "Silver Age" were writing their epics, satires, fables, pastoral and astronomical poetry; while Tiberius bored the Senate with his long-winded, ponderous orations; while Caligula slept with his horse and Claudius played the stuttering buffoon and Nero fiddled as Rome burned and Domitian impaled flies on the tip of his stylus; a Galillean carpenter from Nazareth began his ministry, and one fateful Passover around 30 AD, after about two or three years of preaching in Galilee, he entered Jerusalem, was arrested in the garden of Gethsemane, a grove on the Mount of Olives, and was put on trial for claiming to be "the Messiah, the Son of the Blessed," or "King of the Jews." He was given the death penalty, and wearing a crown of thorns, was executed by the Roman custom of crucifixion on a little hill called Golgatha (Calvary) alongside two common criminals described as "bandits" or insurgents.

This sequence of events is known as the "Passion,"from the Latin verb *pateor*, to suffer, or *passio*, suffering. The location itself is mentioned in all four canonical Gospels:

> *And they bring him unto the place Golgotha, which is, being interpreted, The place of a skull.*
> [Mark 15:22]
> *And when they were come unto a place called Golgotha. that is to say, a place of a skull.*
> [Matthew 27:33]
> *And when they were come to the place, which is called Calvary, there they crucified him, and the malefactors, one on the right hand, and the other on the left.*
> [Luke 23:33]
> *So they took Jesus, and led him away. And he, bearing his own cross, went forth into a place called the place of a skull, which is called in the Hebrew Golgotha.*
> [John 19:17]

It's possible that the biblical gloss is erroneous and the Aramaic name is actually *Gol Goatha*, meaning "mount of execution," possibly the same location as the Goatha mentioned in a Book of Jeremiah describing the geography of Jerusalem:

> And the measuring line shall yet go forth over against it upon the hill Gareb, and shall compass about to Goath.[Jeremiah 31:39]

If it was a place of execution, the name could have referred to the abandoned skulls found there. In some Christian and Jewish traditions, the name refers to the skull of Adam, and other sources have even speculated that the landscape resembled the shape of a skull, thus the name. In the New Testament, the name Gûlgaltâ is the Greek transcription of the Aramaic word. Jerome's *Vulgate* rendered the name in Latin as *Calvariae Locus*. When the King James Version was written, the translators used an anglicised version, Calvary, to refer to Golgotha in the Gospel of Luke, rather than translate it.

According to the Gospels of Matthew and Mark, a darkness at noon came over the earth and lasted until Jesus' death at 3pm (Mark 15.33), when the veil of the Temple was torn in two (Mark 15.38) as the result of an earthquake causing bodies to rise from tombs throughout Jerusalem (Matt. 27.51-53).

Three days after his burial, Jesus is said to have risen from the dead, subsequently making numerous appearances to his followers before ascending to heaven. In one of the finest pieces of storytelling in the New Testament, Jesus appears as the anonymous traveler who engages his followers in conversation on the road to Emmaus, and is recognized only when Cleopas and his companion break bread with him.

> And, behold, two of them went that same day to a village called Emmaus, which was from Jerusalem about threescore furlongs. And it came to pass that, while they communed together and reasoned, Jesus himself drew near, and went with them. But their eyes were holden that they should not know him. And he said unto them, What manner of communications are these that ye have one to another, as ye walk, and are sad? And the one of them, whose name was Cleopas, answering said unto him, Art thou only a stranger in Jerusalem, and hast not known the things which are come to pass there in these days? And he said unto them, What things? And they said unto him, Concerning Jesus of Nazareth, which was a prophet mighty in deed and word before God and all the people: And how the chief priests and our rulers delivered him to be condemned to death, and have crucified him. But we trusted that it had been he which should have redeemed Israel: and beside all this, to day is the third day since these things were done. Yea, and certain women also of our company made us astonished, which were early at the sepulchre; And when they found not his body, they came, saying, that they had also seen a vision of angels, which said that he was alive. And certain of them which were with us went to the sepulchre, and found it even so as the women had said: but him they saw not. Then he said unto them, O fools, and slow of heart to believe all that the prophets have spoken: Ought not Christ to have suffered these things, and to enter into his glory? And beginning at Moses and all the prophets, he expounded unto them in all the scriptures the things concerning himself. And they drew nigh unto the village, whither they went: and he made as though he would have gone further. But they constrained him, saying, Abide with us: for it is toward evening, and the day is far spent. And he went in to tarry with them. And it came to pass, as he sat at meat with them, he took bread, and

blessed it, and brake, and gave to them. And their eyes were opened, and they knew him; and he vanished out of their sight. And they said one to another, Did not our heart burn within us, while he talked with us by the way, and while he opened to us the scriptures? And they rose up the same hour, and returned to Jerusalem and found the eleven gathered together, and them that were with them, Saying, The Lord is risen indeed, and hath appeared to Simon. And they told what things were done in the way, and how he was known of them in breaking of bread. And as they thus spoke, Jesus himself stood in the midst of them, and saith unto them, Peace be unto you.

[Luke 24. 13-36]

[see the first of Caravaggio's two paintings
on this biblical episode, *The Supper at Emmaus*

The story of the journey to Emmaus gives us some idea of what it meant to the early followers of Jesus to experience him as being still in their midst. Maybe there's something mythic about such an experience, a collective consciousness of companionship that occurs when we are transported to the stress of emotional or physical extremitry. When I used to go backpacking with a friend into Devil's Canyon in the Angeles National Forest, or into the Cucamonga Wilderness, or high in the Sierras to Lost Lake, we often experienced moments when we felt that there was someone else present among us. Whether sitting around the campfire in the darkness of the forest or ascending a difficult switchback at twilight, we remarked that it felt as if someone were there with us, keeping us company. I've talked to other hikers over the years who've had a similar experience, that sensation in the middle of the dark forest of another presence. We didn't give it a religious or spiritual interpretation, nor did we think that someone actually was walking with us. We knew it was just a strange sensation, but because we'd experienced it many times on different hiking trips, we wondered if this was something unique, or perhaps a universal experience for all those who trudge into the wilderness. And yesterday, I happened to be flipping through T. S. Eliot's poem *The Waste Land*, a poem I often dip into—whenever I find myself growing grim about the mouth, whenever it is a damp and drizzly November in my soul, whenever I begin to grow hazy around the eyes— and I came across these lines:

Who is the third who walks always beside you?
When I count, there are only you and I together
But when I look ahead up the white road
There is always another one walking beside you
Gliding wrapt in a brown mantle, hooded
I do not know whether a man or a woman
—But who is that on the other side of you?

In Eliot's notes to the poem, he says that these lines call up the journey to Emmaus. Eliot further explains that his lines about the mysterious third companion were "stimulated by the account of one of the Antarctic expeditions . . . : it was related that the party of explorers, at the extremity of their strength, had the constant delusion that there was one more member than could actually be counted." Perhaps those who had heard Jesus speak, who were there when he was executed, who heard the stories of his tomb being empty, needed to meet and, in talking about him, feel his presence and heal their grief, just as Jews do today after someone dies when they "sit shiva" for eight days. Those early Jewish followers of Jesus (they weren't called Christians until sometime afterwards, dubbed so by the authorities in Corinth) continued to meet, singing songs and reciting passages from the prophets that foretold of His coming. Scholars call this process of healing and preaching, these "healing circles or gatherings that took place after Jesus' death, "the *kerygma*" a rather complex word (possibly from the Greek *kérugma,* used in the New Testament to mean preaching, also related to the Greek verb *kerússo,* to cry or proclaim as a herald); the word can mean proclamation, announcement, or preaching. "Kerygmatic" is sometimes used to express the message of Jesus' whole ministry, as "a proclamation" addressed not to the theoretical reason, but to the hearer "as a self," as opposed to the didactic use of Scripture that seeks understanding in the light of what is taught. Some modern scholars use *kerygma* to refer to the entire Gospels as a totally unique literary genre in the ancient world—neither fiction nor non-fiction, neither memoir nor history, neither fable nor biography, neither prose nor poetry. In Biblical and theological discussions, the term *kerygma* has come to denote the irreducible essence of Christian apostolic preaching. Even before Paul's conversion and missionary activities, this preaching may well have begun in these early healing circles in which the faithful kept his memory and teachings alive. Jerusalem had become home to many of the original disciples. In the days, months, and years after the curcifixion, *ekklesiai,* small gatherings of its members, probably spread to the villages of Samaria and Judea as well as in Galilee.

Within a few years of Jesus' death, it is probable that small bands of believers traveled throughout Palestine from Galilee to Judea, wandering Jews who went from village to village, spreading the good news of Christ's resurrection and second coming. Some appeared as prophets, others as charismatics, while many hovered somewhere between a position of grace and a stage of madness. But those living in the countryside were slow to be converted and tenacious of old peasant superstitions and pagan beliefs. Early Christianity actually began as an urban religion, and never quite shrugged off the nature of its origins. Eventually, evangelists went into the larger towns preaching to the urban poor, traveling on roads the Romans had paved with chalky stone that blew into white dust clouds as the pilgrims passed. After a long day on the road, they might have found a friendly house that offered them a meal and lodging. They didn't speak Greek, the language Paul spoke and the language in which the later Gospels were written; they spoke Aramaic, the language spoken by Jesus. Many of the early evangelists were farmers, fisherman, merchants and craftsmen like Paul, who learned from his father craft of weaving goat's hair into tents, carpets, and shoes. Few of the ruling elite of the larger cities heeded the call of these Jewish Christians, though gradually, some did, offering their homes as gathering places. In fact, we really don't know what a "synagogue" looked like, or how the rituals were conducted before the destruction of the Temple in Jerusalem in 70AD. The gatherings of those early Jews who were followers of Christ's Way could be called "church houses". Luke gives us some idea in [quote passage here when Jesus is give the scroll of Isaiah to read before the congreaetion]. But while the majority of those who were converted came from the urban poor, they didn't have a proletarian ethos. From the start (as I Corinthians shows) the followers of Jesus contained a proportion of well-educated people, capable of private Bible study at home—and the Bible they studied as Scripture would have been scrolls from the Old Testament: the Pentateuch, the Prophets, and the Psalms. Even the Jewish Bible had yet to be finalized into a "canon".

In the beginning, they were focused perhaps on creating a new sect within Judaism. The Jesus movement was not the only sect vying for importance within Judaism at that time. But within a century, this small Nazarean movement was to evolve beyond the limits of Judaic Law and ritual and become a new religion in itself, composed of Jews, Gentiles, and other pagans across the Roman Empire—both in the Latin-speaking West and the Greek-speaking East. In those early decades, before the first Gospels, it is doubtful that they stressed Jesus' virgin birth or the humiliation of his crucifixion, or any of the other narrative stories we find in the Gospels of Mark, Matthew, Luke, and John. It was his teachings and resurrection, the promise of the kingdom to come, not the humiliation of his crucifixion, that were important. But much like the *Illiad* and other epic poems, there would have been an oral tradition, three or four decades during which the deeds and sayings of Jesus were being remembered and his words recited. The illiterate population of believers probably outnumbered the literate population, since only 10 percent of those in the Greco-Roman world were literate. The oral tradition held great power, and eyewitnesses to the events of Jesus's life and death would have passed down stories and sayings to others, and eventually, the written forms would have incorporated those oral traditions. Luke, writing as late as ten or fiftenn years after Mark's Gospel, begins with a reference to "many" previously written accounts, indicating that there may have been more than just the gospels of Mark and Matthew.

> For as much as many have taken in hand to set forth in order a declaration of those things which are most surely believed among us, Even as they delivered them unto us, which from the beginning were eye-witnesses, and ministers of the word;
>
> [Luke, I:1-2]

Those "eye-witness" testimonies and sayings of Jesus were passed along orally at first, but at some point, perhaps toward the end of Paul's missionary travels, a collection of these teachings were written down in a book now lost, but a book that probably served as a source for some of the material contained in the books of Mark and Matthew, written in the late 60s and early 70s. Scholars refer to this lost book as the Q *Gospel,* from the German word *quelle,* for source, and it may well have contained the Sermon on the Mount and the Lord's prayer, the story of John the Baptist and the parable of the lost sheep, along with aphorisms and advice on how to live a compassionate life dedicated to God. The first section of the Sermon on the Mount contains the beautifully poetic "Beatitudes."

> Blessed are the poor in spirit,
>   for theirs is the kingdom of heaven.
> Blessed are those who mourn,
>   for they will be comforted.
> Blessed are the meek,
>   for they will inherit the earth.

Blessed are those who hunger and thirst for righteousness,
    for they will be filled.
Blessed are the merciful,
    for they will be shown mercy.
Blessed are the pure in heart,
    for they will see God.
Blessed are the peacemakers,
    for they will be called sons of God.
Blessed are those who are persecuted because of righteousness,
    for theirs is the kingdom of heaven.

Unlike the scrolls written by scribes who were practiced in the art of calligraphy common in Roman times—scrolls that would have been difficult to carry—the *Lost Gospel of Q*, was a codex, a forerunner to the modern-day book. All the Christian books, both canonical and non-canonical, were codices, made by cutting sheets of papyrus, punching holes in them, and using leather thongs to bind the sheets together. The codex was not much bigger than a paperback book, covered with wood or animal hide. It was meant to be functional, a portable handbook of sorts suited to wandering missionaries.

In the beginning, Christianity was a movement too insignificant to leave more than a trace in any writings other than what the Christians themselves wrote. [quote Seutonius and Tacitus] Up to the end of the first century, it is virtually impossible to get any perspective on the first Christian churches or communities other than what we can glean from those writings that were to be judged canonical and eventually called the New Testament, as well as from the non-canonical gospels written during that time. The earliest extant Christian documents were the letters Paul wrote to various congregations during the late 40s and 50s, and since the Gospels didn't even exist at that point, all references by Paul to "scripture" would have meant the scrolls of the Hebrew Bible. Paul was a prolific correspondent, and in many of the letters we get first-hand insights into the problems of setting up and maintaining a church, its structures, hierarchy, and organization. Paul's vigorous, combative personality emerges from these epistles with stunning force; he was a strange addition indeed to those early adherents of the infant church who were not sophisticated but humble and in some cases, uneducated. The letters, despite their erudition and poetic phrasing, could be ambiguous as well, often sending paradoxical messages. Paul was dealing with the current needs of the moment, dashing off these epistles to keep new converts in line, demanding utter obedience. The fanatical Pharisee had not softened, he'd merely changed the object of his fantaical pursuit. The strain of complying with the unrealistic demands of the Law with its legalistic provisions and religious demands proved more than Paul could bear, but he showed remarkable perseverance and endurance in his ability to argue, remonstrate, cajole, and appeal in support of the new sort of Judaism that Jesus's crucifixion had made possible, even necessary, perhaps inevitable. Paul reasoned that after all the miseries endured by the Jewish people in their own homeland, the Torah had failed to bring oppression to an end; only Jesus's suffering and resurrection could bring completion to the Law. There's often a sense of urgency, a relentless missionary zeal that reveals the birth-pangs of the new religion and the conflicts faced by both Jewish converts who were reluctant to abandon

Jewish practices and those Gentile converts tempted to revert to pagan ones. Founding a new community was a difficult enterprise, and in many cases there may have been only half-a-dozen converts to begin with. Scholars estimate that the community in Antioch fluctuated at times from thirty to a hundred members. Left on their own, these early communities were often fragile and vulnerable, with the loss of even a few members enough to dissolve the group. Not all communities lasted, while some grew and spiritually prospered. Initially, Paul's letters were aimed at settling immediate local problems in which there were conflicting issues of doctrine; sometimes the letters dealt with practical aspects of Christian living, such as marriage, communal eating, ethical behavior, and common worship. Paul's followers must have been baffled at times by the profundity and dynamism of his understanding of Christ and his efforts to create an ecclesiastical organization, especially when significant parts of the letters focused more on reminding Jews and Gentiles alike that the end was at hand and that Jesus' return was imminent. Paul's injunction to love one another in these days before the End Times was reported to have allowed for congregant's behavior to degenerate into sexual immorality. A man had married his stepmother; another leader appeared dressed as a woman.

Paul's attempt to convince other Jews (and eventually Gentiles) that the Law had been superseded and replaced by faith in Christ was only the first of his efforts. Once a community had been set up, they had to confront the everyday challenges of living together until Christ returned. It must have felt as if he were keeping several plates spinning simultaneously, and the tone in some of the letters range from compassionate understanding to outright bullying. Much of Paul's teaching is rabbinic in style, which is not surprising, considering his education under Rabbi Gamliel's Pharasiasic school in which he was steeped in Jewish literature and culture. Initially, he would have addressed members of a synagogue, who would have responded to his knowledge of the Hebrew Bible. (In his own use of scriptures in his letters, he always takes quotes from the *Septuagint*, a translation into Greek of the Hebrew scriptures.) Paul's arguments often relied on his own interpretation of those scriptures, which he cited extensively. As part of his education as a youth, it's probable that he studied the art of rhetoric, which included the writing of letters, and probably picked up a smattering of Greek philosophy, Stoicism as well as Platonism. [quote Seneca here] He possessed the remarkable triple qualification of belonging to the Jewish, Greek, and Roman civilizations all at the same time; no one else in ancient history spans, as he does, all those three different worlds. A single city could present an extraordinary cultural diversity between the town and the surrounding country, and even within the town itself. Paul and Barnabas, performing a cure at Lystra in Lycanonia (Asia Minor), were hailed as Zeus and Hermes by the local people shouting "in the Lycaonian langauge" (Acts 12:8ff). Their triumph was short lived, though, when a hostile crowd of Jews from Pisidian Antioch and Iconium pelted them with stones. But more often than not, Paul was able to exploit his social prestige as one who had inherited Roman citizenship. Jesus had confined his mission to villages and townships, meeting his death during his single known visit to Jerusalem as an adult, where he was executed by a penalty reserved for slaves, brigands, and aliens of the lowest social status. Paul, on the other hand, traveled from city to city, attracted particularly to centers where Greek culture, philosophical learning, and Roman officials were to be found. The difference between the social milieux of the Acts of the Apostles and of the Gospels is clearly evident.

Paul preached not only to Jews, but to Gentiles as well, and it's hard to imagine that Gentile audiences would have appreciated the sophistication of his biblical references. That might partly explain Paul's focus, not so much on specific issues of scriptural doctrine or even the events of Jesus' life, but on the fact of Jesus' crucifixion, resurrection, and ascension. Paul is almost totally uninterested in any and every supposed occurence in Jesus' life before the Last Supper. Jesus's death and what followed—that was what counted, that was what was redemptive (by God's grace, besides which all human initiatives were negligible). His letters scarcely refer to the events later recounted in the Gospels, apart from Jesus' death and resurrection. His main aim was to teach that Christ's *passion* had inaugurated a new relationship between man and God: as a consequence of Christ rising from the dead, the age-old cycle of death and decay inaugurated at the Fall had been broken, and those who were incorporated into Christ through baptisim would share with him in a similar resurrection.

> What shall we say then? Shall we continue in sin, that grace may abound? God forbid. How shall we, that are dead to sin, live any longer therein? Know ye not, that so many of us as were baptized into Jesus Christ were baptized into his death? Therefore we are buried with him by baptisim into death: that like as Christ was raised up from the dead by the glory of the Father, even so we also should walk in newness of life. For if we have been planted together *in the likeness* of *his* death, we shall be also *in the likeness* of *his* resurrection: Knowing this, that our old man is crucified with him, that the body of sin might be destroyed, that henceforth we should not serve sin. For he that is dead is freed from sin. Now, if we be dead with Christ, we believe we shall also live with him: Knowing that Christ being raised from the dead dieth no more; death hath no more dominion over him. For in that he died, he died unto sin once: but in that he liveth, he liveth unto God.
>
> (Romans, 6:1-10)

While it is hard to know exactly what those early gatherings consisted of, it appears they read portions from the Hebrew scriptures, especially from the Prophets and Psalms, shared stories of the Crucifixion and Ressurection of Jesus, and shared a communal meal. It is from Paul in his first letter to the Corinthians that we get the earliest mention of Christianity's central ritual meal, the Eucharist, the taking of bread and wine. (One of the points later debated was whether the substance of the bread and wine during Divine Liturgy were merely symbolic of the body and blood of Christ, or whether by "transubstantiation," they became the actual body and blood of the Savoir, despite the "appearance" remaining the same. The earliest known use of the term "transubstantiation" to describe the change from bread and wine to body and blood of Christ was by Hildebert de Lavardin, Archbishop of Tours in the eleventh century and by the end of the twelfth century the term was in widespread use. Other terms such as "trans-elementation" and "re-ordination" are more common among the Orthodox.)

Perhaps an even better description of those early ritual gatherings comes from Justin Martyr, who was flogged and beheaded with six other Christians in 165 AD during the reign of Marcus Aurelius. Brought up as a pagan, Justin converted and became one of the first apologists for the Church. In one of his works, he discussed how early Christians gathered together to worship on Sunday, the day of Jesus' resurrection. They met in private homes, from small apartments to the more elaborate residences of well-to-do Christian converts, such as Priscilla and Aquila (Acts 18. 2-3), who were tentmakers, like Paul. (A tentmaker could mean leather tanner, weaver of tent cloth, one who sews tents, or a tent vendor. Paul could not have tanned leather because working with pig skin would have made him ritually unclean. His biggest market was probably the Roman army, who used leather tents almost exclusively, and since Priscilla was a Gentile, she might have made the tents and Paul was the vendor. Or Paul may have made the cloth tents from goat's hair.) Such "house churches," or assemblies (*ekklesia*), were often identified with their owner who, presumably, presided at the services and held communal meals. Two key elements of worship were the reading and interpretation of scripture (meaning the Old Testament, since as yet there was no New Testament), and the Eucharist. Justin Martyr describes a second-century service, which included by that time the reading of portions of the early Gospels, and perhaps even some of the writings that were later disputed and did not become part of the Christian canon. But in Paul's time, there were no gospels to be read, just those portions of the Hebrew Bible that would have been meaningful in terms of the coming of the Messiah.

> The memoirs of the apostles or the writings of the prophets are read, then the president in a discourse urges and invites the congregation to the imitation of those noble things. Then we all stand up and offer prayers. Bread is brought and wine and water, and the president similarly sends up prayers and thanksgivings, and the congregation assents, saying the Amen; the distribution and reception of the consecrated elements by all takes place, and the deacons send them to the absent.
>
> [from *The Apoligia* by Justin Martyr]

Until the 4th Century AD, Latin literature was secular literature, or from the point of view of the early Christians, pagan literature. Christians were admonished not to read pagan classical poets such as Virgil, Ovid, and Horace, although Juvenal was tolerated because, as a satirist, he mocked the opulance and power of Rome. When Christian authors finally began to create literary works (as opposed to theological tracts), what models could they use if not the great poets of the previous age? Obviously the pagan forms and genres could be used, especially the epic written in dactylic hexameter, but if they were to eschew subject matter from Greek and Roman mythology, legend, or history (myth and history were often the same thing), where would Christian writers interested in writing "literature" find permissable subject matter? They could use the Bible—that is, the Hebrew Bible; the New Testament usually refers to the Jewish scriptures as "The Law and the Prophets," but Luke (24.44) has "the Law, the Prophets, and the Psalms" and New Testament writers also quote from Proverbs and Job. This indicates that the third section of the Old Testament, the Writings, had not yet been settled in New Testament times. In fact, the thirty-nine-book Jewish canon was probably not fixed until later in the 2nd century. It wasn't as if early Christians had a single bound book, as we do today, containing both the Hewbrew Bible and the New Testament. What "bibles" they had were collections of scrolls, and it's probable that not every congregation of early Christians had all the scrolls. Once various gospels began to be circulated later in the first century, each congregation may have had only one or two scrolls, and many of those gospels turned out to be non-canonical. Whenever an early congregation talked about scriptures, they were talking about the Hebrew Bible, the Old Testament, because in the early decades of Christianity, there was no New Testament. When the Gospels and other works began to be collected, they were merely attached to the Hebrew Bible, and it was only later that the Hebrew Bible was considered the Old Testament and the newer writing attributed to the original apostles was considered part of a separate book, a New Testament. Jews in Jesus' day actually had two Bibles: one in Hebrew (called the *Tanakh*) and another in Greek, The *Septuagint*, a translation made in 200 BC to meet the needs of Diaspora Jews who no longer used Hebrew in daily life. The *Septuagint* contained fifteen books that were absent from the Hebrew Bible, and it was this Greek translation that most early Christians used, especially the scrolls of Isaiah, the Psalms, and Zechariah, which contained messianic passages said to predict or interpret Jesus' acts. Such passages were frequently read aloud when early Christians gathered on Sunday (the day of Jesus' resurrection), and included as proof to outsiders that Jesus was the Messiah, that indeed his coming was foretold in the Hebrew scriptures. These passages from the Hebrew prophets expressed Christian conviction that their Lord was the culmination of Old Testament scripture. But by the 4th Century, the Hebrew canon and Christian canon were in the process of being fixed, and for Christianity, the Bible consisted of the Septaugint and the attached gospels and letters.

Paul has often been referred to as "The Apostle to the Gentiles," and "The Second Founder of Christianity." It's not as if Paul single-handedly spread Christianity throughout Asia Minor, Syria, Greece and Palestine. Both apostles James and Peter were active in Jerusalem, and many other evangelists were out spreading the good news and winning converts, not to a new religion, but to the religion of the Jews, with the added element that they were Jews who believed that Jesus was not just a prophet, but the Messiah who had finally come to redeem the people of Israel. But unlike Peter and James, Paul had never actually met Jesus or witnessed the Crucifixion. James and Peter were not trying to convert gentiles (those from other "nations"), but those who were already Jewish into accepting Jesus as part of Judiaism. Paul must have felt left out of that circle of original apostles, so it was easy to make the leap by carving out his own niche and preaching not only to Jews, but to non-Jews as well. His influence on Christian theology proved to be the most permenant and far-reaching of all Christian writers and thinkers.

Born in Tarsus sometime between 1 and 8 AD, Paul would have been anywhere from three to twelve years younger than Jesus, but there is no indication that he ever knew him. (The Vatican has recently settled on 8 AD as his date of birth, and in 2008 commemorated the two thousandth anniversary of Paul's birth.) Tarsus was a provincial capital located in present-day Turkey, one of the leading Hellenistic centers of commerce and Greek philosophy. Paul was brought up in a tradtional, middle-class Jewish family, schooled in Greek and Hebrew. As a youth, he struggled with the demands of the Mosaic Code, and that struggle only intensified when he left for Jerusalem to study at one of the rabbinical academies, probably with the eminent Jewish teacher Rabbi Gamaliel. He would have been there when Jesus was executed, but there is no suggestion in his own writings that the two ever met. Paul was fanatically devoted to the Law, the original Hebrew term, Torah, meaning "teaching" or instruction," contained in the first five books of Moses. As instructed by the Pharisees, the Law was the only path of righteousness, the only way to salvation. The teachings of the Torah was more than just a list of prohibitions, but an ethical approach to life. Nevertheless, the prescriptions and prohibitions were long and complex, governing almost every aspect of daily life, and anyone devoted to following the letter of the Law would have to be extremely pious and almost fanatically observant. The extent to which one followed the Law often determined which sect within Judaism one followed.

Within Judea itself, there were at least four (according to the Jewish historian Josephus, but there may have been more) identities for Judaism: Sadducees, Pharisees, Essenes, and Zealots. The Sadducees were the privileged elite who ran the Temple; they were flexible when it came to everyday life—follow the basic commands of the Law as set forth in the scriptures and you'll be fine. There was no need to get carried away with every detail. For instance, the debate over what one could and couldn't do on the Sabbath proved endless. One could not "work" on the Sabbath, but just what constituted work? The answer to that question could become complicated. When I was twelve years old, I was asked by a very religious man in our synagogue to open a can of soup for him, because using a can opener was "work," and since I was not yet Bar-Mitzvahed, it was okay for me to operate the can opener. There isn't a great deal of mention in Hebrew scripture of the afterlife, but were the subject to come up, the Sadducees would have said, don't worry about the life to come, live a virtuous life in the here and now, that's what counts. They rejected any belief in the resurrection of the body, since there was no mention of it in scripture. (There's a passage in the Book of Daniel (12:2) in which it is written: "And many of them that sleep in the dust of the earth shall awake, some to everlasting life, and some to shame and everlasting contempt." The last few verses of that chapter talks about "the time of the end," and indicates that it will come "a thousand and two hundred and ninety days from the time that the daily sacrifice shall be taken away." But the Sadducees would have dismissed this as not being literal, but a figurative expression of man's need to change his life in the here and now. The Sadducees were also supportive of Roman rule, rendering—even before Jesus said it—to Caesar, what was Caesar's.

The Pharisees were not considered elite; they were of a lower social status, and supported the ideals of the Maccabean rebels who won independence for Judea in 141 BC, an independence that was preserved until the coming of the Romans in 63 BC. The successful revolt of the Maccabees was the first time that Jews had ever risen against any of their varied foreign masters over the previous centuries. The Pharisees were much stricter than the Sadducees. They were dedicated to the Law in its entirety, all the complex additional regulations which governed everyday life. They believed in balancing the study of Torah with oral interpretations, and could spend an entire night debating the meaning of the smallest detail. For instance, when I helped the observant old man with the soup, would it have been okay for that can of soup to be opened with an electric can opener, since one didn't actually have to apply force (labor, work) to the turning of the handle? If these smaller issues proved so vexing, imagine how complex it was interpreting the larger theological questions. Yet, from the Pharisaic perspective, the larger theological issues were no more important than how to open a can of soup. The Pharisees also believed in the resurrection of the body. Jesus and Paul, judging by their backgrounds, were most probably closer to the Pharisees, and Jesus even poked fun at the Sadducees when they asked him a tricky question about marriage that involves the obligation to marry the wife of one's deceased brother. But what if that brother dies, and another brother marries that wife. And so on, through several more brothers. What happens in the afterlife, they taunt him, when all brothers and the one wife reach heaven? Whose wife is she then, if "they all had her?" Jesus needles them for not knowing scripture nor the power of God, then says: "For in the resurrection they neither marry, nor are given in marriage, but are as the angels of God in heaven. . . . God is not the God of the dead, but of the living." The Pharisees who were present gloated that Jesus had put the Sadduces down. One of the Pharisees, who was a lawyer, then asked Jesus, which of all the commandents was the greatest and most important. And Jesus answered: "Thou shalt love the Lord thy God with all thy heart and with all thy soul and with all thy mind [often translated as, with all thy "might"]. This is the first and great commandment. And the second is like unto it, Thou shalt love thy neighbor as thyself. On these two commandments hang all the law and the prophets." Today, Jesus and Paul would more likely attend an orthodox synagogue, rather than a Conservative temple, or even a Reformed one.

There are scholars who think Jesus may have actually been part of the group known as Essenes, who were even stricter when it came to the law. The Essenes believed that strictly following the commandments and living in ordinary society did not protect one from spiritual pollution. So they withdrew from society and established a counter-culture based on an idealization of poverty and asceticism, setting up separate communities with selected scriptures. They were often persecuted by other Jews. Josephus and Philo, Jewish historians at that time, mentioned the Essenes with admiration, acknowledging their piety; even the Roman scholar Pliny the Elder had this to say about them: "They are a unique people and admirable beyond all others in the whole world, without women and renouncing love entirely, without money, and having for company only the palm trees." (The Dead Sea Scrolls, discovered in the late 1940s and 50s were part of the so-called Qumran communtiy which was part of the Essene movement.) The Essenes were celibate and insisted on strict observance of the Law. They believed in the imminent coming of the Messiah, the "Son of David," as foretold in scripture, who would bring the world to an end. It is not uncommon to equate the early Christians with the same impulse that drove the Essenes, but the Essenes separated themselves from the rest of the Jews as a matter of religious principle, with no desire to bring others to their way of thinking, nor were they interested in moving out into the world beyond. Early Christians were concerned with becoming a force within Judaism, and eventually, through the missionary work of Paul and others who reached out to the Geniles, Chrisitanity found itself no longer a Jewish sect, but a new religion.

All three goups had to contend with the strictures of Roman rule, but it was only the Zealots, our fourth group, who were militant enough to advocate violent resistence. It was they who were the driving force behind the disastrous revolts, which by the mid-second century AD had shattered Jewish life in Palestine. (The first was the revolt of 66-70, in which Jewish rebels massacred many of the Sadducee elite, but in the end, were massacred themselves by the Romans and the Temple complex itself went up in flames; the second great Jewish revolt of 132-5 also ended in defeat, with the Romans erasing the name of Jerusalem from the map. In both revolts, Jewish Christians abstained from involvement, many fleeing the city. Their refusal to become associated with resistance to Roman oppression caused most Jews to consider them traitors.)

Paul was probably executed in Rome a few years before the first of these revolts, but he would certainly have been aware of the currents of unrest and the different movements within Judaism. By nature, he would not have sympathized with the Sadducees, nor was he drawn to the isolation of the Essenes. Intensely pious, he endeavored to observe every facet of the Law, but the rules and regulations became so complex and oppressive, that it became almost impossible to observe them all. Obsessed with absolute devotion, Paul may even have been manic-depressive; there's vague mention of a disabilty, perhaps epilepsy. After the death of Jesus, those in the Jesus Movement were regarded as heretics and suffered persecution, and for awhile, perhaps to absolve himself of his own guilt for his inability to achieve greater purity, Paul furiously participated in the persecutions himself, driving many of the followers of Jesus out of Jerusalem during a reign of terror. He may have been present at the stoning of Stephen, who is remembered as the first Christian martyr; he may have held the coats of those who threw stones, and maybe even cast a few stones himself. Perhaps he felt that the purity he was seeking was impossible to attain, either by strict observance of the Law or by participating in the persecution of those Jewish heretics. Either he was going to accept his imperfect nature and align himself with the Sadduces, become an Essene and live a secluded life, or become a Zealot rabble rouser. A psychological crisis was bound to occur. But no one would have guessed that Paul would have become a follower of the Jesus movement, the movement he was so aggressively persecuting. A few years after the death of Jesus, perhaps in 34 AD, something did happen "on the road to Damascas." On his way to persecute more disciples of Jesus, the emotional stress led to a breakdown in which he was thrown to the ground by an explosion of light, temporarily blinding him. (Psychologists describe such experiences under the name of photism, a sensation of light or color accompanying some other kind of sensation, often sound.) Paul had a vision in which Jesus spoke to him, asking him, in Aramaic, "Saul, Saul, why do you persecute me?"

For Paul, it was a moment of revelation. The sound Paul believed that he had heard was the voice of Jesus ordering him to enter Damascus where he would discover an even greater undertaking. In that flash of revelation, Paul realized that his faith didn't have to be a matter of following to perfection the letter (or the seemingly infinite letters) of the Mosaic Law. His torment that he could never achieve spiritual purity through observance of the Law was eased by the realization that if he accepted Jesus as the Son of God, a new path of redemption was laid out before him. In a sense (even though Jesus had said he had not come to do away with the Law), it was the gift of God's grace, freely given through faith, that rendered the Law obsolete.

Despite Paul's revelation, it was not as if this idea sprang full blown from the head of Zeus (to mix pagan and Christian metaphors). As a scholar of the Hebrew scriptures, driven by his Pharisaical orthodoxy, Paul would have been familiar with the story of the Suffering Servant, taken from Isaiah 53, which tells the story of the Man of Sorrows or "The Suffering Servant."

> To whom is the arm of the Lord revealed? . . . . He is despised and rejected of men; a man of sorrows, and acquainted with grief: and we hid as it were our faces from him; he was despised, and we esteemed him not. Surely he hath borne our griefs, and carried our sorrows: yet we did esteem him stricken, smitten of God, and afflicted. Be he was wounded for our transgressions, he was bruised for oue iniquities; the chastisment of our peace was upon him; and with his stripes we are healed. All we like sheep have gone astray; we have turned every one to his own way; and the LORD hath laid on him the iniquity of us all. He was oppressed, and he was afflicted, yet he opened not his mouth: he is brought as a lamb to the slaughter, and as a sheep before her shearers is dumb, so he openeth not his mouth. . . . He shall see of the travail of his soul, and shall be satisfied: by his knowledge shall my righteous servant justify many; for he shall bear their iniquities.
>
> [Isaiah, 53]

As a Jew, Paul would have taken the reference to mean that the servant was the nation of Israel, but the last four of Isaiah's poems were interpreted in medieval and later Christian art as the suffering Jesus faced, not to mention the absolution of sins believed to be made possible by his death. The passage is known for its interpretation by many Christians to be a prophecy of the coming of Jesus, being written over 700 years before his birth. These doctrines were already being espoused by Stephen's Christian community, the very group Paul was on his way to persecute. The irony is obvious: On his way to stamp out the heresy that threatened the salvation of Israel, Paul was spoken to by the Lord, in the person of Jesus. Speaking to his persecutor, Jesus compelled him to tell the story of his resurrection. Faith in Jesus was what mattered, not adherence to the letter of the Law, particularly its dietary restrictions and circumcision. .

This conversion on the road to Damscus was a shattering experience for Paul. How could he spread the good news, though, when he was not much of a charismatic preacher, with no commanding presence like the other prophets and traveling missionaries. He was short, bandy-legged, with a receding hairline and thick eyebrows that met atop a rather prominent nose. He might have been well equipped to persecute followers of Jesus, but he had no evangelical skills at all, and when he spoke, had a tendency to antagonize his audience, especially the local authorities. In his second letter to the Corinthians, he admits that his "bodily presence is weak, and [his] speech is contemptible." [2 Corinthians 10.10] After two or three years of preaching in the desert kingdom of Nabatean Arabia, he was unable to organize a Christian community, and so antagonized the city magistrates there that he had to be smuggled out of the country by his friends.

He went to Jerusalem to meet with Peter and James; Peter had been doing missionary work in Samaria and the Judean coastal cities, while James remained in Jerusalem, the center of the new Jewish cult. James (known as "the Just") was a brother of Jesus and adamantly insisted that those followers of Jesus in the so-called Nazarean movement were required to follow the Mosaic Law in its strictist sense. Obviously, there was tension between Paul and the two apostles, who insisted that new converts had to follow Jewish practices such as circumcision. Paul didn't ask for, nor did he receive approval for the nature of his evangelical work. But his inner struggle was probably not much different from the inevitable tensions of a Jesus follower who was also a Jew. It wasn't a question of a new religion; it was about the acceptance of the Messiah and what that would mean. In the beginning, there was no question that only Jews would be involved in this struggle to accept or reject Jesus. If the Messiah had truly come, wouldn't he have come with a sword, God's warrior bringing salvation to the nation of Isreal and redemption for those who had devoted themselves to the Mosaic Law? Surely, a messiah wouldn't be someone who turned the other cheek, who was so easily arrested and executed in such a humiliating manner as crucifixion? But this man, who claimed to be the Son of God, suffered for those who, like Paul, had failed to achieve the purity that would earn redemption. He suffered for the sins of the unrightous, and his resurrection was a symbol of hope. The time was at hand, the End Days were approaching, and the Messiah's first arrival was a signal to prepare, for when he came a second time, a final time, those who had faith in him as a redeemer would be redeemed, and those who did not, would be cast into the flames of hell. Paul's theological preoccution was his clear conviction that the End Time was imminent. There was no time to waste. As far as Paul was concerned, Jews who accepted Jesus as the Messiah would not have to be rigid about following the Law, and it was even possible for Gentiles to be converted. (The question of whether or not they had to be converted to Judaism first and then to Christianity was a thorny issue taken up much later).

Paul returned to Syria and continued preaching. There is a gap in the record; for the next ten years we know nothing about where he went, nor how successful he was in setting up Christian communities, though it is probable that he worked as a missionary to his fellow Jews in Syria and Cilicia. In 47 AD, he was joined by an old friend from Cyprus, a Jew named Barnabas. (It was to Barnabas that a letter written probably around 130 AD was falsely attributed, probably in order to give it "apostolic" legitimacy. The forged Letter of Barnabas was circulated for centuries to Christian communities, and was even included among the books of the New Testament in a famous Greek manuscript, the *Codex Sinaiticus*. The letter was more of a theological treatise, claiming that Judaism was a false religion, and that Jews had been misled by an evil angel who persuaded them to take the laws of Moses literally. The only way to read the Old Testament, it said, was not as a Jewish book, but as a Christian one.)

Paul went to Jerusalem and worked out an agreement that he would preach to the Gentiles. Barnabas asked Paul to come to the city of Antioch, in Syria, to help settle a dispute that had arisen between two factions. After Rome and Alexandria, Antioch was the third largest metropolis in the Roman Empire. There were several Christian communities there, and the multitude of Jewish splinter groups throughout Palestine called themselves Nazareans or followers of The Way. But the Greeks began to call the Antioch Jewish splinter group the party of *Christianoi*, especially when they built their church onto a cave just outside the city walls. This was perhaps the beginning of Christianity, not as a Jewish splinter group, but as a new religion unto itself.

Paul worked out a compromise between the two factions, then he and Barnabas set off on their first lengthy journey throughout Asia Minor and Cyprus, encountering a rising tide of hostility, partly as a result of the increased tensions between the Jewish community and Rome. Scores of Jewish protestors were captured and crucified or beheaded. In time, Paul and his new traveling companions, Timothy and Silas, had founded churches in numerous cities, and one night, while in Troy, he had a dream in which a voice called him to "come over and help us." So for the first time, Paul crossed the Aegean Sea into Europe. After founding another church in Philippi, and stirring up popular unrest in Athens for using the term "Kingdom of God," Paul left for Corinth, a gathering place for merchants from all over the Mediteranean. Corinth was officially known as the city of the goddess Aphrodite, and a wide variety of religious cults and sacrificial rites were devoted to various dieties, including the Egyptian goddess Isis. The city had the reputation for licentiousness, leading to the coining of the Greek word *korinthiazethai*, "to fornicate."

By this time, Paul's preaching focused not so much on Jesus' ethical teachings, but on the fact of the resurrection. The cross itself, once a symbol of humiliation, had become a sort of magical charm suggesting supernatural powers. Paul turned the dreaded crucifix against the Romans by declaring it the source of salvation. A magical Resurrection redeems a painful and humiliating crucifixion, transforming suffering into hope. Furthermore, Paul elevated Jesus to the status of a diety, not just a prophet. He invoked Isaiah's story of the Suffering Servant sent by God to inaugurate a new covenant that would be sealed at the second coming of Christ at the Last Judgment—an event that was close at hand, any day now. Understanding every demand of the Law could take years of study, but the mere leap of faith in Jesus would ready everyone, Jew and Gentile alike, for the coming Kingdom.

Orthodox Jews reacted to this message with great resentment and hostility. Paul had denigrated the Law, by-passed Jesus' ethical teachings (most of which were philosophically Judaic) by claiming he was the Messiah and raised Jesus to the same level as God, a clear sacrilege in that it violated the concept of a mono-theistic deity. But graver than that was Paul's accusation that the Jews were responsible for murdering the Messiah. But Jesus did not fit the Judaic picture of the expected messiah. As foretold in Isaiah, the Messiah was supposed to punish the enemies of Israel, redeem the faithful and establish his own kingdom, not turn the other cheek and suffer such an ignoble and humiliating death on the cross. How could this man have been the Messiah, they said, if he died. A messiah was pictured as a warrior, someone who would smite the unrighteous and save those who believed in the Lord and followed his commandements. Instead, the man claiming to be the Messiah broke conventional expectations of messiahship by dying. And now, Paul was saying that those responsible for his death were the people of Israel, the ones he had come to save. Most Jews were offended to the core.

Paul continued to preach, going to the great port of Ephesus, visiting the existing churches in Antioch and Galatia, and returning to Ephesus for another two years. Ephesus was a challenge. It was the center of the cult of Artemis, the goddess of fertility, often shown with a dozen or more breasts. Her magnificent temple was one of the Seven

Wonders of the World, four times as large as the Parthenon in Athens, and pilgrims flocked to the city from all over the world, bringing home silver statues of the goddess. Paul was not only offending Jews, but attempting to shut down the city's primary commercial activity. When he was no longer allowed to preach in the synagogue, he preached in a lecture hall owned by one of the converts, every day, from mid-morning to late in the afternoon. He did this for two years. On numerous occasions he was arrested and put in prison for stirring up unrest, and sometimes flogged for refusing to stop preaching. Near the end of the year 55 AD, Paul finally left the city.

In was during this time that he began to write many of the letters that were later included in the New Testament. Only seven of the so-called Pauline letters are now fully accepted as genuine: Romans, 1 and 2 Corinthians, Galatians, 1 Thessalonians, Philippians, and the short Letter to Philemon. The earliest surviving letter, that to the Galatians, was probalby written in 49 AD, while the most mature and influential statement of Paul's theology, the Letter to the Romans, in about 57 AD, and his last surviving letter, to the Philippians in 61 or 62. He may have written letters once he was brought to Rome under house arrest, but none survive. That he was executed within a few years of his being brought there for trial is also speculation, but probably correct. Paul's eloquence in these letters reaches an intensity which place these letters among the finer literary achievements of the ancient world. They showed his erudition and religious zeal, not to mention his literary genius.

Eventually, Paul returned to Jerusalem and was once again embroiled in controversy. Paul was again arrested and kept in jail for two years, awaiting the new Roman procurator who would settle the dispute between Paul and the Jewish Council. At one point, as Paul was explaining his missionary activities, the revelation he had on the road to Damascus, his Pharisaic training, his belief that Jesus was the Son of God sent to save mankind, the procurator burst out in exasperation: "Paul, you are raving! Too much learning is driving you mad!" Paul was given a choice—risk a verdict dictated by political pressure from the Jewish Council, or go to Rome and submit to the Emperor's verdict, a right Paul had since he was a citizen of Rome. Paul's last letter was written before he elected to go to Rome to be tried as a Roman citizen.

He was put on a ship under military guard. In what is one of the best descriptions of a voyage in the ancient world, Luke describes the tortuous journey across the Mediterreranean that followed. It was a rough crossing, in the middle of winter, and the ship encountered a storm so violent they had to throw the cargo overboard, and eventually the ship's tackle as well. The ship ran aground off the coast of Malta, and passengers reached shore by clutching planks and other parts of the broken ship. Once in Rome, Paul was put under house arrest, but for the next two years was allowed to preach the Gospel "quite openly and unhindered." And that's the last we hear of him. In the first letter of Clement, it is suggested that he was allowed to travel to Spain before returning to Rome to his death. Luke abruptly concludes Acts and leaves the question of his death open. Had he been exonerated, there is no question that he would have continued his missionary actitivities, continued writing letters, continued stirring up trouble. Since he was a citizen of Rome, he didn't have to suffer crucifixion, as Peter did a few years later in the persecutions of Nero (described by the historian Tacitus). Paul would have had the honor of being beheaded.

Paul's reputation at his death was at its lowest ebb. His missionary work appeared to be a failure, considering the fact that the churches he set up did not prosper, and many of the Christian communities either ceased to exist, or they followed the Jewish Christian theology and spurned Paul's rejection of the Law. But events were to change all that. The First Jewish Revolt (66-73 AD) ended in the eventual crushing of the insurgents. Vaspasian's son Titus destroyed the Temple in 70 AD, marking the end of the nation's life in Israel for more than two thousand years. The Jews lost any favor they might have been given by the Roman authorities, and the Jewish Christians were unable to prove distance themselves from the more orthodox Jewish sects. Thus, they dwindled gradually into a scattering of insignificant sects, which failed to survivie into the modern world. But the Gentile Christians had not taken part in the rebellion, and avoided falling into total disgrace, at least from the Roman viewpoint. As far as the Jews were concerned, they were traitors. But within the first two decades following the revolt, they distanced themselves from both Jews and Jewish Christians, producing dozens of gospels, four of which were to prove compelling to the followers of Jesus. Eventually, Paul's letters, and the account of his missionary activities in Luke's *Acts of the Apostles* brought Paul's work into a new light. True, much of his teachings still seemed too daring and provocative for the average Christian, and Luke was careful in the *Acts* to say little or nothing at all about Paul's theological principles. But gradually, Paul's eminence increased, though the Church was careful in not letting it focus on his awkward radicalism. Better to praise him for his missionary work, "the greatest example of endurance," while minimizing his true outlook, even though there have been times when Paul's vision was emphasized enough to cause discomfort among Church leaders. Everyone was in agreement, though, about one thing: By extending Christianity to the Gentiles, it was he who had made it into a world religion, and during periods of revivial, Paul's teachings were the greatest single source.

Taken out of their religious and historical context, Paul's letters reveal a poetic sensibility that confirm his literary genius. They reach an eloquence that is both heart-wrenching and uplifting. In his biography of Paul, A.N. Wilson writes that "he was one of the most stupendous religious poets and visionaries whom the world has ever known." Perhaps the most famous poetic passage is from the first letter he wrote to his fellow Christians in Corinth.

> If I speak in the tongues of men and of angels, but have not love, I am noisy gong or a clanging cymbal. And if I have prophetic powers, and understand all mysteries and have all knowledge, and if I have all faith, so as to remove mountains, but have not love, I am nothing. If I give away all I have, and if I deliver my body to be burned, but have not love, I gain nothing. Love is patient and kind: love is not jealous or boastful; it is not arrogant or rude. Love does not insist on its own way; it is not irritable or resentfull it does not rejoice at wrong, but rejoices in the right. Love bears all things, believes all things, hopes all things, endures all things. Love never ends; as for prophecy, it will pass away; as for tongues, they will cease; as for knowledge, it will pass away. For our knowledge is imperfect and our prophecy is imperfect; but when perfect comes, the imperfect will pass away. When I was a child, I spoke like a child;

when I became a man, I gave up childish ways. For now, we see in a mirror darkly, but then face to face. Now I know in part; then I shall understand fully, even as I have been fully understood. So faith, hope, lovef abide, these three; but the greatest of these is love. but when I spoke like a child, I thought like a child.

[1 Corinthians 13]

His letters, as the oldest extant Christian writings, are not only characterized by their poetic eloquence, but by the personality of a flawed human being who showed his rage, his prejudice, his self-obsession, as well as his courage, gentleness, and faith. When Paul was writing his letters, he certainly did not consider that what he was writing was comparable to the Hebrew Scriptures. As a matter of fact, at this point in the evolution of the Jesus movement into the Christian religion, there were no scriptures other than those contained in the Hebrew Bible, and even then the Bible had yet to reach a canonized form comprising the 39 books we know today. That would have come in the following century. But at this point, the various scrolls either from the five books of Moses or the writings of the prophets or the Laws were available and read in synagogues and at those early Jewish-Christian gatherings. The only real difference between traditional Jewish worship and early Christian worship was the belief that Jesus was a messiah who died for their sins, was ressurected then ascended, to come a second time declaring the end of time and establishing a new kingdom for those who believed in him, who would find a place in the afterlife. There was no concept in those early years of Christian scriptures, of a "new" testament (or covenant), and certainly for Paul, no concept that his letters would form an integral part of such new testament scriptures. While the *Gospel of Q* may have existed during the period of Paul's travels (unlikely, but possible), the Synoptic Gospels of Matthew, Mark, and Luke had not yet been written, nor the Gospel of John, nor Luke's Acts of the Apostles, nor the epistles of Jude, James, Peter, and John, nor the Revelation of John the Divine. There was nothing. Paul's letters to the various communities were not circulated, nor were they treated as sacred. The question of identity would have been as important as their belief in Christ. What were they? Jews who were establishing a sect within Judaism, like the Saduccees or Pharisees; Jews who were more like the Zealots, a rebellious force that might cause trouble for the Roman authorities; a hybrid sect composed of Jews and Gentiles, the latter called "God-Fearers," who often attended synagogues and participated in worshipping the one God of the Hebrews but who were not themselves Jews, not circumcised, not followers of the dietary laws; or were they something different, a new religion perhaps. And if so, did they believe in one god, who sent his son as a prophet, or were there two gods, The Lord, and Jesus Christ, thus making the followers of Jesus worshippers of two gods, not one; making them not much different from pagans who workshipped many gods. These early Christian communities were operating in a "no-man's land," and Paul's evangelical work and letters—compassionate and heartfelt, bullying and pedantic, rabbinic and preachy, poetic and lofty—the letters focused on matters of organization and procedure, much like the CEO of a new company bringing various branches into alignment.

Even before the Gospels were known, early Christian communities were developing their own patterns of worship, focused on Christ, re-enacting the last Passover meal, where

Jesus broke bread and declared that the bread and wine were his body and blood, the Eucharist meal. Paul's description is the earliest text to assert that Jesus commanded his disciples to repeat in remembrance what he had done in the Last Supper.

> For I have received of the Lord that which also I delivered unto you, That the Lord Jesus the same night in which he was betrayed took bread: And when he had given thanks, he brake it, and said, Take, eat: this is my body, which is broken for you: this do in remembrance of me. After the same manner also he took the cup, when he had supped, saying, This cup is the new testament in my blood: this do ye, as oft as ye drink it, in remembrance of me. For as often as ye eat this bread, and drink this cup, ye do shew the Lord's death till he come.
>   (I Corinthians, 11: 23-26)

Among the Synoptic Gospels, Luke (22.19) picks up this reference to a command to remember and repeat the actions, which is not present in the earlier parallel descriptions in Mark or Matthew (14.22; 26.26). Thus, the focus of Paul's letters was how to live, how to conduct their church gatherings during this crucial time before Christ's return, which could be anyday now.

But as time went on, Paul had to take into account the fact that the immenent second coming of Jesus may take longer than expected. In the first flush of apocalyptic fervor, it was much easier to work out a simple theology. But in time, the movement's first assumptions were being challenged. If the Christ had not returned as immediately as Paul and other evangelists were saying, would he return at all, was he truly the Son of God? Paul's last few letters struggled with these questions that many in the Christian communities were asking. Paul was, so to speak, in a theological no-man's land, somewhere between traditional Judaism, and Jewish Christianity as it evolved in the communities in Jerusalem and the rest of Palestine. And then, of course, what about that tiny minority of Gentiles who were attracted to the teachings of Jesus?

After Paul's death in 64 AD, his letters, as well as those "gospels" (those supposedly written by the original apostles, as well as those that later proved to be disputed, heretical, non-canonical and not discovered until recently, though many were referred to or quoted) were being written and circulated, read aloud among the early congregations of Christians. The main purpose for establishing a distinctive Christian canon was primarily to limit the number of texts deemed to be correct, especially given the increasing growth in Christian writings in the second and third centuries. Just as the Hebrew biblical canon wasn't finally established until the second or third century, the Christian New Testament slowly took shape over a few hundred years. The letters (epistles) of Paul are the earliest surviving Christian writings and they were the first to be accorded special treatment. By the end of the first century, Paul's letters were already being spoken of in the same breath as "other scriptures."

> And account that the longsuffering of our Lord is salvation; even as our beloved brother Paul also according to the wisdom given unto him hath written unto you; As also in all his epistles, speaking in them of these things; in which are some things hard to be understood, which they that are unlearned and unstable wrest, as they do also

the other scriptures [i.e., the Hebrew Bible], unto their own destruction.
[2 Peter 3.15-17]

The four canonical Gospels themselves were written 40 to 70 years after Jesus' death, and much of it was heavily reliant on oral traditions, some of which may have been written down. Paul's own knowledge of Jesus' life appears to have been very limited. Nevertheless, collections of Paul's letters were made and circulated. But during that time, the *Lost Gospel of Q* was composed, a gospel scholars assume Mark and Matthew used for their own gospels. Mark's gospel was written around 65 AD, Matthew's sometime between 75 and 80 AD. Luke's gospel would have been written around that same time, along with the Acts of the Apostles, and the Gospel of John was written between 90 and 95 AD. Soon the floodgates opened, and Christians of varying theological and ecclesiastical persuasion wrote all kinds of books: gospels recording the words, deeds, and activities of Jesus; accounts of the miraculous lives and teachings of early Christian leaders, personal letters, prophetic revelations, etc. Within a few decades, books began to appear that claimed to be written by the original apostles, which in fact were forgeries written in their name. Many of these books were revered and treated as sacred texts, with different communities of Christians using them as their founding document. Even if we consider what was written in the 2nd century, we have to remember that 85 percent of all texts that make mention of early Christian writings have themselves been lost, and what survives represents only a fraction of what there once was. Paul was probably not the only one to travel throughout the Mediterranean preaching the teachings of Jesus, but except for the Epistles of James, Peter, John and Jude, his letters are the only ones that survive. Below, along with the Four Gospels and the other books of the New Testament, is a list of some of the non-canonical gospels, letters and revelations and approximate date of their composition. Remember, when these non-canonical works were being circulated and read, there was as yet no "canon"—all were considered significant, perhaps sacred, maybe not by every community of Christians, but each community might have chosen different texts as sacred and read them aloud as part of their religious services. Though I list them alongside the major works of poetry discussed earlier in this chapter, we should also keep in mind that these Christian texts were known by very few throughout the Empire. The poets of the Silver Age like Juvenal and Petronius were quite well-known and widely read, while these early Christian texts were hardly known. Today, millions know the letters of Paul or the Gospel of Matthew, while only the well-read know the work of Virgil or Ovid, much less Statius or Lucan. Centuries later, Clement of Alexandria was to compare the Church as a river emerging from the confluence of Biblical faith with Greek philosophy. To adjust that metaphor somewhat, we might say that in time, the small stream of Christian writing became the wide Amazon beside the Nile of Latin poets.

Many of the non-canonical gospels were used by certain congregations for decades, perhaps even a few centuries. There was no official universally accepted canon; if a work was chosen to be read along with Hebrew scriptures as part of church lectionaries, it had the criterion of "canonicity," so to speak. Eventually, most of the gospels, epistles, and revelatory works were not included in the official canon. They were either attacked, suppressed, destroyed or simply lost, not to be rediscovered until modern times in systematic searches through the monasteries and libraries of the Middle East and Europe or in archaeological digs which produced the Dead Sea Scrolls and the papyrus scrolls found at Nag Hammadi in 1946.

In those early decades of Christianity, the copies of Jewish Scriptures as well as the many gospels and other writings by those early followers of Christ would have been scrolls, and most of the house churches would have had one or two such scrolls; eventually, by the second century, these writings were being collected in codices. Scrolls were the dominant medium for literature throughout the Greco-Roman world, and codices were used mainly as school notebooks for making lists and writing practice. The pages might even have been made of wood with wax surfaces added to portions that were hollowed out. When the codices began to be used for literary works, sheets of parchment or papyrus were stacked together and stitched along the fold. Like today's chapbooks, one sheet folded in half made for two "leaves" composing four pages, and four such sheets when folded together made a "quire" of sixteen pages. Quires were then stacked together and bound into a larger book. While this practice took about three centuries to become common, it still amounted to a media revolution of sorts. For awhile, scrolls and codices coexisted, but in time, the book as we know it completely replaced scrolls. The earliest reference to a work of literature being produced as a codex comes from the Roman poet Martial, who recommended that his small, pithy poems be copies onto parchment and made into small codices, easy to carry and read. Perhaps that's why so many of the early Christians preferred the codex, since it was not only easily portable, but cheaper to produce, with text being written on both sides of each sheet, making it possible to hold over 200 pages. A scroll of even 100 pages would be heavy and hard to carry. Judging by the archaeological evidence, these early Christians may have been among the earliest users of this new medium. The oldest Christian codex found dates to the first half of the second century, a tiny fragment of the Gospel of John, a small eight-inch square that would have run about 130 pages. A codex dating to around 200 AD including all of Paul's letters runs to 208 pages. Trying to carry around a scroll of that size would have been impractical. As a matter of fact, many scholars believe that the codex was a Christian innovation, since so much literarture of that period was still copied onto scrolls, and the use of the codex by Christian writers stands out in striking contrast.

Portability and cheapness may not have been the only reason why the codex became a preferred medium for early Christians. For one thing, followers of many of the rabbis during this time probably used the notebook form to write down the sayings of their teachers, and this would have applied to those followers of Jesus. Furthermore, the codex made it easier for this new scriptural culture that must have cross-referenced often as a new practice of reading. A scroll might be fine for a linear reading experience, but it's quite difficult to jump back and forth in a text, and almost impossible to read aloud short passages from different parts of the text in quick succession. Codices accommodated such need for random access to documents that were in the process of becoming scripture, allowing--even encouraging--readers to make connections between disparate passages.

It was still unusual for a codex to run more than 100 pages. Most were shorter. Unlike modern tomes, the codex's "storage capacity" was still limited. It would take centuries before anything resembling today's bibles could be produced. Furthermore, it took several centuries before there was any kind of agreement on what would have constituted such a "bible." Christianity got along quite well in those early centuries without any Bible. Congregations used various collections of codices and boxed scrolls. Some might have used just one gospel or collection of letters, and the gospel they used might not have been one of the four "canonoical" gospels of Matthew, Mark Luke or John, but any one of dozens of other writings. Thus, the closing of the cannon and the binding of it into a single big book seems to have gone hand in hand.

The early history of Christianity included periods of persecution; not only were Christians martyred under Diocletian, but orders were given that all scriptures should be burned. It is impossible to know how many books were lost, or to what lengths the early Christian's went to protect some copies. But perhaps it explains why, even when Constantin's conversion cleared the way for Christian worship, one of hte most important tasks of the Church was to compile accurate copies of its sacred texts, and to get rid of those it considered heretical. After Constantine's conversion and recognition of Christianity as the official religion of the Empire, it took another half-century before the technology of the codex had reached the point that it was possible to produce a single volume that could accomodate a canon of scriptures. The world's oldest Christian Bible, the *Codex Sinaiticus*, is the earliest complete New Testament and one of the two earliest copies of the Old, created in the mid-4th century. Eusebius of Caesarea claimed that in 331 Constantine commissioned him to produce fifty Bibles, one for each of the fifty churches he planned to found. They were to be "sacred Scriptures . . . written on prepared parchment in a legible manner, and in a convenient, portable form, by professional transcribers thoroughly practiced in their art." None of these copies have survived, and chances are they would not have been whole Bibles, but probably a few of the Gospel books. Even at that time, it would have been difficult to produce such a large, portable codex. And as Eusebius makes clear in his catalogue of "undisputed," "disputed," and "heretical" Christian writings, the canon of the New Testament was not yet fixed. Nevertheless, romantically minded scholars have speculated that two of these copies survive today in the shape of the *Codex Sinaiticus* and *Codex Vaticanus*. The Codex Sinaiticus was discovered in 1844 in the library of Saint Catherine's Monastery on Mount Sinai, the world's oldest Christian monastery (founded by Emperor Justinian). At some point during its history, the manuscript was unbound and parts were used to bind other books, but what remained in the library was still enormously impressive. It was seen by Constantine Tischendorf, a visitng German scholar, in 1843, and he was given 43 leaves, which he took home to Leipzig. He was shown almost all of the rest of the manuscript on a later visit, and was lent it so that he could make a copy. In his accounts of finding the *Codex*, Tischendorf claimed that the manuscript was being kept in a basket for the fire and that he therefore "rescued" it. Alternative accounts suggest this was a mistake in Tischendorf's understanding: parchment does not burn well and the monastery traditionally kept, and still keeps, books in baskets in the library rather than on bookshelves. Given that much of the manuscript was put under significant pressure, in 1869 it was agreed to donate the *Codex* to the Tsar of Russia. It was obviously a matter of great personal interest to the imperial government of the time, which went to considerable lengths to obtain the *Codex*, proudly housing it in the Hermitage in St. Petersburg. After the Bolshevik Revolution, many in the West feared for the safety of the precious manuscript, though in fact it remained carefully protected. When Stalin was in need of hard currency to pay for his undustrialization program, he sold it to the British Museum for 100,000 pounds. When the manuscript went on display in 1933, the queue of visitors stretched from the Reading Room all the way to Great Russell Street. Men removed their hats in a gesture of reverence as they approached the book.

From the loose pages found in the waste bin, scholars have reconstructed the Codex and figure it would have contained about 700 pages of parchment. There's a great deal of animal hide, and from an analysis of the handwriting, it appears that three or four scribes wrote the text. It is not totally indentical in contents to the canon as we now have it: its Old Testament includes some Apocryphal Jewish texts but is missing others that eventually were included, and its collection of Christian Scriptures includes two texts that eventually did not make the canonical cut: the Letter to Barnabus and an abbreviated version of an early Christian text known as the Shepherd of Hermes. It wasn't that these extra writings were not regarded as special or edifying for Christians, just that they were not suitable to be read aloud in church worship.

By the 4th Century, Christian literature becomes *the* literature of most of the Middle Ages, but in that first century after the birth of Jesus, that century we call the Silver Age of Latin poetry, it was as if there were two streams feeding the great ocean of poetry, one pagan and mainstream, and the other Christian, a small tributary with hardly any pretension of even being considered literature or poetry. These early Christian writings were almost becoming a genre in themselves for which there was no precedent. Are the *Gospels* history or narrative non-fiction? Is the *Acts of the Apostles* biography or history? We're not even sure who wrote them, even though the names of the early apostles and evangelists (from the Greek word *euangelion*, "Good News") were assigned to them decades later. Despite recent efforts to argue the contrary, they can scarcely have been the real authors, and it's doubtful their authors can ever be truly determined. The *Gospels* reached their final form between 35 and 60 years after Jesus's death, but from the historian's point of view, these works present their main purpose not to give historical accounts, but to edify, to spread belief in the divinity of Jesus; they were not designed primarlity as historical evidence. While some lines of Jesus's career and thinking can be reconstructed, in terms of biography, and some passages can be used for historical information, there are other parts than can only be called narrative non-fiction, or possibly even narrative fiction, whose main purpose was to help legitimize the early Church. And what about Paul's letters; can we compare Paul's letters to those letters Ovid wrote in exile? Do Ovid's letters, in which he practically begs Augustus to rescind his exile, fall into the category of literature, and do Paul's letters to the various Christian congregations fall into the categroy of theological and organizational communications from the CEO of a new company? What about the sayings of Jesus; do they compare to the philosophical precepts of the Greek and Latin philosophers, such as Plato and Lucretius? Or do they fall short in failing to achieve a synthesis and overarching philosophy? Can we compare the philosophic ideas in New Testament writing that dealt with the notion of incarnation and the mutability of the universe with Plato's cosmogony as set forth in the *Timaeus*? Is there a fair philosophic comparison between Plato's treatment of the dialectical problems about being, identity, and difference, with the distinctive features of Chrisitan ethics in the parables of Jesus? Do the miniature stories or parables—the "Wise and Foolish Wives," "The Bad and Good Use of Talents," "The Great Man's Rejected Supper," "The Return of the Prodigal Son," etc.—do they compare to Socrates' explanation of love in the *Symposium* or Plato's metaphor of the cave in chapters six and seven of the *Republic*? (There was nothing like the parables in the writings of Jewish spiritual teachers before Jesus used them, and it was only after his death that they emerge as a literary form in later Judaism, but collectively, do they compare philosophically to Plato's famous metaphors, at least in terms of literary genres?) Can we evaluate these early Christian writings solely as literature, and if so, what into what genre do they fall? Or do we have to wait until the 4th Century when a distinctive Christian literature emerges using classical forms and genres? Many of the non-canonical writings were written in the later second and third century, that "Age of Iron and Rust" that followed the "Silver Age," writings such as: The Gospel of the Savior (150 AD), the Proto-Gospel of James (160 AD), The Coptic Gospel of Peter (3rd century), The Acts of Thomas (3rd century), The Secret Book of John (late 2nd Century), The Hymn of the Pearl (late 2nd century), On the Origin of the World (late 3rd century), The Shepherd of Hermas (2nd century), The Treatise on the Resurrection (late 2nd century), The Acts of Peter (end of 2nd century), The Second Treatise of the Great Seth (3rd century), The Gospel of Mary (late 2nd century) The Gospel According to the Hebrews (mid-2nd century), etc. None of these books made it into the official canon, but during those early centuries they circulated as widely perhaps as the gospels that did become canonical. Are we to treat these early Christian writings as literature in and of themselves, or as something else that nevertheless *influenced* later literature? One could construct two kinds of academic courses: "The Bible *as* Literature," or "The Literature of the Bible." In the former, everything written in both the Old and New Testaments would be considered from a strictly literary point of view, whereas in the latter, only those parts that have literary merit would be studied. Because this study is focused more on poetry than prose literature, only those parts of the Bible written in the form of poetry will be looked at, but the impact of the Bible on world poetry is so great that some consideration of both the Hebrew and Christian Testaments is required. Before moving on to the poetry of the 2nd and 3rd centuries, often called "The Age of Iron and Rust," we'll look at both the Hebrew Bible and the Christian New Testament.

We can hardly imagine that a cultivated citizen of the Empire (both East and West) would have encountered the writings of early Christians as literature, *per se*. Who among the Roman elite was reading these religious texts other than those who had become dissilusioned with the pagan gods and were looking for something else? Though there is great literary value in many parts of the New Testament, as well as parts of the dozens of non-canonical books, they were no more thought of as literature than we would consider a cookbook (apologies to Julia Child) or a How-To book (apologies to Carpentry Made Easy) or any number of self-help books (apologies to The Seven Habits of Highly Efficient People) as literature. But once Constantine officially recognized Christianity as the state religion in 313 AD (via the Edict of Milan), Christian writers were free to create, not just theological tracts and religious books, but works of literature with a capital L. Just as Greek and Roman poets used their myths and legends as background for their literature, Christians began writing epic poems based on the stories in the Old Testament, on the narratives of Jesus' life in the Gospels, and on other writings being circulated, but not yet canonized. Latin and Greek poetry written from the 4th century onwards can now be divided into two distinct types: Christian poetry and Secular poetry, but they are equal in quantity, each just as significant as the other, two broad rivers existing side by side.

Unless we count the poems of Commodian (who some scholars say wrote mid-3rd Century, while others date his writings to the 5th century), the earliest Christian Latin poem (as a poem *per se*, not exclusively a theological tract) was *The Phoenix* by Lactantius, written around the middle of the 3rd Century, 50 years before Constantine's edict. After Lactanius converted to Christianity, all his so-called pagan poems were destroyed, either by the Chruch or by himself. Thus, there is some dispute as to whether *The Phoenix* was written before his conversion or afterwards, since the poem is not specifically Christian and there is nothing in the poem that overtly points to it's theological intention. The story is based on the oriental myth of the phoenix, the bird which is supposed to live for centuries, then consumes itself in flames, only to be reborn from its own ashes. The myth appears in both Greek and Roman writers such as Herodotus and Ovid. From a Christian standpoint, one could easily interpret the phoenix as a symbol of resurrection, and in the centuries that followed, many Christian readers did just that. Furthermore, the description of the phoenix's home in the East parallels the description of paradise in Genesis, and there are many other passages that echo passages in the Bible. So *The Phoenix* serves as a bridge between secular (or pagan) poetry written during Rome's Silver Age (which came to an end around 140 AD, and the Latin secular poetry written in the 2nd and 3rd centuries, an age commonly called "The Age of Iron and Rust." After Constantine, it's possible to separate Secular Latin poetry and Christian Latin Poetry, but before Constantine (except for maybe Lactantius's poem on the phoenix), there is no Christian poetry or literature *per se*, (who would have read it?, since many early Christians tended to be from the urban poor, and perhaps illiterate) except for those few prose works written by influential Christian writers, scholars, and theologians such as Irenaeus of Lyons (c.140-220), Tertullian, "the Father of Latin Christianity" (160-220), Clement of Alexandria (c.150-215), and Origen of Adamantius (185-254), whose audience would have been other theologians debating the often controversial tenents of the young religion. But their works were not intended as literature to be read for pleasure and entertainment. Those writers were attempting to establish an orthodoxy, winnowing out heretical texts. Tertulllian—Quintus Septimius Florens Tertullianus, anglicised as Tertullian—was the first Christian author to produce an extensive corpus of Latin Christian literature. He is perhaps most famous for being the oldest extant Latin writer to use the term "Trinity," giving the oldest extant formal exposition of a Trinitarian theology. Because of certain theological positions he took (including the fact that he became a Montanist), Tertullian was eventually declared a heretic. But except for these theological tracts, and the poems of Lactantius (and maybe Commodian, depending on where we place him chronologically), there was no Christian literature, one reason being that there just wasn't a large enough audience for it. Constantine's toleration and official recognition of Christianity was to change all that. By the 4th and 5th centuries, a distinctly Christian literature emerged, certainly to be read for instruction and edification, but also meant to rival the great works of pagan literature themselves, such as Virgil's *Aenid*, Ovid's *Metamorphosis*, and Homer's two great epics, the *Odyssey* and the *Illiad*.

If we mark the Silver Age of Latin poety as beginning after the death of Augustus in 14 AD (or with the death of Ovid in 17 AD), and ending with the death of Hadrian in 140 AD, (or the death of Juvenal in 138 AD), then we have to ask ourselves the age-old question, what was going on back at the ranch in that period between Christ's crucifixion and the date of the last of the canonical writing, *The Book of Revelation* by John the Divine, written around 120 AD? It may have been a Silver Age for Latin poetry, but it was a Golden Age for Christian writings, considering the fact that out of that period emerged the books that would eventually be canonized into the New Testament. But we should not forget that for some time, at least in the century we are talking about here (that is, Rome's Silver Age, which lasted until about 140 AD), these gospels and other writings were in fact considered sacred books, read and revered by those who considered themselves to be Christian. In terms of literature, then, the left column lists what was going on in the big city, by both the major and minor poets; the column on the right is what was going on back at the ranch.

SILVER AGE:
from approximately death of Augustus (14 AD) or Ovid (17 AD))
to death of Emperor Hadrian (138 AD) or Juvenal (140 AD)

SILVER AGE POETS	CHRISTIAN WRITINGS
Persius, d. 62 AD	The Letters of Paul, 50 AD
Lucan, d. 65 AD	The Gospel of Mark, 65-70 AD
Phaedrus, c. 15 BC - c. 50 AD	The Gospel of Matthew, 80-85 AD
Petronius, d. 66 AD	The Gospel of Luke, 80-85 AD
Abronius Silo, d 50 AD ?	The Acts of the Apostles, 80-90 AD
Marcus Manilius, fl 50s	The Gospel of John, 90-95 AD
Titus Calpurnius Siculus, 40 AD	The Revelation of John, ca.120 AD
Lucillius (fl. 60s AD)	The Gospel of the Nazareans, 90-110 AD
Calpurnius, fl 60s AD	Letter to the Hebrews, 65 AD
Statius, d. 96 AD	The Letter of 1 Clement, 95-100 AD
Martial, d. 102 AD	The Gospel of the Ebionites, 100-120 AD
Juvenal, d. 140 AD	Gospel According to the Egyptians, 110AD
Marcus Manilius, d ca 60 AD	The Gospel of Peter, 110 AD
Phaedrus, 15BC-50AD	The Didache ("The Teaching"), 90-120 AD
Silius Italicus, 28-103 AD	The Coptic Gospel of Thomas, 120 AD
Valerius Flaccus, d. 90 AD	The Apocryphel Letter of Barnabas, 130 AD
	The Preachings of Peter, ca 130-140 AD

The Secret Gospel of Mark, 65-60 AD

The *Shepherd* of Hermas, ca 130 AD

Pauline Letters to Colossians, Thessalonians,
and Ephesians, 85 AD

Epistle of Ignatius, 107 AD

The Apocalypse of Peter, ? 90-140 AD

There were dozens more gospels, epistles, revelatory writings, and narratives written over the course of the next century, many being widely read and accepted as canonical, many contradicting each other, many turning out to be forgeries, and many espousing doctrines that were becoming heretical. As the Church grew and Bishops began to assert their authority over hundreds of congregations from Rome to Asia Minor, it became apparent that there had to be some sort of official statement regarding those writings that were considered "orthodox" (the right belief) and those writings that were considered "heretical" (false belief). In the second half of the second century, Irenaeus, Bishop of Lyons, approved a four-gospel canon in order to ostracize unwanted aprocryphal gospels; he accepted only the familiar gospels of Matthew, Mark, Luke, and John as scripture, justifying this number on the grounds that it was divinely ordained. Various lists of approved writings were drawn up over the next hundred years, but the most significant was that by Athanasius, bishop of Alexandria (ca. 297-373), who wrote a letter listing the twenty-seven books found today in the New Testament. Athanasius' New Testament was generally recognized in 393, at the synod in Hippo Regius, North Africa, but there was no official churchwide pronouncement on the matter until the Council of Trent in the mid-sixteenth century, by which time the 27-book NewTestament had been in use for well over a millenium. But it was in that first century, when Rome had entered its Silver Age, with poets such as Lucan, Statius, Martial, Persius, Petronius, and Juvenal writing their greatest work, that hundreds of gospels, letters, sermons, biographies, narratives, teachings, and other apocalyptic work were circulating throughout the Empire. Many such gospels continued to be written after the *Revelation of John* (120 AD) and the death of Emperor Hadrian (138 AD), when, for all intents and purposes, the Silver Age of Rome came to an end, and "The Age of Iron and Rust" was about to begin. We'll discuss the poetry of that age in a later chapter, but not before we've looked at the literature of both the Old and New Testament, not only for those parts that can be considered "poetry," but because both the Hebrew Bible (The Old Testament) and the Christian Bible (The New Testament) had an influence on Western literature and poetry that was so pervasive as to be almost incalculable.

THE BIBLE

Works of the Old Testament written from 12th to 2nd century BC
Hebrew Bible finally "canonized" around 150 BC
New Testament written between 70-100 AD

Septaugint (Greek) - 250 BC
The Vulgate (Latin) - 400 AD
The Masoretic Text (Hebrew) 6th to 10 centuries AD
King James Authorized Version (English) 1611
Modern translations into English based on above sources

isaiah

jeremiah

psalms

song of songs

proverbs

job

ecclesiastes

Walt Whitman: "Paean to Evolution"
Walter Benton: *This is My Beloved*
Samuel Beckett: *Waiting for Godot*
Charles Bukowski: "The Tragedy of the Leaves"
Weldon Kees: "If This Room is Our World"
William Blake: *Illustrations to the Book of Job*

William Blake from Illustrations to Book of Job

We have no Latin poems on Christian themes dating from the first three centuries of the Christian era, perhaps because those that were written have been lost, or because the language of the Church during this period was Greek rather than Latin, even in the West. It was mainly Jewish and hellenistic sources that had the main influence on the liturgy of the early Church. Even the Christian hymnody that flourished alongisde the psalms were in Greek and Syriac, rather than Latin. It wasn't until the fourth century that we find a Latin hymnody, specifically as developed by Hilary of Poitiers and Ambrose. It's unlikely a Christian in these early centuries would have written poetry because poetry was associated with pagan culture. And there's also the question of literacy, in that early converts to Christianity probably did not have the training in classical Latin to even write poetry, even if they wanted to.

All that changed once Constantine recognized the Christian religion. It not only became tolerated in the 4th century, but gained significant numbers of converts, especially among the nobility, and from the 4th to the 6th century we find a prodigious body of literature in Latin deriving its inspiration and content from both the Old and the New Testament. There were advances in book production, in work on the Biblical text and revision of its translation into Latin from Greek and Hebrew. Poets produced hundreds of poems, epic and lyrical based on the Bible, explaing the meaning of scripture. So before we look at the poetry written in Latin during the 3rd and 4th Centuries by both pagan and Christian poets, now would be a good time to consider the Bible, and the biblical texts that were considered poetry, namely, Psalms, the Book of Job, the Song of Songs, Jeremiah, Isaiah, Proverbs, and Ecclesiastes.

The influence of the Bible on English and European literature has been so pervasive as to be almost incalculable. The spread of Christianity generated an enormous body of writing, which, supplementing and accompanying the Bible, has served as the foundation for much of Western literature and Christian culture. In his *God: A Biography*, Jack Miles writes:

> But whether the ancient writers who wrote the Bible created God or merely wrote down God's revelation of himself, their work has been, in literary terms, a staggering success. It has been read aloud every week for two thousand years to audiences who have received it with utmost seriousness and consciously sought to maximize its influence upon themselves. In this, it is certainly without parallel in Western literature and probably without parallel in all literature. The Qur'an comes immediately to mind, but Muslims do not regard the Qur'an as literature: It occupies, for them, a metaphysical niche all its own. Jews and Christians, by contrast, while revering the Bible as more than mere literature, do not deny that it is *also* literature and generally concede that it may be appreciated as such without blasphemy.

The Bible obviously played a key role in the work of early Christian authors. In the pre-Nicene period (ie., up to 325 CE—Common Era) perhaps only Tertullian (ca. 160-225), that fierce controversialist, moralist, and apologist, has retained an important place in the Western literary canon. During the first few centuries of the Common Era, many poets and writers struggled with the conflict over their love of classical Greek and Roman literature and their duty to supplant that pagan body of writing with Biblical themes and stories. Even into the 17th century, John Milton debated over what subject should be the focus for his planned epic—a Greek or Roman classical story? The national Arthurian myth? or something from the Bible, maybe the story of man's fall and redemption? Perhaps we could point to *Paradise Lost* (1667) and *Paradise Regained* (1671) as representing a high point of Biblical influence on English literature.

In the early centuries after Christ, the conflict was even more pronounced. The Augustinian notion that classical literature ought to be appropriated to Christian use, "baptized" by subordination to biblical and catechetical rewriting, became a strong mandate for poets and writers. And with the decline of the Roman Empire and the subsequent decline in literacy in the centuries that followed, most of those who took up the pen were monks and clerics.

Jerome (ca 342-420) not only produced the first great translation of the Bible, the *Vulgate*, but some of the most brilliantly rhetorical letters in any language. He is generally considered the supreme stylist of Christian Latinity. Unlike other important Christians of the fourth century, he held no great office in the church. He was a scholar and schoolteacher, a private man who might have been a poet or a dramatist in another era. His life revolved around two poles: the Christian church and the love of language. Possessing one of the great literary minds of his day, he was enormously sensitive to the meaning and esthetic of words. Words were beautiful in and of themselves, and their essential meaning was their literary meaning. This must have been difficult for him considering the authority of the church; language has its own internalizing ethic, and individualistic base that can be threatening to any monolithic system that demands a chorus or litany. This sensitivity to the meaning of words was reflected in his early sturggles to find Christian justification for the literary approach, reflected by his famous nightmare. In letter XXII, Jerome tells of a dream in which he saw himself dragged before the judgment seat and asked about his condition. Claiming to be a Christian, he was abruptly contradicted, "You lie. You are a Ciceronian. `Where your treasure is, there will your heart be also.' [Matthew 6.21]" The scene reveals Jerome's ambivalence and guilt (and that of countless Christian intellectuals like him) about his love of classical literature, which persisted, despite this warning from on high.

Another offshoot of Biblical influence was the tradition of hymns and religious poetry in Latin, introducing the use of rhyme, which was then adopted by writers of vernacular verse.

The supreme literary work of the late Middle Ages was Dante's *Divine Comedy*, completed by the second decade of the 14th century. Though his poem drew upon science, philosophy, and history, as well as theology, it was supremely indebted to the Bible, especially in the way he brought important Biblical figures into his epic canvas. What he is unable to avoid is the devil's disconcerting way of having all the best lines: just as Satan ends up the most interesting character in *Paradise Lost*, so Dante's *Inferno* is superior to the *Purgatorio* and *Paradiso* in dramatic power. Some of the most memorable moments come when those who have been damned tell their tragic tales, often with a grandeur of soul not lessened by the fact that they remain eternally condemned by God.

INFLUENCE ON ENGLISH LITERATURE

Since the Christianization of Britain in the 7th century, the Bible has been by far the most important of foundational texts for English literature. In the earliest days of written English, the Bible effectively established the literary canon. Even in the modern period, though this definitive influence has declined dramatically, we may still say that the Bible remains the most widely alluded to of all texts in works by English speaking poets and writers.

The impact of the Bible on vernacular English literature involved a strong tradition of narrative works that may be described as biblical paraphrase and abridgement, including the famous 14th century cycle plays of York, Chester, Wakefield, Lincoln, and Coventry. These plays were presented by the various regions as part of multiday pageants. Covering the biblical history of salvation from creation to the Last Judgement, these plays represent the most extensive adaptation of the Bible to vernacular literary use in the history of English letters. Since very few people had sufficient Latin to read the *Vulgate*, such vernacular works were a principal source of their biblical knowledge. Other writers took individual Bible stories and turned them into romance narratives.

Another stream of biblical influence can be found in the poem *Sir Gawain and the Green Knight* with its emphasis on the search for the Holy Grail. Chaucer reveals rich appreciation of biblical literature in his *Cantebury Tales*, even if used variously for humor and parody.

By the Protestant Reformation and the Renaissance in the 16th century, the influence of the Bible showed itself not only in the emergence of previously neglected themes and narratives such as the stories of Samson and Ruth, but in idiom, phrase, and cadence of the various translations into English, culminating in the *Authorized King James Version*, rightly regarded as the high-water mark in English literary prose. Eventually the power of the prose-cadence of the King James Version worked its way into English poetic diction. Nowhere else has the effect of the Bible on literary language been so all-pervasive. Writers, poets, and playwrights could assume their audiences had an intimate familiarity with the Bible.

Throughout his work, Shakespeare draws heavily on the Geneva Bible (1560) to encode and enrich his plays, whether in romances like the *Winter's Tale*, or history plays like *Henry IV* (Parts 1 and 2). Shakespeare was able to critique the Puritans in *Measure for Measure* by taking the text from Matthew 7 and setting it in a rich context of quotations from Paul's letter to the Romans, which was frequently featured in the Puritans' own sermons.

It's really impossible to summarize the influence of the Bible on the growth of literature in English. Milton made two very significant choices when he wrote *Paradise Lost*: one was the choice of English over Latin, just as Dante chose Italian over Latin when he wrote the *Divine Comedy*; the other was his rejection of a classic Greek tale or English myth such as the Arthurian cycle and choosing instead subject matter from the Bible. But even when religious influence suffered a sharp demise due to the dismal failure of the Puritan Commonwealth under Oliver Cromwell and the Restoration under Charles II, the Bible's influence was still felt at the level of language and allusion, or allegorical devices. Poets commonly used biblical paraphrases, especially from passages in the *Book of Job* or Psalms.

With William Blake, English literature entered another strong period of biblical influence, even though Blake created his own "reading" and "rewriting" of the Bible to suit his myth. A measure of the literary power of the Bible in overcoming religious consideration is the complete dominance of the King James Version from its first publication until well into the 20th century; even James Joyce prefered the cadences of the English translation in making his numerous inversions.

We can find the same use of allusions and parable in the poems of Yeats, Gerard Manley Hopkins, T.S. Eliot (*Ash Wednesday*), Robert Frost (*A Masque of Reason*), Marianne Moore, William Carlos Williams, Langston Hughes, Countee Cullen, and Ted Hughes (*Crow*), not to mention writers such as Gustave Flaubert, Marcel Proust, Franz Kafka, Saul Bellow (*The Adventures of Auggie March*), Walker Percy (*Love in the Ruins*), John Steinbeck (*East of Eden* & *The Grapes of Wrath*), Ernest Hemingway (*The Sun Also Rises, The Old Man and the Sea*, etc), William Faulkner (*Go Down Moses,* etc.), Katherine Anne Porter (*Pale Horse, Pale Rider*), James Baldwin (*Go Tell It On The Mountain*, and *The Fire Next Time*), John Updike, and Isaac Bashevis Singer.

TRANSLATIONS

Few people were put to death for translating the *Aeneid* or Dante's *Commedia* into English. Translations of the Bible have not only been significant for their literary impact, but their political significance as well. Making it possible for the average person to directly access the Bible could be a bloody business, since the wrong word or phrase could be considered heretical by church leaders.

During the Middle Ages, only those who knew Latin well could read the Bible. Most depended upon the explanations, interpretations, and paraphrases of leading churchmen, or in the popular English cycle plays. But with the invention of the printing press and movable type, that limitation was removed and almost anyone could own and read (and even interpret) the Bible. Martin Luther's translation into an earthy and vigorous German was of unparalleled importance. Likewise, the Bible's translation into English by William Tyndale and his successors, culminating in 1611 with the King James Version, re-invigorated its influence on poetry and prose.

THE OLD TESTAMENT

The Old Testament (as it is called by Christians) or the Hebrew Bible is a collection of works composed at various times from the 12th century to the 2nd century BCE. The word "bible" comes from the Latin *biblia* ("little books"), and derives ultimately from the Greek name for an ancient Syrian city renowned for its papyrus industry: Byblos. In a sense, when we speak of the Hebrew Bible we are dealing with a series of books, a library, if you will. Most of the books were written in classical Hebrew, except for brief portions which were written in Aramaic. Very few of these manuscripts (or books) survived the destruction of Jerusalem in 70 CE. The Hebrew Bible finally achieved the form we know today in the 2nd century BCE. Its Books comprise virtually all that has survived of ancient Hebrew Literature to about 150 BCE. A selection process excluded certain books believed not to have been written under divine inspiration. According to Jewish tradition, there were 24 books considered sacred that became part of the "canon" of the Jewish Bible.

Canonization of the Bible

This process of canonization seems to have occurred in three stages over a period of several centuries: first the Five Books of Moses (The Pentateuch), then the Prophets, then the Writings (or Hagiographa—"holy writings). Once the books of the Bible were set in their order, the Bible became one single book, the story of God and His people. While many books of the Bible such as Genesis became the foundation of numerous poems written in the 3rd and 4th Century of the Christian era by Christian poets, the books of the Bible that concern us, as poetry *per se*, are several in the third section, The Writings. They include *Psalms*, *Proverbs*, *Job*, *Song of Songs*, and *Ecclesiastes*. We'll also look at the work of some of the prohets, especially the book of *Isaiah* for its great poetic power.

The Five Books of Moses did not attain their final form until some time after the Babylonian Exile at the end of the 6th century BCE when 90% of the population of the Kingdom of Judah was deported to Babylon. This deportation, and their dispersion generations later to Israel and other parts of the world—called the Diaspora—loomed large as a chronological hinge in biblical composition. The sources and writing for the Hebrew Bible go back as early as 1200-800 BCE, and the oral traditions from which they drew go back even further. The "writing" Prophets flourished from the eighth down to the fifth century BCE, and they employ many devices of powerful rhetoric, often rising to the heights of great poetry. Some of these books were composed after the Babylonian Exile, but probably contain earlier elements. A Greek translation of the First Five Books (the *Pentateuch*) was completed by the close of the third century BCE and the Prophetic books in the second.

By 150 BCE the Hebrew Bible was complete. No original manuscripts have survived, and present versions are based on two primary sources: The *Septaugint*, a Greek translation from the Hebrew, made in Alexandria about 250 BCE, and the *Masoretic Text*, the work of a group of trained Jewish scholars, beginning in the 6th century after Christ, whose purpose was to correct and preserve the Hebrew versions then available. The *Masoretic Text* was completed by the end of the 10th century.

The *Septaugint* became the accepted Christian version of the Old Testament, while the *Masoretic Text* has remained the Hebrew canon.

☛ The Septuagint, Greek Translation (250 BCE)

Most of the Jews in Alexandria spoke Greek. To acquaint the Greeks with the Jewish religious tradition, and to enable the Jews who knew no Hebrew to read the scriptures, a group of Alexandrian Jewish scholars began the Greek translation about 250 BCE. The legend tells how Ptolemy II had an accurate Hebrew manuscript sent from Jerusalem to Alexandria. He then invited seventy-two Jewish scholars from Judea representing the twelve tribes to come to Alexandria, where they were housed each in a separate room and forbidden to communicate until they had finished their translation of the *Pentateuch*. Legend continues that when all seventy versions were done, they were compared and found to agree word for word, proving that the original was divinely inspired, and so were the translators. Thus, the Greek version of the Hebrew Bible came to be known as the *hermeneia kata tous hebdomekonta*—the *Interpretation According to the Seventy*—in Latin, *Interpretatio Septuaginta*—in English, the "Septaugint." This was the Bible used by Philo and St. Paul. It remains to this day the authoritative biblical text of the Greek Orthodox church.

Since the *Septuagint* dates from a time prior to the stabilization of the Hebrew text in the 1st century BCE, it serves as an important witness, alongside the biblical manuscripts found in 1947 near the Dead Sea, to early textual reforms of the Hebrew Bible.

☛ The Masoretic Text (6th - 10th century)

Ancient texts such as the Hebrew Bible were transmitted over the centuries in various forms, at first in scrolls, later in manuscripts of codex format, and in recent centuries in printed editions. The Torah scrolls used today in synagogues resemble the ancient format, sheets of leather sewn together into large scrolls. A codex consists of any number of sheets (leather, parchment) bound together into a book. Scrolls contained individual biblical books, while codices could contain most of all of the Hebrew Bible. The ancient text of the Bible was first transmitted in scrolls; after the use of codices for the New Testament and other ancient literature, the codex form began to be used as well.

Often there were several manuscript copies of a biblical book, each with slight variations. Instead of a single master being preserved, generations of scribes added new details to the manuscript and scrolls they copied, increasing the number of different texts. Many of the texts fell out of use for one reason or another, but by the Roman period there evolved several "families" of texts, and one of these became the basis for the official version of the text of the Hebrew Bible ("the received text"), which in centuries to follow was called the Masoretic Text. From comparison with the Dead Sea Scrolls and other texts found at Qumran since 1947, it appears that there was a tendency to establish a single unified text around the turn of the 2nd century, but this ideal was never fully achieved. At no time did there exist one "Masoretic" text; there always were several different ones.

The *Masoretic Text* known to us today was created in the early Middle Ages. Learned scribes involved in the transmission of the biblical text developed different systems for the vocalization of vowels and other data, but the system finally accepted by all western Jewish communities was the Tiberian system devloped by Moshe Ben-Asher in the tenth century.

☛ **The Vulgate**, 405 (St. Jerome, b. 340)

A Latin translation by St. Jerome was begun in 382 CE. Jerome left Rome and built a monastery at Bethlehem, of which he became head. He made his own cell in a cave, gathered his books and papers there, gave himself up to study, composition, and administration, and lived there the remaining thirty-four years of his life. It took him eighteen years of patient scholarship to finish the *Vulgate*; some of the "barbarisms" of common speech offended the purists. His earliest biblical translations were made from Origen's revision of the *Sepuagint*, but after several years he boldly turned to the Hebrew original as a better source, and turned Hebraic emotion and imagery into poetic Latin expressions. Many consider this translation the greatest and most influential literary accomplishment of the fourth century. Some consider the accomplisment revolutionary in that he successfully overthrew the authority of the *Sepuagint* within the Latin church. Jerome's difficulty integrating his literary genius with the litanistic approach of the church found its true expression in this monumental project. The translation had to communicate the Holy Book written in the Greek of an alien Near Eastern people to the Roman world—from ordinary people as well as to scholars. Had he wanted to, he could easily have used the Ciceronian Latin of intellectuals, but instead found a style that was somewhere between literary Latin and the vulgar language of the streets. His "Vulgate" was grammatically correct in every way, yet stroked the ear of demanding scholars. Anyone, no matter what their class or education, could read it—assuming they were literate in the first place. It wasn't Jerome's fault the schools of 5th century Rome failed and there were no literate masses to benefit from this work until the eleventh or twelfth century. Nevertheless, his translation gave to literature a thousand noble phrases of compact eloquence and force, and the Latin world became acquainted with the Bible as never before. The *Vulgate* is still the authorized Roman Catholic version. (The "Douai Bible" is the English version of the *Vulgate*.)

☛ **The Wyclif Bible**, 1380-82; John Wyclif (1330-1384)
The first complete translation of the Bible into English is credited to John Wyclif, though there are two versions and it is uncertain how much of either is the work of Wyclif himself and how much is the work of his colleagues. The Wyclif Bible is almost a word-for-word equivalent of the Vulgate. For 150 years this was the only bible in English, and some 107 manuscript copies have survived. In 1415 the Wyclif Bible was condemned and burned, and 13 years later Wyclif's body was exhumed and burned. The earliest printed edition of Wyclif's New Testament was published in 160 copies at London in 1731; the first printed edition of the complete Wyclif version was issued at Oxford in 1850.

☛ **Tyndale's Bible**, William Tyndale (1494-1536)
William Tyndale, "the Father of the English Bible," was the first person to translate the Bible into English from its original Greek and Hebrew and the first to print the Bible in

English, which he did in exile from 1526 to 1535. Eighteen thousand copies were printed and sold in England, of which only two are known to survive (many were bought by Cuthbert Tunstall, Bishop of London, who burned them publicly). Giving the laity access to the word of God outraged the clerical establishment in England: he was condemned, hunted, betrayed and lured back to England where he was found guilty of heresy, strangled, then burned at the stake. However, his masterly translation formed the basis of all English bibles—including the King James Bible, many of whose finest passages were taken unchanged, though unacknowledged, from Tyndale's work. It's estimated that 90% of his translation was retained in the King James Authorized Version.

Educated at Cambridge, where he may have studied Greek, he got into debates with various clergy and other "learned men," and was soon accused of espousing heretical ideas. One of his opponents argued that Christians were better off without God's law (the scriptures) than without the Pope's laws (Canon Law), to which Tyndale replied, "If God spares my life, before many years I will cause a boy that drives the plough to know more of the scripture than you do!"

As a translator and expositer, not to mention his influence on writers from Shakespeare to those of the twentieth century, Tyndale made an enormous impact on the theology, literature, and humanism of Renaissance and Reformation Europe.

☛ The Geneva Bible, 1560

During the reign of Queen Mary (1553-1558) all printing of English Bibles in England was stopped, and the English Bible could not be used in church services. Many Protestant leaders sought refuge on the Continent. William Whittingham, pastor of the English Church in Geneva, translated the New Testament and served as editor of the Old Testament translation; the Geneva Bible of 1560 was dedicated to Queen Elizabeth. It was printed in roman type, bound in small octavo size, and was the first Englih bible to have verse numbers. It became immensely popular and was the Bible of William Shakespeare and John Bunyan who wrote *Pilgrim's Progress*. It was the Bible of the pilgrims to the New World and the Mayflower Compact, of Oliver Cromwell and his army. Over 150 editions were published, and it remained popular for nearly a hundred years.

☛ The Authorized King James Version, 1611.

When James I became King of England in 1603, there were two competing Bibles: the Bishops' Bible, preferred by the church authorities, and the Geneva Bible, the favorite of the people. A year later he approved of a plan to make a new translation to replace the two Bibles, and this one was to be based on the original Hebrew and Greek, not the Latin translations of the Middle Ages. Fifty-four "learned men" began work on it in 1606 and it was published in 1611, rapidly going through several editions, and became known as the "Authorized Version."

It took about another half century before the 1611 Bible replaced the Geneva Bible in the affection of the people, but once established it became *the* Bible of the English-speaking people, and continues to be one of the most widely read Bibles in English.

In 1870 the Church of England authorized a revision, and in 1885 the complete Revised Version appeared. The Americans published their edition, the American Standard Edition of the Revised Version, popularly known as the **American Standard Version**, in 1901.

☞ The Revised Standard Version (1952)

In the Tyndale-King James tradition, this was a revision of the American Standard Version, which embodied earlier revisions of the King James Version. The Revised Standard Version gained the distinction of being officially authorized for use by all major Christian churches: Protestant, Anglican, Roman Catholic, and Eastern Orthodox.

The New Revised Standard Version, published in 1990, is a model of what a revision of an existing translation should be. In matters of text, exegesis, and language it goes a long way toward becoming the Bible of English speaking readers for generations to come. It has dropped archaic terms and obsolete language, including the pronouns and verb forms used in addressing God.

☞ The New International Version, *(New Testament*, 1973)

When the RSV was published in 1952 it was received not only with appreciation and gratitude but also with bitter criticism and condemnation, especially from conservative Protestants. Because of its sponsorship by the National Council of Churches, this Bible was seen by some as tainted by liberal, if not heretical beliefs. It was even said that the translation committee included Communist sympathizers. Conservatives felt a strong need for a modern translation that they could trust. Several appeared, including the *New American Standard Bible* (1971) intending to preserve and perpetuate the *American Standard Version* as the most faithful Bible translation in English. All were well received, but none achieved the status of the Bible acceptable to a majority of conservative Protestants, most of whom were still using the King James Version. Finally in 1978 the *New International Version* was published. The intense advertising campaign focused on the trustworthiness of the translators and their high view of Scripture. In its various editions this Bible is now widely used, and bids fair to become the Bible for those who still view the RSV (and other modern translations) with suspicion.

☞ The New English Bible (1970) The Revised English Bible (1989)

What may justly be called a landmark in Bible translation was achieved with the publicaiton of *The New English Bible* in 1970. Representing nearly all major Christian denominations in Great Britain and Ireland, this translation broke away completely from the Tyndale-King James tradition. Using all resources of the English language, the translators produced an Engish Bible whose language is fresh and natural, but not slangy or undignified. At times the vocabulary may seem a bit too British for American taste, and many of its textual decisions, especially in the Hebrew Bible, have been criticized as idiosyncratic. But most have recognized this edition as a stunning achievement, and consider the 1989 *Revised English Bible* a bit of a disappointment because it showed a more conservative restraint in exegetical and linguistic decisions. Where the description of

Genesis 1.1 was fresh and vivid, the rendering in the Revised version seems to be hardly distinguishable from the King James Version.

☞ The New American Bible (1970)

Roman Catholics have produced their share of modern translations. American Roman Catholics began a fresh translation of the *Vulgate* in 1937, but with the publication in 1943 of the encyclical *Divino afflante spiritu*, authorizing vernacular translations made directly from the original Hebrew, Aramaic, and Greek texts, the translation was begun anew, and in 1970 *The New American Bible* was published, the first English Bible translated directly from the original texts by American Catholic scholars. A revised edition of the New Testament was issued in 1989.

☞ The New King James Bible (1986)

☞ The Tanakh (1985)

Under the sponsorship of the Jewish Publication Society of America, a group of Jewish scholars headed by Marcus Jastrow produced a new translation in 1917 which became known as the *Jewish Publication Society Bible*. This translation became the standard Bible of the American Jewish community until the appearance of what is known as the *New Jewish Version*, which was published in stages: the *Torah* appeared in 1962, *The Prophets*, in 1978, and the final volume, *The Writings*, appeared in 1981. The complete translation, under the title *Tanakh*, was publsihed in one volume in 1985.

The word Tanakh is a postbiblical acronym dervied from the Hebrew words *torah*, "treaching"; *nebi'im*, "prophets"; and *ketubim*, "writings." Not since the third century BCE, when seventy-two elders of the tribes of Israel created the Greek translation of Scriptures known as the *Septuagint*, has such a broad-based committee of Jewish scholars produced a major Bible translation. These scholars drew upon the entire range of biblical interpretation, ancient and modern, Jewish and non-Jewish, as well as making use of the latest findings in linguistics and archaeology.

ROGUE BIBLES

Not all translations are significant for their religious impact or political controversy. Some are known for the infamous mistakes, incorrect renderings of certain key words. Here's a few to remind us that while God may be perfect, those of us who transmit his words are not. I imagine an angelic jester including these in his latest stand-up routine, giving God a humorous break from the usual Earthly headlines of man's inhumanity to man, and of man's inhumanity to himself.

☞ The Wicked Bible

An edition in which the word *not* is omitted in the seventh commandment, making it "Thou shalt commit adultery." It was printed in 1632 in London by Baker and Lucas, who were fined 300 pounds for their unfortunate error. It's also called the Adulterous Bible.

☞ The Unrighteous Bible

An edition printed at Cambridge in 1653, containing the printer's error, "Know ye not that the unrighteous shall inherit the Kingdom of God?" (1 Cor. 6:9). It should read "shall *not* inherit." The same edition gave Rom. 6:13 as, "Neither yield ye your members as instruments of righteousness unto sin," in place of *un*righteousness."

☞ The Vinegar Bible

This edition was printed in 1917 at the Clarendon Press, Oxford, with the heading to Luke 20, "Parable of the Vinegar" instead of "Parable of the Vineyard."

☞ The Bug Bible

This is the name that has been given to Coverdale's Bible of 1535, the first complete English Bible to be printed. It was published by Miles Coverdale, but is often called the Bug Bible because Psalm 91:5 is translated, "Thou shalt not nede to be afrayed for eny bugges by night," instead of "terror" by night.

But what about them bugges?

☞ Murderers' Bible

An edition of 1801 in which the misprint *murderers* for *murmurers* makes Jude 16 read, "These are murderers, complainers, walking after their own lusts. . . "

☞ Rebecca's Camels Bible

An edition printed in 1823 in which Gen. 24:61 reads, "Rebecca arose, and her camels," instead of "her damsels."   [Yea, but what about them camels?]

☞ Place-makers' Bible

The second edition of the Geneva bible, 1562, so called from the printer's error in Matt. 5:9, "Blessed are the placemakers, for they shall be called the children of God."

☞ Wife-Hater Bible

An edition of 1810 in which the word *life* in Luke 14:26 is printed *wife*. It reads, "If any man comes to me, and hate not his father . . . yea, and his own wife also. . . . "

The Poems of The Old Testament

The spread of Christianity was also responsible for the great influence in literature of the *Hebrew Bible* or the *Old Testament*, which is made up of numerous books, written by many authors, and it is certainly the most influential text in Western literature.

This is not the place to discuss the rich langauge and poetry of the entire Bible and how it has been used by poets and writers. Our interest for this study guide is in those sections than can rightly be emphasized for their poetry, or to be more specific, that are seen as being written as poems, not as prose. I'm not even sure that this is a legitimate distinction, but it's an easier way to begin. So before launching into the Latin poets of the Middle Ages, I think some mention should be made of a few of the important poetical works of the *Hebrew Bible* or *The Old Testament*, and then do the same for the *Gospels* or *The New Testament*.

What is the poetry of the *Bible*? The King James translation used a typographic procedure faithful to the Hebrew manuscript tradition, which ran everything together in dense, unpunctuated columns (there's a few exceptions). Over the centuries, many perceived *Psalms* as poetry, as well as *The Book of Job* and the *Song of Songs* because of the lyric beauty of the latter and the grandeur of the former. *Proverbs* was also seen as poetry. The Prophets cast much of their messages in the poetics of verse. Many prose narratives were interspersed with verse insets.

Aside from line breaks, what other convention could identify it as poetry? Not rhyme or syllable count. Rhyme was not used as a poetic convention until late in the Middle Ages, and syllabic regularity was a feature of Greek poetry and did not occur in the Bible.

Some have argued for "syntactic parallelism"—2 or 3 lines of verse held together by a common meaning or repetition of words or set phrases. "Harken" in one verset might be followed by "heed" or "listen" in the second verset. Other parallel syntactic patterns can be found.

This parallelism of meaning, which is often joined with a balancing of the number of rhythmic stresses between verset or parallel syntatic patterns, seems to have played a role roughly analogous to that of iambic pentameter in Eizabethan and later English poetry. Many verse sequences of the *Old Testament* use dyadic as well as triadic lines in building a symmetrical structure.

Contemporary translations of the Bible recognize internal evidence and indicate with line breaks that the particular book of the *Bible*, or parts of different books of the *Bible* were meant to be taken as poems. The "Hymn to Wisdom" in Job 28 is dividied into three symmetrical strophes marked by a refrain. Recently, the Hebrew verse of the *Book of Job* was rendered into English by Stephen Mitchell, who has also translated Rilke.

☛ Prophets: Isaiah

There were lots of prophets in biblical times. In contrast to the visionary holy men of Buddhist or Hindu faith or the Christian saints who worked toward a spiritual purification, the Prophets were socratic gadflies with a passion, angry and provocative, questioning man's plight, annoyed with mankind's mistakes and mismanagements, disgusted with their ignornace of God's one, true way. Especially when times were marked by crisis, they rose to the heights of passionate and poetic exhortation. The prophets wanted to rouse people from lethargy and complacency; they wanted them to act as God's chosen and set an example for the rest of mankind. Their idea that Jews were specially chosen to be a "light unto the nations" (in the words of the later Isaiah) was later appropriated by both Christian and Muslim thought for their own use and represents one of the central organizational forces of civilization.

They preached a faith of ideas, not just practice. They spoke of this world and of transcendent visions of a world to come. During periods of prosperity, they raged against temporal power, exposing the uselessness of materialism. Man must overcome dismissal of the power of God and his addiction to waging war in the name of blood-line and nationhood.

The Book of Isaiah is a collection of "prophecies" or sermons by two or more authors ranging in time from the 8th to the 4th century BCE. The "First" Isaiah emerged as one of the great figures of Hebrew history during the seige of Jerusalem by the Assyrians in the 8th century. He was a statesmen who tried to counsel his people in a time when they were besieiged on both sides by mighty kingdoms vying for power. He foresaw the fall of the northern kingdom of Samaria, and felt that all the nations were destined to be struck down by God in time.

> Make thy shadow as the night
> in the midst of the noonday;
> hide the outcasts;
> do not betray the fugitives;
>
> Every one shall howl:
> they will howl for the posperous farmers who face ruin;
> for the vineyards that languish;
> the vines whose red grapes used to overpower
> the lords of the nations;
> and trailed out to the winderness
> and their spreading branches crossed the sea.
>
> Therefore, I will weep for the vines
> as I weep for Jazer;
> I shall drench you with tears,
> for the shouts of the enemy have fallen
> on your summer fruits and harvest.
>
> Joy and gladness will be banished from the fields,
> no more will they tread wine in the winepress;
> I have silenced the shouting of the harvesters.
> Though they come to worship
> and weary themselves at the shrines,
> though they flock to their sanctuaries to pray,
> it shall avail them nothing.

Some believe this ardor for ruination, this litany of curses, mars Isaiah's book, as it mars the entire prophetic literature of the Bible. Yet the denunciations of economic exploitation and greed rise to a powerful eloquence seldom matched by modern poltical poetry.

> The Lord opens the indictment against the elders
> and officers of his people:
>
> "It is you that have ravaged the vineyard;
> in your houses are the spoils taken from the poor.

Is it nothing to you
that you crush my people
and grind the faces of the poor?

Woe betide those who add house to house
and join field to field,
until everyone else is displaced,
and you are left as sole inhabitants of the countryside.

Woe betide those who enact unjust laws
and draft oppresive edicts,
depriving the poor of justice,
robbing the weakest of my people of their rights;
plundering the widow and despoiling the fatherless!
What will you do when called to account,
when devastation from afar confronts you?

To whom will you flee for help,
and where will you leave your glory,
and where will you leave your children
so that they do not cower among the prisoners
or fall among the slain?
For all this anger has not abated;
his hand still threatens."

In the end, he sees the coming of a Redeemer who will end their political divisions, their servitude, and their misery, and bring an era of universal brotherhood and peace.

Then the wolf will live with the lamb,
and the leopard will lie down with the kid;
the calf and the young lion will feed them together,
with the little child to tend them.

And they shall beat their swords into plowshares
And their spears into pruning hooks:
Nations shall not lift up
Sword against nation;
Neither shall they learn war anymore.

The book of Isaiah has made a profound and distinctive impression on Jewish literary and religious tradition, and played a central role in Christian liturgy and theology. It has provided liberation theologians and feminists with many of their key scriptural texts. Isaiah is more often quoted in the *New Testament* than is any other book of the *Hebrew Bible* apart from Psalms.

✳

 Psalms

The poetry of *Psalms* has shown great power to speak to countless readers and has echoed through the work of writers as different as Augustine, John Donne, Paul Claudel, Walt Whitman, and Dylan Thomas, to name a few.

The sense of confessional urgency and the desperation of the speaker characterize these poems of supplication—a rising intensity toward a climax of terror or desperation. The speaker confesses to a feeling of despair, prays to God for rescue from the abyss, or asserts by the end of the poem that such wondrous rescue is already taking place. The poems in *Psalms* are imaginative realizations of the experience of crisis and the dramatic reversal at their conclusion.

The poetical literature of the *Hebrew Bible* reaches its finest moments in the *Psalms*, probably written by several poets after the Babylonian Captivity (though we ascribe them to David). They are among the finest examples of lyric poetry in world literature. Psalm is a Greek word, meaing "song of praise" or "a poem sung to the accompaniment of musical instruments." As songs of praise, many of the psalms lapse into extreme flattery. As expressions of pious ecstasy and faith they often become tiresome in their endless adulation of a God who, despite his "lovingkindness," pours "smoke out of his nostrils, and fire out of his mouth." But beyond the threats of Yahweh and military ardor, there are poems and stanzas unequalled for their tender passion, and humble wisdom. The imagery of religious feeling moves us with the same pulse as any lyric of love, no matter how jaded or skeptical the reader. Even the skepticism of the highest intellect longs somehow for a perfection to which it can dedicate life's philosophic quest.

Psalm 23 A Psalm of David The Divine Shepherd

> The Lord is my shepherd, I shall not want.
> He maketh me to lie down in green pastures:
> He leadeth my beside the still waters.
> He restoreth my soul:
> He leadeth me in the paths of righteousness
> For his name's sake.
> Yea, though I walk through the valley of the shadow of death,
> I will fear no evil:
> For thou are with me;
> Thy rod and thy staff they comfort me.
> Thou preparest a table before me in the presence of mine enemies;
> Thou anointest my head with oil; my cup runneth over.
> Surely goodness and mercy shall follow me all the days of my life:
> And I will dwell in the house of the Lord for ever.

139 The Captives Cry for Vengeance

> By the rivers of Babylon, there we sat down,
> yea, we wept when we remembered Zion.
> We hung our harps upon the willows in the midst thereof.
> For there they that carried us away captive required of us a song;
> and they that wasted us required of us mirth, saying,
> Sing us one of the songs of Zion.
> How shall we sing the Lord's song in a foreign land?
> If I forget thee, O Jerusalem, let my right hand forget her cunning.

If I do not remember thee,
let my tongue cleave to the roof of my mouth,
if I prefer not Jerusalem above my chief joy.

FOOD FOR THOUGHT

Whitman's Song of Myself

[44] [A Paean to Evolution]

It is time to explain myself . . . . let us stand up.
What is known I strip away . . . . I launch all men and women forward with me into the unknown.
Were mankind murderous or jealous upon you my brother or my sister?
I am sorry for you . . . . they are not murderous or jealous upon me;
All has been gentle with me . . . . I keep no account with lamentation;
What have I to do with lamentation?

I am an acme of things accomplished, and I an encloser of things to be.

Rise after rise bow the phantoms behind me,
Afar down I see the huge first Nothing, the vapor from the nostrils of death,
I know I was even there . . . . I watied unseen and always,
And slept while God carried me through the lethargic mist,
And took my time . . . . and took no hurt from the foetid carbon.

Before I was born out of my mother generations guided me,
My embryo has never been torpid . . . . nothing could overlay it.

All forces have been steadily employed to complete and delight me,
Now I stand on this spot with my soul.

☛ **Song Of Solomon**, "*I Am My Beloved's*"

Here we catch a sensual element not often found in the *Old Testament*, perhaps because most of its authors were prophets and priests. *Ecclesiastes* reveals a scepticism not otherwise discernible in the edited literature of the ancient Jews, and *Song of Solomon* is an amorous composition earthy and lustful in its passion. We're not entirely sure where it comes from: it could be a collection of songs Babylonian in origin, or the work of Hebrews influenced by the Hellenistic spirit that entered Judea after Alexander conquered the Persians. It's possible that a poet in Alexandria found the dialogue of Egyptian siblings a point of departure for his lyrics of love. And even more than the mystery of how it got into the Bible is its placement between the prophesies of *Isaiah* and the cynical preachments of *Ecclesiastes*.

> *Bride*
> A bundle of myrrh is my well-beloved unto me; he shall lie all night betwixt my breasts.
> My beloved is unto me as a spray of henna blossom in the vineyards of Engedi.

I am a rose of Sharon, a lily growing in the valley.
For see, the winter is past!
The rains are over and gone; the flowers appear in the countryside;
the season of birdsong is come, and the turtle-dove's cooing is heard in our land.
My beloved is mine, . . .
Night after night on my bed I have sought my true love;

Bridegroom
Your lips are like a scarlet thread, and your mouth is lovely;
your parted lips like a pomegranate cut open.
Your two breasts are like two fawns, grazing among the lilies.
You have stolen my heart, my sister, you have stolen my heart, my bride,
With just one of your eyes, one jewel of your necklace.
How beautiful are your breasts, my sister and bride!
Your love is more fragrant than wine, your perfume sweeter than any spices,
Honey and milk are under your tongue,
Your two cheeks are an orchard of pomegranates, an orchard full of choice fruits:
spikehard and saffron, aromatic cane and cinnamon,
My sister, my bride, is a garden close-locked,
    a garden close-locked, a fountain sealed.

Bride
The fountain in my garden is a spirng of running water.
Awake, north wind, and come, south wind!
Blow upon my garden to spread its spices abroad,
that my beloved may come to his garden and enjoy the choice fruit.

Bridegroom
The curves of your thighs are like ornaments devised by a skilled craftsman.
Your navel is a rounded goblet that will never lack spiced wine,
And your breasts are like clusters of fruit.
May I find your breasts like clusters of grapes on the vine,
your breath sweet-scented like apples, your mouth like fragrant wine
Flowing smoothly to meet my caresses, gliding over my lips and teeth.

Bride
I am my beloved's, his longing is all for me.
Come, my beloved, let us go out into the fields to lie among the henna bushes,
There I shall give you my love, when the mandrakes yield their perfume,
And all choice fruits are ready at our door, fruits new and old
Which I have in store for you, my love.
I should give you mulled wine to drink and the fresh juice of my pomegranates.

FOOD FOR THOUGHT

Walter Benton, This Is My Beloved, 1943

You won't find the poetry of Walter Benton in any antholgies of modern or contemporary
poetry, despite the fact that his book has become one of the most popular and widely sold

books of love poetry since its publication in 1943. Popularity and sales figures do not an important book make. There are numerous books of popular verse that have sold well and reached a wide audience—books by the likes of Rod McKuen, Kathy Pollitt Shultz, Piet Hien, etc.—but which have never enjoyed critical esteem. The verse in these books fall into the category of sappy, inspirational, witty, or love poetry. Poets who write about love walk a fine line between generalized sappy lyrics and heartfelt poetry of deep emotion that rises to the level of greatness. The poems of Sappho and Catullus are good examples of the latter, partly because of their intensity, but also because they explore the darker side of love, and are often specific in their details.

This is not the place to digress into a comprehensive section on love poetry. That's another book altogether. I offer some of the work of Walter Benton as an example of a particular poet whose major output falls under the category of love verse, and who is himself not considered an important poet in the mainstream sense. Yet, like the *Song of Songs,* his poems are wonderfully evocative and beautifully written. *This Is My Beloved,* which takes its title from *Song of Songs,* is a book of poems written during the late 1930s and early 40s as America was struggling through the Great Depression and rearming itself for another global conflict. Underlying the poetry of love is an awareness that the personal lives of the lovers are subject to the darker forces of a contaminated world.

Benton worked on a farm, in a steel mill, as a window washer, as a salesman, and at various other jobs before graduating from Ohio University. He served in the Army during World War II. Some of his poems were published in *Poetry,* the *Yale Review,* and the *New Republic.* His first book, *This Is My Beloved,* was a "diary in verse" published in 1943. The copy I bought in 1960 had already gone through 34 printings, and the copy I saw for sale in Book Soup was in its 53rd printing.

The tone of the poems range from the grateful wonder of love to the dark despair of its loss.

ENTRY April 28

> Because hate is legislated . . . written into
> the primer and the testament,
> shot into our blood and brain like vaccine or vitamins
> Because our day is of time, of hours — and the clock-hand turns,
> closes the circle upon us: and black timeless night
> sucks us in like quicksand, receives us totally —
> without a raincheck or a parachute, a key to heaven or the last long look
>
> I need love now more than ever . . . I need your love,
> I need love more than hope or money, wisdom or a drink
>
> Because slow negative death withers the world — and only yes
> can turn the tide
> Because love has your face and body . . . and your hands are tender
> and your mouth is sweet — and God has made no other eyes like yours.

ENTRY May 4

You rise out of sleep like a growing thing rises
out of the garden soul.
Two leaves part to be your moth, two tender seedleaves —
and your eyes are wonderfully starlike,
your eyes are luminous and soft as the velvet of pansies.

Darling, good morning.

Our arms are empty of each other for a moment only.
How beautifully you turn . . . your mouth tilts to let my kisses in.
Lie still . . . we shall be longer.
We need so little room, we two . . . thus on a single pillow —
as we move nearer,
nearer heaven — until I burst inside you like a screaming rocket.

Then we are quietly apart . . . returning to this earth.

ENTRY May 25

All right, sulk. But as you sit, so . . . knees high —
the wild, spiral feathers accentuating the meeting of your thighs,
like dark grass grown in too rich a soil —

you are beutifully eloquent.

ENTRY June 3

Your eyes never opened after the last kiss.
We had loved hard —
it's all over your throat and hair, it lies on your mouth like a wild
red flower: it's on your cheeks and forehead in waning radiance.

Your nipples contract . . . farther in like blossoms for the night.
Your hand half-sleeping finds me . . . your touch is very dear.

Now you are all asleep, alone with yourself — and a tall blue fence
around you: not a tendon taut, not a secret secret,
you are all sleep and alone in a warm and velvet world —

many an idle dream is looking for a home of sleep like yours to
happen in.

ENTRY June 24

Last night we entered our bed through opposite doors.
Hours we lay awake, entrenched . . . before the trapdoor gave
and we were hurtling down in jerky sleep.

Today . . . your mind moved back into your face, willing away
your last night's beauty.
And the hard mask of reoslution lies dull upon you like a bad make-up.

ENTRY June 27

I stood long where you left me.
Night was all around me
and the stars pecked at it with fierce acetylene silver beaks.
A little thin moon scarred the sky.
Then I walked . . . my arm around the emptiness of you beside me.

ENTRY August 9

Each season of each year I will be forgetting you
all over. Each season, every year.
I will need to forget you each summer, spring . . . autumn and winter.
Each summer I will be forgetting you: forever naked, you brown with the sun's
fire, you moving in massive adagio like a seal turning in water.
Autumn, I will be forgetting meeting you,
and the first long kiss on the green bedlam hill, under the rash of stars—
I could not leave your mouth . . . remember? And the garret rooms
we lived in. The bittersweet we gathered and the rich red sumac in the high
hectic woods where the air was ripe apples and the colors of chrysanthemum.

ENTRY August 29

It was like something done in fever, when nothing fits,
mind into mind nor body into body . . . when nothing
meets or equals—when dimensions lie and perceptions go haywire.

With what an alien sense my fingers curved about her breasts
and searched the tangled dark where love lay hiding!
I closed my eyes better to imagine you—but the rehearsed body would not ratify
the mind's deception.

ENTRY September 12

When all the poems on the theme have been written
and all the night and day dreams dreamt, without prophecy or fulfillment.
When hope sustains us no longer—
nor being drunk or body or therapeutically in love keeps us from remembering.

What will we do to keep madness sulking in the brain?
When we have forgotten even why we parted, if we ever knew it at all—
remembering, however, when we could sleep naked and be warm together,
kiss, though with a cold—
when even baby-talk became you . . . yes,
and everything I said was sweet or funny and everyting you did was beautiful.

ENTRY Novemeber 25

There are no stars tonight to get my bearing by.
What time is it? What season? What year?
The sky sags . . . bellies. The city gargles dust in the streets.
I am lost on an island somewhere between two rivers.
Blind buildings are all around me—
and the earth is covered with flat stones. And over me, the low

dark roof—the harbor's lifted morass and the belchings of many chimneys.

☛ Proverbs

If the *Song of Songs* is the voice of youth, Proverbs is the voice of old age. Some of their influence goes back to Egyptian literature and Greek philsophy, and they were probably compiled in the 2nd century BCE by an Alexandrian Jew with an affinity for Greek thought and ways. The Socratic connection between virtue and wisdom can be found in many of the proverbs, consistent with the melding of Greek philsophy and Hebrew theology, two streams which came together in European, and eventually modern thought.

> Happy is he who has found wisdom,
> he who has acquired understanding,
> for wisdom is more profitable than silver,
> and the gain she brings is better than gold!
>
> Her ways are pleasant ways
> and her paths all lead to prosperity.
> She is a tree of life to those who grasp her,
> and those who hold fast to her are safe.

☛ The Book of Job:

It's said that the *Book of Job* is about the inexplicability of suffering in this world, but it's also about man's right to question God and hold him accountable for his actions. That God refuses to answer, and rages at Job's presumption to question Him at all, goes to the heart of the book's existential dilemma. God implies that His actions are beyond our ability to understand. He refuses to "justify His ways to man."

The drama of Job seems to have been written with uninked fingers, for the author is even more anonymous than Homer. The *Book of Job* is a poem, bracketted by a prose prologue and epilogue. It is also a drama in the form of a debate in which conflicting points of view are put forward. Each side has its merits, neither presented as preferable—perhaps one reason why it is the most intellectually demanding book of the Hebrew Bible. As soon as one finds a workable interpretation or way of explaining the story, the carefully worked out viewpoint suddenly unravels as another possible meaning begins to emerge. Just as God fails to answer Job's questions about the reason for his suffering, The *Book of Job* fails to answer our questions about the meaning of the drama.

Though considerably shorter than Homer's *Illiad* and *Odyssey*, Virgil's *Aeneid*, Dante's *Divine Comedy*, Milton's *Paradise Lost*, Goethe's *Faust*, or Sophocles and Shakespeare's great tragedies, The *Book of Job* is just as much a literary masterpiece as those classics of world literature. The poetry moves—sometimes subtley and sometimes in sudden and surprising bursts—from great delicacy to almost shocking power. It can be seen as a spiritual epic, a drama of the human soul. It's also a tragedy, but not only Job's tragedy. It may also be the tragedy of God.

The legend of Job is old. He was a man of exemplary righteousness, blessed with prosperity, and seven sons and three daughters.

> There was once a man in the land of Uz whose name was Job. That man was blameless and upright, one who feared God and turned away from evil. There were born to him seven sons and three daughters. He had seven thousand sheep, three thousand camels, five hundred yoke of oxen, five hundred donkeys, and very many servants; so that this man was wealthier than anyone in the east. . . . And when the feast days had run their course, Job would send for his children and sanctify them, and he would rise early in the morning and offer burnt offerings, one for each of them; for Job thought, "It may be that my children have sinned, and cursed God in their hearts." This is what Job always did.

In this prose prologue we meet the *dramatis personae*. Job is shown as a pious and virtuous man, blessed by God with material riches and a dutiful family. His scrupulous piety extends to his regular ritual of sanctification.

The second scene of the drama shifts to the court of Heaven where God is visited by divine beings, including Satan, who has not yet become the Prince of Darkness. In the Hebrew text, Satan can also be translated as "The Adversary," or "The Opposer"—if you'll forgive the pun, God's Devil's Advocate. According to traditional exegesis, his role is to oppose men in their pretensions to a right standing with God, and to test their sincerity. Satan is also presented in the *Masoretic Text* as one of the sons of God.

> The Lord asked him where he had been. "I have been roaming all over the earth," said the Adversary, Satan, "from end to end." The Lord asked him, "Have you noticed My servant Job? You will find no one like him on earth, a blameless and upright man who fears God and shuns evil."

Note that it is God, not Satan, who calls attention to the exemplary Job. God is proud, bringing him up to Satan as if to show him off. The Hebrew word for "servant" can also be translated "slave." Here is a man who loves and fears and worships God, unwilling to curse him even in his heart, taking regular steps to purify his own children lest they do. Here is a man God can justly be proud of, and His mention of Job is done with an air of pride. Satan responds by taking God down a peg or two, pointing out that it's easy not to curse God when He has done nothing to provoke it. Look at all Job has.

> "Has not Job good reason to be godfearing?" answered the Adversary. "Why, it is You who have fenced him round on every side with Your protection, him and his household and all that he has. Whatever he does You bless, and everywhere his herds have increased beyond measure. But lay Your hand upon all that he has and see if he will blaspheme You to Your face."

In the original Hebrew, Satan's phrase, "see if he will blaspheme," has the force of a wager: *I bet he will curse you to your face*. God then takes the bet and is willing to put Job to the test. "Very well," said the Lord. "All that he has is in your power; just don't lay a hand on him."

In the third scene we're rushed headlong into the action. With crushing calamity, Job's wealth and his children are taken from him. Four successive messengers bring Job news of disasters, blow after ruinous blow, with each disaster growing in magnitude. Job loses his livestock, his wealth, his servants, and finally his children. "Only I have escaped to tell you," says each messenger in turn. Utterly desolate, Job tears his cloak, shaves his head, and throws himself on the ground, blessing God in one of the Bible's more famous passages.

> Naked I came from the womb,
> naked I shall return whence I came.
> The Lord gives and the Lord takes away;
> blessed be the name of the Lord.

The drama moves forward.

> Once again the day came when the members of the court of heaven took their places in the presence of the Lord, and Satan was there among them. The Lord enquired where he had been. "I have been roaming all over the earth from end to end." The Lord said to the adversary, "Have you noticed My servant Job? There is no one like him on earth, a blameless and upright man who fears God and sets his face against wrongdoing. You incited me to ruin him without cause, but he still holds fast to his integrity.

Not only has God won the bet, not only has His faithful and patient servant refrained from cursing Him, but Job has blessed God for everything—what was given and what was taken away. Satan, however, presses the issue further.

> "Skin for skin! To save himself there is nothing a man will not give up.
> But lay a hand on his bones and his flesh, and see if he will not curse You to Your face."

Satan raises the stakes. God answers, "So be it. He is in your power. Just don't kill him."

The scene shifts back to earth, where Job is smitten with a terrible disease, black leprosy or elephantitus, some have speculated, for his body is covered head to foot with loathesome boils. When patient Job sits among the ash-heap of buried animal dung outside the city, his wife loses her patience and rebukes him for being so submissive and accepting.

> "Why do you still hold fast to your integrity? Curse God, and die!" He answered, "You talk as any impious woman might talk. If we accept good from God, shall we not accept evil?" Throughout all this, Job did not utter one sinful word, nor did he cast reproach on God.

The story from Job's point of view emphasizes his steadfastness. But are we not, as audience, compelled to shake our heads and wonder at the irony of the situation. If Job knew all of this was provoked by a bet between God and Satan, what might Job have said of his sufferings, and of God?

Job's three friends arrive and attempt to comfort and console him. Horrified by the sight of him, they tear their own cloaks and sit beside him, for seven days and nights, unable to speak a word, so great was Job's suffering. Suddenly, Job rouses himself and like Lear on the heath, in a rage he raises a hand to the sky, and curses, not God, but the day of his birth, in one of the great poetic monologues in all drama.

> God damn the day I was born!
> And the night that forced me from the womb.
> Let that day be darkness;
> Let God above not look for it;
> nor light of dawn shine on it.
> Let gloom and deep darkness claim it again,
> let clouds smother that day,
> blackness eclipse the sun.
> Let blind darkness swallow up that night!
> Let it not be counted upon among the days of the year;
> on that night — let no child be born,
> no mother cry out with joy.
> May those who cast spells upon the day damn it,
> those prepared to disable Leviathan.
> Let no star shine out in its twilight;
> let it wait for a dawn that never breaks,
> and never see the eyelids of the morning,
> because it did not shut the doors of my mother's womb
> nor did it keep trouble away from my sight.
>
> Why was I not born stillborn,
> why did I not perish when I came from the womb?
> Why was I ever laid on my mother's knees
> or put to suck at her breasts?
>
> Why should the sufferer be born to see the light?
> Why is life given to those who find it so bitter?
> They long for death but it does not come,
> they seek it more eagerly than hidden treasure.
> They are glad when they reach the grave;
> when they come to the tomb they exult.
> Why should a man be born to wander blindly
> hedged about by God on every side?
>
> My groaning serves as my bread;
> My roaring pours forth like water.
> Every terror that haunted me has caught up with me;
> what I dreaded has overtaken me.

There is no peace of mind, no quiet for me;
trouble comes, and I have no rest.

[The King James Version is really more direct.]

I was not in safety, neither had I rest, neither was I quiet
Yet trouble came.

Job admits that his worst fears have happened; his nightmares have come to life. An interesting admission. If he truly believed he was a righteous man, why would he have feared all along that some great calamity might befall him? In the deepest recesses of his mind, did he have an inkling that God's wrath could strike even the pious and upright. Look how careful he was, sanctifying his children *in case* they had sinful *thoughts*. A man can't be too careful with an unpredictable God. But if Job suspected this, how deep was his faith and trust? For those of us who feel blessed, how often do we look over our shoulders?

With Job's outburst, the drama begins. The symmetrical shape of the body of the poem is composed of three cycles of colloquies, or discourses. In each round of the debate, Job refutes his friends' arguments and pleads for God's response. Job moves from bewilderment to rebellion to rage, though he never actually curses God. His friends make the assumption that—since God is just and would never punish an innocent man—Job must be guilty of some sin. Whatever the arguments, the poetic idioms are vivid and pliable, delighting the reader with their power and beauty. Elephaz the Tamanite speaks:

This is what I have seen:
those who plough mischief and sow trouble
reap no other harvest.
They perish at the blast of God;
they are shrivelled by the breath of his nostrils.
The roar of the lion,
the whimpering of his cubs, fall silent;
the teeth of the young lions are broken;
the lion perishes for lack of prey
and its whelps are scattered.

Can mortals be acquited by God?
Can man be cleared by his Maker?
If He cannot trust His own servants,
and casts reproach on His angels,
How much less those who dwell in houses of clay
whose origin is dust,
who are crushed like the moth,
shattered between daybreak and evening,
perishing forever, unnoticed.
Their cord is pulled up
and they die, and without ever finding wisdom.

Call if you will; is there any to answer you?
To whom among the holy ones will you turn?

The drama aside, this is forceful poetry. I'm reminded of the beginning of Rilke's *Duino Elegies*, "Who, if I cried, would hear me among the angelic orders?" Job lashes out at his friends who accuse him of wrongdoing.

> If only I might have my request
> and God would grant what I hope for:
> that he would be pleased to crush me,
> to sever with his hand and cut me off!
> What end have I to expect,
> that I should be patient?
> Is my strength the strength of stone,
> or is my flesh made of bronze?
>
> Just so unreliable have you now been to me:
> you felt dismay and took fright.
> Did I ever say "Give me this or give me that,"
> or say, "Use your wealth to save my life!"
>
> Tell me plainly, and I shall listen in silence;
> show me where I have been at fault.
> How harsh are the words of the upright!
> But what do your arguments prove?
>
> So months of futility are my portion,
> troubled night are my lot.
> When I lie down, I think,
> When will it be day,
> that I may rise?
> But the night drags on,
> and I do nothing but toss till dawn.
> My body is infested with worms,
> and scabs cover my skin;
> it is cracked and discharging.
> My days pass more swiftly than a weaver's shuttle
> and come to an end as the thread of life runs out.
>
> Remember that my life is but a breath of wind;
> I shall never again see good times.
>
> But I cannot hold my peace;
> I shall speak out in my anguish of spirit
> and complain in my bitterness of soul.

Job protests his innocence and demands an explanation from God for his great suffering. He is not asking why God has forsaken him, but wants to know why his punishment is so severe. Job accuses God of allowing injustice into the world; he is outraged that the innocent and righteous may suffer.

Bildad the Shuhite speaks up, reproaching Job for the "long-winded ramblings of an old man." He counsels him to turn to God for forgiveness. But Job answers:

Indeed, this I know for the truth:
that no one can win his case against God.
If anyone does choose to argue with him,
God will not answer one question in a thousand.
He is wise, he is all-powerful;
who has stood up to him and remained unscathed?
It is God who moves mountains,
overturning them in his wrath;
who makes the earth start from its place
so that its pillars are shaken;
who commands the sun not to rise
and shuts up the stars under his seal.

He goes by me and I do not see him;
he moves on his way undiscerned by me.
If he hurries on, who can bring him back?
Who will ask him what he is doing?
God does not turn back his wrath;
How much less can I answer him
or find words to dispute with him?
Though I am in the right, I get no answer;
He crushes me for a hair.
Though I am in the right,
he condemns me out of my own mouth;
though I am blameless, he makes me out to be crooked.
Blameless, I say;
of myself I reck nothing, I hold my life cheap.
But it is all one; therefore I declare,
"He destroys blameless and wicked alike."
When a sudden flood brings death,
he mocks the plight of the innocent.
When a country is delivered into the power of the wicked,
he blindfolds the eyes of its judges.

Zophar the Naamathite speaks up, mocking Job's assumption of wisdom, and proclaims that God's wisdom is beyond human understanding.

He surely knows who are false,
and when he sees iniquity, does he not take note of it?
But a stupid man will be wise
when a cow gives birth to a zebra!

Job responds in kind, telling his friends that if they take God's part falsely, God's majesty will surely strike them down. They assume that because he suffers, God must have punished him for wrongdoing. Is it possible that God is unjust? Is it not possible that Job is innocent. Should he suffer wrongly in the one life he has to live.

But when a human being dies all his power vanishes;
he expires, and where is he then?
As the waters of a lake dwindle,
or as a river shrinks and runs dry,

so mortal man lies down, never to rise
until the very sky splits open.
If a man dies, can he live again?

Job raises an interesting point here. Many of the questions raised by Job could not be answered, even by the God of the *Book of Job*. The problem of the question of suffering remained and was to have profound effects upon later Jewish thought. In the days of Daniel, it was to be abandoned as insoluble in terms of this world, which was finite. Thinkers from Daniel and Enoch to Kant would say that no answer could be given unless one believed in some other life, beyond the grave, in which all wrongs would be righted, the wicked would be punished, and the just would inherit infinite reward. This was one of the many currents of thought that flowed into Christianity and gave it such powerful appeal. Job's moral outrage demands that the question be answered in the here and now, in the context of a finite life lived on this earth.

The debate continues vigorously, and Job becomes more and more skeptical of his God, until he calls him "Adversary," and wishes that this Adversary would destroy himself by writing a book. He calls upon God to defend him, against God. Job concludes his argument with his "Hymn to Widsom," in Chapter 28.

But where can wisdom be found,
and where is the source of understanding?
No one knows the way to it,
nor is it to be found in the land of the living.
"It is not in us," declares the ocean depths;
the sea declares, "It is not with me."
Red gold cannot buy it,
nor can its price be weighed out in silver;
Where, then, does wisdom come from?
Where is the source of understanding?
No creature on earth can set eyes on it;
even from birds of the air it is concealed.
Destruction and Death declare,
"We know of it only by hearsay."

God alone understands the way to it,
he alone knows its source;
for he can see to the ends of the earth
and observe every place under heaven.
When he regulated the force of the wind
and measured out the waters in proportion,
when he laid down a limit for the rain
and cleared a path for the thunderbolt,
it was then he saw wisdom and took stock of it,
he considered it and fathomed its very depths.
And he said to mankind:
"The fear of the Lord is wisdom,
and to turn from evil, that is understanding!"

Job gives God his due, but will not back down. He wants God to answer him.

Let the Almighty state his case against me!

If my accuser had written out his indictment,
I should not keep silence and remain indoors.
No! I should flaunt it on my shoulder
and wear it like a crown on my head;
I should plead the whole record of my life
and present that in court as my defense.

Job's speeches are finished. Then, in one of the most majestic passages in the Bible, a voice comes down out of the clouds. The Lord answers Job out of the whirlwind.

Who is this whose ignorant words
    smear my design with darkness?
Stand up now like a man;
    I will question you: please, instruct me.

Where were you when I planned the earth?
    Tell me, if you are so wise.
Do you know who took its dimensions,
    measuring its length with a cord?

Were you there when I stopped the waters,
    as they issued gushing from the womb?
when I wrapped the ocean in clouds
    and swaddled the sea in shadows?

Have you ever commanded morning
    or guided dawn to its place—
to hold the corners of the sky
    and shake off the last few stars?

Have you stood at the gates of doom
    or looked through the gates of death?
Have you seen to the edge of the universe?
    Speak up, if you have such knowledge.

Has God's accuser resigned?
    Has my critic swallowed his tongue?

Job Said to the Unnamable:

I am speechless: what can I answer?
    I put my hand on my mouth.
I have said too much already;
    now I will speak no more.

Then the Unnamable again spoke to Job from the Whirlwind:

Do you dare to deny my judgment?
    Am I wrong because you are right?
Is your arm like the arm of God?
    Can your voice bellow like mine?
Unleash your savage justice.
    Cut down the rich and the mighty.

> Make the proud man grovel.
>> Pluck the wicked from their perch.
> Push them into the grave.
>> Throw them, screaming, to hell.
> Then I will admit
>> that your own strength can save you.
>
> Look now: the Beast that I made:
>> created to be my plaything.
> Go ahead: attack him:
>> you will never try it again.
>
> Look: hope is a lie:

Then Job said to the Unnamable:

> I have heard of you with my ears;
>> but now my eyes have seen you.
> Therefore I will be quiet,
>> comforted that I am dust.

The poem ends, but the prose epilogue closes the book with God's final verdict. Job's friends are rebuked for not speaking of God correctly, where Job had. God condemns their theology, that suffering necessarily implies sin, and commends Job in their presence. Once again God stressed the integrity of Job and applauds his intellectual honesty. Confirming once again Job's righteous nature, when God threatens to punish his friends for their mistakes, Job successfully intercedes on their behalf, and they are forgiven. With poetic justice, God rewards Job with twice as much as he had before,

> so the Lord blessed the latter end of Job more than his beginning. . . .
> And after this Job lived a hundred and forty years, and saw his sons, and
> his sons' sons, even four generations. So Job died, being old and full of
> days.

Not only is the *Book of Job* complex, the poetry is some of the richest and most powerful in Western literature. It is also an unsettling story. God loses a bet with Satan, sees Job punished horribly, and has no compassion for Job's pain, or his need to understand the cause of his suffering. God declares that the Beast was "the first of the works of God, created to be my plaything." Man may well be His plaything, too; we can never know, for the ways of God are beyond our logic; all Job can do is fear this vengeful God, and know his awful power and majesty.

From Job's perspective we could interpret the drama thus: Job would have preferred to think of himself as guilty of some sin, for if he was innocent, how could he explain God's punishments. His strong defiance of God was merely to provoke God into speaking. Job wanted to hear God's voice. To know there is a God is enough—even if His ways are unjustifiable. To think one could suffer without meaning in a world without purpose is an intolerable thought. Even if God's purpose is beyond our comprehension, we can find some comfort in knowing there is a higher reason for life's apparent capriciousness.

Even this consolation is not offered us by the Preacher in *Ecclesiastes* who tells us all is futile, all is vanity. Some would have wanted Job to refute God's gift of happiness at the end. In the name of his children, he should have continued to question God, to demand an answer, instead of becoming silent.

But Job's silence is the silence of one who has realized an awful truth, and to press it further would be useless. Job *does* hear God's voice, and it is not the voice of an understanding, consoling God. Afterall, Job's plea for an explanation is reasonable, considering the piousness of his obediance and the extent of his sufferings. Why does God become so upset? Perhaps Job detects in God's admonition that something is amiss. Job didn't know about the wager made with Satan. If he did, might he have cursed God? But the subtext indicates that Job's backing off is not a simple retreat into submission. Job seems to know something, to realize something, and chooses not to push God further. It's not a pat ending. It raises more questions than it answers.

Food for Thought

The Tragedy of God: Samuel Beckett's *Waiting for Godot*

But there's another perspective. Not Job's, but ours, the reader's. Because it's called the *Book of Job*, it's assumed the protagonist is Job. But I'm not so sure. Reading the dramatic poem in which God waits in the wings for Job's summons, I'm reminded of Samuel Beckett's play *Waiting for Godot*, in which Godot, sitting or hovering somewhere in the wings, never makes an appearance. I can't help feeling the *Book of Job* is a tragedy in the classical sense, in which someone of high estate suffers a fall from grace brought upon by their tragic flaw, *hubris*, overweaning pride and arrogance. And the tragic hero is not Job, but God.

When Beckett was asked if Godot was God, Beckett replied somewhat peevishly, "I know how to spell." Yet, the play was written in French, and the name *Godot* is a compound of the English name God and the French diminutive ending *-ot*, the same as *-ie* in English. In French, it's Charlot; in English, it's Charlie. Was Beckett saying that in this existential time, the God we are waiting for is a comic puppeteer named Goddie, who never shows up.

In the two-act play, comic tramps named Vladimir (Didi) and Estragon (Gogo) sit on a mound near a barren tree waiting for someone to show up whose name is Godot. They entertain themselves day after day, doing essentially the same thing. One gets the sense that this first act is merely one of many such acts in which Didi and Gogo wait for Godot. Everything that happens to them has happened before, including the strange antics of Pozzo and Lucky, who are passing through. By the end of day, Pozzo and Lucky are gone. Gogo forgets things from one minute to the next, one day to the next. Didi seems to be puzzling over the succession of events, aware that something is amiss. He's beginning to suffer from a cosmic kind of *deja vu*. Near the end of the first act, Pozzo and Lucky bluster off in a whirlwind of words.

VLADIMIR:	That passed the time.
ESTRAGON:	It would have passed in any case.
VLADIMIR:	Yes, but not so rapidly
Pause	
ESTRAGON:	What do we do now?
VLADIMIR:	I don't know.
ESTRAGON:	Let's go.
VLADIMIR:	We can't.
ESTRAGON:	Why not?
VLADIMIR:	We're waiting for Godot.
ESTRAGON:	(*despairingly*). Ah!

Finally, at the end of the first act, a Boy enters.

VLADIMIR:	What is it?
BOY:	Mr. Godot . . .
VLADIMIR:	Well, what is it?
BOY:	Mr. Godot—
VLADIMIR:	I've seen you before, haven't I?
BOY:	I don't know sir.
VLADIMIR:	You don't know me?
BOY:	No Sir.
VLADIMIR:	It wasn't you came yesterday?
BOY:	No sir.
VLADIMIR:	This is your first time?
BOY:	Yes Sir.
	Silence
VLADIMIR:	Words words. (*Pause.*) Speak.
BOY	(*In a rush*) Mr. Godot told me to tell you he won't come this evening but surely tomorrow.
	Silence
VLADIMIR:	Is that all?
BOY:	Yes Sir.
	Silence
VLADIMIR:	All right, you may go?
BOY:	What am I to tell Mr. Godot, Sir?
VLADIMIR:	Tell him . . . (*he hesitates*) . . . tell him you saw us. (*Pause*) You did see us, didn't you?
Boy:	Yes, Sir.
	He steps back, hesitates, turns and exit running.
VLADIMIR:	We've nothing more to do here.
ESTRAGON:	Nor anywhere else.
VLADIMIR:	Ah Gogo, don't go on like that. Tomorrow everything will be better.
ESTRAGON:	How do you make that out?
VLADIMIR:	Did you not hear what the child said?
ESTRAGON:	No.
VLADIMIR:	He said that Godot was sure to come tomorrow. (*Pause.*) What do you say to that?
ESTRAGON:	Then all we have to do is to wait on here.

VLADIMIR:	Are you mad? We must take cover.
ESTRAGON:	How long have we been together all the time now?
VLADIMIR:	I don't know. Fifty years maybe.
Silence.	
ESTRAGON:	Well, shall we go?
VLADIMIR:	Yes, let's go.

They do not move.

Curtain   [end of first act]

At the opening of act two, it's the next day, same time, same place. The second act is pretty much the same as the first. They pass the time. Pozzo and Lucky come and go. The Boy arrives to tell them that Godot won't be coming, same as he did in the first act, but that Godot will be coming tomorrow for sure. The two tramps sit again on their mound as night falls. And so it goes. Critics called it "the play in which nothing happens." Written in 1948, *Waiting for Godot* had its world premiere in 1953 in the tiny Left Bank Théâtre de Babylone in Paris. It was not an immediate success, and audiences were baffled by this odd, absurdist drama in which nothing seemed to happen. Godot didn't even make an appearance. What did it all mean? *Waiting for Godot* has become a part of theatre history, but the battle of interpretation still rages.

I think something does happen in *Waiting for Godot*, and it's the same thing that happens in Job, except that at the end of Job, God *does* make an appearance. But for all intents and purposes, the idea of the ending is the same. *Waiting for Godot* merely recognizes what Job at the end knew all along. God cannot be called upon for answers. Furthermore, God will not be coming again.

Let's take a look at the end of the second act, which seems to be an exact replica of the end of the first act, thus suggesting to most that "nothing new has happened." Vladimir is becoming increasingly aware that Gogo is not the only one who forgets what happened the day before. And Vladimir is becoming increasingly aware that there's a progression here, the progression of repetition, and it's beginning to disturb him.

BOY:	Mister . . .
VLADIMIR:	Off we go again. (*Pause.*) Do you not recognize me?
BOY:	No sir.
VLADIMIR:	It wasn't you came yesterday.
BOY:	No Sir.
VLADIMIR:	This is your first time.
BOY:	Yes Sir.
	Silence.
VLADIMIR:	You have a message from Mr. Godot.
BOY:	Yes Sir.
VLADIMIR:	He won't be coming this evening.
BOY:	Yes Sir.
VLADIMIR:	But he'll come tomorrow.
BOY:	Yes Sir.
VLADIMIR:	Without fail.
BOY:	Yes Sir.
	Silence.
VLADIMIR:	What does he do, Mr. Godot?

	(*Silence.*)
	Do you hear me?
BOY:	Yes Sir.
VLADIMIR:	Well?
BOY:	He does nothing, Sir.
	Silence.
VLADIMIR:	How's Your brother?
BOY:	He's sick, Sir.
	Silence.
	What am I to tell Mr. Godot, Sir?
VLADIMIR:	Tell him . . . (*he hesitates*) . . . tell him you saw me and that . . . (*he hesitates*) . . . that you saw me.
	(*Pause*)
	Vladimir advances. With sudden violence.)
	You're sure you saw me, you won't come and tell me tomorrow that you never saw me!
	Silence.
	Vladimir makes a sudden spring forward, The Boy avoids him and exits running..
	Silence.
ESTRAGON:	Where shall we go?
VLADIMIR:	Not far.
ESTRAGON:	Oh yes, let's go far away from here.
VLADIMIR:	We can't.
ESTRAGON:	Why not?
VLADIMIR:	We have to come back tomorrow.
ESTRAGON:	What for?
VLADIMIR:	To wait for Godot.
ESTRAGON:	Ah! (*Silence.*) He didn't come?
VLADIMIR:	No.
ESTRAGON:	And now it's too late.
VLADIMIR:	Yes, now it's night.
ESTRAGON:	And if we dropped him? (*Pause.*) If we dropped him?
VLADIMIR:	He'd punish us.
Silence.	
VLADIMIR:	Well? Shall we go?
ESTRAGON:	Yes, let's go.
	They do not move.

Curtain

[End of play]

On the face of it, the ending to both acts are the same. But they're not. Vladimir has had an existential awareness of the futility of it all. Like Job, he falls silent, and pretends to go on with the game. But he's changed, just as Job was. End of day after end of day a young boy will bring a message just before dark that Godot will not appear. When the Boy comes this time (the Boy has been coming for years), Vladimir does not ask any questions. He makes statements, and the boy confirms their truth. Vladimir does it almost by rote, as if he knows the answers anyway. "Godot won't be coming." No. "But he'll come tomorrow." Yes. Vladimir knows that this game will continue forever. Godot will never come. The message will always be the same. Godot's not coming today, but he will be coming tomorrow. On and on and on. Waiting. Waiting with the knowledge that there is nothing to wait for. Sisyphus rolls his rock up the mountain ceaselessly. At least it's a job, a punishment, a burden. Which is why Albert Camus [see page 176] in his famous essay *The Myth of Sisyphus,* posits Sisyphus happy. He has found his burden. "One always finds one's burden." It is only on the way down that Sisyphus experiences the existential nausea that life is a meaningless series of repetitions. The burden of the rock relieves him from the awful nature of consciousness. For Didi, there is only waiting, the awful waiting, with the knowledge that Godot will never come. Perhaps this was the knowledge contained in the apple that God most feared Adam would realize. Job eats of the apple of greater knowledge, that if there is a God, he can not be depended upon. Thus Job's terrible silence.

For Didi or Job to say what they know would demand an existential leap of action too frightening to consider. Didi and Job play the game, but they know the real game is over. Neither Godot nor God will ever show up.

Does God forgive us for knowing that he doesn't exist? One could interpret God's reward of Job in the prose epilogue a kind of forgiveness for realizing the truth about their relationship. When Gogo askes Didi, "And if we dropped him," Didi says, "He'd punish us." Job realizes the same thing. He cannot drop God. He must carry him to the end, worshipping his all powerful wrath. But Job knows the score. God needs us as much as we need him. This is truly the nature of man's fall from grace and exile from Eden, that he knows the true nature of God. And God knows that his pride has been seen through by Job. It's an uneasy truce between God and Man, a tragic arm's-length embrace.

Spelling aside, it's easy to identify Godot with God. Godot will never come, God will never speak again. Who caused it? Job.

The *Book of Job* ends with Job placing his hand over his mouth promising to speak no more. But it is God who is silenced. In the narrative of the Old Testament (using the arrangement of the books in the Hebrew Bible), it is the last we hear from God, directly from his own mouth. In *God: A Biography*, Jack Miles writes:

> The beginning and the end of the Hebrew Bible are not linked by a single, continuous narrative. Well short of the halfway point in the text, the narrative breaks off. What then follows are, first, speeches spoken by God; second, speeches spoken either to or, in some degree, about God; third, a protracted silence; and, last, a brief resumption of the narrative before a closing coda.
>
> After action yields to speech in the Hebrew Bible, however, speech yields in its turn to silence. God's last words are those he speaks to Job, the human being who dares to challenge not his physical power, but his moral authority. Within the Book of Job itself, God's climactic and overwhelming reply seems to silence Job. But reading from the end of the Book of Job onward, we see that it is Job who has somehow silenced God. God never speaks again. . . .

To paraphrase Nietzsche, if God is not dead, he's been silenced. Never again in the Hebrew Bible does God intervene in human affairs. As the prime creator, God is outside of time and space, but when he creates the temporal world and its people, God "enters time and is changed by experience." Were that not the case, he would not be surprised by what happens to his people. But he is often surprised, unpleasantly so. "God is constant; he is not immutable," concludes Miles.

And it is Job who makes him play his last revealing hand. Once God's cards are on the table, Job, like Didi, knows the game is up. And God must know that Job realizes this. Several literary critics have found in the book the likeness of a Greek tragedy, written on the model of Euripedes. The book of Genesis opens with man's creation and fall. In Job, God has his tragic recognition, and exits without a word, except to briefly praise Job for speaking true, and rewarding him with fortune and family. But it's as if he's returned to the old game. God is the fallen hero of the *Book of Job*.

Tragically, we know even more than Job does, and for us, the meaning of the drama has greater significance. We know that Job's suffering was the result of a bet with Satan. It's possible, informed by this discomforting thought, some choose never to wait for God again, nor call upon him for explanation or comfort when suffering is greatest. Both God, and his people, are alone.

In The *Book of Job* we see the full flower of God's destructive or demonic side exposed by his final confrontation with an individual human being. In *Genesis* we saw his anger.

> When the Lord saw how great was the wickedness of human beings on earth, and how their every thought and inclination were always wicked, he bitterly regretted that he had made mankind on earth. He said, "I shall wipe off the face of the earth this human race which I have created—yes, man and beast, creeping things and birds. I regret that I ever made them."   [6:6,7]

In Ezekiel we see his benevolent and malevolent side:

> But the Israelites rebelled against me in the wilderness; they did not conform to my statutes, they rejected my laws, though it is by keeping them that mortals have life, and they totally desecrated my sabbaths. I resolved to pour out my wrath on them in the wilderness to destroy them. But then I acted for the honour of my name, that it might not be profaned in the sight of the nations who had seen me bring them out. . . .
> However, in the wilderness I swore to them with uplifted hand that I would disperse them among the nations and scatter them over the earth. . . . I even imposed on them statutes that were malign and laws which would not lead to life. I let them defile themselves with gifts to idols; I made them surrender their eldest sons to them so that I might fill them with revulsion. Thus they would know that I am the Lord. [20:8, 23]

Even in his first terrifying appearance in Exodus, God was violent and dangerous:

The Lord said to Moses, "I am coming to you in a thick cloud, so that I may speak to you in the hearing of the people, ... Anyone who touches the mountain shall be put to death. No hand may touch him, he is to be stoned to death or shot; neither man nor beast may live." At dawn on the third day there were peals of thunder and flashes of lightning, dense cloud on the mountain, and a loud-trumpet-blast; all the people in the camp trembled.

Mount Sinai was enveloped in smoke because the Lord had come down on it in fire; all the people trembled violently, and the sound of the trumpet grew ever louder. Whenever Moses spoke, God answered him in a peal of thunder. The Lord said to him, "Warn the people solemnly that they must not force their way through to the Lord to see him, or many of them will perish. Even the priests, who may approach the Lord, must hallow themselves, for fear that the Lord may break out against them." [19:1-25]

As Miles puts it: "God is a stormy, volcanic personality who bursts on the scene in the aftermath of the Exodus. No one remotely like this wild and thunderous being has yet been seen or heard in the Bible. God seems like a force on the point of escaping control." As a creator and destroyer, God shows not only his unpredictability, but the danger of his capriciousness. We see many sides of God, his warrior side, a being who demands obediance, a jealous and powerful God. Isaiah makes it clear that he is a God to be feared:

Because this people worship me with empty words
and pay me lip-service
while their hearts are far from me,
and their religion is but a human precept, learnt by rote,
therefore, I shall shock this people yet again,
adding shock to shock:
the wisdom of their wise men will vanish
and the discernment of the discerning will be lost.

The *Book of Job* brings to stirring, awesome culmination the destructive and wrathful God shown earlier in the books of the Bible, as well as the disquieting intuitions and dark doubts His people have come to have of Him. While it is true that the righteous are rewarded and the wicked punished, it's just as possible the opposite can occur, as decreed by God, for no reason at all, or for a reason that is inexplicable and mysterious to man. Ever after the *Book of Job*, no one can point a finger at a suffering person and assume that their punishment was because they committed some sin. Even the innocent may suffer. If nothing else, Job established the right to call upon God for answers, and established the idea that even he who is without sin may be punished. Thus, there is an element of danger and absurdity to the world. Inexplicable punishment can befall anyone, anytime. Job hears the angry, volcanic, wrathful God with a power we've heard before. But it is the sight of the Lord Yahweh that strikes Job almost dumb. Considering what God had said to Moses in Exodus, God must have had a good reason to show himself to Job.

Those of us who read the story from outside of Job's point of view know what that reason was. Here is a God not only capable of great wrath and destruction, but a God susceptible to manipulation by a demon, Satan, his adversary. The Job-narrator tells a story quite blasphemous. Without God, the world can be a fearful place, unpredictable and dangerous. What is worse, the world without God can disregard all we do, and we can fall into the vortex of calamity at the drop of a hat. With God, it's the same. As children, we've crushed under the swatter a fly crawling busily along, stepped on a bug on its way to work, roasted with the concentrated fire of a magnifying glass an ant on its way home. Who's to say—after reading the story in the *Book of Job*—that God has not done the same to us, on a bet, on a whim. Question all we want. His answer is still the same. "I am Who I am."

One of the difficulties in attaching a consistent meaning to the *Book of Job* is the way one's focus shifts from Job to God. The debate between Job and his three friends is overshadowed by the contention between Job and God. Their separate speeches acquire commanding power, but when each is viewed from the other's perspective, the grandeur of God's volcanic outburst pales beside the anguish of Job's lament. Conversely, Job's kvetching complaints take on a trivial air when compared to the rhetoric of God's commanding power. But just who has the last word is hard to say. Job's silence is eloquent; God's, disturbing.

How to cope with this knowledge of God is suggested by the Preacher in *Ecclesiastes*.

Food for Thought

Charles Bukowski, *The Tragedy of the Leaves*

The greatness of Bukowski's poetry has been often overlooked because his publisher has been able to capitalize on his fame by releasing much inferior work, and Bukowski was glad to go along with it. But the best of his work is characterized by a deep human compassion, a beauty of lyric, and a jaded spirituality that confronts the nature of redemption. In "The Priest and the Matador," he drives home from a bullfight, stops at a Mission and notices a priest "staring from the window like a caged bear." He contrasts the image of the matador on his knees in the bullring, "the dead bull his baby," and the image of the priest in his "fort of Christ," and concludes

> I have lived in both their temples,
> believing all and nothing — perhaps, now, they will
> die in mine.

Many of his poems reflect on the nature of the spiritual emptiness in our modern world. But the once heroic proportions have diminished in size. If he is a modern-day Job railing at the world for answers, the God he faces is an angry landlady browbeating her tenant in imitation of God's roar at the end of the *Book of Job*.

> *The Tragedy of The Leaves*
> I awakened to dryness and the ferns were dead,
> the potted plants yellow as corn;
> my woman was gone
> and the empty bottles like bled corpses
> surrounded me with their uselessness;
> the sun was still good, though,
> and my landlady's note cracked in fine and
> undemanding yellowness; what was needed now

was a good comedian, ancient style, a jester
with jokes upon absurd pain; pain is absurd
because it exists, nothing more;
I shaved carefully with an old razor
the man who had once been young and
said to have genius; but
that's the tragedy of the leaves,
the dead ferns, the dead plants;
and I walked into the dark hall
where the landlady stood
execrating and final,
sending me to hell,
waving her fat sweaty arms
and screaming for rent
because the world had failed us
both.

God and Job must forgive each other. The world has not lived up to either of their expectations. We live in an imperfect world created by an imperfect god, and from this knowledge springs the only grace left to live by: in God's case, compassion for what He's created; in Job's case, forgiveness for the inadequacy of God's arrangement with His people. The problem of suffering cannot be explained. It is inexplicable. It is the tragedy of the leaves.

✳

☛ Ecclesiastes

Written between the 3rd and 2nd century BCE, *Ecclesiastes* may seem like the contradictory sayings of folk wisdom, but in spite of what appears to be a lack of sequence and an overlapping of ideas, there is a real unity in the thought pattern. On closer inspection, *Ecclesiastes* is a challenging and sophisticated counsel on how life should be lived. For all its bitterness and cynicism, one wonders how it got into the Bible in the first place. Even more than the *Book of Job*, it seems to overthrow all that went before it. In his penetrating book, *God: A Biography*, Jack Miles calls it the "ringer in the canon, ... the Polonius of the Bible."

While there is much dispute over the number of authors who contributed to it, the repetition of idiosyncractic phrases and the weaving of poetic rhythms may point to a single author. Ecclesiastes is a Greek word frequently rendered "The Preacher," but the editorial epilogue shows the author in the guise of a writer-teacher, and the content of Ecclesiastes displays a skepticism and dry wit incongrous in a formal religious assemby. The "sermon" or address presents a running dialectic: the futility or "vanity of things" is posed against the basic goodness of life. Contradictions are used to instruct the reader. The unorthodox tone comes from this dialectical style, not from the ideas themselves. The book is more a philosophical argument, more an existential tract, than a religious inquiry. It begins with a pessimistic reply to the *Book of Job*, declaring that good fortune and wealth have nothing to do with vice and virtue. Life is basically meaningless and absurd. *The Revised English BIble* renders the well-known opening

> Futility, utter futility, says the speaker;
> Everything is futility.

Here's the King James Version's more familiar translation:

> Vanity of vanities, saith the preacher.
> Vanity of vanities, all is vanity.

> What profit hath man of all his labour
> Wherein he laboureth under the sun?

> One generation passeth away, and another generation cometh;
> And the earth abideth forever.

> The sun also ariseth, and the sun goeth down,
> And hasteth to his place where he ariseth.

This theme is continued throughout:

> All things have I seen in the days of my vanity:
> there is a just man that perisheth in his righteousness,
> and there is a wicked man that prolongeth his life in his wickedness.

> So I returned, and considered all the oppressions
> that are done under the sun:
> and behold the tears of such as were oppressed,
> and they had no comforter;
> and on the side of their oppressors there was power.

> If thou seest the oppression of the poor,
> and violent perverting of judgment and justice in a province,
> marvel not at the matter:
> for he that is higher than the highest regardeth;
> and there be higher than they.

The book begins and ends with this cynical theme, that it is not virtue and vice that determine our lot, but blind and merciless chance.

> I saw under the sun that the race is not to the swift,
> nor the battle to the strong,
> neither yet bread to the wise,
> nor yet riches to men of understanding,
> nor yet favor to men of skill;
> but time and chance happeneth to them all.

Some of this echoes Job, where God says, "Hope is a lie."

Despite the sophistication of argument, the style is different from all the other books of the *Bible* in that its idiom is common speech, not literary composition. Unlike *Prophets*, it argues but doesn't declaim. The supplicant song of the *Psalms* is absent, and there's no historical or narrative accounting. We can't even compare it to other Hebrew thinkers because no other such texts have been preserved.

Ecclesiastes also begins to challenge the hidden premise of Jewish monotheism, that the convenant with God implies a reward for virtue and punishment for sin. Instead, we get a quasi-Platonic notion that God's foreknowledge of events is really a knowledge of what has already happened in the past and what will happen in the future. There is not even a distinction between past, present, and future; in the eyes and mind of God, it's a cycle of events that simultaneously exist as one vast eternal "now."

> I know that whatsoever God doeth,
> it shall be for ever:
> nothing can be added to it,
> nor anything taken from it:
> and God doeth it, that men should feel awe in His presence.
> That which hath been is now;
> and that which is to be
> hath already been;
> and God seeketh that which is pursued.

The second part of *Ecclesiasties* deals with the consequences of this awareness, the lessons of Job: we cannot reason the ways of God, nor make sense of our lot. Therefore, what ends do we pursue, and with what attitude and frame of mind do we pursue those ends, however futuile, fleeting, and ultimately meaningless they may be?

Adopting the mantel of Solomon, and thus vested with perfect wisdom, the author considers the quest for knowledge and concludes that it too comes up short.

> I have seen everything
> that has been done here under the sun;
> it is all futility,
> and a feeding on the wind.
> What is crooked cannot become straight;
> what is not there
> cannot be counted.

> I thought to myself,
> "I have amassed great wisdom . . . .
> I applied my mind to understanding wisdom
> and knowledge, madness, and folly.
> And I came to see that this too
> is a feeding on the wind.
> For in much wisdom is much vexation;
> the more knowledge, the more suffering.

Or as the King James Version puts it, "He that increaseth knowledge, increaseth sorrow."

The author looks for meaning in pleasure, in riches, in work. All end in death. Even wisdom avails nothing. Absurdity remains, and not just in personal experience. "God has given to human beings" the innate urge to reason why, but even this is futile, vanity.

Paradoxically, the inevitability of death focuses the mind on the "here and now," and so human life, with all its limitations and pleasures, remains the one thing we can embrace while it is there within arm's reach.

If there were a subtitle to the text, it would be that life is a "Feeding on the Wind." But while it can be seen as a book that preaches cynicism and life's futility, it is also a practical attitude toward life, reminding us that we move forward by letting go of what's past. The paradox lies in the fact that old cycles renew themselves. What was, shall be again. Therefore, let go. Give in to the fullness—as well as the meaningless and vanity—of life.

The melancholy, skeptical refrain of the opening has a ring of joy as well. Havelock Eliis writes in one of his literary essays that if we are to set our "shoulder joyously to the world's wheel, we can spare ourselves unhappiness if, beforehand, we slip the Book of *Ecclesiastes* beneath our arm." Perhaps, Sisyphus [see p. 176], trudging eternally down the mountain, does just that, before he begins pushing the large stone toward the summit, a summit he is condemned never to reach, locked in a task that will never cease. "All things toil to weariness; Man cannot utter it, the eye is not satisfied with seeing, nor the ear filled with hearing."

The author was a teacher who dared to confront our worst fears: that life is a meaningless journey. He was also a great poet, seeking, through the sad music of his poems, the ruthless truth of existence. And from that search comes a higher synthesis of Faith and Reason, a reverence for God and the dignity of man. Everything shall be as it shall be, and our part in the cosmic order may be small, but it is a part, nonetheless. We give in to the absurdity of the cosmic dance, and find our dignity in knowing that we participate in this dance, each in our own time, each in our own way.

> To every thing there is a season,
> and a time to every purpose under the heaven.
>
> A time to be born, and a time to die;
> A time to plant, and a time to pluck up that which is planted;
>
> A time to kill, and a time to heal;
> A time to break down, and a time to build up;
>
> A time to weep, and a time to laugh;
> A time to mourn, and a time to dance;
> A time to cast away stones, and a time to gather stones together;
> A time to embrace, and a time to refrain from embracing;
>
> A time to seek, and a time to lose;
> A time to keep, and a time to cast away;
>
> A time to rend, and a time to sew;
> A time to keep silence, and a time to speak;
>
> A time to love, and a time to hate;
> A time for war, and a time for peace.

The second half of the book marvels at the mystery of existence as a pattern beautiful in its inscrutability. Fulfillment may not come with success, but neither should we reject the gift of life's pleasures when they do come. Like Aristotle, the Preacher counsels the golden mean of moderation. *Ecclesiastes* becomes a wise dialectic in the service of a humanistic ethic. The awful cloud of death and the capricious lessons of moral retribution lead to the belief that life remains the only good—provided one accepts its elusive nature and lives within the moderate limits of good judgement. On the one hand, God is there to moderate the harsh skepticism and the promise of hope; while on the other hand a belief in free will and human responsibilty mitigates life's determinism.

The book concludes with one of the more famous passages in all literature, an allegory of youth and age that combines the lyric poetry of life's splendor with a reminder, once again, that in the end, nothing can really be counted on to give life an ultimate purpose. I quote from *The Revised English Bible*.

> No one knows when his hour will come,
> like fish caught in the destroying net,
> like a bird taken in a snare. . . .
>
> He who digs a pit may fall into it,
> and he who breaks down a wall may be bitten by a snake.
> He who keeps watching the wind will never sow,
> and he who keeps his eye on the clouds will never reap.
>
> The light of day is sweet,
> and pleasant to the eye is the sight of the sun.
> However many years a person may live,
> he should rejoice in all of them.
>
> But let him remember the days of darkness,
> for they will be many.
> Everything that is to come
> will be futility.
>
> Delight in your youth, young man,   [carpe diem, n'est pas?]
> make the most of your early days;
> let your heart and your eyes show you the way;
> but remember that for all these things
> God will call you to account.
> Banish vexation from your mind
> and shake off the troubles of the body,
> for youth and the prime of life are mere futility.
>
> Remember your Creator in the days of your youth,
> before the bad times come and the years draw near
> when you will say, "I have no pleasure in them,"
> before the sun and the light of day give place to darkness,
> before the moon and the stars grow dim,
> and the clouds return with the rain.
>
> Remember him in the day

when the guardians of the house become unsteady,   [the legs go]
and the strong men stoop,   [then the teeth]
when the women grinding the meal cease work because they are few,
and those who look through the window can see no longer,   [the eyes]
when the street doors are shut,
when the sound of the mill fades,
when the chirping of the sparrow grows faint
and the songbirds fall silent;
when people are afraid of a steep place and the street is full of terrors,
when the blossom whitens on the almond tree
and the locus can only crawl and the caper-buds no longer give zest.
For mortals depart to their everlasting home,
and the mourners go about the street.

Remember your Creator
before the silver cord is snapped
and the golden bowl is broken,
before the pitcher is shattered at the spring
and the wheel broken at the well,
before the dust returns to the earth as it began
and the spirit returns to God who gave it.

Utter futility, says the Speaker,
everything is futile.

All is vanity, meaningless, absurd. Yet, one maintains a sense of humanity despite this despairing vision of the world, and that is the challenge put forth by the Wise One. The truth is driven home "straight as a nail," but it guides us for better or for worse. We accept for the better that in an unpredictable world, one can still preserve a sense of integrity and decency based on human values. If there is meaning to be found, it is in maintaining one's humanity, it is in compassion for the sufferings of others.

Or, we can fall for the worse into the pit of despair that has afflicted many in many an age. *Ecclesiastes* was written at a time when civilization had evidently gone to seed. The vitality of the nation's youth had been exhausted by her struggles against the empires that surrounded her. If God was not pronounced dead, the Yahweh in whom they had trusted seemed unable or unwilling to heed their call. In their desolation and dispersion a bitter voice was raised to express the profoundest of doubts that life was worth living. When we read *Ecclesiastes*, we feel it could have been written by any one of a number of modern poets who have written from the desolation of their own private waste land.

Food For Thought

Weldon Kees (1914-1955), Collected Poems

Little mention is made of Weldon Kees in most histories or anthologies of 20th century American poetry. He began as a writer of fiction, but by the end of the 30s he wrote mainly poetry. Much of his work can be read as a denial of the values of the present civilization. The same kind of cynicism and pessimism that runs through Ecclesiastes also dominates the work of Kees. Few of his poems are flawless; it is only by taking his work as a whole that its power emerges. His is one of a handful of voices that speak to us from the bitter tone of apocalyptic hopelessness.

If This Room Is Our World

> If this room is our world, then let
> This world be damned. Open this roof
> For one last monstrous flood
> To sweep away this floor, these chairs,
> This bed that takes me to no sleep.
> Under the black sky of our circumstance,
> Mumbling of wet barometers, I stare
> At citied dust that soils the glass
> While thunder perishes. The heroes perish
> Miles from here. Their blood runs heavy in the grass,
> Sweet, restless, clotted, sickening,
> Runs to the rivers and the seas, the seas
> That are the source of that devouring flood
> That I await, that I must perish by.

On July 19, 1955, his car was found abandoned on the approach to the Golden Gate Bridge. He has never been seen since.

William Blake's answer to the *Book of Job*

I return here to offer another interpretation of the Book of Job, because it is also an answer to the pessimism of Ecclesiastes. William Blake's Illustrations of the Book of Job was his third attempt to produce a book without text of his own, and the most successful. According to the illustrations and the notes provided by Blake, Job's sons are not killed in the flesh: they are dead only to their father, and they reappear at the end. The devil who destroys them is not an independent angel but the Accuser in Job's own brain. The boils which infect him are not a mere skin desease but a disease of his own soul. In fact, the whole drama is enacted in Job's soul. His wife is his feminine aspect, his children are his creations, his deeds, his joys; the accusing friends speak for his submerged sense of guilt. His devil is the Accuser within him, and even his God is his own creation, his own ideal, made in his image, his Selfhood, and not the true God at all.

Blake was dissatisfied with the usual interpretations of the Book of Job, most of which assumed that Job's punishment was the result of an arrangement made between God and Satan. Who was this Satan who introduced doubt and guilt into Job's Heaven? He was the diabolus, the Accuser of Sin. According to Blake, Job's prime error was admitting this Accuser into his heaven—

> For what I feared has overtaken me;
> What I dreaded has come to pass.

and from this Satan all the disasters proceed. Job did not trust God's blessings. He feared he'd lose everything because of his own unworthiness. Thus he invited this diabolus into the heaven of a false God. Only a false God would ever have listened to someone like Satan. Once these points are settled, everything becomes clear. Job's disasters are not punitive but educational. They rouse Job from his complacent submissiveness to tradition, and start him on his search for the true God.

THE ROMAN AGE OF IRON AND RUST

Caesar's expressed intention to reform and reorganize the Roman government was bitterly opposed by his fellow Senators, who feared for the safety of the Republic. They thought of Caesar as a tyrant and assasinated him on the steps of the Senate house. Though their intention was to restore the Republic, their act plunged the Roman world into another round of civil war, from which Caesar's adopted son, Octavian, emerged victorious in 30 BC, naming himself Augustus Caesar when he became Emperor in 27 BC.

Thus began The Golden Age of Art and Literature, especially poetry, a high water mark that included Virgil and Ovid. The age comes to an end with the death of Augustus around 14 AD, Virgil and Ovid both dying within five years. The Silver Age followed and lasted over a century, ending with the the death of Hadrian, who ruled as Emperor from 117 to 138 AD. Juvenal, whose satires bid farewell to a decaying empire, died about two years later. During these two centuries Rome was at the height of its power. in relative peace, emperors ruled an immense realm that encircled the Mediterranean Sea and extended northward across present day France and England. The so-called *Pax Romana* (Roman Peace) was kept by Roman legions stationed along the wide northern frontier marked by the Rhine-Danube rivers that stretched from the English Channel to the Black Sea. Today, we can still see the great ruins that were built in the classical Roman style in Italy, France, Spain, England, North Africa, the Balkans, and the Near East—temples, public buildings, baths, schools, amphitheaters, and triumphal arches. Imperialistic expansion reached as far as the Parthian Empire in the east (which finally gave way to the new Sassanid Persian Empire in the 3rd century), the Arabian and Sahara Deserts to the south, and the mountains and dense forests beyond the Rhine-Danube rivers from which migrating/invading Germanic tribes were to come. Thus, the great poets and writers who lived in Rome were read throughout a vast empire. On the same roads that all led to Rome, armies were able to reach the ends of a land that extended nearly 3,000 miles, the approximate length of the continental United States. Books and manuscripts were sent along these same, safe roads to those throughout the Empire who ordered them. By the end of the next century, all the symptoms of what must remain the mysterious collapse of Roman civilization had begun to appear. The 3rd century historian Dio Cassius characterized the pierod that followed the prosperous era of the "Good Emperors" that ended with Marcus Aurelius "The Age of Iron and Rust." This century of crisis (180-285) saw numerous corrosive forces gradually weaken the empire.

It was a time when the military dominated political life. 34 men were brought to the throne, each lasting an average of three years, producing a veritable politcal anarchy at a time when the Roman frontiers were hard pressed. If you count the unsuccessful pretenders in the provinces, we're talking nearly a hundred officers vying for control of the empire. Civil war and bloodshed were common. Economic decline led to a drop in population, causing cities to shrink to one-fourth their former size. This in turn led to an increase in taxes, and the persecution of Christians as scapegoats. St. Cyprian of Carthage wrote in a letter:

Behold the roads blocked by brigands, the seas choked by pirates, the bloodshed and horror of universal strife. The world drips with slaughter: murder, considered a crime when privately committed, is regarded as virtuous when publicly perpetrated.

Every great civilization has looked to the example of Rome to legitimize its own power, from the Holy Roman Empire of the European Middle Ages, to the British Empire in the 19th and early 20th Centuries, to the theorists of the *pax Americana* since the Revolution of '76. Rome's economic, social, military, and cultural models have been scrutinized and held up as both mirrors and warnings in every age. The French Revolution elevated the "Roman virtues" of the love of freedom and independence. The Third Reich extoled the virtues of obediance, austerity, and discipline.

In his *Ideas on the Philosophy of Humankind*, Johann Herder saw the collapse of the Roman Empire as just retribution for the arrogance and destructiveness of this "warrior state." Southern Italy, Carthage, Greece, North Africa, and other lands of the Hellenized East and European West were "sucked dry, enervated, depopulated. . . . Thus the Romans who claim to bring light to the world first everywhere make desolating night. Treasures of gold and works of art are extorted; whole regions of the world and whole ages of ancient thought sink into the abyss. The characters of peoples are extinguished, and the provinces under a series of the most detestable emperors are sucked dry, robbed, mishandled."

For Hegel, the Roman state's later development rested on its "robber beginnings—both geographically and historically on the moments of violence." The might that brought her to greatness sowed the seeds of her own collapse. The Empire that came of the Republic, and the decay that caused the Empire's fall, grew out of the desire for domination and military power. "It had no intellectual center in itself for the purposes of mind. It was the cold abstraction of domination and power, the purest self-seeking of will against the rest, with no moral fulfillment in itself but gaining content only through private interests." No wonder we see ourselves in its political and cultural models, in its artists and poets and writers.

We don't have to look to the historians of our time to confirm this assessment. The Augustan historian Livy wrote in the preface to his history:

> . . . . how with gradual crumbling of discipline the state of morals so to speak gave way, then abruptly collapsed, until it finally reached such a pass in our own day that we could no longer endure either our own corruption or the means taken against it. . . . Nowhere did greed and self-indulgence make a later entry. Nowhere were poverty and frugality so long held in honour. For the smaller the possessions, the less the covetousness. Not until recent times did wealth bring greed in its train, and with excess of all enjoyments came the lust to ruin ourselves by extravagance and riotous living and by spreading ruin about us.

Rome began as a city and became nothing less than the whole world of classical antiquity, a historical unit that lasted a thousand years. We continue to marvel at her rise to power and the great Augustan age of art and literature. But we are also fascinated by the crises of its declining centuries, perplexed by its eventual collapse, and the decline of morals and politcal corruption that remind us of our own time. In the 1st century AD Tacitus unfavorably compared Roman decadence and barbarian virtue. In the 2nd century BC, Cato blamed the decay of Rome's traditional, austere values on the corrupting influence of Hellenism. It is hard to find a time when the Romans did *not* think their morals were in dangerous decline.

In this age of "Iron and Rust," we can see the signs of decay in its poets and writers, who lost much of the vigor of earlier times and concentrated instead on extravagant forms and intellectual cleverness, a showy refinement that stroked the tastes of a cultivated class. It was not a heroic age; literature was sophisticated, using a precious mannerism of style that went along with an equally erudite philology. Hadrian, as emperor and poet, best represents this era's taste for Greek culture and Roman rhetoric. It was also an age of imitation, not emulation. Hadrian was the first of the Roman Emperors to wear a beard, and this neatly trimmed archaism is a sign of his support of the rebirth of Greek classicism, with certain "classics" of the 4th century BC serving as a canon. Many of the Greek classic sculptures that fill our museums are copies made by Roman sculptors of the 2nd century AD. Among writers, there was a veritable cult of archaism. Not only was the *how* more important than the *what*, but many poets worked to eliminate the *what* entirely.

Hadrian himself wrote short poems in the neoteric style of the Catullans, and was largely responsible for the establishment of the new literary ideal. We have this short exchange of verses between Hadrian and his literary friend Florus. Though his identity and other names are not known for certain, Florus is variously identified with the author of a history of Rome, written in a style that is markedly rhetorical and sometimes brief to the point of obscurity. He may also have been the author of "The Vigil of Venus." The second stanza is Hadrian's response.

> I'm glad I'm not Caesar
> ranging through Britain,
> hiding in forests,
> freezing to death in Scythia!
>
> I'm glad I'm not Florus,
> ranging through taverns,
> hiding in kitchens,
> bitten to death by mosquitoes!

☛ **Apeluius** (125-ca 170), *The Golden Ass*

While Fronto was noted as one of the most gifted authors of the period, and tutor to the heir-apparant Marcus Aurelius, it was **Apuleius**, the African rhetorician who wrote one of the most popular books of late antiquity, the *Metamorphoseon Libri,* or as it has come to be known, *The Golden Ass,* an early form of the picaresque novel, harking back to Petronius's *Satyricon.* It was Augustine who first referred to the manuscript as *Asinus Aureus*, but we're not sure if he meant the adjective to be taken as a reference to the quality of the text, or to the animal's tawny color. A recent translation deal with the problem more directly by rendering the title as *The Metamorphoses of Apuleius: On Making an Ass of Oneself.* The book relates the adventures of a young man, Lucius, transformed into a donkey and subsequently restored to human shape by Isis. On his way to Thessaly, a land of magic and witchcraft, Lucius meets two other travelers who tell of a horrible murder by a witch in Hypata, the town to which Lucius is going. Despite the warning, his curiousity gets the better of him, and he continues his journey to Thessaly. When he gets there, he finds himself spellbound by the mysterious atmosphere. He is led deeper and deeper into the black arts. He is entertained by Milo, whose wife Pamphile turns out to be a witch. Several of Lucius relatives give him a party, and there he hears another horrible story of mutilation by a witch. Drunk and wary, he makes his way home only to meet three robbers. Forced to defend himself, he kills them, only to discover that they were nothing more than animated wineskins. Next he meets Fotis, Milo's and Pamphile's servant. After he makes love to her, he persuades her to let him witness one of their rites. Pamphile is transformed into an owl by the aid of an unguent. Lucius cannot resist and wants to be transformed too. He persuades Fotis to perform the rite on him, but the maid makes a mistake with the unguent and Lucius becomes an ass, though he retains his human faculties of thought, though not his voice. The servant tells him that he must eat roses if he is to recover his human form. But before he is able to, he falls into the hands of robbers, and becomes an unwilling and much beaten partaker in their exploits. At their hideout, he sees the beautiful Charite, who was kidnapped for ransom on her wedding night. To console the frightened girl, the old lady who cooks for the robbers tells Charite the story of Cupid and Psyche, which is a brilliant piece of narrative. Thus, Apulius's main story is punctuated with many inserted tales, including the well-known and delightful tale, *Cupid and Psyche,* embedded in the *Metamorphoses* like a jewel.

In this way, the principal narrative becomes the frame to tell this famous story of a beautiful maiden, her invisible lover, and jealous sisters, characters which reapper in fairy stories the world over. Venus becomes jealous of Psyche, the extraordinarily beautiful daughter of a king. So Venus uses her powers and orders Psyche married to a horrible monster. Cupid, the god of love, sees Pysche and is struck by her beauty, falling madly in love with her. When Psyche is about to be killed on top of a cliff, Cupid has her transported to a magnificent palace, where she is to meet her husband, whose identity she does not know. Psyche is cautioned not to look upon him or they will immediately become separated. Psyche is goaded by her two envious sisters to disobey the order. When she looks upon the face of Cupid while he sleeps, the prophecy comes true. Only after undergoing various difficult trials and tests, including a trip to the Underworld, is Psyche finally reunited with Cupid. She marries him, and is brought up to heaven as a goddess.

Meanwhile, Lucius suffers his own trials and tribulations, Charite is rescued by her lover, disguised as a robber, but he is subsequently killed by a rival and avenged by Charite. In his asinine form, Lucius then witnesses the obscene orgies of a wandering band of lewd Syrian priests, in the course of which he becomes a famous performing ass. Numerous tragicomic calamities follow. He hears four ribald tales—"The Tale of the

Tub," "The Bakers Wife," "The Lost Slippers," and "The Fuller's Wife." As if these tales were not enough, Lucius hears another story of an amorous stepmother who tries to poison her stepson for not returning her advances. Finally, that is followed by a tale of five murders committed by a sadistic woman, whose punishment consists of public display in sexual union with a donkey (soon to be Lucius). Whether or not the woman would have gone through with it, Lucius finds this prospect so abhorrent that he escapes and eventually falls asleep on a seashore, exhausted.

The last section is a moving religious document and affords us a glimpse of the beauty of holiness in a cult elsewhere described as compounded of superstition and chicanery. As Lucius sleeps, Isis appears and promises to help him. As the spring festival proceeds in which Isis launches her sacred vessel, a priest gives Lucius a garland of roses, which he eats, and he is changed once again into his human form.

Lucius is able to observe human behavior in all it's manifestations, including many unhappy episodes of adultery and death that occupy the last part of the book. Driven by the basic feature of his character, *curiositas*, which got him in trouble in the first place, Lucius is drawn by his curiousity to investigate the nature of the surrounding world and by his desire to find the roses that can free him from the magic spell. When Lucius is transformed back into human shape, he becomes Apuleius, the author himself. Devoting himself to the service of the Goddess, he undergoes arduous preparations for initiation, experiences new visions, and finally, alone in her temple at night, he approaches the borderland of death, experiences rebirth and revelation as he wakes to the brilliant light of the sun. The novel is not exactly a satire, nor is it a comic romance or ribald adventure like Petronius' *Satyricon*. It's a serious novel, using a variety of prose and poetic styles, a sort of "Pilgrim's Progress of the Ass-Man" in quest for knowledge of marvels and the spiritual meaning of life. His hero walks to the beat of his own drum, and the final transformation is not an accident, but a redemption brought about by his mystic worship of the Goddess, Isis. Bawdy and witty, comic and philosophical, the work cannot be easily categorized. Marked by elements of burlesque as well as intimations of an ethical, religious purpose, *The Golden Ass* is an entertaining narrative filled with serio-comic tales embedded in other tales of adventure and suspense, including a final overarching vision of the possibilities of grace and salvation.

Much of classical tradition had spent its creative force and was becoming repetitive and derivative. It is no great exaggeration to say that the only original secular work of the later empire was Apuleius's *Golden Ass*. In Apuleius we encounter the pulsing life, the wit and fantasy and prying curiosity—even an interest in philosophy and religion—which we miss in Fronto and hardly get from other poets of this time. Living in a period of enthusiasm for the archaic, Apuleius liked to use obsolete words in the larger fabric of literariness, as well as the penchant for oratory that characterized this age. His style is marked by the juxtaposition of archaic syntax with vulgarisms and poeticisms, spiced with the technical vocabulary of science and the crafts. He coined words and phrases which we find in no other writing of his time, and no other extant writers has imitated him. If his intent was to distance literary language from the language of speech, he found the perfect way to do it.

Words became evocative, surrounded by the glow of marginal meanings and suggestive innuendo.

It would look as if the virtuosity of Apuleius was carefully calculated to attract the interest of the bored Roman of his day (like some avant-garde writers in the 1920s, and language poets of the post-Vietnam era), which would not have been excited by an ordinary composition in a tongue familiar to readers. Most of the verbal ingenuity is lost in translation into any tongue, though many translators have made the attempt, in part, perhaps, accounting for his continued popularity with them, for they were thus enabled to play amusing tricks with their own languages also. The highly sophisticated and calculated artificiality of the tales of Apuleius renders them sometimes most charming in translation, but is certainly a sign that the creative period of Roman writing was over. Latin literature did not recover its vitality until the descendants of the invading barbarians took up the use of a greatly modified Latin once more in the early Middle Ages.

☼-

A recurring theme in the history of Latin poetry was this recourse to archaic linguistic and literary models, separate from the contemporary language of speech. By the middle of this 2nd century, it became a more marked and organic tendency. The best example of this attitude is exemplified by **Marcus Cornelius Fronto** (ca 100-ca. 167), considered the new Cicero. While he uses a style that sounds new and original, it does not seem modern, drawing instead on the models of pre-Augustan literature. Of course, as expected, in the fragments that have come down to us, we discover that this reverence for rhetoric existed at the expense of content. The body of his writings that have survived show how vacuous form devoid of content can be. His letters to Marcus Aurelius, his pupil, show that Fronto placed greatest emphasis on how something is said or written, not on what is being said or written about. He remained on intimate terms with the heir-apparent, who continued to hold him in high esteem. In their letters, there's a certain amount of flattery on either side—Fronto makes Marcus the peer of Julius Caesar, and Marcus sets Fronto beside Cato and Cicero. Nothing distressed him more deeply than Marcus Aurelius's decision to follow philosophy instead of rhetoric. A distaste for philosophy may be excusable, but for Fronto, neither history nor any other serious discipline had any meaning except as a source for ornamental anecdotes and figures of speech. There are no real ideas in Fronto, just phrases. Much of the prose and poetry of this age was lifeless and had to await the passionate conviction of Christian writers to breathe some vitality into it. After Fronto's death, Marcus Aurelius set his statue up in the senate and kept his bust among his household gods.

☛ **Marcus Aurelius** (121-180) *Meditations*

If there is one main link between the fall of Rome and the literary revival of the 12-13th centuries, perhaps it is *The Confessions* of St. Augustine, who virtually founded the literary genre of romantic and introspective autobiography. But especially from our modern vantage point, we should not forget Marcus Aurelius, the philosopher-poet,

Roman Emperor the last twenty years of his life who kept a journal of philosophical thoughts which was later titled *Meditations*. The most favored genre of poetry in the 20th century is often called "post-romantic lyric meditation," and the most popular among contemporary verse has been labeled "confessional," often a pejorative term. But the lyric meditation and confessional writing is not as new as we think. We can trace the confessional, personal meditation back to Marcus Aurelius and St. Augustine. Actually, Marcus Aurelius did not use the word, meditations. In the orginal Greek manuscripts (he chose not to write in Latin), he used the words *Pros Heauton*, which literally means "To Himself." When he writes "you," he is not talking to the reader or referencing a third person. He is actually talking to himself.

●◆

Begin each day by telling yourself: Today I shall be meeting with interference, ingratitude, insolence, disloyalty, ill-will, and selfishness—all of them due to the offenders' ignorance of what is good or evil. But for my part I have long perceived the nature of good and its nobility, the nature of evil and its meanness, and also the nature of the culprit himself, who is my brother (not in the physical sense, but as a fellow-creature similarly endowed with reason and a share of the divine); therefore none of those things can injure me, for nobody can implicate me in what is degrading. Neither can I be angry with my brother or fall foul of him; for he and I were born to work together, like a man's two hands, feet, or eyelids, or like the upper and lower rows of teeth.

✦

Either the world is a mere hodge-podge of random cohesions and dispersions, or else it is a unity of order and providence. If the former, why wish to survive in such a purposeless and chaotic confusion; why care about anything, save the manner of the ultimate return to dust; why trouble my head at all; since, do what I will, disperson must overtake me sooner or later? But if the contrary be true, then I do reverence, I stand firmly, and I put my trust in the directing Force.

[just for fun, I've arranged the following "meditation" in the form of a poem, to give the reader some idea as to how easily it could pass for a contemporary poem.]

Take Your Stand

An empty pageant;
a stage play;
flocks of sheep, herds of cattle; a tussle of spearmen;
a bone flung among a pack of dogs;
a crumb tossed into a pond of fish;
ants, loaded and labouring; mice, scared and scampering;
puppets, jerking on their strings—
that is life.
In the midst of it all
you must take your stand,
good-temperedly and without disdain,
yet always aware that a man's worth
is no greater than the worth

of his ambitions.

Reflect often how the life of today is a repetition of the past; and observe that it also presages what is to come. Review the many complete dramas and their settings, all so similar, which you have known in your own experience, or from bygone history: the whole court-circle of Hadrian, for example, or the court of Antonius, or the courts of Philip, Alexander, and Croesus. The performance is always the same; it is only the actors who change.

Mislead yourself no longer; you will never read these notebooks again now, nor the annals of bygone Romans and Greeks, nor that choice selection of writings you have put by for your old age. Press on, then, to the finish; cast away vain hopes; and if you have any regard at all for self, see to your own security while still you may.

We also see in this period the creation of a vast religious literature aimed at preserving Christian doctrine from contamination by pagan systems of thought. Already by about 130 AD the doctrinal corpus of the four Gospels and the thirteen epistles of Paul was commonly accepted as the New Testament.

Greek Christian poetry begins with **Clement of Alexandria** who wrote in the late 2nd Century. He used the Greek metrical system of syllabic quantity, long and short syllables counted across the hexameter line. Many of Clement's poems were influenced by the Book of *Psalms*. Christian culture, though seeing itself separate from Roman secular (pagan) culture, actually revitalized many elements of classical literature. The Latin and Greek secular literature written at this time was hardly notable, but Christian writers and poets were fueled by their passion to produce inspiring homilies sermons, letters, and especially devotional poetry and hymns. Despite the hostility some Christian intellectuals developed toward pagan literature, Clement believed that studying the work of Latin poets and Greek philosophers could be beneficial when taken as *propaedentic*, or introductory to the work of Christian authors, similar in function to the pedagogue who brings his students to the schoomaster, Christ.

During the next few centuries, a great number of Greek poets took their cue from Clement, and wrote religious poems based on the *Hebrew Bible* or *The New Testament*, but the best of the lot was Gregory of Nazianzus who wrote several volumes of work. His poems, characterized by vivid and beautiful imagery, addressed his own religous experiences and the ethical demands such faith placed upon him, qualities hardly found in the pagan poetry of the time, nor in much of the Christian didactice and dogmatic verse.

By the 4th Century, Greek poetry began to show the influence of Syriac verse, which was written in a stress rhythm, not syllabic meter. The Syrian poet Ephraim (d. 373) composed the first Christian hymns. When these were translated into Greek verse, the stress rhythms were kept and Greek Christian poets began to use both conventions, often in the same poem: verse based on syllabic quantity, and poems that followed the regular stress rhythms that would soon develop into rhymed accentual verse.

Latin poetry, unlike Greek verse, had always used stress rhythms, which grew out of its folk poetry and the beat of its military legions. By the middle of the 3rd century, Latin poets began to imitate the Greek poets, eschewing their own native verse convention for the more prestigious Greek syllabic meter. (In the 20th Century, a similar event occurred when American poets, on the verge of finding the natural American voice that stemmed from Whitman, suddenly took the European path of Symbolist verse prompted by the influence of Eliot's *Waste Land*. William Carlos Williams lamented that Eliot's poem set American poetry back at least 50 years—[see chapter on Williams]. Ironically, Christianity's influence began among the lower classes, who continued their folk verse tradition of the rhythmic stress beat. When Latin began to be used instead of Greek in Church services, the more popular form of verse rhythm took hold, and thus, rhyme in the Church hymns established itself.

In the field of secular Latin poetry, we also find a great deal of occasional verse, acrostic riddles, eclogues, epigrames, and poeticl epistles; these poems too smack of the schoolroom and the schoolmaster's instructions. Latin secular poetry of the late empire seems weak and weary, a reworking of classical themes and subjects. Poems called attention to themselves in how the clever poet could manipulate old forms from previous centuries. Many of the works have not survived; some were deliberately destroyed in later centuries by the Church; and some by the destructions of war and mere negligence. But what we do have appears shabby and insignificant. There may well have been fewer writers during the declining years of Roman civilization. We should not forget that while Roman classical culture was impressive, it was also narrowly limited, shared only by the Empire's upper-crust. In their desire to escape from the burdens of life in the decadent and overtaxed towns, senators and aristocrats fled to their estates, spacious villas, or country houses and lived a life of sports and leisure amid their dependants. Culture became imitative and lifeless. In a world in the throes of decay and deterioration, there was probably a reduced interest in poetry.

Most Greek and Latin speakers were illiterate peasants and artisans whose varying patois by no means allowed them to appreciate the conservative literary tongue. The privileged, educated classes lost interest perhaps in the inner spirit of the heritage they revered, but they certainly paid attention to the externals of form. The Roman schools of grammar (elementary education) and rhetoric (secondary and advanced education) were designed to prepare the sons of the aristocracy and the more abitious middle class for leadership in government and law. The system of education focused more and more on rhetoric and concentrated the students' attention on declamatory, exaggerated phrases, on the art of spinning sentences to a patient audience. From the age of seven onward, girls and boys together went to private schools to learn the "three R's"—reading, writing, and 'rithmetic. The methods used were primitive and harsh, with continual shouting and caning by the schoolmaster. Many children did not proceed to the next stage where the focus was on learning grammar. The last phase in the schools of rhetoric prepared these young adults for careers of state and politics and the law—they learned to imitate the great Greek and

Latin orators. Upon graduation, young gentlemen of the ruling class often took the "grand tour" to Athens, Asia Minor, and other intellectual centers of Hellenistic culture. They came back able to read and comprehend and to write and speak clearly. Unfortunately, they had very little to say._

☞ The poetae novelli

That thin intellectual strata which had produced the great classics of Western civilization was slowly disappearing. Classical culture came to be dominated by academics—always a bad sign—and those classical texts read in the schools were studied not for their content but as examples of grammar and rhetoric. Among the general populace in town and country, it became an age of signs and wonders, of emotional credulity and vulgar magic. The very dead-weight of unsuperable, unattainable models in literature, thought, and art, all combined to drive western men into themselves, to spin a visionary universe from the unreachable ego.

The second century was a period of cultural liveliness, but flourishing poetic talent began to wane. Poetry became a refined hobby of the upper classes rather than a serious vocation. With the beginning of Hadrian's reign, the unbroken trail of great traditional poetic genres faded into the brush of dilitantism. We have no epics, either historical or mythological; satire ceases with Juvenal; and that genre of personal poetry, the elegy, had feeble successors. Even poetry written for the stage lost its power.

A minor genre of poetry, however, does continue to be practiced. It's main characteristic seems to be an opposition to the grand epic. Many historians and literary critics have called these minor poets poetae novelli, referring back to the neoteric school of the 1st century BC. Thus, the novelli could be seen as a diminuation of poetae novi, which included poets such as Catullus and Lucretius. But unlike those earlier poets, the poets at the end of the 2nd century were not avant-garde or moderns, but used the archaic, obsolete, and old fashioned. By salvaging the remnants of an earlier time, they remind us of the post-moderns of today who mix the bric-a-brac of cultural mediocrity with a parody of discarded classicism. Today we argue about whether the post-modern is a reaction to modernism, an extension of modernism, or a separate parallel development. The same can be said for the poetae novelli. Did they represent a sudden renaissance, or the development of a secondary, but separate stream in Latin verse?

The poetae novelli were mostly concerned with metrical experimentation, inventing new forms, often rendering a traditional subject in purposely awkward and inappropriate meter. Much effort went into the clever manipulation of words, such as following a hexameter line with a line that is the exact reverse of the former, word for word, but in iambic dimeter. Sometimes the poem was composed in such a way that the image of the object being described is shown—today we call this "concrete poetry." A poem about the bomb is shaped to look like a mushroom cloud, etc. As with the postmodern, it is hard to define this genre—further evidence that when poetry is aimed at an audience of academics or a refined upper class, it often deteriorates into the clever and vacuous.

By the end of the second century, pagan and Christian literature began to co-exist, each trying to characterize an age of disintegration and turmoil, dislocation and violence that was not to end for centuries to come.

☞ **The *Anthologia Latina* and its most famous poem, the "Pervigilium Veneris."**

The *Latin Anthology* was a vast collection of poems assembled in Africa in the sixth century. The work focused primarily on African poets of late antiquity but also included authors from earlier periods. The value of this "anthology" lies in the fact that it preserved texts that were lost or destroyed during the barbarian invasions, and would be lost to us as well were it not for this anthology. For some of the poems, no author is indicated.

Vespa writes a satiric poem in which a cook and a baker argue over whose job is the more difficult, and whose calling is the greater. The two use use mythological and philosophical references to defend their respective points of view. In the end, it's the sumptuous dishes and mouth-watering desserts that make the point. Vespa also tells us of his own activity as a lecturer, going from city to city in search of paying spectators. He makes fun of his own calling (implying that the baker's or cook's calling is superior to his own), mocking as futile vanity the lectures and readings which were his only source of livelihood.

Many of the poems in the *Anthologia* were <u>centos</u>. The cento was a genre of poetry where the poet used whole or half-verses taken from classical poems (in the Latin world, Virgil's works were most often used), and joined them to make a new poem. Like a patchwork quilt, the Latin word *cento* comes from a kind of blanket made by stitching various pieces of cloth together. But it's not an easy matter to assign accurate dates to the composition of many of these poems. **Pentadius**, for instance, probably belongs to the third century, but we can't be sure. He wrote "echoing couplets," a form in which the first part of the hexameter is the same as the last part of the pentameter. We're familiar with the palindrome, where the letters actually spell the same sentence forwards and backwards ("Madam, I'm Adam"), but echoing couplets only deal with the beginning and ending phrase, such as the following in Latin:

> *Sentio, fugit hiems*, Zephyrisque moventibus orbem
> iam tepet Eurus aquis; *sentio, fugit hiems*.   [my italics]

Verse using "echoing couplets" was not just a part of literature, but of common graffiti as well. Ancient graffiti has been found all over the excavated walls and monuments of Rome, often expressing a philosophy of life that mocked the nobility who claimed to strive for *virtu*, *honos*, and *gloria*, when what they really wanted was wealth, large families, and social prestige. The following *graffito*, using echoing couplets, was often scribbled on walls of that period.

> *Balnea, vina, Venus corrumpunt corpora nostra,*
> *At vitam faciunt balnea, vina, Venus.*

Baths, wine, and love-making destroy our bodies,

but life's worth living because of bath, wine, and love-making.

Pentadius seems to have no trouble with this form, writing on the theme of spring and the rebirth of the world in graceful vignettes. The theme of nature is taken up by many of the poets in the *Anthologia*, especially in the most famous poem of the collection, the anonymous *Pervigilium Veneris*, or the "Vigil of Venus."

The "Vigil of Venus" is surely one of the loveliest pieces in all Latin literature. It could well have been written at the end of the 3rd or even the middle of the 4th century. Others date it even later, in the 5th, or even 6th century. Because of certain similarities to the style of the *poetae novelli*, many scholars have attributed this poem to Florus, Hadrian's literary friend. And Hadrian had revived the worship of Venus on a grand scale. In his magnificent temple across from the Colosseum, the apses of Venus and of Rome stand in the center of the structure, back to back. The poem's ninety-two trochaic tetrameter lines, exquisite and melodious, are punctuated by the refrain,

> *Cras amet* qui numquam amavit,   [another echoing couplet]
> quique amavit *cras amet.*

> "Tomorrow shall be love for the loveless,
> and for the lover tomorrow shall be love."

The "Vigil of Venus" is unique in Latin literature for its imaginative fancy, and its evocations and blending of nature and love, life and patriotism. Much of the meter recalls the form of the acclamations that soldiers and people used to shout after the triumphs of their victorious generals. The syntax and tone of the popular language blends at times with largely classical vocabulary, though the poem attains an extraordinary freshness because the descriptions are clear and the expressions simple. It's the spring tide of the goddess of love, with the Graces and nymphs, Ceres, Bacchus and Apollo, and Cupid without bows and arrows, all participating in the festival. Everywhere, nature awakes from the sleep of winter, birds chirp loudly and flowers burst from every bud. By the power of the goddess, all creatures mate and insure increase; fertility abounds. At its close, a note of personal elegy is heard:

> The nightengale sings, but we are mute:
> when is *my* spring coming?

Color map of Rome in 3rd & 4th centuries

In the 3rd and 4th Centuries, Rome is threatened on all sides:
Germans from the north, Persians from the east, Scots from the West,
And pirates on the Mediterranean.

3rd and 4th Centuries

The third century was not a prosperous time for the Empire, economically or culturally. After the death of Marcus Aurelius in 180 AD, there began a period of military anarchy and great economic decline. With the assassination of Alexander Severus and his mother, there broke out the formidable crisis which nearly shattered the Roman world to fragments and brought its civilization, still so brilliant at the beginning of the third century, to an end. Of all the reasons for the fall of Rome, one can find in the politcal the fundamental vice of the Empire: It had no constitution. It was the army, not the Senate or the people or a line of succession that made or broke an Emperor. Between 235 and 285 there were 18 emperors, some remaining in power a few months, others only a few days. To accept the title of Caesar was like accepting the death sentence. A man could be a general one day, emperor the next, and dead the day after that. By the time a farmer in Gaul heard there was a new Emperor, chances are that that Emperor had been assassinated, and a new one was proclaimed to take his place. For half a century the men who wore the mantle of emperor played a life and death game of musical chairs. There was a slow but continuous evolution whereby the *principate* ("first citizen") was transformed into a monarchy or quasi-monarcy—the *dominate* ("lord"), but there's no need to retrace the history of the so-called period of the Thirty Tyrants. Recurring civil wars decimated the ruling classes, impoverished the economic system, and weakened the frontier garrisons, the only defense in place to resist invasions by Germanic tribes, the so-called barbarians. On the borders of the Rhine and the Danube, Germanic peoples momentarily broke through. To the East, the new Persian kingdom of the Sassanids began a military expansion. The Emperor Valerian was made prisoner in 260 by the Persian King Sapor, who is said to have used him as a footstool for mounting his horse. A gigantic bas-relief at Nakeh-Rousten near Persepolis shows Valerian kneeling before the Persian King, who is on horseback. Legend has it that at the prisoner's death his skin, after being tanned, dyed red and stuffed, hung for several centuries in a Persian temple. Further west, Scots threatened the English border with incursions beyond Hadrian's Wall. Pirates were active on the inland seas, and the *Pax Romana* was beginning to fail. The countryside was becoming depopulated, the routes of communication were unsafe, and commerce declined. Successive debasements of the coinage caused gold and silver to practically disappear from circulation—indeed, a large proportion of the Roman coins now preserved derive from hoards apparently deposited in the third century. This monetary collapse and inflation hit the cities hardest. And as if this weren't enough, natural catastrophes such as earthquakes and epidemics were more frequent and more deadly than in other periods, contributing to the decline in population, which at certain points was half the average of earlier decades.

Beginning with the murder of Severus in 235 and lasting until the accession of Diocletian in 284, this period in the third century is often seen as a watershed, called by various historians "the third-century crisis," "the age of transition," "the age of the soldier-emperors," "the age of anarchy," "the time of chaos," "the military monarchy," etc. We see in this period the signs of decay, which, despite the recovery under Constantine in the fourth century, led to the collapse and fragmentation of the Roman empire in the west in the fifth century. Gibbon, in his *Decline and Fall of the Roman Empire*, felt that Constantine's adoption of Christianity assisted this process of decline by finally abandoning earlier Roman values. Even during this period Christians were often blamed for the turmoil. Many felt the hard times were caused by turning away from the ancient gods. Persecutions were usually an on-again off-again event—under Decius (249-51), and Diocletian (303-11) , and emperor's who encouraged it believed that neglect of the gods endangered the empire's security, that deviant groups such as Christians had to be brought in line. Of course, the obverse side of this was that more and more people were turning to Christianity, not to mention other religions, for comfort and reassurance in their times of suffering. It's only natural that contemporary writers like **Cyprian of Carthage**, who was martyred in the persecutions under Valerian in 258, would emphasize the evils of this time. But the Christian church also grew stronger during this time, and was able to develop a solid institutional structure which served it well when Constantine made it the religion of the empire. A great deal of the work of Christian poets writing in Latin during this time has been lost, and no good contemporary narrative survives for the critical middle period of this century. Often, we have to depend on fanciful accounts like the *Historia Agusta*, which comes off as tabloid journalism at its best.

Gallienus, Valerian's son and successor, was incapable of ransoming his father. Under his principate the revolt broke out that split the Empire into twenty fragments: Egypt, Greece, Thessaly, Africa, Gaul, to name just a few.

Yet, historians still marvel at the Empire's ability to recover from such crisis before the definitive disintegration still to come in the fifth century. Diocletian brought a measure of unity back to the Empire, but realized that it could no longer be directed by a single ruler in Rome. So he set up a colleague to share the power, but one who would not threaten to become a rival or an enemy. His comrade-in-arms Maximian consented to be the hand that served the brain.

In the reigns of Diocletian and Constantine from 284 to 337 AD, the empire seemed to recover, and once again there was a move back to a centralized government. The notion of the emperor as "the first among equals" transformed over the 3rd century into a theocratic monarchy, which was modified for the Christian Roman Empire of the 4th century and perpetuated into medieval political life. Much of the 4th century is noted for is cultural renaissance and literary revival. Christian poets, writing in both Greek and Latin, began to make significant achievements alongside their pagan counterparts.

Except for a few Christian writers, most Latin texts seemed to be repeating old themes during this period. These were unsteady times, and the establishment of Christianity grew out of the need for religious certainty. The urban poor began to grow weary of pagan gods. As the state became more and more urban in character, the country lost contact with the life out of which the old Italian agricultural deities and rites had sprung.

An attempt was made to bring these gods into line with a growing trend toward mysticism and monotheism. **Plotinus**, the Greek philosopher, was one of the most influential minds of the Roman Imperial era. He incorporated all that was vital in the pagan cults into a new philosophical scheme called Neo-Platonism. In this scheme, there was only one god—infinite, unknowable, and unapproachable except through mystical experience. As the source of everything, God's being radiated outward like concentric circles in a pond. Everything in the world, from objects to people to minor deities, were manifestations of that one, radiating being. Thus, the pagan gods of the Greco-Roman Olympic cult—Jupiter, Juno, Apollo, Minerva, and the rest—were useful symbols, however crude, of the one, true Neoplatonic god. As the dominant philosophical system of the third century, Neoplatonism's belief in one god helped prepare the way among the upper classes for Christianity.

The average person looked to new religions that offered release from individual guilt, and promised, instead, salvation and eternal life. Those who sought spiritual transcendance and personal salvation turned away from the ancient pagan gods and embraced the new mystery religions and cults that had originated in the older, eastern culture of Rome. From Egypt came the cult of the goddess Isis; from Persia came the cult of the savior Mithras; from Asia Minor came the worship of the Great Earth Mother; and from Palestine came Christianity.

Each had its own doctrinal disputes, though none as lively or as intense as the new religion named after Christ and spread by Paul. Numerous heresies were identified. Most sought to simplify the nature of Christ and the Trinity. One group, the Gnostics, insisted that Christ was not truly human, but merely a divine phantom or ghost; they believed that God would not have degraded himself by assuming a flesh and blood body. The doctrine brought forward by Arius, a priest of Alexandria, was a denial of both the absolute divinity and the complete humanity of Christ. In its historical consequences, it is considered the most important of all the variants of orthodox belief that troubled the peace of the early church. Arianism maintained that Christ was not fully divine and therefore could not be equal to God the Father without introducing elements of polytheism. But the Church maintained the substantial indentity between God, the Father and Christ, his only begotten son. This dispute raged on for over a century. Finally, the emperor called the first general or ecumenical council of the church to meet at Nicaea in 325, and a majority of the bishops in attendance condemned the Arians and drew up the Nicene Creed maintaining the full divinity and humanity of Christ. Arias and his followers were sent into exile. Ironically, most Germans were converted to Christianity by the Arian bishops who were exiled. **Ulfilas** not only carried the Arian brand of Christianity to his people, but devised a Gothic alphabet, then translated much of the Bible into Gothic, thereby laying the foundation for a written German literature. When the Germanic tribes were absorbed into the empire after the invasions, the problem first introduced by the priest Arius flared up again.

The Manichian heresy solved the problem of the dualism of good and evil by positing two Gods, instead of one. Since a perfect and good God could not have willed evil, evil must have been introduced into the world by an evil God. Obviously the Church could not allow the concept of a double divinity. (Agustine was himself a follower of Mani before rejecting his teachings.)

The Donatists felt that sacraments administered by a priest who was not spiritually perfect invalidated the sacrament. But acceptance of this notion would have destroyed the power of the Church. Whether or not the priest himself was pure, the sacraments administered were valid merely because the priest's sanction had come from the Church and God.

The heresy of Pelagius, a monk of British origin who knew many of the Christian writers of the day, such as Paulinus of Nola, was so threatening to the early church that Augustine opposed its spread by any means he could muster. Pelagius believed that one could earn salvation merely by good deeds, ethical behavior, and a spiritual life avoiding sin and guilt. The doctrine takes no account of the need for divine grace, which meant the official church was not required to play a mediating role. Human beings could play a direct role in their own salvation, and Christ's role was diminished. This doctrine had special appeal for many of the senatorial aristocracy who did not like the idea of having to answer to the authority of the Church. For them, Christ could be another god, alongside Opollo and Minerva.

Early Christianity had many things in common with other mystery religions: baptism, a sacramental meal, and human brotherhood under a divine god or goddess. Many cults and religions featured the death and resurrection of a savior god; some promised eternal salvation and redemption that would reward those who suffered their life on earth. But Christianity differed from them all in two fundamental ways: (1) unlike Isis and Mithras, its founder and savior was an actual historical personage who made the others seem vague and unreal; and (2) its god was not merely the best of many gods, but the One God, the God of the Hebrews, unique in all antiquity in His claims to exclusiveness and omnipotence, and now detached by Christianity from his association with a chosen people to become the God of all peoples. Thus, Christianity went from being a minority cult to the religion of the majority within the Empire, due in no small part to Constantine's conversion in 324 and his establishment of Christianity as the official state religion.

It was not an age of great literary production. The most competent writing of the age, aside from Christian works, was in the field of jurisprudence and history. The greatest poets of the age are read today only by scholars and other poets or literary historians. But some of these poets provide a nugget that is interesting either for its lyric beauty, or as a model of what not to write in an age that suffers equally from decline and decay.

☛ Nemesianus, the *Cynegetica* (283-84)

The only significant poet of the entire 3rd century was M. Aurelius Nemesianus, a North African, probably from Carthage, who wrote didactic poems on fishing, hunting, and perhaps fowling. The *Cynegetica* opens with Nemesianus's declaration that he does not want and does not know how to write other genres of poetry. This motiff—telling the reader that the author is unable to write on a specific subject or in a specific genre, and then doing it—is actually a genre in itself, the *recusatio*. Didactic poetry on the subject of hunting had a long tradition in Roman literature, and often served as a justification for elegant descriptions of landscapes, usually in a Virgilian style. This genre continues today, where novels and movies show man in contact with the natural world, roaming field and forest, freed from the unhealthy urban environment—a noble creature tasting adventure and getting in touch with primal emotions. Fact was, since the 2nd century AD, the state of agriculture in the Roman world had changed for the worse. By choosing to present landscapes in the Virgilian manner, the poet could conceal this decline in the name of a poetic model of indisputable authority. By drawing a parallel between the present and the Augustan Golden age, readers were comforted with the notion of an idyllic past, and didn't have to face the troubled present. Perhaps that's why Nemesianus's pastoral poems were praised so highly by his contemporaries. But the 325 hexameter lines that have survived do not justify this praise. In a translation by William Somervile made in 1735, English archaisms such as thy and thou, not to mention the tendency to capitalize any word that seems significant, makes the effect even worse.

> From *The Chace*: "Of the Litter of Whelps"

> When now the third revolving Moon appears,
> With sharpen'd Horns, above th'Horizon's Brink;
> Without *Lucina*'s Aid, except thy Hopes   [Lucina: goddess of birth]
> Are amply crown'd; short Pangs produce to Light
> The smoking Litter, crawling, helpless, blind,
> Nature their Guide, they seek the pouting Teat
> That plenteous streams. Soon as the tender Dam
> Has form'd them with her Tongue, with Pleasure view
> The Marks of their renown'd Progenitors,
> Sure Pledge of Triumphs yet to come. All these
> Select with Joy; but to the merc'less Flood
> Expose the dwindling Refuse, nor o'erload
> Th'indulgent Mother.

Food for Thought

Randall Jarrell, *The Next Day*

The first time I read Randall Jarrell's poem "The Next Day," I had just finished a course in 18th Century English literature. I caught a glimpse of the first line

> Moving from Cheer to Joy, from Joy to All,

and closed the book. I came across the poem again several years later, had the same initial reaction, but read on for a few more lines. And it struck me. Jarrell wasn't talking about the grand concepts of Joy and Cheer, or the great oneness of the All; he was writing about a woman shopping in a supermarket the day after attending her best friend's funeral. The Cheer and Joy and All were laundry detergents. The Cornish game hens, wrapped tightly with cord and basketed, "identical food-gathering flocks" are selves she overlooks.

> . . . Wisdom, said William James,
> Is learning what to overlook. And I am wise
> If that is wisdom.
> Yet somehow, as I buy All from these shelves
> And the boy takes it to my station wagon,
> What I've become
> Troubles me even if I shut my eyes.

When I was young and miserable and pretty
and poor, I'd wish what all girls wish: to have a husband,
A house and children. Now that I'm old, my wish
Is womanish:
that the boy putting groceries in my car

See me. It bewilders me he doesn't see me.
For so many years
I was good enough to eat: the world looked at me
And its mouth watered. . . . Now the boy pats my dog
And we start for home. Now I am good.

Driving home, she thinks of her life, "afraid only that it will change, as I am changing."
Looking at her face in the rear-view mirror, she realizes she's old. "That's all, I'm old."
Then she remembers the funeral she went to the day before.

My friend's cold made-up face, granite among its flowers,
Her undressed, operated-on, dressed body
Were my face and body.
As I think of her I hear her telling me

How young I seem; I *am* exceptional;
I think of all I have.
But really no one is exceptional,
No one has anything, I'm anybody,
I stand beside my grave
Confused with my life, that is commonplace and solitary.

"The Next Day" is now one of my favorite poems. So much for judging a book by its cover,
or a poem by its first line and capitalized nouns..

Nemesianus also wrote poems on fishing and navigation, but those have been lost. We
do have four eclogues based on Virgil's *Bucolics*. But the best Nemesianus can manage is a
refrain reminiscent of the *cras amet* of the "Perigilium Veneris":

Let each sing his love
Songs to lighten praise.

Nemesianus' verse exhibits correct technique and form; what is lacking is poetic
inspiration.

The 4th century sees Rome making a slight comeback, called the Great Cultural Renaissance. Diocletian's reforms and Constantine's economic and political policy were responsible for a surprising literary flourishing that is one of the most impressive in the history of Rome. With Constantine's conversion to Christianity, making it the religion of the Empire, paganism was held at bay as it fought for some kind of co-existence with emerging Christian literature.

Christian Poets of the Late Empire

Latin poetry served as a medium of expression for the feelings, appreciations, and idealism of early medieval clerics and monks. Coming more from the heart, many of these poets shed the rhetorical artificiality of later Roman poetry, and wrote in plain direct language about personal issues. Following the rules of classical grammar, so that it was universally understandable, they added new terms and modified the meaning of others, becoming more direct, simple, and "modern." Other poets of this period, Christian and Pagan alike, continued to write in that artificial and ornate style of late classical literature. The evolution of Latin verse over a period of centuries diverged into two separate streams, one adhering to the classical style, often marked by rhetorical formalism and verbosity, and the other widening out, emphasizing certain features which made it more popular, as well as better adapted to catchy music. This was the Latin of popular speech, which changed over the course of centuries into the various vernaculars that were to become French, Spanish, Italian, and other Romance languages. Both languages—written Latin and the evolving Latin vernacular—continued to exist, side by side; Even into the Renaissance of the 16th century, Latin was the universal language of Europe, used for the writing of philosophic and scientific books. In the 14th and 15th centuries, writers such as Dante and Chaucer wrote in both literary Latin and the new languages of their own countries, Italian and English. It was a bold choice for Dante to use Italian (specificaly, his own Tuscan dialect) for the composition of his *Commedia*, and Chaucer directed his *Canterbury Tales* to a new reading public when he chose English (specifically the midland dialect) to bring alive the Wife of Bath and the other pilgrims telling their bawdy and moralistic tales on the way to the shrine of Thomas à Beckett.

There's no easy way to divide the poets of late antiquity from the poets of the early medieval period (or the "dark ages) of these few centuries, nor can one conveniently separate those who wrote in formal, often artifical Latin and those who were choosing the modern path of spoken Latin. In most cases, the poetry speaks for itself.

☛ **Lactantius** (b. mid-3rd century, d. After 324), the *Symposium*

Lucius Caelius Firmianus Lactantius was born in Africa, converted to Christianity, and in 317 Constantine chose him to tutor his son, Crispus. All the writings from his pagan period are completely lost. Maybe they were destroyed, either by the Church, or his own hand. The *Symposium* describes in verse his voyage from Africa to Bithynia. The De Opificio Dei defends the immortality of the soul; the Divinae Institutions attacks paganism, philosophy, and celebrates Christ, the Last Judgment and the destiny of souls; the De Ira Dei makes a case for God's need to punish the wicked as a way to show his love for the good; in the De Mortibus Persecutorum, he also affirms the equilibrium of the world, which is maintained through the divine punishment of the wicked.

☛ **Commodian** (c. 250 ad - mid 4th century)

It's difficult to know exactly where to place him chronologically. What references we have about his life and time are vague and confusing. Some evidence places him as late as the middle of the 5th century, but a more likely date could be the middle of the 3rd century, from the references he makes in his own work to the persecutions of that time.

His most famous works include the *Instructions*, 80 hexameter poems written against the pagans and Jews. The poems are all acrostics. His other important work is the *Carmen Apologeticum*, a history of the world—which meant the history of the *Old Testament* and Rome—seen as a battle between God and the Devil.

Of all the prose writers that also wrote Christian poetry, he was significant in that his interest lay in the poorer classes; he focused on their aspirations and dreams, and he was the only significant poet. His Latin shows the influence of vernacular speech that was gradually moving away from the written classical style. His metrics also lacked continuity with the classical style, often coming off as crude and vulgar.

In the *Instructions*, written about 250, he used stress rhythm in a series of poems that employed the crude grammatical syntax of colloquial barbarisms, attacking Jew and heathen alike for failure to follow the Christian God. From stress rhythm it was a natural step to the use of deliberate rhyme, a practice, as far as we can tell, unknown in previous Latin verse. While such clumsy rhythmical verse can be traced to inscriptions and poems that have no literary merit, they mark the first time this new style of accentual rhyme was used. In the centuries that followed, this new poetic convention was to change poetry completely. This change was not just fostered by poets following new aesthetic theories of verse. The Latin language itself was changing. Long and short vowels began to lose their distinction. By the end of the 4th century, ordinary speech treated long and short sounds alike, and the difference disappeared completely. Poets merely followed suit and used the language and conventions of native speech

What is striking about Commodian's verse is its anomalous prosody, which uses any number of syllabels from line to line, and the tonal effects that run contrary to the long and short vowels of classical Latin. The rhythm is created by the sequence of tonic accents, not quantitative regularity. Commodian thus anticipates the evolution that will lead from quantitative metrics to the accentual poetry of the Romance languages.

After Commodian, poets used both syllabic meter and accentual rhythm. Before 450 A.D., most of the Christian poetry in both Greek and Latin were mediocre at best and failed to achieve the beauty of the great pagan poets of the Augustan and Silver Age of Rome. Written for a Christian readership, these long narrative poems used Biblical stories as subjects, but rarely rose above mediocrity. Some of the Latin hymns of the 4th Century were written in rhythmical prose, *prosa metra*, such as the *Te Deum* and the *Gloria in Excelsius*. **Hilary of Poiters** and **Ambrose of Milan** wrote didactic hymns, intended for congregational singing, and several rose to passionate heights.

● **Juvencus** , *Evangeliorum Libri IV* (329-30).)

Traditionally, poetry and specifically the epic treated of mythological subjects, and therefore most Christian authors had written in prose. The various Latin texts of the Bible were inferior as far as literary product was concerned. By the 3rd century, educated Christians felt a growing need for writings that would tell the story of the Christ's coming and the history of salvation in a genre more elevated than simple prose, a genre that would redo the Bible in verse. The first of the Latin Biblical poets, virtually the founder of this literary form, Gaius Vettius Aquilinus Juvencus published a heroic version of the Gospels in 330. Unfortunately, to give the elegance of poetry to the biblical narrative was an enterprise beyond Juvencus's powers. Written in Virgilian fashion, which at times borders on the ludicrous, God becomes "The High-Thunderer" and "The Lofty-Throned Parent."

> Adiurabo tamen summi per regna tonantis;
>
> Iudex, altithroni genitoris gloria, Christus

In St. Matthew, "morning came." But for Juvencus, morning can't just come. In Juvencus,

Fuderat in terra roseum in bar ignicomus sol.	The fire-tressed sun shook from his rosy mane new light to the earth.

The book was one of the favorite school books of the Middle Ages. Juvencus' example proved contagious. Poets rushed to become the Christian Virgil. If the Gospels were done to death by dozens of poets, there was always a chance to render something from the Old Testament into the great epic of the age. Cyprianus Callicus covered the five books of Moses, then swept into the rest of the Old Testament as far as he could go. Numerous Virgilian renderings of *Sodom* and *Jonah* exist by poets whose names have passed into oblivion.

Another school of Christian poets used Biblical texts to demonstrate their technical dexterity. Their grasp was greater than their reach. Porfyrius wrote learned poetry of great technical refinement, often based on a difficult poetic game, such as aligning the verses in vertical and horizontal patterns similar to a crossword puzzle. These virtuoso displays of patient labor were sent to Constantine in hopes of getting back into his good graces. The geometric or allegoric design was emphasized by using a different ink for each letter. Perhaps the most ambitious display of virtuosity was the cento—a patchwork quilt of verses, or parts of verses, from one or more poems by one or more poets, arranged in such a way so as to create an entirely new poem. The cento gives new meaning to the word plagarism, elevating it to a new art form. The greatest example of this feat was written by Falconia Proba.

☛ Falconia Proba (mid-fourth century)

It's rare to find in Latin literature a poet who was a woman. She belonged to one of the most illustrious families of the aristocracy and was the wife of an important magistrate. Proba is also noted for writing an unusual poem, a long Virgilian *cento* on subjects of the Old and the New Testamenta. The word *cento* is Latin for "patchwork, thus a cento is a patchwork poem made up of verses by different writers. All of her lines come from Virgil, which she used to recount the temptation of Eve. The following translation is basically literal, though it hangs like a mock-Miltonic rendering between Virgil's Latin and Milton's English. With great cleverness, she accomplishes the seemingly impossible—patching phrases and verse directly from Virgil to render this scene from the Bible—however laughable it becomes at times.

> The snake, of slippery spirals sevenfold,
> And hatred on his face, wrath in his soul,
> Hangs from the branches of a leafy tree,
> Breathing out viper-breath in loathsome hisses,
> Brooding on envy, spite, and treacherous war,
> Detestable to God himself.
> "Tell me," quoth he, "oh Virgin, dwell we not
> In shady groves by banks of pleasant streams?
> Under each tree the ripened apples lie;
> What hinders us to know the hidden truths?
> Naught but vain superstition!
> Why should he mock us with eternal life?
>
> Dare but to heed me! Break the accurséd law!
> Thou'rt the man's wife, and thine the privilege
> To melt his purpose with caressing pleas.
> I am your leader. Heed me! We will build
> Soft, sylvan couches round th' inviting feast."
> He said, and they, swift-heeding, spread a store
> Of fruit forbidden.
>
> Unhappy Eve, fulfilling her own doom,
> Eyed the strange leaves and apples not her own,
> Cause of our ill, she touched her lips to them,
> And, fury-driven, daring greater sin,
> Ah me, she offered of the alien fruit
> Unto her consort—and her charms prevailed.
> Straightway the mighty Lord of earth and heaven
> Called in loud tones, "Hence, get ye hence, profane."
> When him they saw advance with awful strides,
> Wrath on his face, they turned in fear and fled
> To distant woods and secret caverns dim,

Shamed of their deed and of the light of day,
And ashamed to raise their faces to the sky.

Her poem was very popular in the Middle Ages and even into the Renaissance, regarded by many as almost a doctrinal text. When Pope Gelasius listed it among the texts that had no authority in the field of faith, it was a tacit admission that the work had acquired the same value as the works of the church Fathers. It inspired other poets to attempt a similar patchwork on different Biblical themes. The idea has survived even into modern times. The May 1922 Harvard Lampoon printed a modified cento from various familiar masterpieces entitled "A Poem Every Child Should Know." The author may or may not have been aware of the ancient tradition that lay behind his parody.

☛ **Prudentius**, (c. 348-410), *The Martyr's Crowns*

Called the Horace and the Virgil of the Christians, Aurelius Prudentius Clemens was the first and ultimately the greatest of the Roman Christian poets. He wrote long hymns that were similiar to classic odes, using material from the Bible instead of classical mythology. His short epics and ballads were among the best of the poetical legends, including *The Martyr's Crowns*—14 poems on the lives and deaths of famous martyrs. Describing a visit to the catacombs, he paints a scene of awesome darkness and the musty odors of that underground street of tombs.

Sunt et muta tamen tacitus claudentia tumbus	Yet some are mute, and on their marble face
Marmora, quae solum significant numerum	Tell but the numbers of the dead within.

Told in a wealth of meters—trochaic, iambic dimeter and trimeter, dactylic tetrameter, sapphic, the 11 syllable Alcaic—*The Martyr's Crowns* was also rendered at times in a simple style, providing a model for both High and Low Latin in Medieval Latin Literature.

Prudentius was also the author of numerous short poems and hymns. In the course of his *Hymn for the Burial of the Dead*, he says:

Each sorrowful mourner keep silent!
Fond mothers stop your weeping lamentation!
None count these loved ones gone forever
when death is life's restoration.

Though shriveled, and lifeless, and buried,
These seeds shall arise in beauty so bright:
Resurrected from the ground where we laid them
Envisioning a new and eternal life!

Now receive him, kind earth, for cherishing,
And take him to your tender breast.
I bring you, the body of man,
Even in decay, noble and finally at rest.

Even his didactic and theological essays were written in verse. One of his most famous long poems, the *Psychomachia* (The Soul's Conflict), was an epic in which the personified virtues, modesty, humility, and patience fight against the vices, lust, and anger. The work became a great favorite of the Middle Ages and deeply influenced medieval literature and art.

Two didactic poems, *Apotheosis* and *Hamartigenia*, deify both Christ and man. For the first time Christians had an imaginative presentation in excellent verse of the inmost mysteries of their faith. Prudentius must have known his Virgil as intimately as Virgil knew his Homer. While not having Virgil's magic touch, he mastered the art of the Virgilian hexameter cast in an originality of expression and intensity of feeling. *Hamartigenia* could be called *Paradise Lost*; it was a poetic treatment of the power of evil. What made it significant was that it did not posit an Evil God versus a Good God, as Marcion did. There was one God, and Evil entered the world through Lucifer first, then through Man, by virtue of his free will. God created the possibility of evil, leaving man with the question of its necessity.

Exemplum dat vita hominum,	Nature takes patterns
quo cetera peccent	from the sins of man.

In other words, people kill, not guns. God gives man the boon of resurrection, but without free will, the prize of attainment is impossible. With it, the way is open for the very course of sin and suffering that man has made his own. Freedom allows us to choose between Heaven and Hell, or between them, Purgatory, a temporary state for souls too stained with sin to enter at once. Prudentius gave the doctrine of Purgatory (toward which Plato and Virgil hadled the way) a Catholic stamp. Conscious of his age and infirmities, Prudentius ends the poem by praying he be granted a comfortable corner of Hell, where he won't have to look upon the face of Lucifer, and where

Lux immensa alios et tempora iuncta coronis	the tempered heat exudes a mild vapor,
Glorificent, me poena leuis clementer adurat.	And where Hell's furnace breathes a gentler blast.

In asking God to have mercy on his sins, Prudentius foreshadows the dusty wind and milder heat of Limbo in Dante's Inferno. Using a verse form based on syllabic quantity, he combined a love for classical pagan culture with an intense Christian fervor, some of his work rises to the level of great writing. In his Latin verse and hymns, we catch a last echo of the achievement and mastery of Rome.

☞ Paulinus of Nola (353-431),

Paulinus was a pupil of the poet Ausonius. He was born into a rich family of Bordeaux and married Therasia, a wealthy Spanish woman of like high lineage. A brilliant political figure, Paulinus became consul in 378 and eventually governor of Campania. It is said that "conversion" came upon him suddenly, in the full sense of a turning away from the world. He sold his property, gave all to the poor, and became a priest, retiring to Nola in Campania. Therasia lived with him as his chaste "sister in Christ" in a private monastery for thirty-five years. But Ausonius felt he had made a mistake withdrawing from the obligations of civic life at a time the empire was most in need of men like himself. Paulinus wrote letters to all his pagan friends, inviting them to come and share his bliss.

Like those of Symmachus, Paulinus' letters are noted for their literary style. In one he discusses the relation between Christianity and pagan culture, taking the same view Augustine took—that as long as pagan literature is used for publicizing the new faith, it is okay to read, preserve, and translate it. The style of his letters is noted for its use of rhetoric, combined with words and phrases lifted from the Bible, creating something like a cento. But the best of his work is his poetry. In simple brief prayers, Paulinus touches on the beauty of a single moment; his style is reserved, but the language he uses reminds one of the epic. These poems were used in sermons, or read simply to his flock, describing popular scenes with directness and honesty. The subjects go from how to avoid getting drunk, to the story of a cow that runs away, then magically reappears on St. Felix's day just in time to be slaughtered for the festival. His poems touch upon the frustrations of peasant life from the point of view of someone who shared their toil.

Most touching though are the verse epistles written to his friend and teacher, Ausonius, who had tried to dissuade him from giving his life to the Church.

> In words of anger and love you reproach me . . .
> For choosing another part of the world . . . ,
> Forgetful of the life of refinement
> Spent with you in former days.
> Cease, I beg you, to wound your friend . . .

Paulinus assures him that a life devoted to politics and power pale in comparison to a life of spiritual affirmation and serving those who follow their faith.

Prudentius used poetry—especially the classical epic—to validate the power of Christianity and help spread it among the literate and intellectual aristocracy of the empire. Paulinus, who came from the senatorial nobility, used poetry to enlighten his people, to awake their faith and devotion, and to express his own faith. But for Prudentius, literature was the central means of exercising his influence. For Paulinus, poetry was only one of many ways of serving his faith; in fact, he believed that he could be more influential by building a church. Prudentius spoke for and to those who constituted the backbone of the late Empire, extoling the virtue of study and professional accomplishment. Paulinus renounced his goods to be closer to the poor, and took part in their celebrations and sorrows of the heart. Both poets looked to Virgil for inspiration. Prudentius took as his model the epic tone and passion of the *Aeneid*; Paulinus looked to Virgil's passion for the fields and the earth, the lives of peasants and the stories of animals. The Virgil he emulated was the Virgil of the *Bucolics* and the *Georgics*.

Despite the chaos and violence of the world, the sack of Rome and the invasion of the Germanic tribes from the north and east, Paulinus kept to a spirit of toleration and simple faith. Pagans and Jews joined Christians at his funeral. Ausonius mourned when Paulinus became a saint; the church's gain was not as monumental as the empire's loss.

☛ **St. Hilary** of Poitiers (d. 367) and **St. Ambrose** of Milan

Much of the poetry written by Christian monks and clerics, especially the hymns, included accentual rhythms, rhyme, assonance, and alliteration. The most outstanding extant examples of Latin religious poetry are hymns and sequences composed for singing at Mass. The Fathers of the Christian Church such as Augustine and Jerome infused new life into both Latin and Greek poetry, especially Jerome's use of rhyme..

In the West, St. Hilary was one of the earliest authors of Latin hymns—often set to existing popular tunes. One of the great bishops of fourth-century Gaul, Hilary actively defended the Nicene Creed and wrote a treatise in twelve books struggling to explain the Trinity. Yet, in his modest see at Poitiers, we see him living the good life of a devoted churchman—rising early, receiving callers, hearing complaints and settling disputes, leading the Mass, preaching, teaching, dictating books and letters, listening to pious readings at his meals, and every day performing some manual labor like cultivating the fields or weaving garments for the poor.

At first all Masses were sung, and the congregation joined in the singing. (Mass probably derived its name from the closing formula—*Ite, missa est*—"Depart, it is dismissal") The hymns sung in the various services of the Church are among the most moving products of medieval sentiment and art. The known history of the Latin hymn begins with Bishop Hilary. Returning to Gaul from exile in Syria, he brought home some Greco-Oriental hymns, translated them into Latin, and composed some of his own; all of these are lost.

The most noted 4th century Latin Christian poet was St. Ambrose, who composed several beautiful hymns in which he popularized new poetic devices. Written in iambic dimeters, these poems have shaped Christian song and music. Augustine tells us that such hymns were originally used by the Arians to lure away the faithful, and by the orthodox to lure them back. One such incident is related by Ambrose in his *Sermo contra Auxentium*, an anti-Arian speech. In 386 the bishop had spearheaded a drive to reclaim all the churches in Milan from the heretics, but the empress Justina decreed that one, the Portian, should be reserved for the woship of the Arians, who until a few years earlier had been half of the Christian population. To prevent opposing forces from restoring the church to the Arians, Ambrose brought a group of the faithful to occupy the church—an ancient form of the modern "sit-in" used by civil rights activists of the 1960s who entertained themselves by singing "We Shall Overcome," and other songs by Bob Dylan, Pete Seeger, Joni Mitchell, Woodie Guthrie, Joan Baez, and Arlo Guthrie. To fortify their resolve and raise their spirits during the long days when the church was under seige, Ambrose thought of having his followers sing his poems, whose rhythms were easy and whose content was edifying. The popularity they had among the faithful and the successful outcome of the battle for the Portian church led to the hymns being made a reguler part of the Milanese liturgy and then of all Christian liturgy.

Instrumental in St. Augustine's conversion were the hymns of Ambrose which stirred him first by their sensous beauty and then by their spiritual meaning. Eighteen of his sonorous hymns survive, including *Aeterne rerum conditor* (the most famous), *Iam surgit hora tertia*, *Deus creator omnium*, and *Veni redemptor gentium*. An oft-quoted hymn of St. Ambrose is his picturesque *Hymn at Cockcrow*, which begins:

O Everlasting Architect, how starts
the change from night to day to night?
By the season's changes you fill our hearts,
Sated and thirsting for fresh delight!

The noble hymn of faith and thanksgiving, *Te Deum laudamus*, was thought to have been written by Ambrose, but later scholarship ascribed it to the Romanian Bishop Nicetas. Ambrose is as much noted for his hymns as for his writings on Church doctrine, and most significant of these was a letter he wrote to the Emperor Valentinian, threatening to excommunicate him if he accepted the plea of Symmachus to restore the pagan Altar of the Statue of Victory to the Roman senate.

☛ St. Augustine of Hippo (d. 430)

The greatest Western Father of the Church, Augustine was also himself the author of snatches of poetry such as

The enamoured soul thirsts
After the fountain of eternal life.
The imprisoned spirit breaks its chains,
and flees from anguished guilt and strife.

In later centuries the Latin hymns were influenced by Moslem and Provençal love poetry of the 12th century, imparting them with a new delicacy of feeling and form. One would expect many of these hymns to show an excess of rhyme verging on doggerel, but by the literary flowering of the twelfth and thirteenth century we find hymns that developed a subtle turn of compact phrase, a melodiousness of frequent rhyme, and a grace and tenderness of thought that rank them with the greatest lyrics in literature.

☛ Dracontius (

At the end of the 5th century, **Dracontius** wrote a Biblical epic, attempting "to justify the ways of God to man." The poem was written while he was in prison. *De Laudibus Dei* begins with the story of creation and includes an account of the first fall of night—he may be the only poet of his time who described the feelings our first parents had when the blackness of that first night came on.

As slow sun set, they in awe looked on,
Thinking its light was never to return.
Their hearts were solaced as th' effulgent moon
Broke through the shadows and a radiant host
Of stars they counted in the cloudless sky.
But when the Day-star, rising from the deep,
Shook his bright mane and called the new-born light
Flushed with the sun, to ride above the stars,
They warmed their souls with yesterday's delight;

Knowing the daily change, they calmed their dread
And cheered night's shaodws with the hope of dawn.

☛ **Avitus**, *The Deeds of Spiritual History* (4th or 5th century)

Some of the Proba and Dracontius is no worse, and in some cases much better, than portions of Milton's *Paradise Lost*. The best of all the biblical epics was written by Alcimus Ecdicius **Avitus**, Bishop of Vienna, who wrote when he was a very young man *De Spiritalis Historicae Gestis*, "The Deeds of Spiritual History." His epic promotes our first man to heroic proportions, and Eve is almost worthy of the tragic stage. Avitus replaces quaint description with the broad sweep of argument, heightened by allegory and mysticism. Satan is not the simple serpent of Genesis, but an expansive evil power, declaring himself the real ruler of mankind, foreshadowing Milton's Satan, called by many the real hero of *Paradise Lost*. Here Satan wants rendered "unto Satan the things that are Satan's."

> For God, who formed you, has no greater right
> Over your souls than I. What he has formed
> That can he keep. What I have taught is mine, —
> The major portion. For ye surely owe
> Much to your Maker; to your Teacher — more.

Pagan Poets of the Late Empire

☛ Quintus Aurelius **Symmachus** (340-c.402), *the Relationes* (384)

The quintissential religious battle was fought over the Altar of Victory, a statue of the goddess that served as a symbol of Empire. It was probably erected by Augustus in 29 BC and stood in the Roman senate house for nearly four centuries. Persuaded that it was a pagan relic, Constantine removed it in 357; Julian the Apostate, so called because he restored paganism and initiated widespread persecutions of Christians, had it returned to its former place. Years later, the new Emperor Gratian, won to a passionate orthodoxy by the eloquent Ambrose, proclaimed the Nicene Creed compulsory. Anyone following another faith was "mad and insane." In 382 he confiscated all lands belonging to pagan temples, and had his agents remove from the Senate House the statue of the goddess Victory, before which twelve generations of senators had taken their vows of allegiance to the emperor. Symmachus was banished from Rome. Gratian was killed the following year, and a delegation of senators sought an audience with Valentinian II. The delegation was headed by Symmachus, a loyal pagan whose famous third *relatio*," or "report," to the young Emperor Valentinian was acclaimed as a masterpiece of eloquent pleading. Why end a religious practice that had through a millenium been associated with the stability of social order and the prestige of the state? Rome herself, he wrote, cries out against the death sentence of the values of which Victory was the symbol and guardian. Rome herself, he pleaded, in the name of a glorious past and of the mystery that surrounds faith, asks that Victory always remain by her side. After all, "What does it matter by what road each man seeks the truth? By no one road can men come to the understanding of so great a mystery." (*uno itinere non potest perveniri ad tam grande secretum*).

Symmachus' formal eloquence was matched by his ability to strike powerful emotional chords. So effective was the third *relatio*, that the great Christian poet Prudentius still felt the need to reply to it twenty years after the speech was made, calling Symmachus the greatest living orator. But Ambrose was firm, almost arrogant, and had no respect at all for the pagan faith. Ambrose disputed each point in Symmachus's letter, and if that wasn't enough, he threatened to excommunicate the emperor if Symmachus's plea should be granted. "You may enter the churches, but you will find no priest there to receive you, or you will find them there to forbid your entrance." The young Valentinian denied the Senate's appeal. Despite Symmachus' masterful speech, it required the energetic intervention of the powerful Ambrose to avert a pagan victory.

Of Symmachus's poems, speeches, and letters (a correspondance in ten books published by his son), the most famous is the third letter about the Altar of Victory, part of a volume of 50 official letters sent to the emperors during the time Symmachus was prefect of Rome from 383 to 385.

This century was even more addicted to rhetoric than was Fronto's. Symmachus's letters paint a pleasant picture of that charming aristocracy which thought itself immortal on the eve of death. But except for his third *relatio*, Symmachus's letters and speeches were confined to petty banalities. Gibbon wrote in his *Delince and Fall* that the works of Symmachus "consisted in barren leaves without fruit or flowers. Few facts and few sentiments can be extracted from his verbose correspondence."

The statue of the Goddess Victory was eventually restored ten years later, but within a year Theodosius marched into Rome and compelled the Senate to decree the abolition of paganism in all its forms. The Altar of Victory was cast out for the last time. The Emperor Theodosius carried the alliance between throne and altar to its logical conclusion by prohibiting all rival faiths, thus making Rome officially Christian. When Alaric sacked Rome 15 years later, pagans saw in this humiliation the fury of their neglected gods. The faiths were at war, and when the tidal wave of barbarian invasion reached them in full force, Christian and pagan curses rang out in one voice, but their prayers were directed toward separate gods.

Despite the so-called cultural renaissance, the gap in society widened between the wealthy large landowners and the poorer classes, the latter composed mostly of urban proletariat, formerly free peasants who became enslaved to the owners of large estates (the beginnings of fuedalism), and artisans who became impoverished as cities declined in importance when the more affluent fled to the country. The Empire came to be ruled by the senatorial class who bent to the needs of the military. The masses became indifferent to politcal machinations and intrigue. The great majority of them were impoverished and undernourished, and vast numbers were enslaved. Writing at the end of the 4th century, the last great historian of the Roman Empire, Ammianus Marcellinus makes these observations on Roman decline:

The misery of these times was further increased by the insatiable covetousness of his [the emperor's] tax collectors who brought him more odium than money . . . . The natives, from weariness of the severe rule under which they were, were eager for any change whatever. . . . Some, becoming weary of life and light, sought a release from their miseries by hanging themselves. The treasury is empty, the cities are exhausted, the finances are stripped bare. The city is declining into old age. Many fall away into error and licentiousness, as if a perfect impunity were granted to vice; those who, sweating under many cloaks, try by continual wriggling of their bodies and especially by the waving of the left hand to make their long fringes and tunics, embroidered in multiform figures of animals and threads of various colors, more conspicuous; men who drive their horses through the wide streets of the city, dragging behind them large bodies of slaves like bands of robbers; women with their hair curled, old enough to have three children, dance on the pavements. When nobles arrive at the bath and find that any unknown female slave has appeared or any worn-out-courtesan, they run up as if to a race, and patting and caressing her with disguising and unseemly blandishments extol her, but when one meets these nobles and speaks to them on the street, they toss their heads like bulls preparing to butt, offering their flatterers their knees or hands to kiss. As for the lazy and idle common people, the lower and most of the indigent class of the populace, they're not much better, spending the whole night in the wine shops. Some lie concealed in the shady arcades of the theatres or else they play at dice so eagerly as to quarrel over them, snuffing up their nostrils and making unseemly noises by drawing back their breath into their noses. The Circus Maximus is their temple, their home, their public assembly, in fact their whole hope or desire. Some are continually crying that the republic cannot stand if, in the contest which is to take place, the skillful charioteer whom some individual backs is not foremost in the race. Among these men are many chiefly addicted to delicate food, and gliding over the ground on tiptoe, they get entrance into the halls, biting their nails while the dishes are getting cool. Others fix their eyes so intently on the tainted meal which is being cooked that you might fancy Democritus with a number of anatomists was gazing into the entrails of sacrificed victims in order to teach poseterity how best to relieve internal pains.

I can't imagine Juvenal's satires being any more acerbic than the above observations. The writing is elegant and devastating all in one sweep, with forceful images and even better similies and metaphors. One could break the prose into lines of poetry and get one hell of a poem, filled with social commentary and stark scenes of the Eternal City, braced for a fall.

The frontiers were hammered repeatedly by barbarians, many penetrating and being absorbed within the Empire. Some cities constructed protective walls. Towns and countryside suffered a degree of local violence and mayhem imaginable only by thinking of the conditions in our own inner cities where the average citizens are often afraid to leave their homes after nightfall.

During the 3rd and 4th centuries, secular or pagan poets spent their time editing the classics and translating what was important into Latin. The study of rhetoric continued to flourish during this period. Panegyrists wrote poems glorifying the deeds of emperors. The most famous of the learned poets active in the last half of the 4th century was a gentle school teacher and professor of rhetoric who was summoned while still in his twenties to teach the future emperor Gratian.

☞ **Ausonius** (310-394), the *Mosella*

> My father was Ausonius, and I bear the same name.
> Who I am, and what is my rank, my family,
> my home, and my native land,
> I have written here, that you might know me,
> whover you are or may have been,
> and when you know me,
> might honour me with a place in your memory.

By the fourth and fifth centuries, Gaul took over the literary leadership of Europe, just as it had become the most prosperous and intellectually advanced of Roman provinces in the West. Decimus Magnus Ausonius was the poet and embodiment of this Gallic Silver Age, and he's been called the first medieval secular poet. His poems, which were mostly short observations respecting some trivial detail, are strongly marked by his work as a school teacher. Born at Bordeaux about 310, son of its leading physician, he received his education there and became a professor of grammar, then of rhetoric. He later held public office, and after Gratian's death in 383, retired to a private life in his exquisitely maintained country estate in Bordeaux. He also kept another equally impressive estate in Aquitaine.

Born a hundred years before the Germans crossed the Rhine and invaded the empire, Ausonius lived a life that typifies the blinders worn by many poets in Roman society, shielding them from the social, economic, and moral decay that led directly to the calamities of the fifth century. He was raised by two battle-axes, a grandmother and an aunt, both named Aemilia. Of Grandmother Aemilia, he writes:

> *et non delicis ignoscere prompta pudendis*
> *ad perpendiculum seque suosque habuit.*

> To questionable pleasures she gave no quarter,
> but held both herself and her houshold rigidly upright.

The aunt must have been big and manly:

> *Aemilia, in cunis Hilari cognomen adepta,*
> *quod laeta et pueri comis ad effigien,*
> *reddebas verum non dissimulanter ephebum*

> Aemilia, nicknamed Lusty in your cradle,
> because you were as much fun as a boy —
> and, without trying, you always looked like a guy.

With a taste for metrical play, he told the world in generous hexameters the virtues of his teachers and wisdom of their lessons. The sincere affection with which he writes of his parents, uncles, wife, children, and pupils suggests a home and a life like that of a professor in a nineteenth-century university town in New England or a Chinese gentlemen of the T'ang dynasty. He says to his wife, in the early years of their marriage: "Let us live always as we live now, and let us not abandon the names that we have given each other in our first love . . . . You and I must always remain young, and you shall always be beautiful to me. We must keep no count of the years." She bore him a son, and died not long after giving birth to their daughter. He was so deeply bound to her that he never again married; and in his old age he described with fresh grief the pain of his loss, and the somber silence of the house that had known the care of her hands and the sound of her footsteps. His poems were known for their tender sentiment, their rural pictures, the purity of their Latin, the almost Virgilian smoothness of their verse.

But many of the poems of praise and homage go on and on, imitations of Virgil and endless word games about the heroes of the Trojan War or the Twelve Caesars. Most of his work is filled with conventional sentiment, neither fresh nor original, what we might find in the inscription of a book or Hallmark greeting (or sympathy) card.

> By such kindness did she rear me — ripped from cradle
> and mother's breast — but under the guise of stern commands.
> Let my grandmother's ashes rest in peace,
> ever silent shades, if I say the proper prayers.

His poetry is filled with *pia verba*, "faithful words" from a dutiful son, husband, and father. Only the "Cento Nuptualis" dares to intrude on the decorum of the age. The poem is a jaded, though clinical account of a bride's deflowering on her wedding night. Racy and titillating as it may be, any pretentions of originality are destroyed when we realize that not one word comes from Ausonius. It's a cento, all the lines and phrases coming directly from Virgil. Instead of sexual provocation we get an impressive showcase of knowledge and technical virtuosity. Content is subsumed by literary formula. The *Loeb* Classical Library, which offers Greek and Latin texts with a facing English translation, includes two volumes on Ausonius, whose one "hot" poem is left untranslated.

His best and most ambitious work is an *epyllion*, a brief epic poem that celebrates the Moselle, the river near which he lived most of his life. In one section, he carries on a rhapsodic litany for the amiable fish to be found in the stream that ran near his home.

> No fish has ever told another of danger
> lurking in those knit fabrics or drawn wire —
> the bite of iron in the soft gullet
> or the pinch of linen cord at the gills —
> the green wand bows to the fish it has caught,
> the dutiful corks bob in pert respect.
>   Unthinking, excited, the hungry boy
> whips his catch from the stream onto the grass
> and I think of a scourge falling on flesh.
> Under the waters a fish is alive,
> but in the sun he will strangle for air.
> The dying body quivers helplessly,
> the tail is feeble, the mouth is open:
> the gills cannot breathe out life in that gasp
> every animal tries to make at death.
> Those shining gill covers once were beating

like a bellows in a blacksmith's workshop.
Now these gills cannot use the air they suck.
Then again I have seen fish almost dead
leap up high in the air like tumblers
and throw themselves back into the water,
swimming off, to the fisherman's surprise.
When this happens, the boy will make a dive
and try to catch them as they swim away.
Glaucus was stunned to see his catch of fish
flip themselves back into the waiting sea.
He tasted the herbs the fish had lain on
and found he could not avoid the ocean
and would be happy to live as a fish.
All these strange things I think of when I see
these young boys try to catch a fleeing fish.

This Whitmanesque passion for cataloguing relatives, teachers, pupils, and fish is not redeemed by Whitman's expansive feeling and lusty philosophy; Ausonius, after thirty years of grammar, could hardly burn with more than literary passions. We can't condemn the poet here, since every poet of that time was doing the same thing. It was an age that had to come to terms with Gothic invaders, yet most of the poets seemed to be completely isolated from the turbulent world of their day. In fact, the "Cento Nuptualis" was written when he was tutor to Gratian, son of Valentinian, emperor of the West. Ausonius was asked to accompany the Emperor and his son on an anti-German expedition, and it was Valentinian who asked him to compose something the legions might enjoy; thus we get a poem of barracks humor. During this time Ausonius was offered the services of a German slave girl, Bissula, and he wrote a short poetic homage to her ability to rouse his sexual ardour.

> Delicium, blanditiae, ludus, amor, voluptas,
> barbara, sed quae Latias vincis alumna pupas.

> Morsel — Blandishment — Sport — Desire — Climax —
> Barbarian! but you, kid, are ahead of all the Latin girls.

It would seem the old boy still has some poetic fire left in him. The nouns parallel his sexual arousal, the tension building to the climax when he moans the word *barbara* (barbarian). Unfortunately, the poem is a close crib of Catullus. But the poem is noted for one distinction: it's the only time he writes of someone not of his own class. His poems show no concern for the decay of the empire going on all around him—the rising taxes which produced a caste as hopeless as any in history, the rising violence, the decline in production, etc. He writes of Bissula, the German slave girl, not to condemn the age, but to show-off his manhood.

Yet, in his day, Ausonius was admired. Symmachus felt the *Moselle* was the equal of Virgil's poems. Paulinus of Nola compared Ausonius to Virgil and Cicero. That Ausonius was so highly praised doesn't say much for the other poets of this age. Writing over a millenium later, Edward Gibbon minced no words. He dismisses Ausonius with a disdainful wave of the hand: "The poetical fame of Ausonius condemns the taste of his own age." Where Nemesianus lacked inspiration, Ausonius lacked vision, without which the people perish. But we can say this for him—his poems preserve a gentleness of friendship and appreciation of life that was rare in its day. He died around 393-94, peacefully cultivating his vineyard in Bordeaux, still known to this day as Château Ausone.

Food For Thought

"Which Way of Life Shall You Follow"

Some would say that analytical geometry was born with the three dreams René Descartes experienced on the night of Nov 10, 1619. But maybe its conception goes back even further, to 4th century Gaul, and the work of Ausonius, that minor poet of the late Roman Empire. How then is Ausonius linked to the man widely regarded as the founder of modern philosophy, whose "I think, therefore, I am," is probably the most famous of all philosophical statements, the "Call me Ishmael," of philosophical literature. When then, do Ausonius and Descartes, a 4th century poet and a 16th century philosopher, have in common?

There are huge gaps in the knowable life of Descartes: He tried to conceal his whereabouts for years, and vital manuscripts are either lost or include stories that were made up in order to fill in the blanks. His major work, *The Discourse on Method* (1637), grounded modern thinking on the ability of the human mind to think clearly and distinctly, and he was the first philosopher to see that the new science of Copernicus and Galileo required a radical reordering of our understanding of physical nature simpy around the concepts of matter and motion. When he died in 1650 from pneumonia while tutoring the Queen of Sweden, he was recognized as having built the most compelling case for seeing nature as a mechanism and for accepting that the Earth was just like any other body, at motion and held in place by the direct pressure of other matter in the universe. For Descartes, discrete bodies had to come into actual contact in order for motion to occur. This was in direct contradiction to the followers of Aristotle, known as schoolmen or scholastics, who thought that immaterial forms, such as the soul in human beings, gave nature it's motion, and that these forms carried with them "tendencies." Thus, an apple would fall to the ground because it had a tendency to seek out that which was heavier. The contest between the Aristotelians and the Cartesians was a bitter contest, but today we believe that nature is composed of atoms which are mathematically knowable, a victory for Cartesian philosophy. In 1687, Newton would prove that universal gravitation operated as a force in a vacuum and not in the filled Cartesian universe, but that's another story.

Descartes came from an old noble family, but at eighteen he left the sobriety of the paternal estate and settled in Paris where he and his fellow companions, hungering for life in the raw, took up drinking and gambling, the lattar being one of the accomplishments of a gentleman in that day. When he grew bored with this dissolute life, he found lodgings in another part of the city and spent the next two years buried in constant mathematical investigation until his friends discovered where he was living and tried to get him to resume his former life-style. "I desire only tranquility and repose," he said. Since he could find no peace in Paris, he went to war in Holland, hoping to see action under the Prince of Orange. But camp life was as boring as Paris was stimulating. So off he went to Germany, witnessing the gaudy spectacle in Frankfort where Ferdinand II was crowned emperor, and once again Descartes enlisted to fight in a war, this time against Bohemia.

While camped with the army in its winter quarters on the banks of the Danube, Descartes found the tranquility and repose he sought, and experienced his co-called "conversion." On the night of November 10, 1619, he had three vivid dreams which changed the course of his life. One could interpret the dreams in a Freudian manner, or as a mystical, religious experience such as Augustine's. But how do we account for the invention of analytic geometry which resulted from those dreams? The first two dreams involved an evil wind and a sudden strom in which Descartes realized that by seeing each with the unsuperstitious eyes of science, they could do him no harm.

In the third dream, he reads aloud the poem of Ausonius which begins *Quod vitae secatabor iter?*—"What way of life shall I follow?" Descartes woke from that third dream with a start. He said it was as if a magic key had unlocked a door leading him into a new life, a life he was meant to follow, and the magical idea came to him to apply algebra to geometry, thus giving birth to analytic geometry and modern mathematics.

The ironies here are subtle but illuminating. Though Descartes continued to live the life of a soldier for years afterwards, Mars, the god of war, spared his life. Three centuries later, in a war that ravished Europe and christened the decline of one empire and the emergence of a new American Empire, scores of young mathematicians died in muddy trenches and on scorched battlefields, partly the result of the advance of that very science which Descartes' dream had inspired. The second irony——that the poem Descartes dreamed he was reading was written over a millenium earlier by a gentle schoolteacher who lived in a time when another great Empire was crumbling. One final irony—that mathematical physics blooms from the mind of a scientist dreaming of a poem. One could say this is Einstein's famous statement—that "the highest physics always evolves into poetry"—turned on its head: that even the simplest poem is capable of evolving into the highest physics.

☞ Claudius Claudianus (370-404)

A poet of refined artificiality, Claudian is usually refered to as the last poet of classical Rome. Unlike Ausonius, who lived in a happy world far from the realities of the time, Claudian was well aware of the problems the world was facing. Born at Alexandria in Egypt, he came to Rome as a young poet and within a short time was the most acclaimed Latin poet of his day. He became a confidante of the barbarian Stilicho, the supreme general, of Vandal origin, who held the highest position in the ranks of power. Coleridge considered Claudian "the first of the moderns." Coleridge was alluding to the tension in his work between the ancient poem of objective narrative and the modern tendency towards the personal and subjective.

Claudian wrote a great number of poetic compositions, including epic poems on mythological subjects, such as *The Rape of Proserpinea*. Full of extensive decriptive passages, especially on the realm of the dead, his work sufferes from a lack of narrative action. He also wrote two invectives against powerful persons who were enemies of Stilicho. One was titled *In Rufinum*, from which I quoted a few lines above on page (_____255?)

He belonged to that group of professional poets who made a living writing poetry. He reclaimed the form of the epic and made it popular among the senatorial classes. But to do so, he had to reduce the scale of the mythical story, and make the message more explicit, since too long a poem could weary the reader, especially the larger public, which hadn't the patience to decode ambiguous allegories.

Most of his work was written during the last decade of the 4th century. His verses are noted for their technical perfection and lyric beauty, reminding us of the poets of the Augustan age. Some of his shorter poems were favorite exercises in schools to teach the skills of translation.

For France

Even as the cattle in the winter woods,
Hearing their master's old familiar shout,
Come shouldering down to the remembered pastures
Deep in the valley, answering faithful lowing,
Each stepping in her turn,
Till the last straggler's horn
Glints through the twilight of the naked branches.
From the uttermost isles of Britain
Came the legions, where they held the Scots in leash,
And those that were a wall against the Ruhr,
And cowed the churls of Hesse and Thuringen,
They've turned the splendid menace of their line
Against the threat to Italy: they're gone.
The right bank's naked of its garrison.
Naught but the terror of the Roman name
Defends an open frontier.
Tonight there is no watch upon the Rhine.

As Claudian pointed out, Roman legions were pulled back to more secure positions, mainly because the cost of maintaining garrisons all along the Rhine and Danube was too costly. Within a decade after this poem was written, Rome was sacked by Alaric. It is doubtful that the barbarian tribes, already in the process of crossing the frontier, were affected by "the terror of the Roman name."

☛ **Sulpicius Lupercus Servasius**, 4th Century AD

Little is known of Servasius except that he lived in the fourth century. Very little of his work survives. From this translation by Kenneth Rexroth, published in 1944, we gather that Servasius had a sharp eye for detail, and an ironic tone. In these six lines, a masterpiece of imagery and ironic inuendo, he sums up the decline of Rome as part of the natural, ongoing process of change.

> Rivers level granite mountains,
> Rains wash the figures from the sundial,
> The plowshare wears thin in the furrow;
> And on the fingers of the mighty,
> The gold of authority is bright
> With the glitter of attrition.

This is as good an imaginstic poem as any poet writing today could hope to write. Rexroth's fine translation reminds us that little has changed. The sun sets, and the sun also rises, but the earth abides forever.

☛ **Avienus**—wrote poems on astronomy, geography, and Roman legends.

☛ **Avianus,** (flourished c 400 AD), *Fables*

He was a fabulist who redid 42 Aesopic fables in elegiac couplets. By translating Babrius's Greek fables into Latin elegiacs, Avianus elevated the stories so that they could be regarded with more respect as literature with a moral purpose. One of their chief concerns is with the power and the relations between slave and master, and may have been considered provocative, if not subversive, during his lifetime. He believed in the pagan gods of the Roman religion, but playfully and sometimes scornfully implied that the gods were no longer in control of the world and that humans must be held accountable for their irresponsibility. In David Slavit's free translation of "The Shopkeeper and the Statue," Bacchus complains that his statue is being mistreated and misinterpreted by mere mortals:

> "Who in the hell are you
> to decide my fate? What kind
> of world is this, when a clerk
> can determine the life of a god?"
>
> What happened then? Does it matter?
> The point is the god's complaint
> chastens us all, that the whole world is
> contingent on such people's whims.

Avianus's fable show a world in change and turmoil, and that the best response may well be cunning, and the only saving grace, humor. These fables were composed not long after the sack of Rome by Vandals (or was it the Visogoths? check this) in 410. Augustine's City of God was a philosophical and religious response to that great calamity. While the Roman world was being transformed by the rise of Christianity, Augustine counseled his flock not to despair, that the world of real importance was not the earthly city of Rome, but the heavenly city of God. Avianus was not one to despair either, but his fables voice a common doubt and skepticism about man's ability to deal with change. Physical survival was often more important than religious escape and acceptance. In the closing lines of "The Oak and the Reed," the reed points out this obvious moral when he says to the oak:

> "There can be safety in weakness.
> See how you were strong, fought the winds, defied them,
> stood tall, and endured their entire awesome strength,
> or tried to, but we were pliable, weak, swayed and gave
> way, agreed with whatever the winds proposed,
> moved this way and that, and, offering almost no
> resistance, baffled its crude might.
> It isn't what you'd call noble, or even particularly
> admirable, but we're still standing, are still here."

The fables were very popular in medieval schools. The difficult metrics and playful rhyme scheme delivered the moral as part of an ironic plot. Avianus' literary ambitions are clear, especially as he tried to imitate Ovid and Virgil. He hoped in his own way to help preserve interest in the Roman customs and religion, since Avianus was a pagan. But we really know little about his life. A contemporary of his described him as a virtuous youth who seldom spoke, but who was admired for his wit and wry commentary.

☛ Aelius Donatus (4th century AD)

Aelius Donatus was a Latin grammarian and teacher of St. Jerome. He wrote two books of Latin grammar which remained in use throughout the Middle Ages, to the extent that "donat" or "donet" was used generally to mean "text-book." He also wrote a commentary on Virgil, part of which survived and was used by Servius in his commentary on Virgil. Most of the commentaries on Virgil and other classical authors were intented for school use, focusing mostly upon grammatical, rhetorical, and stylistic points. Aelius Donatus is not to be confused with the other Donatus—Tiberius Claudius Donatus (late 4th century), who also wrote a commentary in twelve books on Virgil's *Aeneid*, which like its predecessor's, contained some notes on the subject matter, with most of the work devoted to the finer points of grammar and rhetoric and the shaping of an eloquent style of writing.

✠

By the end of the 4th century the West began to face greater pressure from the barbarians—Germanic peoples who were seeking new lands beyond the Rhine and Danube. The word barbarian had been used by the Greeks to designate an alien, and therefore by definition, someone who was culturally inferior to a Greek. The Romans applied this demeaning term to all tribes of peoples who came to live beyond the Rhine-Danube frontier. *Germani* was originally the name for one of these tribes, and the word became the root of the French and Spanish word for German, *Aleman* or *Alemanni*. Most of these tribes referred to themselves as *Theuts*—meaning "the folk" or "the peoples"—and *Theut* became the root of the modern Deutsch and Tueton.

There were actually three successive waves of barbarian invasions, separated from each other by brief periods of stabalization. The first wave, between 200 AD and 600 AD was set in motion by nomadic peoples of the Eurasian steppe, mongolian or Tartar tribes called the Huns. For centuries they had driven their heards in yearly migrations from the northern to the southern steppes of central Asia, following the seasonsal changes in pasturage. Perhaps they were forced by some obscure disturbance among the races of the interior to seek new pastures. The Huns may have been descendants of the Hiung-nu against whom the Chinese had constructed the Great Wall. Successfully held back by the Chinese, the Huns turned in the opposite direction, As they swept westward along the steppe, whole tribes and peoples fled before the assault. The Huns were expert horsemen and could cover large distances, strike rapidly before their victims were aware, and make off before they could retaliate. A contemporary historian said they were "the most famous offspring of the north, fiercer than ferocity itself, invinciple devils" who not only fought on horseback, but conducted business in the saddle as well. They were expert archers, able to catch pursuing foes off guard by suddenly turning upon them and firing their arrows in one swift move. The German barbarians who fled before their assault claimed the Huns did not even dismount to eat, but warmed raw meat under their saddles and kept on riding. To those they invaded, they appeared uncommonly ugly from scars of battle and lacerations purposefully inflicted on their faces as children. The Roman poet Claudian wrote, "with horrid wounds they gash their brutal brows."

> There is a race on Scythia's extreme edge
> Eastward, beyond the Tanais' frigid stream,   [the Don River in Russia]
> The Northern Bear looks down on no uglier crew:
> Their garb is coarse, their bodies foul to view;
> Their souls are never subdued by hoe and rake
> or Ceres arts, their sustenance is what they take.   [agriculture]
> Not even the Centaur-offspring of the cloud
> Were horsed more firmly than this savage crowd;
> Brisk, lithe, in loose array they charge, by terror led,
> Then fly, they turn, attacking the foe who thinks they've fled.

[By not practicing Ceres arts, they are not an agricultural people, but take what they want from others. The Centaur was a mythological being, half-horse, half man. The Huns are pictured above as being more firmly seated on their horses than even the Centaur. The issue of the Huns eating half-raw, or raw meat is one example of historians embroidering what they read in other sources, and in this case, a basic misunderstanding of a wide-spread nomadic custom. Actually, the Huns did put raw meat under their saddles, but only to prevent and heal the horses' wounds caused by the pressure of the saddle and the long, hard ride. Furthermore, the Huns cooked their meat; big copper cauldrons for cooking meat have been found by archeologists at numerous Hunnic camping places. And when Ammianus writes that the Huns "wore clothing that they sewed together from the skins of forest rodents," he was merely copying word for word a sentence in a book on the history of the Scythians written by another historian, Trogus Pompius, a contemporary of the emperor Augustus.]

Through a gateway in the Ural Mountains, this whirlwind appeared in southern Russia and immediately defeated the Ostrogoths, who fled southward, triggering the flight of

Visogoths, Burgundians, Vandals, Franks, Anglo-Saxons, and other Germanic peoples between 375 and 450 AD.

These German invaders originally came from the north, from Scandinavia. In later centuries, tribes who were ethnically the same peoples as the ones whom the Romans called Germans invaded western Europe and Brittain, and even reached Greenland and the shores of North America. We called them Vikings, and they were immortalized in this century by Hollywood in a movie of the same name starring Burt Lancaster and Tony Curtis. Tony and Burt later worked together in a circus picture, *Trapeze,* which featured Gina Lollabridgida, who gave a fine performance. From epic poetry to the epic film, history has always furnished the events to be grist in the artistic mill.

The Battle of Adrianople, 378

The Germans along the Rhine were dominated by the two great divisions of the Gothic nation, the Visogoths (West Goths) and the Ostrogoths (East Goths). Shortly after the Huns defeated the Ostrogoths, they broke into the land of the Visogoths and were so quickly loaded down with booty that they had to break off the attack. In the summer of 376, tens of thousands of Visogoths were encamped on the northern bank of the lower Danube anxiously waiting for permission to cross the river. They had once been part of a proud nation, and now, defeated by the Huns and starving, they were scared lest their enemies fall upon them again before they were admitted into the empire. A Roman historian, Ammianus Marcellinus (330-400 AD), perhaps "the greatest literary genius which the world has seen between Tacitus and Dante," wrote an account of the German invasions which was a stylistic masterpiece. Once the Visogoths got permission to cross,

> They poured across the Danube river day and night without ceasing, . . .
> on board ships and rafts, as well as in canoes hollowed out of the trunks
> of trees. . . . A great many drowned because, finding no room in the
> vesssels, they tried to swim across. . . . So numerous were the barbarians
> that one might as well have tried to count the waves of the African sea or
> the grains of sand driven by the wind.

Unfortunately, the Roman administrators appointed to provide for the needs of the Visogoths diverted much of the money allotted by the government for their provisions, and subjected them to various forms of extortion. The oppressed Visogoths revolted and began to ravage the countryside. The Emperor Valens himself set out from Constantinople and led a Roman army to face them at Adrianople. While the Visogoths were far superior in numbers, they were not exactly an army; they were a whole people: women, children, sick people, old people. Outnumbered, Valens waited for reinforcements. But he grew impatient. On the afternoon of August 9, 378, Valens launched the fierce attack of his Roman cavalry. The Germans were driven back to their wagons, hard pressed by the advancing legions. Suddenly the Ostrogoths arrived with their cavalry, joined the battle, and turned the tide by its charge. This sudden Ostrogoth attack threw the Romans into confusion, then into panic, and what followed was a massacre. The Roman army was annihilated and the Emperor Valens killed. In the words of Ammianus, "Hardly a third of the Roman army escaped. Not since the battle of Cunnae [a crushing defeat by Hannibal centuries earlier] has there been so destructive a slaughter in our history." The Battle of Adrianople was the first defeat of Rome by Germans; it marked the beginning of the ascendance of heavy cavalry in European warfare, as well as the real beginning of the barbarian invasions. The Roman military was no longer considered invincible. On the events which led to the disaster of Adrianople, Ambrose wrote: "The Huns threw themselves upon the Alemanni, the Alemanni upon the Goths, and the Goths, exiled from their own country, made us exiles as well, and the end is not yet."

410 The Sack of Rome

Seasonal crossings continued, as families and tribes sought greener pastures. In December of 406, New Year's Eve, the Rhine froze over, allowing thousands to cross the natural bridge of ice. Roman soldiers were weary of stopping the flow, as more and more Visogoths entered the empire. As the Ostrogoths approached the frontier, the Visogoths moved on, invading Italy from the east, led by Alaric the Bold, their crafty, aggressive leader who was seeking land for his people. Alaric was no wild barbarian chieftan, but a soldier trained in the Roman army who had risen to the rank of commander. The failure of the military to give him a higher command probably caused him to turn against the empire. He decided to lead his people in their search for productive land. Initially, he hoped to get land peacefully and fairly through negotiations with Roman leadership. In hindsight, the Romans should have worked something out, as they had been doing for centuries with individual farmers and families who had crossed the frontier and were absorbed productively into the Empire. Others had been allowed to enter by tribes as *foederati* or allies, and given grants of land by the government within the frontiers on the condition that they would aid in repelling further invasions. But not only was the emperor ill-advised, he was foolish not to grant their modest requests. With his back to the wall, Alaric was forced to the only recourse left, a military assault upon a Roman people he had greatly respected.

At first, this so-called invasion was no more than a picketing demonstration, with Alaric hesitant to inflict damage upon Roman power, and Stilicho, the head of the Roman army—himself a German—reluctant to engage his forces. Had a workable solution been found, the shattering of the imperial power may have been prevented. But Honorius was jealous and suspicious of Stilicho, and had him put to death in 408, allowing Alaric to march into Italy unopposed. After prolonged pillaging and plundering of northern Italy, Alaric eventually took and sacked Rome in 410, robbing, killing, and burning with abandon (though they spared Christian churches). Vandals, and other peoples began crossing the frontier and devastated all of Gaul (France) and reached into Spain.

The Visogoth's capture and the sack of Rome in 410 shocked the civilized world. Many believed the end of the world had come, or at least the end of a world upon which the standards of value and the guiding principles of their existence had been based. Christians thought the glorious end prophesied by *Revelations* was at hand. Yet Jerome—whose greatest work was the translation of the Bible into Latin, *The Vulgate*, and whose moral force filled his anti-pagan writings with controversial vigor—accused himself in a famous dream of loving Cicero and the pagan writers more than the new Christian literature; his writings were fully in the tradition of Rome, and he loved the ancient capital. When the news reached him that Alaric had sacked Rome, Jerome wept in his cell in Bethlehem.

> I was desirous of setting to work today studying Ezekiel, but at the very moment I began to dictate I felt such anguish in thinking of the catastrophe in the west that the words ceased to come to me. For long I remained silent, bethinking me well that this was a time for weeping.
>
> My voice left me and sobs choked my speech. The city which had conquered the whole world is herself captive. What can I say? . . . . That famous city, head of the Roman Empire, is laid waste by fire. There is no spot which is not receiving refugees from Rome.

A bitter polemic exploded between pagans and Christians. Pagans blamed Christians who had rejected the tradtional Roman gods. For this, the old pagan gods were bringing retribution to all. In order to refute pagan attacks, Augustine began writing his *City of God* soon after the capture of Rome. One of the greatest efforts of Christian speculation, the book was a response to a question which had been broached as early as the third century and which had become urgent in the fifth: why, with the advent of Christianity, had so many calamities befallen the empire. While it was true that throughout its history Rome had suffered misfortune, why should fifth-century Rome, where godly men held the true concerning the Trinity, suffer at the hands of blasphemous Arian heretics? Augustine tells his readers that the key to human history is the coexistence of two cities—a City of God, founded by the creation of angels, and an earthly city, founded by the angels who fell. Earthly glory and prosperity were not necessary for true happiness. Christians should not worry, he wrote, about this city of man that had fallen to the barbarians. It was the city of God that really mattered. Those who cherish the earthly city, filled with the sin of Adam, will find their end in death and the fires of hell—a literal fire in which the vast majority of his fellow beings would be tormented throughout eternity. In this last epoch of human history, says Augustine, Christians will witness the triumph of the heavenly city and the eternal rest of its citizens.

☛ **St. Augustine** (Aurelius Agustinus, 354-430), *Confessions* (401)

Unlike Marcus Aurelius, Augustine was not fluent in Greek (though he was much influenced by Greek neoplatonic philosophy), but he is one of the masters of Latin prose. His *City of God*, written as a reaction to the sack of Rome in 410, is one of the great works of the early Church. St. Augustine merged Platonic philsophy with the teaching of the Church, just as Thomas Aquinas was to do with Aristotelian philosopy centuries later, in writing the monumental *Summa Theologica*. Augustine was thirty-three when he underwent his dramatic conversion to Christianity. He tells the story of his long and painful path to final acceptance in his *Confessions,* one of the great works of literature. Setting aside for the moment the *Meditations* of Marcus Aurelius, we can also consider it the first genuine autobiography in human history. Poets such as Sappho, Catullus, and Propertius revealed something of their sexual longings and misdemeanors, but their work hardly descended into the confessional anguish and despair expressed by Augustine. The *Confessions* begins with several pages of praise to God; then Augustine does something no writer before him had ever done.

> O Lord, my God, but that I know not where I came into this dying life (shall I call it?) or living death. . . . but I was welcomed by the consolations of human milk; . . . . Afterwards I began to smile, first in my sleep, then when awake. That at least is what I was told, and I believed it since that is what we see other infants doing.
> Little by little I began to be aware where I was and wanted to manifest my wishes to those who could fulfill them as I could not. . . . .

The subject of childhood had been almost entirely ignored by other ancient writers. In the fifty biographies of great men, Greek and Roman, written by Plutarch, for example, there is hardly a mention of childhood; it is as if the ancient world thought of it as a pre-human stage. For Augustine, however, the infant's exhibition of greed and jealousy was one more proof of the doctrine of Original Sin, a doctrine he was to develop to the full and hand on to the Church for the ages.

> . . . . My desires were internal; adults were external to me and had no means of entering my soul. When I did not get my way I used to be indignant with my seniors for their disobedience and would revenge myself upon them by weeping.

As a schoolboy, Augustine dreaded the school exercises in "reading, writing, and arithmetic, the repititious memorization: " 'One and one are two; two and two are four'—what hateful singsong." After being forced to study Greek, having to endure the teacher's "punishments and cruel threats," he was introduced to the magnificent Latin of Virgil's *Aeneid*, the literary masterpiece of the Roman world. The language and the story captivates the young Augustine. He is touched by Dido, queen of Carthage, who fell madly in love with Aeneas, only to be plunged into despair when he leaves her, as he must, since his destiny was to found the City of Rome. In one of the most haunting and memorable images in classical literature, Dido "mounts in madness that high pyre, unsheathes [Aeneas'] sword," and kills herself. Augustine weeps as he reads this. But his feeling for the *Aeneid* is diminished when his teachers use the text for rhetorical exercises. Underlying his criticism is a disgust with the privileged class of lawyers and bureaucrats trained in this kind of rhetoric. Augustine had risen high into this class, only to abandon it and become first a priest and then a bishop of the Church.

> Even now I have not yet discovered the reasons why I hated Greek literature when I was being taught it as a small boy. Latin I deeply loved, not at the stage of my primary teachers but at the secondary level taught by the teachers of literature called "grammarians." The initial elements, where one learns the three R's of reading, writing, and arithmetic, I felt to be no less a burden and an infliction than the entire series of Greek classes. . . . This was better than the poetry I was later forced to learn about the wanderings of some legendary fellow named Aeneas (forgetful of my own wanderings) and to weep over the death of a Dido who took her own life from love.
>
> > [Compare the following complaint with Hamlet's soliloquoy quoted on page 346 of this study guide.—"What's Hecuba to him, or he to Hecuba that he should weep for her!"]
>
> What is more pitiable than a wretch without pity for himself who weeps over the death of Dido dying for love of Aeneas, but not weeping over himself dying for his lack of love for you, My God, light of my heart, bread of the inner mouth of my soul, the power which begat life in my mind and in the innermost recesses of my thinking. I had no love for you and "committed fornication against you" and in my fornications I heard all round me the cries "Well done, well done" and "Well done" is what they say to shame a man who does not go along with them. Over this I wept not a tear. I wept over Dido who "died in pursuing her ultimate end with a sword." I abandoned you to pursue the lowest things of your creation. I was dust going to dust. Had I been forbidden to read this story, I would have been sad that I could not read what made me sad. Such madness is considered a higher and more fruitful literary education than being taught to read and write. . . .

Augustine tells us of his infant jealousies, youthful stealing, fights with his mother, Monica, who wanted him to change his ways a become a good Christian lad. He lusts after a peasant woman, takes her, then sends her away. Filled with shame and disgust, he is unable to change.

> I carried inside me a cut and bleeding soul, and how to get rid of it I just
> didn't know. I sought every pleasure—the countryside, sports, fooling
> around, the peace of a garden, friends and good company, sex, reading.
> My soul floundered in the void—and came back upon me. For where
> could my heart flee from my heart? Where could I escape from myself. "

We do not find this kind of personal revelation and anguish elsewhere in classical literature. The author is ruthless, as he plumbs the depth of his despair. Homer's characters spoke eloquently of their inner conflicts and plans for action, but this is something new. The "I" of the protagonist and the "I" of the author are one and the same; the journey is not an epic adventure over land and stormy sea, but a descent into the self. Augustine makes his way to Carthage, Dido's city on the northern coast of Africa. He continues his studies and remains there until he is twenty, enjoying the life of the capital, especially the theater, and settling into a regular liason with a woman. The city is boiling with vice, riotous living, and cultural depravit, and it is here that Augustine feels the turmoil of his errant and lustful ways. In a famous passage noted for its opening line, the author uses rhyme and other rhetorical devices. *Carthago* rhymes with the Latin word for cauldron, *sartago;* while rhyme had been used by poets writing in the classical style, here was the vulgar Latin taking a first step toward the rhythmic accentual rhyme that characterized the "common" literature and poetry of the Latin Middle Ages.

> **To Carthage then I came** and all around me hissed a cauldron of illicit
> loves. I polluted the spring water of friendship with the filth of
> concupiscence. I muddied its clear stream by the hell of lust, and yet,
> though foul and immoral, in my excessive vanity, I used to carry on in
> the manner of an elegant man about town. I rushed headlong into love,
> by which I was longing to be captured. My love was returned and in
> secret I attained the joy that enchains. I was glad to be in bondage, tied
> with troublesome chains, with the result that I was flogged with the
> red-hot iron rods of jealousy, suspicion, fear, anger, and contention.
> As yet I loved no one, yet I loved to love, and out of a deep-seated
> need, I hated myself for not being needy. I pursued whoever-whatever
> might be lovable, in love with love. I hated safety and any course
> without danger. For within me was a famine.

Speak clearly, speak poignantly, speak ruthlessly, and your voice will be heard across the ages. Published in 401, Augustine's confessional prose has the same power today that it had over 1500 years ago. And yet, the sensibility is modern, not modern with a capital M, as in 20th century Modern, but modern in the sense that it is timely and present, shocking us with the truth of the here and now. Modern for all time, modern for the ages. Augustine's "I" is different from the "I" of Marcus Aurelius, who, as the title in Greek (*Pro Heuton*) of his *Meditations* suggests, was speaking to himself; and different from the "I" of Socrates, who was speaking to an inner spirit, his *daimon*. Augustine is grabbing us by the shirt collar and speaking directly to us, his reader.

I carried inside me a cut and bleeding soul, and how to get rid of it I just didn't know. I sought every pleasure—the countryside, sports, fooling around, the peace of a garden, friends and good company, sex, reading. My soul floundered in the void—and came back upon me. For where could my heart flee from my heart? Where could I escape from myself.

In another passage, Augustine touches upon the nature of theatrical events, and brings up the issue of "alienation," that Bertold Brecht was to make the cornerstone of his concept of epic theatre.

I was captivated by theatrical shows. They were full of representations of my own miseries and fuelled my fire. Why is it that a person should wish to experience suffering by watching grievous and tragic events which he himself would not wish to endure? Nevertheless he wants to suffer the pain given by being a spectator of these sufferings, and the pain itself is his pleasure. What is this but amazing folly? For the more anyone is moved by these scenes, the less free he is from similar passions. Only, when he himself suffers, it is called misery; when he feels compassion for others, it is called mercy. But what quality of mercy is it in fictitious and theatrical inventions? A member of the audience is not excited to offer help, but invited only to grieve. The greater his pain, the greater his approval of the actor in these presentations. If the human calamities, whether in ancient histories or fictitious myths, are so presented that the theatregoer is not caused pain, he walks out of the theatre disgusted and highly critical. But if he feels pain, he stays riveted in his seat enjoying himself.

Food for Thought

Bertold Brecht's Epic Theatre & the Alienation Affect

Here's a passage in a book of religious confessions by a 5th century writer that not only looks back to the nature of Greek literature and the emergence of Latin as the language of the West, but looks forward to our own century. It anticipates the very problem with Aristotelian theatre that Brecht attempted to change with his Epic Theatre and the "alienation effect." Augustine points out that if the audience doesn't feel grief and pity and sorrow, they walk out of the theatre disgusted. If, however, they do feel the catharsis called for by Aristotle, they leave without feeling compelled to act on their own problems; or, as Brecht would have wanted, to act on the political problems of the world. Brecht wanted the director to create a separation between actor and character, between the world of the play and the experience of seeing the play—an "alienation effect." How to create this "alienation effect" is still not fully understood, and seldom used in theatre or film. Years ago I played the role of Tiger Brown in Beacht's Three Penny Opera. The director had us scowl at the audience in order to "alienate" them. This is not what Brecht meant. It's a very difficult and complicated effect, which requires actors and directors trained in the dialectics of Brecht's method. When it works, it can have a powerful and often unsettling effect on the audience. One wonders if Augustine would have approved of Brecht's Epic Theatre in light of his criticism above.

★

In Milan, Augustine's mother arranged a marriage for him, hoping that the break with his longtime mistress (who was the mother of his son) might bring about his conversion.

> Meanwhile my sins multiplied. The woman with whom I habitually slept was torn away from my side because she was a hindrance to my marriage. My heart which was deeply attached was cut and wounded, and left a trail of blood. She left with me the natural son I had by her. I was unhappy, incapable of following a woman's example, and impatient of delay. I was to get the girl I had proposed to only at the end of two years. As I was not a lover of marriage but a slave of lust, I procured another woman, not of course as wife.

Augustine has been called the greatest poet of the early Chruch, and in all but meter the *Confessions* is indeed a continuous lyric, charged with the author's particular emotions, recounting his intimate perceptions, interconnected by lyric impulses that progress from one emotional thrust to another. The reader is left with a sense of having undergone the experience vicariously. Never before had the rhetorical tradtion been put to such hearfelt use, a device justified by the book's lyric quality. This genre of personal writing, which can be called meditative or confessional, began with Marcus Aurelius' *Meditations* and continues through Augustine's *Confessions.* It is taken up again in the 12th century with Peter Abelard's *History of My Calamities*, an account of his affair with Heloise and subsequent castration by her Uncle's henchmen. Using Augustine's *Confessions* and Abelard's *History* as springboard, we come to the 18th century writer Jean Jacques Rousseau, whose novel *La Nouvelle Heloise* was a model for generations of "confessional" writers, and whose *Confessions* inaugurated autobiography as a literary genre. Rousseau's *Confessions* fueled the fires of individual emancipation that burst into flames with the French Revolution of 1789. Rousseau rejected classical restraint in favor of inwardness and the truths of feeling, which became the core impulse of the Romantic Movement of the 19th century. Romanticism marked a profound shift in European culture. In art and literature, self-expression became the third major critical definition of a work of art and its purpose. Aristotle's theory of *mimesis*, calls for the writer to mirror reality, mimick what's already there in nature; Horace (in his *Ars Poetica*), allowed its mimetic ability, but added that art should instruct and/or entertain. The Romantic movement took up a new torch: art doesn't have to reflect the outside world, nor does it have to entertain or instruct. It is enough to express the inner world of feelings and imagination. Today, we live in a post-Romantic age, despite the notions of Modernism and Post-Modernism. Ninety percent of poetry written in this century is romantic, and most of it lyric, despite the efforts of the "high-modernists" (Eliot, Pound, etc.) who emphasize fragmentation and dislocation (mimetic, in that they see the world as fragmented and non-linear), and the attempts of Language Poets, who eschew personal communication altogether in order to freshen perception. The Romantic Movement looked to nature as a way of evoking human feelings. The power of the imagination was exalted, viewed as a spiritual faculty, creative not imitative. Poets embraced a poetics of memory as a way of beginning the reconstruction of selfhood. It challenged expectations, combined personal lyricism with political commitment, exuding energy and desire. The disintegration of classical intellectualism became a hymn to metamorphosis and transformation, sometimes uncovering unsettling truths about the unconscious and its workings. Out of this came a belief in the goodness of (human) nature and an ability to achieve synthesis and unity through the challenges of art. Rousseau's great work has remained unchallenged for two hundred years as the classic text on self-revelation. (Not that others haven't been written—F. Scott Fitzgerald's *The Crack Up,* Jean Paul Sartre's *Words*, and Simone de Bouvair's *The Second Sex* come to mind, not to mention great autobiographical novels such as Samuel Butler's *The Way of All Flesh*, Louis-Ferdinand Céline's *Journey to the End of the Night*, etc.

The opening paragraph of Rousseau's *Confessions* (quoted below) contains the philosophic underpinning of most of the poetry written in our century, especially that poetry often dismissed under the banner of "confessionalism." If confessionalism is a fad. it's a fad that has passed through every great age of literature in one form or another from Sappho through Catallus to Ovid, from Augustine through Abelard to Rousseau, from the Romantic poets to the Confessional poets. As Rousseau declared—

> Myself alone! I know the feelings of my heart, and I know men. I am not made like any of those I have seen; I venture to believe that I am not made like any of those who are in existence. If I am not better, at least I am different.

∝⁊

A minor production of a work by Augustine marked a revolution in European prosody. His *Psalm against the Donatists* is the first authentic example of poetry based on rhythm, constructed on the principle of *numbering* syllables, with fixed caesure (pause) and a more or less developed rhyme. There's a refrain which includes interal rhyme as well as end rhyme. The only other consistent device is the accent on the penultimate syllable of each half line, and the rhyme endings on the vowel *e* (or *ae*). The syllabic principle became standard in Christian poetry when the humanist impulse was spent, and from Christian poetry spread to the secular poetry of all Europe.

While modern literary history can be said to begin with the Renaissance around 1500, medieval literary history is usually said to have begun around 1000, with the rise of universities in the 12th century spurring a renaissance of its own. Yet, it is in the darker ages of early medieval times—400 to 1000—that many of the seeds of modernism can be found. It was an age in which the breakdown of antique literature and culture fused with Latin rhetoric and Christian passion. Many poets and writers of this period took part in the creation and dissemination of its principles, but Augustine caught its total nature in one work that exemplifies literary impulses and attitudes that seem as modern to us as they were to the readers of his own day.

To the ancients, the second of the seven liberal arts was rhetoric ("the craft of speech"), an indispensable complement to the life of regulated beauty and freedom of their lives, their arts, and their poetry. The student of rhetoric was taught how to artificially construct a discourse. Almost half of the *Iliad* and more than two thirds of the *Odyssey* are devoted to speeches (rhetoric) by its characters, often quite long speeches. The centuries that followed the Latin Silver Age, an age marking a decline in literary excellence; rhetoric was often over-used, and became the be-and-end all for a speech, poem, or any piece of writing. Through the influence of Latin church hymns, rhyme became part of rhetorical effect. It's practically impossible to determine just when, where, and how rhyme became a part of poetry, though many historians and literary critics point to a particular event or person as an innovator. One such notable was the Sicilian writer and poet Gorgias, who came to Athens an ambassador in 427 and consciously employed rhyming words to achieve a musico-poetic effect.

Where Jerome brought humanism and a distrust of allegory to his letters and translation of the Bible (not to mention his influential introductions), Augustine had qualities that Jerome lacked: a most delicate emotional life and spiritual fire; and a longing to know an essence that soars above science. But as a student of rhetoric and a pupil of the Platonists, Augustine's conversion convinced him that all education must be endeavored at the service of Faith, and he used the rhetoric of the Bible as his own. Where Jerome saw no allegory in the Bible, Augustine believed that everything in the Bible that is not directly concerned with faith and morals has a hidden meaning. He may have misused allegory in his exegeses, but his theory became a permanent possession of the Middle Ages. His *Confessions* was written in a style called *antique artistic prose* where the methods of rhetoric were made to serve the new spiritual world of Christianity. One of those methods was syntactic parallelism and the coupling of phrases of equal length, or contrasting ideas; the other was the use of rhyme within or at the end of a passage (remember his *Psalm Against the Donatist*, and the famous paragraph in the *Confessions* in which he uses the inner rhymes *carthago* and *sartago*).

Arranged in the form of a poem, the opening sentences of that paragraph have the *sound* of a modern poem.

> To Carthage then I came
> and all around me hissed a cauldron of illicit loves.
> I polluted the spring water of friendship
> with the filth of concupiscence.
> I muddied its clear stream
> by the hell of lust,
> and yet, though foul and immoral, in my excessive vanity,
> I used to carry on in the manner of an elegant man about town.
> I rushed headlong into love,
> by which I was longing to be captured.
> My love was returned
> and in secret I attained the joy that enchains.

I was glad to be in bondage,
tied with troublesome chains, . . .

And here again, the sound of modernism in the closing sentences of the *Confessions*, rendered as a prayer. I give the Latin alongside the English to better show the passionate rhythms and parallel constructions of the original.

Thou art ever quiet	Semper quietus
because thou thyself art thy quiet.	es quoniam tua quies tu ipse es.
And comprehension of this,	Et hoc intellegere
what man shall give it to any man?	quis hominium dabit homini?
What angel to any angel?	Quis engelus angelo?
What angel to any man?	Quis angelus homini?
Of thee must it be asked,	A te petatur,
in thee sought,	in te quaeratur,
at thy gate knocked for;	ad te pulsetur:
thus, thus will it be received,	sic, sic accipietur,
thus found,	sic invenietur,
thus will the grave be opened.	sic aperietur.

No modern prose can reproduce these solemn parallelisms and assonances. Here rhetoric becomes poetry, even in its original prose form. Breaking these sentences into lines of poetry doesn't change the rhetorical effect, but does make clear how the use of the breath line as exemplified by contemporary (if not modern) poetry, is the very thing that gives structural form to the rhetoric underlying the prose. Where rhyme—and especially end-stopped rhyme—became the structural determinant for centuries of poetry and song, it is the rhetorical component, going back to the great Latin writers of the Middle Ages, that gives it a modern stamp. Poets of the medeival age used the rhetorical devices of the Latin poets of the Golden Age, and before them, the rhythms and pulses found in the ancient Greek poets from Callimachus to Sappho to Homer. In one fell swoop, Augustine linked those ancient rhetorical devices to the poetic impulses of modern poetry. His *Confessions* begins a new form of literary expression, expanded by writers like Abelard and Rousseau, that became one of the dominant impulses of 20th century modern and contemporary verse.

❧❧

☛ **Martianus Capella**, *The Weding of Philology and Mercury*

Pagan literature continued; poets and writers extended the classical tradition, though most of the work written in the 2nd to 5th centuries was, at best, mediocre. An excess of creative energy went into the writing of panagyrics that celebrated the inefficient and ineffectual emperors that came and went. Most of these poets come off as skilled performers and rhetoricians rather than as great poets. They rarely go beyond technical cleverness.

It's easy to make generalizations but difficult to prove their applicability. There are those who would charge that anytime the production of literature is left to those who teach it, the literature and poetry produced will smack of the schoolroom and lack the breath of life. But literature has been a school subject since the 6th century BC when the Greeks equated Homer with "tradition," in whom they believed their essential nature and the essence of their past could be found. Since then, poetry has always had a pedagogical function, along with its natural role to elevate and inspire. The Romans, great imitators that they were, followed the Greek model—Roman poetry begins with the translation of the *Odyssey* into Latin by Livius Andronicus. Subsequently, Roman poets like Naevius and Ennius strove to write the national epic—something that could stand alongside the *Iliad*. Finally, Virgil did the trick, and the *Aeneid* became the schoolbook taken by the Middle Ages to provide the connection between them and antiquity, between them and Homer, between epic and school. Yet, as we have seen, despite their inspirational fire, the Christian epics written in these centuries designed to stand alongside the *Aeneid* are tedious reading today, and part of the reason must lie in their chief purpose, which was to instruct, not entertain.

If Plato had had his way, Homer would have been banished forever from the educational curriculm—but that was because Plato thought all poets were liars, inimical to the nature of philosophy, which Plato felt should be not just the core of all education, but the only education necessary. Plato rejected the idea of a general "liberal artes" education. Like his politics, his pedagogical theories foundered. It was Isocrates who bridged the gap between opposing educational forces by arranging the curriculm in a hierarchical manner—general education would serve as a *propaedentics*, or preparation, for the study of philosophy. The arts—as a branch of learning—were divided between the *liberal artes*, studies worthy of a free man and therefore not designed to make money, and the practical arts, *artes mechanicae*.

By the 5th century, philosophy in the Greek sense ceased to be an educational force, and therefore the liberal arts were no longer seen as representing the propaedentics of philosophy, though Christian intellectuals felt they could serve a similar function in relation to religious education. In this, writers like Augustine felt the pagan classics could be studied as a prepatory approach to the study of the Bible, and other Christian texts.

What were the subjects that made up the liberal arts curriculm? Originally, there were nine [see page 227], but by late antiquity, the number had been reduced to seven—in a sequence they would retain throughout the Middle Ages: grammar, dialectic, rhetoric, arithmetic, geometry, music, and astronomy. The authoritative description of the seven liberal arts was produced by Martianus Capella, a North African scholar, who wrote a widely used pedagogical allegory dressed up as a romance, *The Wedding of Philology and Mercury* (De nuptiis Philolgiae et Mercurii). Written in the years following the sack of Rome in 410, much of it is prose, but verse sections alternate with prose throughout. The form calls to mind Menippean satire, which alternates prose and poetry, and the model for its first two books was Apuleius's "Marriage of Cupid and Psyche" told in his *Metamorphoses* (or *The Golden Ass*, see page _____).

At 500 pages, it's not a book you'd want to plow through today, but it has its charming moments. It begins with a poem to Hymen as the matchmaker among the gods. After talking things over with the gods Natura and Virtus, they try to fix up Mercury, who is yet unmarried. Who'd make the best match? they wonder. Apollo suggests the learned maiden Philologia, who embraces all knowledge. So—like Dorothy, the Scarecrow, the Tin Man, and the Cowardly Lion—Philologia, Mercury, Apollo, Virtus, Hymen, and Natura, escorted by the Muses, make their way through the celestial spheres to Jupiter's palace, where an assembly of all the gods consent to admitting a deserving mortal such as Philologia, and grant Mercury's wish. In order to become worthy of immortality, though, Philologia is instructed by Athanasia that she must vomit up a number of books before ascending to heaven. There she meets all the inhabitants of Olympus—somewhat different from the Greek version—including demons, demigods, poets and philsophers. Finally, the wedding takes place and Philologia is presented with her wedding present, the seven liberal arts, personified as women and dressed accordingly.

Grammar is a gray-haired woman, carrying a knife and a file for surgical work on children's grammatical mistakes. Rhetoric is a tall, beautiful woman, magnificently dressed, holding the weapons she'll use to wound her adversaries. Capella's book was influential throughout the Middle Ages, especailly for the use of the allegorial figures which appeared again and again in medieval art and poetry. The theme of a journey taken through the celestial spheres to heaven also became a common image, the most notable example being Dante's trek down into hell, and upward through Purgatory toward the heavenly stars of Paradise.

☛ Rutilius Namatianus,

One of the "New Poets" of the 5th century known for his elegiac couplets, Rutilius was born in Gaul in the late 4th century AD, moved to Rome as a young man and held high office at the court of Honorius. In 410 Rome was sacked by Alaric. Rutilius stayed to become prefect a few years later, but in 417 he returned to his native country to check on his properties after hearing of the barbarian attacks in Gaul. His *De Reditu Suo* recounts his sea voyage from Ostia to the northern part of Tuscany on his way home. In this work, he bears witness to a crumbling civilization marked by temples and buildings that lay in ruins as the result of a century of invasions by Goths and Vandals. Much of the countrside was abandoned, cities had been ravaged, and everywhere he went there was poverty and desolation. By the end of the 2nd Book, the reader realizes that Rutilius is not returning to Gaul, where he was born, but fleeing Rome,

> a city that had previously been the world.

> *Urben fecisti quod prius orbis erat*

Namatianus mourns for a world that is ending. A pagan poet, he is not consoled by the Christian hope for a better, future life; his melancholy heart looks to the past, to a glorious empire and an eternal city, which he praises for its historical role,

> For the various nations, you made a single homeland.

> *Fecisti patriam diversis gentibus unam*

Namatianus was often compared to Claudian as the last poet of the Empire and the pagan world, but Claudian was a professional poet who needed to satisfy his patrons and backers. Namatianus was a wealthy landowner and officer of the state who wrote for himself and became the champion of a dying paganism.

His famous tribute to the city of Rome was translated in this century by Ezra Pound. Reading the poem today is a moving experience, because the poem not only expresses the ideals and feelings of the poet, but of the translator as well. It's a classic example of the way art, literature, and poetry continue to speak to us across centuries, even millennia. The American poet Ezra Pound had found his voice and calling in Venice when he was in his early twenties. He lived in London for awhile, becoming the nucleus and driving force of the modern movement, launching poets as diverse as T.S. Eliot and Robert Frost. But after seeing so many of his contemporaries killed in the First World War, he became disillusioned and moved back to Italy, where he developed some crack-pot economic ideas and believed that Mussolini would return Italy to the glory of its classical age. During the Second World War he made a series of treasonous broadcasts, and when the Allies finally advanced up the boot of Italy, he was found dazed and half-mad, walking the streets of Rome. He was arrested by partisans in 1945, and held for execution in a wire cage in a detention camp in Pisa. While Pound worked on his *Pisan Cantos*, he could hear the firing squads executing traitors and deserters. Luckily for him, he was turned over to US Forces and then repatriated to the United States to stand trial. But he was found unfit to plead on grounds of insanity. So he was then incarcerated in St. Elizabeth's Hospital in Washington DC from 1946 to 1958. Upon his release, he returned to Italy. A central figure in modern poetry, Pound also had a genius for translation, practically reinventing the art in modern times.

Namatianus wrote his poem as he left the Rome he loved, praising a city he hoped would last forever, and mourning an empire on the verge of extinction. Fifteen centuries later, Pound turned to Namatianus's poem and rendered it into English, using biblical diction to capture the sense of his own loss, saying farewell to a city he thought he'd never see again. It's as if two voices, separated by fifteen hundred years, are finally speaking as one.

        Roma

Again and again I kiss thy gates at departing
And against our will leave thy holy door-stone,
Praying in tears and with praises
   such words as can pierce our tears.

Hear us, Queen, fairest in all the earth, ROMA,
Taking post twixt the sky's poles,
Nurse of men! Mother of Gods,
              do thou hear us.
Ever we hymn thee and will, while the Fates can have power.
No guest can forget thee.
  It were worse crime than forgetting the sun
If we ceased holding thy honor in heart,
Thou impartial as sunlight to the splash of all outer sea-bords.
All that Apollo over-rides in his quadriga

Hast thou combined into equity:
Many strange folk in one fatherland,
To their good, not seeking to dominate;
Gravest law to the conquered as consorts;
Made city what had been world.

They say that Venus was thy mother, that is by Aeneas,
Mars for father hadst'ou through Romulus,
Making mild armed strength, she in conquest:
One god in two natures;
                    Joy out of strife by sparing
O'ercamest the sources of terror
In love with all that remains.

⚬⚬

The Huns, led by their great leader, Atilla, entered Italy in 452 and descended to the edge of Rome. But Atilla was dissauded from plundering the city by the diplomatic intercession of Pope Leo I who was well aware of the impending collapse of the Roman state and went out himself to negotiate with him. The Emperor of the Roman Empire abdicated his responsibility and let the Bishop of Rome represent the Eternal City—an event of great significance because it prepared the way for the transformation of leadership in the West from the Roman state to the Holy See of Rome. Within a few years Atilla died, and the Hunnic confederacy broke up as quickly as it had arisen. Divided among themselves, some tribes drifted eastward, disappearing into the shadows that for the modern historian veil eastern Europe and the Asiatic steppes. The Visogoths, who had sacked Rome in 410, moved further West and set up a kingdom in Spain that lasted until Moslems took over in 711.

Vandals unsucessfully engaged the Visogoths & Romans in Spain, crossed the Straits of Gibralter, and set up new kingdoms in Northern Africa. Under Gaeseric, they plundered Carthage, and from that strategic base, began to raid Roman commerical ships. If Gaeseric and his Vandal army could not get to Rome from the top of the boot, perhaps he could enter through the toe. He kept his eye open for an opportunity, and it finally came in 454 when Valentinian was assassinated, ending the dynasty of the great Theodosius and sending the imperial government into a state of paralysis. Sailing across from Carthage, the Vandals entered Rome without opposition. Again, Leo I interceded with the barbarian, gaining a promise from Gaeseric that the lives of the inhabitants would be spared. For two weeks they "vandalized" private and public property, looting the still wealthy city at leisure, then returned to Carthage. Rome was left impoverished.

The two decades following the sack of Rome by Vandals in 454 saw the final disintegration of the empire in the West. The real rulers were the barbarian generals who controlled the imperial government, as Stilicho had done, creating and deposing emperors at will. Odovacer was a Scirian German and leader of the barbarian soldiers from beyond the Danube who now made up the greater part of the Roman army in Italy. He sought land for his own troops and direct rule of Italy for himself. Less committed to the Roman tradition than his predecessors, Odovacer decided to forego the pretense of creating a puppet emperor and in 476 took the government openly into his own hands. He deposed the last emperor of the West, Romulus Augustulus. The boy emperor was nicknamed "the little emperor," and it's a curious irony of history that the last Roman emperor should bear the names of the founder of Rome (Romulus) and the founder of the Empire (Augustus). Odovacer was now the Ostrogothic king of Italy, claiming to rule as an agent of the Eastern Empire. In fact, he was on his own. The Western empire was partitioned among the barbarians.

Though we commonly give the date 476 as the end of the empire, the greater part had long since fallen prey to barbarian kingdoms and Italy itself had been ruled for twenty years by barbarian generals. Gaul (modern day France) was loosely divided between Burgundians in the southwest, Franks in the north and northwest, and Alamani in the northeast. The Vandals controlled North Africa. This kingdom, centered on ancient Carthage, had been the Empire's breadbasket, but the Vandal conquest cost Rome much of its grain supply. Like Barbary pirates, they devastated Mediterranean shipping, and sacked coastal cities, including Rome itself. In Spain, the Visogothic kingdom stood until the Muslim conquests of the eighth century. And Ostrogoths, free of Hunnish control, moved into Italy and defeated Odovacer. Led by their great king Theodoric, the Ostrogoths established their own powerful state. The shattering of the Western Empire took hundreds of years to accomplish, but by the end of the 5th century, it was complete. Europe was in the process of being transformed as a result of this first wave of barbarian invasions. In time, these Germanic invaders developed into great nations; in France and Spain they were to shape the fate of the Western World.

☛ Sidonius Apollinaris (431-486), *The Letters*

Ausonius died fifteen years before the Goths sacked Rome in 410. His world in southwestern France in the latter half of the fourth century was an "Indian summer between ages of storm and wreckage." Ausonius was nearly fifty when the Germans crossed the Rhine in 357, pillaging forty-five flourishing cities, and pitching their camps on the banks of the Moselle. He was nearly sixty when he heard of the disastrous Battle of Adrianople in the East, when the Goths defeated a Roman army and killed an emperor. But the last two decades of his life were peaceful; he was an old man contentedly living on his estates. He died in 395, and within twelve years of his death the host of Germans had burst across the Rhine and "all Gaul was a smoking funeral pyre." The Goths were at the gates of Rome. Comb through the writings of Ausonius and Symmachus and you'll find little mention of what was happening to the world around them, just as the novels of Jane Austen touch not a whit upon the Napoleonic wars.

Sidonius Apollinaris, Gallo-Roman aristocrat, son-in-law to one emperor, father-in-law to another, sometime prefect of Rome, and in the end Bishop of Clermont, was born twenty years after the sack of Rome, but as a writer he was unable to ignore the collapse of the empire. He was twenty when Attila and the Huns swooped down from the north and invaded Italy. He was twenty-four when the Vandals sailed from North Africa across the Meditteranean, drove up the Italian coast and sacked Rome in 454. Where Namatianus had witnessed the fall of the Empire, this notable Gallo-Roman poet lived through its last years and learned to compromise with the new Gothic order. A wealthy landed aristocrat, proud that he was still officially a Roman senator, Sidonius wrote verse that bridged classical tradition and Christianity. He was a man of the world, and even though he longed to return to tranquil times, he also took part in the reality of German conquest and the new Gothic rulers.

He married the daughter of Avitus, who had been proclaimed Roman emperor in the West in 455. For his panegyric in verse celebrating Avitus, he was rewarded by a statue in the Ulpian Library of Trajan at Rome. He wrote panegyrics for Majorian, who succeeded his father in 458, and when Majorian was overthrown three years later, Sidonius withdrew to Gaul and wrote a third panegyric for a later emperor, Anthemius. Sidonius was considered the chief literary figure of 5th century Rome. In the seclusion of his estates, he wrote poems that today are noted mostly for their literary escapism. In an age of chaos and transition, he tried to assemble in his writings all the formal refinements accumulated during centuries of rhetorical tradition. Between 460 and 470, he lived on his estate in Auvergne. What was left of Gaul was squeezed between three barbarian kingdoms—but for the rumblings in the distance, we could be back in the days of Ausonius. Most mornings, Sidonius rose to a view of the lake adjacent to his luxurious villa with its baths and swimming pool. He sent poems and letters to fellow professors and bishops, and invited the neighboring country gentlemen to hunt and play sports. "There are games of tennis on the lawn before breakfast or backgammon for the older men," he writes a friend in Rome. "There is an hour or two in the library before we sit down to an excellent luncheon followed by a siesta. Then we go out riding and return for a hot bath and a plunge in the river." Sidonius confesses that he'd like to "describe our luscious dinner parties, but I have no more paper." But unlike Ausonius, he does not pretend that all is well. The Visogoths were pressing against the borders, and the Burgundians ruled Lyons, the city of his birth. By 475, when Sidonius was forty-four, Euric, the new king of the Visogoths, was preparing to cross the Rhône.

Perhaps Sidonius had grown bored with his politcal duties, perhaps the turmoil of the times lessened his confidence in the government. Whatever the reason, he abandoned politics unexpectedly in order to devote himself to an ecclesiastical career. As Bishop of Clermont, he turned to conscientious activity and resisted the invasion of Visogoths with courage and devotion. He organized the people of Auvergne, who vowed to defend this last stronghold of Rome in Gaul. But they were little match for Euric's army. Sidonius appealed to Rome for help, telling the quaestor Licinianus, who had come to Gaul on a fact-finding mission, to bring reinforcements. When no response came, Sidonius began to suspect political intrigue. Would Rome commit its resources to risk another defeat defending a land on the outskirts of its empire? Centuries earlier, the people of Britain had appealed to Rome for help against northern invaders, but Rome abandoned Britain and pulled back its troops, unwilling to defend a land so far from its borders. By Sidonius's time, Britain was a cultural backwater; its half-barbarian people camped in abandoned villas and cooked food on the floors of their bedrooms. Was this to be the fate of Gaul as well? A council was finally held in Rome where it was decided to cede the whole territory to Euric, no strings attached. The Visogoths under Euric settled in the region and took possession of it, sending Sidonius to prison. In one of his famous letters, he bitterly condemns the bishop who took part in the negotiations.

> The state of our unhappy region is miserable indeed. Everyone declares that things were better in wartime than they are now after peace has been concluded. Our enslavement was made the price of security for a third party; the enslavement, ah—the shame of it! Of those Avernians . . . . Who in our own time stood forth alone to stay the advance of the common enemy . . . These are the men whose common soldiers were as good as captains, but who never reaped the benefit of their victories; that was handed over for your consolation, while all the crushing burden of defeat they had to bear themselves . . . . This is to be our reward for braving destitution, fire, sword and pestilence, for fleshing our swords in the enemy's blood and going ourselves starved into battle. This is the famous peace we dreamed of, when we tore the grass from the crannies in the walls to eat . . . . For all these proofs of our devotion, it would seem that we are to be made a sacrifice. If it be so, may you live to blush for a peace without either honour or advantage.

Sidonius was released from prison a year later, the same year that Odovacer deposed the last Roman emperor (476), thus bringing the Western half of the Empire to a close. Thereafter, Sidonius devoted himself to his diocese and literature until his death a decade later. He wrote poems to friends replete with mythological allusions. In his letters he inserted graceful verse compositions marked by their attention to minute details and the combination of classical meter & new words culled from the living Latin being spoken during the last years of the Empire. The nine books of the *Letters*, published during his lifetime, is his most important work. In the letters and poems of this scholar-aristocrat, we catch glimpses of the difficulties faced by senators in adjusting to the new realities encountered as a result of the Germanic invasions and the establishment of Germanic kingdoms across regions of Western Europe. In order to recover his estates, he had to write a panegyric for King Euric, but life in his country villa was not the same. Gone were the days of heaven. While he expressed admiration for Euric, a cultivated Visogothic king who played backgammon, he also expressed dismay and exasperation at the "gluttonous" barbarians billeted on his estate "who spread rancid butter on their hair." In one of his letters, he complained that to Roman or Greek ears, the barbarian language did not sound like the speech of humans, but more like stammering and noise. How could a poet write classical meter with its flowing hexameters six-beats to the line, he wondered, when all day long he was assaulted by a barage of barbarian songs.

> How can I artfully construct verse
> with a six-foot line
> When outside my house
> stomps a seven-foot Burgundian.

Another letter contains a classic example of a palindrome (a phrase which reads the same forwards and backwards):

Roma tibi subito motibus ibit amor

Rome, your love, will suddenly collapse in disturbances.

Shortly before his death, Sidonius grieves, in a beautiful three-line poem, for all that was lost.

O necessitas abjecta nascendi,
Vivendi misera,
Dura moriendi.

O the humiliating necessity of birth,
The wretched necessity of living,
The harsh necessity of dying.

The Roman Empire had raised science, prosperity and power to their ancient peaks. In these last centuries of Roman decline and decay, men sought relief from poverty and violence by looking toward some new ideal that would give them hope, something to console them in their suffering and toil. An age of power slowly gave way to an age of faith. Reflecting a widespread process of clericalization, Sidonius's episcopal election was one way a disoriented aristocracy maintained its traditional leadership, and it was through men like Sidonious that Roman customs and culture were preserved and finally transformed in the new institutions of the Dark Ages.

Historians have long debated the various causes for the decline and fall of the Roman Empire. Some have marveled that it lasted as long as it did. They point to the fundamental stability of many of its institutions and the minor economic and cultural revivals during the 2nd to the 5th century, before it finally succumbed to the force of Germanic invasions that began in the 4th century.

The *Cambridge Medieval History* begins its account of the Middle Ages with the "double revolution" initiated by Constantine, who adopted Christianity as the dominant religion of the Empire. Before the battle at Milvian Bridge in 312, Constantine saw a blazing cross with the words, in Greek, "By this, conquer." In 324, he stood on the western plain across the Bosphorus, took a stick, and traced a line in the sand where he would erect the walls of a New Rome, with its capital situated on the site of the old Greek colony of Byzantium, thus reuniting east and west. This new city he called Constantinople—Constantine's city—although its old name never went out of use. Thus, a Latin Roman Empire remained in the west and the Hellenized Greek part to the east. When Agustulus Romulus—the "little emperor" who became the last emperor—was deposed in 476 by the Gothic King Odovacer, the semblance of emperial government that had limped along for centuries in the west finally came to an end. (It's somewhat ironic that Rome began with the legend of Romulus being the mythical founder, and ended with an Emperor also named Romulus.)

By the end of the fifth century the Western Roman Empire had disintegrated, not to revive until the mid-eleventh century. But the image of the Empire persisted; the continuation of the idea of Rome in the Middle Ages is one of the fundamental themes of medieval history.

A favorite game of historians is marking the date of Rome's fall. The Battle of Adrianople (378 AD) in which a Roman legion lost a major battle was a portent of things to come, but the sack of Rome by Alaric's Visogoths in 410 AD sent shock waves through the empire. Pagan critics blamed the disaster on Christianity and those who had abandoned the old pagan gods. Augustine answered those critics by writing *The City of God*. While the Empire was being punished for its heathen sins, Augustine wrote, Christians could look forward to the greater, eternal city of God. Edward Gibbon's influential book, *The Decline and Fall of the Roman Empire*, was a mostly narrative account, like all 18th century historical works, but in Chapter 38 he interrupts the flow of the narrative to offer two main reasons for the Empire's disintegration: 1) the weight of its massive bureaucratic institutions and social structures, and 2) the "success of Christianity," which, Gibbon reminded his readers, taught non-resistance and a belief in a greater world beyond the one fraught with the violence of barbarians. Yet it was the very sufferings of the times that prompted Augustine to claim that it was the moral lapse of a sinful Rome that caused the collapse, and in so doing, prepared mankind for the triumph of the other great city, the one of God. Other factors contributing to Rome's collapse were the decline in trade after 200, the crushing burden of taxation and the economic deterioration that followed. Historians have suggested numerous other possibilities: 1) the decline in population caused by the outbreak of bubonic plague in the 3rd and 4th centuries; 2) weakened political unity caused by separate regions becoming isolated and provincial in the face of barbaric invasions; 3) the debasement of the coinage used to pay military and civil expenditures—contributing further to the economic decline; and 4) the institution of slavery, which precluded the development of industrial technology. Even the Greeks knew the principle of the steam engine, but as long as slave power was available, there was no compelling need to increase productivity through technology; all one had to do was create more manpower using readily available slave labor. Thus, historians say, Rome failed to undergo an industrial revolution

Montesquieu claimed that the republican principles that helped the republic of Rome conquer the world were changed to fit the demands of Empire, and that it was the principles of empire, not the republican virtues, that caused its fall,.

The racial theories of the late 19th century led some historians to attribute Rome's fall to racial mixing, with the vigor of the Roman race diminished by "outbreeding" with "inferior" subject races and barbarians who had moved across her frontiers by migration or invasion. Other historians theorize that they didn't "outbreed" enough. The Roman aristocracy, after centuries of "inbreeding," became weak and ineffectual, unable to meet the challenges of a new age. Rome disintegrated, they maintained, because of her failure to outbreed centuries before the crisis came.

Food ꜰoꞃ Thought

C.D. Darlington, The Evolution of Man and Society

My wife Lori and I were discussing the poets and artists of late antiquity and the unsettling times in which they created their works. With language poetry and post-modernism flourishing today around us, there's a great temptation to abandon the deep voice of communication and follow the path of rhetoric or clever manipulation of the creative product based on an academic theoretical premise. Could an individual possibly affect significant change in the historical process, she wondered. In shallow times, what happens if one continues to swim upstream? While I agreed with her that one should—as my acting teacher once told me—"give them the best you've got, whether they want it or not," I wasn't sure a single artist *could* change or redirect the forces of history. But I didn't mean to imply that the loss of faith in our power to affect change meant that we should not try. Like Pascal's wager on the existence of God, the best choice an artist can make is to act *as if* she can change history.

But let's concede the point anyway; let's say we cannot influence the course of history. We still do not have to write only for those of our own time. We can direct our best at the gods themselves, and the ages. Great works of art are not focused only on form, but on the deep voice speaking of the great and difficult truths of our experience here on earth. Ultimately, it is content that matters most. Or, at least, form and content should be

---

inextricably linked. Homer, Ovid, Juvenal, Dante, Shakespeare, Goethe, etc., all speak to us across the ages and we are one.

Perhaps my wife's faith in the power of a single individual is more important than I thought. Her position in the debate reminded me of the influence that concept once had on me. I remembered C. D. Darlington's book, *The Evolution of Man and Society*, which describes how war, religion, migration, and the rise and fall of empires (not to mention our own natures and the nature of our institutions) are determined by humankind's breeding patterns and the laws of genetics. His chapters on Greece and Rome were especially pertinent. Darlington admits that inbred races can have great historical success, as long as they live in a stable world. But, he continues, in a changing world inbreeding can bring disaster. Some psuedo-Darwinian historians blamed the fall of Rome on racial mixing with inferior peoples, or outbreeding, while other historians maintained the opposite: that Rome's disintegration was due more to the fact that her ruling class had inbred for so long, that it lost it's ability to meet the challenge when the crisis of instability came.

Historians such as Lord Acton and Henri Pirenne, the great Belgium economic historian who wrote *Medieval Cities,* and probably the best short work on the subject, *Economic and Social History of Medieval Europe*, recognized that the stratified societies of cities were derived from the co-operation of different races. This genetic principle underlies the studies of numerous sociologists as well, not to mention, the archaeologist, Flinders Petrie, who turned this idea into a working hypothesis. Petrie, reviewing problems of civilization from the point of view of artistic creation wrote: "The rise of the new civilization is conditioned by an immigration of a different people . . . it arises from a mixture of two or more different stocks." He acknowledges that change doesn't take place all at once. The barriers of antipathy, creed, social standing, and racial identity, in fact "every barrier to race fusion gives way in time." Written in 1911, Petrie's assessment brings together the principles of the religious breeding group, of assortative mating, of social stratification, of racial differentiation and of genetic recombination: all principles with which he was familiar through his association with W. Bateson and other rival exponents of genetics and biometry at that time.

In the field of anthropology, there have been exponents of both theories, each side obsessed with either the avoidance of outbreeding, or the avoidance of inbreeding. But it is the two together which govern the course of human evolution.

This brings me to Darlington's landmark work. After talking to my wife, I searched among my books and found the copy I'd read 25 years ago. Thumbing through it, re-reading underlined passages and notes I'd made in the margins, I came across the following section which I had boldly highlighted.

The Hero and the Misfit

. . . all of the interactions of individuals with society and the world arise from the genetic character of individuals and the genetic structures of society. From their changing effects in turn arises the changing pattern of human activity.

It is a pattern which changes most rapidly in the divided society of the large cities, and in countries where movement is easiest, least restricted by poverty, or by religious or linguistic distinctions. Then the degree of outbreeding is highest. And with the high degree of outbreeding comes a higher proportion of individuals at both our extremes: the creative and the defective.

First, consider the defective, the unfit recombination. He lies in the field of sociology and raises the greatest problem. The misfit may be a mental, social or sexual misfit. He may be the delinquent or criminal. He is the price that has to be paid for hybridization. He is the burden that has to be carried by society as a whole in return for the most adaptable breeding system. Usually, he is, as a rule, of reduced viability and fertility. Natural selection has in this way so far prevented the burden from becoming intolerable.

Next, consider the creative recombination: the inventor, the artist, or the hero. He lies in the field of history and raises its greatest problem. Does he in fact change the course of history? The answer is that in terms of the ultimate destiny of man, which is probably extinction, he does not. But on a shorter view, where the events of a few hundred years or the fate of only a few nations seem to matter, he may alter it. For what we call great men are due to unique genetic recombinations and occur at particular times and places. What they do affects the prospects of every other man who follows them.

The coming of the great man [or woman] is not predictable. In his origin, there are two sources of uncertainty, one genetic, the other environmental. The genetic source is that the creative individual is always a unique recombination arising from outbreeding, arising indeed from the organized uncertainty of recombination on whose exploitation organic evolution depends. . . . Man's future prospects are proportionate to the amount of genetic diversity he maintains among the interfertile members of his own species.

Race is always a touchy issue, and arguments invoking such theories are often taken out of context, or applied in the wrong way. Either way, they make us uncomfortable. We were talking about one of the reasons given for the decline and collapse of the Roman Empire. One theory is it had to do with alterante theories of inbreeding or outbreeding. We will probably never know whether Rome fell because she failed to outbreed, or because she mixed blood with "inferior" barbarians crossing her borders, or for reasons which have nothing at all to do with genetics.

To Marxist historians, the shattered Roman Empire was the result of class conflict. Contemporary historians cite the changing environment—soil depletion, deforestation, climate change and drought. Others seek a simpler answer: the Romans lost their morals, then their lands, and finally, they lost their minds. Orgies and homosexuality, for instance, were regarded as symptomatic of the general moral decline resulting from the greed and self-indulgence of the Roman upper classes. The loss of land and the spread of the desert caused by ecological damage, degraded farming (soil depletion), and deforestation adversely affected agriculture. These problems may have begun centuries earlier when small farms began to give way to the *latifunda*—large estates worked by slaves, the precursors of the medieval manor. The small citizen-farmer had once been the backbone of the republican army and early imperial legions. By the 2nd century AD, the loss of solid citizen-soldiers combined with the drainage of gold to the east, created not only a shortage of soldiers, but of money to pay the soldiers they already had. Emperors were afraid to staff their legions with aristocrats lest they attempt to take over the government, and the bourgeoisie didn't want to leave their businesses to join the military. The only men left were slaves, dispossesed peasants, the city proletariat (notoriously bad soldiers because they were undernourished), and Germanic barbarians along the northern and western frontiers who had peacefully migrated into the empire. These tribes were not interested in conquest; they wanted to cross the river and settle down. The Romans made treaties with certain Germanic chieftans who became mercenary allies fighting to defend Rome against their own kinsmen. In many cases the barbarian occupation and the transition to complete German control were so gradual and quasi-legal that often the native Roman subjects hardly realized what was taking place. Depopulation had actually begun in Italy and Greece in the 3rd century BC, and before long even Gaul was affected.

The civil powers were no longer able to control the army. As the Empire's population declined, the proportion of Germans in the army went from 5-10 percent in 200 AD to as much as 50 percent by 400 AD. Many of these so-called barbarians rose to high positions of command, such as the Vandal Stilicho, the Roman general who faced Alaric before he sacked Rome. When it came to a crisis, the military men on whom Rome depended knew and cared little for Roman history, law, literature, or tradition.

And finally, so the charge goes, Roman citizens lost their minds as a result of lead poisoning, drinking water supplied via lead pipes and crockery which caused a wide range of health problems including impaired intelligence and brain damage. Lead pipes were concentrated in public baths and the homes of the rich. But many experts contend that the threat posed by lead pipes has been exaggerated. Much of the water supplied to Roman cities came from masonry aqueducts from mountains rich in limestone—calcium carbonate. Thus, any lead pipes bringing water into the city would be coated with calcium, which would render the amount of lead negligible. Nevertheless, many workers would have been susceptible to lead poisoning, especially lead miners, pot-makers, plumbers, and those who processed grapes for decanting in lead vessels, who would have been exposed to the lead acetates formed from the acetic acid in vinegar. Lead acetate was also used to sweeten poor-quality wine. Heavy drinkers would thus have taken in large amounts of toxic lead. A study of 46 skeletons exhumed from Herculaneum showed high concentrations of lead in only two, and medium concentration in six. Of course, the Romans of Herculaneum lived centuries before the fall of the Empire. Nevertheless, none of the theories accounting for its fall have been proven, and no single factor can adequately explain the fall of the western empire. Arnold Toynbee, in his monumental *Study of History,* actually traces the decline of ancient civilization to the Peloponnesian War between Athens and Sparta in 431 BC. The whole history of the Roman Empire, he declares, is but an epilogue to the failure of Greek civilization to "respond" to a "challenge" that every civilization eventually must face. Toynbee's account can be termed the "biological-cyclical- mystical" answer, which treats an empire as a living organism that must pass through various stages—birth, growth, adulthood, old age, decline, and death.

Suffice it to say that the decline and fall of the Roman Empire, and thus the decay of classical literature and culture, was due to a complex interaction of external pressure by the barbarians, and internal and political weakness exacerbated by the high cost of defense.

ॐ

The Last Gasp

Cities shrank in size as the population decreased, municipal services were practically abandoned, and much of the farm land reverted to waste and marsh. The glory days of gold and art had been propped up by conquest, tribute, and slavery. All the money now went to pay for a military that was being used to defend the empire by waging expensive wars that brought little booty. The last days of the Empire were characterized by fear and indecision, a failure of nerve and a loss of moral fiber.

Within this long period of cultural stagnation and darkness, there were bright spots, such as the great cultural renaissance of the later 4th and early 5th centuries. Imperial courts of the Empire were important centers of poetry. There was a large educated public among the nobility and court functionaries, and rulers wanted writers and especially poets to disseminate the culture of the ruling classes among the people. Writers were usually wealthy men who didn't have to tend their estates (such as Symmachus & Sidonius), or they were school teachers distinguished by their learning and talents (Ausonius), or a few professional poets who lived from their own vese. **Claudian** (370-404) was one of those. Coleridge called him "the first of the moderns." Finally, taking up the slack were true wandering poets and ballad singers. These writers and poets shared one great accomplishment: the renewed interest in the classic of the Augustan era.

The other great current, poetry of religious insipiration, set pagan poets apart, many of them blaming Christianity for the Empire's fall. Despite the flowering of literature among the upper classes, the empire continued to disintegrate. **Rutilius Namatianus** (see pages _____) wrote a new kind of poetry, blunt and to the point. He was a pagan poet who lamented the world that was ending and took refuge in the past. His travel journals written during his return to Gaul, present descriptions of places he saw during his jouney, an unbroken series of ruins and devastation: ravaged cities, abandoned countryside, desolation and poverty.

With the decline of cities and the emergence of feudal society over the course of the next few centuries, there was a general decline in higher education, except for the learning one acquired in monasteries or in planning for a life in the church. The decline in learning and literature could also be attributed to the fact that organized book-selling came to an end. The book trade, dependent upon an effective system of communication and transportation, required the well-built and guarded roads of the empire. It also needed a cultivated leisure class, a class which disappeared during the periods of civil war and barbaric invasions. Long before the reign of the last of the Roman emperors, original literary production and the book trade had, for the most part, ceased. By 476, when Augustulus was driven out by the triumphant Odovacar, the literary activities of the capital had pretty much come to an end.

Monasteries were then to become the repository of learning; most of the writers were monks and other churchmen who wrote for each other and circulated their books through the offices of the Church. Thus, most of what was written had a religious tone; even criticisms of the church were written by churchmen. The average lay person was unable to read or write, and so literature became religious in nature, or philosophical (and the great philosophical debates of the time were Christian in nature). The great writers of this period were Latin poets composing epics on biblical themes or writing long philosophical examinations on the Church and Christian theory. To the modern reader, these tracts seem dry, boring, or badly written, or written in a style that rings false to our more sophisticated ears.

Overall, the dark period from the fall of Rome to the Carolingian ***[define this] revival of learning in the 8th century was a transitional age in art and literature caused by the interaction of Christiantiy and Paganism as well as by the confluence of Roman, Greek, and Oriental cultures. From our standpoint, the most significant factor was the transformation of literature and language.

The metrical evolution of poetry from the Greek syllabic to the stressed accentual verse was partly the result of the effects of natural speech rhythms on the writers of the time. The aristocracy of Greek meters with its delicate music of quantitative syllables had maintained a precarious hold over Latin verse, whose natural roots were more connected to the stressed peasant rhythms of folk song and dance and the heavy tramp of marching legions. During the 2nd Century this accentual verse began to take hold due to a weakening of cultural standards and because it was a congenial vehicle of self-expression with its strongly stressed rhythms. The regular beat captured the clockwork rhythm of the popular trochiac meter, and the rhyme and assonance was typical of folk poetry of the time.

The spoken language itself underwent a parallel transformation. "Vulgar Latin" can be distinguished from High Literary Latin. The latter was held prisoner by the external force of Literary Greek, but the spoken, "vulgar Latin" remained dynamic on the tongues of common people, and eventually became differentiated into the various Romance languages: French, Italian, and Spanish. "Hellenized Latin," thanks to its literary mummification, could neither live nor die after the fall of the Roman state. It melted into "Middle Latin," where it led a rather supernatural existence in the Church, in schools, in official documents, and scholarly discourse. It floated like a cloud above the currents of everyday speech, which were the effective forces in the development of language and the evolution of literature. Eventually, literary Latin lost all its power. It took a millenium, but by the 14th century, the local, vernacular language became the language chosen for composing literature and poetry—in England, France, Spain, and Italy. The greatest of these works was Dante's *Commedia*, written at the end of the 13th century in Italian, not Latin, and marked the beginning of a new era in poetry.

We also see three other significant developments during the early medieval period: there was a revival of local traditions due to the passing of city life; changes in vocabulary and syntax; and the substitution of prose for poetry which enlarged the scope for greater artistry.

All in all, this age was a dark time of retrenchment, not a time of surplus wealth which could be put into vast public works and gardens, the expansion of the city, and lavish funding for all the arts. Fuedal life among the educated classes was marked by a simpler grandeur. The wealthier landed class took refuge in rock-perched castles or huge country homes where they dined amid great purple drapes, clouds of incense, massive silver plates, and rose-wreathed cups. They were entertained by flute players and Corinthian dancing girls. Removed from the stimulus and pace of a large, city pulsing with numerous diversions, their social life turned inward to the "neighborhood" and the home. Manored men of the feudal age visited friends in nearby villages, took baths, played ball-games, hunted, and read in their libraries. In their poems, we can see the varied life of the decline of Rome—the monks, the merchants, the farmers, the travelers, the robbers, and the pastoral setting of a family picnic.

This transition from the central government and wide horizen of the Roman days to the local groupings and restricted outlook of the early Middle Ages was almost complete by the time of St. Augustine. The old city life was gone. Temples and amphitheaters lay in ruins. Churches were rising everywhere. The spoken tongue was changing rapidly. Various dialects were already in the process of formation. Germanic words were borrowed and infiltrated French and Latin and eventually English. Literature was practically confined to the lives of the Saints. Stock phrases were used again and again; clumsy sentences followed one after another. No writer mastered a singular voice or his words.

Creative literature lessened in favor of anthologies, grammars, reference works, religious instruction manuals and essays of theologic interpretation. The literary epitaph began as a simple tombstone inscription and grew to a poetical narrative or biography, and from there to the epic—if the hero was heroic—and finally to the full-fledged poetical legend if the hero was a Saint, and the life contained a bit of the miraculous.

The classical heritage was strong enough to inspire Latin works of learning like Boethius's *Consolations of Philosophy*, written while he awaited execution for conspiring against the emperor Theodoric. This classical tradition gradually faded, however, while the vernacular modern languages had not yet achieved a literary existence.

Ultimately, by the age of Boethius, the most original contribution made by the Church to poetry was in the Christian Hymn. Nowhere do we see the reason for throwing off the Virgilian hexameter more than in the **rhymed verse of the Latin Church Hymns,** especially those written by **St. Hilary** and **St. Ambrose**. The regular iambic dimeter was better able to express great emotion and despair, which quivered differently in the medieval hymn from any movement of the spirit in classic measures. The Christian Hymn vibrated, shuddered, and expressed the utter terror and love of the penitant in this darker age, and it was **the rhymed Latin metric that used the iambic dimeter** that was best able to summon the supplicant to despair and enlightenment. When wedded to the music of the Church, the effect was often sublime. It is not easy today to follow the pious doggerel of somebody else's translation of these hymns. Instead, listen to the Latin words, hear the deep voice of the organ, glance upwards at the Gothic vaulting of Amiens or Chartres, see the light sifting in through the flaming windows and the purer flame of the candles shining on the altar where the holy scarifice is made. To get a feeling for the power and majesty of the Latin hymns, listen to Beethoven's magnificent *Mass in C*, Op 86, and you'll get an inkling of the emotion these verses can stir.

***[do France and Theodoric around here]
***[define Menippean Satire—see Mennippus in Greek Poetry p._____]]

By the end of this period, religous poetry was to give up entirely the ancient syllabic metres. The two forms of rhythmic verse and prose sequence were to merge in the rhymed verse of a new age. This new poetry of the early Medieval Period had a great influence on the French Symbolists of the late 19th century, especially Baudelaire, who scorned the classicalities of the ancient poets and revelled in the barbarisms and nonstandard grammatical constructions of the vernacular Latin, those "negligences forced by a passion that forgets itself and mocks at rules."

☛ **Boëthius** (475-524), *The Consolation of Philosophy*

While awaiting execution in his cell, did Boethius look back across a span of centuries and realize that he was the last link to the glories of classical literature? His efforts to translate so much of Greek philosophy into Latin must have been prompted by his understanding that the age he was living through was sliding into a great darkness that would last for centuries. Italy was now ruled by Theodoric, a barbarian king who knew that at any time he might be swallowed up by the forces of the Eastern Empire in Constantinople. To the west of Italy, Theodoric faced several barbarian tribes, each vying for control of Gaul, and ultimately, for dominance in western Europe. Could Theodoric revive the economy and culture of the western empire, and lead Europe into a new era? Or would an entirely new civilization rise out of the barbarian kingdoms, and if so, from which kingdom would it come, the Visogoths in Spain, the Franks in Gaul, the Burgundians in Burgundy, the Ostrogoths in Italy, the Vandals in north Africa, or the former Empire in the East, now centered on Constantinople, a Greek-speaking, Byzantine culture?

Contrary to popular belief, the Gothic conquest of Italy did not put an end to Roman civilization. Theodoric, King of Italy and of the Goths, kept the civil administration Roman, and allowed pagan literary culture and the ancient Gothic culture to exist side by side. Out of a century of barbarism that swept like a wave over Roman civilization, there appeared the most original philosopher that Rome ever produced, second only to St. Augustine: Ancius Manlius Severinus Boëthius, whose *Consolation of Philosophy* was written in that cold jail cell while awaiting execution.

Boethius was born four years after Odovacer deposed the last of the Roman emperors. Boethius came from a noble family. Among his ancestors and kinsmen were two emperors and a pope. His father, a consul under Odovacer, died when Boethius was a boy. Symmachus the Younger took the boy in and steered him toward literature and philosophy. Symmachus became consul and later Prefect of Rome and Head of the Senate. His daughter Rusticiana fell in love with Boethius, and they were married. Theodoric murdered Odovacer in 493, when Boethius was eighteen, and already known for his eloquence and style. One of the reasons Boethius entered public service under Theodoric was because he felt an obligation to his people and his country. His perfect command of Greek made him a valuable man to have in government, and he soon came to Theodoric's attention. Boethius was commissioned to construct a water clock and sundial for Gundobad, king of the Burgundians. Theodoric also asked Boethius to choose a lyre player for Clovis, King of the Franks. With the Ostrogoths in Italy and the Visogoths in Spain, it looked as if the Merovingian Franks under Clovis were going to control much of France and Germany. Named for Clovis's grandfather Merowech, the Merovingian dynasty was to be the dominant power in western Europe for over a century. It was only natural that Theodoric made attempts to establish amicable relations with the Franks.

Boethius became Consul without companion in 510, at the age of thirty. It was the most illustrious of all the Roman offices, and Boethius followed in his father's footsteps, becoming Theodoric's favorite minister. Boëthius was also a man of great administrative skills. As Theodoric's minister, he reformed the coinage and worked tirelessly for the public good. In any age he would have been unusual; in this age of disintegration and decay, his accomplishments were simply amazing. But Theodoric feared a plot involving men in his own government, and imprisoned his minister when Boethius defended a senator accused of conspiring with the Emperor in the East (Byzantium). Theodoric suspected Boëthius of treachery and sentenced him to death without a trial.

The Consolation of Philosophy is one of the most famous of medieval books, written in 524 while Boethius was awaiting execution. The book follows the form of a dialogue in the style of Menippean satire, which alternated poetry and prose. The 39 short poems are written in various metres and styles. Boëthius speaks in prose. Philosophy, in the guise of a woman—"Dame Philosophy"—consoles the prisoner and answers in verse. She recalls the sufferings of other thinkers such as Socrates and encourages Boëthius to speak freely of his troubles. He complains of the ingratitude he's faced and how often it is in life that injustice triumphs. Dame Philosophy reminds him of the vanity of worldly things and the fickelness of fortune. Only God is the real and constant Good.

We can see how this work influenced Dante, especially in his *Vita Nuova*, which had prose sections interspersed with poems, and in the *Commedia*, which featured, if you will, a "Dame Philosophy"—except in the *Commedia*, Beatrice did not symbolize the consolations of Philosophy, but Divine wisdom and love. One of the remarkable things about the tone of the *Consolation* is its lack of whining and superstition. Even the dark thoughts that come with age and impending death are absent. There's such an even philosophic calm, that if we didn't realize Boethius was writing under the duress of imminent death, we'd think his stoic resignation was nothing more than complacent self-righteousness.

No worldly thing
Can have continuance
Unless love bring it back again
To the cause which first gave it essence.

The *Consolation of Philosophy,* a moving work written from the heart, provided comfort to innumerable readers throughout the Middle Ages.

A century earlier, in *The Wedding of Philologia and Mercury*, Martianus Capella had fixed the seven liberal *artes*. Boethius was responsible for further dividing the curriculm of seven into the *quadrivium* (four roads)—music, arithmetic, geometry, and astronomy—and the *triuvium* (three roads)—grammar, dialectic, and rhetoric. Of the seven *artes*, those of the *trivium* were more thoroughly cultivated than those of the *quadrivium*, and grammar the most thorough of all. In the "Paradiso," Dante listed grammar as *la prima arte*. Lest we get the wrong impression, grammar often meant the study of literature and poetry. Grammar was further divided into two parts: "the science of correct speech and the interpretation of the poets" (*recte loquendi scientiam et poetarum enarrationem*). Numerous passages from the ancient classics were used to teach the elements of grammar, which involved concepts no longer relevant today. In studying the different categories of errors, or "barbarisms," were a class of errors in vocabulary and pronounciation brought in by the Germanic corruption of the Latin, as well as errors in construction. In our own century many consider the American corruption of British English a kind of "barbarism," not to mention those American purists who shake their heads at the slang and colloquialisms that have invaded American English, such as Spanglish and Eubonics. Much of what became proper French, Italian, and Spanish began as grammatical barbarisms of Latin. Metaplasm was another kind of deviation from the grammatical norm, but this was allowed by poets concerned with metrical regularity, who thus were given *licentia poeterum* to invert the normal order of words or phrases in a sentence in order to produce metrical or rhymed effects at the expense of a natural spoken sentence structure. Poetry could also be studied as part of Rhetoric, which had to do not so much with grammatical correctness as with syntactical and dictional persuasiveness, an aspect of poetry that is prominent even today.

Much of Boethius's importance derives from his being the last Latin-speaking scholar of the ancient world to have a genuine mastery of Greek. After him, no one in the West had first hand acquaintance with Greek philosophy until the rediscovery of Aristotle in the 12th Century. In this final fling of Latin literature in Italy, Boëthius carried classical philosophy and literature into the Middle Ages with his numerous translations of Aristotle, as well as his commentaries and interpretations of other philosophical works that were read and treasured for a thousand years.

Today, few would plow through the pages of those dreary books. But the *Consolation* is another matter. For almost a millenium it was one of those top 100 books that anyone calling themselves educated would have read. It's one of the few philosophic works written between Augustine and the 12th century which still has anything to say to contemporary readers. Hundreds of manuscript copies of the *Consolation* have survived, a fact which attests to its popularity and influence. It was translated into more European languages than any book other than the Bible. Alfred the Great translated it into Old English for his Anglo-Saxon subjects. Chaucer translated it into Middle English, and almost all substantial passages of philosophical reflection in Chaucer's works can be traced to Boethius. Queen Elizabeth claimed it took her only 27 hours to translate the entire text. Other versions appeared in Greek, Middle Dutch, Old Provençal, and Spanish. Jean de Meung, who completed the second part of *The Romance of the Rose* begun by William de Lorris, translated the *Consolation* into Old French, and Notker Labeo and Peter von Kastle turned it into Medieval German. After the death of Beatrice, Dante found his greatest consolation in Boethius, which he translated into Italian. In the *Paradiso*, Dante placed Boethius among the 12 lights in the heaven of the Sun, calling him

> The holy soul who shows anyone
> Who listens attentively, how deceitful the world is.

We can find many echoes of Boethius in Dante's *Commedia*, including its closing line—*l'amor che move il sole e l'altre stelle*—"the love that moves the sun and the other stars"—which recalls Boethius's—*caelo imperitans amor*, "the love which rules the skies." In many passages, Dante does more than merely echo Boethius, he paraphrases or copies phrases outright. Tthe entire *Commedia*, in fact, extends Boethius's concept of the soul ascending in stages to the contemplation of the mind of God, thus finding its true place at home in the world.

If Augustine is the link between Virgil and Dante, it is doubtful if the connection would have been made without Boethius, who restored the simplicity of Plato's idealism at a time when the literary style of medieval rhetoric worked against clarity of thought. His restraint and simplicity is a breath of fresh air compared to the plodding and elaborate diffuseness of his contemporaries.

Though written in a dungeon, possibly between beating or episodes of torture, the *Consolation* cannot be simply classified as prison-literature. In the solitude of his cell, Boëthius had access to none of the beloved books that comprised his library. He was forced in the end to rely on the vast wealth of knowledge his reading had brought him, and his vivid memories of a blessed life. Like Ezra Pound in the 20th century, who wrote his finest poetry while awaiting execution as a traitor at the end of World War II (see 441-55), Boëthius drew upon the literature and philosophy that had sustained him throughout his life.

The book represents a skillful combination of several literary genres: the dialogue, the allegory, the poetic-elegy, and as the title indicates, that ancient form referred to as the "consolation monologue." And like Petronius's *Satyricon*, which uses the form of Menippean satire where prose sections alternate with verse, the structure of the *Consolation* calls to mind the *satura*—a literary form that has no equal for its Protean changes of content throughout its long history. The poems are written in many different forms and function throughout the text in different ways. Sometimes, they sum up the argument of the previous prose sections, other times they continue with a verse response. Sometimes Boethius (the imprisoned one) is the speaker, sometimes Dame Philosophy, and sometimes the poems come from Boethius as the omniscient narrator. Often, the poems operate in a way similar to the chorus in Greek tragedy or the meditative passages in Lucretius. We are also reminded of the form Martianus Capella chose for his *Marriage of Philology and Mercury*.

Book I begins with a poetic lament, bordering on self-pity, for his turn of bad Fortune, consoled only by the Muses of Poetry.

> I who once composed with eager zest
> Am driven by grief to shelter in sad songs;
> All torn the Muses' cheeks who spell the words
> For elegies that wet my face with tears.
> No terror could discourage them at least
> From coming with me on my way.
> They were the glory of my happy youth
> And still they comfort me in hapless age.
> Old age came suddenly by suffering sped,
> And grief then bade her government begin:
> My hair untimely white upon my head,
> And I a worn out bone-bag hung with flesh.
> Death would be happy if it spared the glad
> But heeded invocations from the wretch.
> But now Death's ears are deaf to hopeless cries,
> His hands refuse to close poor weeping eyes.
> First fickle Fortune gave me wealth short-lived,
> Then in a moment all but ruined me.
> Since Fortune changed her trustless countenance,
> Small welcome to the days prolonging life.
> Foolish the friends who called me happy then
> Whose fall shows how unsure my foothold was .

In the prose section that follows, Dame Philosophy makes her appearance.

> While I was quietly thinking these thoughts over to myself and giving vent to my sorrow with the help of my pen, I became aware of a woman standing over me. She was of awe-inspiring appearance, her eyes burning and keen beyond the usual power of men. She was so full of years that I could hardly think of her as of my own generation, and yet she possessed a vivid colour and undiminished vigour. It was difficult to be sure of her height, for sometimes she was of average human size, while at other times she seemed to touch the very sky with the top of her head, and when she lifted herself even higher, she pierced it and was lost to human sight.

His description of her clothes includes symbolic references and allegorical commentary. Though made of imperishable material of the finest threads, the color of her garments was obscured by the dust of long neglect.

> On the bottom hem could be read the embroidered Greek letter Pi, and on the top hem the Greek letter Theta. Her dress had been torn by the hands of marauders who had each carried off such pieces as he could get.

The Greek letters stand for the two kinds of philosophy—practical (ethics), and contemplative (theology, metaphysics, etc)., respectively. When Dame Philosophy notices the Muses of Poetry dictating words to him, she becomes angry.

"Who," she demanded, her piercing eyes alight with fire, "has allowed these hysterical sluts to approach this sick man's bedside? They have no medicine to ease his pains, only sweetened poisons to make them worse. These are the very women who kill the rich and fruitful harvest of Reason with the barren thorns of Passion. They habituate men to their sickness of mind instead of curing them. . . . [T]his man has been nourished on the philosophies of Zeno and Plato. Sirens is a better name for you and your deadly enticements: be gone, and leave him for my own Muses to heal and cure."

At first Boethius does not know who she is, and shamefully looks down at the floor. Dame Philosophy offers a poem about his confusion of mind, then, in prose, continues.

"But it is time for healing, not lamenting. . . . You are the man, are you not, who was brought up on the milk of my learning. . . . Surely you recognize me? And yet you do not speak. Is it shame or is it astonishment that keeps you silent?" . . . . When she saw that I was dumbstruck, she gently laid her hand on my breast and said, "It is nothing serious, only a touch of amnesia that he is suffering, the common disease of deluded minds. He has forgotten for awhile who he is, but he will soon remember once he has recognized me."

In the 20th century, there are two major literary works whose underlying theme is the act of remembering. When Ezra Pound was incarcerated inside a wire cage at a detention center in Pisa, awaiting execution for treason after World War II, he, like Boethius, he had no access to his library and the books that had consoled him over a lifetime. The poems he wrote during this time made up a crucial section of his lifelong work, *The Cantos*, and were called *The Pisan Cantos*. As a separate work, they won the Bollington Prize, a controversial cedision considering Pound's anti-semitic opinions. Many readers feel the *Pisan Cantos* are his finest work. Its basic theme is the act of remembering, of recollection as a way of fueling the soul's ascent toward God. The other great work is Proust's *Remembrance of Things Past*, the literal French being *To Recapture Lost Time*, not as poetic as Shakespeare's phrase from which Proust's translator, C. K. Scott Moncrieff took his title (from Sonnet # ___), but more accurate. The act of remembering is a vital act. The Platonic influence in the *Consolation* is obvious throughout, but here is Plato's concept of *anamnesis*, or recollection, used in connection with his concept of the ascent of the soul toward illumination and salvation. In Plato's dialogues *Protagoras* and *Meno*, he talks about the teacher, whose job it is to "bring up from within" what is already inside the student, the knowledge of something learned prior to birth and now forgotten. *Anamnesis* is the reawakening of such memory. Boethius refers to this in the third poem of Book III of the *Consolation*.

> Not all its light is banished from the mind
> By body's matter which makes me forget.
> The seed of truth lies hidden deep within,
> And teaching fans the spark to take new life;
> Why else unaided can man answer true,
> Unless deep in the heart the touchwood burns?

And if the muse of Plato speaks the truth,
Man but recalls what once he knew and lost.

Add that to Plato's concept of the ascension of the soul by stages as shown in the allegory of the Cave. What we get is the healing of the soul by remembering; therefore moving toward divine illumination. In the prose section of chapter 6, Book I, Dame Philosophy diagnoses his condition.

"Now I know the other cause, or rather the major cause of your illness: you have forgotten your true nature. . . . It is because you are confused by loss of memory that you wept and claimed you had been banished and robbed of all your possessions. . . . And because you have forgotten the means by which the world is governed you believe these ups and downs of fortune happen haphazardly. . . . [But] the nature of the mind is such that for every true belief it rejects, it assumes a false one from which the fog of distraction rises to blot out its true insight. I will try to lessen this particular fog little by little by applying gentle remedies of only medium strength. In this way the darkness of the ever treacherous passions may be dispelled, and you will be able to see the resplendent light of truth."

Then follows another poem in a form William Carlos Williams and Robert Creeley made popular, using short, irregular lines.

In dark clouds
Hidden
The stars can shed
No light.
If boisterous winds
Stir the sea
Causing a storm,
Waves once crystal
Like days serene
Soon turn opaque
And thick with mud
Prevent the eye
Piercing the water.
Streams that wander
From tall hills
Down descending
Often dash
Against a rock
Torn from the hillside.
If you desire
To look on truth
and follow the path
With unswerving course,
Rid yourself
Of joy and fear,
Put hope to flight,
And banish grief.
The mind is clouded

and bound in chains
Where these hold sway.

Boethius goes on to consider the nature of good and evil, and of happiness itself, and the nature of God, Fate, and Free Will. He asks Dame Philosophy: If God determines everything that happens in the world, and knows everything that will happen in the world, how is it possible for a human being to have Free Will?

> You are urging me to the greatest of all questions, a question that can never be exhausted. The subject is of such a kind that when one doubt has been removed, countless others spring up in its place, like the Hydra's heads. The only way to check them is with a really lively intellectual fire. The usual subjects of inquiry concern the oneness of providence, the course of fate, the haphazard nature of the random events of chance, divine knowledge and predestination, and the freedom of the will; you can see for yourself how difficult they are.

Boethius describes the nature of God as being the "still point of the turning world," an idea found not only in Plotinus, but in Confusious, who called it the "unwobbling pivot." Pound invokes this concept in his *Cantos* as well: It would be impossible for the world to exhibit such diversity were it not for a power that could brings and holds everything together. Boethius tells Dame Philosophy what he means by God.

> Nature's fixed order could not proceed on its path and the various kinds of change could not exhibit motions so orderly in place, time, effect, distance from one another, and nature, unless there was one unmoving and stable power to regulate them. For this power, whatever it is, through which creation remains in existence and in motion, I use the word which all people use, namely, God.

Boethius's genius lay in his ability to fuse various concepts into a single original idea. The Providence of God is the whole shebang at once, the "still point in the middle" of a moving circle. Fate involves the motion of the parts, and the further from the center, the greater the apparent motion, the greater the apparent randomness. God is the still point of peace and love, and exists *outside* of time and motion. Man perceives cause and effect, the linear movement of events in time. For God, all has already happened, yet all is still happening, in motion around the fixed center. From our perspective, we see randomness, the bad and good of Fate. But Providence is larger and includes Fate. Man is not only free to move as he pleases, his acts have consequences. He can chose good, or he can choose evil, but God's Providence is not obvious to the mind of man, who, through contemplative stages—through the act of remembering his true nature—can approach the mind of God. To approach the mind of God, man's soul must first free itself from material things, which move with random constancy far from the stability and simplicity of the still and peaceful center of the universe.

Boethius works much of this out in Book III and IV. Book III includes the poem about the famous story of Orpheus and Eurydice, which was known to readers of the Middle Ages from two other sources: Virgil's *Georgics* (IV, 453-527) and Ovid's *Metamorphoses*

(X-XI). Boethius's version was probably the most influential. The translation below (by V.E. Watts, Penguin) distorts the natural syntax of the Latin in order to render the rhyme. I'd prefer a better rhymed translation or the natural diction of the original without the rhyme.

> Then she replied, "The form of the divine substance is such that it does not spread out into outside things or take up into itself anything from them. As Parmenides says of it,
>
> > like the mass of a sphere well-rounded in all ways
>
> it rotates the moving sphere of the universe while remaining itself unmoved.

Happy the man whose eyes once could
Perceive the shining fount of good;
Happy he whose unchecked mind
Could leave the chains of earth behind.
Once when sad Orpheus mourned
for his wife beyond death's bourn,
His tearful melody begun
Made the moveless trees to run,
Made the rivers halt their flow,
Made the lion, hind's fell foe,
side by side with her to go,
Made the hare accept the hound
Subdued now by the music's sound.
But his passions unrepressed
Burned more fiercely in his breast;
Though his song all things subdued,
It could not calm its master's mood.
Complaining of the gods above,
Down to hell he went for love.
There on sweetly sounding strings
Songs that soothe he plays and sings;
All the draughts once drawn of song
From the springs the Muses throng,
All the strength of helpless grief,
And of love which doubled grief,
give their weight then to his weeping,
As he stands the lords beseeching
Of the underworld for grace.
The triform porter stands amazed,   [Cerberus, the three headed dog]
By Orpheus' singing tamed and dazed;
The Furies who avenge men's sin,
Who at the guilty's terror grin,
Let tears of sorrow from them steal;
No longer does the turning wheel
Ixion's head send whirling round;
Old Tantalus upon the sound
Forges the waters and his thirst,
And while the music is rehearsed
The vulture ceases flesh to shred.
At last the monarch of the dead   [Pluto, god of the lower world]

In tearful voice, "We yield," he said:
"Let him take with him his wife,
by song redeemed and brought to life.
but let him, too, this law obey,
Look not on her by the way
Until from night she reaches day."
But who to love can give a law?
Love unto itself is law.
Alas, close to the bounds of night
Orpheus backwards turned his sight
And, looking, lost and killed her there.
For you I sing the sad affiar,
Whoever seek the upward way
To lift the mind into the day;
For who gives in and turns his eye
Back to darkness from the sky,
Loses while he looks below
All that up with him may go.

from Book IV, Boethius continues the dialogue with Dame Philosophy:

. . . . I would be less surprised if I could believe that the confusion of things is due to the fortuitous operations of chance. But my wonder is only increased by the knowledge that the ruling power of the universe is God. Sometimes He is pleasant to the good and unpleasant to the bad, and other time He grants the bad their wishes and denies the good. But since He often varies between these two alternatives, what grounds are there for distinguishing between God and the haphazards of chance?"

"It is not surprising," she said, "if ignorance of the principle of its order makes people think a thing is unplanned and chaotic. But even if you don't know the reason behind the great plan of the universe, there is no need for you to doubt that a good power rules the world and that everything happens aright.

"If you knew not the stars of Arcturus
Sail near the highest pole of heaven, or why
The Waggoner is late to take his wain
And late to dip his flames into the sea
Although his rising comes again with haste,
The law observed in heaven would leave you dazed.
. . . .
But hidden cause confounds the human heart,
Perplexed by things that rarely come to pass,
For unexpected things the people dread.
Then let clouds of ignorance give way
And these events will no more wondrous seem."

Then, as if she were starting a fresh argument, she spoke as follows.

"The generation of all things, the whole progress of things subject to change and whatever moves in any way, receive their causes, their due order and their form from the unchanging mind of God. . . . When this plan is thought of as in the purity of God's understanding, it is called Providence, and when it is thought of with reference to all things, whose motion and order it controls, it is called by the name the ancients gave it, Fate. . . . Providence is the divine reason itself. It is set at the head of all things and disposes all things. Fate, on the other hand, is the planned order inherent in things subject to change through the medium of which Providence binds everything in its own alloted place. Providence includes all things at the same time, however diverse or infinite, while Fate controls the motion of different individual things in different places and in different times. So this unfolding of the plan in time when brought together as a unified whole in the foresight of God's mind is Providence; and the same unified whole when dissolved and unfolded in the course of time is Fate.

"They are different, but one depends on the other. The order of Fate is derived from the simplicity of Providence. . . . [O]ne thing is clear: the simple and unchanging plan of events is Providence, and Fate is the ever-changing web, the disposition in and through time of all the events which God has planned in His simplicity. . . . the relationship between the ever-changing course of Fate and the stable simplicity of Providence is like that between reasoning and understanding, between that which is coming into being and that which is, between time and eternity, or between the moving circle and the still point in the middle. . . .

"It is because you men are in no position to contemplate this order that everything seems confused and upset.

. . . . Let it be enough that we have seen that God, the author of all natures, orders all things and directs them towards goodness. . . . Evil is thought to abound on earth. But if you could see the plan of Providence, you would not think there was evil anywhere.

"If you desire to see and understand
In purity of mind the laws of God,
Your sight must on the highest point of heaven
Where through the lawful covenant of things
The wandering stars preserve their ancient peace:
. . . .
Unless He call them home to their true path,
And force them back their orbits to perfect,
Those things which stable order now protects,
Divorced from their true source would fall apart.
This is the love of which all things partake,
The end of good their chosen goal and close:
No other way can they expect to last,
Unless with love for love repaid they turn
And seek again the cause that gave them birth.

We find a similar passage in the *Commedia*, [Paradise, Canto I], where Beatrice explains the workings of the universe to Dante.

She sighed with pity when she heard my question
    and looked at me the way a mother might
    hearing her child in his delirium:

"Among all things, however disparate,
    there reigns an order, and this gives the form
    that makes the universe resemble God,"

she said; "therein God's higher creatures see
the imprint of Eternal Excellence —
that goal for which the system is created,

and in this order all created things,
according to their bent, maintain their place,
disposed in proper distance from their Source;

therefore, they move, all to a different port,
across the vast ocean of being, and each
endowed with its own instinct as its guide.

This is what carries fire toward the moon,
this is the moving force in mortal hearts,
this is what binds the earth and makes it one.

Not only living creatures void of reason
prove the empelling strength of instinct's bow,
but also those with intellect and love.

The Providence that regulates the whole
becalms forever with its radiance
the heaven wherein revolves the swiftest sphere;

to there, to that predestined place, we soar,
propelled there by the power of that bow
which always shoots stright to its happy mark.

Finally, it is love which brings to the world a divine peace. We forget who we are, and, as in Dante's beautiful play on words in the opening of the *Commedia*, we can only find ourselves when lost in a dark wood. It may be that love for the wrong things, or the wrong kind of love has led us astray, far out to the edge of the moving sphere. Boethius implies that he himself lost his way because of a perverse love, but through love he can be brought back to himself.

Unless with love for love repaid they turn
And seek again the cause that gave them birth.

God's knowledge is perfect. Through the divinity of love, man's freedom increases. God is eternal; the world, merely perpetual. In our journey through the world, we'd best raise our eyes skyward, toward the stars, toward the unmoving mover. Like Orpheus, one look down and we lose our way.

Dame Philosophy reminds him that all God's justice is Good, though we may not be able to understand how it is all directed. The wise man takes any clash with fortune as an opportunity to increase his wisdom.

"You are engaged in a bitter but spirited struggle against fortune of every kind, to avoid falling victim to her when she is adverse or being corrupted by her when when she is favourable. Hold to the middle way with unshakeable strength.

In Latin, virtus means *virtue*, and *vires* means strength. There's an obvious play on words in the last sentence of the above quoted passage that cannot be imitated in English. Boethius calls forth Aristotle's concept of the Golden Mean, the middle path. Then there's the story of the Babylonian king who awarded a fabulous prize to the man who would make a ring bearing an inscription that would keep him to the middle path, consoling him in times of tragedy, and preventing overweening pride from overtaking him in times of great joy. The inscription that won read: "And this too shall pass."

In one somber poem, Boëthius broods over the transitory glories of this world. The famous passage begins: *Ubi nunc fidelis ossa Fabricii manent.**

> Who knows where faithful Fabricé bones may lie,
> Where Brutus and strict Cato are resting.
> A thin fame is all there is
> Consigning their vain titles to the few letters that are left.
> Because we read their famous names in books,
> Does that mean we come by them to know the dead?
> You dying, then, are remembered by none,
> Nor can any fame make you really known.
> But if you think that life outstrips death,
> With your mortal breath going up to heaven,
> So will go your name, when length of time
> Is all that is needed to take it away as well,
> And you shall then be surprised by a second death.

*[The opening line of this stanza was translated by King Alfred as "Where are the bones of Weland?" See page #___ for the reason]

Fame is fleeting. When even our name is forgotten after death, it is as if we've died a second time.

Within days of finishing the *Consolation of Philosophy*, his executioners burst into his cell, tightened a cord around his head until his eyes burst from their sockets, then clubbed him to death. A few months later, his father-in-law Symacchus was executed. Shortly thereafter, Theodoric put the Pope in prison and he died there in the spring of 526.

Despite such acts of futility and violence, Theodoric's reign was considered one of the most enlightened in history. Long before Boethius' heyday, Atilla's empire fell apart and the Ostrogoths regained their independence. In order to keep the Ostrogoth's faithful to the Emperor in the East, King Theodemir's seven-year-old son Theodoric was brought to Constantinople as hostage, where he was schooled in the arts of war and government. He never learned to write, however, and all his life he signed his name by stencilling it through a perforated gold plate. When he succeeded his father as leader of the Eastern Goths, he dedicated the next two decades to finding a permanent home for his people. After twenty years of fighting, he made an agreement with the Emperor in Constantinople that he'd lead his entire people into Italy, overthrow Odovacer, and rule the land as an Ostrogothic Kingdom under Emperor Zeno's sovereignty. Initially, he agreed to rule Italy jointly, with Ocavacer sharing the palace of Ravenna. Ten days after Theodoric's entrance into Italy, a banquet was held in his wing of the palace to honor Odovacer. Before desert, Theodoric stepped forward and, with one tremendous stroke of his sword, sliced Odovacer down from collarbone to thigh. The blade penetrated so cleanly and quickly that Theodoric exclaimed in surprise, "The wretch canot have had a bone in his body."

We don't know if this act of bloodshed haunted Theodoric during his thirty-three year reign of peace and prosperity, but with the executions of Boethius and Symmachus, his hands were bloody once again. Theodoric wept for the wrong he had done and followed them both to the grave within two years. A generation later, the Byzantine historian Procopius summed up the episode in his history of the Goths.

> And he [Theodoric] died in the following manner. Symmachus and his son-in-law Boethius were men of noble and ancient lineage, and both had been leading men in the Roman senate and had been consuls. But because they practiced philosophy and were mindful of justice in a manner surpassed by no other men, relieving the destitution of both citizens and strangers by generous gifts of money, they attained great fame and thus led men of the basest sort to envy them. Now such persons slandered them to Theodoric, and he, believing their slanders, put these two men to death, on the ground that they were setting about a revolution, and confiscated their property for the public treasury. And a few days later, while he was dining, their servants set before him the head of a great fish. This seemed to Theodoric the head of Symmachus newly slain. Indeed, with its teeth set in its lower lip and its eyes looking at him with a grim and insane stare, it did resemble exceedingly a person threatening him. And becoming greatly frightened at the extraordinary prodigy and shivering excessively, he retired running to his own chamber, and bidding them place many covers upon him, remained quiet. But afterward he disclosed to his physician all that had happened and wept for the wrong he had done Symmachus and Boethius. Then, having lamented and grieved over the unfortunate occurrence, he died not long afterward.

The two Christian nations west of Constantinople—the Franks under Clovis and the Ostrogoths under Theodoric—faced each other with different designs for a Roman-German synthesis. Clovis embraced the Catholic orthodoxy of the Christian faith, while Theodoric, though tolerating non-Arian Christians, was an Arian, and therefore failed to attain the full support of the Church, a crucial factor in their demise. Theodoric's kingdom of Arian Goths was too close to be tolerated as an alternative to the Catholic Church, either in religious terms or as a public state divided into barbarians and Romans and thus, on its own terms, a contradiction. As part of the Merovingian line which ruled the Franks till 751, Clovis provided Charlemagne with a foundation for the reestablishment of a western empire, which some have even seen as the template of modern Europe. In a sense, Clovis founded France, or the idea of it, and considering the fact that Chlodwig, Ludwig, Clovis and Louis are one name, one could say he gave his name to eighteen French kings.

Centuries later, the monastery of Saint Mary was built next to Theodoric's royal tomb, the famous mausoleum in Ravenna, that perfectly symbolizes, in its half-classical, half barbaric style, this collossus who strode two cultures, but failed in his attempt to fuse East and West. Even if the monks of later centuries chose to dispose of the bones of this heretic king, they'd have discovered that someone beat them to it. By the ninth century, the tomb was already empty. No one knows who removed Theodoric's bones from his final resting place. Rumors and stories circulated that it was the spirits of the senators he had persecuted and killed who threw him into the crater of the volcano on the island of Lipara. Either way, most Catholics were sure that the Gothic king had gone to hell. But with his death in 526, Italy lost the greatest of her early medieval rulers, unequalled until the days of Charlemagne.

Several centuries after Boethius's death in Pavia, a local cult devoted to his work emerged and by the 13th century attained great popularity. Dante knew of Boethius' resting place in the church of San Pietro in Cielo d'Oro. Along with Symmachus and Pope John, Boethius was venerated as an orthodox martyr of Arianism. In 1883 the Sacred Congregation of Rites in Rome approved the local cult and canonized Boethius as "St. Severinus." The irony is obvious. The *Consolation of Philosophy* can be regarded as the last work of pagan philosophy. It was written by a Christian who took his final comfort from the Olympian philosophers of Athens, not from the God on Golgotha.

Echoing the *Book of Job*, Boëthius attempted to justify the tragedies of good men with the intentions of a benevolent God. In a line that Dante practically stole, [see *Commedia*, page 311], Boëthius admits to Dame Philosophy that

Boethius:	Dante:
Nam in omni adversitate forunae	*"Nessun maggior dolore*
infelicissimum est genus infortunii	*che ricordarsi del temp felice*
fuisse felicem.	*ne la miseria;*
In all adversity of fortune,	There is no greater pain
it is the most unhappy kind of misfortune	Than to remember a happy time
to have been happy.	In wretchedness.

☞ **Cassiodorus** (490-580),

Cassiodorus and Boethius had much in common: Both came from aristocratic families. Both led public lives in the service of Theodoric, the Gothic King; Cassiodorus actually replaced Boethius as *magister officiorum* after the latter's execution. Both wrote books that became proverbial best-sellers throughout the Middle Ages. And both held similar cultural theories, committing themselves to the preservation of classical culture and making it relevant to a new era.

Born in Calabria to an aristocratic family, Cassiodorus followed in the family footsteps. His grandfather was a tribune under the Roman Emperor Valentinian III and took part in a diplomatic mission to placate Atilla the Hun. His father was a financial officer for Ocdovacer, the barbarian king of Italy, who had deposed the last Roman Emperor, Romulus Augustulus in 476. When the Ostrogoth Theodoric seized Italy from Odovacer in 493, becoming the most powerful monarch in the western Mediterranean, Cassiodorus's father became his praetorian prefect. Like Boethius, Cassiodorus was a Roman who clearly saw that the Empire was finished and that it was necessary to help build a new state and a new civilization. Toward that end, he tried to understand the world of their German victors. He knew that it was better for Roman civilization to survive under the Goths than to die with its cultural purity intact.

In the course of his political life, Cassiodorus wrote 468 official letters which were later collected in 12 books, called the *Variae*. Like most poets of this age, he wrote in a formal style marked by an elegance and eloquence that verged on the pompous. One after the other, those stuffy documents were passed along for Theodoric's signature. What could this Ostrogothic King have made of such purple prose, except that he knew it would dazzle his Roman subjects with the complexity of his mind while impressing his own people with the wonder of his erudition. Reading these letters today, one comes away stupfied by the complex metaphors brought to bear on some minor, bureaucratic memo, like the one quoted below, to "Maximian, Vir Illustris and Andreas, Vir Spectabilis.

> If the people of Rome will beautify their City we will help them.
>
> Institute a strict audit (of which no one need be ashamed) of the money given by us to the different workmen for the beautifuication of the City. See that we are receiving money's worth for the money spent. If there is embezzlement anywhere, cause the fund so embezzled to be disgorged. We expect the Romans to help fromn their own resources in this patriotic work, and certainly not to intercept our contributions for the purpose.
>
> The wandering birds love their own nests; the beasts haste to their own lodgings in the brake; voluptuous fish, roaming the fields of ocean, returns to its own well-known cavern. How much more should Rome be loved by her children! Most worthy of Roayl attention is the rebuilding of ancient cities, an adornment in time of peace, a precaution for time of war.

Cassiodorus was 50 years old when the Byzantines under Justinian conquered Ravenna, taking it from the Goths as Theodoric had feared. Cassiodorus went to Constantinople and remained there until the Eastern Empire won its decisive victory a few years later. He was 54 and could have continued serving the empire in some official capacity, but he chose to retire to the family estate to devote himself to scholarship and the Christian life. In other words, he was done choosing sides. It was time to loaf about in his gardens for a well-earned rest. Cassiodorus turned his back to the world completely. His estate was located at the bottom of the boot of Italy, on the Gulf of Squillace. A small, rippling stream meandered through orchards and well-kept flower and vegetable gardens, dovecotes, and beehives. Travelers in need of rest could stop for the night, and the poor and indigent were given shelter from the storm. Amidst a time of upheaval, it was a peaceful retreat that "hung like a cluster of grapes" on the mountain slope.

Having witnessed the destruction of Rome, Cassiodorus realized that classical literature was viewed with some suspicion in many quarters, and in others, was virtually unknown. As a youth, he no doubt talked with people who had seen Atilla with their own eyes. When the Ostrogothic monarchy was created at the disposition of Odovacer, Cassiodorus rocked the cradle of a new era. When that kingdom fell to the Byzantine Emperor Justinian, Cassiodorus wept over its grave. But his real work was just beginning.

He was 60 years old, but the 35 years that lay ahead proved to be the most significant of his life. Several years earlier, Cassiodorus had planned with Pope Agapetas to found a Christian university at Rome on the model of the ancient universities where liberal arts were taught as a precursor to sacred learning. But the ancient ideal of education had become distorted. Rhetoric displaced Philosophy; students were taught to display the flashy excess of eloquence instead of the reasoned simplicity of clear writing. Cassiodorus, like Boethius before him, had envisioned a restoration of true Philosophy and Poetry, relegating the false charm of Rhetoric to its proper place. Such a university would have resembled such humnanistic institutions of learning as Harvard College when originally founded.

Agapetus died the year after Cassiodorus made his proposal, and the times were not right for such an enterprise. Four years later, Cassiodorus began the second phase of his career by establishing two monasteries on his estate, one for ascetic retirement and the other devoted to a more active life of service. He called it *Vivarium* because of its fishponds, in which live fish were kept in seawater for the use of the monastery. Like his friend Boethius, Cassiodorus believed that classic Greek and Roman thought should be preseved in the Christian era; as an orthodox Christian, however, he wasn't above censoring heretical writings, such as the supposedly anonymous commentary on thirteen letters of the apostle Paul, which looked more like Pelagian writings. The offending passages were expurgated. A valuable library was assembled under his guidance, anticipating the *scriptoria* of the great abbeys during the following centuries.

For the next 40 years, Cassiodorus assembled manuscripts and books to be copied, amended, collated, summarized, translated, and popularized. He borrowed, he bought, he smuggled texts from as far away as North Africa. Under his supervision, monks followed his rules for transcription and the proper treatment of corrupt texts. Where letters had been miscopied by former scribes, corrections were made. When translating Scriptures, however, care was taken not to render the divine message into smoother, vernacular idioms.

In his last years, he devoted himself to writing the *Institutiones, A Manual of Instruction in Divine and Human Readings*, an encyclopedic handbook in two volumes devoted to sacred and profane literature, with a good bibliography on its various subjects. What he was unable to accomplish as a politician in public service, he now tried to accomplish with a cultural enterprise comparable to Boethius's. Where Boethius focused on the philosophic, theoretical aspects of classical literature, Cassiodorus concerned himself with the practical content of the various arts, teaching letter writing, agriculture, medicine, and natural history. The title Cassiodorus chose recalled the *Divine Institutions* of Lactantius, but made explicit the union of both Christian and pagan cultures. In treating the liberal arts, he first gives a sketch of the seven arts, done more succinctly and in clearer language than did Martinius Capella or Boethius. He also included reading lists of Christian and pagan literature he deemed suitable for monks. These lists, or library catalogues, broadened over time, and were drawn up by other scholars such as Alcuin and Theodulph centuries later. Before his death at the age of 94, Cassiodorus composed a work on spelling, *De Orthographia,* for the use of the monks of Vivarium. He praises the monks responsible for the copying of books. "By their fingers divine, treasures are scattered abroad."

> Oh blessed the perseverance,
> laudable the undustry which preaches
> to men with the hand,
> starts tongues with the fingers,
> gives an unspoken salvation to mortals,
> and against the iniquitious deceits
> of the Devil
> fights with pen and ink.
> For Satan receives as many wounds
> as the scribe copies words of the Lord.

The monk, in copying page after page in the cold *scriptorium*, could believe he was weilding a mighty sword in the battle against ignorance and evil. The preservation of such works of classical Latin literature we have today we owe in large part to Cassiodorus and his creation of the monastic *scriptorium*. (This is not altogether different from 20th century film preservationists. Except in the case of film, there's no force that is specifically lobbying against efforts to save the only copies of certain older films from deteriorating—only the apathy of those who fail to realize what is being lost.)

The forces working to eradicate the pagan literature of the classical past were formidable. Pope Gregory the Great was a force unto himself. After Justinian had reconquered Italy and made it part of the Eastern Empire, Lombard invaders following the tracks of earlier Germanic tribes, invaded an Italy that Justinian's reconquest had bled to exhaustion. Firmly establishing their domination in the north, the Lombards occupied the great plain between the Alps and the Apennines, ever since called Lombardy. Unlike the Ostrogoths under Theodoric, they seized the Roman estates of the conquered Italians and made no pretense of alliance with the empire. Whatever continuity of Roman civilization had survived after the fall was finally broken. The Lombards severed the connection between Rome and Ravenna, the Byzantine administrative center on the Adriatic coast. The unity of Italy was completely destroyed. Slowly, the Roman institutions and civilization that Theodoric had tried to maintain disappeared. The power of Byzantium was too distant, and from this time on Italy was largely left to fend for itself. Pope Gregory the Great lamented the destruction of Rome's great glory.

> What has become of Rome, who seemed formerly to be the mistress of the world? Where is the Senate? Where are the people? Where are all those who used to relish in her glory? Where are their attendants, their pride?

He may have felt that the end of the world had come, but it was only the end of one small part of the world. New ones were rising. While Clovis and the Merovingians were building a Frankish empire in Gaul, and the Angles and Saxons were conquering Britain, the Roman papacy rose out of the turmoil of this last barbarian invasion as a new power, led by Gregory the Great. He organized the defense of Rome, negotiated with the Lombards, and became the practical ruler of the lands surrounding the former capital of the Roman Empire. He sent missionaries to Britain to convert the heathen Anglo-Saxons, following up on the work already begun by missionaries from the Celtic church in Ireland.

The three other Church Fathers had respected the importance of pagan literature. Augustine felt the classical works could be used to bolster Biblical thought, and Jerome, who translated the Bible into Latin, accused himself in a dream of being a classicist. St. Ambrose was a poet who composed some of the Church's earliest and noblest hymns. But Gergory's appreciation for classical literature did not match the other western Church Fathers'. His writings, such as a long commentary on the *Book of Job*, instructions to the clergy and numerous letters, earned him the title of Father of the Church, along with Augustine, Jerome, and Ambrose, but his works were full of mystic ramblings and provincial superstitions. There's no comparison between the philosophical, literary, and intellectual erudition of the other Fathers and him. He knew no Greek, and his Latin was awkward and pedestrian when compared to the classical Latin of Augustine. It was Gregory's vision of the fate of classical literature against which Cassiodorus had to contend.

Gregory's prescriptions for the literature of the future excluded the classics, closing the doors of those collectors of ancient books and caring little if those literary treasures turned to dust. His vision of a Christian literature did not include comic irreverence or Horatian urbanities. Men like Ausonius, Sidonius, and Boethius spoke for a Christian humanism that embraced the full spectrum of classical pagan literature, and ironically, it was those monks from Italy to Britain who kept the classical heritage alive and ensured that the programme of Cassiodorus would ultimately triumph over Gergory's provincial view.

Eventually, the great library Cassiodorus created was dispersed, some items surviving in the distant northern parts of the monastic world. We know that a Bible that had once belonged to Cassiodorus found its way to the British Isles where the Venerable Bede used it for prayer and research. Who knows what other books Bede may have gotten from the labors of Cassiodorus. Bede certainly was familiar with classical literature, and according to medieval tradition, the manuscript of the Durham edition of the works of Cassiodorus were written down by Bede. Perhaps the connecting link between Bede and Cassiodorus was the Northumbrian abbot Benedict Biscop, who traveled throughout Gaul and Italy in search of literary treasures that he could bring back with him to the monasteries of Wearmouth and Jarrow in the British Isles.

To Cassiodorus goes the credit for preserving humanist culture, for he introduced the copying of manuscripts as a monastic occupation. It was his work at Vivarium which makes him, along with Boethius, a significant transition figure from Rome to the Middle Ages. Their works helped keep classical culture alive during the Dark Ages, works that carried the literary ideals of Homer and Virgil to the Carolingian Revival of the 8th century, through the 12th Century Renaissance, and into the work of Dante that marks the end of the Middle Ages and the beginnings of the Italian Renaissance. Perhaps there would have been no way to completely fuse Christianity and humanism, but the pattern established at Vivarium, and of Cassiodorus' *Institutiones*, at least made it possible for each to survive without destroying the other.

Rome never actually recovered from the disasters of the civil wars of the third century AD and the Empire was never truly reconstituted after the great barbarian breakthroughs of the 4th thru 6th centuries (375-525 AD). With its capital in Constantinople, it was still refered to as the Roman Empire. But the western half had disintegrated, though the fiction carried on. The ideal of a universal Roman Empire still cast its spell over the imagination of men. Its memory was kept alive by the Roman Catholic Church, a universal spiritual empire, ruled by the pope at Rome, employing Latin as its official speech and with a hierarchical government modeled after the imperial administration. There had been no emperors in the West for three centuries when Charlemagne, the King of the Franks, knelt before the altar of Saint Peter's Church on Christmas day in 800. Pope Leo III placed an imperial crown on his head and hailed him emperor amidst the shouts of the people. It was an amazing and epoch-making scene and established a precedent for the crowning of all future emperors by the Pope, thus setting the church up as equal, if not superior to the secular realm. By the 10th century Otto the Great officially founded the Holy Roman Empire, which recognized the two great traditions that medieval people had inherited from Roman antiquity—that of a universal empire and a universal church. Even in 14th-century Italy there were German kings who claimed to be Roman emperors. They drew on the notion that the Roman empire had continued from antiquity to their day. Yet, the Holy Roman Empire was—as the joke goes—neither holy, nor Roman, nor an empire. When scholars after Petrarch (1304-74) built on his humanist principals, they took a serious look at the history of Rome and realized for the first time that at some point in the distant past it had entered a decline in its fortunes. The Renaissance that followed was a result of their attempts to recover the lost spirit of classical antiquity. If this marked a "rebirth," then what could they call the period between it's decline (they never thought it had fallen), and its modern revival? Thus began the notion of a Middle Age, an age looked down upon by the superior Latinists of the Renaissance as a period of barbarism. But those who lived through those ten centuries never thought they were living in a "middle age." As far as they were concerned, the imperial Roman ideal was still alive, and they were part of its extension.

This unity and continuance of the empire was not all a fiction. Even the barbarian invasions of the fifth century failed to mark a decisive ending to the structures and values of classical Greece and Rome. The Roman Senate remained active under Odovacer and the Roman civil administration survived. Roman civilization, in spite of loss and deterioration, was still living in Italy and dominated by Catholic Christianity—and it was the monks and clerics of the Catholic Church who were responsible for preserving much of classical literature by their copying and translating the written body of a culture the Chruch itself considered pagan. Until the Arab invasions of the seventh century, the peoples of the Mediterranean world did not feel they were inhabiting a Gothic world, but a Roman one. The Arab conquest of Syria, Egypt, north Africa, and then southern Spain and Sicily, ended the unity of the old Roman world as no other factor did. In reality, the Mediterranean was no longer a Roman lake. But the idea remained, partly because Greek-speaking Roman emperors reigned uninterruptedly from the "New Rome" of Constantinople until 1204. These Roman emperors are commonly termed Byzantine, but they referred to themselves as *Rhomaioi* (Romans). The last claimant to the title disappeared only in 1453, when the Turks conquered Constantinople. However the Holy Roman Empire of Western Europe and its Christian emperors continued down to the beginning of the 19th century when the French Revolution and Napolean swept it all away. In 1806, when Napoleon asserted that he no longer recognized a Holy Roman Emperor, Francis II agreed to abandon that title and called himself Francis I, Emperor of Austria instead. Such was the ignominious end of that impressive medieval empire, the rulers of which had traced their authority to Charlemagne and Augustus Caesar.

But if by "the end of the ancient world" we mean the loss of a uniquely privileged position for Greek and Latin classics in Western education and culture, then the shift cannot be described as decisive until the late twentieth century, an age in which powerful forces were inimical to the very notion of a "classic" of the past providing a model or criterion of judgment over the present. Monks of a different order began setting themselves the task of preserving what they could for the brave new world of the coming century.

What's the difference between poetry and prose?

From antiquity through the Middle Ages and into the beginnings of the Renaissance a millenium later, there was no one word generally available for poetry. In Homer, the poet is the "divine singer," or "maker" or "fabricator," and by Roman times he was called *vates*, "soothsayer," though all prophecy was rendered in rhythmical speech. Thus, even the Romans said the poet's work was "to sing." Remember how Virgil begins the *Aeneid*:

> *Arma virumque cano*
> Arms and the Man I sing

Antiquity did not always separate poetry and prose. Both forms of expression fell within the idea of "discourse." The schools of rhetoric that flourished in Roman times and into the Middle Ages commonly used exercises that turned poetry into prose, or "artistic prose." Metrical and non-metrical discourse were felt to be interchangable arts. This reciprocal relation between rhetoric and poetry had its foundation in the rhetorization of Roman poetry which began with Ovid.

By the Middle Ages, two poetic systems were current—the syllable measuring, or metric, and the accentual, or rhythmic. To these were added prose *dictamina*, and a fourth, rhymed prose, *mixtum sive compositum*—or ordinary prose, which was rhymed at the end line. The boundaries between poetry and prose became more and more blurred. There were several levels of prose:

artistic prose, "*rhetoricus sermo*"—medieval scholars often referred to the style of Isaiah as "*eloquentiae prosa*."
the **plain prose** of factual communication—*sermo simplex* as opposed to sermo artifex. From the 5th century onwards, the literary language became more and more artificial (*sermo artifex*), until finally it was incomprehensible to all but the scholars. A writer or poet who hoped to reach a wider public was compelled to use "*sermo simplex,*" which approached ordinary speech.
Prosa was also used to mean "rhythmic poem."

Actually, each of these categories had several levels, and it's almost impossible to give a complete picture of the variety of linguistic art-forms in the Middle Ages. Mixed prose texts—called *prosimetra*—in which prose alternates with verse inserts, was also common. *Poesis* could refer to a long poem; *poema* meant a short one.

The terminologies of poetry and prose were easily interchanged, especially with the introduction of the Roman rhythmical cadence into the Greek syllabic/metrical verse. But this should come as no surprise, since writers and poets of the Middle Ages (as well as our own age) were fond of uniting and crossing stylistic devices, especially the cross between meter and rhyme. Those with a living feeling for their art indulge in a childlike delight in play, and from play comes the mingling of jest and profundity, the sacred and the burlesque, Latin eloquence with vernacular verse so popular in the later Middle Ages, and also common in our own time.

The crumbling Roman road that goes from the ancient classics to the doorstep of the *Divine Comedy*, and from there into the modern world, travels a bumpy route through the complex terrain of the Latin Middle Ag

www.ingramcontent.com/pod-product-compliance
Lightning Source LLC
Chambersburg PA
CBHW081138020726
47504CB00009B/1908